Android Recipes

A Problem-Solution Approach
Third Edition

Dave Smith

with Jeff Friesen

Apress®

Android Recipes: A Problem-Solution Approach

ISBN-13 (pbk): 978-1-4302-6322-7

ISBN-13 (electronic): 978-1-4302-6323-4

President and Publisher: Paul Manning
Lead Editor: Steve Anglin
Development Editor: Douglas Pundick
Technical Reviewer: Chád Darby
Editorial Board: Steve Anglin, Mark Beckner, Ewan Buckingham, Gary Cornell, Louise Corrigan, Jim DeWolf, Jonathan Gennick, Jonathan Hassell, Robert Hutchinson, Michelle Lowman, James Markham, Matthew Moodie, Jeff Olson, Jeffrey Pepper, Douglas Pundick, Ben Renow-Clarke, Dominic Shakeshaft, Gwenan Spearing, Matt Wade, Steve Weiss
Coordinating Editor: Mark Powers
Copy Editor: Sharon Wilkey
Compositor: SPi Global
Indexer: SPi Global
Artist: SPi Global
Cover Designer: Anna Ishchenko

Distributed to the book trade worldwide by Springer Science+Business Media New York, 233 Spring Street, 6th Floor, New York, NY 10013. Phone 1-800-SPRINGER, fax (201) 348-4505, e-mail orders-ny@springer-sbm.com, or visit www.springeronline.com. Apress Media, LLC is a California LLC and the sole member (owner) is Springer Science+Business Media Finance Inc. (SSBM Finance Inc.). SSBM Finance Inc. is a Delaware corporation.

For information on translations, please e-mail rights@apress.com, or visit www.apress.com.

Apress and friends of ED books may be purchased in bulk for academic, corporate, or promotional use. eBook versions and licenses are also available for most titles. For more information, reference our Special Bulk Sales–eBook Licensing web page at www.apress.com/bulk-sales.

Any source code or other supplementary material referenced by the author in this text is available to readers at www.apress.com/9781430263227. For detailed information about how to locate your book's source code, go to www.apress.com/source-code/.

Contents at a Glance

Contents

Foreword

The Android landscape has dramatically changed since the first publication of this book in 2011. The capability of the devices and quality of the software has significantly improved. Since that time, Dave Smith has continued to ship some of the top Android applications in the Google Play store, improving his repertoire of information. In this book, you'll learn from a doer, and one of the most experienced in the Android development community.

Dave is the go-to Android dev around our company, so if you are ready to take your Android skills to the next level, you've picked the right resource. Obsess on the details; your users will appreciate it—and remember, "Real Artists Ship."

Ben Reubenstein (@benr75)

CEO, Double Encore

About the Authors

 Dave Smith is a professional engineer developing hardware and software for mobile and embedded platforms. Dave's engineering efforts are currently focused full-time on Android development. Since 2009, Dave has worked on developing at all levels of the Android platform, from writing user applications using the SDK to building and customizing the Android source code for embedded devices. Dave also frequently shares ideas via his development blog (http://wiresareobsolete.com) and Twitter stream @devunwired.

 Jeff Friesen is a freelance tutor and software developer with an emphasis on Java (and now Android). In addition to writing Android Recipes, Jeff has written numerous articles on Java and other technologies for JavaWorld (JavaWorld.com), InformIT (InformIT.com), and Java.net.

About the Technical Reviewer

Chád Darby is an author, instructor, and speaker in the Java development world. As a recognized authority on Java applications and architectures, he has presented technical sessions at software development conferences worldwide. In his 15 years as a professional software architect, he has had the opportunity to work for Blue Cross and Blue Shield, Merck, Boeing, Northrop Grumman, and a handful of startup companies.

Chád is a contributing author to several Java books, including *Professional Java E-Commerce* (Wrox Press), *Beginning Java Networking* (Wrox Press), and *XML and Web Services Unleashed* (Sams Publishing). Chád has Java certifications from Sun Microsystems and IBM. He holds a BS in computer science from Carnegie Mellon University. You can read Chád's blog at www.luv2code.com and follow him on Twitter @darbyluvs2code.

Acknowledgments

First and foremost, I would like to thank my wife, Lorie, for her eternal patience and support during the long hours I spent compiling and constructing the materials for this book. To my friend and colleague Ben Reubenstein, thank you for taking time to provide the foreword for the book *and still put up with me every day*. Finally, I send a huge thank you to the editorial team that Apress brought together to work with me and make the book the best it could possibly be; *you guys are the ones who make me look good*. Without your time and effort, this project would not even exist.

—Dave Smith

Introduction

Welcome to the third edition of *Android Recipes*!

If you are reading this book, you probably don't need to be told of the immense opportunity that mobile devices represent for software developers and users. In recent years, Android has become one of the top mobile platforms for device users. This means that you, as a developer, must know how to harness Android so you can stay connected to this market and the potential that it offers. But any new platform brings with it uncertainty about best practices and solutions to common needs and problems.

What we aim to do with *Android Recipes* is give you the tools to write applications for the Android platform through direct examples targeted at the specific problems you are trying to solve. This book is not a deep dive into the Android SDK, NDK, or any of the other tools. We don't weigh you down with all the details and theory behind the curtain. That's not to say that those details aren't interesting or important. You should take the time to learn them, as they may save you from making future mistakes. However, more often than not, they are simply a distraction when you are just looking for a solution to an immediate problem.

This book is not meant to teach you Java programming or even the building blocks of an Android application. You won't find many basic recipes in this book (such as how to display text with TextView, for instance), as we feel these are tasks easily remembered once learned. Instead, we set out to address tasks that developers, once comfortable with Android, need to do often but find too complex to accomplish with a few lines of code.

Treat *Android Recipes* as a reference to consult, a resource-filled cookbook that you can always open to find the pragmatic advice you need to get the job done quickly and well.

What Will You Find in the Book?

Although this book is not a beginner's guide to Android, Chapter 1 offers an overview of those Android fundamentals that are necessary for understanding the rest of the book's content. Specifically, it shows you how to install the Android SDK and get up and running with the library code, including the Android Support Library and Google Play Services.

Performance matters if you want your applications to succeed. Most of the time, this isn't a problem because the Android runtime engines get progressively better at compiling bytecode into the device's native code. However, you might need to leverage the Android NDK to boost performance. Chapter 8 offers you an introduction to the NDK and integrating native code into your application using Java Native Interface (JNI) bindings.

The NDK is a complex technology, which can also reduce your application's portability. Also, while good at increasing performance, the NDK doesn't address multicore processing very well for heavy workloads. Fortunately, Google has eliminated this tedium and simplified the execute-on-multiple-cores task while achieving portability by introducing RenderScript. Chapter 8 introduces you to RenderScript and shows you how to use its compute engine (and automatically leverage CPU cores) to process images.

In the intervening chapters, we dive into using the Android SDK to solve real problems. You will learn tricks for effectively creating a user interface that runs well across device boundaries. You will become a master at incorporating the collection of hardware (radios, sensors, and cameras) that makes mobile devices unique platforms. We'll even discuss how to make the system work for you by integrating with the services and applications provided by Google and various device manufacturers.

Keep a Level Eye on the Target

Throughout the book, you will see that we have marked most recipes with the minimum API level that is required to support them. Most of the recipes in this book are marked API Level 1, meaning that the code used can be run in applications targeting any version of Android since 1.0. However, where necessary, we use APIs introduced in later versions. Pay close attention to the API level marking of each recipe to ensure that you are not using code that doesn't match up with the version of Android your application is targeted to support.

Chapter 1

Getting Started with Android

Android is hot, and many people are developing Android applications (*apps* for short). Perhaps you too would like to develop apps but are unsure about how to get started. Although you could study Google's online *Android Developer's Guide* (http://developer.android.com/index.html) to acquire the needed knowledge, you might be overwhelmed by the guide's vast amount of information. In contrast, this chapter presents just enough theory to help you grasp the basics. Following this theory are recipes that teach you how to develop apps and prepare them for publication on Google Play (https://play.google.com/store).

1-1. What Is Android?

The *Android Developer's Guide* formally defines Android as a *software stack*—a set of software subsystems needed to deliver a fully functional solution—for mobile devices. This stack includes an operating system (a modified version of the Linux kernel), *middleware* (software that connects the low-level operating system to high-level apps) that's partly based on Java, and key apps (written in Java) such as a web browser (known as Browser) and a contact manager (known as Contacts).

Android offers the following features:

- Application framework enabling reuse and replacement of app components (discussed later in this chapter)

- Bluetooth, EDGE, 3G, and WiFi support (hardware dependent)

- Camera, GPS, compass, and accelerometer support (hardware dependent)

- Dalvik virtual machine optimized for mobile devices

- GSM telephony support (hardware dependent)

- Integrated browser based on the open source WebKit engine

- Media support for common audio, video, and still-image formats (MPEG-4, H.264, MP3, AAC, AMR, JPG, PNG, GIF)

- Optimized graphics powered by a custom 2D graphics library; 3D graphics based on the OpenGL ES 1.0, 1.1, or 2.0 specification (hardware acceleration optional)

- SQLite for structured data storage

Although not part of an Android device's software stack, Android's rich development environment—including a device emulator and plug-ins for many mainstream integrated development environments (IDEs)—could also be considered an Android feature.

1-2. Exploring the History of Android

Contrary to what you might expect, Android did not originate with Google. Instead, Android was initially developed by Android, Inc., a small Palo Alto, California–based startup company. Google bought this company in the summer of 2005 and released a beta version of the Android Software Development Kit (SDK) in November 2007.

On September 23, 2008, Google released Android 1.0, whose core features included a web browser, camera support, Google Search, and more. Table 1-1 outlines subsequent releases. (Starting with version 1.5, each major release comes under a code name that's based on a dessert item.)

Table 1-1. Android Releases

Version	Release Date and Changes
1.1	Google released SDK 1.1 on February 9, 2009. Changes included showing/hiding the speakerphone dialpad and saving attachments in messages.
1.5 (Cupcake) Based on Linux Kernel 2.6.27	Google released SDK 1.5 on April 30, 2009. Changes included recording and watching videos in MPEG-4 and 3GP formats, populating the *home screen* (a special app that is a starting point for using an Android device) with *widgets* (miniature app views), and providing animated screen transitions.
1.6 (Donut) Based on Linux Kernel 2.6.29	Google released SDK 1.6 on September 15, 2009. Changes included an expanded Gesture framework and the new GestureBuilder development tool, an integrated camera/camcorder/gallery interface, support for WVGA screen resolutions, and an updated search experience.
2.0/2.1 (Éclair) Based on Linux Kernel 2.6.29	Google released SDK 2.0 on October 26, 2009. Changes included live wallpapers, numerous new camera features (including flash support, digital zoom, scene mode, white balance, color effect, and macro focus), improved typing speed on the virtual keyboard, a smarter dictionary that learns from word usage and includes contact names as suggestions, improved Google Maps 3.1.2, and Bluetooth 2.1 support.
	Google subsequently released SDK update 2.0.1 on December 3, 2009, and SDK update 2.1 on January 12, 2010. Version 2.0.1 focused on minor API changes, bug fixes, and framework behavioral changes. Version 2.1 presented minor amendments to the API and bug fixes.

(continued)

Table 1-1.   *(continued)*

Version	Release Date and Changes
2.2 (Froyo) Based on Linux Kernel 2.6.32	Google released SDK 2.2 on May 20, 2009. Changes included the integration of Chrome's V8 JavaScript engine into the Browser app, voice dialing and contact sharing over Bluetooth, Adobe Flash support, additional app speed improvements through Just-In-Time (JIT) compilation, and USB tethering and WiFi hotspot functionality. Google subsequently released SDK update 2.2.1 on January 18, 2011, to offer bug fixes, security updates, and performance improvements. It then released SDK update 2.2.2 on January 22, 2011, to provide minor bug fixes, including SMS routing issues that affected the Nexus One. Finally, Google released SDK update 2.2.3 on November 21, 2011, and this contained two security patches.
2.3 (Gingerbread) Based on Linux Kernel 2.6.35	Google released SDK 2.3 on December 6, 2010. Changes included a new concurrent garbage collector that improves an app's responsiveness, support for gyroscope and barometer sensing, support for WebM/VP8 video playback and AAC audio encoding, support for near-field communication, and enhanced copy/paste functionality that lets users select a word by press-hold, copy, and paste. Google subsequently released SDK update 2.3.3 on February 9, 2011, offering improvements and API fixes. SDK update 2.3.4 on April 28, 2011, added support for voice or video chat via Google Talk. SDK update 2.3.5 on July 25, 2011, offered system enhancements, shadow animations for list scrolling, improved battery efficiency, and more. SDK update 2.3.6 on September 2, 2011, fixed a voice search bug. SDK update 2.3.7 on September 21, 2011, brought support for Google Wallet to the Nexus S 4G.
3.0 (Honeycomb) Based on Linux Kernel 2.6.36	Google released SDK 3.0 on February 22, 2011. Unlike previous releases, version 3.0 focuses exclusively on tablets, such as Motorola XOOM, the first tablet to be released (on February 24, 2011). In addition to an improved user interface, version 3.0 improves multitasking, supports multicore processors, supports hardware acceleration, and provides a 3D desktop with redesigned widgets. Google subsequently released SDK updates 3.1, 3.2, 3.2.1, 3.2.2, 3.2.4, and 3.2.6 throughout 2011 and in February 2012.
4.0 (Ice Cream Sandwich) Based on Linux Kernel 3.0.1	Google released SDK 4.0.1 on October 19, 2011. SDK 4.0.1 and 4.x successors unify the 2.3.x smartphone and 3.x tablet SDKs. Features include 1080p video recording and a customizable launcher. Google subsequently released SDK updates 4.0.2, 4.0.3, and 4.0.4 in late 2011 and in March 2012.

(continued)

Table 1-1.   *(continued)*

Version	Release Date and Changes
4.1/4.2/4.3 (Jelly Bean) Based on Linux Kernel 3.1	Google released SDK 4.1 on June 27, 2012. Features include vsync timing, triple buffering, automatically resizable app widgets, improved voice search, multichannel audio, and expandable notifications. An over-the-air update (version 4.1.1) was released later in July.
	In early October, Google released SDK 4.1.2, which offers lock/home screen rotation support for the Nexus 7, one-finger gestures to expand/collapse notifications, and bug fixes/performance enhancements. Then, in late October, Google released SDK 4.2, which offers Photo Sphere panorama photos, multiple user accounts (tablets only), a Daydream screen saver that activates when the device is idle or docked, notification power controls, support for a wireless display (Miracast), and more.
	On July 24, 2013, Google released SDK 4.3, which added restricted profile controls for multiple user accounts, Bluetooth LE (Smart) support, and additional API enhancements for the Digital rights management (DRM) and media-encoding features added in the first Jelly Bean release.
4.4 (KitKat) Based on Linux Kernel 3.4	Google released SDK 4.4 on October 31, 2013. The primary focus of this release was to enable Android on low-memory devices, and several new developer tools were provided to help applications better manage memory. Major features of this release include frameworks for printing view contents and serving all documents on the device from a common provider.

1-3. Installing the Android SDK

Problem

You've read the previous introduction to Android and are eager to develop your first Android app. However, you must install the Android SDK before you can develop apps.

Solution

Google provides the latest release of an Android SDK distribution file for each of the Windows, Intel-based Mac OS X, and i386-based Linux operating systems. Download and unarchive the appropriate file for your platform and move its unarchived home directory to a convenient location. You might also want to update your PATH environment variable so that you can access the SDK's command-line tools from anywhere in your filesystem.

Before downloading and installing this file, you must be aware of SDK requirements. You cannot use the SDK when your development platform doesn't meet these requirements.

The Android SDK supports the following operating systems:

- Windows XP (32-bit), Vista (32- or 64-bit), or Windows 7 (32- or 64-bit).

- Mac OS X 10.5.8 or later (x86 only).

- Linux (tested on Ubuntu Linux, Lucid Lynx). GNU C Library (glibc) 2.7 or later is required. On Ubuntu Linux, version 8.04 or later is required. 64-bit distributions must be able to run 32-bit applications. To learn how to add support for 32-bit applications, see the Ubuntu Linux installation notes at http://developer. android.com/sdk/installing/index.html#Troubleshooting.

You'll quickly discover that the Android SDK is organized into various separately downloadable components, which are known as *packages*. You will need to ensure that you have enough disk storage space to accommodate the various packages that you want to install. Plan for around 2 gigabytes of free storage. This figure takes into account the Android API documentation and multiple *Android platforms* (also known as Android software stacks).

Finally, you should ensure that the following additional software is installed:

- *JDK 6 or JDK 7*: You need to install one of these Java Development Kits (JDKs) to compile Java code. It's not sufficient to have only a Java Runtime Environment (JRE) installed.

- *Apache Ant*: You need to install Ant version 1.8 or later so that you can build Android projects from the command line using the current build system.

- *Gradleware Gradle*: Although it's currently in beta, you may need to install Gradle version 1.6 or later to experiment with the new command-line build system that will be replacing Ant.

Note   If a JDK is already installed on your development platform, take a moment to ensure that it meets the previously listed version requirement (6 or 7). Some Linux distributions may include JDK 1.4, which is not supported for Android development. Also, GNU Compiler for Java is not supported.

How It Works

Point your browser to http://developer.android.com/sdk/index.html and download one of the android-sdk_r22-windows.zip (Windows), android-sdk_r22-macosx.zip (Mac OS X), or android-sdk_r22-linux.tgz (Linux) distribution archives for Release 22 of the Android SDK. (Release 22 is the latest release at the time of this writing.)

Note   Windows developers have the option of downloading and running installer_r20-windows.exe. This tool automates most of the installation process.

For example, if you run Windows (the assumed platform in this chapter), you might choose to download `android-sdk_r22-windows.zip`. After unarchiving this file, move the unarchived `android-sdk-windows` home directory to a convenient location in your filesystem; for example, you might move the unarchived `C:\unzipped\android-sdk_r22-windows\android-sdk-windows` home directory to the root directory on your C: drive, resulting in `C:\android-sdk-windows`.

> **Note**   It is recommended that you rename `android-sdk-windows` to `android` to avoid a potential emulator crash when attempting to run an app from within Eclipse. Although this problem may no longer exist, it has been encountered in the past, and it most likely results from the hyphen (-) between `android` and `sdk`, and between `sdk` and `windows`.

To complete the installation, add the `tools` and `platform-tools` subdirectories to your `PATH` environment variable so that you can access the SDK's command-line tools from anywhere in your filesystem.

A subsequent examination of `android-sdk-windows` (or `android`) shows that this home directory contains the following subdirectories and files:

- `add-ons`: This initially empty directory stores *add-ons* (additional SDKs beyond the core platform that apps can target) from Google and other vendors; for example, the Google APIs add-on is stored here.

- `platforms`: This initially empty directory stores Android platforms in separate subdirectories. For example, Android 4.1 would be stored in one `platforms` subdirectory, whereas Android 2.3.4 would be stored in another `platforms` subdirectory.

- `tools`: This directory contains a set of platform-independent development tools, such as the emulator. The tools in this directory, known as *basic tools*, may be updated at any time and are independent of Android platform releases.

- `platform-tools`: This directory contains the Android Debug Bridge (ADB), the utility used to connect to a device or emulator for the purposes of installing applications, pushing/pulling files, and accessing the device shell.

- `AVD Manager.exe`: This tool is used to manage *Android Virtual Devices (AVDs)*, device configurations that are run with the Android emulator.

- `SDK Manager.exe`: This tool is used to manage SDK packages and runs AVD Manager in response to a menu selection.

- `SDK Readme.txt`: This text file welcomes you to the Android SDK and tells you that, in order to start developing apps, you need to use SDK Manager to install platform tools and at least one Android platform.

The `tools` directory contains various useful basic tools, including the following:

- `android`: Creates and updates Android projects; updates the Android SDK with new Android platforms and more; and creates, deletes, and views AVDs.

- ■ `emulator`: Runs a full Android software stack down to the kernel level; includes a set of preinstalled apps (such as Browser) that you can access.

- ■ `hierarchyviewer`: Provides a visual representation of a layout's view hierarchy (the Layout view) and a magnified inspector of the display (the Pixel Perfect view) so that you can debug and optimize your activity screens.

- ■ `sqlite3`: Manages SQLite databases created by Android apps.

- ■ `zipalign`: Performs archive alignment optimization on APK files.

You will look at many of these tools in greater detail throughout the book.

1-4. Installing an Android Platform

Problem

Installing the Android SDK is insufficient for developing Android apps; you must also install at least one Android platform.

Solution

Use the `SDK Manager` tool to install an Android platform. If `SDK Manager` doesn't display its Android SDK Manager dialog box, you probably need to create a `JAVA_HOME` environment variable that points to your JDK's home directory (for example, set `JAVA_HOME=C:\Program Files\Java\jdk1.7.0_04`) and try again.

Alternatively, you can use the `android` tool to install an Android platform. If `android` shows `Failed to convert path to a short DOS path: C:\Windows\system32\java.exe`, locate a file named `find_java.bat` (see `C:\android\tools\lib\find_java.bat`) and remove `-s` from each of the following lines:

```
for /f %%a in ('%~dps0\find_java.exe -s') do set java_exe=%%a
for /f %%a in ('%~dps0\find_java.exe -s -w') do set javaw_exe=%%a
```

How It Works

Run `SDK Manager` or `android`. Either tool presents the Android SDK Manager dialog box that is shown in Figure 1-1.

Figure 1-1. *Use this dialog box to install, update, and remove Android packages and to access the AVD Manager*

The Android SDK Manager dialog box presents a menu bar and a content area. The menu bar presents Packages and Tools menus:

- *Packages*: Use this menu to display a combination of updates/new packages, installed packages, and obsolete packages; to show archive details (or not); to sort packages by API level or repository; and to reload the list of packages shown in the content area.

- *Tools*: Use this menu to manage AVDs and add-on sites, to specify the proxy server and other options, and to display an About dialog box.

The content area shows you the path to the SDK, a table of information on packages, check boxes for choosing which packages to display, radio buttons for sorting packages by API level or repository, buttons for installing and deleting packages, and a progress bar that shows the progress of a scan of repositories for package information.

The Packages table classifies packages as tools, specific Android platforms, or extras. Each of these categories is associated with a check box that, when checked, selects all of the items in the category. Individual items can be deselected by unchecking their corresponding check boxes.

Tools are classified as SDK tools or SDK platform tools:

- *SDK tools* are the basic tools that are included in the SDK distribution file and that are stored in the `tools` directory. This fact is borne out by the Installed message in the status column for the Android SDK Tools item.

- *SDK platform tools* are platform-dependent tools for developing apps. These tools support the latest features of the Android platform and are typically updated only when a new platform becomes available. They are always backward-compatible with older platforms, but you must make sure that you have the latest version of these tools when you install a new platform. If you don't select the Android SDK Platform tools item (which is not selected by default), the platform tools will be installed automatically.

The only platform that you need to install for this book is Android 4.4 (Level 19). This category and all of its items are selected, so leave them as is. As well as this platform, you will install the documentation, samples, ARM and/or x86 *system image* (for creating emulator instances), Google APIs, and source code.

Finally, you can install *extras*, which are external libraries or tools that can be included or used when building an app. For example, the Google USB Driver item is already selected in the Extras section. However, you need to install this component only when developing on a Windows platform and testing your apps on an actual Android device.

Click the Install Packages button (the number will differ should you choose to install more or fewer packages). You'll encounter the Choose Packages to Install dialog box shown in Figure 1-2.

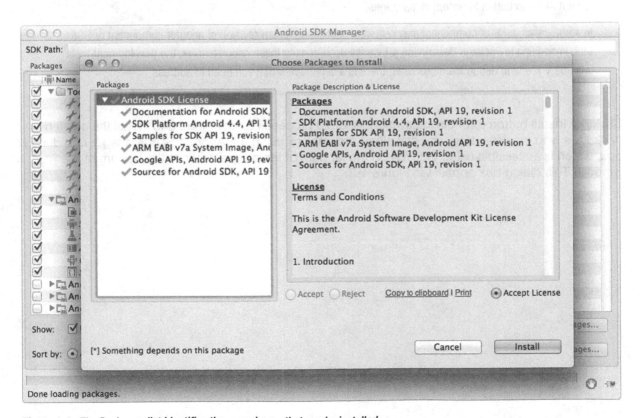

Figure 1-2. The Packages list identifies those packages that can be installed

The Choose Packages to Install dialog box shows a Packages list that identifies those packages that can be installed. It displays green check marks beside packages that have been accepted for installation, and it displays question marks beside those packages that have not yet been selected.

> **Note**   Although Google APIs and Google USB Driver were initially selected, they are indicated as not having been selected. (Perhaps this is an example of a bug, where information is not being carried forward.) You will need to highlight and accept these packages if you still want them.

For the highlighted package, Package Description & License presents a package description, a list of other packages that are dependent on this package being installed, information on the archive that houses the package, and additional information. Click the Accept or Reject radio button to accept or reject the package.

> **Note**   A red X appears beside the package name in the Packages list when you reject the package. Click the Accept All radio button to accept all packages.
>
> In some cases, an SDK component may require a specific minimum revision of another component or SDK tool. In addition to Package Description & License documenting these dependencies, the development tools will notify you with debug warnings when there is a dependency that you need to address.

Click the Install button to begin installation. Android proceeds to download and install the chosen packages; you may also track the download progress by using the Android SDK Manager Log dialog box, which is accessible using the icon on the far right of the progress bar at the bottom of the window. This dialog box appears in Figure 1-3.

Figure 1-3. The log window reveals the progress of downloading and installing each selected package archive

Upon completion, you should observe a "Done loading packages" message at the bottom of the Android SDK Manager Log and Android SDK Manager dialog boxes. Click the Close button on the former dialog box; the Status column in the Packages table on the latter dialog box will tell you which packages have been installed.

You should also observe several new subdirectories of the home directory, including the following:

- `platform-tools` (in android)
- `android-19` (in android/platforms)

1-5. Creating an Android Virtual Device

Problem

After installing the Android SDK and an Android platform, you're ready to start creating Android apps. However, you won't be able to run those apps via the `emulator` tool until you create an Android Virtual Device (AVD), a device configuration that represents an Android device.

Solution

Use the AVD Manager or android tool to create an AVD.

How It Works

Run AVD Manager (or select Manage AVDs from the Android SDK Manager dialog box's Tools menu). Figure 1-4 shows the Android Virtual Device Manager dialog box.

Figure 1-4. No AVDs are initially installed

Click the New button. Figure 1-5 shows the resulting Create New Android Virtual Device (AVD) dialog box.

Figure 1-5. An AVD consists of a name, a target Android platform, and more

Figure 1-5 reveals that an AVD has a name, targets a specific Android platform, targets a specific CPU/ABI (Application Binary Interface, such as ARM/armeabi-v7a), can emulate an SD card, provides a skin with a certain screen resolution, and has various hardware properties.

Enter a name, target device, target platform (you may have only one choice), and any other device options you would like. If your machine has an attached or built-in webcam, this can be used to emulate the device's front or rear cameras as well.

> **Tip**   You can select the Enabled check box in the Use Host GPU section to enable hardware acceleration of graphics. This will greatly improve the animations in the UI, but it is not supported on all system images.

After making all the appropriate selections, finish the AVD creation by clicking Create AVD. Figure 1-4's AVD pane now includes an entry for your new AVD.

Caution   When creating an AVD that you plan to use to test compiled apps, make sure that the target platform has an API level greater than or equal to the API level required by your app. In other words, if you plan to test your app on the AVD, your app typically cannot access platform APIs that are more recent than those APIs supported by the AVD's API level.

Although it's easier to use AVD Manager to create an AVD, you can also accomplish this task via the android tool by specifying android create avd -n *name* -t *targetID* [-option *value*].... Given this syntax, *name* identifies the device configuration (such as target_AVD), *targetID* is an integer ID that identifies the targeted Android platform (you can obtain this integer ID by executing android list targets), and [-option *value*]... identifies a series of options (such as SD card size).

If you don't specify sufficient options, android prompts to create a custom hardware profile. Press the Enter key when you don't want a custom hardware profile and prefer to use the default hardware emulation options. For example, the android create avd -n AVD1 -t 1 command line causes an AVD named AVD1 to be created. This command line assumes that 1 corresponds to the Android 4.1 platform and prompts to create a custom hardware profile.

Note   Each AVD functions as an independent device with its own private storage for user data, its own SD card, and so on. When you launch the emulator tool with an AVD, this tool loads user data and SD card data from the AVD's directory. By default, emulator stores user data, SD card data, and a cache in the directory assigned to the AVD.

1-6. Starting the AVD

Problem

You must start the emulator with the AVD so that you can install and run apps. You want to know how to accomplish this task.

Solution

Use the AVD Manager tool to start the AVD. Or start the AVD by using the emulator tool.

How It Works

Refer to Figure 1-4 and you'll notice a disabled Start button. This button is no longer disabled after an AVD entry is created (and highlighted). Click Start to run the emulator tool with the highlighted AVD entry as the emulator's device configuration.

A Launch Options dialog box appears. This dialog box identifies the AVD's skin and screen density. It also provides unchecked check boxes for scaling the resolution of the emulator's display to match the physical device's screen size, for wiping user data, for launching from a previously saved snapshot, and for saving device state to a snapshot upon device exit.

> **Note** As you update your apps, you'll periodically package and install them on the emulator, which preserves the apps and their state data across AVD restarts in a user-data disk partition. To ensure that an app runs properly as you update it, you might need to delete the emulator's user-data partition, which is accomplished by selecting Wipe User Data.

Click the Launch button to launch the emulator with AVD1. AVD Manager responds by briefly displaying a Starting Android Emulator dialog box followed by the emulator window. See Figure 1-6.

Figure 1-6. *The emulator window presents the home screen on its left, and it presents phone controls on its right*

Figure 1-6 shows that the emulator window is divided into a left pane, which displays the Android logo on a black background followed by the home screen, and a right pane, which displays phone controls. If, when creating the AVD, you unchecked the box for including hardware controls, the emulator will start up showing just the device display.

A status bar appears above the home screen (and every app screen). The *status bar* presents the current time, amount of battery power remaining, and other information; it also provides access to notifications.

The home screen initially appears in locked mode. To unlock this screen, drag the lock icon to its right until it touches an unlock icon. You should end up with the unlocked home screen shown in Figure 1-7.

Figure 1-7. The home screen now reveals the app launcher and more

The home screen presents the following items:

- *Wallpaper background*: Wallpaper appears behind everything else and can be dragged to the left or right. To change this background, press and hold down the left mouse button over the wallpaper, which causes a wallpaper-oriented pop-up menu to appear.

- *Widgets*: The Google Search widget appears near the top, the Clock widget appears upper-centered, and the Camera widget appears near the bottom left. A widget is a miniature app view that can be embedded in the home screen and other apps, and receives periodic updates.

- *App launcher*: The app launcher (along the bottom) presents icons for launching the commonly used Browser, Contacts, Messaging, and Phone apps; it also displays a rectangular grid of all installed apps, which are subsequently launched by single-clicking their icons. Figure 1-8 shows some of these icons.

Figure 1-8. Drag this screen to the left to reveal more icons

The app launcher organizes apps and widgets according to the tabs near the top left of the screen. You can run apps from the APPS tab, and select additional widgets to display on the home screen from the WIDGETS tab. (If you need more room for widgets on the home screen, drag its wallpaper in either direction.)

> **Tip** The API Demos app demonstrates a wide variety of Android APIs. If you are new to Android app development, you should run the individual demos to acquaint yourself with what Android has to offer. You can view each demo's source code by accessing the source files that are located in the `android/samples/android-19/ApiDemos` folder.

The phone controls include the following commonly used buttons:

- The house icon phone control button takes you from wherever you are to the home screen.
- The MENU phone control button presents a menu of app-specific choices for the currently running app.
- The curved arrow icon phone control button takes you back to the previous activity in the activity stack.

While the AVD is running, you can interact with it by using your mouse to "touch" the touch screen, and your keyboard to "press" the AVD keys. Table 1-2 shows you the mappings between AVD keys and keyboard keys.

Table 1-2. *Mappings Between AVD Keys and Keyboard Keys*

AVD Key	Keyboard Key
Home	Home
Menu (left softkey)	F2 or Page Up
Star (right softkey)	Shift-F2 or Page Down
Back	Esc
Call/dial button	F3
Hang up/end call button	F4
Search	F5
Power button	F7
Audio volume up button	Keypad_Plus, Ctrl-5
Audio volume down button	Keypad_Minus, Ctrl-F6
Camera button	Ctrl-Keypad_5, Ctrl-F3
Switch to previous layout orientation (for example, portrait or landscape)	Keypad_7, Ctrl-F11
Switch to next layout orientation	Keypad_9, Ctrl-F12
Toggle cell networking on/off	F8
Toggle code profiling	F9 (only with -trace startup option)
Toggle full-screen mode	Alt-Enter
Toggle trackball mode	F6
Enter trackball mode temporarily (while key is pressed)	Delete
DPad left/up/right/down	Keypad_4/8/6/2
DPad center click	Keypad_5
Onion alpha increase/decrease	Keypad_Multiply (*) / Keypad_Divide (/)

> **Tip** You must first disable NumLock on your development computer before you can use keypad keys.

Table 1-2 refers to the -trace startup option in the context of toggle code profiling. This option lets you store profiling results in a file when starting the AVD via the emulator tool.

For example, emulator -avd AVD1 -trace results.txt starts the emulator for device configuration AVD1, and it also stores profiling results in results.txt when you press F9—press F9 again to stop code profiling.

Figure 1-6 displays 5554:AVD on the title bar. The 5554 value identifies a console port that you can use to dynamically query and otherwise control the environment of the AVD.

Note   Android supports up to 16 concurrently executing AVDs. Each AVD is assigned an even-numbered console port number starting with 5554.

You can connect to the AVD's console by specifying telnet localhost *console-port*. For example, specify telnet localhost 5554 to connect to AVD1's console. Listing 1-1 shows you the resulting commands.

Listing 1-1. Typing a Command Name by Itself for Command-Specific Help

```
Android Console: type 'help' for a list of commands
OK
help
Android console command help:

    help|h|?          print a list of commands
    event             simulate hardware events
    geo               Geo-location commands
    gsm               GSM related commands
    cdma              CDMA related commands
    kill              kill the emulator instance
    network           manage network settings
    power             power related commands
    quit|exit         quit control session
    redir             manage port redirections
    sms               SMS related commands
    avd               control virtual device execution
    window            manage emulator window
    qemu              QEMU-specific commands
    sensor            manage emulator sensors

try 'help <command>' for command-specific help
OK
```

Tip   The telnet command is disabled on Windows 7 by default (to help make the OS more secure). To enable telnet on Windows 7, start the Control Panel, select Programs and Features, select Turn Windows Features On or Off, and (from the Windows Features dialog box), select the Telnet Client check box.

1-7. Migrating to Eclipse

Problem

You prefer to develop apps by using the Eclipse IDE.

Solution

To develop apps with Eclipse, you need to install an IDE such as Eclipse Classic 4.2. Furthermore, you need to install the Android Development Tools (ADT) plug-in.

How It Works

Before you can develop Android apps with Eclipse, you must complete at least the first two of the following three tasks:

1. Install the Android SDK and at least one Android platform. JDK 6 or JDK 7 must also be installed.

2. Install a version of Eclipse that's compatible with the Android SDK and the ADT plug-in for the Eclipse IDE.

3. Install the ADT plug-in.

You should complete these tasks in the order presented. You cannot install the ADT plug-in before installing Eclipse, and you cannot configure or use the ADT plug-in before installing the Android SDK and at least one Android platform.

THE BENEFICIAL ADT PLUG-IN

Although you can develop Android apps in Eclipse without using the ADT plug-in, it's much faster and easier to create, debug, and otherwise develop these apps with this plug-in. The ADT plug-in offers the following features:

- It gives you access to other Android development tools from inside the Eclipse IDE. For example, ADT lets you access the many capabilities of the Dalvik Debug Monitor Server (DDMS) tool, allowing you to take screenshots, manage port-forwarding, set breakpoints, and view thread and process information directly from Eclipse.

- It provides a New Project Wizard, which helps you quickly create and set up all of the basic files you'll need for a new Android app.

- It automates and simplifies the process of building your Android app.

- It provides an Android code editor that helps you write valid XML for your Android manifest and resource files.

- It lets you export your project into a signed APK, which can be distributed to users.

You'll learn how to install the ADT plug-in after learning how to install Eclipse.

The `Eclipse.org` website makes available for download several IDE packages that meet different requirements. Google places the following stipulations on which IDE package you should download and install:

- Install an Eclipse 3.6.2 (Helios) or greater IDE package.

- Make sure that the Eclipse package being downloaded includes the Eclipse Java Development Tools (JDT) plug-in. Most packages include this plug-in.

Complete the following steps to install Eclipse Classic 4.2, which is the latest version of this IDE at the time of this writing:

1. Point your browser to the Eclipse Classic 4.2 page at `http://eclipse.org/downloads/packages/eclipse-classic-42/junor`.

2. Select the appropriate distribution file by clicking one of the links in the Download Links box on the right side of this page. For example, you might click Windows 64-bit platform.

3. Click a download link and save the distribution file to your hard drive. For example, you might save `eclipse-SDK-4.2-win32-x86_64.zip` to your hard drive.

4. Unarchive the distribution file and move the `eclipse` home directory to a convenient location. For example, on 64-bit Windows 7, you would move `eclipse` to your `C:\Program Files` directory, which organizes 64-bit programs.

5. You might also want to create a desktop shortcut to the `eclipse` application located in the `eclipse` home directory.

Complete the following steps to install the latest revision of the ADT plug-in:

1. Start Eclipse.

2. The first time you start Eclipse, you will discover a Workspace Launcher dialog box following the splash screen. You can use this dialog box to select a workspace folder in which to store your projects. You can also tell Eclipse to not display this dialog box on subsequent startups. Change or keep the default folder setting and click OK.

3. Once Eclipse displays its main window, select Install New Software from the Help menu.

4. Click the Add button in the resulting Install dialog box's Available Software pane.

5. In the resulting Add Repository dialog box, enter a name for the remote site (for example, **Android Plugin**) in the Name field, and enter `https://dl-ssl.google.com/android/eclipse/` into the Location field. Click OK.

6. You should now see Developer Tools and NDK Plugins in the list that appears in the middle of the Install dialog box.

7. Select the check box next to these categories, which will automatically select the nested items underneath. Click Next.

8. The resulting Install Details pane lists Android DDMS, Android Development Tools, Android Hierarchy Viewer, Android Native Development Tools, Android Traceview, and Tracer for OpenGL ES. Click Next to read and accept the various license agreements, and then click Finish.

9. An Installing Software dialog box appears and takes care of installation. If you encounter a Security Warning dialog box, click OK.

10. Finally, Eclipse presents a Software Updates dialog box that prompts you to restart this IDE. Click Yes to restart.

> **Tip**   If you have trouble acquiring the plug-in in step 5, try specifying `http` instead of `https` (`https` is preferred for security reasons) in the Location field.

To complete the installation of the ADT plug-in, you may have to configure it by modifying the ADT preferences in Eclipse to point to the Android SDK home directory. Accomplish this task by completing the following steps:

1. Select Preferences from the Window menu to open the Preferences dialog box. For Mac OS X, select Preferences from the Eclipse menu.

2. Select Android from the left panel.

3. If the SDK Location text field presents the SDK's home directory (such as `C:\android`), close the Preferences dialog box. You have nothing further to do.

4. If the SDK Location text field does not present the SDK's home directory, click the Browse button beside this text field and locate your downloaded SDK's home directory on the resulting Browse For Folder dialog box. Select this location, click OK to close this dialog box, and click Apply in the Preferences dialog box to confirm this location, which should result in a list of SDK Targets (such as Android 4.1) appearing below the text field.

> **Note**   For more information on installing the ADT plug-in, which includes helpful information in case of difficulty, check out the "Installing the Eclipse Plugin" page (`http://developer.android.com/sdk/installing/installing-adt.html`) in Google's online Android documentation.

1-8. Creating Java Library JARs

Problem

You want to create a library that stores Android-agnostic code and that can be used in your Android and non-Android projects.

Solution

Create a JAR-based library that accesses only Java 5 (and earlier) APIs via JDK command-line tools or Eclipse.

How It Works

Suppose you plan to create a simple library of math-oriented utilities. This library will consist of a single MathUtils class with various static methods. Listing 1-2 presents an early version of this class.

Listing 1-2. MathUtils Implementing Math-Oriented Utilities via static Methods

```
package com.androidrecipes.lib;

public class MathUtils {
   public static long factorial(long n) {
      if (n <= 0)
         return 1;
      else
         return n*factorial(n-1);
   }
}
```

MathUtils currently consists of a single long factorial(long n) class method for computing and returning factorials (perhaps for use in calculating permutations and combinations). You might eventually expand this class to support fast Fourier transforms and other math operations not supported by the java.lang.Math class.

> **Caution**   When creating a library that stores Android-agnostic code, make sure to access only standard Java APIs (such as the collections framework) that are supported by Android. Don't access unsupported Java APIs (such as Swing) or Android-specific APIs (such as Android widgets).

Creating MathUtils with the JDK

Developing a JAR-based library with the JDK is easy. Complete the following steps to create a mathutils.jar file that contains the MathUtils class:

1.   Within the current directory, create a package directory structure consisting of a com subdirectory that contains an androidrecipes subdirectory that contains a lib subdirectory.

2. Copy Listing 1-2's `MathUtils.java` source code to a `MathUtils.java` file stored in `lib`.

3. Assuming that the current directory contains the `com` subdirectory, execute `javac com/androidrecipes/lib/MathUtils.java` to compile `MathUtils.java`. A `MathUtils.class` file is stored in `com/androidrecipes/lib`.

4. Create `mathutils.jar` by executing `jar cfv mathutils.jar com/androidrecipes/lib/*.class`. The resulting `mathutils.jar` file contains a `com/androidrecipes/lib/MathUtils.class` entry.

Note   If you're using JDK 7, execute one of the following command lines to compile `MathUtils.java`:

`javac -source 1.5 -target 1.5 com/androidrecipes/lib/MathUtils.java`

`javac -source 1.6 -target 1.6 com/androidrecipes/lib/MathUtils.java`

Each command line results in a harmless "bootclasspath" warning message that is explained at https://blogs.oracle.com/darcy/entry/bootclasspath_older_source.

Fail to do this and you will see the following warning messages when executing ant debug to build an APK that references this library:

`[dx] trouble processing:`

`[dx] bad class file magic (cafebabe) or version (0033.0000)`

`[dx] ...while parsing com/androidrecipes/lib/MathUtils.class`

`[dx] ...while processing com/androidrecipes/lib/MathUtils.class`

`[dx] 1 warning`

Creating MathUtils with Eclipse

Developing a JAR-based library with Eclipse is a bit more involved. Complete the following steps to create a `mathutils.jar` file that contains the `MathUtils` class:

1. Assuming that you've installed the Eclipse version discussed previously in this chapter, start this IDE if it is not already running.

2. From the File menu, choose New ➤ Java Project.

3. In the resulting New Java Project dialog box, enter **mathutils** into the Project name text field. If the execution environment JRE setting (in the JRE section) is set to JavaSE-1.7, change this setting to JavaSE-1.6. Click the Finish button.

4. Expand Package Explorer's `mathutils` node. Then right-click the `src` node (underneath `mathutils`) and choose New ➤ Package.

5. In the resulting New Java Package dialog box, enter **com.androidrecipes.lib** into the Name text field and click Finish.

6. Right-click the resulting com.androidrecipes.lib node and choose New ➤ Class.

7. In the resulting New Java Class dialog box, enter **MathUtils** into the Name field and click Finish.

8. Replace the skeletal contents in the resulting MathUtils.java editor window with Listing 1-2.

9. Right-click the mathutils project node and choose Build Project. (You might have to deselect Build Automatically from the project menu first.) Ignore any "Build path specifies execution environment JavaSE-1.6. There are no JREs installed in the workspace that are strictly compatible with this environment" warning message.

10. Right-click the mathutils project node and choose Export.

11. In the resulting Export dialog box, select JAR file under the Java node (if not selected), and click the Next button.

12. In the resulting JAR Export dialog box, keep the defaults but enter **mathutils.jar** into the JAR file text field. Click Finish. (At this point, you will see a Save Modified Resources dialog box if you have not saved the source code entered in step 8. Click OK to dismiss this dialog box.) The resulting mathutils.jar file is created in your Eclipse workspace's root directory.

1-9. Creating Android Library Projects

Problem

You want to create a library that stores Android-specific code, such as custom widgets or activities with or without resources.

Solution

You can create *Android library projects*, which are projects containing shareable Android source code and resources and which you can reference in other Android projects. This is useful when you want to reuse common code. Library projects cannot be installed onto a device. They are pulled into the APK file at build time.

> **Note** The Android 4.0 SDK (r14) includes changes to Android library projects. Previously, library projects were handled as extra resource and source code folders for use when compiling the resources and the app's source, respectively. Because developers wanted to distribute a library as one JAR file of compiled code and resources, and because library project implementations were extremely fragile in Eclipse, r14 based Android library projects on a compiled-code library mechanism.
>
> Check out the "Changes to Library Projects in Android SDK Tools, r14" blog post (http://android-developers.blogspot.ca/2011/10/changes-to-library-projects-in-android.html) for more information.

How It Works

Suppose you want to create a library that contains a single reusable custom view describing a game board (for playing chess, checkers, or even tic-tac-toe). Listing 1-3 reveals this view's GameBoard class.

Listing 1-3. GameBoard Describing a Reusable Custom View for Drawing Different Game Boards

```
public class GameBoard extends View {
   private int nSquares, colorA, colorB;

   private Paint paint;
   private int squareDim;

   public GameBoard(Context context, int nSquares, int colorA,
         int colorB) {
      super(context);
      this.nSquares = nSquares;
      this.colorA = colorA;
      this.colorB = colorB;
      paint = new Paint();
   }

   @Override
   protected void onDraw(Canvas canvas) {
      for (int row = 0; row < nSquares; row++) {
         paint.setColor(((row & 1) == 0) ? colorA : colorB);
         for (int col = 0; col < nSquares; col++) {
            int a = col*squareDim;
            int b = row*squareDim;
            canvas.drawRect(a, b, a+squareDim, b+squareDim,
                  paint);
            paint.setColor(
                  (paint.getColor() == colorA) ? colorB : colorA);
         }
      }
   }
```

```
@Override
protected void onMeasure(int widthMeasuredSpec,
        int heightMeasuredSpec) {
    // keep the view squared
    int width = MeasureSpec.getSize(widthMeasuredSpec);
    int height = MeasureSpec.getSize(heightMeasuredSpec);
    int d = (width == 0) ? height : (height == 0) ? width :
            (width < height) ? width : height;
    setMeasuredDimension(d, d);
    squareDim = width/nSquares;
}
}
```

In Android, a custom view extends android.view.View or one of its subclasses (such as android.widget.TextView). GameBoard extends View directly because it doesn't need any subclass functionality. We'll talk more about creating custom views in Chapter 2.

GameBoard declares the following fields:

- nSquares stores the number of squares on each side of the game board. Typical values include 3 (for a 3-by-3 board) and 8 (for an 8-by-8 board).

- colorA stores the color of even-numbered squares on even-numbered rows, and the color of odd-numbered squares on odd-numbered rows—row and column numbering starts at 0.

- colorB stores the color of odd-numbered squares on even-numbered rows, and the color of even-numbered squares on odd-numbered rows.

- paint stores a reference to an android.graphics.Paint object that is used to specify the square color (colorA or colorB) when the game board is drawn.

- squareDim stores the dimension of a square—the number of pixels on each side.

GameBoard's constructor initializes this widget by storing its nSquares, colorA, and colorB arguments in same-named fields, and it also instantiates the Paint class for use in drawing.

Creating GameBoard with the Android SDK

You create an Android library project in much the same way as you create a standard app project. However, instead of specifying a command line beginning with android create project, you specify a command line starting with android create lib-project, according to the following syntax:

```
android create lib-project --target target_ID
                --name your_project_name
                --path /path/to/your/project/project_name
                --package your_library_package_namespace
```

This command creates a standard project structure, adding the following line to the project's project.properties file to indicate that the project is a library:

```
android.library=true
```

Once the command completes, the library project is created, and you can begin moving source code and resources into it.

> **Tip** To convert an existing app project to a library project for other apps to use, add the `android.
> library=true` property to the app's `project.properties` file.

Execute the following command (spread across two lines for readability) to create a `GameBoard` library project:

```
android create lib-project -t 1 -p <path/to/project/directory>
                        -k com.androidrecipes.gameboard
```

Continue by creating a `com/androidrecipes/gameboard` hierarchy under the `src` directory, and store a `GameBoard.java` source file containing Listing 1-3's code in this directory.

Although you can build the library by executing `ant debug` or `ant release` (it doesn't matter which command you use, because the same `classes.jar` file is created in the `bin` directory), there is no need to do so because this library will be built automatically when referenced from another project (as demonstrated in the next recipe).

Creating GameBoard with Eclipse

Complete the following steps to create the `GameBoard` project in Eclipse:

1. Assuming that you've installed the Eclipse version discussed earlier in this chapter, start this IDE if it is not already running.

2. Select New from the File menu, and select Project from the resulting pop-up menu.

3. In the resulting New Project dialog box, expand the `Android` node in the wizard tree (if not expanded), select the `Android Application Project` branch below this node (if not selected), and click the Next button.

4. In the resulting New Android App dialog box, enter **GameBoard** into the Application Name text field. This entered name also appears in the Project Name text field, and it identifies the folder/directory in which the `GameBoard` project is stored.

5. Enter **com.androidrecipes.gameboard** into the Package Name text field.

6. Via Build SDK, select the appropriate Android SDK to target. This selection identifies the Android platform you'd like your library to be built against. Assuming that you've installed only the Android 4.1 platform, only this choice should appear and be selected.

7. Via Minimum SDK, select the minimum Android SDK on which your library runs, or keep the default setting.

8. Uncheck the Create Custom Launcher Icon check box, because a custom launcher icon is not used with a library.

9. Select the Mark This Project as a Library check box.

10. Leave the Create Project in Workspace check box selected, and click Next.

11. In the resulting Create Activity pane, uncheck the Create Activity check box and click Finish.

The GameBoard project is marked as an Android library project. However, it doesn't yet contain a GameBoard.java source file containing Listing 1-3's contents.

Introduce a com.androidrecipes.gameboard node under Package Explorer's GameBoard/src node (right-click src, choose New ➤ Package from the resulting pop-up menus, enter **com.androidrecipes. gameboard** into the Name text field in the resulting New Java Package dialog box, and click the Finish button). Introduce a GameBoard.java node under com.androidrecipes.gameboard (right-click com. androidrecipes.gameboard, choose New ➤ Class from the resulting pop-up menus, enter **GameBoard** into the Name text field on the resulting New Java Class dialog box, and click the Finish button). Double-click the GameBoard.java node, and replace its skeletal contents with Listing 1-3.

Although you can build the library by right-clicking the GameBoard node and selecting Build Project from the pop-up menu (a gameboard.jar file is created in the bin directory), there is no need to do so because this library will be built automatically when referenced from another project (as demonstrated in the next recipe).

1-10. Using Core Libraries in Applications
Problem

Google keeps improving Android by offering new features (such as fragments) in SDK upgrades. Furthermore, Google lets you use some of these features on older Android platforms where they are not supported. You want to use Google's solution to retrofit your apps to support fragments and/or other previously unsupported features.

Solution
Android Support Library

Google has anticipated the need for apps to access newer Android features on older versions of Android by introducing the Support Library. This collection of static support libraries can be added to an app to use APIs that are not available on older Android platforms or to use utility APIs that are not part of the framework APIs.

The Support Library introduces various new capabilities, including the following:

- Fragments
- Recommended Android user-interface navigation patterns
- Support classes that ease the implementation of Android Dreams in a backward-compatible fashion. First introduced in Android 4.0 (Ice Cream Sandwich), Android Dreams (also known as Rocket Launcher) is a new screen-saver feature.

Google discusses the Support Library on its page at `http://developer.android.com/tools/extras/support-library.html`. This page points out that each of the static support libraries has a specific minimum API level. (An app using a specific library will not work on Android platforms with a lower API level.)

Three libraries are currently targeted:

- *Level 4*: This level corresponds to Android 1.6 (Donut). An app including this library has access to all capabilities except for those belonging to Level 7 and Level 13.
- *Level 7*: This level corresponds to Android 2.1 (Éclair). An app including this library has access to an equivalent `android.widget.GridLayout` class, which was introduced in Level 14.
- *Level 13*: This level corresponds to Android 3.2 (Honeycomb). An app including this library has access to fragment features introduced after Level 13 and Android Dreams.

Google Play Services

Google provides developer access to many of their proprietary technology APIs through Google Play Services, an additional application running on devices with Google Play that exposes services to third-party applications, such as Maps or Google+.

The Services application on the device is regularly updated via Google Play, so new APIs can be added to users' devices immediately as they are released by Google. Similar to the Support Library, this means that new features can be included in Android applications regardless of the platform version that device may be running.

Google further discusses how Google Play Services works on its page at `http://developer.android.com/google/play-services/index.html`.

Installation

You need to run the SDK Manager tool to download and install the Support Library and Google Play Services. Run this tool from the command line (as shown earlier in this chapter) or from within Eclipse (by selecting Android SDK Manager from the Window menu). Figure 1-9 shows the Android Support Library and Google Play Services entries selected in the Extras section.

Figure 1-9. Android Support Library and Google Play Services

Click the Install 2 Packages button, followed by the Install button in the subsequent Choose Packages to Install dialog box. The Support Library revision 18 (current at the time of this writing) is installed to the *<Android_home_directory>*/extras/android/support directory, which includes text files along with samples, v4, v7, and v13 directories. The v4 directory contains an android-support-v4.jar file. Similarly, the v13 directory contains an android-support-v13.jar file. In contrast, the v7 directory contains a series of library projects whose libs subdirectories contain the core library and whose res subdirectory contains accompanying required resource files.

Google Play Services revision 9 (current at the time of this writing) is installed to *<Android_home_directory>*/extras/google/google_play_services, which includes documentation along with samples and libproject directories. Similar to v7 of the Support Library, the libproject directory contains a library project whose libs subdirectory contains the core libraries and whose res subdirectory contains accompanying required resource files.

How It Works

JAR Libraries

To incorporate JAR libraries in your application, simply copy the JAR file to your project's `libs` directory. If that directory does not already exist in your project, then create it first. If you are using a recent version of the SDK tools (r17 or later, including the ADT plug-in if you are using Eclipse), the tools will handle integrating the JAR files into the build path as long as they are in the `libs` directory.

Important   If you are using the new beta build system based on Gradle to build your application, you will need to add the JAR files as dependencies in your project's `build.gradle` file. Something like the following will be necessary:

```
dependencies {
    compile files("libs/library1.jar",
        "libs/library2.jar")
}
```

Library Projects

Integrating a library project is a bit more involved. For this reason, we'll focus a bit more on referencing one from a command line–based and Eclipse-based project. We will use the `GridLayout` project from the v7 Support Library for this example.

Listing 1-4 presents the source code to this project's `UseGridLayout.java` file. (For brevity, there are no other files except for `AndroidManifest.xml`.)

Listing 1-4. UseGridLayout Presenting a Grid of Buttons

```java
public class UseGridLayout extends Activity {
    @Override
    public void onCreate(Bundle savedInstanceState) {
        super.onCreate(savedInstanceState);

        GridLayout gl = new GridLayout(this);
        gl.setRowCount(2);
        gl.setColumnCount(2);

        Button btn = new Button(this);
        btn.setText("1");
        gl.addView(btn);

        btn = new Button(this);
        btn.setText("2");
        gl.addView(btn);
```

```
        btn = new Button(this);
        btn.setText("3");
        gl.addView(btn);

        btn = new Button(this);
        btn.setText("4");
        gl.addView(btn);

        setContentView(gl);
    }
}
```

Also for brevity, Listing 1-4 hard-codes the layout and includes literal text. After instantiating GridLayout, it invokes this class's void setRowCount(int rowCount) and void setColumnCount(int columnCount) methods to establish the grid dimensions. Finally, it sets the activity's view hierarchy to the grid layout and its child view.

Creating and Running UseGridLayout with the Android SDK

Execute the following command (spread across two lines for readability) to create a UseGridLayout project:

```
android create project -t 2 -p <path/to/project/directory>
-a UseGridLayout -k com.androidrecipes.usegridlayout
```

This command assumes an Android 2.3.3 target identified as ID 2. It is also assumed that you have created an AVD2 device with Android 2.3.3 as the target platform.

Now replace the skeletal src/com/androidrecipes/usegridlayout/UseGridLayout.java source file with the contents of Listing 1-4.

Continue by executing the following command (spread across two lines for readability) to reference the GridLayout library project:

```
android update project -t 2 -p <path/to/project/directory>
-l <path/to/android-sdk>/extras/android/support/v7/gridlayout
```

At this point, execute the following command to build this project in debug mode:

```
ant debug
```

The output should reveal the following error message:

```
Invalid file: <androidsdk>/extras/android/support/v7/gridlayout/build.xml
```

The error message results from the absence of a build.xml file in the directory of the Support Library's project.

To create this file, switch to this directory and execute the following command:

```
android update lib-project -t 2 -p.
```

You could replace `lib-project` with `project` for this example. Assuming that `build.xml` is created, re-execute `ant debug`.

Assuming success, execute the following command from the project's `bin` subdirectory to install the `UseGridLayout-debug.apk` file onto AVD2, which should be running:

```
adb install UseGridLayout-debug.apk
```

Finally, launch the app. You should see the output shown in Figure 1-10.

Figure 1-10. The buttons appear small because the default values of `gridlayout`'s width and height properties are each set to WRAP_CONTENT

Creating and Running UseGridLayout with Eclipse

Complete the following steps to create the `UseGridLayout` project that references the `GridLayout` library project in Eclipse:

1. Assuming that you've installed the Eclipse version discussed earlier in this chapter, start this IDE if it is not already running.

2. Select Import from the File menu, followed by Existing Android Code Into Workspace in the resulting Import dialog box. Click Next.

3. In the resulting dialog box, click the Browse button and locate your Android SDK directory, then `extras/android/support/v7/gridlayout`. Exit these dialog boxes by clicking OK, followed by Finish.

4. From the File menu, choose New ➤ Project.

5. In the resulting New Project dialog box, expand the `Android` node in the wizard tree (if not expanded), select the `Android Application Project` branch below this node (if not selected), and click the Next button.

6. In the resulting New Android App dialog box, enter **UseGridLayout** into the Application Name text field. This entered name also appears in the Project Name text field, and it identifies the folder/directory in which the `UseGridLayout` project is stored.

7. Enter **com.androidrecipes.usegridlayout** into the Package Name text field.

8. Via Build SDK, select the appropriate Android SDK to target. This selection identifies the Android platform you'd like your app to be built against. Assuming that you've installed Android 2.3.3, select this platform.

9. Via Minimum SDK, select the minimum Android SDK on which your app runs, or keep the default setting. (Do not select an SDK whose API level is less than Level 10.)

10. Leave the Create Custom Launcher Icon check box checked if you want a custom launcher icon to be created. Otherwise, uncheck this check box when you supply your own launcher icon.

11. Leave the Mark This Project as a Library check box unchecked because you are not creating a library.

12. Leave the Create Project in Workspace check box checked, and click Next.

13. In the resulting Configure Launcher Icon pane, make suitable adjustments to the custom launcher icon; click Next.

14. In the resulting Create Activity pane, leave the Create Activity check box checked, make sure that BlankActivity is selected, and click Next.

15. In the resulting New Blank Activity pane, enter **UseGridLayout** into the Activity Name text field. Keep all other settings and click Finish.

Eclipse creates a UseGridLayout node in the Package Explorer window. Complete the following steps to set up all files:

16. Expand the UseGridLayout node (if not expanded), followed by the src node, followed by the com.androidrecipes.usegridlayout node.

17. Double-click the UseGridLayout.java node (underneath com.androidrecipes. usegridlayout) and replace the skeletal contents in the resulting window with Listing 1-4. Ignore any error messages; they will disappear shortly.

18. Right-click the UseGridLayout node and select Properties from the resulting pop-up menu.

19. In the resulting Properties for UseGridLayout dialog box, select the Android category and click the Add button.

20. In the resulting Project Selection dialog box, select gridlayout and click OK.

21. Click Apply, and then OK to close Properties for UseGridLayout.

To build and run this project, select Run from the menu bar, followed by Run from the drop-down menu. (Click OK if the Save Resources dialog box appears.) If a Run As dialog box appears, select Android Application and click OK. Eclipse starts the emulator, installs this project's APK, and runs the app, whose output appears in Figure 1-11.

Figure 1-11. `UseGridLayout`'s *user interface looks different because of an Eclipse-generated custom theme*

Summary

Android has excited many people who are developing (and even selling) apps for this platform. It's not too late to join in the fun, and this chapter got you started.

You first learned that Android is a software stack for mobile devices and that this stack consists of apps, middleware, and the Linux operating system. You also learned about Android's history, including the various SDK updates that have been made available.

You then focused on installing the Android SDK and an Android platform, creating an AVD, and starting the emulator with this AVD.

Finally, you learned how to create and use external libraries in an Android application. Specifically, you were exposed to the Android Support Library and Google Play Services, both of which you will use throughout this book in a number of recipes.

In Chapter 2, you will learn how to begin crafting your application's user interface by looking at how Android handles views, graphics, and drawing.

Views, Graphics, and Drawing

The Android platform is designed to operate on a variety of device types, screen sizes, and screen resolutions. To assist developers in meeting this challenge, Android provides a rich toolkit of user interface (UI) components to utilize and customize to the needs of their specific applications. Android also relies very heavily on an extensible XML framework and set resource qualifiers to create liquid layouts that can adapt to these environmental changes. In this chapter, we take a look at some practical ways to shape this framework to fit your specific development needs.

2-1. Customizing the Window

Problem

You want to create a consistent look and feel for your application across all the versions of Android your users may be running. Your application may also need to toggle the system elements to obtain more screen real estate.

Solution

(API Level 1)

Customize the window attributes and features by using themes and the WindowManager. Without any customization, an activity in an Android application will load with the default system theme. Depending on the version of Android you have targeted, this may be the standard flat-black theme common in Android 2.x, the Holo theme prominent in Android 3.x and 4.x, or a manufacturer-defined skin that has replaced the Android device's default theme. In order to guarantee that your application looks the way you want across all devices, you need to declare use of a system or custom theme.

How It Works

Customizing Window Attributes with a Theme

A *theme* in Android is a type of appearance style that is applicable to an entire application or activity. There are two choices when applying a theme: use a system theme or create a custom one. In either case, a theme is applied in the AndroidManifest.xml file, as shown in Listing 2-1.

Listing 2-1. AndroidManifest.xml

```
<?xml version="1.0" encoding="utf-8"?>
<manifest xmlns:android="http://schemas.android.com/apk/res/android"
    ...>
    <!--Apply to the application tag for a global theme -->
    <application android:theme="THEME_NAME"
        ...>
        <!--Apply to the activity tag for an individual theme -->
        <activity android:name=".Activity"
            android:theme="THEME_NAME"
            ...>
            <intent-filter>
                ...
            </intent-filter>
        </activity>
    </application>
</manifest>
```

System Themes

The styles.xml and themes.xml files packaged with the Android framework include a few options for themes with some useful custom properties. Referencing R.style in the SDK documentation will provide the full list, but here are a few useful examples:

- Theme.Light: Variation on the standard theme that uses an inverse color scheme for the background and user elements. This is the default recommended base theme for applications prior to Android 3.0.

- Theme.NoTitleBar.Fullscreen: Removes the title bar and status bar, filling the entire screen (minus any onscreen controls that may be present).

- Theme.Dialog: A useful theme to make an activity look like a dialog.

- Theme.Holo.Light: (API Level 11) Theme that uses an inverse color scheme and that has an Action Bar by default. This is the default recommended base theme for applications on Android 3.0.

- Theme.Holo.Light.DarkActionBar: (API Level 14) Theme with an inverse color scheme but a dark solid Action Bar. This is the default recommended base theme for applications on Android 4.0.

Listing 2-2 is an example of a system theme applied to the entire application by setting the android:theme attribute in the AndroidManifest.xml file.

Listing 2-2. Manifest with Theme Set on Application

```xml
<?xml version="1.0" encoding="utf-8"?>
<manifest xmlns:android="http://schemas.android.com/apk/res/android"
    ...>
    <!--Apply to the application tag for a global theme -->
    <application android:theme="Theme.NoTitleBar"
        ...>
        ...
    </application>
</manifest>
```

Custom Themes

Sometimes the provided system choices aren't enough. After all, some of the customizable elements in the window are not even addressed in the system options. Defining a custom theme to do the job is simple.

If there is not one already, create a `styles.xml` file in the `res/values` path of the project. Remember, themes are just styles applied on a wider scale, so they are defined in the same place. Theme aspects related to window customization can be found in the `R.attr` reference of the SDK, but here are the most common items:

- `android:windowNoTitle`: Governs whether to remove the default title bar; set to `true` to remove the title bar.

- `android:windowFullscreen`: Governs whether to remove the system status bar; set to `true` to remove the status bar and fill the entire screen.

- `android:windowBackground`: Color or `Drawable` resource to apply as a background.

- `android:windowContentOverlay`: `Drawable` placed over the window content foreground. By default, this is a shadow below the status bar. Set to any resource to use in place of the default status bar shadow, or `null` (@null in XML) to remove it.

- `android:windowTitleBackgroundStyle`: Style to apply to the window's title view; set to any style resource.

- `android:windowTitleSize`: Height of the window's title view; set to any dimension or dimension resource.

- `android:windowTitleStyle`: Style to apply to the window's title text; set to any style resource.

- `android:actionBarStyle` attribute: Style to apply to the window's action bar; set to any style resource.

Listing 2-3 is an example of a `styles.xml` file that creates two custom themes:

- `MyTheme.One`: No title bar and the default status bar shadow removed.

- `MyTheme.Two`: Full-screen with a custom background image.

Listing 2-3. res/values/styles.xml with Two Custom Themes

```xml
<?xml version="1.0" encoding="utf-8"?>
<resources>
    <style name="MyTheme.One" parent="@android:style/Theme">
        <item name="android:windowNoTitle">true</item>
        <item name="android:windowContentOverlay">@null</item>
    </style>
    <style name="MyTheme.Two" parent="@android:style/Theme">
        <item name="android:windowBackground">
            @drawable/window_bg</item>
        <item name="android:windowFullscreen">true</item>
    </style>
</resources>
```

Notice that a theme (or style) may also indicate a parent from which to inherit properties, so the entire theme need not be created from scratch. In the example, we chose to inherit from Android's default system theme, customizing only the properties that we needed to differentiate. All platform themes are defined in res/values/themes.xml of the Android package. Refer to the SDK documentation on styles and themes for more details.

Listing 2-4 shows how to apply these themes to individual activity instances in the AndroidManifest.xml.

Listing 2-4. Manifest with Themes Set on Each Activity

```xml
<?xml version="1.0" encoding="utf-8"?>
<manifest xmlns:android="http://schemas.android.com/apk/res/android"
    ...>
    <!--Apply to the application tag for a global theme -->
    <application
        ...>
        <!--Apply to the activity tag for an individual theme -->
        <activity android:name=".ActivityOne"
            android:theme="MyTheme.One"
            ...>
            <intent-filter>
                ...
            </intent-filter>
        </activity>
        <activity android:name=".ActivityTwo"
            android:theme="MyTheme.Two"
            ...>
            <intent-filter>
                ...
            </intent-filter>
        </activity>

    </application>
</manifest>
```

Customizing Window Features in Code

In addition to using XML styles, window properties may also be customized from the Java code in an activity. This method opens up a slightly different feature set to the developer for customization, although there is some overlap with the XML styling.

Customizing the window through coding involves making requests of the system using the `Activity.requestWindowFeature()` method for each feature change prior to setting the content view for the activity.

> **Note**   All requests for extended window features with `Activity.requestWindowFeature()` must be made *prior* to calling `Activity.setContentView()`. Any changes made after this point will not take place.

The features you can request from the window, and their meanings, are defined in the following:

- `FEATURE_CUSTOM_TITLE`: Sets a custom layout resource as the activity title view
- `FEATURE_NO_TITLE`: Removes the title view from the activity
- `FEATURE_PROGRESS`: Utilizes a determinate (0–100 percent) progress bar in the title
- `FEATURE_INDETERMINATE_PROGRESS`: Utilizes a small indeterminate (circular) progress indicator in the title view
- `FEATURE_LEFT_ICON`: Includes a small title icon on the left side of the title view
- `FEATURE_RIGHT_ICON`: Includes a small title icon on the right side of the title view

FEATURE_CUSTOM_TITLE

Use this window feature to replace the standard title with a completely custom layout resource (see Listing 2-5).

Listing 2-5. Activity Setting a Custom TitleLayout

```
protected void onCreate(Bundle savedInstanceState) {
    super.onCreate(savedInstanceState);
    //Request window features before setContentView
    requestWindowFeature(Window.FEATURE_CUSTOM_TITLE);
    setContentView(R.layout.main);

    //Set the layout resource to use for the custom title
    getWindow().setFeatureInt(Window.FEATURE_CUSTOM_TITLE,
            R.layout.custom_title);

}
```

> **Note**   Because this feature completely replaces the default title view, it cannot be combined with any of the other window feature flags.

FEATURE_NO_TITLE

Use this window feature to remove the standard title view (see Listing 2-6).

Listing 2-6. Activity Removing the Standard Title View

```
protected void onCreate(Bundle savedInstanceState) {
    super.onCreate(savedInstanceState);
    //Request window features before setContentView
    requestWindowFeature(Window.FEATURE_NO_TITLE);
    setContentView(R.layout.main);

}
```

> **Note**   Because this feature completely removes the default title view, it cannot be combined with any of the other window feature flags.

FEATURE_PROGRESS

Use this window feature to access a determinate progress bar in the window title. This is an indicator that shows finite progress. The progress can be set to any value from 0 (0 percent) to 10000 (100 percent). See Listing 2-7.

Listing 2-7. Activity Using Window's Progress Bar

```
protected void onCreate(Bundle savedInstanceState) {
    super.onCreate(savedInstanceState);
    //Request window features before setContentView
    requestWindowFeature(Window.FEATURE_PROGRESS);
    setContentView(R.layout.main);

    //Set the progress bar visibility
    setProgressBarVisibility(true);
    //Control progress value with setProgress
    setProgress(0);
    //Setting progress to 100% will cause it to disappear
    setProgress(10000);

}
```

FEATURE_INDETERMINATE_PROGRESS

Use this window feature to access an indeterminate progress indicator, also known as a *spinning progress indicator*, to show background activity. Because this indicator is indeterminate, it can only be shown or hidden (see Listing 2-8).

Listing 2-8. Activity Using Window's Indeterminate Progress Bar

```java
protected void onCreate(Bundle savedInstanceState) {
    super.onCreate(savedInstanceState);
    //Request window features before setContentView
    requestWindowFeature(Window.FEATURE_INDETERMINATE_PROGRESS);
    setContentView(R.layout.main);

    //Show the progress indicator
    setProgressBarIndeterminateVisibility(true);

    //Hide the progress indicator
    setProgressBarIndeterminateVisibility(false);
}
```

FEATURE ICONS

(API Level 8)

Use this window feature to place a small drawable icon on the left or right side of the title view (see Listing 2-9).

Listing 2-9. Activity Using Feature Icons

```java
protected void onCreate(Bundle savedInstanceState) {
    super.onCreate(savedInstanceState);
    //Request window features before setContentView
    requestWindowFeature(Window.FEATURE_LEFT_ICON);
    requestWindowFeature(Window.FEATURE_RIGHT_ICON);

    setContentView(R.layout.main);

    //Set the layout resource to use for the custom icons
    setFeatureDrawableResource(Window.FEATURE_LEFT_ICON,
            R.drawable.icon);
    setFeatureDrawableResource(Window.FEATURE_RIGHT_ICON,
            R.drawable.icon);

}
```

Note   These features were available prior to API Level 8, but a bug kept FEATURE_RIGHT_ICON from being placed on the right side of the title text.

FEATURE_ACTION_BAR

(API Level 11)

This window feature is enabled by default if your application is targeting an SDK version of 11 or higher as part of the default style. However, it can also be requested in code if you are using an older style theme but want to enable the Action Bar in certain specific cases. See Listing 2-10.

Listing 2-10. Activity Using ActionBar Overlay

```java
protected void onCreate(Bundle savedInstanceState) {
    super.onCreate(savedInstanceState);
    //Request window features before setContentView
    requestWindowFeature(Window.FEATURE_ACTION_BAR);
    setContentView(R.layout.main);

    //Access the ActionBar to modify it
    ActionBar actionBar = getActionBar();
}
```

FEATURE_ACTION_BAR_OVERLAY

(API Level 11)

Use this window feature to request that the Action Bar element be laid out over the top of your view content, rather than above it. This can be advantageous in applications where you want to temporarily hide and show the Action Bar and when you don't want the overall layout to change each time you do so (more on this in the next section). See Listing 2-11.

Listing 2-11. Activity Using ActionBar Overlay

```java
protected void onCreate(Bundle savedInstanceState) {
    super.onCreate(savedInstanceState);
    //Request window features before setContentView
    requestWindowFeature(Window.FEATURE_ACTION_BAR_OVERLAY);
    setContentView(R.layout.main);
}
```

Figure 2-1 shows an activity with all the icon and progress features enabled simultaneously and another with the Action Bar feature enabled.

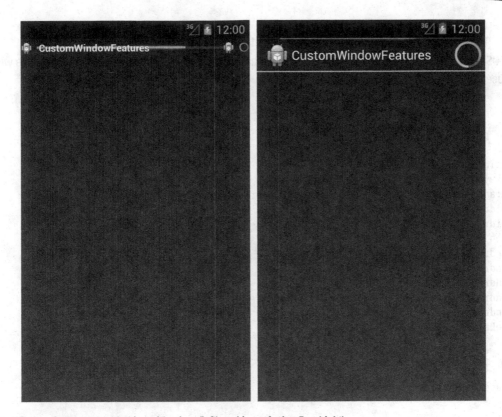

Figure 2-1. Window features enabled in a title view (left) and in an Action Bar (right)

Dynamically Toggling System UI Components

Many applications that target a more immersive content experience (such as readers or video players) can benefit from temporarily hiding the system's UI components to provide as much screen real estate as possible to the application when the content is visible. Beginning with Android 3.0, developers are able to adjust many of these properties at runtime without the need to statically request a window feature or declare values inside a theme.

Dark Mode

(API Level 11)

Dark mode is also often called *lights-out mode*. It refers to dimming the onscreen navigation controls (and the system status bar in later releases) without actually removing them to relieve any system elements onscreen that might distract the user from the current view in the application.

To enable this mode, we simply have to call setSystemUiVisibility() on any View in our hierarchy with the SYSTEM_UI_FLAG_LOW_PROFILE flag. To set the mode back to default, call the same method with SYSTEM_UI_FLAG_VISIBLE instead. We can determine which mode we are in by calling getSystemUiVisibility() and checking the current status of the flags (see Listings 2-12 and 2-13).

> **Note**   These flag names were introduced in API Level 14 (Android 4.0); prior to that they were named
> STATUS_BAR_HIDDEN and STATUS_BAR_VISIBLE. The values of each are the same, so the new flags will
> produce the same behavior on Android 3.x devices.

Listing 2-12. res/layout/main.xml

```xml
<?xml version="1.0" encoding="utf-8"?>
<RelativeLayout
    xmlns:android="http://schemas.android.com/apk/res/android"
    android:layout_width="match_parent"
    android:layout_height="match_parent" >
    <Button
        android:layout_width="match_parent"
        android:layout_height="wrap_content"
        android:layout_centerVertical="true"
        android:text="Toggle Mode"
        android:onClick="onToggleClick" />
</RelativeLayout>
```

Listing 2-13. Activity Toggling Dark Mode

```java
public class DarkActivity extends Activity {

    @Override
    protected void onCreate(Bundle savedInstanceState) {
        super.onCreate(savedInstanceState);
        setContentView(R.layout.main);
    }

    public void onToggleClick(View v) {
        int currentVis = v.getSystemUiVisibility();
        int newVis;
        if ((currentVis & View.SYSTEM_UI_FLAG_LOW_PROFILE)
                == View.SYSTEM_UI_FLAG_LOW_PROFILE) {
            newVis = View.SYSTEM_UI_FLAG_VISIBLE;
        } else {
            newVis = View.SYSTEM_UI_FLAG_LOW_PROFILE;
        }
        v.setSystemUiVisibility(newVis);
    }
}
```

The methods setSystemUiVisibility() and getSystemUiVisibility() can be called on any view
currently visible inside the window where you want to adjust these parameters.

Hiding Navigation Controls

(API Level 14)

SYSTEM_UI_FLAG_HIDE_NAVIGATION removes the onscreen HOME and BACK controls for devices that do not have physical buttons. While Android gives developers the ability to do this, it is with caution because these functions are extremely important to the user. If the navigation controls are manually hidden, any tap on the screen will bring them back. Listing 2-14 shows an example of this in practice.

Listing 2-14. Activity Toggling Navigation Controls

```
public class HideActivity extends Activity {

    @Override
    protected void onCreate(Bundle savedInstanceState) {
        super.onCreate(savedInstanceState);
        setContentView(R.layout.main);

    }

    public void onToggleClick(View v) {
        //Here we only need to hide the controls on a tap because
        // Android will make the controls reappear automatically
        // anytime the screen is tapped after they are hidden.
        v.setSystemUiVisibility(
                View.SYSTEM_UI_FLAG_HIDE_NAVIGATION);
    }
}
```

Notice also when running this example that the button will shift up and down to accommodate the changes in content space because of our centering requirement in the root layout. If you plan to use this flag, make note of the fact that any views being laid out relative to the bottom of the screen will move as the layout changes.

Full-Screen UI Mode

(API Level 11)

Prior to Android 4.1, there is no method of hiding the system status bar dynamically; it has to be done with a static theme. To hide and show the Action Bar, however, ActionBar.show() and ActionBar.hide() will animate the element in and out of view. If FEATURE_ACTION_BAR_OVERLAY is requested, this change will not affect the content of the activity; otherwise, the view content will shift up and down to accommodate the change.

(API Level 16)

Listing 2-15 illustrates an example of how to hide all system UI temporarily.

Listing 2-15. Activity Toggling All System UI

```java
public class FullActivity extends Activity {

    @Override
    protected void onCreate(Bundle savedInstanceState) {
        super.onCreate(savedInstanceState);
        //Request this feature so the ActionBar will hide
        requestWindowFeature(Window.FEATURE_ACTION_BAR_OVERLAY);
        setContentView(R.layout.main);
    }

    public void onToggleClick(View v) {
        //Here we only need to hide the UI on a tap because
        // Android will make the controls reappear automatically
        // anytime the screen is tapped after they are hidden.
        v.setSystemUiVisibility(
                /* This flag tells Android not to shift
                 * our layout when resizing the window to
                 * hide/show the system elements
                 */
                View.SYSTEM_UI_FLAG_LAYOUT_STABLE
                /* This flag hides the system status bar.  If
                 * ACTION_BAR_OVERLAY is requested, it will hide
                 * the ActionBar as well.
                 */
                | View.SYSTEM_UI_FLAG_FULLSCREEN
                /* This flag hides the onscreen controls
                 */
                | View.SYSTEM_UI_FLAG_HIDE_NAVIGATION);
    }
}
```

Similar to the example of hiding only the navigation controls, we do not need to show the controls again because any tap on the screen will bring them back. As a convenience beginning in Android 4.1, when the system clears the SYSTEM_UI_FLAG_HIDE_NAVIGATION in this way, it will also clear the SYSTEM_UI_FLAG_FULLSCREEN, so the top and bottom elements will become visible together. Android will hide the Action Bar as part of the full-screen flag only if we request FEATURE_ACTION_BAR_OVERLAY; otherwise, only the status bar will be affected.

We have added one other flag of interest in this example: SYSTEM_UI_LAYOUT_STABLE. This flag tells Android not to shift our content view as a result of adding and removing the system UI. Because of this, our button will stay centered as the elements toggle.

2-2. Creating and Displaying Views
Problem
Your application needs view elements in order to display information and interact with the user.

Solution

(API Level 1)

Whether using one of the many views and widgets available in the Android SDK or creating a custom display, all applications need views to interact with the user. The preferred method for creating user interfaces in Android is to define them in XML and inflate them at runtime.

The view structure in Android is a tree, with the root typically being the activity or window's content view. ViewGroups are special views that manage the display of one or more child views, which could be another ViewGroup, and the tree continues to grow. All the standard layout classes descend from ViewGroup, and they are the most common choices for the root node of the XML layout file.

How It Works

Let's define a layout with two Button instances and an EditText to accept user input. We can define a file in res/layout/ called main.xml with the following contents (see Listing 2-16).

Listing 2-16. res/layout/main.xml

```xml
<LinearLayout
    xmlns:android="http://schemas.android.com/apk/res/android"
    android:layout_width="fill_parent"
    android:layout_height="fill_parent"
    android:orientation="vertical">
    <EditText
        android:id="@+id/editText"
        android:layout_width="fill_parent"
        android:layout_height="wrap_content"
    />
    <LinearLayout
        android:layout_width="fill_parent"
        android:layout_height="wrap_content"
        android:orientation="horizontal">
        <Button
            android:id="@+id/save"
            android:layout_width="wrap_content"
            android:layout_height="wrap_content"
            android:text="Save"
        />
        <Button
            android:id="@+id/cancel"
            android:layout_width="wrap_content"
            android:layout_height="wrap_content"
            android:text="Cancel"
        />
    </LinearLayout>
</LinearLayout>
```

LinearLayout is a ViewGroup that lays out its elements one after the other in either a horizontal or vertical fashion. In main.xml, the EditText and inner LinearLayout are laid out vertically in order. The contents of the inner LinearLayout (the buttons) are laid out horizontally. The view elements with an android:id value are elements that will need to be referenced in the Java code for further customization or display.

To make this layout the display contents of an activity, it must be inflated at runtime. The Activity. setContentView() method is overloaded with a convenience method to do this for you, requiring only the layout ID value. In this case, setting the layout in the activity is as simple as this:

```
public void onCreate(Bundle savedInstanceState) {
    super.onCreate(savedInstanceState);
    setContentView(R.layout.main);
    //Continue Activity initialization
}
```

Nothing beyond supplying the ID value (main.xml automatically has an ID of R.layout.main) is required. If the layout needs a little more customization before it is attached to the window, you can inflate it manually and do some work before adding it as the content view. Listing 2-17 inflates the same layout and adds a third button before displaying it.

Listing 2-17. Layout Modification Prior to Display

```
public void onCreate(Bundle savedInstanceState) {
    super.onCreate(savedInstanceState);
    //Inflate the layout file
    LinearLayout layout = (LinearLayout)getLayoutInflater()
            .inflate(R.layout.main, null);
    //Add a new button
    Button reset = new Button(this);
    reset.setText("Reset Form");
    layout.addView(reset,
        new LinearLayout.LayoutParams(LayoutParams.FILL_PARENT,
                LayoutParams.WRAP_CONTENT));

    //Attach the view to the window
    setContentView(layout);
}
```

In this instance, the XML layout is inflated in the activity code with a LayoutInflater, whose inflate() method returns a handle to the inflated View. Since LayoutInflater.inflate() returns a View, we must cast it to the specific subclass in the XML in order to do more than just attach it to the window.

> **Note** The root element in the XML layout file is the View element returned from
> LayoutInflater.inflate().

The second parameter to inflate() is the parent ViewGroup, and this is extremely important because it defines how the LayoutParams from the inflated layout are interpreted. Whenever possible, if you know the parent of this inflated hierarchy, it should be passed here; otherwise, the LayoutParams from the root view of the XML will be ignored. When passing a parent, also note that the third parameter of inflate() controls whether the inflated layout is automatically attached to the parent. We will see in future recipes how this can be useful for doing custom views. In this instance, however, we are inflating the top-level view of our activity, so we pass null here.

Completely Custom Views

Sometimes, the widgets available in the SDK just aren't enough to provide the output you need. Or perhaps you want to reduce the number of views you have in your hierarchy by combining multiple display elements into a single view to improve performance. For these cases, you may want to create your own View subclass. In doing so, there are two main interaction points between your class and the framework that need to be observed: measurement and drawing.

Measurement

The first requirement that a custom view must fulfill is to provide a measurement for its content to the framework. Before a view hierarchy is displayed, Android calls onMeasure() for each element (both layouts and view nodes), and passes it two constraints the view should use to govern how it reports the size that it should be. Each constraint is a packed integer known as a MeasureSpec, which includes a mode flag and a size value. The mode will be one of the following values:

- AT_MOST: This mode is typically used when the layout parameters of the view are match_parent, or there is some other upper limit on the size. This tells the view it should report any size it wants, as long as it doesn't exceed the value in the spec.

- EXACTLY: This mode is typically used when the layout parameters of the view are a fixed value. The framework expects the view to set its size to match the spec—no more, no less.

- UNSPECIFIED: This value is often used to figure out how big the view wants to be if unconstrained. This may be a precursor to another measurement with different constraints, or it may simply be because the layout parameters were set to wrap_content and no other constraints exist in the parent. The view may report its size to be whatever it wants in this case. The size in this spec is often zero.

Once you have done your calculations on what size to report, those values *must* be passed in a call to setMeasuredDimension() before onMeasure() returns. If you do not do this, the framework will be quite upset with you.

Measurement is also an opportunity to configure your view's output based on the space available. The measurement constraints essentially tell you how much space has been allocated inside the layout, so if you want to create a view that orients its content differently when it has, say, more or less vertical space, onMeasure() will give you what you need to make that decision.

> **Note**   During measurement, your view doesn't *actually* have a size yet; it has only a measured dimension. If you want to do some custom work in your view after the size has been assigned, override onSizeChanged() and put your code there.

Drawing

The second, and arguably most important, step for your custom view is drawing content. Once a view has been measured and placed inside the layout hierarchy, the framework will construct a Canvas instance, sized and placed appropriately for your view, and pass it via onDraw() for your view to use. The Canvas is an object that hosts individual drawing calls so it includes methods such as drawLine(), drawBitmap(), and drawText() for you to lay out the view content discretely. Canvas (as the name implies) uses a painter's algorithm, so items drawn last will go on top of items drawn first.

Drawing is clipped to the bounds of the view provided via measurement and layout, so while the Canvas element can be translated, scaled, rotated, and so on, you cannot draw content outside the rectangle where your view has been placed.

Finally, the content supplied in onDraw() does not include the view's background, which can be set with methods such as setBackgroundColor() or setBackgroundResource(). If a background is set on the view, it will be drawn for you, and you do not need to handle that inside onDraw().

Listing 2-18 shows a very simple custom view template that your application can follow. For content, we are drawing a series of concentric circles to represent a bull's-eye target.

Listing 2-18. Custom View Example

```java
public class BullsEyeView extends View {

    private Paint mPaint;

    private Point mCenter;
    private float mRadius;

    /*
     * Java Constructor
     */
    public BullsEyeView(Context context) {
        this(context, null);
    }

    /*
     * XML Constructor
     */
    public BullsEyeView(Context context, AttributeSet attrs) {
        this(context, attrs, 0);
    }
```

```java
/*
 * XML Constructor with Style
 */
public BullsEyeView(Context context, AttributeSet attrs,
        int defStyle) {
    super(context, attrs, defStyle);
    //Do any initialization of your view in this constructor

    //Create a paintbrush to draw with
    mPaint = new Paint(Paint.ANTI_ALIAS_FLAG);
    //We want to draw our circles filled in
    mPaint.setStyle(Style.FILL);
    //Create the center point for our circle
    mCenter = new Point();
}


@Override
protected void onMeasure(int widthMeasureSpec,
        int heightMeasureSpec) {
    int width, height;
    //Determine the ideal size of your content, unconstrained
    int contentWidth = 200;
    int contentHeight = 200;

    width = getMeasurement(widthMeasureSpec, contentWidth);
    height = getMeasurement(heightMeasureSpec, contentHeight);
    //MUST call this method with the measured values!
    setMeasuredDimension(width, height);
}


/*
 * Helper method to measure width and height
 */
private int getMeasurement(int measureSpec, int contentSize) {
    int specSize = MeasureSpec.getSize(measureSpec);
    switch (MeasureSpec.getMode(measureSpec)) {
        case MeasureSpec.AT_MOST:
            return Math.min(specSize, contentSize);
        case MeasureSpec.UNSPECIFIED:
            return contentSize;
        case MeasureSpec.EXACTLY:
            return specSize;
        default:
            return 0;
    }
}
```

```java
    @Override
    protected void onSizeChanged(int w, int h,
            int oldw, int oldh) {
        if (w != oldw || h != oldh) {
            //If there was a change, reset the parameters
            mCenter.x = w / 2;
            mCenter.y = h / 2;
            mRadius = Math.min(mCenter.x, mCenter.y);
        }
    }

    @Override
    protected void onDraw(Canvas canvas) {
        //Draw a series of concentric circles,
        // smallest to largest, alternating colors
        mPaint.setColor(Color.RED);
        canvas.drawCircle(mCenter.x, mCenter.y, mRadius, mPaint);

        mPaint.setColor(Color.WHITE);
        canvas.drawCircle(mCenter.x, mCenter.y, mRadius * 0.8f,
            mPaint);

        mPaint.setColor(Color.BLUE);
        canvas.drawCircle(mCenter.x, mCenter.y, mRadius * 0.6f,
            mPaint);

        mPaint.setColor(Color.WHITE);
        canvas.drawCircle(mCenter.x, mCenter.y, mRadius * 0.4f,
            mPaint);

        mPaint.setColor(Color.RED);
        canvas.drawCircle(mCenter.x, mCenter.y, mRadius * 0.2f,
            mPaint);
    }
}
```

The first thing you may notice is that View has three constructors:

- View(Context context): This version is used when a view is constructed from within Java code.

- View(Context, AttributeSet): This version is used when a view is inflated from XML. AttributeSet includes all the attributes attached to the XML element for the view.

- View(Context, AttributeSet, int): This version is similar to the previous one, but is called when a style attribute is added to the XML element.

It is a common pattern to chain all three together and implement customizations in only the final constructor, which is what we have done in the example view.

From onMeasure(), we use a simple utility method to return the correct dimension based on the measurement constraints. We basically have a choice between the size we want our content to be (which is arbitrarily selected here, but should represent your view content in a real application) and the size given to us. In the case of AT_MOST, we pick the value that is the lesser of the two; thus saying the view will be the size necessary to fit our content as long as it doesn't exceed the spec. We use onSizeChanged(), called after measurement is finished, to gather some basic data we will need to draw our target circles. We wait until this point to ensure we use the values that exactly match how the view is laid out.

Inside onDraw() is where we construct the display. Five concentric circles are painted onto the Canvas with a steadily decreasing radius and alternating colors. The Paint element controls information about the style of the content being drawn, such as stroke width, text sizes, and colors. When we declared the Paint for this view, we set the style to FILL, which ensures that the circles are filled in with each color. Because of the painter's algorithm, the smaller circles are drawn on top of the larger, giving us the target look we were going for.

Adding this view to an XML layout is simple, but because the view doesn't reside in the android.view or android.widget packages, we need to name the element with the fully qualified package name of the class. So, for example, if our application package were com.androidrecipes.customwidgets, the XML would be as follows:

```
<com.androidrecipes.customwidgets.BullsEyeView
    android:layout_width="match_parent"
    android:layout_height="match_parent" />
```

Figure 2-2 shows the result of adding this view to an activity.

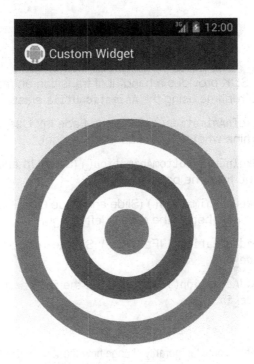

Figure 2-2. Bull's-eye custom view

2-3. Animating a View

Problem

Your application needs to animate a view object, either as a transition or for effect.

Solution

(API Level 1)

An `Animation` object can be applied to any view and can be run using the `View.startAnimation()` method; this will run the animation immediately. You may also use `View.setAnimation()` to schedule an animation and attach the object to a view but not run it immediately. In this case, the `Animation` must have its start time parameter set. Modifications made through this API will modify where the view is temporarily drawn onscreen, but not the view itself.

(API Level 12)

An `ObjectAnimator` instance, such as `ViewPropertyAnimator`, can be used to manipulate the properties of a `View`, such as its position or rotation. `ViewPropertyAnimator` is obtained through `View.animate()`, and then modified with the specifics of the animation. Modifications made through this API will alter the actual properties of the `View` itself.

How It Works

System Animations

For convenience, the Android SDK provides a handful of transition animations that you can apply to views, which can be loaded at runtime using the `AnimationUtils` class:

- `AnimationUtils.makeInAnimation()` (Slide and Fade In): Use the boolean parameter to determine whether the slide is left or right.

- `AnimationUtils.makeInChildBottomAnimation()` (Slide Up and Fade In): The view always slides up from the bottom.

- `AnimationUtils.makeOutAnimation()` (Slide and Fade Out): Use the boolean parameter to determine whether the slide is left or right.

- `AnimationUtils.loadAnimation()` (Fade Out): Set the `int` parameter to `android.R.anim.fade_out`.

- `AnimationUtils.loadAnimation()` (Fade In): Set the `int` parameter to `android.R.anim.fade_in`.

> **Note**   These transition animations only temporarily change how the view is drawn. The visibility parameter of the view must also be set if you mean to permanently add or remove the object.

Listing 2-19 animates the appearance and disappearance of a view with each button click event.

Listing 2-19. res/layout/main.xml

```xml
<?xml version="1.0" encoding="utf-8"?>
<LinearLayout
    xmlns:android="http://schemas.android.com/apk/res/android"
    android:orientation="vertical"
    android:layout_width="fill_parent"
    android:layout_height="fill_parent">
    <Button
        android:id="@+id/toggleButton"
        android:layout_width="fill_parent"
        android:layout_height="wrap_content"
        android:text="Click to Toggle"
    />
    <View
        android:id="@+id/theView"
        android:layout_width="fill_parent"
        android:layout_height="wrap_content"
        android:background="#AAA"
    />
</LinearLayout>
```

In Listing 2-20, each user action on the button toggles the visibility of the gray view below it with an animation.

Listing 2-20. Activity Animating View Transitions

```java
public class AnimateActivity extends Activity
        implements View.OnClickListener {

    View viewToAnimate;

    @Override
    public void onCreate(Bundle savedInstanceState) {
        super.onCreate(savedInstanceState);
        setContentView(R.layout.main);

        Button button = (Button)findViewById(R.id.toggleButton);
        button.setOnClickListener(this);

        viewToAnimate = findViewById(R.id.theView);
    }

    @Override
    public void onClick(View v) {
        if(viewToAnimate.getVisibility() == View.VISIBLE) {
            //If the view is visible, slide it out to the right
            Animation out =
                    AnimationUtils.makeOutAnimation(this, true);
```

```
                viewToAnimate.startAnimation(out);
                viewToAnimate.setVisibility(View.INVISIBLE);
        } else {
            //If the view is hidden, do a fade_in in-place
            Animation in = AnimationUtils.loadAnimation(this,
                    android.R.anim.fade_in);
            viewToAnimate.startAnimation(in);
            viewToAnimate.setVisibility(View.VISIBLE);
        }
    }
}
```

We hide the view by sliding it off to the right and fading it out simultaneously, whereas the view simply fades into place when it is shown. We chose a simple View as the target here to demonstrate that any UI element (since they are all subclasses of View) can animate in this way.

Custom Animations

Creating custom animations to add an effect to views by scaling, rotation, and transforming them can provide invaluable additions to a UI as well. In Android, we can create the following animation elements:

- AlphaAnimation: Animates changes to a view's transparency.

- RotateAnimation: Animates changes to a view's rotation. The point about which rotation occurs is configurable. The top-left corner is chosen by default.

- ScaleAnimation: Animates changes to a view's scale (size). The center point of the scale change is configurable. The top-left corner is chosen by default.

- TranslateAnimation: Animates changes to a view's position.

Let's illustrate how to construct and add a custom animation object by creating a sample application that creates a coin-flip effect on an image (see Listings 2-21 and 2-22).

Listing 2-21. res/layout/main.xml

```
<?xml version="1.0" encoding="utf-8"?>
<RelativeLayout
    xmlns:android="http://schemas.android.com/apk/res/android"
    android:layout_width="fill_parent"
    android:layout_height="fill_parent">
    <ImageView
        android:id="@+id/flip_image"
        android:layout_width="wrap_content"
        android:layout_height="wrap_content"
        android:layout_centerInParent="true"
    />
</RelativeLayout>
```

Listing 2-22. Activity with Custom Animations

```java
public class Flipper extends Activity {

    boolean isHeads;
    ScaleAnimation shrink, grow;
    ImageView flipImage;

    @Override
    public void onCreate(Bundle savedInstanceState) {
        super.onCreate(savedInstanceState);
        setContentView(R.layout.main);

        flipImage = (ImageView)findViewById(R.id.flip_image);
        flipImage.setImageResource(R.drawable.heads);
        isHeads = true;

        shrink = new ScaleAnimation(1.0f, 0.0f, 1.0f, 1.0f,
                        ScaleAnimation.RELATIVE_TO_SELF, 0.5f,
                        ScaleAnimation.RELATIVE_TO_SELF, 0.5f);
        shrink.setDuration(150);
        shrink.setAnimationListener(
        new Animation.AnimationListener() {
            @Override
            public void onAnimationStart(Animation animation) {}

            @Override
            public void onAnimationRepeat(Animation animation) {}

            @Override
            public void onAnimationEnd(Animation animation) {
                if(isHeads) {
                    isHeads = false;
                    flipImage.setImageResource(R.drawable.tails);
                } else {
                    isHeads = true;
                    flipImage.setImageResource(R.drawable.heads);
                }
                flipImage.startAnimation(grow);
            }
        });
        grow = new ScaleAnimation(0.0f, 1.0f, 1.0f, 1.0f,
                    ScaleAnimation.RELATIVE_TO_SELF, 0.5f,
                    ScaleAnimation.RELATIVE_TO_SELF, 0.5f);
        grow.setDuration(150);
    }
```

```
    @Override
    public boolean onTouchEvent(MotionEvent event) {
        if(event.getAction() == MotionEvent.ACTION_DOWN) {
            flipImage.startAnimation(shrink);
            return true;
        }
        return super.onTouchEvent(event);
    }
}
```

This example includes the following pertinent components:

- Two image resources for the coin's head and tail (we named them heads.png and tails.png). These images may be any two-image resources placed in res/drawable. The ImageView defaults to displaying the heads image.

- Two ScaleAnimation objects:

  1. Shrink: Reduces the image width from full to nothing, about the center.

  2. Grow: Increases the image width from nothing to full, about the center.

- Anonymous AnimationListener to link the two animations in sequence.

Custom animation objects can be defined either in XML or code. In the next section, we will look at making the animations as XML resources. Here we created the two ScaleAnimation objects by using the following constructor:

```
ScaleAnimation(
    float fromX,
    float toX,
    float fromY,
    float toY,
    int pivotXType,
    float pivotXValue,
    int pivotYType,
    float pivotYValue
)
```

The first four parameters are the horizontal and vertical scaling factors to apply. Notice in Listing 2-22 that X went from 100 percent to 0 percent to shrink, and from 0 percent to 100 percent to grow, while leaving Y alone at 100 percent always.

The remaining parameters define an anchor point for the view while the animation occurs. In this case, we tell the application to anchor the midpoint of the view, and we then bring both sides in toward the middle as the view shrinks. The reverse is true for expanding the image: the center stays in place, and the image grows outward toward its original edges.

Android does not inherently have a way to link multiple animation objects together in a sequence, so we use an Animation.AnimationListener for this purpose. The listener has methods to notify when an animation begins, repeats, and completes. In this case, we are interested in only the latter so that when the shrink animation is done, we can automatically start the grow animation after it.

The final method used in the example is the `setDuration()` method to set the animation duration of time. The value supplied here is in milliseconds, so our entire coin flip would take 300ms to complete (150ms for each `ScaleAnimation`).

AnimationSet

Many times the custom animation you are searching to create requires a combination of the basic types described previously; this is where `AnimationSet` becomes useful. `AnimationSet` defines a group of animations that should be run simultaneously. By default, all animations will be started together and will complete at their respective durations.

In this section, we will also expose how to define custom animations by using Android's preferred method of XML resources. XML animations should be defined in the `res/anim/` folder of a project. The following tags are supported, and all of them can be either the root or child node of an animation:

- `<alpha>`: An `AlphaAnimation` object

- `<rotate>`: A `RotateAnimation` object

- `<scale>`: A `ScaleAnimation` object

- `<translate>`: A `TranslateAnimation` object

- `<set>`: An `AnimationSet`

Only the `<set>` tag, however, can be a parent and contain other animation tags.

In this example, let's take our coin-flip animations and add another dimension. We will pair each `ScaleAnimation` with a `TranslateAnimation` as a set. The desired effect will be for the image to slide up and down the screen as it "flips." To do this, in Listings 2-23 and 2-24, we will define our animations in two XML files and place them in `res/anim/`. The first will be `grow.xml`. This is followed by `shrink.xml`.

Listing 2-23. res/anim/grow.xml

```xml
<?xml version="1.0" encoding="utf-8"?>
<set xmlns:android="http://schemas.android.com/apk/res/android">
    <scale
        android:duration="150"
        android:fromXScale="0.0"
        android:toXScale="1.0"
        android:fromYScale="1.0"
        android:toYScale="1.0"
        android:pivotX="50%"
        android:pivotY="50%"
    />
    <translate
        android:duration="150"
        android:fromXDelta="0%"
        android:toXDelta="0%"
        android:fromYDelta="50%"
        android:toYDelta="0%"
    />
</set>
```

Listing 2-24. res/anim/shrink.xml

```xml
<?xml version="1.0" encoding="utf-8"?>
<set xmlns:android="http://schemas.android.com/apk/res/android">
    <scale
        android:duration="150"
        android:fromXScale="1.0"
        android:toXScale="0.0"
        android:fromYScale="1.0"
        android:toYScale="1.0"
        android:pivotX="50%"
        android:pivotY="50%"
    />
    <translate
        android:duration="150"
        android:fromXDelta="0%"
        android:toXDelta="0%"
        android:fromYDelta="0%"
        android:toYDelta="50%"
    />
</set>
```

Defining the scale values isn't any different than previously when using the constructor in code. One thing to note, however, is the definition style of units for the pivot parameters. All animation dimensions that can be defined as ABSOLUTE, RELATIVE_TO_SELF or RELATIVE_TO_PARENT use the following XML syntax:

- ABSOLUTE: Use a float value to represent an actual pixel value (for example, "5.0").

- RELATIVE_TO_SELF: Use a percentage value from 0 to 100 (for example, "50%").

- RELATIVE_TO_PARENT: Use a percentage value with a p suffix (for example, "25%p").

With these animation files defined, we can modify the previous example to now load these sets (see Listings 2-25 and 2-26).

Listing 2-25. res/layout/main.xml

```xml
<?xml version="1.0" encoding="utf-8"?>
<RelativeLayout
    xmlns:android="http://schemas.android.com/apk/res/android"
    android:layout_width="fill_parent"
    android:layout_height="fill_parent">
    <ImageView
        android:id="@+id/flip_image"
        android:layout_width="wrap_content"
        android:layout_height="wrap_content"
        android:layout_centerInParent="true"
    />
</RelativeLayout>
```

Listing 2-26. Activity Using Animation Sets

```java
public class Flipper extends Activity {

    boolean isHeads;
    Animation shrink, grow;
    ImageView flipImage;

    @Override
    public void onCreate(Bundle savedInstanceState) {
        super.onCreate(savedInstanceState);
        setContentView(R.layout.main);

        flipImage = (ImageView)findViewById(R.id.flip_image);
        flipImage.setImageResource(R.drawable.heads);
        isHeads = true;

        shrink = AnimationUtils.loadAnimation(this,
                R.anim.shrink);
        shrink.setAnimationListener(
        new Animation.AnimationListener() {
            @Override
            public void onAnimationStart(Animation animation) {}

            @Override
            public void onAnimationRepeat(Animation animation) {}

            @Override
            public void onAnimationEnd(Animation animation) {
                if(isHeads) {
                    isHeads = false;
                    flipImage.setImageResource(R.drawable.tails);
                } else {
                    isHeads = true;
                    flipImage.setImageResource(R.drawable.heads);
                }
                flipImage.startAnimation(grow);
            }
        });
        grow = AnimationUtils.loadAnimation(this, R.anim.grow);
    }

    @Override
    public boolean onTouchEvent(MotionEvent event) {
        if(event.getAction() == MotionEvent.ACTION_DOWN) {
            flipImage.startAnimation(shrink);
            return true;
        }
        return super.onTouchEvent(event);
    }
}
```

The result is a coin that flips, but it also slides down and then up the y-axis of the screen slightly with each flip.

ViewPropertyAnimator

(API Level 12)

Starting with Android 3.2, a much more convenient method of animating views was introduced with ViewPropertyAnimator. The API works similarly to a builder, where the calls to modify the different properties can be chained together to create a single animation. Any calls made to the same ViewPropertyAnimator during the same iteration of the current thread's Looper will be lumped into a single animation. Listing 2-27 illustrates our same view transition example, modified to use the new API.

Listing 2-27. Activity Using ViewPropertyAnimator

```java
public class AnimateActivity extends Activity implements View.OnClickListener {

    View viewToAnimate;

    @Override
    public void onCreate(Bundle savedInstanceState) {
        super.onCreate(savedInstanceState);
        setContentView(R.layout.main);

        Button button = (Button)findViewById(R.id.toggleButton);
        button.setOnClickListener(this);

        viewToAnimate = findViewById(R.id.theView);
    }

    @Override
    public void onClick(View v) {
        if(viewToAnimate.getAlpha() > 0f) {
            //If the view is visible, slide it out to the right
            viewToAnimate.animate().alpha(0f).translationX(1000f);
        } else {
            //If the view is hidden, do a fade-in in place
            //Property Animations actually modify the view, so
            // we have to reset the view's location first
            viewToAnimate.setTranslationX(0f);
            viewToAnimate.animate().alpha(1f);
        }
    }
}
```

In this example, the slide and fade-out transition is accomplished by chaining together a modification of the alpha and translationX properties, with a translation value sufficiently large to go offscreen. We do not have to chain these methods together for them to be considered a single animation. If we had called them on two separate lines, they would still execute together because they were both set in the same iteration of the main thread's Looper.

Notice that we have to reset the translation property for our View to fade in without a slide. This is because property animations manipulate the actual View, rather than where it is temporarily drawn (which is the case with the older animation APIs). If we did not reset this property, it would fade in but would still be 1,000 pixels off to the right.

ObjectAnimator

(API Level 11)

While ViewPropertyAnimator is convenient for animating simple properties quickly, you may find it a bit limiting if you want to do more-complex work such as chaining animations together. For this purpose, we can go to the parent class, ObjectAnimator. With ObjectAnimator we can set listeners to be notified when the animation begins and ends; also, they can be notified with incremental updates as to what point of the animation we are in. Listing 2-28 shows how we can use this to update our Flipper animation code.

Listing 2-28. Flipper Animation with ObjectAnimator

```java
public class Flipper extends Activity {

    boolean isHeads;
    ObjectAnimator flipper;
    Bitmap headsImage, tailsImage;
    ImageView flipImage;

    @Override
    public void onCreate(Bundle savedInstanceState) {
        super.onCreate(savedInstanceState);
        setContentView(R.layout.main);

        headsImage = BitmapFactory.decodeResource(getResources(),
                R.drawable.heads);
        tailsImage = BitmapFactory.decodeResource(getResources(),
                R.drawable.tails);

        flipImage = (ImageView)findViewById(R.id.flip_image);
        flipImage.setImageBitmap(headsImage);
        isHeads = true;

        flipper = ObjectAnimator.ofFloat(flipImage,
                "rotationY", 0f, 360f);
        flipper.setDuration(500);
        flipper.addUpdateListener(flipperListener);
    }

    private AnimatorUpdateListener flipperListener =
            new AnimatorUpdateListener() {
        @Override
        public void onAnimationUpdate(ValueAnimator animation) {
            if (animation.getAnimatedFraction() >= 0.25f
                    && isHeads) {
                flipImage.setImageBitmap(tailsImage);
                isHeads = false;
            }
```

```
                    if (animation.getAnimatedFraction() >= 0.75f
                            && !isHeads) {
                        flipImage.setImageBitmap(headsImage);
                        isHeads = true;
                    }
                }
            };

            @Override
            public boolean onTouchEvent(MotionEvent event) {
                if(event.getAction() == MotionEvent.ACTION_DOWN) {
                    flipper.start();
                    return true;
                }
                return super.onTouchEvent(event);
            }
        }
```

Property animations provide transformations that were not previously available with the older animation system, such as rotations about the x and y axes that create the effect of a three-dimensional transformation. In this example, we don't have to fake the rotation by doing a calculated scale; we can just tell the view to rotate about the y axis. Because of this, we no longer need two animations to flip the coin; we can just animate the rotationY property of the view for one full rotation.

Another powerful addition is the AnimationUpdateListener, which provides regular callbacks while the animation is going on. The getAnimatedFraction() method returns the current percentage to completion of the animation. You can also use getAnimatedValue() to get the exact value of the property at the current point in time.

In the example, we use the first of these methods to swap the heads and tails images when the animation reaches the two points where the coin should change sides (90 degrees and 270 degrees, or 25 percent and 75 percent of the animation duration). Because there is no guarantee that we will get called for every degree, we just change the image as soon as we have crossed the threshold. We also set a boolean flag to avoid setting the image to the same value on each iteration afterward, which would slow performance unnecessarily.

ObjectAnimator also supports a more traditional AnimationListener for major animation events such as start, end, and repeat, if chaining multiple animations together is still necessary for the application.

2-4. Animating Layout Changes

Problem

Your application dynamically adds or removes views from a layout, and you would like those changes to be animated.

Solution

(API Level 11)

Use the LayoutTransition object to customize how modifications to the view hierarchy in a given layout should be animated. In Android 3.0 and later, any ViewGroup can have changes to its layout animated by simply enabling the android:animateLayoutChanges flag in XML or by adding a LayoutTransition object in Java code.

There are five states during a layout transition that each View in the layout may incur. An application can set a custom animation for each one of the following states:

- APPEARING: An item that is appearing in the container

- DISAPPEARING: An item that is disappearing from the container

- CHANGING: An item that is changing because of a layout change, such as a resize, that doesn't involve views being added or removed

- CHANGE_APPEARING: An item changing because of another view appearing

- CHANGE_DISAPPEARING: An item changing because of another view disappearing

How It Works

Listings 2-29 and 2-30 illustrate an application that animates changes on a basic LinearLayout.

Listing 2-29. res/layout/main.xml

```xml
<?xml version="1.0" encoding="utf-8"?>
<LinearLayout
    xmlns:android="http://schemas.android.com/apk/res/android"
    android:layout_width="match_parent"
    android:layout_height="match_parent"
    android:gravity="center_horizontal"
    android:orientation="vertical" >

    <Button
        android:id="@+id/button_add"
        android:layout_width="wrap_content"
        android:layout_height="wrap_content"
        android:onClick="onAddClick"
        android:text="Click To Add Item" />

    <LinearLayout
        android:id="@+id/verticalContainer"
        android:layout_width="match_parent"
        android:layout_height="match_parent"
        android:animateLayoutChanges="true"
        android:orientation="vertical" />

</LinearLayout>
```

Listing 2-30. Activity Adding and Removing Views

```
public class MainActivity extends Activity {

    LinearLayout mContainer;

    @Override
    public void onCreate(Bundle savedInstanceState) {
        super.onCreate(savedInstanceState);
        setContentView(R.layout.main);
        mContainer =
            (LinearLayout) findViewById(R.id.verticalContainer);
    }

    //Add a new button that can remove itself
    public void onAddClick(View v) {
        Button button = new Button(this);
        button.setText("Click To Remove");
        button.setOnClickListener(new View.OnClickListener() {
            @Override
            public void onClick(View v) {
                mContainer.removeView(v);
            }
        });

        mContainer.addView(button, new LinearLayout.LayoutParams(
                LayoutParams.MATCH_PARENT,
                LayoutParams.WRAP_CONTENT));
    }
}
```

This simple example adds `Button` instances to a `LinearLayout` when the Add Item button is tapped. Each new button is outfitted with the ability to remove itself from the layout when it is tapped. In order to animate this process, all we need to do is set `android:animateLayoutChanges="true"` on the `LinearLayout`, and the framework does the rest. By default, a new button will fade in to its new location without disturbing the other views, and a removed button will fade out while the surrounding items slide in to fill the gap.

We can customize the transition animations individually to create custom effects. Take a look at Listing 2-31, where we add some custom transitions to the previous activity.

Listing 2-31. Activity Using Custom LayoutTransition

```
public class MainActivity extends Activity {

    LinearLayout mContainer;

    @Override
    public void onCreate(Bundle savedInstanceState) {
        super.onCreate(savedInstanceState);
        setContentView(R.layout.main);
```

```java
        // Layout Changes Animation
        mContainer = (LinearLayout) findViewById(R.id.verticalContainer);
        LayoutTransition transition = new LayoutTransition();
        mContainer.setLayoutTransition(transition);

        // Override the default appear animation with a flip in
        Animator appearAnim = ObjectAnimator.ofFloat(null,
            "rotationY", 90f, 0f).setDuration(
            transition.getDuration(LayoutTransition.APPEARING));
        transition.setAnimator(LayoutTransition.APPEARING, appearAnim);

        // Override the default disappear animation with a flip out
        Animator disappearAnim = ObjectAnimator.ofFloat(null,
            "rotationX", 0f, 90f).setDuration(
            transition.getDuration(LayoutTransition.DISAPPEARING));
        transition.setAnimator(LayoutTransition.DISAPPEARING,
            disappearAnim);

        // Override the default change with a more animated slide
        // We animate several properties at once, so we create an
        // animation out of multiple PropertyValueHolder objects.
        // This animation slides the views in and temporarily shrinks
        // the view to half size.
        PropertyValuesHolder pvhSlide =
            PropertyValuesHolder.ofFloat("y", 0, 1);
        PropertyValuesHolder pvhScaleY =
            PropertyValuesHolder.ofFloat("scaleY", 1f, 0.5f, 1f);
        PropertyValuesHolder pvhScaleX =
            PropertyValuesHolder.ofFloat("scaleX", 1f, 0.5f, 1f);
        Animator changingAppearingAnim =
            ObjectAnimator.ofPropertyValuesHolder(
                this, pvhSlide, pvhScaleY, pvhScaleX);
        changingAppearingAnim.setDuration(
            transition.getDuration(LayoutTransition.CHANGE_DISAPPEARING)
        );
        transition.setAnimator(LayoutTransition.CHANGE_DISAPPEARING,
                changingAppearingAnim);
    }

    public void onAddClick(View v) {
        Button button = new Button(this);
        button.setText("Click To Remove");
        button.setOnClickListener(new View.OnClickListener() {
            @Override
            public void onClick(View v) {
                mContainer.removeView(v);
            }
        });

        mContainer.addView(button, new LinearLayout.LayoutParams(
                LayoutParams.MATCH_PARENT, LayoutParams.WRAP_CONTENT));
    }
}
```

In this example, we have modified the APPEARING, DISAPPEARING, and CHANGE_DISAPPEARING transition animations for our Button layout. The first two transitions affect the item being added or removed. When the Add Item button is clicked, the new item horizontally rotates into view. When any of the Remove buttons are clicked, that item will vertically rotate out of view. Both of these transitions are created by making a new ObjectAnimator for the custom rotation property, setting its duration to the default duration for that transition type and attaching it to our LayoutTransition instance along with a key for the specific transition type. The final transition is a little more complicated; we need to create an animation that slides the surrounding views into their new location, but we also want to apply a scale animation during that time.

> **Note**   When customizing a change transition, it is important to add a component that moves the location of the view, or you will likely see flickering as the view moves to create or fill the view gap.

In order to do this, we need to create an ObjectAnimator that operates on several properties, in the form of PropertyValuesHolder instances. Each property that will be part of the animation becomes a separate PropertyValuesHolder, and all of them are added to the animator by using the ofPropertyValuesHolder() factory method. This final transition will cause the remaining items below any removed button to slide up and shrink slightly as they move into place.

2-5. Creating Drawables as Backgrounds
Problem

Your application needs to create custom backgrounds with gradients and rounded corners, and you don't want to waste time scaling lots of image files.

Solution

(API Level 1)

Use Android's most powerful implementation of the XML resources system: creating shape drawables. When you are able to do so, creating these views as an XML resource makes sense because they are inherently scalable, and they will fit themselves to the bounds of the view when set as a background.

When defining a drawable in XML by using the <shape> tag, the actual result is a GradientDrawable object. You may define objects in the shape of a rectangle, oval, line, or ring, although the rectangle is the most commonly used for backgrounds. In particular, when working with the rectangle, the following parameters can be defined for the shape:

- Corner radius: Define the radius to use for rounding all four corners or individual radii to round each corner differently.

- Gradient: Linear, radial, or sweep gradient that supports two or three color values. Orientation may be any multiple of 45 degrees (0 is left to right, 90 bottom to top, and so on).

- Solid color: Single color to fill the shape. This doesn't play nice with the gradient also defined.

- Stroke: Border around the shape. You may define both the width and color of the stroke.

- Size and padding.

How It Works

Creating static background images for views can be tricky, given that the image must often be created in multiple sizes to display properly on all devices. This issue is compounded if it is expected that the size of the view may dynamically change based on its contents.

To avoid this problem, we create an XML file in res/drawable to describe a shape that we can apply as the android:background attribute of any view.

Gradient ListView Row

Our first example for this technique will be to create a gradient rectangle that is suitable to be applied as the background of individual rows inside a ListView. The XML for this shape is defined in Listing 2-32.

Listing 2-32. res/drawable/backgradient.xml

```xml
<?xml version="1.0" encoding="utf-8"?>
<shape xmlns:android="http://schemas.android.com/apk/res/android"
    android:shape="rectangle">
    <gradient
        android:startColor="#EFEFEF"
        android:endColor="#989898"
        android:type="linear"
        android:angle="270"
    />
</shape>
```

Here we chose a linear gradient between two shades of gray, moving from top to bottom. If we wanted to add a third color to the gradient, we would add an android:middleColor attribute to the <gradient> tag.

Now this drawable can be referenced by any view or layout used to create the custom items of your ListView (we will discuss more about creating these views in Recipe 2-11). The drawable would be added as the background by including the attribute android:background="@drawable/backgradient" to the view's XML or by calling View.setBackgroundResource(R.drawable.backgradient) in Java code.

Advanced tip   The limit on colors in XML is three, but the constructor for GradientDrawable takes an int[] parameter for colors, and you may pass as many as you like.

When we apply this drawable as the background to rows in a `ListView`, the result will be similar to Figure 2-3.

Figure 2-3. Gradient Drawable as a row background

Rounded View Group

Another popular use of XML drawables is to create a background for a layout that visually groups a handful of widgets together. For style, rounded corners and a thin border are often applied as well. This shape defined in XML would look like Listing 2-33.

Listing 2-33. `res/drawable/roundback.xml`

```xml
<?xml version="1.0" encoding="utf-8"?>
<shape xmlns:android="http://schemas.android.com/apk/res/android"
    android:shape="rectangle">
    <solid
        android:color="#FFF"
    />
    <corners
        android:radius="10dip"
    />
```

```
<stroke
    android:width="5dip"
    android:color="#555"
/>
</shape>
```

In this case, we chose white for the fill color and gray for the border stroke. As mentioned in the previous example, this drawable can be referenced by any view or layout as the background by including the attribute android:background="@drawable/roundback" to the view's XML or by calling View.setBackgroundResource(R.drawable.roundback) in Java code.

When applied as the background to a view, the result is shown in Figure 2-4.

Figure 2-4. Rounded rectangle with border as view background

Drawable Patterns

The next category of drawables we are going to look at is patterns. Using XML, we can define some rules around which a smaller image should be stepped and repeated to make a pattern. This can be a great way to make full-screen background images that don't require a large Bitmap to be loaded into memory.

Applications can create a pattern by setting the `tileMode` attribute on a `<bitmap>` element to one of the following values:

- `clamp`: The source bitmap will have the pixels along its edges replicated.
- `repeat`: The source bitmap will be stepped and repeated in both directions.
- `mirror`: The source bitmap will be stepped and repeated, alternating between normal and flipped images on each iteration.

Figure 2-5 illustrates two small square images that will become the source for our patterns.

Figure 2-5. Source bitmaps for patterns

Listings 2-34 and 2-35 show examples of how to define an XML pattern as a background.

Listing 2-34. res/drawable/pattern_checker.xml

```xml
<?xml version="1.0" encoding="utf-8"?>
<bitmap xmlns:android="http://schemas.android.com/apk/res/android"
    android:src="@drawable/checkers"
    android:tileMode="repeat" />
```

Listing 2-35. res/drawable/pattern_stripes.xml

```xml
<?xml version="1.0" encoding="utf-8"?>
<bitmap xmlns:android="http://schemas.android.com/apk/res/android"
    android:src="@drawable/stripes"
    android:tileMode="mirror" />
```

> **Tip**   Patterns can be made only with a `bitmap` that has intrinsic bounds, such as external images. XML shapes cannot be used as the source for a pattern.

Figure 2-6 reveals the result of applying each of these patterns as view backgrounds.

Figure 2-6. Background patterns

You can see that the checkerboard image is repeated unmodified, while the stripe pattern image is reflected both horizontally and vertically as it is repeated across the screen, creating the diamond effect you see in Figure 2-6.

Nine-Patch Images

The NinePatchDrawable is one of Android's greatest strengths when it comes to designing user interfaces that are flexible across devices. The nine-patch is a special image that is designed to stretch in only certain areas by designating sections of the image that are stretchable and areas that are not. In fact, the image type gets its name from the nine stretch zones that are created when an image is mapped (more on this in a moment).

Let's take a look at an example to better understand how this works. Figure 2-7 shows two images; the image on the left is the original, and the image on the right has been converted into a nine-patch.

Figure 2-7. Speech bubble source image, speech_background.png (left) and nine-patch conversion, speech_background.9.png (right)

Notice the black markings on each side of the image on the right. A valid nine-patch image file is simply a PNG image in which the outer 1 pixel contains only either black or transparent pixels. The black pixels on each side define something about how the image will stretch and wrap the content inside:

- *Left side*: Black pixels here define areas where the image should stretch vertically. The pixels in these areas will be stepped and repeated to accomplish the stretch. The example image in Figure 2-7 has one of these areas.

- *Top side*: Black pixels here define areas where the image should stretch horizontally. The pixels in these areas will be stepped and repeated to accomplish the stretch. The example image in Figure 2-7 has two of these areas.

- *Right side*: Black pixels here define the vertical content area, which is the area where the view's content will display. In effect, it is defining the top and bottom padding values, but inherent to the background image.

- *Bottom side*: Black pixels here define the horizontal content area, which is the area where the view's content will display. In effect, it is defining the left and right padding values, but inherent to the background image. This must contain a single line of solid pixels defining the area.

This image was created using the draw9patch tool that is part of the Android SDK. To better visualize how these markings affect the resulting image, let's take a look at the image when loaded into this tool. See Figure 2-8.

Figure 2-8. Speech bubble inside draw9patch

You can now start to see where the nine-patch gets its name. The areas of the image that are not highlighted will not be stretched. The highlighted areas of each image will stretch in a single direction (either horizontal or vertical, based on their orientation), and the areas where the highlights intersect will stretch in both directions. In an image with the minimum of one stretchable zone in each direction, this would create nine individual mapped zones in the image: four corners that aren't modified, four middle areas that stretch once, and the single center section that stretches twice.

There isn't any special code required to create a NinePatchDrawable and use it as a background; the image file just needs to be named with the special .9.png extension so Android can package it correctly. Listing 2-36 shows how you might set this image as a background, and Figure 2-9 reveals what this image looks like when set as the background for a TextView.

Listing 2-36. res/layout/main.xml

```xml
<?xml version="1.0" encoding="utf-8"?>
<RelativeLayout
    xmlns:android="http://schemas.android.com/apk/res/android"
    android:layout_width="match_parent"
    android:layout_height="match_parent" >
    <TextView
        android:layout_width="match_parent"
        android:layout_height="wrap_content"
        android:layout_centerVertical="true"
        android:gravity="center"
        android:text="This is a text speech bubble"
        android:background="@drawable/speech_background"/>
</RelativeLayout>
```

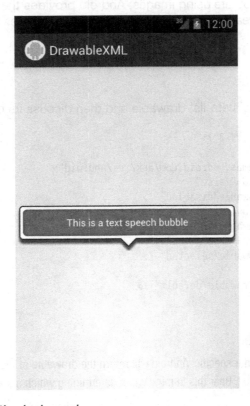

Figure 2-9. Speech bubble as TextView background

Note how the two 3-pixel-wide horizontal stretch zones evenly distributed the excess space between them, centering the origin point of the speech bubble. If you would like to create an offset between two stretch points, this can be done by varying their distance from the image center or by varying their size. If one zone is 3 pixels wide and the other is only 1 pixel wide, the wider zone will take up three times as much space when stretched.

2-6. Creating Custom State Drawables

Problem

You want to customize an element such as a `Button` or `CheckBox` that has multiple states (default, pressed, selected, and so on).

Solution

(API Level 1)

Create a state-list drawable to apply to the element. Whether you have defined your drawable graphics yourself in XML, or you are using images, Android provides the means via another XML element, the `<selector>`, to create a single reference to multiple images and the conditions under which they should be visible.

How It Works

Let's take a look at an example state-list drawable and then discuss its parts:

```xml
<?xml version="1.0" encoding="utf-8"?>
<selector
    xmlns:android="http://schemas.android.com/apk/res/android">
    <item android:state_enabled="false"
        android:drawable="@drawable/disabled" />
    <item android:state_pressed="true"
        android:drawable="@drawable/selected" />
    <item android:state_focused="true"
        android:drawable="@drawable/selected" />
    <!-- Default State -->
    <item android:drawable="@drawable/default" />
</selector>
```

> **Note**   The `<selector>` is order specific. Android will return the drawable of the first state it matches completely as it traverses the list. Bear this in mind when determining which state attributes to apply to each item.

Each item in the list identifies the state(s) that must be in effect for the referenced drawable to be the one chosen. Multiple state parameters can be added for one item if multiple state values need to be matched. Android will traverse the list and pick the first state that matches all criteria of the current view the drawable is attached to. For this reason, it is considered good practice to put your normal, or default, state at the bottom of the list with no criteria attached.

Here is a list of the most commonly useful state attributes. All of these are boolean values:

- state_enabled: Value the view would return from isEnabled()
- state_pressed: View is pressed by the user on the touch screen
- state_focused: View has focus
- state_selected: View is selected by the user using keys or a D-pad
- state_checked: Value a checkable view would return from isChecked()

Now let's look at how to apply these state-list drawables to different views.

Button and other Clickable Widgets

Widgets such as Button are designed to have their background drawable change when the view moves through the preceding states. As such, the android:background attribute in XML or the View. setBackgroundDrawable() method are the proper methods for attaching the state list. Listing 2-37 is an example with a file defined in res/drawable/ called button_states.xml.

Listing 2-37. res/drawable/button_states.xml

```xml
<?xml version="1.0" encoding="utf-8"?>
<selector
    xmlns:android="http://schemas.android.com/apk/res/android">
    <item android:state_enabled="false"
        android:drawable="@drawable/disabled" />
    <item android:state_pressed="true"
        android:drawable="@drawable/selected" />
    <!-- Default State -->
    <item android:drawable="@drawable/default" />
</selector>
```

The three @drawable resources listed here are images in the project that the selector is meant to switch between. As we mentioned in the previous section, the last item will be returned as the default if no other items include matching states to the current view; therefore, we do not need to include a state to match on that item. Attaching this to a view defined in XML looks like the following:

```xml
<Button
    android:layout_width="wrap_content"
    android:layout_height="wrap_content"
    android:text="My Button"
    android:background="@drawable/button_states" />
```

CheckBox and other Checkable Widgets

Many of the widgets that implement the Checkable interface, such as CheckBox and other subclasses of CompoundButton, have a slightly different mechanism for changing their state. In these cases, the background is not associated with the state, and customizing the drawable to represent the "checked" states is done through another attribute called the button. In XML, this is the android:button attribute, and in code the CompoundButton.setButtonDrawable() method should do the trick.

Listing 2-38 is an example with a file defined in res/drawable/ called check_states.xml. Again, the @drawable resources listed are meant to reference images in the project to be switched.

Listing 2-38. res/drawable/check_states.xml

```
<?xml version="1.0" encoding="utf-8"?>
<selector
    xmlns:android="http://schemas.android.com/apk/res/android">
    <item android:state_enabled="false"
        android:drawable="@drawable/disabled" />
    <item android:state_checked="true"
        android:drawable="@drawable/checked" />
    <!-- Default State -->
    <item android:drawable="@drawable/unchecked" />
</selector>
```

And here they are attached to a CheckBox in XML:

```
<CheckBox
    android:layout_width="wrap_content"
    android:layout_height="wrap_content"
    android:button="@drawable/check_states" />
```

2-7. Applying Masks to Images

Problem

You need to apply one image or shape as a clipping mask to define the visible boundaries of a second image in your application.

Solution

(API Level 1)

Using 2D graphics and a PorterDuffXferMode, you can apply any arbitrary mask (in the form of another bitmap) to a bitmap image. The basic steps to this recipe are as follows:

1. Create a mutable Bitmap instance (blank), and a Canvas to draw into it.

2. Draw the mask pattern onto the Canvas first.

3. Apply a PorterDuffXferMode to the Paint.

4. Draw the source image on the Canvas using the transfer mode.

The key ingredient is the `PorterDuffXferMode`, which considers the current state of both the source and destination objects during a paint operation. The destination is the existing `Canvas` data, and the source is the graphic data being applied in the current operation.

There are many mode parameters that can be attached to this, which create varying effects on the result, but for masking we are interested in using the `PorterDuff.Mode.SRC_IN` mode. This mode will draw only at locations where the source and destination overlap, and the pixels drawn will be from the source; in other words, the source is clipped by the bounds of the destination.

The same effect can also be accomplished using the image as a `BitmapShader` to draw the content into another element. In this way, we are treating the image pixels as the "color" to be used to draw whatever shape or element we have that makes up the image mask. We will explore both options in this recipe.

How It Works

Rounded Corner Bitmap

One extremely common use of image masking is to apply rounded corners to a bitmap image before displaying it. For this example, Figure 2-10 is the original image we will be masking.

Figure 2-10. *Original source image*

To illustrate this, we have created a custom view that receives an image and draws it as a rounded rectangle to the provided `Canvas` with a `BitmapShader`. This view also manages the sizing math necessary to center the image inside the custom view.

Listings 2-39 and 2-40 show our custom view and its use inside an activity.

Listing 2-39. View Applying a Rounded Rectangle Mask to a Bitmap

```java
public class RoundedCornerImageView extends View {

    private Bitmap mImage;
    private Paint mBitmapPaint;

    private RectF mBounds;
    private float mRadius = 25.0f;

    public RoundedCornerImageView(Context context) {
        super(context);
        init();
    }

    public RoundedCornerImageView(Context context,
            AttributeSet attrs) {
        super(context, attrs);
        init();
    }

    public RoundedCornerImageView(Context context,
            AttributeSet attrs, int defStyle) {
        super(context, attrs, defStyle);
        init();
    }

    private void init() {
        //Create image paint
        mBitmapPaint = new Paint(Paint.ANTI_ALIAS_FLAG);
        //Create rect for drawing bounds
        mBounds = new RectF();
    }

    @Override
    protected void onMeasure(int widthMeasureSpec,
            int heightMeasureSpec) {
        int height, width;
        height = width = 0;

        //Requested size is the image content size
        int imageHeight, imageWidth;
        if (mImage == null) {
            imageHeight = imageWidth = 0;
        } else {
            imageHeight = mImage.getHeight();
            imageWidth = mImage.getWidth();
        }
        //Get the best measurement and set it on the view
        width = getMeasurement(widthMeasureSpec, imageWidth);
        height = getMeasurement(heightMeasureSpec, imageHeight);

        setMeasuredDimension(width, height);
    }
```

```java
/*
 * Helper method to measure width and height
 */
private int getMeasurement(int measureSpec, int contentSize) {
    int specSize = MeasureSpec.getSize(measureSpec);
    switch (MeasureSpec.getMode(measureSpec)) {
        case MeasureSpec.AT_MOST:
            return Math.min(specSize, contentSize);
        case MeasureSpec.UNSPECIFIED:
            return contentSize;
        case MeasureSpec.EXACTLY:
            return specSize;
        default:
            return 0;
    }
}


@Override
protected void onSizeChanged(int w, int h,
        int oldw, int oldh) {
    if (w != oldw || h != oldh) {
        //We want to center the image, so we offset our
        //values whenever the view changes size
        int imageWidth, imageHeight;
        if (mImage == null) {
            imageWidth = imageHeight = 0;
        } else {
            imageWidth = mImage.getWidth();
            imageHeight = mImage.getHeight();
        }
        int left = (w - imageWidth) / 2;
        int top = (h - imageHeight) / 2;
        //Set the bounds to offset the rounded rectangle
        mBounds.set(left, top, left+imageWidth,
                top+imageHeight);
        //Offset the shader to draw the Bitmap inside the rect
        // Without this, the bitmap will be at 0,0 in the view
        if (mBitmapPaint.getShader() != null) {
            Matrix m = new Matrix();
            m.setTranslate(left, top);
            mBitmapPaint.getShader().setLocalMatrix(m);
        }
    }
}

public void setImage(Bitmap bitmap) {
    if (mImage != bitmap) {
        mImage = bitmap;
        if (mImage != null) {
            BitmapShader shader = new BitmapShader(mImage,
                    TileMode.CLAMP, TileMode.CLAMP);
            mBitmapPaint.setShader(shader);
```

```
            } else {
                mBitmapPaint.setShader(null);
            }
            requestLayout();
        }
    }

    @Override
    protected void onDraw(Canvas canvas) {
        //Let the view draw backgrounds, etc.
        super.onDraw(canvas);
        //Draw the image with the calculated values
        if (mBitmapPaint != null) {
            canvas.drawRoundRect(mBounds, mRadius, mRadius,
                    mBitmapPaint);
        }
    }
}
```

Listing 2-40. Activity Displaying RoundedCornerImageView

```
public class ShaderActivity extends Activity {

    @Override
    protected void onCreate(Bundle savedInstanceState) {
        super.onCreate(savedInstanceState);
        RoundedCornerImageView iv =
                new RoundedCornerImageView(this);
        Bitmap source = BitmapFactory.decodeResource(
                getResources(), R.drawable.dog);

        iv.setImage(source);
        setContentView(iv);
    }
}
```

Inside our custom view, when a new image is passed in via setImage(), we create a new BitmapShader to wrap the image pixels and set it on the paintbrush we will use to draw. Later, when the view is measured and laid out, we will get a call in onSizeChanged() when the view has a size; at this point, we measure the bounds the image needs to have to be centered inside the view. We must also offset the shader by using a Matrix. Otherwise, the rounded rectangle mask will draw in the center, but our image will still be in the top-left corner of the view.

Now, when the view is ready to draw, we can simply call drawRoundRect() on our Canvas with the bounds we calculated and the paintbrush configured earlier. This draws a rounded rectangle in the view, but uses the pixels from the bitmap to color, or shade, the shape. The result of these efforts is shown in Figure 2-11.

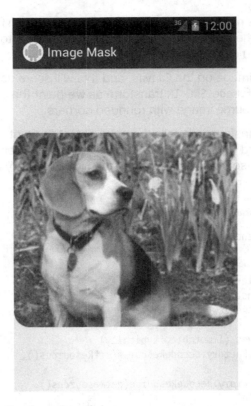

Figure 2-11. Image with a rounded rectangle mask applied

Arbitrary Mask Image

Let's look at an example that's a little more interesting. Here we take two images: the source image and an image representing the mask we want to apply (in this case, an upside-down triangle). See Figure 2-12.

 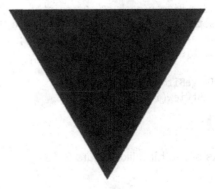

Figure 2-12. Original source image (left) and arbitrary mask image to apply (right)

The chosen mask image does not have to conform to the style chosen here, with black pixels for the mask and transparent everywhere else. However, it is the best choice to guarantee that the system draws the mask exactly as you expect it to be.

We will first draw the triangle image on the Canvas, and this will serve as our mask for the image. Then, applying the PorterDuff.Mode.SRC_IN transform as we paint the source image into the same Canvas, the result will be the source image with rounded corners.

This is because the SRC_IN transfer mode tells the paint object to paint pixels only on the Canvas locations where the source and destination (the triangle we already drew) overlap, and the pixels that are drawn come from the source. Listing 2-41 is the simple activity code to mask the image and display it in a view.

Listing 2-41. Activity Applying an Arbitrary Mask to a Bitmap

```
public class MaskActivity extends Activity {

    @Override
    public void onCreate(Bundle savedInstanceState) {
        super.onCreate(savedInstanceState);
        ImageView iv = new ImageView(this);

        //Create and load images (immutable, typically)
        Bitmap source = BitmapFactory.decodeResource(getResources(),
            R.drawable.dog);
        Bitmap mask = BitmapFactory.decodeResource(getResources(),
            R.drawable.triangle);

        //Create a *mutable* location, and a Canvas to draw into it
        Bitmap result = Bitmap.createBitmap(source.getWidth(),
            source.getHeight(), Config.ARGB_8888);
        Canvas canvas = new Canvas(result);
        Paint paint = new Paint(Paint.ANTI_ALIAS_FLAG);

        //Draw the mask image first, then paint the source
        // using the transfer mode
        canvas.drawBitmap(mask, 0, 0, paint);
        paint.setXfermode(new PorterDuffXfermode(Mode.SRC_IN));
        canvas.drawBitmap(source, 0, 0, paint);
        paint.setXfermode(null);

        iv.setImageBitmap(result);
        setContentView(iv);
    }
}
```

The result looks something like Figure 2-13.

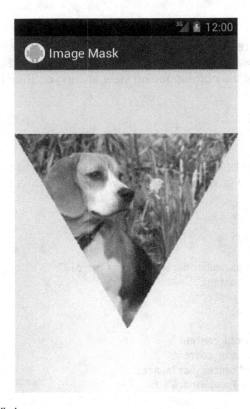

Figure 2-13. Image with a mask applied

Please Try This at Home

Applying the `PorterDuffXferMode` in this fashion to blend two images can create lots of interesting results. Try taking this same example code, but changing the `PorterDuff.Mode` parameter to one of the many other options. Each of the modes will blend the two bitmaps in a slightly different way. Have fun with it!

2-8. Drawing over View Content

Problem

You want to display content on top of what is currently visible, but without inserting or otherwise modifying the existing view hierarchy.

Solution

(API Level 1)

Place your content into a `PopupWindow`, which is a new temporary window in which you can place views that will be displayed on top of the current activity window. `PopupWindow` can be shown anywhere onscreen, either by providing an explicit location or by providing an existing view that the `PopupWindow` should be anchored to.

(API Level 18)

You may also use the newer `ViewOverlay` to draw content on top of your views. `ViewOverlay` allows you to add any number of `Drawable` objects to a private layer managed by the parent view. Those objects will be drawn on top of the corresponding view as long as their bounds are within the bounds of the parent.

How It Works

In order to draw content on top of our view hierarchy, we first need to create the content to display. Listing 2-42 constructs a simple group of views that will be the content of our `PopupWindow`.

Listing 2-42. `res/layout/popup.xml`

```xml
<?xml version="1.0" encoding="utf-8"?>
<LinearLayout
    xmlns:android="http://schemas.android.com/apk/res/android"
    android:layout_width="wrap_content"
    android:layout_height="wrap_content"
    android:orientation="vertical">
    <TextView
        android:layout_width="wrap_content"
        android:layout_height="wrap_content"
        android:layout_gravity="center_horizontal"
        android:text="This is a PopupWindow" />
    <EditText
        android:layout_width="250dp"
        android:layout_height="wrap_content"
        android:layout_gravity="center_horizontal" />
    <Button
        android:layout_width="wrap_content"
        android:layout_height="wrap_content"
        android:layout_gravity="center_horizontal"
        android:text="Close" />
</LinearLayout>
```

When we display this content in a pop-up anchored to a view, by default the `PopupWindow` will display just below the view, left-aligned. However, if there is not enough space below the view to display the `PopupWindow`, it will be displayed above the anchor view instead. To make the pop-up visually distinct in both cases, we can provide a custom background drawable that switches on the `android:state_above_anchor` attribute. Listing 2-43 and Figure 2-14 illustrate the custom drawables we will be using for this example.

Listing 2-43. `res/drawable/popup_background.xml`

```xml
<?xml version="1.0" encoding="utf-8"?>
<selector
    xmlns:android="http://schemas.android.com/apk/res/android" >
    <item android:state_above_anchor="true"
        android:drawable="@drawable/speech_background_top" />
```

```
<!-- Default State -->
<item
    android:drawable="@drawable/speech_background_bottom" />
</selector>
```

Figure 2-14. Background nine-patch drawables

You may recognize these background images from the speech bubble nine-patch example in Recipe 2-5. We've slightly modified the stretch zones so that the extension point is always on the same side.

Listings 2-44 and 2-45 illustrate an example activity and layout that construct and display a PopupWindow in response to a button click. In this example, the PopupWindow will be shown anchored to the button that was clicked.

Listing 2-44. res/layout/activity_main.xml

```xml
<?xml version="1.0" encoding="utf-8"?>
<FrameLayout
    xmlns:android="http://schemas.android.com/apk/res/android"
    android:layout_width="match_parent"
    android:layout_height="match_parent">
    <Button
        android:id="@+id/button"
        android:layout_width="match_parent"
        android:layout_height="wrap_content"
        android:text="Show PopupWindow"
        android:onClick="onShowWindowClick" />
    <Button
        android:layout_width="match_parent"
        android:layout_height="wrap_content"
        android:layout_gravity="bottom"
        android:text="Show PopupWindow"
        android:onClick="onShowWindowClick" />
</FrameLayout>
```

Listing 2-45. Activity Displaying a PopupWindow

```java
public class MainActivity extends Activity
        implements View.OnTouchListener {
    private PopupWindow mOverlay;
```

```java
@Override
protected void onCreate(Bundle savedInstanceState) {
    super.onCreate(savedInstanceState);
    setContentView(R.layout.activity_main);

    //Inflate the popup content layout; we do not have access
    // to the parent view yet, so we pass null as the
    // container view parameter.
    View popupContent =
            getLayoutInflater().inflate(R.layout.popup, null);

    mOverlay = new PopupWindow();
    //Popup should wrap content view
    mOverlay.setWindowLayoutMode(
            WindowManager.LayoutParams.WRAP_CONTENT,
            WindowManager.LayoutParams.WRAP_CONTENT);
    //Set content and background
    mOverlay.setContentView(popupContent);
    mOverlay.setBackgroundDrawable(getResources()
            .getDrawable(R.drawable.popup_background));

    //Default behavior is not to allow any elements in
    // the PopupWindow to be interactive, but to enable
    // touch events to be delivered directly to the
    // PopupWindow. All outside touches will be delivered
    // to the main (Activity) window.
    mOverlay.setTouchInterceptor(this);

    //Call setFocusable() to enable elements in the
    // PopupWindow to take focus, which will also enable
    // the behavior of dismissing the PopupWindow on any
    // outside touch.
    mOverlay.setFocusable(true);

    //Call setOutsideTouchable() if you want to enable
    // outside touches to auto-dismiss the PopupWindow
    // but don't want elements inside the PopupWindow to
    // take focus
    mOverlay.setOutsideTouchable(true);
}

@Override
protected void onPause() {
    super.onPause();
    //PopupWindow is like Dialog, it will leak
    // if left visible while the Activity finishes.
    mOverlay.dismiss();
}
```

```
@Override
public boolean onTouch(View v, MotionEvent event) {
    //Handle direct touch events passed to the PopupWindow
    return true;
}

public void onShowWindowClick(View v) {
    if (mOverlay.isShowing()) {
        //Dismiss the pop-up
        mOverlay.dismiss();
    } else {
        //Show the PopupWindow anchored to the button we
        // pressed. It will be displayed below the button
        // if there's room, otherwise above.
        mOverlay.showAsDropDown(v);
    }
}
}
```

In this example, we create a simple layout with two buttons, both set to trigger the same action. When either button is clicked, the PopupWindow will be displayed anchored to that view by using the showAsDropDown() method.

> **Reminder**   A PopupWindow can also be shown at a specific location by using its showAtLocation() method instead. Similar to showAsDropDown(), this method takes a View parameter, but it is used only to get window information.

The results of this example, when the button is pressed, can be seen in Figure 2-15.

Figure 2-15. *Activity with* `PopupWindow` *shown*

When the activity is first created, the `PopupWindow` is initialized and the layout mode is set to `WRAP_CONTENT`. We must do this in code, even though it was defined in our layout XML, because the layout parameters in the XML are erased during manual inflation with a null parent view container. We then supply the content view and custom background we created. We will discuss the other flags set on the overlay shortly.

For now, if you were to try to run this application as is, you might notice that the `PopupWindow` doesn't display when the bottom button is tapped. This is because of the `WRAP_CONTENT` layout mode we set. Remember that if no space is available below the anchor view, the pop-up should display above it. However, that is determined by how big the pop-up is vs. how much space is left in the main window. If we don't give the window a defined size, it will measure to whatever space remains and try to scrunch the content inside. In order to fix this, we are going to add a `dimens.xml` file to the project and modify `onCreate()` for our activity, as in Listings 2-46 and 2-47.

Listing 2-46. `res/values/dimens.xml`

```xml
<?xml version="1.0" encoding="utf-8"?>
<resources>
    <dimen name="popupWidth">350dp</dimen>
    <dimen name="popupHeight">250dp</dimen>
</resources>
```

Listing 2-47. Modified onCreate() for Fixed Size

```java
@Override
protected void onCreate(Bundle savedInstanceState) {
    super.onCreate(savedInstanceState);
    setContentView(R.layout.activity_main);

    //Inflate the popup content layout; we do not have access
    // to the parent view yet, so we pass null as the
    // container view parameter.
    View popupContent =
            getLayoutInflater().inflate(R.layout.popup, null);

    mOverlay = new PopupWindow();
    //Popup should wrap content view
    mOverlay.setWindowLayoutMode(
            WindowManager.LayoutParams.WRAP_CONTENT,
            WindowManager.LayoutParams.WRAP_CONTENT);
    mOverlay.setWidth(getResources()
            .getDimensionPixelSize(R.dimen.popupWidth));
    mOverlay.setHeight(getResources()
            .getDimensionPixelSize(R.dimen.popupHeight));
    //Set content and background
    mOverlay.setContentView(popupContent);
    mOverlay.setBackgroundDrawable(getResources()
            .getDrawable(R.drawable.popup_background));

    //Default behavior is not to allow any elements in
    // the PopupWindow to be interactive, but to enable
    // touch events to be delivered directly to the
    // PopupWindow. All outside touches will be delivered
    // to the main (Activity) window.
    mOverlay.setTouchInterceptor(this);

    //Call setFocusable() to enable elements in the
    // PopupWindow to take focus, which will also enable
    // the behavior of dismissing the PopupWindow on any
    // outside touch.
    mOverlay.setFocusable(true);

    //Call setOutsideTouchable() if you want to enable
    // outside touches to auto-dismiss the PopupWindow
    // but don't want elements inside the PopupWindow to
    // take focus
    mOverlay.setOutsideTouchable(true);
}
```

Now our overlay window has a defined size, which we've pulled from a dimension resource to preserve pixel density independence across devices. When we run the example and click the buttons, we can see the PopupWindow display below the top button and above the bottom button, as shown in Figure 2-16.

Figure 2-16. *Activity with* PopupWindow *anchored to each button*

Working with PopupWindow Behavior

PopupWindow has a number of useful flags we can set to govern its behavior and interaction points. By default, the pop-up is touchable, meaning it can receive direct touch events. In order to act on those events, we call setTouchInterceptor() to provide an OnTouchListener as the destination for those touch events.

By default, the pop-up is *not* focusable, which means views inside it cannot receive focus (as an EditText or a Button can). We have these widgets in our content view, so we have set the focusable flag to true to enable the user to interact with these elements. The final flag is setOutsideTouchable(), which we have also enabled. By default, this value is false, but we can set it to true to send touch events outside the pop-up content area to the PopupWindow rather than the main window underneath. Doing so enables the PopupWindow to dismiss itself on any outside touch events. It is most common to use this flag when you do not want to enable focus on the pop-up, but still want the dismiss behavior it provides.

There are a handful of constructors available to create a new PopupWindow. We used the basic version without any parameters, but there are a few versions that also take a Context parameter. When passing a Context to the constructor, the framework creates a PopupWindow that has a default system background included, whereas the version we used does not. We did not need the system background because we supplied our own custom drawable. It is interesting to note that, when either case occurs (either the framework or the application supplies a background for the pop-up), the content view you give to PopupWindow is actually wrapped in another private ViewGroup to manage that background instance. This is important because that extra container also slightly modifies how the overlay behaves.

Based on the combination of choices made for flags and creation options of PopupWindow, a number of user interaction behaviors will change. The behaviors we will explore are as follows:

1. Receive touch events: Events will be received and processed in the OnTouchListener supplied via setTouchInterceptor().

2. Allow inside view interaction: Focusable widgets (for example, a Button) inside the content view will be interactive and able to receive focus.

3. Auto-dismiss on outside touches: Any touch event outside the content view area will automatically dismiss the pop-up.

4. Dismiss on the Back button: Tapping the device's Back button will dismiss the pop-up rather than finish the current activity.

5. Allow outside touches to the main window: When a touch occurs outside the content view area, it is delivered to the main activity window rather than being consumed.

Table 2-1 outlines which of these actions will apply to a PopupWindow based on how it was initialized prior to being shown. These values are not static; they can be modified after the initial display takes place. If a flag is modified while the PopupWindow is visible, the change will not take effect until the next time it is shown or its update() method is called.

Table 2-1. PopupWindow Behaviors

	Created with Context or Background			Standard *PopupWindow*	
Action	Default	Focusable	OutsideTouch	Default	Focusable
1	X	X	X		
2		X			X
3		X	X		
4		X			
5	X		X	X	

In addition to what we've already discussed, you can see from this information that if your content overlay needs to process touch events, you will need to ensure that a Context or background image is supplied.

Animating the PopupWindow

After playing with the previous example, you may have noticed that the PopupWindow has a default animation associated with it when it is shown or dismissed. This can be customized or removed, by passing a new resource via setAnimationStyle(). This method takes a resource ID referencing a style that defines a pair of animations, one for the window entrance and another for the window exit. Listing 2-48 illustrates the style resource we need to create in order to customize the PopupWindow animation.

Listing 2-48. res/values/styles.xml

```
<resources>
    <!-- Define this element below any existing themes -->
    <style name="PopupAnimation">
        <item name="android:windowEnterAnimation">
            @android:anim/slide_in_left</item>
        <item name="android:windowExitAnimation">
            @android:anim/slide_out_right</item>
    </style>
</resources>
```

> **Tip**   It is not necessary to define your own animation styles to customize the transition. There are a host of styles defined within android.R.style that the framework uses to transition other standard window types such as dialog boxes or toasts. To use these animations, just pass the associated ID such as android.R.style.Animation_Dialog or android.R.style.Animation_Toast.

Each of these items can be a reference to animations you define in XML or animations already available in the framework. Here, we have chosen to reference the slide-in and slide-out animations already present in the framework. In Listing 2-49, we then modify our example activity's onCreate() to apply our custom animations. For brevity, we have also removed the configuration flags.

Listing 2-49. Activity onCreate() showing PopupWindow with Custom Animation

```
@Override
protected void onCreate(Bundle savedInstanceState) {
    super.onCreate(savedInstanceState);
    setContentView(R.layout.activity_main);

    //Inflate the popup content layout; we do not have access
    // to the parent view yet, so we pass null as the
    // container view parameter.
    View popupContent =
            getLayoutInflater().inflate(R.layout.popup, null);
```

```
    mOverlay = new PopupWindow();
    //Popup should wrap content view
    mOverlay.setWindowLayoutMode(
            WindowManager.LayoutParams.WRAP_CONTENT,
            WindowManager.LayoutParams.WRAP_CONTENT);
    mOverlay.setWidth(getResources()
            .getDimensionPixelSize(R.dimen.popupWidth));
    mOverlay.setHeight(getResources()
            .getDimensionPixelSize(R.dimen.popupHeight));
    //Set content and background
    mOverlay.setContentView(popupContent);
    mOverlay.setBackgroundDrawable(getResources()
            .getDrawable(R.drawable.popup_background));

    //Set a custom animation enter/exit pair, or 0 to
    // disable animations. You can also use animation
    // styles defined in the platform, such as
    // android.R.style.Animation_Toast
    mOverlay.setAnimationStyle(R.style.PopupAnimation);

    //Default behavior is not to allow any elements in
    // the PopupWindow to be interactive, but to enable
    // touch events to be delivered directly to the
    // PopupWindow. All outside touches will be delivered
    // to the main (Activity) window.
    mOverlay.setTouchInterceptor(this);
}
```

> **Tip** You can also remove the animation completely by calling setAnimationStyle(0), or reset the default animation with setAnimationStyle(-1).

Now when we run the application again, the custom slide animations are used to transition the PopupWindow on and off screen.

Using ViewOverlay

(API Level 18)

Another simple way to draw content over your views is to use the more recent ViewOverlay implementation. ViewOverlay, and its cousin ViewGroupOverlay, allows you to add any number of drawable objects to be drawn on top of the view. Applications cannot create a ViewOverlay directly, and instead obtain a ViewOverlay by calling getOverlay() on any view in the hierarchy. Views are constrained to drawing within their bounds, so any content in an overlay whose location extends outside the hosting view's bounds will be clipped.

To illustrate this capability, we have created a simple application that draws markup content on top of the main view in an activity. The view we are drawing on is purposefully generic to point out that any View subclass (whether it displays text, HTML, an image, or some custom content) can work with an overlay. The application will place either an arrow flag or a resizeable box over the interactive view at the location the user touches. The flag can be moved or the box resized as long as the user holds a finger down and drags. Once the touch is released, the marker is permanent on the view until it is tapped a second time, which will remove the marker completely.

First, let's have a look at the resources used via Listing 2-50 and Figure 2-17.

Listing 2-50. res/drawable/box.xml

```xml
<?xml version="1.0" encoding="utf-8"?>
<shape xmlns:android="http://schemas.android.com/apk/res/android"
    android:shape="rectangle">
    <solid
        android:color="@android:color/transparent"/>
    <stroke
        android:width="3dp"
        android:color="#F00" />
</shape>
```

Figure 2-17. res/drawable/arrow.png

Listing 2-51 shows the layout used for the main activity. We have created a main view containing some text (@+id/textview) that we will be drawing on, and a selector at the bottom to determine which type of marker to place.

Listing 2-51. res/layout/activity_main.xml

```xml
<LinearLayout
    xmlns:android="http://schemas.android.com/apk/res/android"
    android:layout_width="match_parent"
    android:layout_height="match_parent"
    android:orientation="vertical" >

    <TextView
        android:id="@+id/textview"
        android:layout_width="match_parent"
        android:layout_height="0dp"
```

```
            android:layout_weight="1"
            android:gravity="center"
            android:text="Android Recipes" />

    <RadioGroup
        android:id="@+id/container_options"
        android:layout_width="match_parent"
        android:layout_height="wrap_content"
        android:orientation="horizontal"
        android:background="#CCC">
        <RadioButton
            android:id="@+id/option_box"
            android:layout_width="0dp"
            android:layout_height="wrap_content"
            android:layout_weight="1"
            android:text="Box" />
        <RadioButton
            android:id="@+id/option_arrow"
            android:layout_width="0dp"
            android:layout_height="wrap_content"
            android:layout_weight="1"
            android:text="Arrow" />
    </RadioGroup>

</LinearLayout>
```

Finally, we have the activity in Listing 2-52. This activity finds the main view and sets an OnTouchListener to monitor the touch events going through that view. We will look in more detail at custom touch handling in Chapter 3, so for now suffice it to say that this causes the onTouch() method to be called for each touch event, which we then use to determine whether the user has touched, dragged, or released a finger on the main view.

Listing 2-52. Activity with Interactive ViewOverlay

```
public class MainActivity extends Activity implements View.OnTouchListener {

    private RadioGroup mOptions;

    private ArrayList<Drawable> mMarkers;
    private Drawable mTrackingMarker;
    private Point mTrackingPoint;

    @Override
    protected void onCreate(Bundle savedInstanceState) {
        super.onCreate(savedInstanceState);
        setContentView(R.layout.activity_main);

        //Receive touch events for the view we want to draw on
        findViewById(R.id.textview).setOnTouchListener(this);
```

```java
        mOptions =
            (RadioGroup)findViewById(R.id.container_options);

        mMarkers = new ArrayList<Drawable>();
    }

    /*
     * Touch events from the view we are monitoring
     * will be delivered here.
     */
    @Override
    public boolean onTouch(View v, MotionEvent event) {
        switch (mOptions.getCheckedRadioButtonId()) {
            case R.id.option_box:
                handleEvent(R.id.option_box, v, event);
                break;
            case R.id.option_arrow:
                handleEvent(R.id.option_arrow, v, event);
                break;
            default:
                return false;
        }
        return true;
    }

    /*
     * Process touch events when user has selected to draw a box
     */
    private void handleEvent(int optionId, View v,
            MotionEvent event) {
        int x = (int) event.getX();
        int y = (int) event.getY();
        switch (event.getAction()) {
            case MotionEvent.ACTION_DOWN:
                Drawable current = markerAt(x, y);
                if (current == null) {
                    //Add a new marker on a new touch
                    switch(optionId) {
                        case R.id.option_box:
                            mTrackingMarker = addBox(v, x, y);
                            mTrackingPoint = new Point(x, y);
                            break;
                        case R.id.option_arrow:
                            mTrackingMarker = addFlag(v, x, y);
                            break;
                    }
                } else {
                    //Remove the existing marker
                    removeMarker(v, current);
                }
                break;
```

```java
        case MotionEvent.ACTION_MOVE:
            //Update the current marker as we move
            if (mTrackingMarker != null) {
                switch(optionId) {
                    case R.id.option_box:
                        resizeBox(v, mTrackingMarker,
                                mTrackingPoint, x, y);
                        break;
                    case R.id.option_arrow:
                        offsetFlag(v, mTrackingMarker, x, y);
                        break;
                }

            }
            break;
        case MotionEvent.ACTION_UP:
        case MotionEvent.ACTION_CANCEL:
            //Clear state when gesture is over
            mTrackingMarker = null;
            mTrackingPoint = null;
            break;
    }
}

/*
 * Add a new resizable box at the given coordinate
 */
private Drawable addBox(View v, int x, int y) {
    Drawable box = getResources().getDrawable(R.drawable.box);

    //Start with a zero size box at the touch point
    Rect bounds = new Rect(x, y, x, y);
    box.setBounds(bounds);

    //Add to the ViewOverlay
    mMarkers.add(box);
    v.getOverlay().add(box);

    return box;
}


/*
 * Update an existing box to resize based on the given
 * coordinate.
 */
private void resizeBox(View v, Drawable target,
        Point trackingPoint, int x, int y) {
    Rect bounds = new Rect(target.getBounds());
    //If the new touch point is to the left of the tracking
    // point, grow left. Otherwise, grow to the right
```

```java
            if (x < trackingPoint.x) {
                bounds.left = x;
            } else {
                bounds.right = x;
            }

            //If the new touch point is above the tracking point,
            // grow up. Otherwise, grow down
            if (y < trackingPoint.y) {
                bounds.top = y;
            } else {
                bounds.bottom = y;
            }

            //Update drawable bounds and redraw
            target.setBounds(bounds);
            v.invalidate();
    }

    /*
     * Add a new flag marker at the given coordinate
     */
    private Drawable addFlag(View v, int x, int y) {
        //Make a new marker drawable
        Drawable marker =
            getResources().getDrawable(R.drawable.flag_arrow);

        //Create bounds to match image size
        Rect bounds = new Rect(0, 0,
                marker.getIntrinsicWidth(),
                marker.getIntrinsicHeight());
        //Center marker bottom around coordinate
        bounds.offset(x - (bounds.width() /2),
                y - bounds.height());
        marker.setBounds(bounds);
        //Add to the overlay
        mMarkers.add(marker);
        v.getOverlay().add(marker);

        return marker;
    }

    /*
     * Update the position of an existing flag marker
     */
    private void offsetFlag(View v, Drawable marker,
            int x, int y) {
        Rect bounds = new Rect(marker.getBounds());
        //Move drawable bounds to align with the new coordinate
        bounds.offset(x - bounds.left - (bounds.width() / 2),
                y - bounds.top - bounds.height());
```

```
        //Update and redraw
        marker.setBounds(bounds);
        v.invalidate();
    }

    /*
     * Remove the requested marker item
     */
    private void removeMarker(View v, Drawable marker) {
        mMarkers.remove(marker);
        v.getOverlay().remove(marker);
    }

    /*
     * Find the first marker that contains the requested
     * coordinate, if one exists.
     */
    private Drawable markerAt(int x, int y) {
        //Return the first marker found containing the given point
        for (Drawable marker : mMarkers) {
            if (marker.getBounds().contains(x, y)) {
                return marker;
            }
        }

        return null;
    }
}
```

Inside onTouch(), the selection from the RadioGroup is checked to determine the marker type. For the initial ACTION_DOWN, we call either addBox() or addFlag() to create a new Drawable, set its size and location with setBounds(), and apply it to the main view's ViewOverlay. To add the marker to the overlay, we simply call add(). Since ViewOverlay doesn't provide any good method of tracking the items added, we also maintain a list of our own, which will be useful in finding a marker based on touch later.

As the finger moves around in ACTION_MOVE, we either update the location of the flag, or resize the box to fit between the initial touch point and our current touch location. In both cases, this is accomplished by again updating the bounds Rect of the Drawable. Once the finger is released, we clear all tracking state, and the marker is now in its permanent home.

> **Note** Drawable elements get their size and location from the bounds Rect. Bitmap content that comes from an image resource such as a PNG has an intrinsic height and width that we can use to generate the size portion of the bounds, but content taken from XML has no intrinsic size and must be explicitly set. Regardless, especially when used in a ViewOverlay, bounds are used to place the content at the right location, so it is key to remember to call setBounds() at least once for each element you add.

If a new touch comes down at the location of an existing marker (checked using the `markerAt()` helper method), we simply delete the marker by removing it from the `ViewOverlay`. Figure 2-18 shows the initial layout on the left, with some markers added to the overlay on the right.

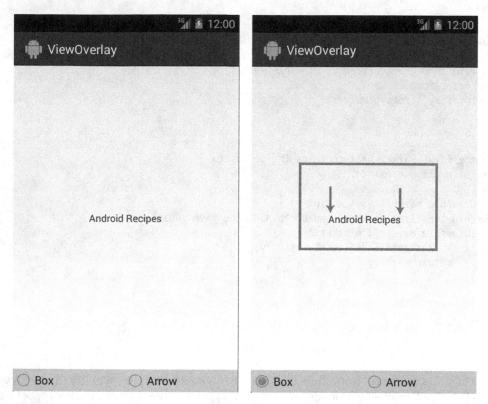

Figure 2-18. *Activity with drawable content inside the* `ViewOverlay`

Caution   Calling `getOverlay()` on a `ViewGroup` will return a `ViewGroupOverlay` instead, which has additional `add()` and `remove()` methods to work with a view instead of a drawable. Beware that this does not work the same way as described in this section. This cannot be used to add a new view on top of the existing hierarchy; it can be used to elevate only an existing view already inside that container to the overlay. It also has the consequence of removing that view from its container when added to the overlay, which will modify the layout of the `ViewGroup`. If you want to place views on top of the main window, use the `PopupWindow` technique described earlier in this section.

2-9. Implementing Situation-Specific Layouts

Problem

Your application must be universal, running on different screen sizes and orientations. You need to provide different layout resources for each of these instances.

Solution

(API Level 4)

Build multiple layout files, and use resource qualifiers to let Android pick what's appropriate. We will look at using resources to create layouts specific for different screen orientations and sizes. We will also explore using layout aliases to reduce duplication in cases where multiple configurations share the same layout.

How It Works

Orientation-Specific

In order to create different resources for an activity to use in portrait vs. landscape orientations, use the following qualifiers:

- resource-land
- resource-port

Using these qualifiers works for all resource types, but they are most commonly found with layouts. Therefore, instead of a res/layout/ directory in the project, there would be a res/layout-port/ and a res/layout-land/ directory.

> **Note**   It is good practice to include a default resource directory without a qualifier. This gives Android something to fall back on if it is running on a device that doesn't match any of the specific criteria you list.

Size-Specific

There are also screen-size qualifiers (physical size, not to be confused with pixel density) that we can use to target large-screen devices such as tablets. In most cases, a single layout will suffice for all physical screen sizes of mobile phones. However, you may want to add more features to a tablet layout to assist in filling the noticeably larger screen real estate the user has to operate.

Prior to Android 3.2 (API Level 13), the following resource qualifiers were acceptable for physical screen sizes:

- `resource-small`: Screen measuring at least 426dp×320dp
- `resource-medium`: Screen measuring at least 470dp×320dp
- `resource-large`: Screen measuring at least 640dp×480dp
- `resource-xlarge`: Screen measuring at least 960dp×720dp

As larger screens became more common on both handset devices and tablets, it was apparent that the four generalized buckets weren't enough to avoid overlap in defining resources. In Android 3.2, a new system based on the screen's actual dimensions (in dp units) was introduced. With the new system, the following resource qualifiers are acceptable for physical screen sizes:

- Smallest Width (`resource-sw___dp`): Screen with at least the noted density-independent pixels in the shortest direction (meaning irrespective of orientation).
    - A 640dp×480dp screen always has a smallest width of 480dp
- Width (`resource-w___dp`): Screen with at least the noted density-independent pixels in the current horizontal direction.
    - A 640dp×480dp screen has a width of 640dp when in landscape and 480dp when in portrait.
- Height (`resource-h___dp`): Screen with at least the noted density-independent pixels in the current vertical direction.
    - A 640dp×480dp screen has a height of 640dp when in portrait and 480dp when in landscape.

So, to include a tablet-only layout to a universal application, we could add a `res/layout-large/` directory for older tablets and a `res/layout-sw720dp/` directory for newer tablets as well.

Layout Aliases

There is one final concept to discuss when creating universal application UIs, and that is layout aliases. Often the same layout should be used for multiple device configurations, but chaining multiple resource qualifiers together (such as a smallest width qualifier and a traditional size qualifier) on the same resource directory can be problematic. This can often lead developers to create multiple copies of the same layout in different directories, which is a maintenance nightmare.

We can solve this problem with aliasing. By creating a single layout file in the default resource directory, we can create multiple aliases to that single file in resource-qualified values directories for each configuration that uses the layout. The following snippet illustrates an alias to the `res/layout/main_tablet.xml` file:

```
<resources>
    <item name="main" type="layout">@layout/main_tablet</item>
</resources>
```

The name attribute represents the aliased name, which is the resource this alias is meant to represent in the selected configuration. This alias links the main_tablet.xml file to be used when R.layout.main is requested in code. This code could be placed into res/values-xlarge/layout.xml and res/values-sw720dp/layout.xml, and both configurations would link to the same layout.

Tying It Together

Let's look at a quick example that puts this into practice. We'll define a single activity that loads a single layout resource in code. However, this layout will be defined differently in the resources to produce different results in portrait, in landscape, and on tablet devices. First, the activity is shown in Listing 2-53.

Listing 2-53. Simple Activity Loading One Layout

```
public class UniversalActivity extends Activity {

    @Override
    public void onCreate(Bundle savedInstanceState) {
        super.onCreate(savedInstanceState);
        setContentView(R.layout.main);
    }
}
```

We'll now define three separate layouts to use for this activity in different configurations. Listings 2-54 through 2-56 show layouts to be used for the default, landscape, and tablet configurations of the UI.

Listing 2-54. res/layout/main.xml

```xml
<?xml version="1.0" encoding="utf-8"?>
<!-- DEFAULT LAYOUT -->
<LinearLayout xmlns:android="http://schemas.android.com/apk/res/android"
    android:layout_width="match_parent"
    android:layout_height="match_parent"
    android:orientation="vertical" >
    <TextView
        android:layout_width="match_parent"
        android:layout_height="wrap_content"
        android:text="This is the default layout" />
    <Button
        android:layout_width="match_parent"
        android:layout_height="wrap_content"
        android:text="Button One" />
    <Button
        android:layout_width="match_parent"
        android:layout_height="wrap_content"
        android:text="Button Two" />
    <Button
        android:layout_width="match_parent"
        android:layout_height="wrap_content"
        android:text="Button Three" />
</LinearLayout>
```

Listing 2-55. res/layout-land/main.xml

```xml
<?xml version="1.0" encoding="utf-8"?>
<!-- LANDSCAPE LAYOUT -->
<LinearLayout
    xmlns:android="http://schemas.android.com/apk/res/android"
    android:layout_width="fill_parent"
    android:layout_height="fill_parent"
    android:orientation="vertical" >
    <TextView
        android:layout_width="wrap_content"
        android:layout_height="wrap_content"
        android:text="This is a horizontal layout for LANDSCAPE"
    />
    <!-- Three buttons to fill screen equally using weight -->
    <LinearLayout
        android:layout_width="match_parent"
        android:layout_height="wrap_content"
        android:orientation="horizontal" >
        <Button
            android:layout_width="0dp"
            android:layout_height="wrap_content"
            android:layout_weight="1"
            android:text="Button One" />
        <Button
            android:layout_width="0dp"
            android:layout_height="wrap_content"
            android:layout_weight="1"
            android:text="Button Two" />
        <Button
            android:layout_width="0dp"
            android:layout_height="wrap_content"
            android:layout_weight="1"
            android:text="Button Three" />
    </LinearLayout>
</LinearLayout>
```

Listing 2-56. res/layout/main_tablet.xml

```xml
<?xml version="1.0" encoding="utf-8"?>
<!-- TABLET LAYOUT -->
<LinearLayout xmlns:android="http://schemas.android.com/apk/res/android"
    android:layout_width="match_parent"
    android:layout_height="match_parent"
    android:orientation="horizontal" >
    <!-- Group of user buttons taking 25% of screen width -->
    <LinearLayout
        android:layout_width="0dp"
        android:layout_height="match_parent"
        android:layout_weight="1"
        android:orientation="vertical">
```

```
    <TextView
        android:layout_width="match_parent"
        android:layout_height="wrap_content"
        android:text="This is the layout for TABLETS" />
    <Button
        android:layout_width="match_parent"
        android:layout_height="wrap_content"
        android:text="Button One" />
    <Button
        android:layout_width="match_parent"
        android:layout_height="wrap_content"
        android:text="Button Two" />
    <Button
        android:layout_width="match_parent"
        android:layout_height="wrap_content"
        android:text="Button Three" />
    <Button
        android:layout_width="match_parent"
        android:layout_height="wrap_content"
        android:text="Button Four" />
    </LinearLayout>


    <!-- Extra view to show detail content -->
    <TextView
        android:layout_width="0dp"
        android:layout_height="match_parent"
        android:layout_weight="3"
        android:text="Detail View"
        android:background="#CCC" />
</LinearLayout>
```

One option would have been to create three files with the same name and to place them in qualified directories, such as res/layout-land for landscape and res/layout-large for tablet. That scheme works great if each layout file is used only once, but we will need to reuse each layout in multiple configurations, so in this example we will create qualified aliases to these three layouts. Listings 2-57 through 2-60 reveal how we link each layout to the correct configuration.

Listing 2-57. res/values-large-land/layout.xml

```
<?xml version="1.0" encoding="utf-8"?>
<resources
    xmlns:android="http://schemas.android.com/apk/res/android">
    <item name="main" type="layout">@layout/main_tablet</item>
</resources>
```

Listing 2-58. `res/value-sw600dp-land/layout.xml`

```xml
<?xml version="1.0" encoding="utf-8"?>
<resources
    xmlns:android="http://schemas.android.com/apk/res/android">
    <item name="main" type="layout">@layout/main_tablet</item>
</resources>
```

Listing 2-59. `res/values-xlarge/layout.xml`

```xml
<?xml version="1.0" encoding="utf-8"?>
<resources
    xmlns:android="http://schemas.android.com/apk/res/android">
    <item name="main" type="layout">@layout/main_tablet</item>
</resources>
```

Listing 2-60. `res/values-sw720dp/layout.xml`

```xml
<?xml version="1.0" encoding="utf-8"?>
<resources
    xmlns:android="http://schemas.android.com/apk/res/android">
    <item name="main" type="layout">@layout/main_tablet</item>
</resources>
```

We have defined configuration groups to accommodate three classes of devices: handsets, 7-inch tablet devices, and 10-inch tablet devices. Handset devices will load the default layout when in portrait mode, and the landscape layout when the device is rotated. Because this is the only configuration using these files, they are placed directly into the res/layout and res/layout-land directories, respectively.

The 7-inch tablet devices in the previous size scheme were typically defined as large screens, and in the new scheme they have a smallest width, of around 600dp. In portrait mode, we have decided that our application should use the default layout, but in landscape mode we have significantly more real estate, so we load the tablet layout instead. To do this, we create qualified directories for the landscape orientation that match this device size class. Using both smallest-width and bucket-size qualifiers ensures we are compatible with older and newer tablets.

The 10-inch tablet devices in the previous size scheme were considered extra-large screens, and in the new scheme they have a smallest width, of around 720dp. For these devices, the screen is large enough to use the tablet layout in both orientations, so we create qualified directories that call out only the screen size. Again, as with the smaller tablets, using both smallest-width and bucket-size qualifiers ensures we are compatible with all tablet versions.

In all cases in which the tablet layout was referenced, we had to create only one layout file to manage, thanks to the power of using aliases. Now when we run the application, you can see how Android selects the appropriate layout to match our configuration. Figure 2-19 shows default and landscape layouts on a handset device.

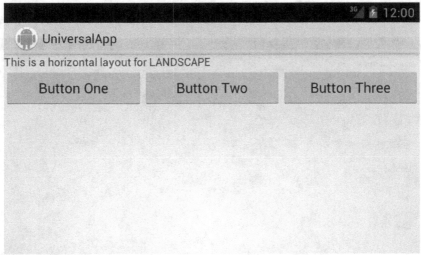

Figure 2-19. Handset portrait and landscape layouts

The same application on a 7-inch tablet device displays the default layout in portrait orientation, but we get the full tablet layout in landscape (see Figure 2-20).

Figure 2-20. *Default portrait and tablet landscape layout on a 7-inch tablet*

Finally, in Figure 2-21 we can see the larger screen on the 10-inch tablet running the full tablet layout in both portrait and landscape orientations.

Figure 2-21. Full tablet layout in both orientations on a 10-inch tablet

With the extensive capabilities of the Android resource selection system, the difficulty of supporting different UI layouts optimized for each device type is greatly reduced.

2-10. Customizing AdapterView Empty Views

Problem

You want to display a custom view when an AdapterView (ListView, GridView, and the like) has an empty data set.

Solution

(API Level 1)

Lay out the view you would like displayed in the same tree as the AdapterView and call AdapterView.setEmptyView() to have the AdapterView manage it. The AdapterView will switch the visibility parameters between itself and its empty view based on the result of the attached ListAdapter's isEmpty() method.

> **Important**   Be sure to include both the AdapterView and the empty view in your layout. The AdapterView changes *only* the visibility parameters on the two objects; it does not insert or remove them in the layout tree.

How It Works

Here is how this would look with a simple TextView used as the empty view. First, a layout includes both views, shown in Listing 2-61.

Listing 2-61. Layout Containing AdapterView and an Empty View

```xml
<?xml version="1.0" encoding="utf-8"?>
<FrameLayout
    xmlns:android="http://schemas.android.com/apk/res/android"
    android:layout_width="fill_parent"
    android:layout_height="fill_parent">
    <TextView
        android:id="@+id/myempty"
        android:layout_width="fill_parent"
        android:layout_height="wrap_content"
        android:text="No Items to Display"
    />
    <ListView
        android:id="@+id/mylist"
        android:layout_width="fill_parent"
        android:layout_height="fill_parent"
    />
</FrameLayout>
```

Then, in the activity, give the ListView a reference to the empty view so it can be managed (see Listing 2-62).

Listing 2-62. Activity Connecting the Empty View to the List

```
public void onCreate(Bundle savedInstanceState) {
    super.onCreate(savedInstanceState);
    ListView list = (ListView)findViewById(R.id.mylist);
    TextView empty = (TextView)findViewById(R.id.myempty);
    //Attach the reference
    list.setEmptyView(empty);

    //Continue adding adapters and data to the list

}
```

Make Empty Interesting

Empty views don't have to be simple and boring like the single TextView. Let's try to make things a little more useful for the user and add a Refresh button when the list is empty (see Listing 2-63).

Listing 2-63. Interactive Empty Layout

```xml
<?xml version="1.0" encoding="utf-8"?>
<FrameLayout
    xmlns:android="http://schemas.android.com/apk/res/android"
    android:layout_width="fill_parent"
    android:layout_height="fill_parent">
    <LinearLayout
        android:id="@+id/myempty"
        android:layout_width="fill_parent"
        android:layout_height="wrap_content"
        android:orientation="vertical">
        <TextView
            android:layout_width="fill_parent"
            android:layout_height="wrap_content"
            android:text="No Items to Display"
        />
        <Button
            android:layout_width="fill_parent"
            android:layout_height="wrap_content"
            android:text="Tap Here to Refresh"
        />
    </LinearLayout>
    <ListView
        android:id="@+id/mylist"
        android:layout_width="fill_parent"
        android:layout_height="fill_parent"
    />
</FrameLayout>
```

Now, with the same activity code from before, we have set an entire layout as the empty view and have added the ability for users to do something about their lack of data.

2-11. Customizing ListView Rows

Problem

Your application needs to use a more customized look for each row in a ListView.

Solution

(API Level 1)

Create a custom XML layout and pass it to one of the common adapters, or extend your own. You can then apply custom state drawables for overriding the background and selected states of each row.

How It Works

Starting Simple

If your needs are simple, create a layout that can connect to an existing ListAdapter for population; we'll use ArrayAdapter as an example. The ArrayAdapter can take parameters for a custom layout resource to inflate and the ID of one TextView in that layout to populate with data. Let's create some custom drawables for the background and a layout that meets these requirements (see Listings 2-64 through 2-66).

Listing 2-64. res/drawable/row_background_default.xml

```xml
<?xml version="1.0" encoding="utf-8"?>
<shape xmlns:android="http://schemas.android.com/apk/res/android"
    android:shape="rectangle">
    <gradient
        android:startColor="#EFEFEF"
        android:endColor="#989898"
        android:type="linear"
        android:angle="270"
    />
</shape>
```

Listing 2-65. res/drawable/row_background_pressed.xml

```xml
<?xml version="1.0" encoding="utf-8"?>
<shape xmlns:android="http://schemas.android.com/apk/res/android"
    android:shape="rectangle">
    <gradient
        android:startColor="#0B8CF2"
        android:endColor="#0661E5"
```

```
        android:type="linear"
        android:angle="270"
    />
</shape>
```

Listing 2-66. *res/drawable/row_background.xml*

```xml
<?xml version="1.0" encoding="utf-8"?>
<selector
    xmlns:android="http://schemas.android.com/apk/res/android">
    <item android:state_pressed="true"
        android:drawable="@drawable/row_background_pressed"/>
  <item android:drawable="@drawable/row_background_default"/>
</selector>
```

Listing 2-67 shows a custom layout with the text fully centered in the row instead of aligned to the left.

Listing 2-67. *res/layout/custom_row.xml*

```xml
<?xml version="1.0" encoding="utf-8"?>
<LinearLayout
    xmlns:android="http://schemas.android.com/apk/res/android"
    android:layout_width="fill_parent"
    android:layout_height="wrap_content"
    android:padding="10dip"
    android:background="@drawable/row_background">
    <TextView
        android:id="@+id/line1"
        android:layout_width="wrap_content"
        android:layout_height="wrap_content"
        android:layout_gravity="center"
    />
</LinearLayout>
```

This layout has the custom gradient state-list set as its background, and this sets up the default and pressed states for each item in the list. Now, because we have defined a layout that matches up with what an ArrayAdapter expects, we can create one and set it on our list without any further customization (see Listing 2-68).

Listing 2-68. *Activity Using the Custom Row Layout*

```java
public void onCreate(Bundle savedInstanceState) {
    super.onCreate(savedInstanceState);
    ListView list = new ListView(this);
    ArrayAdapter<String> adapter = new ArrayAdapter<String>(this,
                R.layout.custom_row,
                R.id.line1,
                new String[] {"Bill","Tom","Sally","Jenny"});
    list.setAdapter(adapter);

    setContentView(list);
}
```

Adapting to a More Complex Choice

Sometimes customizing the list rows means extending a ListAdapter as well. This is usually the case if you have multiple pieces of data in a single row or if any of them are not text. In this example, let's utilize the custom drawables again for the background, but we'll make the layout a little more interesting (see Listing 2-69).

Listing 2-69. res/layout/custom_row.xml Modified

```xml
<?xml version="1.0" encoding="utf-8"?>
<RelativeLayout
    xmlns:android="http://schemas.android.com/apk/res/android"
    android:layout_width="fill_parent"
    android:layout_height="wrap_content"
    android:orientation="horizontal"
    android:padding="10dip">
    <ImageView
        android:id="@+id/leftimage"
        android:layout_width="32dip"
        android:layout_height="32dip"
    />
    <ImageView
        android:id="@+id/rightimage"
        android:layout_width="32dip"
        android:layout_height="32dip"
        android:layout_alignParentRight="true"
    />

    <TextView
        android:id="@+id/line1"
        android:layout_width="fill_parent"
        android:layout_height="wrap_content"
        android:layout_toLeftOf="@id/rightimage"
        android:layout_toRightOf="@id/leftimage"
        android:layout_centerVertical="true"
        android:gravity="center_horizontal"
    />
</RelativeLayout>
```

This layout contains the same centered TextView but bordered with an ImageView on each side. In order to apply this layout to the ListView, we will need to extend one of the ListAdapters in the SDK. Which one you extend depends on the data source you are presenting in the list. If the data is still just a simple array of strings, an extension of ArrayAdapter is sufficient. If the data is more complex, a full extension of the abstract BaseAdapter may be necessary. The only required method to extend is getView(), which governs how each row in the list is presented.

In our case, the data is a simple array of strings, so we will create a simple extension of ArrayAdapter (see Listing 2-70).

Listing 2-70. Activity and Custom ListAdapter to Display the New Layout

```java
public class MyActivity extends Activity {

    public void onCreate(Bundle savedInstanceState) {
        super.onCreate(savedInstanceState);
        ListView list = new ListView(this);
        setContentView(list);

        CustomAdapter adapter = new CustomAdapter(this,
                R.layout.custom_row,
                R.id.line1,
                new String[] {"Bill","Tom","Sally","Jenny"});
        list.setAdapter(adapter);

    }

    private static class CustomAdapter extends ArrayAdapter<String> {

        public CustomAdapter(Context context, int layout, int resId,
                String[] items) {
            //Call through to ArrayAdapter implementation
            super(context, layout, resId, items);
        }

        @Override
        public View getView(int position, View convertView,
                ViewGroup parent) {
            View row = convertView;
            //Inflate a new row if one isn't recycled
            if(row == null) {
                row = LayoutInflater.from(getContext())
                        .inflate(R.layout.custom_row, parent, false);
            }
            String item = getItem(position);
            ImageView left =
                    (ImageView)row.findViewById(R.id.leftimage);
            ImageView right =
                    (ImageView)row.findViewById(R.id.rightimage);
            TextView text = (TextView)row.findViewById(R.id.line1);

            left.setImageResource(R.drawable.icon);
            right.setImageResource(R.drawable.icon);
            text.setText(item);

            return row;
        }
    }
}
```

Notice that we use the same constructor to create an instance of the adapter as before, because it is inherited from ArrayAdapter. We have overridden the view display mechanism of the adapter, and the only reason the R.layout.custom_row and R.id.line1 are now passed into the constructor is that they are required parameters of the constructor; they don't serve a useful purpose in this example anymore.

Now, when the ListView wants to display a row, it will call getView() on its adapter, which we have customized so we can control how each row returns. The getView() method is passed a parameter called the convertView, which is very important for performance. Layout inflation from XML is an expensive process: to minimize its impact on the system, ListView recycles views as the list scrolls. If a recycled view is available to be reused, it is passed into getView() as the convertView. Whenever possible, reuse these views instead of inflating new ones to keep the scrolling performance of the list fast and responsive.

In this example, we use getItem() to get the current value at that position in the list (our array of strings), and then later on we set that value on the TextView for that row. We can also set the images in each row to something significant for the data, although here they are set to the app icon for simplicity.

2-12. Making ListView Section Headers

Problem

You want to create a list with multiple sections, each with a header at the top.

Solution

(API Level 1)

Use the SimplerExpandableListAdapter code defined here and an ExpandableListView. Android doesn't officially have an extensible way to create sections in a list, but it does offer the ExpandableListView widget and associated adapters designed to handle a two-dimensional data structure in a sectioned list. The drawback is that the adapters provided with the SDK to handle this data are cumbersome to work with for simple data structures.

How It Works

Enter the SimplerExpandableListAdapter (see Listing 2-71), an extension of the BaseExpandableListAdapter that, as an example, handles an array of string arrays, with a separate string array for the section titles.

Listing 2-71. SimplerExpandableListAdapter

```
public class SimplerExpandableListAdapter extends BaseExpandableListAdapter {
    private Context mContext;
    private String[][] mContents;
    private String[] mTitles;
```

```java
public SimplerExpandableListAdapter(Context context, String[] titles,
        String[][] contents) {
    super();
    //Check arguments
    if(titles.length != contents.length) {
        throw new IllegalArgumentException(
                "Titles and Contents must be the same size.");
    }

    mContext = context;
    mContents = contents;
    mTitles = titles;
}

//Return a child item
@Override
public String getChild(int groupPosition, int childPosition) {
    return mContents[groupPosition][childPosition];
}

//Return an item's id
@Override
public long getChildId(int groupPosition, int childPosition) {
    return 0;
}

//Return view for each item row
@Override
public View getChildView(int groupPosition, int childPosition,
        boolean isLastChild, View convertView, ViewGroup parent) {
    TextView row = (TextView)convertView;
    if(row == null) {
        row = new TextView(mContext);
    }
    row.setText(mContents[groupPosition][childPosition]);
    return row;
}

//Return number of items in each section
@Override
public int getChildrenCount(int groupPosition) {
    return mContents[groupPosition].length;
}

//Return sections
@Override
public String[] getGroup(int groupPosition) {
    return mContents[groupPosition];
}
```

```
    //Return the number of sections
    @Override
    public int getGroupCount() {
        return mContents.length;
    }

    //Return a section's id
    @Override
    public long getGroupId(int groupPosition) {
        return 0;
    }

    //Return a view for each section header
    @Override
    public View getGroupView(int groupPosition, boolean isExpanded,
            View convertView, ViewGroup parent) {
        TextView row = (TextView)convertView;
        if(row == null) {
            row = new TextView(mContext);
        }
        row.setTypeface(Typeface.DEFAULT_BOLD);
        row.setText(mTitles[groupPosition]);
        return row;
    }

    @Override
    public boolean hasStableIds() {
        return false;
    }

    @Override
    public boolean isChildSelectable(int groupPosition, int childPosition) {
        return true;
    }

}
```

Now we can create a simple data structure and use it to populate an ExpandableListView in an example activity (see Listing 2-72).

Listing 2-72. Activity Using the SimplerExpandableListAdapter

```
public void onCreate(Bundle savedInstanceState) {
    super.onCreate(savedInstanceState);
    //Set up an expandable list
    ExpandableListView list = new ExpandableListView(this);
    list.setGroupIndicator(null);
    list.setChildIndicator(null);

    //Set up simple data and the new adapter
    String[] titles = {"Fruits","Vegetables","Meats"};
    String[] fruits = {"Apples","Oranges"};
```

```
String[] veggies = {"Carrots","Peas","Broccoli"};
String[] meats = {"Pork","Chicken"};
String[][] contents = {fruits,veggies,meats};
SimplerExpandableListAdapter adapter =
        new SimplerExpandableListAdapter(this, titles, contents);

list.setAdapter(adapter);
setContentView(list);
}
```

That Darn Expansion

There is one catch to utilizing ExpandableListView in this fashion: it expands. ExpandableListView is designed to expand and collapse the child data underneath the group heading when the heading it tapped. Also, by default all the groups are collapsed, so you can see only the header items.

In some cases, this may be desirable behavior, but often it is not if you just want to add section headers. In that case, there are two additional steps to take:

1. In the activity code, expand all the groups:

   ```
   for(int i=0; i < adapter.getGroupCount(); i++) {
       list.expandGroup(i);
   }
   ```

2. In the adapter, override onGroupCollapsed() to force a re-expansion. This will require adding a reference to the list widget to the adapter.

   ```
   @Override
   public void onGroupCollapsed(int groupPosition) {
       list.expandGroup(groupPosition);
   }
   ```

2-13. Creating Compound Controls

Problem

You need to create a custom widget that is a collection of existing elements.

Solution

(API Level 1)

Create a custom widget by extending a common ViewGroup and adding functionality. One of the simplest and most powerful ways to create custom or reusable UI elements is to create compound controls leveraging the existing widgets provided by the Android SDK.

How It Works

ViewGroup(and its subclasses LinearLayout, RelativeLayout, and so on) gives you the tools to make this simple by assisting you with component placement, so you can be more concerned with the added functionality.

TextImageButton

Let's create an example by making a widget that the Android SDK does not have natively: a button containing either an image or text as its content. To do this, we are going to create the TextImageButton class, which is an extension of FrameLayout. It will contain a TextView to handle text content as well as an ImageView for image content (see Listing 2-73).

Listing 2-73. Custom TextImageButton Widget

```java
public class TextImageButton extends FrameLayout {

    private ImageView imageView;
    private TextView textView;

    /* Constructors */
    public TextImageButton(Context context) {
        this(context, null);
    }

    public TextImageButton(Context context, AttributeSet attrs) {
        this(context, attrs, 0);
    }

    public TextImageButton(Context context, AttributeSet attrs,
            int defaultStyle) {
        //Initialize the parent layout with the system's button style
        // This sets the clickable attributes and button background
        // to match the current theme.
        super(context, attrs, android.R.attr.buttonStyle);
        //Create the child views
        imageView = new ImageView(context, attrs, defaultStyle);
        textView = new TextView(context, attrs, defaultStyle);
        //Create LayoutParams for children to wrap content and center
        FrameLayout.LayoutParams params = new FrameLayout.LayoutParams(
                LayoutParams.WRAP_CONTENT,
                LayoutParams.WRAP_CONTENT,
                Gravity.CENTER);
        //Add the views
        this.addView(imageView, params);
        this.addView(textView, params);

        //If an image is present, switch to image mode
        if(imageView.getDrawable() != null) {
            textView.setVisibility(View.GONE);
            imageView.setVisibility(View.VISIBLE);
```

```
        } else {
            textView.setVisibility(View.VISIBLE);
            imageView.setVisibility(View.GONE);
        }
    }

    /* Accessors */
    public void setText(CharSequence text) {
        //Switch to text
        textView.setVisibility(View.VISIBLE);
        imageView.setVisibility(View.GONE);
        //Apply text
        textView.setText(text);
    }

    public void setImageResource(int resId) {
        //Switch to image
        textView.setVisibility(View.GONE);
        imageView.setVisibility(View.VISIBLE);
        //Apply image
        imageView.setImageResource(resId);
    }

    public void setImageDrawable(Drawable drawable) {
        //Switch to image
        textView.setVisibility(View.GONE);
        imageView.setVisibility(View.VISIBLE);
        //Apply image
        imageView.setImageDrawable(drawable);
    }
}
```

All of the widgets in the SDK have at least two, and often three, constructors. The first constructor takes only Context as a parameter and is generally used to create a new view in code. The remaining two are used when a view is inflated from XML, where the attributes defined in the XML file are passed in as the AttributeSet parameter. Here we use Java's this() notation to drill the first two constructors down to the one that really does all the work. Building the custom control in this fashion ensures that we can still define this view in XML layouts. Without implementing the attributed constructors, this would not be possible.

In order to make the FrameLayout look like a standard button, we pass the attribute android.R.attr.buttonStyle to the constructor. This defines the style value that should be pulled from the current theme and applied to the view. This sets up the background to match other button instances, but it also makes the view clickable and focusable, as those flags are also part of the system's style. Whenever possible, you should load your custom widget's look and feel from the current theme to allow easy customization and consistency with the rest of your application.

The constructor also creates a TextView and ImageView, and it places them inside the layout. Each child constructor is passed the same set of attributes so that any XML attributes that were set specific to one or the other (such as text or image state) are properly read. The remaining code sets the default display mode (either text or image) based on the data that was passed in as attributes.

The accessor functions are added as a convenience to later switch the button contents. These functions are also tasked with switching between text and image mode if the content change warrants it.

Because this custom control is not in the android.view or android.widget packages, we must use the fully qualified name when it is used in an XML layout. Listings 2-74 and 2-75 show an example activity displaying the custom widget.

Listing 2-74. res/layout/main.xml

```xml
<?xml version="1.0" encoding="utf-8"?>
<LinearLayout
    xmlns:android="http://schemas.android.com/apk/res/android"
    android:layout_width="fill_parent"
    android:layout_height="fill_parent"
    android:orientation="vertical" >
    <com.examples.customwidgets.TextImageButton
        android:layout_width="match_parent"
        android:layout_height="wrap_content"
        android:text="Click Me!"
        android:textColor="#000" />
    <com.examples.customwidgets.TextImageButton
        android:layout_width="match_parent"
        android:layout_height="wrap_content"
        android:src="@drawable/ic_launcher" />
</LinearLayout>
```

Listing 2-75. Activity Using the New Custom Widget

```java
public class MyActivity extends Activity {

    @Override
    public void onCreate(Bundle savedInstanceState) {
        super.onCreate(savedInstanceState);
        setContentView(R.layout.main);
    }
}
```

Notice that we can still use traditional attributes to define properties such as the text or image to display. This is because we construct each item (the FrameLayout, TextView, and ImageView) with the attributed constructors, so each view sets the parameters it is interested in and ignores the rest.

If we define an activity to use this layout, the result looks like Figure 2-22.

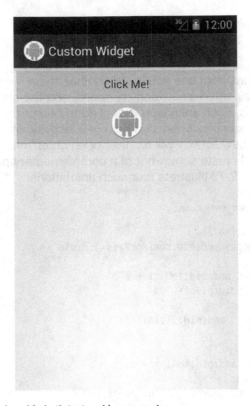

Figure 2-22. `TextImageButton` *displayed in both text and image modes*

2-14. Customizing Transition Animations

Problem

Your application needs to customize the transition animations that happen when moving from one activity to another or between fragments.

Solution

(API Level 5)

To modify an activity transition, use the `overridePendingTransition()` API for a single occurrence, or declare custom animation values in your application's theme to make a more global change. To modify a fragment transition, use the `onCreateAnimation()` or `onCreateAnimator()` API methods.

How It Works

Activity

When customizing the transitions from one activity to another, there are four animations to consider: the enter and exit animation pair when a new activity opens, and the entry and exit animation pair when the current activity closes. Each animation is applied to one of the two activity elements involved in the transition. For example, when starting a new activity, the current activity will run the "open exit" animation and the new activity will run the "open enter" animation. Because these are run simultaneously, they should create somewhat of a complementary pair or they may look visually incorrect. Listings 2-76 through 2-79 illustrate four such animations.

Listing 2-76. res/anim/activity_open_enter.xml

```xml
<?xml version="1.0" encoding="utf-8"?>
<set xmlns:android="http://schemas.android.com/apk/res/android">
    <rotate
        android:fromDegrees="90" android:toDegrees="0"
        android:pivotX="0%" android:pivotY="0%"
        android:fillEnabled="true"
        android:fillBefore="true" android:fillAfter="true"
        android:duration="500"  />
    <alpha
        android:fromAlpha="0.0" android:toAlpha="1.0"
        android:fillEnabled="true"
        android:fillBefore="true" android:fillAfter="true"
        android:duration="500" />
</set>
```

Listing 2-77. res/anim/activity_open_exit.xml

```xml
<?xml version="1.0" encoding="utf-8"?>
<set xmlns:android="http://schemas.android.com/apk/res/android">
    <rotate
        android:fromDegrees="0" android:toDegrees="-90"
        android:pivotX="0%" android:pivotY="0%"
        android:fillEnabled="true"
        android:fillBefore="true" android:fillAfter="true"
        android:duration="500"  />
    <alpha
        android:fromAlpha="1.0" android:toAlpha="0.0"
        android:fillEnabled="true"
        android:fillBefore="true" android:fillAfter="true"
        android:duration="500" />
</set>
```

Listing 2-78. res/anim/activity_close_enter.xml

```xml
<?xml version="1.0" encoding="utf-8"?>
<set xmlns:android="http://schemas.android.com/apk/res/android">
    <rotate
        android:fromDegrees="-90" android:toDegrees="0"
        android:pivotX="0%p" android:pivotY="0%p"
        android:fillEnabled="true"
        android:fillBefore="true" android:fillAfter="true"
        android:duration="500"  />
    <alpha
        android:fromAlpha="0.0" android:toAlpha="1.0"
        android:fillEnabled="true"
        android:fillBefore="true" android:fillAfter="true"
        android:duration="500" />
</set>
```

Listing 2-79. res/anim/activity_close_exit.xml

```xml
<?xml version="1.0" encoding="utf-8"?>
<set xmlns:android="http://schemas.android.com/apk/res/android" >
    <rotate
        android:fromDegrees="0" android:toDegrees="90"
        android:pivotX="0%p" android:pivotY="0%p"
        android:fillEnabled="true"
        android:fillBefore="true" android:fillAfter="true"
        android:duration="500" />
    <alpha
        android:fromAlpha="1.0" android:toAlpha="0.0"
        android:fillEnabled="true"
        android:fillBefore="true" android:fillAfter="true"
        android:duration="500" />
</set>
```

What we have created are two "open" animations that rotate the old activity out and the new activity in clockwise. The complementary "close" animations rotate the current activity out and the previous activity in counterclockwise. Each animation also has with it a fade-out or fade-in effect to make the transition seem more smooth. To apply these custom animations at a specific moment, we can call the method overridePendingTransition() immediately after either startActivity() or finish() like so:

```java
//Start a new Activity with custom transition
Intent intent = new Intent(...);
startActivity(intent);
overridePendingTransition(R.anim.activity_open_enter,
        R.anim.activity_open_exit);

//Close the current Activity with custom transition
finish();
overridePendingTransition(R.anim.activity_close_enter,
        R.anim.activity_close_exit);
```

This is useful if you need to customize transitions in only a few places. But suppose you need to customize every activity transition in your application; calling this method everywhere would be quite a hassle. Instead it would make more sense to customize the animations in your application's theme. Listing 2-80 illustrates a custom theme that overrides these transitions globally.

Listing 2-80. res/values/styles.xml

```xml
<resources>
    <style name="AppTheme" parent="android:Theme.Holo.Light">
        <item name="android:windowAnimationStyle">
            @style/ActivityAnimation</item>
    </style>

    <style name="ActivityAnimation"
        parent="@android:style/Animation.Activity">
        <item name="android:activityOpenEnterAnimation">
            @anim/activity_open_enter</item>
        <item name="android:activityOpenExitAnimation">
            @anim/activity_open_exit</item>
        <item name="android:activityCloseEnterAnimation">
            @anim/activity_close_enter</item>
        <item name="android:activityCloseExitAnimation">
            @anim/activity_close_exit</item>
    </style>

</resources>
```

By supplying a custom attribute for the android:windowAnimationStyle value of the theme, we can customize these transition animations. It is important to also refer back to the parent style in the framework because these four animations are not the only ones defined in this style, and you don't want to erase the other existing window animations inadvertently.

Support Fragments

Customizing the animations for fragment transitions is different, depending on whether you are using the Support Library. The variance exists because the native version uses the new Animator objects, which are not available in the Support Library version.

When using the Support Library, you can override the transition animations for a single FragmentTransaction by calling setCustomAnimations(). The version of this method that takes two parameters will set the animation for the add/replace/remove action, but it will not animate on popping the back stack. The version that takes four parameters will add custom animations for popping the back stack as well. Using the same Animation objects from our previous example, the following snippet shows how to add these animations to a FragmentTransaction:

```java
FragmentTransaction ft = getSupportFragmentManager().beginTransaction();
    //Must be called first!
    ft.setCustomAnimations(R.anim.activity_open_enter,
            R.anim.activity_open_exit,
            R.anim.activity_close_enter,
            R.anim.activity_close_exit);
```

```
    ft.replace(R.id.container_fragment, fragment);
    ft.addToBackStack(null);
ft.commit();
```

> **Important** setCustomAnimations() *must* be called before add(), replace(), or any other
> action method, or the animation will not run. It is good practice to simply call this method first in the
> transaction block.

If you would like the same animations to run for a certain fragment all the time, you may want
to override the onCreateAnimation() method inside the fragment instead. Listing 2-81 reveals a
fragment with its animations defined in this way.

Listing 2-81. Fragment with Custom Animations

```java
public class SupportFragment extends Fragment {

    @Override
    public View onCreateView(LayoutInflater inflater,
            ViewGroup container, Bundle savedInstanceState) {
        TextView tv = new TextView(getActivity());
        tv.setText("Fragment");
        tv.setBackgroundColor(Color.RED);
        return tv;
    }

    @Override
    public Animation onCreateAnimation(int transit, boolean enter,
            int nextAnim) {
        switch (transit) {
        case FragmentTransaction.TRANSIT_FRAGMENT_FADE:
            if (enter) {
                return AnimationUtils.loadAnimation(getActivity(),
                        android.R.anim.fade_in);
            } else {
                return AnimationUtils.loadAnimation(getActivity(),
                        android.R.anim.fade_out);
            }
        case FragmentTransaction.TRANSIT_FRAGMENT_CLOSE:
            if (enter) {
                return AnimationUtils.loadAnimation(getActivity(),
                        R.anim.activity_close_enter);
            } else {
                return AnimationUtils.loadAnimation(getActivity(),
                        R.anim.activity_close_exit);
            }
```

```
            case FragmentTransaction.TRANSIT_FRAGMENT_OPEN:
            default:
                if (enter) {
                    return AnimationUtils.loadAnimation(getActivity(),
                            R.anim.activity_open_enter);
                } else {
                    return AnimationUtils.loadAnimation(getActivity(),
                            R.anim.activity_open_exit);
                }
            }
        }
    }
}
```

How the fragment animations behave has a lot to do with how the `FragmentTransaction` is set up. There are a number of different transition values that can be attached to the transaction with `setTransition()`. If no call to `setTransition()` is made, the fragment cannot determine the difference between an open or close animation set, and the only data we have to determine which animation to run is whether this is an entry or exit.

To obtain the same behavior as we implemented previously with `setCustomAnimations()`, the transaction should be run with the transition set to `TRANSIT_FRAGMENT_OPEN`. This will call the initial transaction with this transition value, but it will call the pop back stack action with `TRANSIT_FRAGMENT_CLOSE`, allowing the fragment to provide a different animation in this case. The following snippet illustrates constructing a transaction in this way:

```
FragmentTransaction ft = getSupportFragmentManager().beginTransaction();
    //Set the transition value to trigger the correct animations
    ft.setTransition(FragmentTransaction.TRANSIT_FRAGMENT_OPEN);
    ft.replace(R.id.container_fragment, fragment);
    ft.addToBackStack(null);
ft.commit();
```

Fragments also have a third state that you won't find on activity, and it is defined by the `TRANSIT_FRAGMENT_FADE` transition value. This animation should occur when the transition is not part of a change, such as add or replace, but rather the fragment is just being hidden or shown. In our example, we use the standard system-fade animations for this case.

Native Fragments

If your application is targeting API Level 11 or later, you do not need to use fragments from the Support Library, and in this case the custom animation code works slightly differently. The native fragment implementation uses the newer `Animator` object to create the transitions rather than the older `Animation` object.

This requires a few modifications to the code; first of all, we need to define all our XML animations with `Animator` instead. Listings 2-82 through 2-85 show this.

Listing 2-82. res/animator/fragment_exit.xml

```xml
<?xml version="1.0" encoding="utf-8"?>
<set xmlns:android="http://schemas.android.com/apk/res/android" >
    <objectAnimator
        android:valueFrom="0" android:valueTo="-90"
        android:valueType="floatType"
        android:propertyName="rotation"
        android:duration="500"/>
    <objectAnimator
        android:valueFrom="1.0" android:valueTo="0.0"
        android:valueType="floatType"
        android:propertyName="alpha"
        android:duration="500"/>
</set>
```

Listing 2-83. res/animator/fragment_enter.xml

```xml
<?xml version="1.0" encoding="utf-8"?>
<set xmlns:android="http://schemas.android.com/apk/res/android" >
    <objectAnimator
        android:valueFrom="90" android:valueTo="0"
        android:valueType="floatType"
        android:propertyName="rotation"
        android:duration="500"/>
    <objectAnimator
        android:valueFrom="0.0" android:valueTo="1.0"
        android:valueType="floatType"
        android:propertyName="alpha"
        android:duration="500"/>
</set>
```

Listing 2-84. res/animator/fragment_pop_exit.xml

```xml
<?xml version="1.0" encoding="utf-8"?>
<set xmlns:android="http://schemas.android.com/apk/res/android" >
    <objectAnimator
        android:valueFrom="0" android:valueTo="90"
        android:valueType="floatType"
        android:propertyName="rotation"
        android:duration="500"/>
    <objectAnimator
        android:valueFrom="1.0" android:valueTo="0.0"
        android:valueType="floatType"
        android:propertyName="alpha"
        android:duration="500"/>
</set>
```

Listing 2-85. res/animator/fragment_pop_enter.xml

```xml
<?xml version="1.0" encoding="utf-8"?>
<set xmlns:android="http://schemas.android.com/apk/res/android" >
    <objectAnimator
        android:valueFrom="-90" android:valueTo="0"
        android:valueType="floatType"
        android:propertyName="rotation"
        android:duration="500"/>
    <objectAnimator
        android:valueFrom="0.0" android:valueTo="1.0"
        android:valueType="floatType"
        android:propertyName="alpha"
        android:duration="500"/>
</set>
```

Apart from the slightly different syntax, these animations are almost identical to the versions we created previously. The only other difference is that these animations are set to pivot around the center of the view (the default behavior) rather than the top-left corner.

As before, we can customize a single transition directly on a `FragmentTransaction` with `setCustomAnimations()`; however, the newer version takes our `Animator` instances. The following snippet shows this with the newer API:

```java
FragmentTransaction ft = getFragmentManager().beginTransaction();
    //Must be called first!
    ft.setCustomAnimations(R.animator.fragment_enter,
            R.animator.fragment_exit,
            R.animator.fragment_pop_enter,
            R.animator.fragment_pop_exit);
    ft.replace(R.id.container_fragment, fragment);
    ft.addToBackStack(null);
ft.commit();
```

If you prefer to set the same transitions to always run for a given `subclass`, we can customize the fragment as before. However, a native fragment will not have `onCreateAnimation()`, but rather an `onCreateAnimator()` method instead. Have a look at Listing 2-86, which redefines the fragment we created using the newer API.

Listing 2-86. Native Fragment with Custom Transitions

```java
public class NativeFragment extends Fragment {

@Override
    public View onCreateView(LayoutInflater inflater,
            ViewGroup container, Bundle savedInstanceState) {
        TextView tv = new TextView(getActivity());
        tv.setText("Fragment");
        tv.setBackgroundColor(Color.BLUE);
        return tv;
    }
}
```

```
@Override
public Animator onCreateAnimator(int transit, boolean enter,
        int nextAnim) {
    switch (transit) {
    case FragmentTransaction.TRANSIT_FRAGMENT_FADE:
        if (enter) {
            return AnimatorInflater.loadAnimator(
                    getActivity(),
                    android.R.animator.fade_in);
        } else {
            return AnimatorInflater.loadAnimator(
                    getActivity(),
                    android.R.animator.fade_out);
        }
    case FragmentTransaction.TRANSIT_FRAGMENT_CLOSE:
        if (enter) {
            return AnimatorInflater.loadAnimator(
                    getActivity(),
                    R.animator.fragment_pop_enter);
        } else {
            return AnimatorInflater.loadAnimator(
                    getActivity(),
                    R.animator.fragment_pop_exit);
        }
    case FragmentTransaction.TRANSIT_FRAGMENT_OPEN:
    default:
        if (enter) {
            return AnimatorInflater.loadAnimator(
                    getActivity(),
                    R.animator.fragment_enter);
        } else {
            return AnimatorInflater.loadAnimator(
                    getActivity(),
                    R.animator.fragment_exit);
        }
    }
}
```

Again, we are checking for the same transition values as in the support example; we are just returning Animator instances instead. Here is the same snippet of code to properly begin a transaction with the transition value set:

```
FragmentTransaction ft = getFragmentManager().beginTransaction();
    //Set the transition value to trigger the correct animations
    ft.setTransition(FragmentTransaction.TRANSIT_FRAGMENT_OPEN);
    ft.replace(R.id.container_fragment, fragment);
    ft.addToBackStack(null);
ft.commit();
```

The final method you can use to set these custom transitions globally for the entire application is to attach them to your application's theme. Listing 2-87 shows a custom theme with our fragment animations applied.

Listing 2-87. res/values/styles.xml

```xml
<resources>
    <style name="AppTheme" parent="android:Theme.Holo.Light">
        <item name="android:windowAnimationStyle">
            @style/FragmentAnimation</item>
    </style>

    <style name="FragmentAnimation"
        parent="@android:style/Animation.Activity">
        <item name="android:fragmentOpenEnterAnimation">
            @animator/fragment_enter</item>
        <item name="android:fragmentOpenExitAnimation">
            @animator/fragment_exit</item>
        <item name="android:fragmentCloseEnterAnimation">
            @animator/fragment_pop_enter</item>
        <item name="android:fragmentCloseExitAnimation">
            @animator/fragment_pop_exit</item>
        <item name="android:fragmentFadeEnterAnimation">
            @android:animator/fade_in</item>
        <item name="android:fragmentFadeExitAnimation">
            @android:animator/fade_out</item>
    </style>
</resources>
```

As you can see, the attributes for a theme's default fragment animations are part of the same windowAnimationStyle attribute. Therefore, when we customize them, we make sure to inherit from the same parent so as not to erase the other system defaults, such as activity transitions. You must still properly request the correct transition type in your FragmentTransaction to trigger the animation.

If you wanted to customize both the activity and fragment transitions in the theme, you could do so by putting them all together in the same custom style (see Listing 2-88).

Listing 2-88. res/values/styles.xml

```xml
<resources>
    <style name="AppTheme" parent="android:Theme.Holo.Light">
        <item name="android:windowAnimationStyle">
            @style/TransitionAnimation</item>
    </style>

    <style name="TransitionAnimation"
        parent="@android:style/Animation.Activity">
        <item name="android:activityOpenEnterAnimation">
            @anim/activity_open_enter</item>
        <item name="android:activityOpenExitAnimation">
            @anim/activity_open_exit</item>
```

```xml
        <item name="android:activityCloseEnterAnimation">
            @anim/activity_close_enter</item>
        <item name="android:activityCloseExitAnimation">
            @anim/activity_close_exit</item>
        <item name="android:fragmentOpenEnterAnimation">
            @animator/fragment_enter</item>
        <item name="android:fragmentOpenExitAnimation">
            @animator/fragment_exit</item>
        <item name="android:fragmentCloseEnterAnimation">
            @animator/fragment_pop_enter</item>
        <item name="android:fragmentCloseExitAnimation">
            @animator/fragment_pop_exit</item>
        <item name="android:fragmentFadeEnterAnimation">
            @android:animator/fade_in</item>
        <item name="android:fragmentFadeExitAnimation">
            @android:animator/fade_out</item>
    </style>
</resources>
```

> **Caution**   Adding fragment transitions to the theme will work only for the native implementation. The Support Library cannot look for these attributes in a theme because they did not exist in earlier platform versions.

2-15. Creating View Transformations

Problem

Your application needs to dynamically transform how views look in order to add visual effects such as perspective.

Solution

(API Level 1)

The API for static transformations that is available on ViewGroup provides a simple method of applying visual effects such as rotation, scale, or alpha changes without resorting to animations. It can also be a convenient place to apply transforms that are easier to apply from the context of a parent view, such as a scale that varies with position.

Static transformations can be enabled on any ViewGroup by calling setStaticTranformationsEnabled(true) during initialization. With this enabled, the framework will regularly call getChildStaticTransformation() for each child view to allow your application to apply the transform.

How It Works

Let's first take a look at an example where the transformations are applied once and don't change (see Listing 2-89).

Listing 2-89. Custom Layout with Static Transformations

```java
public class PerspectiveLayout extends LinearLayout {

    public PerspectiveLayout(Context context) {
        super(context);
        init();
    }

    public PerspectiveLayout(Context context, AttributeSet attrs) {
        super(context, attrs);
        init();
    }

    public PerspectiveLayout(Context context, AttributeSet attrs,
            int defStyle) {
        super(context, attrs, defStyle);
        init();
    }

    private void init() {
        // Enable static transformations so each child will
        // have getChildStaticTransformation() called.
        setStaticTransformationsEnabled(true);
    }

    @Override
    protected boolean getChildStaticTransformation(View child,
            Transformation t) {
        // Clear any existing transformation
        t.clear();

        if (getOrientation() == HORIZONTAL) {
            // Scale children based on distance from left edge
            float delta = 1.0f - ((float) child.getLeft() / getWidth());

            t.getMatrix().setScale(delta, delta, child.getWidth() / 2,
                    child.getHeight() / 2);
        } else {
            // Scale children based on distance from top edge
            float delta = 1.0f - ((float) child.getTop() / getHeight());

            t.getMatrix().setScale(delta, delta, child.getWidth() / 2,
                    child.getHeight() / 2);
            //Also apply a fade effect based on its location
            t.setAlpha(delta);
        }
        return true;
    }
}
```

This example illustrates a custom LinearLayout that applies a scale transformation to each of its children, based on that child's location from the beginning edge of the view. The code in getChildStaticTransformation() calculates the scale factor to apply by figuring out the distance from the left or top edge as a percentage of the full parent size. The return value from this method notifies the framework when a transformation has been set. In any case where your application sets a custom transform, you must also return true to ensure that it gets attached to the view.

Most of the visual effects such as rotation or scale are actually applied to the Matrix of the Transformation. In our example, we adjust the scale of each child by calling getMatrix().setScale() and passing in the scale factor and the pivot point. The pivot point is the location about which the scale will take place; we set this to the midpoint of the view so that the scaled result is centered.

If the layout orientation is vertical, we also apply an alpha fade to the child view based on the same distance value, which is set directly on the Transformation with setAlpha(). See Listing 2-90 for an example layout that uses this view.

Listing 2-90. res/layout/main.xml

```xml
<?xml version="1.0" encoding="utf-8"?>
<LinearLayout
    xmlns:android="http://schemas.android.com/apk/res/android"
    android:layout_width="match_parent"
    android:layout_height="match_parent"
    android:orientation="vertical">
    <!-- Horizontal Custom Layout -->
    <com.examples.statictransforms.PerspectiveLayout
        android:layout_width="match_parent"
        android:layout_height="wrap_content"
        android:orientation="horizontal" >
        <ImageView
            android:layout_width="wrap_content"
            android:layout_height="wrap_content"
            android:src="@drawable/ic_launcher" />
        <ImageView
            android:layout_width="wrap_content"
            android:layout_height="wrap_content"
            android:src="@drawable/ic_launcher" />
        <ImageView
            android:layout_width="wrap_content"
            android:layout_height="wrap_content"
            android:src="@drawable/ic_launcher" />
        <ImageView
            android:layout_width="wrap_content"
            android:layout_height="wrap_content"
            android:src="@drawable/ic_launcher" />
    </com.examples.statictransforms.PerspectiveLayout>
    <!-- Vertical Custom Layout -->
    <com.examples.statictransforms.PerspectiveLayout
        android:layout_width="wrap_content"
        android:layout_height="match_parent"
        android:orientation="vertical" >
```

```
        <ImageView
            android:layout_width="wrap_content"
            android:layout_height="wrap_content"
            android:src="@drawable/ic_launcher" />
        <ImageView
            android:layout_width="wrap_content"
            android:layout_height="wrap_content"
            android:src="@drawable/ic_launcher" />
        <ImageView
            android:layout_width="wrap_content"
            android:layout_height="wrap_content"
            android:src="@drawable/ic_launcher" />
        <ImageView
            android:layout_width="wrap_content"
            android:layout_height="wrap_content"
            android:src="@drawable/ic_launcher" />
    </com.examples.statictransforms.PerspectiveLayout>
</LinearLayout>
```

Figure 2-23 shows the results of the example transformation.

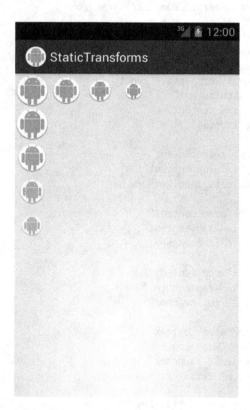

Figure 2-23. *Horizontal and vertical perspective layouts*

In the horizontal layout, as the views move to the right, they have a smaller scale factor applied to them. Similarly, the vertical views reduce in scale as they move down. Additionally, the vertical views begin to fade out because of the additional alpha change.

Now let's look at an example that provides a more dynamic change. Listing 2-91 shows a custom layout that is meant to be housed within a HorizontalScrollView. This layout uses static transformations to scale the child views as they scroll. The view in the center of the screen is always normal size, and each view scales down as it approaches the edge. This provides the effect that the views are coming closer and moving away as they scroll.

Listing 2-91. Custom Perspective Scroll Content

```java
public class PerspectiveScrollContentView extends LinearLayout {

    /* Adjustable scale factor for child views */
    private static final float SCALE_FACTOR = 0.7f;
    /* Anchor point for transformation.  (0,0) is top left,
     * (1,1) is bottom right.  This is currently set for
     * the bottom middle (0.5, 1)
     */
    private static final float ANCHOR_X = 0.5f;
    private static final float ANCHOR_Y = 1.0f;

    public PerspectiveScrollContentView(Context context) {
        super(context);
        init();
    }

    public PerspectiveScrollContentView(Context context,
            AttributeSet attrs) {
        super(context, attrs);
        init();
    }

    public PerspectiveScrollContentView(Context context,
            AttributeSet attrs, int defStyle) {
        super(context, attrs, defStyle);
        init();
    }

    private void init() {
        // Enable static transformations so each child will
        // have getChildStaticTransformation() called.
        setStaticTransformationsEnabled(true);
    }

    /*
     * Utility method to calculate the current position of any
     * View in the screen's coordinates
     */
```

```
    private int getViewCenter(View view) {
        int[] childCoords = new int[2];
        view.getLocationOnScreen(childCoords);
        int childCenter = childCoords[0] + (view.getWidth() / 2);

        return childCenter;
    }

    @Override
    protected boolean getChildStaticTransformation(View child,
            Transformation t) {
        HorizontalScrollView scrollView = null;
        if (getParent() instanceof HorizontalScrollView) {
            scrollView = (HorizontalScrollView) getParent();
        }
        if (scrollView == null) {
            return false;
        }

        int childCenter = getViewCenter(child);
        int viewCenter = getViewCenter(scrollView);

        // Calculate the delta between this and our parent's center.
        // That will determine the scale factor applied.
        float delta = Math.min(1.0f, Math.abs(childCenter - viewCenter)
                / (float) viewCenter);
        //Set the minimum scale factor to 0.4
        float scale = Math.max(0.4f, 1.0f - (SCALE_FACTOR * delta));
        float xTrans = child.getWidth() * ANCHOR_X;
        float yTrans = child.getHeight() * ANCHOR_Y;

        //Clear any existing transformation
        t.clear();
        //Set the transformation for the child view
        t.getMatrix().setScale(scale, scale, xTrans, yTrans);

        return true;
    }
}
```

In this example, the custom layout calculates the transformation for each child based on its location with respect to the center of the parent HorizontalScrollView. As the user scrolls, each child's transformation will be recalculated so the views will grow and shrink dynamically as they move. The example sets the anchor point of the transformation at the bottom center of each child, which will create the effect of each view growing vertically by remaining centered horizontally. Listing 2-92 shows an example activity that puts this custom layout into practice.

Listing 2-92. Activity Using `PerspectiveScrollContentView`

```java
public class ScrollActivity extends Activity {

    @Override
    protected void onCreate(Bundle savedInstanceState) {
        super.onCreate(savedInstanceState);

        HorizontalScrollView parentView = new HorizontalScrollView(this);
        PerspectiveScrollContentView contentView =
                new PerspectiveScrollContentView(this);

        //Disable hardware acceleration for this view, dynamic adjustment
        // of child transformations does not currently work in hardware.
        //You can also disable for the entire Activity or Application
        // with android:hardwareAccelerated="false" in the manifest,
        // but it is better to disable acceleration in as few places
        // as possible for best performance.
        if (Build.VERSION.SDK_INT >= Build.VERSION_CODES.HONEYCOMB) {
            contentView.setLayerType(View.LAYER_TYPE_SOFTWARE, null);
        }

        //Add a handful of images to scroll through
        for (int i = 0; i < 20; i++) {
            ImageView iv = new ImageView(this);
            iv.setImageResource(R.drawable.ic_launcher);
            contentView.addView(iv);
        }
        //Add the views to the display
        parentView.addView(contentView);
        setContentView(parentView);
    }
}
```

This example creates a scrolling view and attaches a custom `PerspectiveScrollContentView` with several images to scroll through. The code here isn't much to look at, but there is one very important piece worth mentioning. While static transformations in general are supported, dynamically updating the transform when the view is invalidated does not work with hardware acceleration in the current versions of the SDK. As a result, if your application has a target SDK of 11 or higher, or has enabled hardware acceleration in some other way, it will need to be disabled for this view.

This is done globally in the manifest via `android:hardwareAccelerated="false"` on any `<activity>` or the entire `<application>`, but we can also set it discretely in Java code for just this custom view by calling `setLayerType()` and setting it to `LAYER_TYPE_SOFTWARE`. If your application is targeting an SDK lower than this, hardware acceleration is disabled by default for compatibility reasons, even on newer devices, so this code may not be necessary.

2-16. High-Performance Drawing

Problem

Your application needs to render and draw a complex scene or animation to the screen, often from a background thread.

Solution

(API Level 1)

Use `SurfaceView` or `TextureView` to render content from a background thread to the screen. The general rule in developing Android user interfaces is to never modify any properties associated with a `View` from any thread other than the main thread. These two classes are the exception to this rule, and they are designed specifically to take draw commands from a background thread and post them to the screen. You will also see in later chapters how these two classes are used by the framework to render camera preview data and video output. However, for now we are going to focus on doing our own drawing.

`SurfaceView` is rather unique in that it doesn't really behave like a traditional `View`. When one is instantiated, a secondary `Window` is actually created at the location of the `View` but underneath the current `Window`, and the `View` component simply "punches a hole" in the top-level `Window` by displaying transparently. The advantage to this approach is that it allows us to do this high-performance drawing without any assistance from hardware acceleration. However, it also means that `SurfaceView` is fairly static and does not respond well to being animated or transformed in any way.

`TextureView` is available in Android 4.0 and later and in most cases can be a drop-in replacement for `SurfaceView`. It behaves more like a traditional `View` in that it can be animated and transformed while content is being drawn to it. However, it requires the context it is running in to be hardware accelerated, which may cause compatibility issues in some applications.

How It Works

Let's take a look at an example application where a background thread continuously renders a series of objects to a `SurfaceView`. In this example, we create a display that animates the motion of several icons continuously on the screen. See Listings 2-93 and 2-94.

Listing 2-93. res/layout/main.xml

```xml
<FrameLayout
    xmlns:android="http://schemas.android.com/apk/res/android"
    android:layout_width="match_parent"
    android:layout_height="match_parent"
    android:orientation="vertical" >
    <Button
        android:id="@+id/button_erase"
        android:layout_width="match_parent"
        android:layout_height="wrap_content"
        android:text="Erase" />
```

```
<SurfaceView
    android:id="@+id/surface"
    android:layout_width="300dp"
    android:layout_height="300dp"
    android:layout_gravity="center" />

</FrameLayout>
```

Listing 2-94. Surface Drawing Activity

```
public class SurfaceActivity extends Activity implements
        View.OnClickListener, View.OnTouchListener,
        SurfaceHolder.Callback {

    private SurfaceView mSurface;
    private DrawingThread mThread;

    @Override
    public void onCreate(Bundle savedInstanceState) {
        super.onCreate(savedInstanceState);
        setContentView(R.layout.main);
        //Attach listener to button
        findViewById(R.id.button_erase).setOnClickListener(this);

        //Set up the surface with a touch listener and callback
        mSurface = (SurfaceView) findViewById(R.id.surface);
        mSurface.setOnTouchListener(this);
        mSurface.getHolder().addCallback(this);
    }

@Override
    public void onClick(View v) {
        mThread.clearItems();
    }

    public boolean onTouch(View v, MotionEvent event) {
        if (event.getAction() == MotionEvent.ACTION_DOWN) {
            mThread.addItem((int) event.getX(),
                    (int) event.getY());
        }
        return true;
    }

    @Override
    public void surfaceCreated(SurfaceHolder holder) {
        mThread = new DrawingThread(holder,
                BitmapFactory.decodeResource(getResources(),
                        R.drawable.ic_launcher));
        mThread.start();
    }
```

```java
@Override
public void surfaceChanged(SurfaceHolder holder, int format,
        int width, int height) {
    mThread.updateSize(width, height);
}

@Override
public void surfaceDestroyed(SurfaceHolder holder) {
    mThread.quit();
    mThread = null;
}

private static class DrawingThread extends HandlerThread
        implements Handler.Callback {
    private static final int MSG_ADD = 100;
    private static final int MSG_MOVE = 101;
    private static final int MSG_CLEAR = 102;

    private int mDrawingWidth, mDrawingHeight;

    private SurfaceHolder mDrawingSurface;
    private Paint mPaint;
    private Handler mReceiver;
    private Bitmap mIcon;
    private ArrayList<DrawingItem> mLocations;

    private class DrawingItem {
        //Current location marker
        int x, y;
        //Direction markers for motion
        boolean horizontal, vertical;

        public DrawingItem(int x, int y, boolean horizontal,
                boolean vertical) {
            this.x = x;
            this.y = y;
            this.horizontal = horizontal;
            this.vertical = vertical;
        }
    }

    public DrawingThread(SurfaceHolder holder, Bitmap icon) {
        super("DrawingThread");
        mDrawingSurface = holder;
        mLocations = new ArrayList<DrawingItem>();
        mPaint = new Paint(Paint.ANTI_ALIAS_FLAG);
        mIcon = icon;
    }
```

```java
@Override
protected void onLooperPrepared() {
    mReceiver = new Handler(getLooper(), this);
    //Start the rendering
    mReceiver.sendEmptyMessage(MSG_MOVE);
}

@Override
public boolean quit() {
    // Clear all messages before dying
    mReceiver.removeCallbacksAndMessages(null);
    return super.quit();
}

@Override
public boolean handleMessage(Message msg) {
    switch (msg.what) {
    case MSG_ADD:
        //Create a new item at the touch location,
        //with a randomized start direction
        DrawingItem newItem =
                new DrawingItem(msg.arg1, msg.arg2,
                    Math.round(Math.random()) == 0,
                    Math.round(Math.random()) == 0);
        mLocations.add(newItem);
        break;
    case MSG_CLEAR:
        //Remove all objects
        mLocations.clear();
        break;
    case MSG_MOVE:
        //Render a frame
        Canvas c = mDrawingSurface.lockCanvas();
        if (c == null) {
            break;
        }
        //Clear Canvas first
        c.drawColor(Color.BLACK);
        //Draw each item
        for (DrawingItem item : mLocations) {
            //Update location
            item.x += (item.horizontal ? 5 : -5);
            if ( item.x >=
                    (mDrawingWidth - mIcon.getWidth()) ) {
                item.horizontal = false;
            } else if (item.x <= 0) {
                item.horizontal = true;
            }
```

```
                item.y += (item.vertical ? 5 : -5);
                if ( item.y >=
                        (mDrawingHeight - mIcon.getHeight()) ) {
                    item.vertical = false;
                } else if (item.y <= 0) {
                    item.vertical = true;
                }
                //Draw to the Canvas
                c.drawBitmap(mIcon, item.x, item.y, mPaint);
            }
            //Release to be rendered to the screen
            mDrawingSurface.unlockCanvasAndPost(c);
            break;
        }
        //Post the next frame
        mReceiver.sendEmptyMessage(MSG_MOVE);
        return true;
    }

    public void updateSize(int width, int height) {
        mDrawingWidth = width;
        mDrawingHeight = height;
    }

    public void addItem(int x, int y) {
        //Pass the location into the Handler using arguments
        Message msg =
                Message.obtain(mReceiver, MSG_ADD, x, y);
        mReceiver.sendMessage(msg);
    }

    public void clearItems() {
        mReceiver.sendEmptyMessage(MSG_CLEAR);
    }
    }
}
```

This example constructs a simple background DrawingThread to render and draw content to a SurfaceView. This thread is a subclass of HandlerThread, which is a convenient framework helper for generating background workers that process incoming messages. We talk in more detail about this pattern in Chapter 6, but for now suffice it to say that our background thread operates by responding to messages sent to the Handler it owns inside of handleMessage(). SurfaceView is really two components: a Surface underneath the Window and a clear View in the hierarchy. To do drawing, we really need access to the underlying Surface, which is wrapped in a SurfaceHolder.

The construction of the Surface doesn't actually happen until the view gets attached to the current window, so we can't just grab it right away. Instead, SurfaceHolder has a callback interface when the Surface is created, destroyed, or changed so that we can use it to manage the life cycle of the components that depend on it (in this case the DrawingThread). Here we wait for surfaceCreated() to construct a new DrawingThread and start rendering, and in surfaceDestroyed() we need to stop rendering to the Surface as it is no longer valid. The final callback, surfaceChanged(), is the only place where the dimensions of the Surface are supplied, so we make sure to update our drawing code with those values whenever they are available.

We have defined three commands for the thread to react to: add, clear, and move. The add method will be triggered when the user taps on the SurfaceView by adding a drawing item to the display list with its initial location set to the location of the touch. The clear method will remove all items from the display list, which is triggered when the button is pressed.

Inside the move method, the thread renders each frame to the SurfaceView. Every drawing operation should be prefaced with lockCanvas(), which provides a Canvas to apply drawing calls. Then the thread iterates through each item in its display list, updates it to a new position, and draws an icon to the Canvas at that location. It also checks whether any item has hit a boundary of the Surface, so it can reverse direction in those cases. We must preface each frame with drawColor() to clear the previous frame's contents. Without this, as the icons move, you would see a trail behind them of the icon's previous locations. In some applications, this may be desirable (such as a painting application where each event should be added to the others), but not for our example. After all the drawing calls are made, the application must call unlockCanvasAndPost() to render the data to the screen.

By continuously posting MSG_MOVE to itself, the DrawingThread runs through this process indefinitely until the thread is quit by the application. An advantage to doing this processing via HandlerThread is that the operations can be cancelled at any time with quit() and the thread can die cleanly, rather than trying to interrupt the thread execution.

You can see the results of this application running in Figure 2-24. The user can tap on the black box an indefinite number of times and watch the number of flying icons stack up. Because the drawing code uses only one bitmap for all the icons, the number of items the view can support is very high without running into any memory concerns.

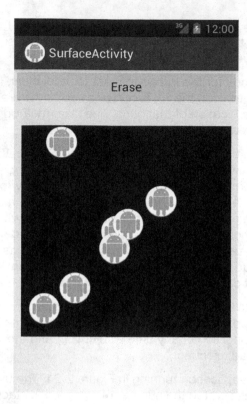

Figure 2-24. SurfaceView *drawing scene*

TextureView

(API Level 14)

If your application is targeting Android 4.0 and later, you can also use TextureView, which has a few additional properties that may make it ideal for your application; the most useful is that it can be transformed. Have a look at Listings 2-95 and 2-96, where we have modified the previous example to use TextureView.

Listing 2-95. res/layout/main.xml

```
<FrameLayout
    xmlns:android="http://schemas.android.com/apk/res/android"
    android:layout_width="match_parent"
    android:layout_height="match_parent">
    <Button
        android:id="@+id/button_transform"
        android:layout_width="match_parent"
        android:layout_height="wrap_content"
        android:text="Rotate" />
```

```
    <TextureView
        android:id="@+id/surface"
        android:layout_width="300dp"
        android:layout_height="300dp"
        android:layout_gravity="center" />

</FrameLayout>
```

Listing 2-96. *Texture Drawing Activity*

```
public class TextureActivity extends Activity implements View.OnClickListener,
        View.OnTouchListener, TextureView.SurfaceTextureListener {

    private TextureView mSurface;
    private DrawingThread mThread;

    @Override
    public void onCreate(Bundle savedInstanceState) {
        super.onCreate(savedInstanceState);
        setContentView(R.layout.texture);
        //Attach listener to button
        findViewById(R.id.button_transform)
                .setOnClickListener(this);

        //Set up the surface with a touch listener and callback
        mSurface = (TextureView) findViewById(R.id.surface);
        mSurface.setOnTouchListener(this);
        mSurface.setSurfaceTextureListener(this);
    }

    @Override
    public void onClick(View v) {
        mSurface.animate()
            .rotationBy(180.0f)
            .setDuration(750);
    }

    public boolean onTouch(View v, MotionEvent event) {
        if (event.getAction() == MotionEvent.ACTION_DOWN) {
            mThread.addItem((int) event.getX(),
                    (int) event.getY());
        }
        return true;
    }

    @Override
    public void onSurfaceTextureAvailable(SurfaceTexture surface,
            int width, int height) {
        mThread = new DrawingThread(new Surface(surface),
                BitmapFactory.decodeResource(getResources(),
                        R.drawable.ic_launcher));
```

```java
        mThread.updateSize(width, height);
        mThread.start();
    }

    @Override
    public void onSurfaceTextureSizeChanged(
            SurfaceTexture surface, int width, int height) {
        mThread.updateSize(width, height);
    }

    @Override
    public void onSurfaceTextureUpdated(SurfaceTexture surface) {
        //Do any processing that needs to happen on each frame
    }

    @Override
    public boolean onSurfaceTextureDestroyed(
            SurfaceTexture surface) {
        mThread.quit();
        mThread = null;

        //Return true to allow the framework to release
        // the surface
        return true;
    }

    private static class DrawingThread extends HandlerThread
            implements Handler.Callback {
        private static final int MSG_ADD = 100;
        private static final int MSG_MOVE = 101;
        private static final int MSG_CLEAR = 102;

        private int mDrawingWidth, mDrawingHeight;

        private Surface mDrawingSurface;
        private Rect mSurfaceRect;
        private Paint mPaint;

        private Handler mReceiver;
        private Bitmap mIcon;
        private ArrayList<DrawingItem> mLocations;

        private class DrawingItem {
            //Current location marker
            int x, y;
            //Direction markers for motion
            boolean horizontal, vertical;
```

```java
    public DrawingItem(int x, int y, boolean horizontal,
            boolean vertical) {
        this.x = x;
        this.y = y;
        this.horizontal = horizontal;
        this.vertical = vertical;
    }
}

public DrawingThread(Surface surface, Bitmap icon) {
    super("DrawingThread");
    mDrawingSurface = surface;
    mSurfaceRect = new Rect();
    mLocations = new ArrayList<DrawingItem>();
    mPaint = new Paint(Paint.ANTI_ALIAS_FLAG);
    mIcon = icon;
}

@Override
protected void onLooperPrepared() {
    mReceiver = new Handler(getLooper(), this);
    //Start the rendering
    mReceiver.sendEmptyMessage(MSG_MOVE);
}

@Override
public boolean quit() {
    // Clear all messages before dying
    mReceiver.removeCallbacksAndMessages(null);
    return super.quit();
}

@Override
public boolean handleMessage(Message msg) {
    switch (msg.what) {
    case MSG_ADD:
        // Create a new item at the touch location,
        // with a randomized start direction
        DrawingItem newItem =
                new DrawingItem(msg.arg1, msg.arg2,
                    Math.round(Math.random()) == 0,
                    Math.round(Math.random()) == 0);
        mLocations.add(newItem);
        break;
    case MSG_CLEAR:
        //Remove all objects
        mLocations.clear();
        break;
```

```java
        case MSG_MOVE:
            //Render a frame
            try {
                Canvas c =
                    mDrawingSurface.lockCanvas(mSurfaceRect);
                if (c == null) {
                    break;
                }
                //Clear Canvas first
                c.drawColor(Color.BLACK);
                //Draw each item
                for (DrawingItem item : mLocations) {
                    //Update location
                    item.x += (item.horizontal ? 5 : -5);
                    if ( item.x >=
                        (mDrawingWidth - mIcon.getWidth()) )
                    {
                        item.horizontal = false;
                    } else if (item.x <= 0) {
                        item.horizontal = true;
                    }
                    item.y += (item.vertical ? 5 : -5);
                    if ( item.y >=
                        (mDrawingHeight - mIcon.getHeight()) )
                    {
                        item.vertical = false;
                    } else if (item.y <= 0) {
                        item.vertical = true;
                    }
                    //Draw to the Canvas
                    c.drawBitmap(mIcon, item.x, item.y,
                            mPaint);
                }
                //Release the surface to be rendered
                mDrawingSurface.unlockCanvasAndPost(c);
            } catch (Exception e) {
                e.printStackTrace();
            }
            break;
        }
        //Post the next frame
        mReceiver.sendEmptyMessage(MSG_MOVE);
        return true;
    }

    public void updateSize(int width, int height) {
        mDrawingWidth = width;
        mDrawingHeight = height;
        mSurfaceRect.set(0, 0, mDrawingWidth, mDrawingHeight);
    }
```

```
    public void addItem(int x, int y) {
        //Pass the location into the Handler using arguments
        Message msg =
                Message.obtain(mReceiver, MSG_ADD, x, y);
        mReceiver.sendMessage(msg);
    }

    public void clearItems() {
        mReceiver.sendEmptyMessage(MSG_CLEAR);
    }
  }
}
```

In this modified example, our layout has a TextureView instance. Similar to SurfaceView, the underlying surface to draw on is not created until the view is attached to the Window, so we must rely on a callback before accessing it. For TextureView, this callback is a SurfaceTextureListener. For the most part, the functionality mirrors SurfaceHolder.Callback with onSurfaceTextureAvailable(), onSurfaceTextureChanged(), and onSurfaceTextureDestroyed(). However, there is one additional callback method we aren't currently using in this example called onSurfaceTextureUpdated(). This method will be called anytime the SurfaceTexture renders a new frame.

The drawing surface that TextureView provides is slightly different, in that there is no SurfaceHolder wrapping it to access. Instead, we can access a SurfaceTexture instance, which we can wrap in a new Surface to do our drawing. This, in turn, requires one small modification of our DrawingThread. SurfaceHolder has a convenience version of lockCanvas() that takes no parameters and marks the entire Surface as dirty. When working with Surface directly, this method does not exist, so we need to pass a Rect into lockCanvas() that tells it which section of the Surface to return as a Canvas for new rendering. Because we still want this to be the entire surface, we maintain the size of the Rect in updateSize(), which will get called by the listener whenever the surface changes.

To showcase the ability to transform the SurfaceTexture live while it is rendering, we have replaced the Erase button with a Rotate button. Clicking this button will cause the TextureView to do a half-circle rotation animation each time. Clicking the button while the current animation is running will cancel it and start a new rotation from the current point, so if you click the button rapidly, you can get the view to rotate into some pretty odd angles. The entire time the SurfaceTexture will continue to animate without skipping a beat. You can see in Figure 2-25 the application with the TextureView rotated upside-down.

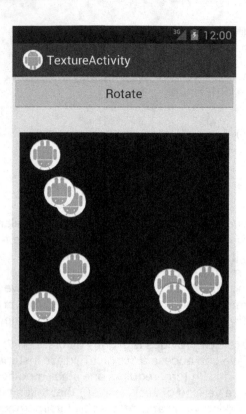

Figure 2-25. `TextureView` *drawing scene*

Summary

In this chapter, you saw many of the tools that the Android framework provides to display content to the user. We explored techniques for creating, customizing, and animating views, as well as ways to draw discrete content directly to the screen using elements such as Canvas and Surface. You were exposed to the many customizations available in the application window, including custom transition animations from one screen to another. Finally, we looked at how you can leverage the resource qualifier system to create optimized view layouts for different screen configurations.

In the next chapter, we will examine some more of the elements in the UI toolkit that are focused on interacting with the user and implementing common patterns for app navigation.

User Interaction Recipes

A great-looking application design means nothing if users do not find the application easy to use and its features easy to discover. The user interaction patterns found in most Android applications are designed to engineer experiences that are consistent for users from one application to another. By maintaining consistency with the platform, users will feel familiar with your application's functionality even if they have never used it before. In this chapter, you'll investigate some of the common implementation patterns for presenting information to users and retrieving their input.

3-1. Leveraging the Action Bar

Problem

You want to use the latest action bar patterns in your application, while staying backward-compatible with older devices, and you want to customize the look and feel to match your application's theme.

Solution

(API Level 7)

The action bar was introduced to the SDK in Android 3.0 (API Level 11), but was back-ported to earlier versions via the `ActionBarActivity` within the AppCompat component of the Android Support Library. Using `ActionBarActivity`, along with the included styles and resources from AppCompat, we can put an action bar into any application targeting Android 2.1 and later.

> **Important** `ActionBarActivity` is available only in the AppCompat Library, found as part of the Android Support Library; it is not part of the native SDK at any platform level. However, any application targeting API Level 7 or later can make use of the widget with the Support Library included. For more information on including the Support Library in your project, reference our guide in Chapter 1.

Action Bar Elements

To help visualize the primary elements of the action bar, Figure 3-1 illustrates an activity with the action bar in standard navigation mode. On the right side of the bar are interactive elements called *action items*, which can be displayed with an icon or a title. The most important actions are typically shown directly in the bar, while action items used less often can be collected into an overflow pop-up menu that displays as the rightmost action. Action items are typically added to the activity via an options menu, which we will discuss in more detail later in this chapter.

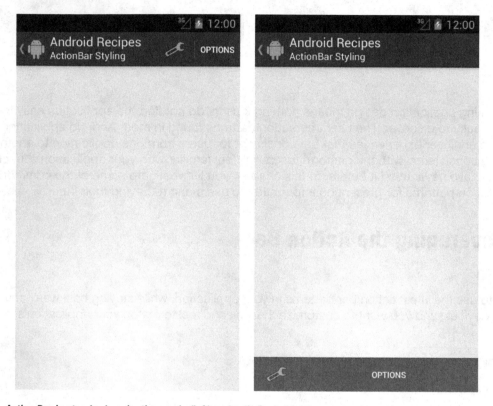

Figure 3-1. Action Bar in standard navigation mode (left) and split mode (right)

By default, all action items and menus are displayed on the right of the bar in both orientations. However, it is common that you may want to display more action items than a portrait screen has room to display. To handle this case, Android employs the *split* navigation mode, in which the action items move to a secondary bar at the bottom of the screen when the screen is "narrow," meaning there is less room to display everything in a single action bar.

This feature can be enabled only statically for an activity inside `AndroidManifest.xml` by setting the `splitActionBarWhenNarrow` flag on the `android:uiOptions` attribute:

```
<activity
    android:name=".MainActivity"
    android:label="@string/app_name"
    android:theme="@android:style/Theme.Holo.Light"
    android:uiOptions="splitActionBarWhenNarrow">
```

The second screenshot in Figure 3-1 shows the split mode of the action bar, with the action items relocated to a secondary bar at the bottom of the display. This is only the case in portrait mode. When the display is in landscape and is no longer "narrow," all the actions are moved back up to the main bar.

Home/Up Button

The upper-left corner of the action bar is the area designated for the Home/Up button. By default, this section displays the application's icon and is not interactive. Many of the common navigation paradigms that Android applications implement involve this button being used to move back through previous screens or displaying menus. We discuss some of these later in this chapter, and others in Chapter 6. To use these, we must enable the button to be interactive. The following snippet of code activates the Home/Up functionality in an activity:

```
//Enable taps on the home logo
getActionBar().setHomeButtonEnabled(true);
//Display home with the "up" arrow indicator
getActionBar().setDisplayHomeAsUpEnabled(true);
```

The second method enables the visual *up* arrow, which is a cue to the user that this button should be used to navigate backward (although it doesn't actually enable any of that functionality inherently).

> **Tip** You can also customize the content of the Home button area. If you would prefer that your activity display the android:logo attribute defined in your AndroidManifest.xml <application> element instead of the launcher icon, simply call setDisplayUseLogoEnabled(true) in your activity code. You may also customize the icon to display per activity with setIcon() and setLogo().

Title and Subtitle

The text area to the right of the Home/Up button is where the action bar displays a title and optional subtitle when in standard navigation mode. By default, the android:label value from the <application> or <activity> element in AndroidManifest.xml will be displayed as the title with no subtitle. The following code snipped allows an activity to customize both of these:

```
//Set the title text
getActionBar().setTitle("Android Recipes");
//Set the subtitle text
getActionBar().setSubtitle("ActionBar Styling");
```

If you want to hide the title completely, which will be beneficial when you start using some of the other navigation modes to be described, you can call these same methods and pass in either null or the empty string.

Custom Views

The action bar supports placement of a custom view along the right side of the title area. This can be any view subclass that you would like to display. In common practice, it often makes sense to eliminate the title views if you would like to apply a custom view instead for real estate reasons. The following snippet places an ImageView displaying the application icon in place of the titles:

```
//Clear the title text
getActionBar().setTitle(null);
//Clear the subtitle text (if shown)
getActionBar().setSubtitle(null);
//Set custom view
ImageView iv = new ImageView(this);
iv.setImageResource(R.drawable.ic_launcher);
getActionBar().setCustomView(iv,
        new ActionBar.LayoutParams(
                LayoutParams.MATCH_PARENT,
                LayoutParams.MATCH_PARENT) );
//Enable custom view display
getActionBar().setDisplayShowCustomEnabled(true);
```

As you can see, an additional display option must be set to enable a custom view via setDisplayShowCustomEnabled(true), and then we call setCustomView() to apply the view we want shown. This method can be called with or without passing discrete layout parameters; if none are passed, typically the view is set to horizontally wrap content and vertically match the parent. Figure 3-2 shows the result of this in our standard action bar example.

Figure 3-2. Action Bar with custom view

Tabs

The second primary navigation mode of the action bar is tab navigation. In this mode, a secondary bar for tabs is displayed below the action bar when the device is in portrait orientation. In landscape orientation, the tabs move up into the main action bar. In both cases, however, if there are more tabs than the screen can display at once, the tab section of the bar can be horizontally scrolled to reveal the remaining tabs. In addition, as tabs are selected, they scroll themselves into a more centered location of the view, allowing the user to discover the remaining tabs.

Figure 3-3 shows an example of this navigation mode in use.

Figure 3-3. *Action Bar with tab navigation*

Lists

The final action bar navigation mode is list navigation. With list navigation enabled, a drop-down spinner widget is in place of the title and subtitle text elements. This is only convention; the action bar will allow a title and navigation list to be displayed at the same time side by side, but there is often not enough visible real estate (at least on a handset device) to effectively display both items.

Figure 3-4 shows an action bar implementing list navigation.

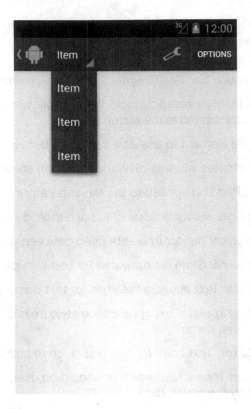

Figure 3-4. Action Bar with list navigation

Action Bar Styles

The action bar is a complex widget with many configuration modes. Because of this, a wealth of styles are available to configure the look of all those associated elements. The following is a list of the most common attributes available on the application's theme to style the action bar and its associated elements. For a complete list, examine the R.attr package in the SDK documentation, specifically looking for attributes with the prefix of actionBar.

- actionBarSize: Size (height) of the action bar

- actionBarStyle: Style resource defining the following attributes of the action bar:

  - background: Background to display on the action bar.

  - backgroundStacked: Background to display on stacked bars such as the tab bar.

  - backgroundSplit: Background to display when the action bar is in split mode.

  - titleTextStyle: Text appearance style for the title element.

  - subtitleTextStyle: Text appearance style for the subtitle element.

- progressBarStyle: Style resource for the determinate progress indicator in the action bar. See Chapter 2 for more on enabling this element.

- indeterminateProgressBarStyle: Style resource for the indeterminate progress indicator in the action bar. See Chapter 2 for more on enabling this element.

- actionBarTabBarStyle: Style resource including the following elements for the stacked tab bar, when included in the action bar:

  - divider: Drawable element to use as a separator between each tab

  - showDividers: Indicates whether dividers should be shown at all between tabs

  - dividerPadding: Padding applied to the tab separators

- actionBarTabStyle: Style resource applied to each individual tab view

- actionBarDivider: Vertical divider Drawable used between action menu items

- actionBarItemBackground: State list drawable for use with clickable action items

- actionBarTabTextStyle: Text appearance style for text displayed in stacked tabs

- actionBarMenuTextAppearance: Text appearance style (minus color) for text displayed in action menu items

- actionBarMenuTextColor: Text color for text displayed in action menu items

- actionBarWidgetTheme: Theme resource that should be used for any view dynamically inflated by the action bar

  - The action bar often uses a different base style from the rest of the activity, and this may cause visual problems with widgets it may inflate (like submenus on certain action items). This allows you to apply a theme to just those widgets without changing the action bar theme.

- actionDropDownStyle: Style resource applied to a drop-down list spinner when included in the action bar

These attributes should be placed into a custom theme that is applied to a specific activity, set of activities, or the application as a whole inside AndroidManifest.xml.

How It Works

> **Note**   The examples in this section use native APIs, but they can easily be modified to work with AppCompat as well. The only changes are that each activity must extend ActionBarActivity, and each call to getActionBar() should be replaced with getSupportActionBar().

Tab Navigation

Listing 3-1 implements the activity by using the tab navigation in the action bar shown previously in Figure 3-3.

Listing 3-1. Activity with Action Bar Tabs

```
public class MainActivity extends Activity implements
       ActionBar.TabListener {

   @Override
   protected void onCreate(Bundle savedInstanceState) {
       super.onCreate(savedInstanceState);

       ActionBar actionBar = getActionBar();

       //Enable taps on the home logo
       actionBar.setHomeButtonEnabled(true);
       //Display home with the "up" arrow indicator
       actionBar.setDisplayHomeAsUpEnabled(true);

       //Tabs Navigation
       actionBar.addTab(getActionBar().newTab()
               .setText("Tab One")
               .setTabListener(this) );
       actionBar.addTab(getActionBar().newTab()
               .setText("Tab Two")
               .setTabListener(this) );
       actionBar.addTab(getActionBar().newTab()
               .setText("Tab Three")
               .setTabListener(this) );
       actionBar.addTab(getActionBar().newTab()
               .setText("Tab Four")
               .setTabListener(this) );

       //Must set the navigation mode for tabs to display
       actionBar.setNavigationMode(
               ActionBar.NAVIGATION_MODE_TABS);
   }

   /* React to Home Button Presses */
   @Override
   public boolean onOptionsItemSelected(MenuItem item) {
       if (item.getItemId() == android.R.id.home) {
           //Select the next tab, or first if we are
           // at the end currently
           int current = getActionBar()
                   .getSelectedTab().getPosition();
           if (++current >= getActionBar().getTabCount()) {
               current = 0;
           }
```

```
        getActionBar().selectTab(
                getActionBar().getTabAt(current) );
        return true;
    }
    return super.onOptionsItemSelected(item);
}

/* TabListener Callback Methods */

@Override
public void onTabReselected(ActionBar.Tab tab,
        FragmentTransaction ft) { }

@Override
public void onTabSelected(ActionBar.Tab tab,
        FragmentTransaction ft) { }

@Override
public void onTabUnselected(ActionBar.Tab tab,
        FragmentTransaction ft) { }

}
```

You can see that inside onCreate(), we use the addTab() method to add four tabs to our action bar. Notice also that to create a tab instance, there is a factory method on ActionBar called newTab(), off of which we can then subsequently chain configuration methods such as setText() to set up each tab.

Your application can react to user tab selections by implementing an ActionBar.TabListener and passing that instance to each created tab. This interface provides the following methods:

- onTabReselected: Called when a tab is selected again
- onTabSelected: Called when a tab is selected the first time
- onTabUnselected: Called when a tab is no longer selected

You may be wondering why there are separate methods for selection and reselection. As you may notice from the method signatures, these are designed primarily to work with fragment instances for transitioning the UI. There may often be conditions where you have to initialize the fragment the first time it is needed, but only redisplay it on subsequent selections. This separation encourages lazy loading of the fragment rather than setting everything possible up upon activity creation. This pattern is common in Android to improve loading of the UI by splitting out the tasks to different times.

It is also possible to programmatically select a tab. In the preceding example, we override onOptionsItemSelected() to react to the user tapping the Home/Up button in the action bar. Each time the button is pressed, we find the next tab in line based on the position of the currently selected tab (accessed via the getSelectedTab() method) and select it by using selectTab().

List Navigation

Listing 3-2 implements the activity by using the list navigation in the action bar shown previously in Figure 3-4.

Listing 3-2. Activity with Action Bar List

```java
public class MainActivity extends Activity implements
        ActionBar.OnNavigationListener {

    @Override
    protected void onCreate(Bundle savedInstanceState) {
        super.onCreate(savedInstanceState);

        ActionBar actionBar = getActionBar();

        //Enable taps on the home logo
        actionBar.setHomeButtonEnabled(true);
        //Display home with the "up" arrow indicator
        actionBar.setDisplayHomeAsUpEnabled(true);
        //Set the title text
        actionBar.setTitle("Android Recipes");
        //Set the subtitle text
        actionBar=.setSubtitle("ActionBar Styling");

        //List Navigation
        //Apply the appropriate theme to ActionBar item views
        Context context = getActionBar().getThemedContext();
        ArrayAdapter<String> adapter =
                new ArrayAdapter<String>(context,
                    android.R.layout.simple_spinner_item,
                    new String[] {"Item", "Item", "Item"} );
        adapter.setDropDownViewResource(
                android.R.layout.simple_spinner_dropdown_item);

        //Attach a selection listener
        getActionBar().setListNavigationCallbacks(adapter, this);
        //Must set the navigation mode to enable the list
        getActionBar().setNavigationMode(
                ActionBar.NAVIGATION_MODE_LIST);
    }

    /* OnNavigationListener Callback Methods */

    @Override
    public boolean onNavigationItemSelected(int itemPosition,
            long itemId) {
        //Handle changes in the list item selection here
        return true;
    }
}
```

In this example, we create a drop-down spinner by using the standard adapters and resources from the framework, and we create a simple static list of three creatively named items. Take note of the Context we pass into the ArrayAdapter instance. Normally, we would just use the activity and pass a this pointer into the constructor. However, it is common that the action bar uses a slightly different set of themes or styles to display itself (one such theme is Theme.Holo.Light.DarkActionBar) than the rest of the activity uses. This can create visual elements that don't look correct as action bar elements. To avoid this problem, we pass the Context offered by getThemedContext(), which provides the appropriate styles for widgets inflated into the action bar.

> **Tip**   The primary use that widgets have for a Context is to obtain resource, theme, and style information. You can often modify how widgets are displayed by passing them a custom Context that references a different resource set. The framework provides the ContextThemeWrapper class for just this purpose.

To enable the list, we must only pass the adapter we've created and an OnNavigationListener callback to react to selection events, and then set the navigation mode on the action bar.

Native Styles

(API Level 11)

Now let's look at an example of applying custom styles to the action bar inside an activity by using the native APIs available in Android 3.0 and later. In the next section, we will look at how this needs to be modified to use the Support Library for older versions. First, we need to define some drawable resources we have created to customize the action bar look. See Listings 3-3 through 3-6.

Listing 3-3. res/drawable/actionbar_background.xml

```xml
<?xml version="1.0" encoding="utf-8"?>
<shape xmlns:android="http://schemas.android.com/apk/res/android"
    android:shape="rectangle">
    <gradient
        android:startColor="#700"
        android:endColor="#FAA"
        android:type="linear"
        android:angle="270"/>
</shape>
```

Listing 3-4. res/drawable/actionbar_item_background.xml

```xml
<?xml version="1.0" encoding="utf-8"?>
<selector
  xmlns:android="http://schemas.android.com/apk/res/android" >
  <item
    android:state_pressed="true"
    android:state_enabled="true"
    android:drawable="@drawable/actionbar_item_background_pressed"
  />
```

```
<!-- Default State -->
<item android:drawable="@android:color/transparent" />
</selector>
```

Listing 3-5. res/drawable/actionbar_item_background_pressed.xml

```xml
<?xml version="1.0" encoding="utf-8"?>
<shape xmlns:android="http://schemas.android.com/apk/res/android"
    android:shape="rectangle">
    <solid
        android:color="#7CCC" />
</shape>
```

Listing 3-6. res/drawable/divider.xml

```xml
<?xml version="1.0" encoding="utf-8"?>
<shape xmlns:android="http://schemas.android.com/apk/res/android"
    android:shape="rectangle">
    <solid
        android:color="#00A"/>
    <size
        android:width="1dp"
        android:height="1dp" />
</shape>
```

What we have defined here is a custom gradient background for the action bar, a selector drawable for the action menu items that highlights gray when pressed, and a blue divider line to go between each action menu item. Listings 3-7 and 3-8 show these changes, among others, applied to a custom activity theme.

Listing 3-7. AndroidManifest.xml Snippet

```xml
<activity
    android:name=".MainActivity"
    android:label="@string/app_name"
    android:theme="@style/AppTheme">
    <intent-filter>
        <action android:name="android.intent.action.MAIN" />
        <category android:name="android.intent.category.LAUNCHER" />
    </intent-filter>
</activity>
```

Listing 3-8. res/values/styles.xml

```xml
<?xml version="1.0" encoding="utf-8"?>
<resources
    xmlns:android="http://schemas.android.com/apk/res/android">

    <style name="AppTheme"
        parent="@android:style/Theme.Holo.Light.DarkActionBar">
        <!-- Style for the action bar -->
```

```xml
        <item name="android:actionBarStyle">
            @style/ActionBarStyle</item>
        <!-- TextAppearance for the action items -->
        <item name="android:actionMenuTextAppearance">
            @style/MenuTextStyle</item>
        <item name="android:actionMenuTextColor">#0A0</item>
        <!-- Divider image between action items -->
        <item name="android:actionBarDivider">
            @drawable/divider</item>
        <!-- Background for action items -->
        <item name="android:actionBarItemBackground">
            @drawable/actionbar_item_background</item>
        <!-- Style a tab bar -->
        <item name="android:actionBarTabBarStyle">
            @style/TabBarStyle</item>
        <!-- Style for a navigation list in the action bar -->
        <item name="android:actionDropDownStyle">
            @android:style/Widget.Holo.Light.Spinner</item>
    </style>

    <style name="ActionBarStyle"
        parent="@android:style/Widget.ActionBar">
        <!-- Backgrounds for each possible bar -->
        <item name="android:background">
            @drawable/actionbar_background</item>
        <item name="android:backgroundStacked">#CCC</item>
        <item name="android:backgroundSplit">
            @android:color/black</item>
        <!-- TextAppearance styles for titles -->
        <item name="android:titleTextStyle">
            @style/TitleTextStyle</item>
        <item name="android:subtitleTextStyle">
            @style/SubtitleTextStyle</item>
    </style>
    <style name="TabBarStyle"
        parent="@android:style/Widget.Holo.ActionBar.TabBar">
        <!-- Indication to hide tab dividers in the tab bar -->
        <item name="android:showDividers">none</item>
    </style>

    <!-- TextAppearance Styles -->
    <style name="MenuTextStyle"
        parent="@android:style/TextAppearance.Small">
        <item name="android:textSize">8sp</item>
        <item name="android:textStyle">italic</item>
        <!-- Setting text color here has no effect -->
    </style>
    <style name="TitleTextStyle"
        parent="@android:style/TextAppearance.Large">
        <item name="android:textColor">#0AA</item>
        <item name="android:textStyle">bold|italic</item>
    </style>
```

```
    <style name="SubtitleTextStyle"
        parent="@android:style/TextAppearance.Small">
        <item name="android:textSize">10sp</item>
    </style>
</resources>
```

The basic flow of this example is to define a custom theme that inherits from the base framework theme you want to start from (in this case, we've chosen Theme.Holo.Light.DarkActionBar) and apply that theme to the activity you wish to customize in your AndroidManifest.xml; in fact, if you prefer, you can apply it to the entire application here as well. Notice that, when defining custom styles, we always begin with a parent style from the framework. This allows us to focus on just the elements we want to change rather than supplying an attribute for every element that makes up a system theme.

Inside our custom AppTheme, we override the attributes we want to customize in the action bar. Many of these are just custom colors or drawables, but some point to other style resources that we define further down in the file. The ActionBarStyle resource, for example, is where the custom backgrounds are defined and the text styles for the title and subtitle—each of which is yet again a pointer to another style we've defined.

Be aware that in some cases, the thing we want to style may live in multiple locations within the theme. For instance, to customize the tab dividers, we had to create the TabBarStyle, but to customize the background of the tab bar, we must set a value on the android:backgroundStacked attribute of the ActionBarStyle.

With our changes applied, the resulting action bar now looks like Figure 3-5. We have re-enabled tabs and split mode together from the previous example so you can see all the style changes made at once.

Figure 3-5. Action Bar with custom styles

Support Styles

Modifying our style customizations to work with an `ActionBarActivity` from the AppCompat Library is straightforward. Listing 3-9 shows the modified theme and styles.

Listing 3-9. res/values/styles.xml

```xml
<?xml version="1.0" encoding="utf-8"?>
<resources
    xmlns:android="http://schemas.android.com/apk/res/android">
    <style name="AppTheme"
        parent="@style/Theme.AppCompat.Light.DarkActionBar">
        <!-- Style for the action bar -->
        <item name="actionBarStyle">@style/ActionBarStyle</item>
        <!-- TextAppearance for the action items -->
        <item name="actionMenuTextAppearance">
            @style/MenuTextStyle</item>
        <item name="actionMenuTextColor">#0A0</item>
        <!-- Divider image between action items -->
        <item name="actionBarDivider">@drawable/divider</item>
        <!-- Background for the action items -->
```

```xml
            <item name="actionBarItemBackground">
                @drawable/actionbar_item_background</item>
            <!-- Style a Tab Bar -->
            <item name="actionBarTabBarStyle">
                @style/TabBarStyle</item>
            <!-- Style for a navigation list in the action bar -->
            <item name="actionDropDownStyle">
              @style/Widget.AppCompat.Light.Spinner.DropDown.ActionBar
            </item>
        </style>

        <style name="ActionBarStyle"
            parent="@style/Widget.AppCompat.ActionBar">
            <!-- Backgrounds for each possible bar -->
            <item name="background">
                @drawable/actionbar_background</item>
            <item name="backgroundStacked">
                @drawable/actionbar_background</item>
            <item name="backgroundSplit">
                @drawable/actionbar_background</item>
            <!-- TextAppearance styles for titles -->
            <item name="titleTextStyle">@style/TitleTextStyle</item>
            <item name="subtitleTextStyle">
                @style/SubtitleTextStyle</item>
        </style>
        <style name="TabBarStyle"
            parent="@style/Widget.AppCompat.ActionBar.TabBar">
            <!-- Indication to hide tab dividers in the tab bar -->
            <item name="showDividers">none</item>
        </style>

        <!-- TextAppearance Styles -->
        <style name="MenuTextStyle"
            parent="@android:style/TextAppearance.Small">
            <item name="android:textSize">8sp</item>
            <item name="android:textStyle">italic</item>
            <!-- Setting text color here has no effect -->
        </style>
        <style name="TitleTextStyle"
            parent="@android:style/TextAppearance.Large">
            <item name="android:textColor">#0AA</item>
            <item name="android:textStyle">bold|italic</item>
        </style>
        <style name="SubtitleTextStyle"
            parent="@android:style/TextAppearance.Small">
            <item name="android:textSize">10sp</item>
        </style>
</resources>
```

In order to use the AppCompat Library, we have to inherit all the styles and themes in our application from one of the AppCompat variants. So the first major change to our example is that the custom theme now inherits from `Theme.AppCompat.Light.DarkActionBar`, which is a version of the same system theme that has been copied into our application via the library project. Our custom widget styles also inherit from AppCompat variants.

In addition, all the attributes specific to action bar items, which are available only in later versions of the framework, are now referenced directly from our application package. As such, the `android:` namespace prefix is removed from these attributes.

3-2. Locking Activity Orientation

Problem

A certain activity in your application should not be allowed to rotate, or rotation requires more-direct intervention from the application code.

Solution

(API Level 1)

Using static declarations in the `AndroidManifest.xml` file, you can modify each individual activity to lock into either portrait or landscape orientation. This can be applied only to the `<activity>` tag, so it cannot be done once for the entire application scope. Simply add `android:screenOrientation="portrait"` or `android:screenOrientation="landscape"` to the `<activity>` element, and the activity will always display in the specified orientation, regardless of how the device is positioned.

There is also an option you can pass in the XML entitled `behind`. If an activity element has `android:screenOrientation="behind"` set, it will take its settings from the previous activity in the stack. This can be a useful way for an activity to match the locked orientation of its originator for some slightly more dynamic behavior.

How It Works

The example `AndroidManifest.xml` depicted in Listing 3-10 has three activities. Two of them are locked into portrait orientation (`MainActivity` and `ResultActivity`), while the `UserEntryActivity` is allowed to rotate, presumably because the user may want to rotate and use a physical keyboard.

Listing 3-10. Manifest with Some Activities Locked in Portrait

```
<?xml version="1.0" encoding="utf-8"?>
<manifest
    xmlns:android="http://schemas.android.com/apk/res/android"
    package="com.examples.rotation"
    android:versionCode="1"
    android:versionName="1.0">
    <application android:icon="@drawable/icon"
        android:label="@string/app_name">
        <activity android:name=".MainActivity"
```

```
            android:label="@string/app_name"
            android:screenOrientation="portrait">
            <intent-filter>
                <action
                    android:name="android.intent.action.MAIN" />
                <category
                    android:name="android.intent.category.LAUNCHER" />
            </intent-filter>
        </activity>

        <activity android:name=".ResultActivity"
            android:screenOrientation="portrait" />

        <activity android:name=".UserEntryActivity" />
    </application>
</manifest>
```

3-3. Performing Dynamic Orientation Locking

Problem

Conditions exist during which the screen should not rotate, but the condition is temporary or dependent on user wishes.

Solution

(API Level 1)

Using the requested orientation mechanism in Android, an application can adjust the screen orientation used to display the activity, fixing it to a specific orientation or releasing it to the device to decide. This is accomplished through the use of the `Activity.setRequestedOrientation()` method, which takes an integer constant from the `ActivityInfo.screenOrientation` attribute grouping.

By default, the requested orientation is set to `SCREEN_ORIENTATION_UNSPECIFIED`, which allows the device to decide for itself which orientation should be used. This is a decision typically based on the physical orientation of the device. The current requested orientation can be retrieved at any time as well by using `Activity.getRequestedOrientation()`.

How It Works

User Rotation Lock Button

As an example of this, let's create a `ToggleButton` instance that controls whether to lock the current orientation, allowing the user to control at any point whether the activity should change orientation.

Somewhere in the `main.xml` layout, a `ToggleButton` instance is defined:

```
<ToggleButton
    android:id="@+id/toggleButton"
    android:layout_width="wrap_content"
```

```
        android:layout_height="wrap_content"
        android:textOff="Lock"
        android:textOn="LOCKED"
/>
```

In the activity code, we will create a listener to the button's state that locks and releases the screen orientation based on its current value (see Listing 3-11).

Listing 3-11. Activity to Dynamically Lock/Unlock Screen Orientation

```
public class LockActivity extends Activity {

    protected void onCreate(Bundle savedInstanceState) {
        super.onCreate(savedInstanceState);
        setContentView(R.layout.main);

        //Get handle to the button resource
        ToggleButton toggle =
                (ToggleButton)findViewById(R.id.toggleButton);
        //Set the default state before adding the listener
        if( getRequestedOrientation() !=
                ActivityInfo.SCREEN_ORIENTATION_UNSPECIFIED ) {
            toggle.setChecked(true);
        } else {
            toggle.setChecked(false);
        }
        //Attach the listener to the button
        toggle.setOnCheckedChangeListener(listener);
    }

    OnCheckedChangeListener listener =
            new OnCheckedChangeListener() {
        public void onCheckedChanged(CompoundButton buttonView,
                boolean isChecked) {
            int current = getResources()
                    .getConfiguration().orientation;
            if(!isChecked) {
                setRequestedOrientation(
                    ActivityInfo.SCREEN_ORIENTATION_UNSPECIFIED);
                return;
            }

            switch(current) {
            case Configuration.ORIENTATION_LANDSCAPE:
                setRequestedOrientation(
                    ActivityInfo.SCREEN_ORIENTATION_LANDSCAPE);
                break;
            case Configuration.ORIENTATION_PORTRAIT:
                setRequestedOrientation(
                    ActivityInfo.SCREEN_ORIENTATION_PORTRAIT);
                break;
```

```
            default:
                setRequestedOrientation(
                    ActivityInfo.SCREEN_ORIENTATION_UNSPECIFIED);
                break;
        }
    }
  }
}
```

The code in the listener is the key ingredient to this recipe. If the user presses the button and it toggles to the ON state, the current orientation is read by storing the `orientation` parameter from `Resources.getConfiguration()`. The Configuration object and the requested orientation use different constants to map the states, so we switch on the current orientation and call `setRequestedOrientation()` with the appropriate constant.

> **Note**   If an orientation is requested that is different from the current state, and your activity is in the foreground, the activity will change immediately to accommodate the request.

If the user presses the button and it toggles to the OFF state, we no longer want to lock the orientation, so `setRequestedOrientation()` is called with the `SCREEN_ORIENTATION_UNSPECIFIED` constant again to return control back to the device. This may also cause an immediate change to occur if the device's physical orientation differs from the activity orientation when the lock is removed.

> **Note**   Setting a requested orientation does not keep the default activity life cycle from occurring. If a device configuration change occurs (the keyboard slides out or the device orientation changes), the activity will still be destroyed and re-created, so all rules about persisting activity state still apply.

3-4. Manually Handling Rotation

Problem

The default behavior destroying and re-creating an activity during rotation causes an unacceptable performance penalty in the application.

Without customization, Android will respond to configuration changes by finishing the current activity instance and creating a new one in its place, appropriate for the new configuration. This can cause undue performance penalties because the UI state must be saved and then completely rebuilt.

Solution

(API Level 1)

Utilize the android:configChanges manifest parameter to instruct Android that a certain activity will handle rotation events without assistance from the runtime. This reduces the amount of work required not only from Android, destroying and re-creating the activity instance, but also from your application. With the activity instance intact, the application does not have to necessarily spend time to save and restore the current state in order to maintain consistency for the user.

An activity that registers for one or more configuration changes will be notified via the Activity.onConfigurationChanged() callback method, where it can perform any necessary manual handling associated with the change.

There are two configuration change parameters the activity should register for in order to handle rotation completely: orientation and keyboardHidden. The orientation parameter registers the activity for any event when the device orientation changes. The keyboardHidden parameter registers the activity for the event when the user slides a physical keyboard in or out. While the latter may not be directly of interest, if you do not register for these events, Android will re-create your activity when they occur, which may subvert your efforts in handling rotation in the first place.

How It Works

These parameters are added to any <activity> element in AndroidManifest.xml, like so:

```
<activity android:name=".MyActivity"
    android:configChanges="orientation|keyboardHidden|screenSize" />
```

Multiple changes can be registered in the same assignment statement, using a pipe (|) character between them. Because these parameters cannot be applied to an <application> element, each individual activity must register in the AndroidManifest.xml file.

With the activity registered, a configuration change results in a call to the activity's onConfigurationChanged() method. Listing 3-12 is a simple activity definition that can be used to handle the callback received when the changes occur.

Listing 3-12. Activity to Manage Rotation Manually

```
public class MyActivity extends Activity {

    @Override
    protected void onCreate(Bundle savedInstanceState) {
        //Calling super is required
        super.onCreate(savedInstanceState);
        //Load view resources
        loadView();
    }
```

```
@Override
public void onConfigurationChanged(Configuration newConfig) {
    //Calling super is required
    super.onConfigurationChanged(newConfig);
    //Store important UI state
    saveState();
    //Reload the view resources
    loadView();
}

private void saveState() {
    //Implement any code to persist the UI state
}

private void loadView() {
    setContentView(R.layout.main);

    //Handle other required UI changes on a new configuration
    //Including restoring any stored state
}
}
```

> **Note** Google does not recommend handling rotation in this fashion unless it is necessary for the application's performance. All configuration-specific resources must be loaded manually in response to each change event.

Google recommends allowing the default re-creation behavior on activity rotation unless the performance of your application requires circumventing it. Primarily, this is because you lose all assistance Android provides for loading alternative resources if you have them stored in resource-qualified directories (such as res/layout-land/ for landscape layouts).

In the example activity, all code dealing with the view layout is abstracted to a private method, loadView(), called from both onCreate() and onConfigurationChanged(). In this method, code such as setContentView() is placed to ensure that the appropriate layout is loaded to match the configuration.

Calling setContentView() will completely reload the view, so any UI state that is important still needs to be saved, without the assistance of life-cycle callbacks such as onSaveInstanceState() and onRestoreInstanceState(). The example implements a method called saveState() for this purpose.

3-5. Creating Pop-up Menu Actions
Problem
You want to provide the user with multiple actions to take as a result of them selecting some part of the UI.

Solution

Display a ContextMenu or ActionMode in response to the user action.

How It Works

ContextMenu

(API Level 1)

Using a ContextMenu is a useful solution, particularly when you want to provide a list of actions based on an item click in a ListView or other AdapterView. This is because the ContextMenu.ContextMenuInfo object provides useful information about the specific item that was selected, such as ID and position, which may be helpful in constructing the menu.

First, create an XML file in res/menu/ to define the menu itself; we'll call this one contextmenu.xml (see Listing 3-13).

Listing 3-13. res/menu/contextmenu.xml

```xml
<?xml version="1.0" encoding="utf-8"?>
<menu xmlns:android="http://schemas.android.com/apk/res/android">
    <item
        android:id="@+id/menu_delete"
        android:icon="@android:drawable/ic_menu_delete"
        android:title="Delete Item"
    />
    <item
        android:id="@+id/menu_edit"
        android:icon="@android:drawable/ic_menu_edit"
        android:title="Edit Item"
    />
</menu>
```

Then utilize onCreateContextMenu() and onContextItemSelected() in the activity to inflate the menu and handle user selection (see Listing 3-14).

Listing 3-14. Activity Utilizing Custom Menu

```java
@Override
public void onCreateContextMenu(ContextMenu menu, View v,
        ContextMenu.ContextMenuInfo menuInfo) {
    super.onCreateContextMenu(menu, v, menuInfo);
    getMenuInflater().inflate(R.menu.contextmenu, menu);
    menu.setHeaderTitle("Choose an Option");
}
```

```
@Override
public boolean onContextItemSelected(MenuItem item) {
    //Switch on the item's ID to find the action the user selected
    switch(item.getItemId()) {
    case R.id.menu_delete:
        //Perform delete actions
        break;
    case R.id.menu_edit:
        //Perform edit actions
        break;
    default:
        return super.onContextItemSelected(item);
    }
    return true;
}
```

In order for these callback methods to fire, you must register the view that will trigger the menu. In effect, this sets the View.OnCreateContextMenuListener for the view to the current activity:

```
protected void onCreate(Bundle savedInstanceState) {
        super.onCreate(savedInstanceState);
    //Register a button for context events
    ListView list = new ListView(this);
    ArrayAdapter<String> adapter = new ArrayAdapter<String>(this,
            android.R.layout.simple_list_item_1, ITEMS);
    list.setAdapter(adapter);
    registerForContextMenu(list);

    setContentView(list);
}
```

The default user behavior in Android is for many views to show a ContextMenu when a long-press occurs as an alternate to the main click action. Following suit, in our example, long-pressing the items in the ListView will display our options menu.

> **Tip**   You can also trigger a ContextMenu for any arbitrary view by calling the Activity.openContextMenu() method, passing it the view you had previously registered.

Tying all the pieces together, we have a simple activity that registers a button to show our menu when tapped (see Listing 3-15).

Listing 3-15. Activity Utilizing Context Action Menu

```
public class ContextActivity extends Activity {

    private static final String[] ITEMS =
            {"Mom", "Dad", "Brother", "Sister", "Uncle", "Aunt"};
```

```
protected void onCreate(Bundle savedInstanceState) {
    super.onCreate(savedInstanceState);
    //Register a button for context events
    ListView list = new ListView(this);
        ArrayAdapter<String> adapter = new ArrayAdapter<String>(this,
                android.R.layout.simple_list_item_1, ITEMS);
        list.setAdapter(adapter);
        registerForContextMenu(list);

        setContentView(list);
}

@Override
public void onCreateContextMenu(ContextMenu menu, View v,
        ContextMenu.ContextMenuInfo menuInfo) {
    super.onCreateContextMenu(menu, v, menuInfo);
    getMenuInflater().inflate(R.menu.contextmenu, menu);
    menu.setHeaderTitle("Choose an Option");
}

@Override
public boolean onContextItemSelected(MenuItem item) {
    //You can obtain the item that was clicked from the
    // bundled ContextMenuInfo object, which is an instance
    // of AdapterContextMenuInfo in the case of a ListView
    AdapterContextMenuInfo info =
            (AdapterContextMenuInfo) item.getMenuInfo();
    int listPosition = info.position;

    //Switch on the item's ID to find the action the user selected
    switch(item.getItemId()) {
    case R.id.menu_delete:
        //Perform delete actions
        break;
    case R.id.menu_edit:
        //Perform edit actions
        break;
    default:
        return super.onContextItemSelected(item);
    }
    return true;
}
}
```

When the user makes a selection, you can determine which action they took by checking the
MenuItem passed in. In addition, this MenuItem has with it a ContextMenuInfo object, which contains
data about the item in the original list that was selected. This can also be quite useful in order for
you to actually perform the requested action on the data item. The resulting application is shown in
Figure 3-6.

Figure 3-6. Context action menu

ActionMode

(API Level 11)

The ActionMode API solves a similar problem to ContextMenu, allowing the user to take actions on specific items in your user interface; however, it does so in a slightly different way. Activating an ActionMode overtakes the system action bar with an overlay that includes menu options you provide and an extra option to exit the ActionMode. It also allows you to select multiple items at once on which to apply a single action. Listing 3-16 illustrates this feature.

Listing 3-16. Activity Utilizing Context ActionMode

```
public class ActionActivity extends Activity implements
        AbsListView.MultiChoiceModeListener {

    private static final String[] ITEMS =
            {"Mom", "Dad", "Brother", "Sister", "Uncle", "Aunt"};

    private ListView mList;

    protected void onCreate(Bundle savedInstanceState) {
        super.onCreate(savedInstanceState);
        //Register a button for context events
        mList = new ListView(this);
```

```java
    ArrayAdapter<String> adapter = new ArrayAdapter<String>(
            this,
            android.R.layout.simple_list_item_activated_1,
            ITEMS);
    mList.setAdapter(adapter);
    //Set up this list with a contextual ActionMode
    mList.setChoiceMode(ListView.CHOICE_MODE_MULTIPLE_MODAL);
    mList.setMultiChoiceModeListener(this);

    setContentView(mList);
}

@Override
public boolean onPrepareActionMode(ActionMode mode,
        Menu menu) {
    //You can do extra work here to update the menu if the
    // ActionMode is ever invalidated
    return true;
}

@Override
public void onDestroyActionMode(ActionMode mode) {
    //This is called when the ActionMode has been exited
}

@Override
public boolean onCreateActionMode(ActionMode mode,
        Menu menu) {
    MenuInflater inflater = mode.getMenuInflater();
    inflater.inflate(R.menu.contextmenu, menu);
    return true;
}

@Override
public boolean onActionItemClicked(ActionMode mode,
        MenuItem item) {
    //List of checked item locations to do the operation
    SparseBooleanArray items =
            mList.getCheckedItemPositions();
    //Switch on the item's ID to find the selected action
    switch(item.getItemId()) {
    case R.id.menu_delete:
        //Perform delete actions
        break;
    case R.id.menu_edit:
        //Perform edit actions
        break;
    default:
        return false;
    }
    return true;
}
```

```
    @Override
    public void onItemCheckedStateChanged(ActionMode mode,
            int position, long id, boolean checked) {
        int count = mList.getCheckedItemCount();
        mode.setTitle(String.format("%d Selected", count));
    }
}
```

To use our ListView to activate a multiple selection ActionMode, we set its choiceMode attribute to CHOICE_MODE_MULTIPLE_MODAL. This is different from the traditional CHOICE_MODE_MULTIPLE, which will provide selection widgets on each list item to make the selection. The modal flag applies this selection mode only while an ActionMode is active.

There are a series of callbacks required to implement an ActionMode that are not built directly into an activity like the ContextMenu. We need to implement the ActionMode.Callback interface to respond to the events of creating the menu and selecting options. ListView has a special interface called MultiChoiceModeListener, which is a subinterface of ActionMode.Callback, which we implement in the example.

In onCreateActionMode(), we respond similarly to onCreateContextMenu(), just inflating our menu options for the overlay to display. Your menu does not need to contain icons; ActionMode can display the item names instead. The onItemCheckedStateChanged() method is where we will get feedback for each item selection. Here, we use that change to update the title of the ActionMode to display how many items are currently selected.

The onActionItemClicked() method will be called when the user has finished making selections and taps an option item. Because there are multiple items to work on, we go back to the list to get all the items selected with getCheckedItemPositions() so we can apply the selected operation. Figure 3-7 shows how the ActionMode looks with our previous list.

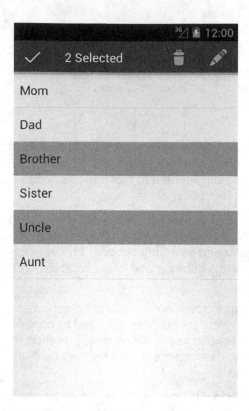

Figure 3-7. ActionMode with two selections made

3-6. Displaying a User Dialog

Problem

You need to display a simple pop-up dialog to the user to either notify of an event or present a list of selections.

Solution

(API Level 1)

AlertDialog is the most efficient method of displaying important modal information to your user quickly. The content it displays is easy to customize, and the framework provides a convenient AlertDialog.Builder class to construct a pop-up quickly.

How It Works

When you use AlertDialog.Builder, you can construct a similar alert dialog but with some additional options. AlertDialog is a very versatile class for creating simple pop-ups to get feedback from the user. With AlertDialog.Builder, a single or multichoice list, buttons, and a message string can all be easily added into one compact widget.

To illustrate this, let's create the same pop-up selection as before by using AlertDialog. This time, we will add a Cancel button to the bottom of the options list (see Listing 3-17).

Listing 3-17. Action Menu Using AlertDialog

```java
public class DialogActivity extends Activity implements
        DialogInterface.OnClickListener,
        View.OnClickListener {

    private static final String[] ZONES = {
            "Pacific Time", "Mountain Time",
            "Central Time", "Eastern Time",
            "Atlantic Time"};

    Button mButton;
    AlertDialog mActions;

    @Override
    protected void onCreate(Bundle savedInstanceState) {
        super.onCreate(savedInstanceState);
        setTitle("Activity");
        mButton = new Button(this);
        mButton.setText("Click for Time Zones");
        mButton.setOnClickListener(this);

        AlertDialog.Builder builder =
                new AlertDialog.Builder(this);
        builder.setTitle("Select Time Zone");
        builder.setItems(ZONES, this);
        //Cancel action does nothing but dismiss, we could
        // add another listener here to do something extra
        // when the user hits the Cancel button
        builder.setNegativeButton("Cancel", null);
        mActions = builder.create();

        setContentView(mButton);
    }

    //List selection action handled here
    @Override
    public void onClick(DialogInterface dialog, int which) {
        String selected = ZONES[which];
        mButton.setText(selected);
    }
```

```
//Button action handled here (pop up the dialog)
@Override
public void onClick(View v) {
    mActions.show();
}
}
```

In this example, we create a new `AlertDialog.Builder` instance and use its convenience methods to add the following items:

- A title, using `setTitle()`
- The selectable list of options, using `setItems()` with an array of strings (also works with array resources)
- A Cancel button, using `setNegativeButton()`

The listener that we attach to the list items returns which list item was selected as a zero-based index into the array we supplied, so we use that information to update the text of the button with the user's selection. We pass in `null` for the Cancel button's listener, because in this instance we just want Cancel to dismiss the dialog. If there is some important work to be done upon pressing Cancel, another listener could be passed in to the `setNegativeButton()` method.

The builder provides several other options for you to set the content of the dialog to something other than a selectable list:

- `setMessage()` applies a simple text message as the body content.
- `setSingleChoiceItems()` and `setMultiChoiceItems()` create a list similar to this example but with selection modes applied so that the items will appear as being selected.
- `setView()` applies any arbitrary custom view as the dialog's content.

The resulting application looks like Figure 3-8 when the button is pressed.

Figure 3-8. Alert dialog with items list

Custom List Items

AlertDialog.Builder allows for a custom ListAdapter to be passed in as the source of the list items the dialog should display. This means we can create custom row layouts to display more-detailed information to the user. In Listings 3-18 and 3-19, we enhance the previous example by using a custom row layout to display extra data for each item.

Listing 3-18. res/layout/list_item.xml

```xml
<?xml version="1.0" encoding="utf-8"?>
<RelativeLayout
    xmlns:android="http://schemas.android.com/apk/res/android"
    android:layout_width="match_parent"
    android:layout_height="wrap_content"
    android:paddingLeft="10dp"
    android:paddingRight="10dp"
    android:minHeight="?android:attr/listPreferredItemHeight">
    <TextView
        android:id="@+id/text_name"
        android:layout_width="wrap_content"
        android:layout_height="wrap_content"
        android:layout_centerVertical="true"
        android:textAppearance="?android:attr/textAppearanceMedium"
    />
```

```xml
    <TextView
        android:id="@+id/text_detail"
        android:layout_width="wrap_content"
        android:layout_height="wrap_content"
        android:layout_alignParentRight="true"
        android:layout_centerVertical="true"
        android:textAppearance="?android:attr/textAppearanceSmall"
    />
</RelativeLayout>
```

Listing 3-19. AlertDialog with Custom Layout

```java
public class CustomItemActivity extends Activity implements
        DialogInterface.OnClickListener,
        View.OnClickListener {

    private static final String[] ZONES = {
            "Pacific Time", "Mountain Time",
            "Central Time", "Eastern Time",
            "Atlantic Time"};

    private static final String[] OFFSETS = {
            "GMT-08:00", "GMT-07:00", "GMT-06:00",
            "GMT-05:00", "GMT-04:00"};

    Button mButton;
    AlertDialog mActions;

    @Override
    protected void onCreate(Bundle savedInstanceState) {
        super.onCreate(savedInstanceState);
        setTitle("Activity");
        mButton = new Button(this);
        mButton.setText("Click for Time Zones");
        mButton.setOnClickListener(this);

        ArrayAdapter<String> adapter = new ArrayAdapter<String>(
                this,
                R.layout.list_item) {
            @Override
            public View getView(int position, View convertView,
                    ViewGroup parent) {
                View row = convertView;
                if (row == null) {
                    row = getLayoutInflater().inflate(R.layout.list_item,
                            parent, false);
                }

                TextView name =
                        (TextView) row.findViewById(R.id.text_name);
                TextView detail =
                        (TextView) row.findViewById(R.id.text_detail);
```

```
                name.setText(ZONES[position]);
                detail.setText(OFFSETS[position]);

                return row;
            }

            @Override
            public int getCount() {
                return ZONES.length;
            }
        };

        AlertDialog.Builder builder = new AlertDialog.Builder(this);
        builder.setTitle("Select Time Zone");
        builder.setAdapter(adapter, this);
        //Cancel action does nothing but dismiss, we could add
        // another listener here to do something extra when the
        // user hits the Cancel button
        builder.setNegativeButton("Cancel", null);
        mActions = builder.create();

        setContentView(mButton);
    }

    //List selection action handled here
    @Override
    public void onClick(DialogInterface dialog, int which) {
        String selected = ZONES[which];
        mButton.setText(selected);
    }

    //Button action handled here (pop up the dialog)
    @Override
    public void onClick(View v) {
        mActions.show();
    }
}
```

Here we have provided an ArrayAdapter to the builder instead of simply passing the array of items. This adapter has a custom implementation of getView() that returns a custom layout we've defined in XML to display two text labels: one aligned left and the other aligned right. With this custom layout, we can now display the Greenwich Mean Time (GMT) offset value alongside the time-zone name. We'll talk more about the specifics of custom adapters later in this chapter. Figure 3-9 displays our new, more useful pop-up dialog.

Figure 3-9. AlertDialog with custom items

3-7. Customizing Menus and Actions

Problem

Your application needs to provide a set of actions to the user that you don't want to have taking up screen real estate in your view hierarchy.

Solution

(API Level 7)

Use the options menu functionality in the framework to provide commonly used actions inside the action bar, and additional options in an overflow pop-up menu. Additionally, menus can be attached to any existing view and shown as a floating drop-down by using PopupMenu. This feature allows you to place menus anywhere in your application besides just the action bar, but still keep them out of view until the user requires them.

The menu functionality in Android varies, depending on the device. In early releases, all Android devices had a physical MENU key that would trigger this functionality. Starting with Android 3.0, devices without physical buttons started to emerge, and the menu functionality became part of the action bar.

Action items resident in the action bar can also expand to reveal a custom widget known as an *action view*. This is helpful for providing features such as a search field that requires additional user input, but that you want to hide behind a single action item until the user taps to reveal it.

> **Note** All of these features are available to devices running Android 2.1 (API Level 7) and later via the AppCompat portion of the Android Support Library.

How It Works

Listing 3-20 defines the options menu we will use in XML.

Listing 3-20. res/menu/options.xml

```xml
<menu xmlns:android="http://schemas.android.com/apk/res/android">
    <item android:id="@+id/menu_add"
        android:title="Add Item"
        android:icon="@android:drawable/ic_menu_add"
        android:showAsAction="always|collapseActionView"
        android:actionLayout="@layout/view_action" />
    <item android:id="@+id/menu_remove"
        android:title="Remove Item"
        android:icon="@android:drawable/ic_menu_delete"
        android:showAsAction="ifRoom" />
    <item android:id="@+id/menu_edit"
        android:title="Edit Item"
        android:icon="@android:drawable/ic_menu_edit"
        android:showAsAction="ifRoom" />
    <item android:id="@+id/menu_settings"
        android:title="Settings"
        android:icon="@android:drawable/ic_menu_preferences"
        android:showAsAction="never" />
</menu>
```

The `title` and `icon` attributes define how each item will be displayed; older platforms will show both values, while newer versions will show one or the other based on placement. Only Android 3.0 and later devices will recognize the `showAsAction` attribute, which defines whether the item should be promoted to an action on the action bar or placed into the overflow menu. The most common values for this attribute are as follows:

- `always`: Always display as an action by its icon

- `never`: Always display in the overflow menu by its name

- `ifRoom`: Display as an action if there is room on the action bar; otherwise, place in overflow

The first item in our menu also defines an `android:actionLayout` resource that points to the widget we want to expand into when this item is tapped, and an additional display flag, `collapseActionView`, to tell the framework this item has a collapsible action view to display. Listing 3-21 shows the action view layout, which is just a simple layout with two `CheckBox` instances.

Listing 3-21. res/layout/view_action.xml

```xml
<?xml version="1.0" encoding="utf-8"?>
<LinearLayout
    xmlns:android="http://schemas.android.com/apk/res/android"
    android:layout_width="match_parent"
    android:layout_height="wrap_content"
    android:orientation="horizontal">
    <CheckBox
        android:id="@+id/option_first"
        android:layout_width="0dp"
        android:layout_height="wrap_content"
        android:layout_weight="1"
        android:text="First"/>
    <CheckBox
        android:id="@+id/option_second"
        android:layout_width="0dp"
        android:layout_height="wrap_content"
        android:layout_weight="1"
        android:text="Second"/>
</LinearLayout>
```

Listings 3-22 and 3-23 show the full activity in which we are inflating our options menu into the action bar, displaying that same menu via PopupMenu, and housing an expandable action view inside one of our action items.

Listing 3-22. res/layout/main.xml

```xml
<?xml version="1.0" encoding="utf-8"?>
<RelativeLayout
    xmlns:android="http://schemas.android.com/apk/res/android"
    android:layout_width="match_parent"
    android:layout_height="match_parent" >
    <TextView
        android:id="@+id/anchor"
        android:layout_width="match_parent"
        android:layout_height="wrap_content"
        android:text="Menu Will Show Here" />
    <Button
        android:layout_width="match_parent"
        android:layout_height="wrap_content"
        android:layout_centerVertical="true"
        android:text="Show Menu"
        android:onClick="onShowMenuClick"/>
</RelativeLayout>
```

Listing 3-23. Activity Overriding Menu Action

```java
public class OptionsActivity extends Activity implements
        PopupMenu.OnMenuItemClickListener,
        CompoundButton.OnCheckedChangeListener {

    /* Action Item with the custom Action View */
    private MenuItem mOptionsItem;
    private CheckBox mFirstOption, mSecondOption;
    /* Explicit PopupMenu */
    private PopupMenu mPopup;

    @Override
    public void onCreate(Bundle savedInstanceState) {
        super.onCreate(savedInstanceState);
        setContentView(R.layout.main);

        //Create a PopupMenu to display just below our TextView
        mPopup = new PopupMenu(this, findViewById(R.id.anchor));
        mPopup.setOnMenuItemClickListener(this);
        //Use the same options menu as our Activity
        mPopup.inflate(R.menu.options);
    }

    public void onShowMenuClick(View v) {
        mPopup.show();
    }

    @Override
    public boolean onCreateOptionsMenu(Menu menu) {
        //Use this callback to create the menu and do any
        // initial setup necessary
        getMenuInflater().inflate(R.menu.options, menu);

        //Find and initialize our action item
        mOptionsItem = menu.findItem(R.id.menu_add);
        mOptionsItem.setOnActionExpandListener(
                new MenuItem.OnActionExpandListener() {

                    @Override
                    public boolean onMenuItemActionExpand(
                            MenuItem item) {
                        // Must return true to have item expand
                        return true;
                    }

                    @Override
                    public boolean onMenuItemActionCollapse(
                            MenuItem item) {
                        mFirstOption.setChecked(false);
                        mSecondOption.setChecked(false);
```

```
                            // Must return true to have item collapse
                            return true;
                    }
                });

        mFirstOption = (CheckBox) mOptionsItem
                .getActionView()
                .findViewById(R.id.option_first);
        mFirstOption
                .setOnCheckedChangeListener(this);
        mSecondOption = (CheckBox) mOptionsItem
                .getActionView()
                .findViewById(R.id.option_second);
        mSecondOption
                .setOnCheckedChangeListener(this);

        return true;
    }

    /* CheckBox Callback Methods */

    @Override
    public void onCheckedChanged(CompoundButton buttonView,
            boolean isChecked) {
        if (mFirstOption.isChecked()
                && mSecondOption.isChecked()) {
            //Hide the action view
            mOptionsItem.collapseActionView();
        }
    }

    @Override
    public boolean onPrepareOptionsMenu(Menu menu) {
        //Use this callback to do setup that needs to happen
        // each time the menu opens
        return super.onPrepareOptionsMenu(menu);
    }

    //Callback from the PopupMenu click
    public boolean onMenuItemClick(MenuItem item) {
        menuItemSelected(item);
        return true;
    }

    //Callback from a standard options menu click
    @Override
    public boolean onOptionsItemSelected(MenuItem item) {
        menuItemSelected(item);
        return true;
    }
```

```java
//Private helper so each callback can trigger the same actions
private void menuItemSelected(MenuItem item) {
    //Get the selected option by id
    switch (item.getItemId()) {
    case R.id.menu_add:
        //Do add action
        break;
    case R.id.menu_remove:
        //Do remove action
        break;
    case R.id.menu_edit:
        //Do edit action
        break;
    case R.id.menu_settings:
        //Do settings action
        break;
    default:
        break;
    }
}
}
```

When the user presses the MENU key on the device, or an activity loads with an action bar present, the onCreateOptionsMenu() method is called to set up the menu. There is a special LayoutInflater object called MenuInflater that is used to create menus from XML. We use the instance already available to the activity with getMenuInflater() to return our XML menu.

If there are any actions you need to take each time the user opens the menu, you can do so in onPrepareOptionsMenu(). Be advised that any actions promoted to the action bar will not trigger this callback when the user selects them; actions in the overflow menu, however, will still trigger it.

When the user makes a selection, the onOptionsItemSelected() callback will be triggered with the selected menu item. Since we defined a unique ID for each item in our XML menu, we can use a switch statement to check which item the user selected and take the appropriate action.

This same menu is attached to a PopupMenu inside onCreate(). When the PopupMenu is created, it is passed an *anchor* view, which is the view alongside which the menu will display. We passed the TextView inside the main layout, so when the user clicks the button in the layout, the same menu from the action bar will show as a floating drop-down just below the text. These anchors work the same as with PopupWindow in the previous chapter, in that if there is not enough room below the view to show the menu, it will display above the view instead.

Finally, we find some additional setup for our expandable action view inside onCreateOptionsMenu(). Here we obtain a reference to the menu item that includes the action view layout and attach an OnActionExpandListener callback. The callback is used here simply to clear both selected elements in the action view whenever the item collapses.

Important If you provide an OnActionExpandListener, you will need to return true inside onMenuItemActionExpand(), or the expansion will never occur!

We can use the getActionView() method from MenuItem to get a reference to the inflated action layout set in the menu XML. In our example, we use this to set a selected listener on each CheckBox inside the layout. Whenever the case occurs where both items are selected inside the action view, we call collapseActionView() to turn the view back into a single action item icon.

Figure 3-10 shows how this menu is displayed across different device versions and configurations. Devices that have physical keys will display the promoted actions in the action bar, but the overflow menu is still triggered by the MENU key. Devices with soft keys will display the overflow menu as a button next to the action bar actions.

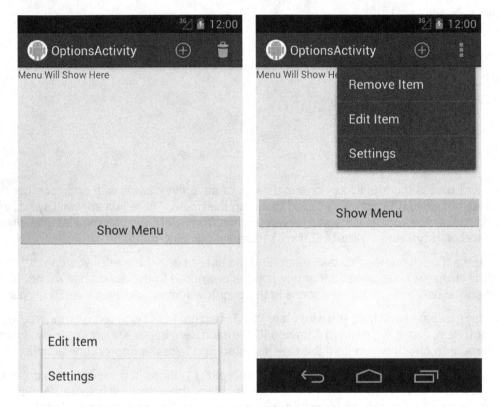

Figure 3-10. Android 4.1 with physical keys (left), and Android 4.0 with soft keys (right)

Figure 3-11 shows the same menu triggered by a button click and shown via PopupMenu below the text content.

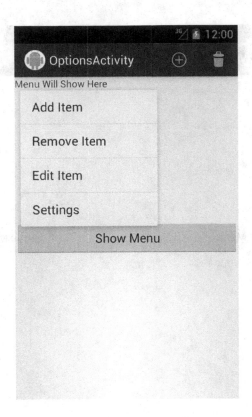

Figure 3-11. *PopupMenu displayed*

Figure 3-12 shows the expandable action view that is displayed when the Add action is tapped in the action bar.

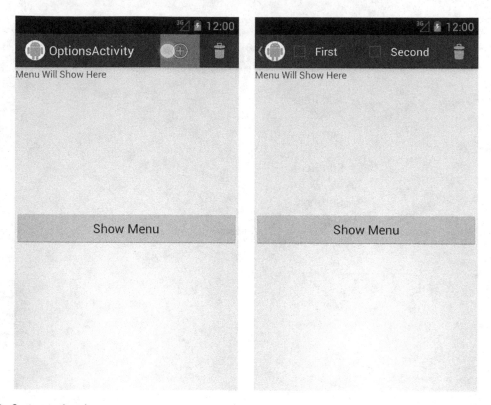

Figure 3-12. Custom action view

AppCompat Changes

The previous example requires a few modifications if you want to use it with AppCompat rather than strictly with the native APIs. Listing 3-24 shows that the options menu XML has to change slightly.

Listing 3-24. res/menu/support.xml

```xml
<menu xmlns:android="http://schemas.android.com/apk/res/android"
    xmlns:appcompat="http://schemas.android.com/apk/res-auto">
    <item android:id="@+id/menu_add"
        android:title="Add Item"
        android:icon="@android:drawable/ic_menu_add"
        appcompat:showAsAction="always|collapseActionView"
        appcompat:actionLayout="@layout/view_action" />
    <item android:id="@+id/menu_remove"
        android:title="Remove Item"
        android:icon="@android:drawable/ic_menu_delete"
        appcompat:showAsAction="ifRoom" />
    <item android:id="@+id/menu_edit"
        android:title="Edit Item"
        android:icon="@android:drawable/ic_menu_edit"
        appcompat:showAsAction="ifRoom" />
```

```
    <item android:id="@+id/menu_settings"
        android:title="Settings"
        android:icon="@android:drawable/ic_menu_preferences"
        appcompat:showAsAction="never" />
</menu>
```

On older versions, the attributes used to control where the menu items display in the action bar, as well as those dealing with a custom action view, do not exist in the framework. Instead, they must be read from the AppCompat library included in the project, so we need to create a new XML namespace prefix that points to the attributes built into our APK (we chose appcompat as our prefix, but you can choose anything you like). Listing 3-25 shows the modified activity.

Listing 3-25. Support Activity for Options Menu

```
public class SupportActivity extends ActionBarActivity implements
        PopupMenu.OnMenuItemClickListener,
        CompoundButton.OnCheckedChangeListener {

    private MenuItem mOptionsItem;
    private CheckBox mFirstOption, mSecondOption;

    private PopupMenu mPopup;

    @Override
    public void onCreate(Bundle savedInstanceState) {
        super.onCreate(savedInstanceState);
        setContentView(R.layout.main);

        //Create a PopupMenu to display just below our TextView
        mPopup = new PopupMenu(this, findViewById(R.id.anchor));
        mPopup.setOnMenuItemClickListener(this);
        //Use the same options menu as our Activity
        mPopup.inflate(R.menu.support);
    }

    public void onShowMenuClick(View v) {
        mPopup.show();
    }

    @Override
    public boolean onCreateOptionsMenu(Menu menu) {
        //Use this callback to create the menu and do any
        // initial setup necessary
        getMenuInflater().inflate(R.menu.support, menu);

        //Find and initialize our action item
        mOptionsItem = menu.findItem(R.id.menu_add);
        MenuItemCompat.setOnActionExpandListener(mOptionsItem,
                new MenuItemCompat.OnActionExpandListener() {

                    @Override
                    public boolean onMenuItemActionExpand(
```

```
                               MenuItem item) {
                           //Must return true to have item expand
                           return true;
                       }

                       @Override
                       public boolean onMenuItemActionCollapse(
                               MenuItem item) {
                           mFirstOption.setChecked(false);
                           mSecondOption.setChecked(false);
                           //Must return true to have item collapse
                           return true;
                       }
                   });

        mFirstOption = (CheckBox) MenuItemCompat
                .getActionView(mOptionsItem)
                .findViewById(R.id.option_first);
        mFirstOption.setOnCheckedChangeListener(this);
        mSecondOption = (CheckBox) MenuItemCompat
                .getActionView(mOptionsItem)
                .findViewById(R.id.option_second);
        mSecondOption.setOnCheckedChangeListener(this);

        return true;
    }

    /* CheckBox Callback Methods */

    @Override
    public void onCheckedChanged(CompoundButton buttonView,
            boolean isChecked) {
        if (mFirstOption.isChecked()
                && mSecondOption.isChecked()) {
            MenuItemCompat.collapseActionView(mOptionsItem);
        }
    }

    @Override
    public boolean onPrepareOptionsMenu(Menu menu) {
        //Use this callback to do setup that needs to happen
        // each time the menu opens
        return super.onPrepareOptionsMenu(menu);
    }

    //Callback from the PopupMenu click
    public boolean onMenuItemClick(MenuItem item) {
        menuItemSelected(item);
        return true;
    }
```

```java
//Callback from a standard options menu click
@Override
public boolean onOptionsItemSelected(MenuItem item) {
    menuItemSelected(item);
    return true;
}

//Private helper so each callback can trigger the same actions
private void menuItemSelected(MenuItem item) {
    //Get the selected option by id
    switch (item.getItemId()) {
    case R.id.menu_add:
        //Do add action
        break;
    case R.id.menu_remove:
        //Do remove action
        break;
    case R.id.menu_edit:
        //Do edit action
        break;
    case R.id.menu_settings:
        //Do settings action
        break;
    default:
        break;
    }
}
}
```

Besides inheriting from the `ActionBarActivity`, the primary modification necessary in this example revolves around access to the newer `MenuItem` APIs for the action view. The newer features of `MenuItem` are provided via static methods on `MenuItemCompat` rather than an extended compatibility class. So everywhere we called methods such as `getActionView()` or `collapseActionView()` in the previous example, we must now call from `MenuItemCompat`, passing in as an additional parameter the `MenuItem` we wish to act on.

3-8. Customizing BACK Behavior

Problem

Your application needs to handle the user pressing the hardware BACK button in a custom manner.

Solution

(API Level 5)

Use the `onBackPressed()` callback inside an activity, or manipulate the back stack inside a fragment.

How It Works

If you need to be notified when the user presses BACK on your activity, you can override onBackPressed() as follows:

```
@Override
public void onBackPressed() {
    //Custom back button processing

    //Call super to do normal processing (like finishing Activity)
    super.onBackPressed();
}
```

The default implementation of this method will pop any fragments currently on the back stack and then finish the activity. If you are not intending to interrupt this workflow, you will want to make sure to call the super class implementation when you are done to ensure this processing still happens normally.

> **Caution**   Overriding hardware button events should be done with care. All hardware buttons have consistent functionality across the Android system, and adjusting the functionality to work outside these bounds will be confusing and upsetting to users.

BACK Behavior and Fragments

When working with fragments in your UI, there are further opportunities to customize the behavior of the devices' BACK button. By default, the action of adding or replacing fragments in your UI is not something added to the task's back stack, so when the user presses the BACK button, they won't be able to step backward through those actions. However, any FragmentTransaction can be added as an entry in the back stack by simply calling addToBackStack() before the transaction is committed.

By default, the activity will call FragmentManager.popBackStackImmediate() when the user presses BACK, so each FragmentTransaction added in this way will unravel with each tap until there are none left; then the activity will finish. There are variations on this method, however, that allow you to jump directly to places in the stack as well. Let's take a look at Listings 3-26 and 3-27.

Listing 3-26. res/layout/main.xml

```xml
<?xml version="1.0" encoding="utf-8"?>
<LinearLayout xmlns:android="http://schemas.android.com/apk/res/android"
    android:layout_width="match_parent"
    android:layout_height="match_parent"
    android:orientation="vertical">
    <Button
        android:layout_width="match_parent"
        android:layout_height="wrap_content"
        android:text="Go Home"
        android:onClick="onHomeClick" />
```

```
    <FrameLayout
        android:id="@+id/container_fragment"
        android:layout_width="match_parent"
        android:layout_height="match_parent"/>
</LinearLayout>
```

Listing 3-27. Activity Customizing Fragment Back Stack

```java
public class MyActivity extends FragmentActivity {

    @Override
    protected void onCreate(Bundle savedInstanceState) {
        super.onCreate(savedInstanceState);
        setContentView(R.layout.main);
        //Build a stack of UI fragments
        FragmentTransaction ft =
                getSupportFragmentManager().beginTransaction();
        ft.add(R.id.container_fragment,
                MyFragment.newInstance("First Fragment"));
        ft.commit();

        ft = getSupportFragmentManager().beginTransaction();
        ft.add(R.id.container_fragment,
                MyFragment.newInstance("Second Fragment"));
        ft.addToBackStack("second");
        ft.commit();

        ft = getSupportFragmentManager().beginTransaction();
        ft.add(R.id.container_fragment,
                MyFragment.newInstance("Third Fragment"));
        ft.addToBackStack("third");
        ft.commit();

        ft = getSupportFragmentManager().beginTransaction();
        ft.add(R.id.container_fragment,
                MyFragment.newInstance("Fourth Fragment"));
        ft.addToBackStack("fourth");
        ft.commit();
    }

    public void onHomeClick(View v) {
        getSupportFragmentManager().popBackStack("second",
                FragmentManager.POP_BACK_STACK_INCLUSIVE);
    }

    public static class MyFragment extends Fragment {
        private CharSequence mTitle;

        public static MyFragment newInstance(String title) {
            MyFragment fragment = new MyFragment();
            fragment.setTitle(title);
```

```
            return fragment;
        }

        @Override
        public View onCreateView(LayoutInflater inflater,
                ViewGroup container, Bundle savedInstanceState) {
            TextView text = new TextView(getActivity());
            text.setText(mTitle);
            text.setBackgroundColor(Color.WHITE);

            return text;
        }

        public void setTitle(CharSequence title) {
            mTitle = title;
        }
    }
}
```

> **Note**   We are using the Support Library in this example to allow the use of fragments prior to Android 3.0.
> If your application is targeting API Level 11 or higher, you can replace FragmentActivity with Activity,
> and getSupportFragmentManager() with getFragmentManager().

This example loads four custom fragment instances into a stack, so the last one added is displayed
when the application runs. With each transaction, we call addToBackStack() with a tag name to
identify this transaction. This is not required, and if you do not wish to jump to places in the stack,
it is easier to just pass null here. With each press of the BACK button, a single fragment is removed
until only the first remains, at which point the activity will finish normally.

Notice the first transaction was not added to the stack; this is because here we want the first
fragment to act as the root view. Adding it to the back stack as well would cause it to pop off the
stack before finishing the activity, leaving the UI in a blank state.

This application also has a button marked Go Home, which immediately takes the user back to
the root fragment no matter where they currently are. It does this by calling popBackStack() on
FragmentManager, taking the tag of the transaction we want to jump back to. We also pass the flag
POP_BACK_STACK_INCLUSIVE to instruct the manager to also remove the transaction we've indicated
from the stack. Without this flag, the example would jump to the "second" fragment, rather than
the root.

> **Note**   Android pops back to the first transaction that matches the given tag. If the same tag is used multiple
> times, it will pop to the first transaction added, not the most recent.

We cannot go directly to the root with this method because we do not have a back stack tag associated with that transaction to reference. There is another version of this method that takes a unique transaction ID (the return value from commit() on FragmentTransaction). Using this method, we could jump directly to the root without requiring the inclusive flag.

3-9. Emulating the HOME Button

Problem

Your application needs to take the same action as if the user pressed the hardware HOME button.

Solution

(API Level 5)

When the user hits the HOME button, this sends an Intent to the system telling it to load the Home activity. This is no different from starting any other activity in your application; you just have to construct the proper Intent to get the effect.

How It Works

Add the following lines wherever you want this action to occur in your activity:

```
Intent intent = new Intent(Intent.ACTION_MAIN);
intent.addCategory(Intent.CATEGORY_HOME);
startActivity(intent);
```

A common use of this function is to override the BACK button to go home instead of to the previous activity. This is useful when everything underneath the foreground activity may be protected (by a login screen, for instance), and letting the default BACK button behavior occur could allow unsecured access to the system.

> **Important**   Whenever you are modifying the behavior of a system button, be extremely sure you are not disrupting what the user's expectation of that action should be.

Here is an example of using the two in concert to make a certain activity bring up the home screen when BACK is pressed:

```
@Override
public void onBackPressed() {
    Intent intent = new Intent(Intent.ACTION_MAIN);
    intent.addCategory(Intent.CATEGORY_HOME);
    startActivity(intent);
}
```

3-10. Monitoring TextView Changes

Problem

Your application needs to continuously monitor for text changes in a TextView widget (for example, EditText).

Solution

(API Level 1)

Implement the android.text.TextWatcher interface. TextWatcher provides three callback methods during the process of updating text:

```
public void beforeTextChanged(CharSequence s, int start, int count, int after);
public void onTextChanged(CharSequence s, int start, int before, int count);
public void afterTextChanged(Editable s);
```

The beforeTextChanged() and onTextChanged() methods are provided mainly as notifications, as you cannot actually make changes to the CharSequence in either of these methods. If you are attempting to intercept the text entered into the view, changes may be made when afterTextChanged() is called.

How It Works

To register a TextWatcher instance with a TextView, call the TextView.addTextChangedListener() method. Notice from the syntax that more than one TextWatcher can be registered with a TextView.

Character Counter Example

A simple use of TextWatcher is to create a live character counter that follows an EditText as the user types or deletes information. Listing 3-28 is an example activity that implements TextWatcher for this purpose, registers with an EditText widget, and prints the character count in the activity title.

Listing 3-28. Character Counter Activity

```
public class MyActivity extends Activity implements TextWatcher {

    EditText text;
    int textCount;

    @Override
    protected void onCreate(Bundle savedInstanceState) {
        super.onCreate(savedInstanceState);
        //Create an EditText widget and add the watcher
        text = new EditText(this);
        text.addTextChangedListener(this);

        setContentView(text);
    }
```

```
/* TextWatcher Implemention Methods */
@Override
public void beforeTextChanged(CharSequence s, int start, int count,
        int after) { }

@Override
public void onTextChanged(CharSequence s, int start, int before,
        int count) {
    textCount = text.getText().length();
    setTitle(String.valueOf(textCount));
}

@Override
public void afterTextChanged(Editable s) { }

}
```

Because our needs do not include modifying the text being inserted, we can read the count from onTextChanged(), which happens as soon as the text change occurs. The other methods are unused and left empty.

Currency Formatter Example

The SDK has a handful of predefined TextWatcher instances to format text input; PhoneNumberFormattingTextWatcher is one of these. Their job is to apply standard formatting for users while they type, reducing the number of keystrokes required to enter legible data.

In Listing 3-29, we create a CurrencyTextWatcher to insert the currency symbol and separator point into a TextView.

Listing 3-29. Currency Formatter

```
public class CurrencyTextWatcher implements TextWatcher {

    boolean mEditing;

    public CurrencyTextWatcher() {
        mEditing = false;
    }

    @Override
    public synchronized void afterTextChanged(Editable s) {
        if(!mEditing) {
            mEditing = true;

            //Strip symbols
            String digits = s.toString().replaceAll("\\D", "");
            NumberFormat nf = NumberFormat.getCurrencyInstance();
            try{
                String formatted =
                        nf.format(Double.parseDouble(digits)/100);
```

```
                s.replace(0, s.length(), formatted);
            } catch (NumberFormatException nfe) {
                s.clear();
            }

            mEditing = false;
        }
    }

    @Override
    public void beforeTextChanged(CharSequence s, int start, int count,
            int after) { }

    @Override
    public void onTextChanged(CharSequence s, int start, int before,
            int count) { }

}
```

> **Note**   Making changes to the `Editable` value in `afterTextChanged()` will cause the `TextWatcher`
> methods to be called again (after all, you just changed the text). For this reason, custom `TextWatcher`
> implementations that edit should use a boolean or some other tracking mechanism to track where the
> editing is coming from, or you may create an infinite loop.

We can apply this custom text formatter to an `EditText` in an activity (see Listing 3-30).

Listing 3-30. Activity Using Currency Formatter

```
public class MyActivity extends Activity {

    EditText text;

    @Override
    protected void onCreate(Bundle savedInstanceState) {
        super.onCreate(savedInstanceState);
        text = new EditText(this);
        text.addTextChangedListener(new CurrencyTextWatcher());

        setContentView(text);
    }

}
```

If you are formatting user input with this formatter, it is handy to define the `EditText` in XML so you
can apply the `android:inputType` and `android:digits` constraints to easily protect the field against
entry errors. In particular, adding `android:digits="0123456789."` (notice the period at the end for a
decimal point) to the `EditText` will protect this formatter as well as the user.

3-11. Customizing Keyboard Actions

Problem

You want to customize the appearance of the soft keyboard's Enter key, the action that occurs when a user taps it, or both.

Solution

(API Level 3)

Customize the input method (IME) options for the widget in which the keyboard is entering data.

How It Works

Custom Enter Key

When the keyboard is visible onscreen, the text on the Enter key typically indicates its action based on the order of focusable items in the view. While unspecified, the keyboard will display a "next" action if there are more focusables in the view to move to, or a "done" action if the last item is currently focused on. In the case of a multiline field, this action is a line return. This value is customizable, however, for each input view by setting the android:imeOptions value in the view's XML. The values you may set to customize the Enter key are listed here:

- actionUnspecified: Default. Displays action of the device's choice
  - Action event is IME_NULL
- actionGo: Displays Go as the Enter key
  - Action event is IME_ACTION_GO
- actionSearch: Displays a search glass as the Enter key
  - Action event is IME_ACTION_SEARCH
- actionSend: Displays Send as the Enter key
  - Action event is IME_ACTION_SEND
- actionNext: Displays Next as the Enter key
  - Action event is IME_ACTION_NEXT
- actionDone: Displays Done as the Enter key
  - Action event is IME_ACTION_DONE

Let's look at an example layout with two editable text fields, shown in Listing 3-31. The first will display the search magnifying glass on the Enter key, and the second will display Go.

Listing 3-31. Layout with Custom Input Options on EditText Widgets

```
<LinearLayout
    xmlns:android="http://schemas.android.com/apk/res/android"
    android:layout_width="fill_parent"
    android:layout_height="fill_parent"
    android:orientation="vertical">
    <EditText
        android:id="@+id/text1"
        android:layout_width="fill_parent"
        android:layout_height="wrap_content"
        android:singleLine="true"
        android:imeOptions="actionSearch" />
    <EditText
        android:id="@+id/text2"
        android:layout_width="fill_parent"
        android:layout_height="wrap_content"
        android:singleLine="true"
        android:imeOptions="actionGo" />
</LinearLayout>
```

The resulting display of the keyboard will vary somewhat, as some manufacturer-specific UI kits include different keyboards, but the results on a pure Google UI will show up as in Figure 3-13.

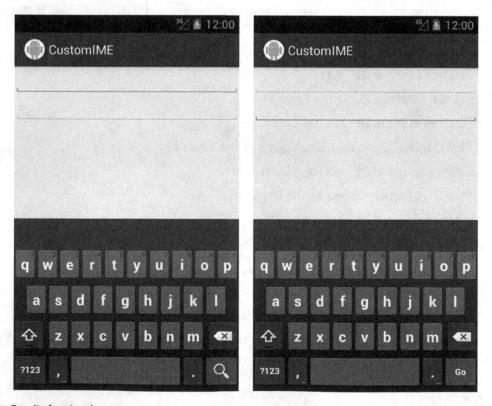

Figure 3-13. Result of custom input options on Enter key

> **Note**   Custom editor options apply only to the soft input methods. Changing this value will not affect the events that get generated when the user presses Enter on a physical hardware keyboard.

Custom Action

Customizing what happens when the user presses the Enter key can be just as important as adjusting its display. Overriding the default behavior of any action simply requires that a `TextView.OnEditorActionListener` be attached to the view of interest. Let's continue with the preceding example layout, and this time we'll add a custom action to both views (see Listing 3-32).

Listing 3-32. Activity Implementing a Custom Keyboard Action

```
public class MyActivity extends Activity implements
        OnEditorActionListener {

    @Override
    public void onCreate(Bundle savedInstanceState) {
        super.onCreate(savedInstanceState);
        setContentView(R.layout.main);

        //Add the listener to the views
        EditText text1 = (EditText)findViewById(R.id.text1);
        text1.setOnEditorActionListener(this);
        EditText text2 = (EditText)findViewById(R.id.text2);
        text2.setOnEditorActionListener(this);
    }

    @Override
    public boolean onEditorAction(TextView v, int actionId,
            KeyEvent event) {
        if(actionId == IME_ACTION_SEARCH) {
            //Handle search key click
            return true;
        }
        if(actionId == IME_ACTION_GO) {
            //Handle go key click
            return true;
        }
        return false;
    }
}
```

The boolean return value of `onEditorAction()` tells the system whether your implementation has consumed the event or whether it should be passed on to the next possible responder, if any. It is important for you to return `true` when your implementation handles the event so no other processing occurs. However, it is just as important for you to return `false` when you are not handling the event so your application does not steal key events from the rest of the system.

> **Note** If your application customizes the `actionId` value returned for a certain keyboard, be aware that this will happen only on soft keyboard IMEs. If the device has a physical keyboard attached, the Enter key on that keyboard will always return an `actionId` of 0 or `IME_NULL`.

3-12. Dismissing the Soft Keyboard

Problem

You need an event on the UI to hide or dismiss the soft keyboard from the screen.

Solution

(API Level 3)

Tell the Input Method Manager explicitly to hide any visible input methods by using the `InputMethodManager.hideSoftInputFromWindow()` method.

How It Works

Here is an example of how to call this method inside a `View.OnClickListener`:

```
public void onClick(View view) {
    InputMethodManager imm = (InputMethodManager)getSystemService(
            Context.INPUT_METHOD_SERVICE);
    imm.hideSoftInputFromWindow(view.getWindowToken(), 0);
}
```

The `hideSoftInputFromWindow()` takes an `IBinder` window token as a parameter. This can be retrieved from any `View` object currently attached to the window via `View.getWindowToken()`. In most cases, the callback method for the specific event will either have a reference to the `TextView` where the editing is taking place or the view that was tapped to generate the event (for example, a button). These views are the most convenient objects to call on to get the window token and pass it to the `InputMethodManager`.

3-13. Handling Complex Touch Events

Problem

Your application needs to implement customized single or multitouch interactions with the UI.

Solution

(API Level 3)

Use the GestureDetector and ScaleGestureDetector in the framework, or just manually handle all touch events passed to your views by overriding onTouchEvent() and onInterceptTouchEvent(). Working with the former is a very simple way to add complex gesture control to your application. The latter option is extremely powerful, but it has some pitfalls to be aware of.

Android handles touch events on the UI by using a top-down dispatch system, which is a common pattern in the framework for sending messages through a hierarchy. Touch events originate at the top-level window and are delivered to the activity first. From there, they are dispatched to the root view of the loaded hierarchy and subsequently passed down from parent to child view until something consumes the event or the entire chain has been traversed.

It is the job of each parent view to validate which children a touch event should be sent to (usually by checking the view's bounds) and to dispatch the event in the correct order. If multiple children are valid candidates (such as when they overlap), the parent will deliver the event to each child in the reverse order that they were added, so as to guarantee that the child view with the highest z-order (visibly layered on top) gets a chance first. If no children consume the event, the parent itself will get a chance to consume it before the event is passed back up the hierarchy.

Any view can declare interest in a particular touch event by returning true from its onTouchEvent() method, which consumes the event and stops it from being delivered elsewhere. Any ViewGroup has the additional ability to intercept or steal touch events being delivered to its children via the onInterceptTouchEvent() callback. This is helpful in cases where the parent view needs to take over control for a particular use case, for example, a ScrollView taking control of touches after it detects that the user is dragging their finger.

There are several action identifiers that touch events will have during the course of a gesture:

- ACTION_DOWN: Initial event when the first finger hits the screen. This event is always the beginning of a new gesture.

- ACTION_MOVE: Event that occurs when one of the fingers on the screen has changed location.

- ACTION_UP: Final event, when the last finger leaves the screen. This event is always the end of a gesture.

- ACTION_CANCEL: Received by child views when their parent has intercepted the gesture they were currently receiving. Like ACTION_UP, this should signal the view that the gesture is over from their perspective.

- ACTION_POINTER_DOWN: Event that occurs when an additional finger hits the screen. Useful for switching into a multitouch gesture.

- ACTION_POINTER_UP: Event that occurs when an additional finger leaves the screen. Useful for switching out of a multitouch gesture.

For efficiency, Android will not deliver subsequent events to any view that did not consume ACTION_DOWN. Therefore, if you are doing custom touch handling and want to do something interesting with later events, you must return true for ACTION_DOWN.

If you are implementing a custom touch handler inside a parent `ViewGroup`, you will probably also need to have some code in `onInterceptTouchEvent()`. This method works in a similar fashion to `onTouchEvent()` in that, if you return `true`, your custom view will take over receiving all touch events for the remainder of that gesture (that is, until `ACTION_UP`). This operation cannot be undone, so do not intercept these events until you are sure you want to take them all!

Finally, Android provides a number of useful threshold constants that are scaled for device screen density and should be used to build custom touch interaction. These constants are all housed in the `ViewConfiguration` class. In this example, we will use the minimum and maximum fling velocity values and the touch slop constant, which denotes how far `ACTION_MOVE` events should be allowed to vary before considering them as an actual move of the user's finger.

How It Works

Listing 3-33 illustrates a custom `ViewGroup` that implements pan-style scrolling, meaning it allows the user to scroll in both horizontal and vertical directions, assuming the content is large enough to do so. This implementation uses `GestureDetector` to handle the touch events.

Listing 3-33. Custom `ViewGroup` with `GestureDetector`

```
public class PanGestureScrollView extends FrameLayout {

    private GestureDetector mDetector;
    private Scroller mScroller;

    /* Positions of the last motion event */
    private float mInitialX, mInitialY;
    /* Drag threshold */
    private int mTouchSlop;

    public PanGestureScrollView(Context context) {
        super(context);
        init(context);
    }

    public PanGestureScrollView(Context context, AttributeSet attrs) {
        super(context, attrs);
        init(context);
    }

    public PanGestureScrollView(Context context, AttributeSet attrs,
            int defStyle) {
        super(context, attrs, defStyle);
        init(context);
    }

    private void init(Context context) {
        mDetector = new GestureDetector(context, mListener);
        mScroller = new Scroller(context);
        // Get system constants for touch thresholds
        mTouchSlop = ViewConfiguration.get(context).getScaledTouchSlop();
    }
```

```java
/*
 * Override measureChild... implementations to guarantee the child
 * view gets measured to be as large as it wants to be. The default
 * implementation will force some children to be only as large as
 * this view.
 */
@Override
protected void measureChild(View child, int parentWidthMeasureSpec,
        int parentHeightMeasureSpec) {
    int childWidthMeasureSpec;
    int childHeightMeasureSpec;

    childWidthMeasureSpec = MeasureSpec.makeMeasureSpec(0,
            MeasureSpec.UNSPECIFIED);
    childHeightMeasureSpec = MeasureSpec.makeMeasureSpec(0,
            MeasureSpec.UNSPECIFIED);

    child.measure(childWidthMeasureSpec, childHeightMeasureSpec);
}


@Override
protected void measureChildWithMargins(View child,
        int parentWidthMeasureSpec, int widthUsed,
        int parentHeightMeasureSpec, int heightUsed) {
    final MarginLayoutParams lp =
            (MarginLayoutParams) child.getLayoutParams();

    final int childWidthMeasureSpec = MeasureSpec.makeMeasureSpec(
            lp.leftMargin + lp.rightMargin, MeasureSpec.UNSPECIFIED);
    final int childHeightMeasureSpec = MeasureSpec.makeMeasureSpec(
            lp.topMargin + lp.bottomMargin, MeasureSpec.UNSPECIFIED);

    child.measure(childWidthMeasureSpec, childHeightMeasureSpec);
}


// Listener to handle all the touch events
private SimpleOnGestureListener mListener =
        new SimpleOnGestureListener() {
    public boolean onDown(MotionEvent e) {
        // Cancel any current fling
        if (!mScroller.isFinished()) {
            mScroller.abortAnimation();
        }
        return true;
    }

    public boolean onFling(MotionEvent e1, MotionEvent e2,
            float velocityX, float velocityY) {
        // Call a helper method to start the scroller animation
        fling((int) -velocityX / 3, (int) -velocityY / 3);
        return true;
    }
```

```java
    public boolean onScroll(MotionEvent e1, MotionEvent e2,
            float distanceX, float distanceY) {
        // Any view can be scrolled by simply calling scrollBy()
        scrollBy((int) distanceX, (int) distanceY);
        return true;
    }
};

@Override
public void computeScroll() {
    if (mScroller.computeScrollOffset()) {
        // This is called at drawing time by ViewGroup. We use
        // this method to keep the fling animation going through
        // to completion.
        int oldX = getScrollX();
        int oldY = getScrollY();
        int x = mScroller.getCurrX();
        int y = mScroller.getCurrY();

        if (getChildCount() > 0) {
            View child = getChildAt(0);
            x = clamp(x,
                    getWidth() - getPaddingRight() - getPaddingLeft(),
                    child.getWidth());
            y = clamp(y,
                    getHeight() - getPaddingBottom() - getPaddingTop(),
                    child.getHeight());
            if (x != oldX || y != oldY) {
                scrollTo(x, y);
            }
        }

        // Keep on drawing until the animation has finished.
        postInvalidate();
    }
}

// Override scrollTo to do bounds checks on any scrolling request
@Override
public void scrollTo(int x, int y) {
    // we rely on the fact the View.scrollBy calls scrollTo.
    if (getChildCount() > 0) {
        View child = getChildAt(0);
        x = clamp(x,
                getWidth() - getPaddingRight() - getPaddingLeft(),
                child.getWidth());
        y = clamp(y,
                getHeight() - getPaddingBottom() - getPaddingTop(),
                child.getHeight());
```

```
            if (x != getScrollX() || y != getScrollY()) {
                super.scrollTo(x, y);
            }
        }
    }

    /*
     * Monitor touch events passed down to the children and intercept
     * as soon as it is determined we are dragging
     */
    @Override
    public boolean onInterceptTouchEvent(MotionEvent event) {
        switch (event.getAction()) {
        case MotionEvent.ACTION_DOWN:
            mInitialX = event.getX();
            mInitialY = event.getY();
            // Feed the down event to the detector so it has
            // context when/if dragging begins
            mDetector.onTouchEvent(event);
            break;
        case MotionEvent.ACTION_MOVE:
            final float x = event.getX();
            final float y = event.getY();
            final int yDiff = (int) Math.abs(y - mInitialY);
            final int xDiff = (int) Math.abs(x - mInitialX);
            // Verify that either difference is enough to be a drag
            if (yDiff > mTouchSlop || xDiff > mTouchSlop) {
                // Start capturing events
                return true;
            }
            break;
        }

return super.onInterceptTouchEvent(event);
    }

    /*
     * Feed all touch events we receive to the detector for processing.
     */
    @Override
    public boolean onTouchEvent(MotionEvent event) {
        return mDetector.onTouchEvent(event);
    }

    /*
     * Utility method to initialize the Scroller and start redrawing
     */
    public void fling(int velocityX, int velocityY) {
        if (getChildCount() > 0) {
            int height =
                    getHeight() - getPaddingBottom() - getPaddingTop();
```

```
        int width =
                getWidth() - getPaddingLeft() - getPaddingRight();
        int bottom = getChildAt(0).getHeight();
        int right = getChildAt(0).getWidth();

        mScroller.fling(getScrollX(), getScrollY(),
                velocityX, velocityY,
                0, Math.max(0, right - width),
                0, Math.max(0, bottom - height));

        invalidate();
    }
}


/*
 * Utility method to assist in doing bounds checking
 */
private int clamp(int n, int my, int child) {
    if (my >= child || n < 0) {
        // The child is beyond one of the parent bounds
        // or is smaller than the parent and can't scroll
        return 0;
    }
    if ((my + n) > child) {
        // Requested scroll is beyond right bound of child
        return child - my;
    }
    return n;
}
}


}
```

Similar to ScrollView or HorizontalScrollView, this example takes a single child and scrolls its contents based on user input. Much of the code in this example is not directly related to touch handling; instead it scrolls and keeps the scroll position from going beyond the bounds of the child.

As a ViewGroup, the first place where we will see any touch event will be onInterceptTouchEvent(). This method is where we must analyze the user touches and see whether they are actually dragging. The interaction between ACTION_DOWN and ACTION_MOVE in this method is designed to determine how far the user has moved their finger, and if it's greater than the system's touch slop constant, we call it a *drag event* and intercept subsequent touches. This implementation allows simple tap events to go on to the children, so buttons and other widgets can safely be children of this view and still get click events. If no interactive widgets were children of this view, the events would pass directly to our onTouchEvent() method, but since we want to allow that possibility, we have to do this initial checking here.

The onTouchEvent() method here is straightforward because all events simply get forwarded to our GestureDetector, which does all the tracking and calculations to know when the user is doing specific actions. We then react to those events through the SimpleOnGestureListener, specifically the onScroll() and onFling() events. To ensure that the GestureDetector has the initial point of the gesture correctly set, we also forward the ACTION_DOWN event from onInterceptTouchEvent() to it.

The onScroll() method is called repeatedly as the user moves their finger with the distance traveled. Conveniently, we can pass these values directly to the view's scrollBy() method to move the content while the finger is dragging.

The onFling() method requires slightly more work. For those unaware, a *fling* is an operation where the user rapidly moves their finger on the screen and lifts it. The resulting expected behavior of this is an animated inertial scroll. Again, the work of calculating the velocity of the user's finger when it is lifted is done for us, but we must still do the scrolling animation. This is where Scroller comes in. Scroller is a component of the framework designed to take the user input values and provide the time-interpolated animation slices necessary to animate the view's scrolling. The animation is started by calling fling() on the Scroller and invalidating the view.

> **Note**   If you are targeting API Level 9 and higher, you can drop OverScroller in place of Scroller, and it will provide more-consistent performance on newer devices. It will also allow you to include the overscroll glow animations. You can spice up the fling animation by passing a custom Interpolator to either one.

This starts a looping process in which the framework will call computeScroll() regularly as it draws the view. We use this opportunity to check the current state of the Scroller and to nudge the view forward if the animation is not complete. This is something many developers can find confusing about Scroller. It is a component designed to animate the view, but it doesn't actually do any animation. It simply provides the timing and calculations for how far the view should move on each draw frame. The application must both call computeScrollOffset() to get the new locations and then actually call a method to incrementally change the view, which in our example is scrollTo().

The final callback we use in the GestureDetector is onDown(), which gets called with any ACTION_DOWN the detector receives. We use this callback to abort any currently running fling animation if the user presses their finger back onto the screen. Listing 3-34 shows how we can use this custom view inside an activity.

Listing 3-34. Activity Using PanGestureScrollView

```java
public class PanScrollActivity extends Activity {

    @Override
    protected void onCreate(Bundle savedInstanceState) {
        super.onCreate(savedInstanceState);

        PanGestureScrollView scrollView =
                new PanGestureScrollView(this);

        LinearLayout layout = new LinearLayout(this);
        layout.setOrientation(LinearLayout.VERTICAL);
        for(int i=0; i < 5; i++) {
            ImageView iv = new ImageButton(this);
            iv.setImageResource(R.drawable.ic_launcher);
```

```
              //Make each view large enough to require scrolling
            layout.addView(iv,
                    new LinearLayout.LayoutParams(1000, 500) );
        }

        scrollView.addView(layout);
        setContentView(scrollView);
    }
}
```

We use a handful of `ImageButton` instances to fill up the custom scroller view on purpose to illustrate that you can click any one of these buttons and the event will still go through, but as soon as you drag or fling your finger, the scrolling will take over. To illustrate just how much work `GestureDetector` does for us, take a look at Listing 3-35, which implements the same functionality but by manually handling all touches in `onTouchEvent()`.

Listing 3-35. PanScrollView Using Custom Touch Handling

```java
public class PanScrollView extends FrameLayout {

    // Fling components
    private Scroller mScroller;
    private VelocityTracker mVelocityTracker;

    /* Positions of the last motion event */
    private float mLastTouchX, mLastTouchY;
    /* Drag threshold */
    private int mTouchSlop;
    /* Fling Velocity */
    private int mMaximumVelocity, mMinimumVelocity;
    /* Drag Lock */
    private boolean mDragging = false;

    public PanScrollView(Context context) {
        super(context);
        init(context);
    }

    public PanScrollView(Context context, AttributeSet attrs) {
        super(context, attrs);
        init(context);
    }

    public PanScrollView(Context context, AttributeSet attrs,
            int defStyle) {
        super(context, attrs, defStyle);
        init(context);
    }

    private void init(Context context) {
        mScroller = new Scroller(context);
        mVelocityTracker = VelocityTracker.obtain();
```

```java
        // Get system constants for touch thresholds
        mTouchSlop = ViewConfiguration.get(context).getScaledTouchSlop();
        mMaximumVelocity = ViewConfiguration.get(context)
                .getScaledMaximumFlingVelocity();
        mMinimumVelocity = ViewConfiguration.get(context)
                .getScaledMinimumFlingVelocity();
    }

    /*
     * Override measureChild... implementations to guarantee the child
     * view gets measured to be as large as it wants to be. The default
     * implementation will force some children to be only as large as
     * this view.
     */
    @Override
    protected void measureChild(View child, int parentWidthMeasureSpec,
            int parentHeightMeasureSpec) {
        int childWidthMeasureSpec;
        int childHeightMeasureSpec;

        childWidthMeasureSpec = MeasureSpec.makeMeasureSpec(0,
                MeasureSpec.UNSPECIFIED);
        childHeightMeasureSpec = MeasureSpec.makeMeasureSpec(0,
                MeasureSpec.UNSPECIFIED);

        child.measure(childWidthMeasureSpec, childHeightMeasureSpec);
    }

    @Override
    protected void measureChildWithMargins(View child,
            int parentWidthMeasureSpec, int widthUsed,
            int parentHeightMeasureSpec, int heightUsed) {
        final MarginLayoutParams lp =
                (MarginLayoutParams) child.getLayoutParams();

        final int childWidthMeasureSpec = MeasureSpec.makeMeasureSpec(
                lp.leftMargin + lp.rightMargin, MeasureSpec.UNSPECIFIED);
        final int childHeightMeasureSpec = MeasureSpec.makeMeasureSpec(
                lp.topMargin + lp.bottomMargin, MeasureSpec.UNSPECIFIED);

        child.measure(childWidthMeasureSpec, childHeightMeasureSpec);
    }

    @Override
    public void computeScroll() {
        if (mScroller.computeScrollOffset()) {
            // This is called at drawing time by ViewGroup. We use
            // this method to keep the fling animation going through
            // to completion.
            int oldX = getScrollX();
            int oldY = getScrollY();
```

```java
        int x = mScroller.getCurrX();
        int y = mScroller.getCurrY();

        if (getChildCount() > 0) {
            View child = getChildAt(0);
            x = clamp(x,
                    getWidth() - getPaddingRight() - getPaddingLeft(),
                    child.getWidth());
            y = clamp(y,
                    getHeight() - getPaddingBottom() - getPaddingTop(),
                    child.getHeight());
            if (x != oldX || y != oldY) {
                scrollTo(x, y);
            }
        }

        // Keep on drawing until the animation has finished.
        postInvalidate();
    }
}

// Override scrollTo to do bounds checks on any scrolling request
@Override
public void scrollTo(int x, int y) {
    // we rely on the fact the View.scrollBy calls scrollTo.
    if (getChildCount() > 0) {
        View child = getChildAt(0);
        x = clamp(x,
            getWidth() - getPaddingRight() - getPaddingLeft(),
            child.getWidth());
        y = clamp(y,
            getHeight() - getPaddingBottom() - getPaddingTop(),
            child.getHeight());
        if (x != getScrollX() || y != getScrollY()) {
            super.scrollTo(x, y);
        }
    }
}

/*
 * Monitor touch events passed down to the children and
 * intercept as soon as it is determined we are dragging.
 * This allows child views to still receive touch events
 * if they are interactive (i.e., Buttons)
 */
@Override
public boolean onInterceptTouchEvent(MotionEvent event) {
    switch (event.getAction()) {
    case MotionEvent.ACTION_DOWN:
        // Stop any flinging in progress
```

```
                if (!mScroller.isFinished()) {
                    mScroller.abortAnimation();
                }
                // Reset the velocity tracker
                mVelocityTracker.clear();
                mVelocityTracker.addMovement(event);
                // Save the initial touch point
                mLastTouchX = event.getX();
                mLastTouchY = event.getY();
                break;
            case MotionEvent.ACTION_MOVE:
                final float x = event.getX();
                final float y = event.getY();
                final int yDiff = (int) Math.abs(y - mLastTouchY);
                final int xDiff = (int) Math.abs(x - mLastTouchX);
                // Verify that either difference is enough for a drag
                if (yDiff > mTouchSlop || xDiff > mTouchSlop) {
                    mDragging = true;
                    mVelocityTracker.addMovement(event);
                    // Start capturing events ourselves
                    return true;
                }
                break;
            case MotionEvent.ACTION_CANCEL:
            case MotionEvent.ACTION_UP:
                mDragging = false;
                mVelocityTracker.clear();
                break;
        }

        return super.onInterceptTouchEvent(event);
    }

    /*
     * Feed all touch events we receive to the detector
     */
    @Override
    public boolean onTouchEvent(MotionEvent event) {
        mVelocityTracker.addMovement(event);

        switch (event.getAction()) {
        case MotionEvent.ACTION_DOWN:
            // We've already stored the initial point,
            // but if we got here a child view didn't capture
            // the event, so we need to.
            return true;
        case MotionEvent.ACTION_MOVE:
            final float x = event.getX();
            final float y = event.getY();
            float deltaY = mLastTouchY - y;
            float deltaX = mLastTouchX - x;
```

```java
            // Check for slop on direct events
            if ( (Math.abs(deltaY) > mTouchSlop
                    || Math.abs(deltaX) > mTouchSlop)
                    && !mDragging) {
                mDragging = true;
            }
            if (mDragging) {
                // Scroll the view
                scrollBy((int) deltaX, (int) deltaY);
                // Update the last touch event
                mLastTouchX = x;
                mLastTouchY = y;
            }
            break;
        case MotionEvent.ACTION_CANCEL:
            mDragging = false;
            // Stop any flinging in progress
            if (!mScroller.isFinished()) {
                mScroller.abortAnimation();
            }
            break;
        case MotionEvent.ACTION_UP:
            mDragging = false;
            // Compute the current velocity and start a fling if
            // it is above the minimum threshold.
            mVelocityTracker.computeCurrentVelocity(1000,
                    mMaximumVelocity);
            int velocityX = (int) mVelocityTracker.getXVelocity();
            int velocityY = (int) mVelocityTracker.getYVelocity();
            if (Math.abs(velocityX) > mMinimumVelocity
                    || Math.abs(velocityY) > mMinimumVelocity) {
                fling(-velocityX, -velocityY);
            }
            break;
        }
        return super.onTouchEvent(event);
    }

    /*
     * Utility method to initialize the Scroller and
     * start redrawing
     */
    public void fling(int velocityX, int velocityY) {
        if (getChildCount() > 0) {
            int height =
                getHeight() - getPaddingBottom() - getPaddingTop();
            int width =
                getWidth() - getPaddingLeft() - getPaddingRight();
            int bottom = getChildAt(0).getHeight();
            int right = getChildAt(0).getWidth();
```

```
            mScroller.fling(getScrollX(), getScrollY(),
                    velocityX, velocityY,
                    0, Math.max(0, right - width),
                    0, Math.max(0, bottom - height) );

            invalidate();
        }
    }

    /*
     * Utility method to assist in doing bounds checking
     */
    private int clamp(int n, int my, int child) {
        if (my >= child || n < 0) {
            // The child is beyond one of the parent bounds
            // or is smaller than the parent and can't scroll
            return 0;
        }
        if ((my + n) > child) {
            // Requested scroll is beyond right bound of child
            return child - my;
        }
        return n;
    }
}
```

In this example, both onInterceptTouchEvent() and onTouchEvent() have a bit more going on. If a child view is currently handling initial touches, ACTION_DOWN and the first few move events will be delivered through onInterceptTouchEvent() before we take control; however, if no interactive child exists, all those initial events will go directly to onTouchEvent(). Therefore, we must do the slop checking for the initial drag in both places and set a flag to indicate when a scroll event has truly started. Once we have flagged the user dragging, the code to scroll the view is the same as before, with a call to scrollBy().

Tip   As soon as a ViewGroup returns true from onTouchEvent(), no more events will be delivered to onInterceptTouchEvent(), even if an intercept was not explicitly requested.

To implement the fling behavior, we must manually track the user's scroll velocity by using a VelocityTracker object. This object collects touch events as they occur with the addMovement() method, and it then calculates the average velocity on demand with computeCurrentVelocity(). Our custom view calculates this value each time the user's finger is lifted and determines, based on the ViewConfiguration minimum velocity, whether to start a fling animation.

Tip   In cases where you don't need to explicitly return true to consume an event, return the super implementation rather than false. Often there is a lot of hidden processing for View and ViewGroup that you don't want to override.

Listing 3-36 shows our example activity again, this time with the new custom view in place.

Listing 3-36. Activity Using PanScrollView

```java
public class PanScrollActivity extends Activity {

    @Override
    protected void onCreate(Bundle savedInstanceState) {
        super.onCreate(savedInstanceState);

        PanScrollView scrollView = new PanScrollView(this);

        LinearLayout layout = new LinearLayout(this);
        layout.setOrientation(LinearLayout.VERTICAL);
        for(int i=0; i < 5; i++) {
            ImageView iv = new ImageView(this);
            iv.setImageResource(R.drawable.ic_launcher);
            layout.addView(iv,
                    new LinearLayout.LayoutParams(1000, 500));
        }

        scrollView.addView(layout);
        setContentView(scrollView);
    }
}
```

We have also changed the content to be ImageView instead of ImageButton to illustrate the contrast when the child views are not interactive.

Multitouch Handling

(API Level 8)

Now let's take a look at an example of handling multitouch events. Listing 3-37 contains a customized ImageView with some multitouch interactions added in.

Listing 3-37. ImageView with Multitouch Handling

```java
public class RotateZoomImageView extends ImageView {

    private ScaleGestureDetector mScaleDetector;
    private Matrix mImageMatrix;
    /* Last Rotation Angle */
    private int mLastAngle = 0;
    /* Pivot Point for Transforms */
    private int mPivotX, mPivotY;

    public RotateZoomImageView(Context context) {
        super(context);
        init(context);
    }
```

```java
public RotateZoomImageView(Context context, AttributeSet attrs) {
    super(context, attrs);
    init(context);
}

public RotateZoomImageView(Context context, AttributeSet attrs,
        int defStyle) {
    super(context, attrs, defStyle);
    init(context);
}

private void init(Context context) {
    mScaleDetector = new ScaleGestureDetector(context,
            mScaleListener);

    setScaleType(ScaleType.MATRIX);
    mImageMatrix = new Matrix();
}

/*
 * Use onSizeChanged() to calculate values based on the view's size.
 * The view has no size during init(), so we must wait for this
 * callback.
 */
@Override
protected void onSizeChanged(int w, int h, int oldw, int oldh) {
    if (w != oldw || h != oldh) {
        //Shift the image to the center of the view
        int translateX =
                Math.abs(w - getDrawable().getIntrinsicWidth()) / 2;
        int translateY =
                Math.abs(h - getDrawable().getIntrinsicHeight()) / 2;
        mImageMatrix.setTranslate(translateX, translateY);
        setImageMatrix(mImageMatrix);
        //Get the center point for future scale and rotate transforms
        mPivotX = w / 2;
        mPivotY = h / 2;
    }
}

private SimpleOnScaleGestureListener mScaleListener =
        new SimpleOnScaleGestureListener() {
    @Override
    public boolean onScale(ScaleGestureDetector detector) {
        // ScaleGestureDetector calculates a scale factor based on
        // whether the fingers are moving apart or together
        float scaleFactor = detector.getScaleFactor();
        //Pass that factor to a scale for the image
```

```
            mImageMatrix.postScale(scaleFactor, scaleFactor,
                    mPivotX, mPivotY);
            setImageMatrix(mImageMatrix);

            return true;
        }
    };

    /*
     * Operate on two-finger events to rotate the image.
     * This method calculates the change in angle between the
     * pointers and rotates the image accordingly.  As the user
     * rotates their fingers, the image will follow.
     */
    private boolean doRotationEvent(MotionEvent event) {
        //Calculate the angle between the two fingers
        float deltaX = event.getX(0) - event.getX(1);
        float deltaY = event.getY(0) - event.getY(1);
        double radians = Math.atan(deltaY / deltaX);
        //Convert to degrees
        int degrees = (int)(radians * 180 / Math.PI);

        switch (event.getAction()) {
        case MotionEvent.ACTION_DOWN:
            //Mark the initial angle
            mLastAngle = degrees;
            break;
        case MotionEvent.ACTION_MOVE:
            // ATAN returns a converted value between +/-90deg
            // which creates a point when two fingers are vertical
            // where the angle flips sign.  We handle this case by
            // rotating a small amount (5 degrees) in the
            // direction we were traveling

            if ((degrees - mLastAngle) > 45) {
                //Going CCW across the boundary
                mImageMatrix.postRotate(-5, mPivotX, mPivotY);
            } else if ((degrees - mLastAngle) < -45) {
                //Going CW across the boundary
                mImageMatrix.postRotate(5, mPivotX, mPivotY);
            } else {
                //Normal rotation, rotate the difference
                mImageMatrix.postRotate(degrees - mLastAngle,
                        mPivotX, mPivotY);
            }
            //Post the rotation to the image
            setImageMatrix(mImageMatrix);
            //Save the current angle
            mLastAngle = degrees;
            break;
        }
```

```
        return true;
    }

    @Override
    public boolean onTouchEvent(MotionEvent event) {
        if (event.getAction() == MotionEvent.ACTION_DOWN) {
            // We don't care about this event directly, but we
            // declare interest to get later multitouch events.
            return true;
        }

        switch (event.getPointerCount()) {
        case 3:
            // With three fingers down, zoom the image
            // using the ScaleGestureDetector
            return mScaleDetector.onTouchEvent(event);
        case 2:
            // With two fingers down, rotate the image
            // following the fingers
            return doRotationEvent(event);
        default:
            //Ignore this event
            return super.onTouchEvent(event);
        }
    }
}
```

This example creates a custom `ImageView` that listens for multitouch events and transforms the image content in response. The two events this view will detect are a two-finger rotate and a three-finger pinch. The rotate event is handled manually by processing each `MotionEvent`, while a `ScaleGestureDetector` handles the pinch events. The `ScaleType` of the view is set to `MATRIX`, which will allow us to modify the image's appearance by applying different `Matrix` transformations.

Once the view is measured and laid out, the `onSizeChanged()` callback will trigger. This method can get called more than once, so we make changes only if the values from one instance to the next have changed. We take this opportunity to set up some values based around the view's size that we will need to center the image content inside the view and later perform the correct transformations. We also perform the first transformation here, which centers the image inside the view.

We decide which event to process by analyzing the events we receive in `onTouchEvent()`. By checking the `getPointerCount()` method of each `MotionEvent`, we can determine how many fingers are down and can deliver the event to the appropriate handler. As we've said before, we must also consume the initial `ACTION_DOWN` event here; otherwise, the subsequent event for the user's other fingers will never get delivered to this view. While we don't have anything interesting to do in this case, it is still necessary to explicitly return true.

`ScaleGestureDetector` operates by analyzing each touch event the application feeds to it and calling a series of `OnScaleGestureListener` callback methods when scale events occur. The most important callback is `onScale()`, which gets called regularly as the user's fingers move, but developers can also use `onScaleBegin()` and `onScaleEnd()` to do processing before and after the gesture.

`ScaleGestureDetector` provides a number of useful calculated values that the application can use in modifying the UI:

- `getCurrentSpan()`: Gets the distance between the two pointers being used in this gesture.

- `getFocusX()`/`getFocusY()`: Gets the coordinates of the focal point for the current gesture. This is the average location about which the pointers are expanding and contracting.

- `getScaleFactor()`: Gets the ratio of span changes between this event and the previous event. As fingers move apart, this value will be slightly larger than 1, and as they move together, it will be slightly less than 1.

This example takes the scale factor from the detector and uses it to scale up or down the image content of the view by using `postScale()` on the image's `Matrix`.

Our two-finger rotate event is handled manually. For each event that is passed in, we calculate the x and y distance between the two fingers with `getX()` and `getY()`. The parameter these methods take is the pointer index, where 0 would be the initial pointer, and 1 would be the secondary pointer.

With these distances, we can do a little trigonometry to figure out the angle of the invisible line that would be formed between the two fingers. This angle is the control value we will use for our transformation. During `ACTION_DOWN`, we take whatever that angle is to be the initial value and simply store it. On subsequent `ACTION_MOVE` events, we post a rotation to the image based on the difference in angle between each touch event.

There is one edge case this example has to handle, and it has to do with the `Math.atan()` trig function. This method will return an angle in the range of –90 degrees to +90 degrees, and this rollover happens when the two fingers are vertically one above the other. The issue this creates is that the touch angle is no longer a gradual change: it jumps from +90 to –90 immediately as the fingers rotate, making the image jump. To solve this issue, we check for the case where the previous and current angle values cross this boundary, and then apply a small 5-degree rotation in the same direction of travel to keep the animation moving smoothly.

Notice that in all cases we are transforming the image with `postScale()` and `postRotate()`, rather than the `setXXX` versions of these methods as we did with `setTranslation()`. This is because each transformation is meant to be additive, meaning it should augment the current state rather than replace it. Calling `setScale()` or `setRotate()` would erase the existing state and leave that as the only transformation in the `Matrix`.

We also do each of these transformations around the pivot point that we calculated in `onSizeChanged()` as the midpoint of the view. We do this because, by default, the transformations would occur with a target point of (0,0), which is the top-left corner of the view. Because we have centered the image, we need to make sure all transformations also occur at the same center.

3-14. Forwarding Touch Events

Problem

You have views or other touch targets in your application that are too small for the average finger to reliably activate.

Solution

(API Level 1)

Use TouchDelegate to designate an arbitrary rectangle to forward touch events to your small views. TouchDelegate is designed to attach to a parent ViewGroup for the purpose of forwarding touch events it detects within a specific space to one of its children. TouchDelegate modifies each event to look to the target view as if it had happened within its own bounds.

How It Works

Listings 3-38 and 3-39 illustrate the use of TouchDelegate within a custom parent ViewGroup.

Listing 3-38. Custom Parent Implementing TouchDelegate

```
public class TouchDelegateLayout extends FrameLayout {

    public TouchDelegateLayout(Context context) {
        super(context);
        init(context);
    }

    public TouchDelegateLayout(Context context, AttributeSet attrs) {
        super(context, attrs);
        init(context);
    }

    public TouchDelegateLayout(Context context, AttributeSet attrs,
            int defStyle) {
        super(context, attrs, defStyle);
        init(context);
    }

    private CheckBox mButton;
    private void init(Context context) {
        //Create a small child view we want to forward touches to.
        mButton = new CheckBox(context);
        mButton.setText("Tap Anywhere");

        LayoutParams lp = new FrameLayout.LayoutParams(
                LayoutParams.WRAP_CONTENT,
                LayoutParams.WRAP_CONTENT,
                Gravity.CENTER);
        addView(mButton, lp);
    }


    /*
     * TouchDelegate is applied to this view (parent) to delegate all
     * touches within the specified rectangle to the CheckBox (child).
```

```
 * Here, the rectangle is the entire size of this parent view.
 *
 * This must be done after the view has a size so we know how big
 * to make the Rect, thus we've chosen to add the delegate in
 * onSizeChanged()
 */
@Override
protected void onSizeChanged(int w, int h, int oldw, int oldh) {
    if (w != oldw || h != oldh) {
        //Apply the whole area of this view as the delegate area
        Rect bounds = new Rect(0, 0, w, h);
        TouchDelegate delegate = new TouchDelegate(bounds, mButton);
        setTouchDelegate(delegate);
    }
  }
}
```

Listing 3-39. Example Activity

```
public class DelegateActivity extends Activity {

    @Override
    protected void onCreate(Bundle savedInstanceState) {
        super.onCreate(savedInstanceState);
        TouchDelegateLayout layout =
                new TouchDelegateLayout(this);

        setContentView(layout);
    }
}
```

In this example, we create a parent view that contains a centered check box. This view also contains a TouchDelegate that will forward touches received anywhere inside the bounds of the parent to the check box. Because we want to pass the full size of the parent layout as the rectangle to forward events, we wait until onSizeChanged() is called on the view to construct and attach the TouchDelegate instance. Doing so in the constructor would not work, because at that point, the view has not been measured and will not have a size we can read.

The framework automatically dispatches unhandled touch events from the parent through TouchDelegate to its delegate view, so no additional code is needed to forward these events. You can see in Figure 3-14 that this application is receiving touch events far away from the check box, and the check box reacts as if it has been touched directly.

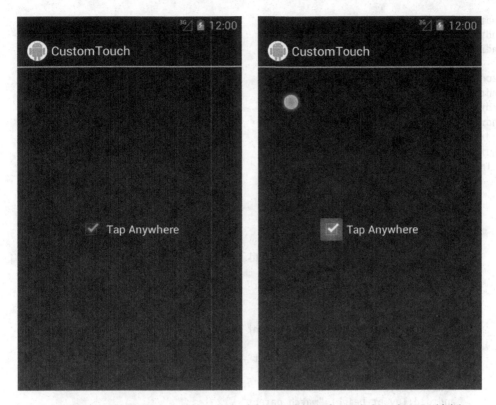

Figure 3-14. Sample application with check box (left), and check box receiving a forwarded touch event (right)

Custom Touch Forwarding (Remote Scroller)

TouchDelegate is great for forwarding tap events, but it has one drawback: each event forwarded to the delegate first has its location reset to the exact midpoint of the delegate view. This means that if you attempt to forward a series of ACTION_MOVE events through TouchDelegate, the results won't be what you expect, because they will look to the delegate view as if the finger isn't really moving at all.

If you need to reroute touch events in a more pure form, you can do so by manually calling the dispatchTouchEvent() method of the target view. Have a look at Listings 3-40 and 3-41 to see how this works.

Listing 3-40. res/layout/main.xml

```
<LinearLayout
    xmlns:android="http://schemas.android.com/apk/res/android"
    android:layout_width="match_parent"
    android:layout_height="match_parent"
    android:orientation="vertical" >

    <TextView
        android:id="@+id/text_touch"
        android:layout_width="match_parent"
        android:layout_height="0dp"
```

```
            android:layout_weight="1"
            android:gravity="center"
            android:text="Scroll Anywhere Here" />

    <HorizontalScrollView
            android:id="@+id/scroll_view"
            android:layout_width="match_parent"
            android:layout_height="0dp"
            android:layout_weight="1"
            android:background="#CCC">
        <LinearLayout
            android:layout_width="wrap_content"
            android:layout_height="match_parent"
            android:orientation="horizontal" >
            <ImageView
                android:layout_width="250dp"
                android:layout_height="match_parent"
                android:scaleType="fitXY"
                android:src="@drawable/ic_launcher" />
            <ImageView
                android:layout_width="250dp"
                android:layout_height="match_parent"
                android:scaleType="fitXY"
                android:src="@drawable/ic_launcher" />
            <ImageView
                android:layout_width="250dp"
                android:layout_height="match_parent"
                android:scaleType="fitXY"
                android:src="@drawable/ic_launcher" />
            <ImageView
                android:layout_width="250dp"
                android:layout_height="match_parent"
                android:scaleType="fitXY"
                android:src="@drawable/ic_launcher" />
        </LinearLayout>
    </HorizontalScrollView>
</LinearLayout>
```

Listing 3-41. Activity Forwarding Touches

```
public class RemoteScrollActivity extends Activity implements
        View.OnTouchListener {

    private TextView mTouchText;
    private HorizontalScrollView mScrollView;

    @Override
    protected void onCreate(Bundle savedInstanceState) {
        super.onCreate(savedInstanceState);
        setContentView(R.layout.main);
```

```
        mTouchText = (TextView) findViewById(R.id.text_touch);
        mScrollView =
            (HorizontalScrollView) findViewById(R.id.scroll_view);
        //Attach a listener for touch events to the top view
        mTouchText.setOnTouchListener(this);
    }

    @Override
    public boolean onTouch(View v, MotionEvent event) {
        // You can massage the event location if necessary.
        // Here we set the vertical location for each event to
        // the middle of the HorizontalScrollView.

        // View's expect events to be relative to their
        // local coordinates.
        event.setLocation(event.getX(),
                mScrollView.getHeight() / 2);

        // Forward each event from the TextView to the
        // HorizontalScrollView
        mScrollView.dispatchTouchEvent(event);
        return true;
    }
}
```

This example displays an activity that is divided in half. The top half is a TextView that prompts you to touch and scroll around, and the bottom half is a HorizontalScrollView with a series of images contained inside. The activity is set as the OnTouchListener for the TextView so that we can forward all touches it receives to the HorizontalScrollView.

We want the events that the HorizontalScrollView sees to look, from its perspective, as if they were originally inside the view bounds. So before we forward the event, we call setLocation() to change the x/y coordinates. In this case, the x coordinate is fine as is, but we adjust the y coordinate to be in the center of the HorizontalScrollView. Now the events look as if the user's finger is moving back and forth along the middle of the view. We then call dispatchTouchEvent() with the modified event to have the HorizontalScrollView process it.

> **Note** Avoid calling onTouchEvent() directly to forward touches. Calling dispatchTouchEvent() allows the event processing of the target view to take place the same way it does for normal touch events, including any intercepts that may be necessary.

3-15. Blocking Touch Thieves

Problem

You have designed nested touch interactions in your application views that don't work well with the standard flow of touch hierarchy, in which higher-level container views handle touch events directly by stealing them back from child views.

Solution

(API Level 1)

ViewGroup, which is the base class for all layouts and containers in the framework, provides the descriptively named method requestDisallowTouchIntercept() for just this purpose. Setting this flag on any container view indicates to the framework that, for the duration of the current gesture, we would prefer they not intercept the events coming into their child views.

How It Works

To showcase this in action, we have created an example in which two competing touchable views live in the same space. The outer containing view is a ListView, which responds to touch events that indicate a vertical drag by scrolling the content. Inside the ListView, added as a header, is a ViewPager, which responds to horizontal drag touch events for swiping between pages. In and of itself, this creates a problem in that any attemps to horizontally swipe the ViewPager that even remotely vary in the vertical direction will be cancelled in favor of the ListView scrolling, because ListView is monitoring and intercepting those events. Since humans are not very capable of dragging in an exactly horizontal or vertical motion, this creates a usability problem.

To set up this example, we first have to declare a dimension resource (see Listing 3-42), and then the full activity is found in Listing 3-43.

Listing 3-42. res/values/dimens.xml

```
<?xml version="1.0" encoding="utf-8"?>
<resources>
    <dimen name="header_height">150dp</dimen>
</resources>
```

Listing 3-43. Activity Managing Touch Intercept

```
public class DisallowActivity extends Activity implements
        ViewPager.OnPageChangeListener {
    private static final String[] ITEMS = {
            "Row One", "Row Two", "Row Three", "Row Four",
            "Row Five", "Row Six", "Row Seven", "Row Eight",
            "Row Nine", "Row Ten"
    };

    private ViewPager mViewPager;

    private ListView mListView;

    @Override
    protected void onCreate(Bundle savedInstanceState) {
        super.onCreate(savedInstanceState);

        //Create a header view of horizontal swiping items
        mViewPager = new ViewPager(this);
        //As a ListView header, ViewPager must have a fixed height
```

```java
        mViewPager.setLayoutParams(new ListView.LayoutParams(
                ListView.LayoutParams.MATCH_PARENT,
                getResources().getDimensionPixelSize(
                        R.dimen.header_height)) );
        // Listen for paging state changes to disable
        // parent touches
        mViewPager.setOnPageChangeListener(this);
        mViewPager.setAdapter(new HeaderAdapter(this));

        // Create a vertical scrolling list
        mListView = new ListView(this);
        // Add the pager as the list header
        mListView.addHeaderView(mViewPager);
        // Add list items
        mListView.setAdapter(new ArrayAdapter<String>(this,
                android.R.layout.simple_list_item_1, ITEMS));

        setContentView(mListView);
    }

    /* OnPageChangeListener Methods */

    @Override
    public void onPageScrolled(int position,
            float positionOffset, int positionOffsetPixels) { }

    @Override
    public void onPageSelected(int position) { }

    @Override
    public void onPageScrollStateChanged(int state) {
        //While the ViewPager is scrolling, disable the
        // ScrollView touch intercept so it cannot take over and
        // try to vertical scroll. This flag must be set for each
        // gesture you want to override.
        boolean isScrolling =
                state != ViewPager.SCROLL_STATE_IDLE;
        mListView.requestDisallowInterceptTouchEvent(isScrolling);
    }

    private static class HeaderAdapter extends PagerAdapter {
        private Context mContext;

        public HeaderAdapter(Context context) {
            mContext = context;
        }

        @Override
        public int getCount() {
            return 5;
        }
```

```java
    @Override
    public Object instantiateItem(ViewGroup container,
            int position) {
        // Create a new page view
        TextView tv = new TextView(mContext);
        tv.setText(String.format("Page %d", position + 1));
        tv.setBackgroundColor((position % 2 == 0) ? Color.RED
                : Color.GREEN);
        tv.setGravity(Gravity.CENTER);
        tv.setTextColor(Color.BLACK);

        // Add as the view for this position, and return as
        // the object for this position
        container.addView(tv);
        return tv;
    }

    @Override
    public void destroyItem(ViewGroup container,
            int position, Object object) {
        View page = (View) object;
        container.removeView(page);
    }

    @Override
    public boolean isViewFromObject(View view,
            Object object) {
        return (view == object);
    }
    }
}
```

In this activity, we have a ListView that is the root view with a basic adapter included to display a static list of string items. Also in onCreate(), a ViewPager instance is created and added to the list as its header view. We will talk in more detail about how ViewPager works later in this chapter, but suffice it to say here that we are creating a simple ViewPager instance with a custom PagerAdapter that displays a handful of colored views as its pages for the user to swipe between.

When the ViewPager is created, we construct and apply a set of ListView.LayoutParams to govern how it should be displayed as the header. We must do this because the ViewPager itself has no inherent content size and list headers don't work well with a view that isn't explicit about its height. The fixed height is applied from our dimension's resource so we can easily get a properly scaled dp value that is device independent. This is simpler than attempting to fully construct a dp value completely in Java code.

The key to this example is in the OnPageChangeListener the activity implements (which is then applied to the ViewPager). This callback is triggered as the user interacts with ViewPager and swipes left and right. Inside the onPageScrollStateChanged() method, we are passed a value that indicates whether the ViewPager is idle, actively scrolling, or settling to a page after being scrolled. This is a perfect place to control the touch intercept behavior of the parent ListView. Whenever the scrolling state of the ViewPager is not idle, we don't want the ListView to steal the touch events ViewPager is using, so we set the flag in requestDisallowTouchIntercept().

There is another reason we continuously trigger this value. We mentioned in the original solution that this flag is valid *for the current gesture*. This means that each time a new ACTION_DOWN event occurs, we need to set the flag again. Rather than adding touch listeners just to look for specific events, we continuously set the flag based on the scrolling behavior of the child view and we get the same effect.

3-16. Making Drag-and-Drop Views

Problem

Your application's UI needs to allow the user to drag views around on the screen and to possibly drop them on top of other views.

Solution

(API Level 11)

Use the drag-and-drop APIs available in the Android 3.0 framework. The View class includes all the enhancements necessary to manage a drag event on the screen, and the OnDragListener interface can be attached to any View that needs to be notified of drag events as they occur. To begin a drag event, simply call startDrag() on the view you would like the user to begin dragging. This method takes a DragShadowBuilder instance, which will be used to construct what the dragging portion of the view should look like, and two additional parameters that will be passed forward to the drop targets and listeners.

The first of these is a ClipData object to pass forward a set of text or a Uri instance. This can be useful for passing a file location or a query to be made on a ContentProvider. The second is an Object referred to as the *local state* of the drag event. This can be any object and is designed to be a lightweight instance describing something application-specific about the drag. The ClipData will be available only to the listener where the dragged view is dropped, but the local state will be accessible to any listener at any time by calling getLocalState() on the DragEvent.

The OnDragListener.onDrag() method will get called for each specific event that occurs during the drag-and-drop process, passing in a DragEvent to describe the specifics of each event. Each DragEvent will have one of the following actions:

- ACTION_DRAG_STARTED: Sent to all views when a new drag event begins with a call to startDrag()

  - The location can be obtained with getX() and getY().

- ACTION_DRAG_ENTERED: Sent to a view when the drag event enters its bounding box

- ACTION_DRAG_EXITED: Sent to a view when the drag event leaves its bounding box

- ACTION_DRAG_LOCATION: Sent to a view between ACTION_DRAG_ENTERED and ACTION_DRAG_EXITED with the current location of the drag inside that view

  - The location can be obtained with getX() and getY().

- ■ ACTION_DROP: Sent to a view when the drag terminates and is still currently inside the bounds of that view
  - ■ The location can be obtained with getX() and getY().
  - ■ ClipData passed with the event can be obtained with getClipData() for this action only.
- ■ ACTION_DRAG_ENDED: Sent to all views when the current drag event is complete
  - ■ The result of the drag operation can be obtained here with getResult().
  - ■ This return value is based on whether the target view of the drop had an active OnDragListener that returned true for the ACTION_DROP event.

This method works in a similar way to custom touch handling, in that the value you return from the listener will govern how future events are delivered. If a particular OnDragListener does not return true for ACTION_DRAG_STARTED, it will not receive any further events for the remainder of the drag except for ACTION_DRAG_ENDED.

How It Works

Let's look at an example of the drag-and-drop functionality, starting with Listing 3-44. Here we have created a custom ImageView that implements the OnDragListener interface.

Listing 3-44. Custom View Implementing OnDragListener

```
public class DropTargetView extends ImageView implements OnDragListener {

    private boolean mDropped;

    public DropTargetView(Context context) {
        super(context);
        init();
    }

    public DropTargetView(Context context, AttributeSet attrs) {
        super(context, attrs);
        init();
    }

    public DropTargetView(Context context, AttributeSet attrs,
            int defaultStyle) {
        super(context, attrs, defaultStyle);
        init();
    }

    private void init() {
        //We must set a valid listener to receive DragEvents
        setOnDragListener(this);
    }
```

```java
@Override
public boolean onDrag(View v, DragEvent event) {
    PropertyValuesHolder pvhX, pvhY;
    switch (event.getAction()) {
    case DragEvent.ACTION_DRAG_STARTED:
        //React to a new drag by shrinking the view
        pvhX = PropertyValuesHolder.ofFloat("scaleX", 0.5f);
        pvhY = PropertyValuesHolder.ofFloat("scaleY", 0.5f);
        ObjectAnimator.ofPropertyValuesHolder(this,
                pvhX, pvhY).start();
        //Clear the current drop image on a new event
        setImageDrawable(null);
        mDropped = false;
        break;
    case DragEvent.ACTION_DRAG_ENDED:
        // React to a drag ending by resetting the view size
        // if we weren't the drop target.
        if (!mDropped) {
            pvhX = PropertyValuesHolder.ofFloat("scaleX", 1f);
            pvhY = PropertyValuesHolder.ofFloat("scaleY", 1f);
            ObjectAnimator.ofPropertyValuesHolder(this,
                    pvhX, pvhY).start();
            mDropped = false;
        }
        break;
    case DragEvent.ACTION_DRAG_ENTERED:
        //React to a drag entering this view by growing slightly
        pvhX = PropertyValuesHolder.ofFloat("scaleX", 0.75f);
        pvhY = PropertyValuesHolder.ofFloat("scaleY", 0.75f);
        ObjectAnimator.ofPropertyValuesHolder(this,
                pvhX, pvhY).start();
        break;
    case DragEvent.ACTION_DRAG_EXITED:
        //React to a drag leaving by returning to previous size
        pvhX = PropertyValuesHolder.ofFloat("scaleX", 0.5f);
        pvhY = PropertyValuesHolder.ofFloat("scaleY", 0.5f);
        ObjectAnimator.ofPropertyValuesHolder(this,
                pvhX, pvhY).start();
        break;
    case DragEvent.ACTION_DROP:
        // React to a drop event with a short keyframe animation
        // and setting this view's image to the drawable passed along
        // with the drag event

        // This animation shrinks the view briefly down to nothing
        // and then back.
        Keyframe frame0 = Keyframe.ofFloat(0f, 0.75f);
        Keyframe frame1 = Keyframe.ofFloat(0.5f, 0f);
        Keyframe frame2 = Keyframe.ofFloat(1f, 0.75f);
        pvhX = PropertyValuesHolder.ofKeyframe("scaleX",
                frame0, frame1, frame2);
```

```
            pvhY = PropertyValuesHolder.ofKeyframe("scaleY",
                    frame0, frame1, frame2);
            ObjectAnimator.ofPropertyValuesHolder(this,
                    pvhX, pvhY).start();
            //Set our image from the Object passed with the DragEvent
            setImageDrawable((Drawable) event.getLocalState());
            //We set the dropped flag so the ENDED animation will
            // not also run
            mDropped = true;
            break;
        default:
            //Ignore events we aren't interested in
            return false;
        }
        //Declare interest in all events we have noted
        return true;
    }

}
```

This ImageView is set up to monitor incoming drag events and animate itself accordingly. Whenever a new drag begins, the ACTION_DRAG_STARTED event will be sent here, and this view will scale itself down to 50 percent size. This is a good indication to the user where they can drag this view they've just picked up. We also make sure that this listener is structured to return true from this event so that it receives other events during the drag.

If the user drags their view onto this one, ACTION_DRAG_ENTERED will trigger the view to scale up slightly, indicating it as the active recipient if the view were to be dropped. ACTION_DRAG_EXITED will be received if the view is dragged away, and this view will respond by scaling back down to the same size as when we entered "drag mode." If the user releases the drag over the top of this view, ACTION_DROP will be triggered, and a special animation is run to indicate the drop was received. We also read the local state variable of the event at this point, assume it is a Drawable, and set it as the image content for this view.

ACTION_DRAG_ENDED will notify this view to return to its original size because we are no longer in drag mode. However, if this view was also the target of the drop, we want it to keep its size, so we ignore this event in that case.

Listings 3-45 and 3-46 show an example activity that allows the user to long-press an image and then drag that image to our custom drop target.

Listing 3-45. res/layout/main.xml

```xml
<?xml version="1.0" encoding="utf-8"?>
<RelativeLayout
    xmlns:android="http://schemas.android.com/apk/res/android"
    android:layout_width="match_parent"
    android:layout_height="match_parent" >

    <!-- Top Row of Draggable Items -->
    <LinearLayout
        android:layout_width="match_parent"
```

```xml
        android:layout_height="wrap_content"
        android:orientation="horizontal" >
        <ImageView
            android:id="@+id/image1"
            android:layout_width="0dp"
            android:layout_height="wrap_content"
            android:layout_weight="1"
            android:src="@drawable/ic_send" />
        <ImageView
            android:id="@+id/image2"
            android:layout_width="0dp"
            android:layout_height="wrap_content"
            android:layout_weight="1"
            android:src="@drawable/ic_share" />
        <ImageView
            android:id="@+id/image3"
            android:layout_width="0dp"
            android:layout_height="wrap_content"
            android:layout_weight="1"
            android:src="@drawable/ic_favorite" />
    </LinearLayout>

    <!-- Bottom Row of Drop Targets -->
    <LinearLayout
        android:layout_width="match_parent"
        android:layout_height="wrap_content"
        android:layout_alignParentBottom="true"
        android:orientation="horizontal" >
        <com.examples.dragtouch.DropTargetView
            android:id="@+id/drag_target1"
            android:layout_width="0dp"
            android:layout_height="100dp"
            android:layout_weight="1"
            android:background="#A00" />
        <com.examples.dragtouch.DropTargetView
            android:id="@+id/drag_target2"
            android:layout_width="0dp"
            android:layout_height="100dp"
            android:layout_weight="1"
            android:background="#0A0" />
        <com.examples.dragtouch.DropTargetView
            android:id="@+id/drag_target3"
            android:layout_width="0dp"
            android:layout_height="100dp"
            android:layout_weight="1"
            android:background="#00A" />
    </LinearLayout>

</RelativeLayout>
```

Listing 3-46. Activity Forwarding Touches

```
public class DragTouchActivity extends Activity implements
        OnLongClickListener {

    @Override
    public void onCreate(Bundle savedInstanceState) {
        super.onCreate(savedInstanceState);
        setContentView(R.layout.main);
        //Attach long-press listener to each ImageView
        findViewById(R.id.image1).setOnLongClickListener(this);
        findViewById(R.id.image2).setOnLongClickListener(this);
        findViewById(R.id.image3).setOnLongClickListener(this);
    }

    @Override
    public boolean onLongClick(View v) {
        DragShadowBuilder shadowBuilder =
                new DragShadowBuilder(v);
        // Start a drag, and pass the View's image along as
        // the local state
        v.startDrag(null, shadowBuilder,
                ((ImageView) v).getDrawable(), 0);

        return true;
    }

}
```

This example displays a row of three images at the top of the screen, along with three of our custom drop target views at the bottom of the screen. Each image is set up with a listener for long-press events, and the long-press triggers a new drag via startDrag(). The DragShadowBuilder passed to the drag initializer is the default implementation provided by the framework. In the next section, we'll look at how this can be customized, but this version just creates a slightly transparent copy of the view being dragged and places it centered underneath the touch point.

We also capture the image content of the view the user selected with getDrawable() and pass that along as the local state of the drag, which the custom drop target will use to set as its image. This will create the appearance that the view was dropped on the target. Figure 3-15 shows how this example looks when it loads, during a drag operation, and after the image has been dropped on a target.

Figure 3-15. Drag example before the drag (top), while the user is dragging and hovering over a target (bottom left), and after the view has been dropped (bottom right)

Customizing DragShadowBuilder

The default implementation of DragShadowBuilder is extremely convenient, but it may not be what your application needs. Let's take a look at Listing 3-47, which is a customized builder implementation.

Listing 3-47. Custom DragShadowBuilder

```
public class DrawableDragShadowBuilder extends DragShadowBuilder {
    private Drawable mDrawable;

    public DrawableDragShadowBuilder(View view, Drawable drawable) {
        super(view);
        // Set the Drawable and apply a green filter to it
        mDrawable = drawable;
        mDrawable.setColorFilter( new PorterDuffColorFilter(
                Color.GREEN, PorterDuff.Mode.MULTIPLY) );
    }

    @Override
    public void onProvideShadowMetrics(Point shadowSize,
            Point touchPoint) {
        // Fill in the size
        shadowSize.x = mDrawable.getIntrinsicWidth();
        shadowSize.y = mDrawable.getIntrinsicHeight();
```

```
        // Fill in the location of the shadow relative to the touch.
        // Here we center the shadow under the finger.
        touchPoint.x = mDrawable.getIntrinsicWidth() / 2;
        touchPoint.y = mDrawable.getIntrinsicHeight() / 2;

        mDrawable.setBounds(new Rect(0, 0, shadowSize.x, shadowSize.y));
    }

    @Override
    public void onDrawShadow(Canvas canvas) {
        //Draw the shadow view onto the provided canvas
        mDrawable.draw(canvas);
    }
}
```

This custom implementation takes in the image that it will display as the shadow as a separate
Drawable parameter rather than making a visual copy of the source view. We also apply a green
ColorFilter to it for added effect. It turns out that DragShadowBuilder is a fairly straightforward class
to extend. There are two primary methods that are required to effectively override it.

The first is onProvideShadowMetrics(), which is called once initially with two Point objects for the
builder to fill in. The first should be filled with the size of the image to be used for the shadow, where
the desired width is set as the x value and the desired height is set as the y value. In our example,
we have set this to be the intrinsic width and height of the image. The second should be filled with
the desired touch location for the shadow. This defines how the shadow image should be positioned
in relation to the user's finger; for example, setting both x and y to zero would place it at the top-
left corner of the image. In our example, we have set it to the image's midpoint so the image will be
centered under the user's finger.

The second method is onDrawShadow(), which is called repeatedly to render the shadow image.
The Canvas passed into this method is created by the framework based on the information contained
in onProvideShadowMetrics(). Here you can do all sorts of custom drawing as you might with any
other custom view. Our example simply tells Drawable to draw itself on the Canvas.

3-17. Building a Navigation Drawer

Problem

Your application needs a top-level navigation menu, and you want to implement one that animates in
and out from the side of the screen in compliance with the latest Google design guidelines.

Solution

(API Level 4)

Integrate the DrawerLayout widget to manage menu views that slide in from the left or right of the
screen, available in the Android Support Library. DrawerLayout is a container widget that manages
each of the first child views in its hierarchy with a specified Gravity value of LEFT or RIGHT (or
START/END if supporting RTL layouts) as an animated content drawer. By default, each view is hidden,

but will be animated in from its respective side when either the openDrawer() method is called or a finger swipe occurs inward from the appropriate side bezel. To help indicate the presence of a drawer, DrawerLayout will also peek the appropriate view if a finger is held down on the appropriate side of the screen.

DrawerLayout supports multiple drawers, one for each gravity setting, and they can be placed anywhere in the layout hierarchy. The only soft rule is that they should be added after the main content view in the layout (that is, placed after that view element in the layout XML). Otherwise, the z-ordering of the views will keep the drawer(s) from being visible.

Integration with the action bar is also supported by way of the ActionBarDrawerToggle element. This is a widget that monitors taps on the Home button area of the action bar and toggles the visibility of the "main" drawer (the drawer with Gravity.LEFT or Gravity.START set).

> **Important**   DrawerLayout is available only in the Android Support Library; it is not part of the native SDK at any platform level. However, any application targeting API Level 4 or later can use the widget with the Support Library included. For more information on including the Support Library in your project, reference our guide in Chapter 1.

How It Works

While it is not required for you to use an action bar at all with DrawerLayout, it is the most common use case. The following examples show how to create navigation drawers with DrawerLayout as well as do the action bar integration. We will look at doing this on both a native action bar (for API Level 11 and later) and using the Support Library's AppCompat action bar.

The following example creates an application with two navigation drawers: a main drawer on the left with a list of options to select from, and a secondary drawer on the right with some additional interactive content. Selecting an item from the list in the main drawer will modify the background color of the primary content view.

Native Action Bar

In Listing 3-48, we have a layout that includes a DrawerLayout. Notice that because this widget is not a core element, we must use its fully qualified class name in the XML.

Listing 3-48. res/layout/activity_main.xml

```
<?xml version="1.0" encoding="utf-8"?>
<android.support.v4.widget.DrawerLayout
    xmlns:android="http://schemas.android.com/apk/res/android"
    android:id="@+id/container_drawer"
    android:layout_width="match_parent"
    android:layout_height="match_parent" >
```

```
<!-- Main Content Pane -->
<FrameLayout
    android:id="@+id/container_root"
    android:layout_width="match_parent"
    android:layout_height="match_parent">

    <!-- Put your main contents here -->

</FrameLayout>

<!-- Main Drawer Content -->
<!--
  Can be any View or ViewGroup content
  Standard drawer width is 240dp
  You MUST set the gravity
  Needs a solid background to be visible overtop the content.
  -->
<ListView
    android:id="@+id/drawer_main"
    android:layout_width="240dp"
    android:layout_height="match_parent"
    android:layout_gravity="left"
    android:background="#555" />

<!--
  You can create additional drawers, this one, for example
  will show up with a swipe from the right of the screen.
  -->
<LinearLayout
    android:id="@+id/drawer_right"
    android:layout_width="240dp"
    android:layout_height="match_parent"
    android:layout_gravity="right"
    android:orientation="vertical"
    android:background="#CCC">
    <Button
        android:layout_width="match_parent"
        android:layout_height="wrap_content"
        android:text="Click Here!" />
    <TextView
        android:layout_width="match_parent"
        android:layout_height="match_parent"
        android:gravity="center"
        android:text="Tap Anywhere Else, Drawer will Hide" />
</LinearLayout>
</android.support.v4.widget.DrawerLayout>
```

We have included two views that will be drawers in our application, one on the left and another on the right; we control the alignment by setting their android:layout_gravity attributes. DrawerLayout does the rest, mapping each view by inspecting the gravity, so we do not need to link them in any other way. Before we get to the activity, our project has one more resource in it; we have created an options menu to display some actions inside the action bar (see Listing 3-49).

Listing 3-49. `res/menu/main.xml`

```xml
<menu xmlns:android="http://schemas.android.com/apk/res/android" >
    <item
        android:id="@+id/action_delete"
        android:orderInCategory="100"
        android:showAsAction="always"
        android:icon="@android:drawable/ic_menu_delete"/>
    <item
        android:id="@+id/action_settings"
        android:orderInCategory="200"
        android:showAsAction="always"
        android:icon="@android:drawable/ic_menu_preferences"/>
</menu>
```

Finally, we have the activity in Listing 3-50. In addition to the DrawerLayout, this example includes an ActionBarDrawerToggle to provide integration with the action bar Home button.

Listing 3-50. Activity with DrawerLayout Integrated

```java
public class NativeActivity extends Activity
        implements AdapterView.OnItemClickListener {

    private static final String[] ITEMS =
        {"White", "Red", "Green", "Blue"};
    private static final int[] COLORS =
        {Color.WHITE, Color.RED, Color.GREEN, Color.BLUE};

    private DrawerLayout mDrawerContainer;
    /* Root content pane in layout */
    private View mMainContent;
    /* Main (left) sliding drawer */
    private ListView mDrawerContent;
    /* Toggle object for ActionBar */
    private ActionBarDrawerToggle mDrawerToggle;

    @Override
    protected void onCreate(Bundle savedInstanceState) {
        super.onCreate(savedInstanceState);
        setContentView(R.layout.activity_main);

        mDrawerContainer =
            (DrawerLayout) findViewById(R.id.container_drawer);
        mDrawerContent =
            (ListView) findViewById(R.id.drawer_main);
        mMainContent = findViewById(R.id.container_root);

        //Toggle indicator must also be the drawer listener,
        // so we extend it to listen for the events ourselves.
```

```java
    mDrawerToggle  = new ActionBarDrawerToggle(
            this,                  //Host Activity
            mDrawerContainer,      //Container to use
            R.drawable.ic_drawer,  //Drawable for action icon
            0, 0) {                //Content descriptions

        @Override
        public void onDrawerOpened(View drawerView) {
            super.onDrawerOpened(drawerView);
            //Update the options menu
            invalidateOptionsMenu();
        }

        @Override
        public void onDrawerStateChanged(int newState) {
            super.onDrawerStateChanged(newState);
            //Update the options menu
            invalidateOptionsMenu();
        }

        @Override
        public void onDrawerClosed(View drawerView) {
            super.onDrawerClosed(drawerView);
            //Update the options menu
            invalidateOptionsMenu();
        }
    };
    //Set the toggle as the drawer's event listener
    mDrawerContainer.setDrawerListener(mDrawerToggle);

    //Enable home button actions in the ActionBar
    getActionBar().setDisplayHomeAsUpEnabled(true);
    getActionBar().setHomeButtonEnabled(true);

    //Our application uses Holo.Light, which defaults to
    // dark text; ListView also has a dark background.
    // Create a custom context so the views inflated by
    // ListAdapter use Holo, to display them with light text
    ContextThemeWrapper wrapper =
            new ContextThemeWrapper(this,
                    android.R.style.Theme_Holo);
    ListAdapter adapter = new ArrayAdapter<String>(wrapper,
            android.R.layout.simple_list_item_1, ITEMS);
    mDrawerContent.setAdapter(adapter);
    mDrawerContent.setOnItemClickListener(this);
}

@Override
protected void onPostCreate(Bundle savedInstanceState) {
    super.onPostCreate(savedInstanceState);
    //Synchronize the state of the drawer after any instance
```

```java
        // state has been restored by the framework
        mDrawerToggle.syncState();
    }

    @Override
    public void onConfigurationChanged(Configuration newConfig) {
        super.onConfigurationChanged(newConfig);
        //Update state on any configuration changes
        mDrawerToggle.onConfigurationChanged(newConfig);
    }

    @Override
    public boolean onCreateOptionsMenu(Menu menu) {
        // Create the ActionBar actions
        getMenuInflater().inflate(R.menu.main, menu);
        return true;
    }

    @Override
    public boolean onPrepareOptionsMenu(Menu menu) {
        //Display the action options based on main drawer state
        boolean isOpen =
                mDrawerContainer.isDrawerVisible(mDrawerContent);
        menu.findItem(R.id.action_delete).setVisible(!isOpen);
        menu.findItem(R.id.action_settings).setVisible(!isOpen);

        return super.onPrepareOptionsMenu(menu);
    }

    @Override
    public boolean onOptionsItemSelected(MenuItem item) {
        //Let the drawer have a crack at the event first
        // to handle home button events
        if (mDrawerToggle.onOptionsItemSelected(item)) {
            //If this was a drawer toggle, we need to update the
            // options menu, but we have to wait until the next
            // loop iteration for the drawer state to change.
            mDrawerContainer.post(new Runnable() {
                @Override
                public void run() {
                    //Update the options menu
                    invalidateOptionsMenu();
                }
            });
            return true;
        }

        //...Handle other options selections here as normal...
        switch (item.getItemId()) {
            case R.id.action_delete:
                //Delete Action
                return true;
```

```
            case R.id.action_settings:
                //Settings Action
                return true;
            default:
                return super.onOptionsItemSelected(item);
        }
    }

    //Handle click events from items in the main drawer list
    @Override
    public void onItemClick(AdapterView<?> parent, View view,
            int position, long id) {
        //Update the background color of the main content
        mMainContent.setBackgroundColor(COLORS[position]);

        //Manually close the drawer
        mDrawerContainer.closeDrawer(mDrawerContent);
    }
}
```

When the activity is initialized, we create an `ActionBarDrawerToggle` instance and set it as the `DrawerListener` of the `DrawerLayout`. This is required so the toggle can listen for events, but it also means we cannot listen for those events in our application unless we extend `ActionBarDrawerToggle` to override the listener method, which we've done here. The toggle is linked to the hosting activity, the `DrawerLayout` it should control, and the icon it should display in the action bar corner. This last item is an icon displayed next to the application logo in the action bar, and it is animated slightly as the drawer opens and closes.

> **Note** You can supply any icon resource you like to `ActionBarDrawerToggle`, but the standard icon that Google recommends you use, which is the one we used in this project, can be downloaded from `http://developer.android.com/downloads/design/`.

There is a fair amount of boilerplate code required to get `ActionBarDrawerToggle` integrated, as it does not hook itself directly into any of the life-cycle methods of the activity. The methods `syncState()`, `onConfigurationChanged()`, and `onOptionsItemSelected()` all need to be called from their appropriate activity callbacks to allow the toggle widget to receive input and maintain state along with the activity instance. In order to trigger Home button events in the action bar, we must also enable it by calling `setHomeButtonEnabled()`. Finally, adding `setDisplayHomeAsUpEnabled()` enables the icon (an arrow by default) to be displayed next to the Home logo; this icon is what the drawer toggle customizes with its own version.

`DrawerLayout` is designed to close an open drawer when the main content view receives touch events (that is, the user touches outside the drawer). Touch events inside the layout (such as tapping an item in our main list or the button in our secondary drawer) require us to close the drawer manually when necessary. Inside the OnItemClickListener registered to our list, after changing the background color of the content view, we call closeDrawer() to do just that. It is interesting to note that even if the user taps on a noninteractive view inside a drawer (for example, a TextView), those touch events will be delivered to the next child view in line. If that child is the main content view (most common), then the drawer will close in the same fashion as if the user touched outside it.

> **Tip**   You can use a ContextThemeWrapper to customize the theme resources used to display certain pieces of your UI. Supplying one of these wrappers rather than the base Context causes the widget receiving it to load resources from a theme other than that defined for your application or the current activity. In our example here, we are using one to ensure the rows in the ListView are loaded with Theme.Holo rather than Theme.Holo.Light. This is because Theme.Holo is a dark theme with light text, which more closely matches our dark ListView than the main theme. This handy trick allowed us to customize the row items' look and feel without creating a custom layout for each one.

Notice how methods such as openDrawer() and closeDrawer() take a view as an argument. Since DrawerLayout can manage more than one drawer, we have to tell it which drawer widget to act on. These methods can also be triggered using the Gravity parameter associated with the drawer if your application doesn't have a reference to the drawer view itself.

Recall that we extended the ActionBarDrawerToggle in order to override the drawer's event listener methods. Inside each method we call invalidateOptionsMenu(), which simply tells the activity to update the menu and call its setup methods again. Recall also that we created some actions to display inside the action bar by using an XML menu, and inside onPrepareOptionsMenu(), we control whether those actions are visible by the visibility state of the drawer. This way, the actions are shown only when the main drawer is not. The purpose of invalidating the menu in each event callback is to allow the menu visibility to update based on changes in the drawer.

Figure 3-16 shows how tapping the Home button in the action bar expands the main drawer to expose the options list; notice also that the actions are gone when the drawer is open. Figure 3-17 illustrates the secondary drawer peeking in from a bezel swipe on the right side of the screen, and then fully open.

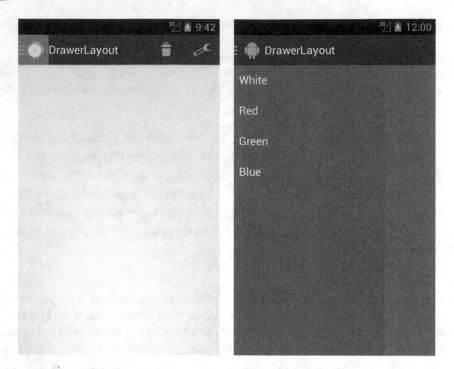

Figure 3-16. *Activity with main drawer*

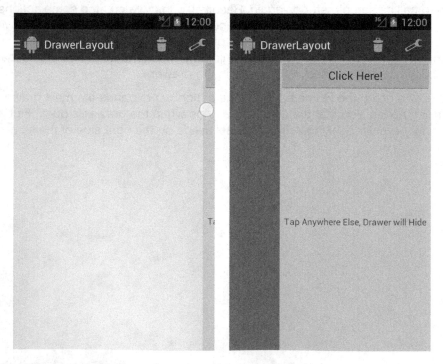

Figure 3-17. *Activity with secondary drawer*

Support Action Bar

(API Level 7)

Adapting the previous example to use the AppCompat library from the Android Support Library is fairly straightforward. We need to only change the theme our activity uses, inherit from the `ActionBarActivity` support class, and modify some of the method calls that refer to newer APIs.

> **Important**   `ActionBarActivity` is available only in the AppCompat Library, found as part of the Android Support Library; it is not part of the native SDK at any platform level. However, any application targeting API Level 7 or later can use the widget with the Support Library included. For more information on including the Support Library in your project, reference our guide in Chapter 1.

Listing 3-51 gets us started by showing an `AndroidManifest.xml` entry that might be used to apply the appropriate theme.

Listing 3-51. Portion of AndroidManifest.xml for the Activity

```
<activity
  android:name=".SupportActivity"
  android:label="@string/app_name"
  android:theme="@style/Theme.AppCompat.Light.DarkActionBar" >
  <intent-filter>
    <action android:name="android.intent.action.MAIN" />
    <category android:name="android.intent.category.LAUNCHER" />
  </intent-filter>
</activity>
```

Notice when using AppCompat, we must include one of the `Theme.AppCompat` theme options. We need not modify any of the resource files, so they are not repeated here. Listing 3-52 shows us the modified activity code.

Listing 3-52. Support Activity with DrawerLayout Integrated

```
public class SupportActivity extends ActionBarActivity
        implements AdapterView.OnItemClickListener {

    private static final String[] ITEMS =
        {"White", "Red", "Green", "Blue"};
    private static final int[] COLORS =
        {Color.WHITE, Color.RED, Color.GREEN, Color.BLUE};

    private DrawerLayout mDrawerContainer;
    /* Root content pane in layout */
    private View mMainContent;
    /* Main (left) sliding drawer */
    private ListView mDrawerContent;
    /* Toggle object for ActionBar */
    private ActionBarDrawerToggle mDrawerToggle;
```

```java
@Override
protected void onCreate(Bundle savedInstanceState) {
    super.onCreate(savedInstanceState);
    setContentView(R.layout.activity_main);

    mDrawerContainer =
        (DrawerLayout) findViewById(R.id.container_drawer);
    mDrawerContent =
        (ListView) findViewById(R.id.drawer_main);
    mMainContent = findViewById(R.id.container_root);

    //Toggle indicator must also be the drawer listener,
    // so we extend it to listen for the events ourselves.
    mDrawerToggle  = new ActionBarDrawerToggle(
            this,                    //Host Activity
            mDrawerContainer,        //Container to use
            R.drawable.ic_drawer, //Drawable for action icon
            0, 0) {                  //Content description

        @Override
        public void onDrawerOpened(View drawerView) {
            super.onDrawerOpened(drawerView);
            //Update the options menu
            supportInvalidateOptionsMenu();
        }

        @Override
        public void onDrawerStateChanged(int newState) {
            super.onDrawerStateChanged(newState);
            //Update the options menu
            supportInvalidateOptionsMenu();
        }

        @Override
        public void onDrawerClosed(View drawerView) {
            super.onDrawerClosed(drawerView);
            //Update the options menu
            supportInvalidateOptionsMenu();
        }
    };

    //Our application uses Holo.Light, which defaults to
    // dark text; ListView also has a dark background.
    // Create a custom context so the views inflated by
    // ListAdapter use Holo, to display them with light text
    ContextThemeWrapper wrapper =
            new ContextThemeWrapper(this,
                    android.R.style.Theme_Black);
    ListAdapter adapter = new ArrayAdapter<String>(wrapper,
            android.R.layout.simple_list_item_1, ITEMS);
```

```
        mDrawerContent.setAdapter(adapter);
        mDrawerContent.setOnItemClickListener(this);

        //Set the toggle as the drawer's event listener
        mDrawerContainer.setDrawerListener(mDrawerToggle);

        //Enable home button actions in the ActionBar
        getSupportActionBar().setDisplayHomeAsUpEnabled(true);
        getSupportActionBar().setHomeButtonEnabled(true);
    }

    @Override
    protected void onPostCreate(Bundle savedInstanceState) {
        super.onPostCreate(savedInstanceState);
        //Synchronize the state of the drawer after any instance
        // state has been restored by the framework
        mDrawerToggle.syncState();
    }

    @Override
    public void onConfigurationChanged(Configuration newConfig) {
        super.onConfigurationChanged(newConfig);
        //Update state on any configuration changes
        mDrawerToggle.onConfigurationChanged(newConfig);
    }

    @Override
    public boolean onCreateOptionsMenu(Menu menu) {
        // Create the ActionBar actions
        getMenuInflater().inflate(R.menu.main, menu);
        return true;
    }

    @Override
    public boolean onPrepareOptionsMenu(Menu menu) {
        //Display the action options based on main drawer state
        boolean isOpen =
                mDrawerContainer.isDrawerVisible(mDrawerContent);
        menu.findItem(R.id.action_delete).setVisible(!isOpen);
        menu.findItem(R.id.action_settings).setVisible(!isOpen);

        return super.onPrepareOptionsMenu(menu);
    }

    @Override
    public boolean onOptionsItemSelected(MenuItem item) {
        //Let the drawer have a crack at the event first
        // to handle home button events
        if (mDrawerToggle.onOptionsItemSelected(item)) {
            //If this was a drawer toggle, we need to update the
            // options menu, but we have to wait until the next
            // loop iteration for the drawer state to change.
```

```
            mDrawerContainer.post(new Runnable() {
                @Override
                public void run() {
                    //Update the options menu
                    supportInvalidateOptionsMenu();
                }
            });
            return true;
        }

        //...Handle other options selections here as normal...
        switch (item.getItemId()) {
            case R.id.action_delete:
                //Delete Action
                return true;
            case R.id.action_settings:
                //Settings Action
                return true;
            default:
                return super.onOptionsItemSelected(item);
        }
    }

    //Handle click events from items in the main drawer list
    @Override
    public void onItemClick(AdapterView<?> parent, View view,
            int position, long id) {
        //Update the background color of the main content
        mMainContent.setBackgroundColor(COLORS[position]);

        //Manually close the drawer
        mDrawerContainer.closeDrawer(mDrawerContent);
    }
}
```

Besides now inheriting from ActionBarActivity, there are only two changes necessary. First, all calls to invalidateOptionsMenu() are replaced by supportInvalidateOptionsMenu(). Second, all calls to getActionBar() are replaced by getSupportActionBar(). With these changes in place, the DrawerLayout is now fully functional with an action bar on devices back to API Level 7.

THE REAL STAR OF THE SHOW

The drag and edge-swipe behavior provided in DrawerLayout is actually the work of another class also available in the Support Library: ViewDragHelper. This class can be quite helpful if you need to do any custom view manipulation based on user dragging.

ViewDragHelper is a touch event processor (similar to GestureDetector), so it needs to be fed events from your views. Typically, every event received in onTouchEvent() of your view must be handed directly to processTouchEvent() on the helper.

```
@Override
public boolean onTouchEvent(MotionEvent event) {
    mHelper.processTouchEvent(event);
}
```

When a `ViewDragHelper` is instantiated, an instance of a `ViewDragHelper.Callback` must be passed as the handler for all events the helper will pass to your application. The most important of these is `tryCaptureView()`, which will be called when the helper starts seeing a drag over a given view; returning `true` causes the view to become "captured," meaning its position will begin to follow the subsequent touch events in the gesture.

`ViewDragHelper` also supports swipes from the view edges if `setEdgeTrackingEnabled()` has been called with one or more valid edge flags. When edge events occur, `onEdgeTouched()` and `onEdgeDragStarted()` will be triggered on the `Callback`.

One final tip: A single `ViewDragHelper` is designed to capture and manage only one view at a time. Problems will occur if you attempt to use the same instance to slide two views at the same time. `DrawerLayout`, for example, has one `ViewDragHelper` for each drawer it supports to avoid this very issue.

3-18. Swiping Between Views

Problem

You need to implement paging with a swipe gesture in your application's UI in order to move between views or fragments.

Solution

(API Level 4)

Implement the `ViewPager` widget to provide paging with swipe scroll gestures. `ViewPager` is a modified implementation of the `AdapterView` pattern that the framework uses for widgets such as `ListView` and `GridView`. It requires its own adapter implementation as a subclass of `PagerAdapter`, but it is conceptually very similar to the patterns used in `BaseAdapter` and `ListAdapter`. It does not inherently implement recycling of the components being paged, but it does provide callbacks to create and destroy the items on the fly so that only a fixed number of content views are in memory at a given time.

> **Important**   `ViewPager` is available only in the Android Support Library; it is not part of the native SDK at any platform level. However, any application targeting API Level 4 or later can use the widget with the Support Library included. For more information on including the Support Library in your project, reference our guide in Chapter 1.

How It Works

Most of the heavy lifting in working with `ViewPager` is in the `PagerAdapter` implementation you provide. Let's start with a simple example, shown in Listing 3-53, that pages between a series of images.

Listing 3-53. Custom PagerAdapter for Images

```java
public class ImagePagerAdapter extends PagerAdapter {
    private Context mContext;

    private static final int[] IMAGES = {
        android.R.drawable.ic_menu_camera,
        android.R.drawable.ic_menu_add,
        android.R.drawable.ic_menu_delete,
        android.R.drawable.ic_menu_share,
        android.R.drawable.ic_menu_edit
    };

    private static final int[] COLORS = {
        Color.RED,
        Color.BLUE,
        Color.GREEN,
        Color.GRAY,
        Color.MAGENTA
    };

    public ImagePagerAdapter(Context context) {
        super();
        mContext = context;
    }

    /*
     * Provide the total number of pages
     */
    @Override
    public int getCount() {
        return IMAGES.length;
    }

    /*
     * Override this method if you want to show more than one page
     * at a time inside the ViewPager's content bounds.
     */
    @Override
    public float getPageWidth(int position) {
        return 1f;
    }

    @Override
    public Object instantiateItem(ViewGroup container, int position) {
        // Create a new ImageView and add it to the supplied container
```

```
        ImageView iv = new ImageView(mContext);
        // Set the content for this position
        iv.setImageResource(IMAGES[position]);
        iv.setBackgroundColor(COLORS[position]);

        // You MUST add the view here, the framework will not
        container.addView(iv);
        //Return this view also as the key object for this position
        return iv;
    }

    @Override
    public void destroyItem(ViewGroup container, int position,
            Object object) {
        //Remove the view from the container here
        container.removeView((View) object);
    }

    @Override
    public boolean isViewFromObject(View view, Object object) {
        // Validate that the object returned from instantiateItem()
        // is associated with the view added to the container in
        // that location.  Our example uses the same object in
        // both places.
        return (view == object);
    }

}
```

In this example, we have an implementation of PagerAdapter that serves up a series of ImageView instances for the user to page through. The first required override in the adapter is getCount(), which, just like its AdapterView counterpart, should return the total number of items available.

ViewPager works by keeping track of a *key* object for each item alongside a view to display for that object; this keeps the separation between the adapter items and their views that developers are used to with AdapterView. However, the implementation is a bit different. With AdapterView, the adapter's getView() method is called to construct and return the view to display for that item. With ViewPager, the callback's instantiateItem() and destroyItem() will be called when a new view needs to be created, or when one has scrolled outside the bounds of the pager's limit and should be removed; the number of items that any ViewPager will keep hold of is set by the setOffscreenPageLimit() method.

> **Note**   The default value for the offscreen page limit is 3. This means ViewPager will track the currently visible page, one to the left, and one to the right. The number of tracked pages is always centered around the currently visible page.

In our example, we use `instantiateItem()` to create a new `ImageView` and then apply the properties for that particular position. Unlike `AdapterView`, the `PagerAdapter` must attach the `View` to display to the supplied `ViewGroup` in addition to returning the unique key object to represent this item. These two things don't have to be the same, but they can be in a simple example like this. The callback `isViewFromObject()` is a required override on `PagerAdapter` so the application can provide the link between which key object goes with which view. In our example, we attach the `ImageView` to the supplied parent and then also return the same instance as the key from `instantiateItem()`. The code for `isViewFromObject()` becomes simple, then, as we return `true` if both parameters are the same instance.

Complementary to instantiate, `PagerAdapter` must also remove the specified view from the parent container in `destroyItem()`. If the views displayed in the pager are heavyweight and you wanted to implement some basic view recycling in your adapter, you could hold on to the view after it was removed so it could be handed back to `instantiateItem()` to attach to another key object. See Listing 3-54, which shows an example activity using our custom adapter with a `ViewPager`. The resulting application is shown in Figure 3-18.

Listing 3-54. Activity Using `ViewPager` and `ImagePagerAdapter`

```java
public class PagerActivity extends Activity {

    @Override
    protected void onCreate(Bundle savedInstanceState) {
        super.onCreate(savedInstanceState);
        ViewPager pager = new ViewPager(this);
        pager.setAdapter(new ImagePagerAdapter(this));

        setContentView(pager);
    }
}
```

Figure 3-18. ViewPager dragging between two pages

Running this application, the user can horizontally swipe a finger to page between all the images provided by the custom adapter, and each page displays full-screen. There is one method defined in the example we did not mention: getPageWidth(). This method allows you to define for each position how large the page should be as a percentage of the ViewPager size. By default it is set to 1, and the previous example didn't change this. But let's say we wanted to display multiple pages at once; we can adjust the value this method returns.

If we modify getPageWidth() as in the following snippet, we can display three pages at once:

```
/*
 * Override this method if you want to show more than one page
 * at a time inside the ViewPager's content bounds.
 */
@Override
public float getPageWidth(int position) {
    //Page width should be 1/3 of the view
    return 0.333f;
}
```

You can see in Figure 3-19 how this modifies the resulting application.

Figure 3-19. `ViewPager` *showing three pages at once*

Adding and Removing Pages

Listing 3-55 illustrates a slightly more complex adapter for use with `ViewPager`. This example uses `FragmentPagerAdapter` as a base, which is another class in the framework where each page item is a fragment instead of a simple view.

This example is designed to take a long list of data and break it into smaller sections that display on each page. The `Fragment` this adapter displays is a custom inner implementation that receives a `List` of items and displays them in a `ListView`.

Listing 3-55. FragmentPagerAdapter to Display a List

```
public class ListPagerAdapter extends FragmentPagerAdapter {

    private static final int ITEMS_PER_PAGE = 3;

    private List<String> mItems;

    public ListPagerAdapter(FragmentManager manager,
            List<String> items) {
        super(manager);
        mItems = items;
    }
```

```
/*
 * This method will only get called the first time a
 * fragment is needed for this position.
 */
@Override
public Fragment getItem(int position) {
    int start = position * ITEMS_PER_PAGE;
    return ArrayListFragment.newInstance(
            getPageList(position), start);
}


@Override
public int getCount() {
    // Get whole number
    int pages = mItems.size() / ITEMS_PER_PAGE;
    // Add one more page for any remaining values if list size
    // is not divisible by page size
    int excess = mItems.size() % ITEMS_PER_PAGE;
    if (excess > 0) {
        pages++;
    }

    return pages;
}


/*
 * This will get called after getItem() for new Fragments, but
 * also when Fragments beyond the offscreen page limit are added
 * back; we need to make sure to update the list for these elements.
 */
@Override
public Object instantiateItem(ViewGroup container, int position) {
    ArrayListFragment fragment =
            (ArrayListFragment) super.instantiateItem(container,
                    position);
    fragment.updateListItems(getPageList(position));
    return fragment;
}


/*
 * Called by the framework when notifyDataSetChanged() is called,
 * we must decide how each Fragment has changed for the new data set.
 * We also return POSITION_NONE if a Fragment at a particular
 * position is no longer needed so the adapter can remove it.
 */
@Override
public int getItemPosition(Object object) {
    ArrayListFragment fragment = (ArrayListFragment)object;
    int position = fragment.getBaseIndex() / ITEMS_PER_PAGE;
    if(position >= getCount()) {
        //This page no longer needed
        return POSITION_NONE;
```

```java
        } else {
            //Refresh fragment data display
            fragment.updateListItems(getPageList(position));

            return position;
        }
    }

    /*
     * Helper method to obtain the piece of the overall list that
     * should be applied to a given Fragment
     */
    private List<String> getPageList(int position) {
        int start = position * ITEMS_PER_PAGE;
        int end = Math.min(start + ITEMS_PER_PAGE, mItems.size());
        List<String> itemPage = mItems.subList(start, end);

        return itemPage;
    }

    /*
     * Internal custom Fragment that displays a list section inside
     * of a ListView, and provides external methods for updating the list
     */
    public static class ArrayListFragment extends Fragment {
        private ArrayList<String> mItems;
        private ArrayAdapter<String> mAdapter;
        private int mBaseIndex;

        //Fragments are created by convention using a Factory
        static ArrayListFragment newInstance(List<String> page,
                int baseIndex) {
            ArrayListFragment fragment = new ArrayListFragment();
            fragment.updateListItems(page);
            fragment.setBaseIndex(baseIndex);
            return fragment;
        }

        public ArrayListFragment() {
            super();
            mItems = new ArrayList<String>();
        }

        @Override
        public void onCreate(Bundle savedInstanceState) {
            super.onCreate(savedInstanceState);
            //Make a new adapter for the list items
            mAdapter = new ArrayAdapter<String>(getActivity(),
                    android.R.layout.simple_list_item_1, mItems);
        }
```

```
        @Override
        public View onCreateView(LayoutInflater inflater,
                ViewGroup container, Bundle savedInstanceState) {
            //Construct and return a ListView with our adapter
            ListView list = new ListView(getActivity());
            list.setAdapter(mAdapter);
            return list;
        }

        //Save the index in the global list where this page starts
        public void setBaseIndex(int index) {
            mBaseIndex = index;
        }

        //Retrieve the index where this page starts
        public int getBaseIndex() {
            return mBaseIndex;
        }
        public void updateListItems(List<String> items) {
            mItems.clear();
            for (String piece : items) {
                mItems.add(piece);
            }

            if (mAdapter != null) {
                mAdapter.notifyDataSetChanged();
            }
        }
    }
}
```

FragmentPagerAdapter implements some of the underlying requirements of PagerAdapter for us. Instead of implementing instantiateItem(), destroyItem(), and isViewFromObject(), we only need to override getItem() to provide the Fragment for each page position. This example defines a constant for the number of list items that should display on each page. When we create the Fragment in getItem(), we pass in a subsection of the list based on the index offset and this constant. The number of pages required, returned by getCount(), is determined by the total size of the items list divided by the constant number of items per page.

> **Tip** FragmentPagerAdapter retains all fragment instances as active whether or not they are actively within the offscreen page limit. If your pager needs to hold a larger number of fragments, or some are more heavyweight, look at using FragmentStatePagerAdapter instead. The latter destroys fragments outside the offscreen page limit while maintaining their saved state—similar to a rotation operation.

This adapter also overrides one more method we did not see in the simple example, which is getItemPosition(). This method will get called when notifyDataSetChanged() gets called externally by the application. Its primary function is to sort out whether page items should be moved or removed as a result of the change. If the item's position has changed, the implementation should return the new position value. If the item should not be moved, the implementation should return the constant value PagerAdapter.POSITION_UNCHANGED. If the page should be removed, the application should return PagerAdapter.POSITION_NONE.

The example checks the current page position (which we have to re-create from the initial index data) against the current page count. If this page is greater than the count, we have removed enough items from the list so that this page is no longer needed, and we return POSITION_NONE. In any other case, we update the list of items that should now be displayed for the current fragment and return the new calculated position.

The method getItemPosition() will get called for every page currently being tracked by the ViewPager, which will be the number of pages returned by getOffscreenPageLimit(). However, even though ViewPager doesn't track a fragment that scrolls outside the limit, FragmentManager still does. So when a previous fragment is scrolled back in, getItem() will not be called again because the fragment exists. But, because of this, if a data set change occurs during this time, the fragment list data will not update. This is why we have overridden instantiateItem(). While it is not required to override instantiateItem() for this adapter, we do need to update fragments that are outside the offscreen page limit when modifications to the list take place. Because instantiateItem() will get called each time a fragment scrolls back inside the page limit, it is an opportune place to reset the display list.

Let's look at an example application that uses this adapter. See Listings 3-56 and 3-57.

Listing 3-56. res/layout/main.xml

```xml
<?xml version="1.0" encoding="utf-8"?>
<LinearLayout xmlns:android="http://schemas.android.com/apk/res/android"
    android:layout_width="match_parent"
    android:layout_height="match_parent"
    android:orientation="vertical" >
    <Button
        android:layout_width="match_parent"
        android:layout_height="wrap_content"
        android:text="Add Item"
        android:onClick="onAddClick" />
    <Button
        android:layout_width="match_parent"
        android:layout_height="wrap_content"
        android:text="Remove Item"
        android:onClick="onRemoveClick" />

    <!-- ViewPager is a support widget, it needs the full name -->
    <android.support.v4.view.ViewPager
        android:id="@+id/view_pager"
        android:layout_width="match_parent"
        android:layout_height="match_parent" />
</LinearLayout>
```

Listing 3-57. Activity with `ListPagerAdapter`

```java
public class FragmentPagerActivity extends FragmentActivity {

    private ArrayList<String> mListItems;
    private ListPagerAdapter mAdapter;

    @Override
    protected void onCreate(Bundle savedInstanceState) {
        super.onCreate(savedInstanceState);
        setContentView(R.layout.main);
        //Create the initial data set
        mListItems = new ArrayList<String>();
        mListItems.add("Mom");
        mListItems.add("Dad");
        mListItems.add("Sister");
        mListItems.add("Brother");
        mListItems.add("Cousin");
        mListItems.add("Niece");
        mListItems.add("Nephew");
        //Attach the data to the pager
        ViewPager pager =
                (ViewPager) findViewById(R.id.view_pager);
        mAdapter = new ListPagerAdapter(
                getSupportFragmentManager(),
                mListItems);

        pager.setAdapter(mAdapter);
    }

    public void onAddClick(View v) {
        //Add a new unique item to the end of the list
        mListItems.add("Crazy Uncle "
                + System.currentTimeMillis());
        mAdapter.notifyDataSetChanged();
    }

    public void onRemoveClick(View v) {
        //Remove an item from the head of the list
        if (!mListItems.isEmpty()) {
            mListItems.remove(0);
        }
        mAdapter.notifyDataSetChanged();
    }
}
```

This example consists of two buttons to add and remove items from the data set as well as a ViewPager. Notice that the `ViewPager` must be defined in XML using its fully qualified package name because it is only part of the Support Library and does not exist in the `android.widget` or `android.view` packages. The activity constructs a default list of items, and it passes it to our custom adapter, which is then attached to the `ViewPager`.

Each Add button click appends a new item to the end of the list and triggers ListPagerAdapter to update by calling notifyDataSetChanged(). Each Remove button click removes an item from the front of the list and again notifies the adapter. With each change, the adapter adjusts the number of pages available and updates the ViewPager. If all the items are removed from the currently visible page, that page is removed and the previous page will be displayed.

Using Other Helpful Methods

There are a few other methods on ViewPager that can be useful in your applications:

- setPageMargin() and setPageMarginDrawable() allow you to set some extra space between pages and optionally supply a Drawable that will be used to fill the margin spaces.

- setCurrentItem() allows you to programmatically set the page that should be shown, with an option to disable the scrolling animation while it switches pages.

- OnPageChangeListener can be used to notify the application of scroll and change actions.

    - onPageSelected() will be called when a new page is displayed.

    - onPageScrolled() will be called continuously while a scroll operation is taking place.

    - onPageScrollStateChanged() will be called when the ViewPager toggles from being idle, to being actively scrolled by the user, to automatically scrolling to snap to the closest page.

3-19. Creating Modular Interfaces
Problem

You want to increase code reuse in your application's UI between multiple device configurations.

Solution

(API Level 4)

Use fragments to create reusable modules that can be inserted into your activity code to tailor your UI to different device configurations or apply common interface elements to multiple activities. Fragments were originally introduced to the Android SDK in 3.0 (API Level 11) but are a main part of the Support Library that allows them to be used in applications targeting any platform version after Android 1.6 (API Level 4).

When using fragments with the Support Library, you must use the FragmentActivity class instead of the default Activity implementation. This version has the necessary functionality built into it, such as a local FragmentManager, that the newer platforms have natively. If your application is targeting Android 3.0 or later, you will not need the Support Library for this purpose, and you can use Activity instead.

Fragments have a life cycle just like an activity, so the same callback methods, such as onCreate(), onResume(), onPause(), and onDestroy() exist on Fragment. There are a few additional life-cycle callbacks as well, such as onAttach() and onDetach() when a fragment is connected to its parent activity. In place of a setContentView() method, the method onCreateView() is called by the framework to obtain the content to display.

A fragment is not required to have a UI component like an activity does. By not overriding onCreateView(), a fragment can exist purely as a data source or other module in your application. This can be a great way to modularize the model portion of your application, because FragmentManager provides simple ways for one fragment to access another. A fragment can also be retained by FragmentManager, which allows fragments that may be housing your data or obtaining it from the network to avoid getting re-created on device configuration changes.

How It Works

This example illustrates a simple master-detail application that uses three fragments. The MasterFragment displays a list of web sites the user can visit, while the DetailFragment contains a WebView to display the URL of the selected list item. A third DataFragment does not have a UI component to it, and it exists purely to serve the model data to the other fragments. Depending on the orientation configuration of the device, we will display these elements differently to best use the screen real estate.

Let's first look at the DataFragment in Listing 3-58.

Listing 3-58. Data Fragment

```
public class DataFragment extends Fragment {
    /*
     * This is an example of a fragment that does not have a UI.
     * It exists solely to encapsulate the data logic for the
     * application in a way that is friendly for other
     * fragments to access.
     */

    public static final String TAG = "DataFragment";

/*
     * Custom data model class to house our application's data
     */
    public static class DataItem {
        private String mName;
        private String mUrl;

        public DataItem(String name, String url) {
            mName = name;
            mUrl = url;
        }

        public String getName() {
            return mName;
        }
```

```
        public String getUrl() {
            return mUrl;
        }
    }

    /*
     * Factory method to create new instances
     */
    public static DataFragment newInstance() {
        return new DataFragment();
    }

    private ArrayList<DataItem> mDataSet;

    @Override
    public void onCreate(Bundle savedInstanceState) {
        super.onCreate(savedInstanceState);
        //Construct the initial data set
        mDataSet = new ArrayList<DataFragment.DataItem>();
        mDataSet.add(new DataItem("Google",
                "http://www.google.com"));
        mDataSet.add(new DataItem("Yahoo",
                "http://www.yahoo.com"));
        mDataSet.add(new DataItem("Bing",
                "http://www.bing.com"));
        mDataSet.add(new DataItem("Android",
                "http://www.android.com"));
    }

    //Accessor to serve the current data the application
    public ArrayList<DataItem> getLatestData() {
        return mDataSet;
    }
}
```

This fragment defines a custom model class for our list data, and it constructs the data set for the application to use. This example is simplified and the data set is static, but you could place the logic to download feed data from a web service or obtain database information from a `ContentProvider` (both of which we will describe in great detail in the coming chapters). It has no view component to it, but we can still attach it to the `FragmentManager` for other modules of the application to access.

Next, see Listing 3-59, which defines the `MasterFragment`.

Listing 3-59. Master View Fragment

```
public class MasterFragment extends DialogFragment implements
        AdapterView.OnItemClickListener {

    /*
     * Callback interface to feed data selections up to the
     * parent Activity
     */
```

```java
public interface OnItemSelectedListener {
    public void onDataItemSelected(DataItem selected);
}

/*
 * Factory method to create new instances
 */
public static MasterFragment newInstance() {
    return new MasterFragment();
}

private ArrayAdapter<DataItem> mAdapter;
private OnItemSelectedListener mItemSelectedListener;

/*
 * Using onAttach to connect the listener interface, and guarantee
 * that the Activity we attach to supports the interface.
 */
@Override
public void onAttach(Activity activity) {
    super.onAttach(activity);
    try {
        mItemSelectedListener = (OnItemSelectedListener) activity;
    } catch (ClassCastException e) {
        throw new IllegalArgumentException(
                "Activity must implement OnItemSelectedListener");
    }
}

/*
 * Construct a custom adapter to display the name field from
 * our data model.
 */
@Override
public void onCreate(Bundle savedInstanceState) {
    super.onCreate(savedInstanceState);

    mAdapter = new ArrayAdapter<DataFragment.DataItem>(getActivity(),
            android.R.layout.simple_list_item_1) {
        @Override
        public View getView(int position, View convertView,
                ViewGroup parent) {
            View row = convertView;
            if (row == null) {
                row = LayoutInflater.from(getContext())
                        .inflate(android.R.layout.simple_list_item_1,
                                parent, false);
            }

            DataItem item = getItem(position);
            TextView tv =
                    (TextView) row.findViewById(android.R.id.text1);
```

```java
                    tv.setText(item.getName());

                    return row;
                }
            };
        }

        @Override
        public View onCreateView(LayoutInflater inflater,
                ViewGroup container, Bundle savedInstanceState) {
            ListView list = new ListView(getActivity());
            list.setOnItemClickListener(this);
            list.setAdapter(mAdapter);
            return list;
        }

        /*
         * onCreateDialog is the opportunity to directly access the dialog
         * that will be shown.  We use this callback to set the title of
         * the dialog.
         */
        @Override
        public Dialog onCreateDialog(Bundle savedInstanceState) {
            Dialog dialog = super.onCreateDialog(savedInstanceState);
            dialog.setTitle("Select a Site");

            return dialog;
        }

        /*
         * When we resume, get the latest model information from our
         * DataFragment
         */
        @Override
        public void onResume() {
            super.onResume();
            //Get the latest data list
            DataFragment fragment = (DataFragment) getFragmentManager()
                    .findFragmentByTag(DataFragment.TAG);
            if (fragment != null) {
                mAdapter.clear();
                for (DataItem item : fragment.getLatestData()) {
                    mAdapter.add(item);
                }
                mAdapter.notifyDataSetChanged();
            }
        }

        @Override
        public void onItemClick(AdapterView<?> parent, View v,
                int position, long id) {
            // Notify the Activity
```

```
        mItemSelectedListener.onDataItemSelected(
                mAdapter.getItem(position));

        // Hide the dialog, if shown.  This returns false when the
        // fragment is embedded in the view.
        if (getShowsDialog()) {
            dismiss();
        }
    }
}
```

This component inherits from DialogFragment, which is a special instance in the SDK that has a secret power. DialogFragment can display its contents embedded in an activity or it can display them inside a dialog box. This will allow us to use the same code to display the list, but it will embed itself in the UI only when there is room to do so. In onCreate(), we implement a custom ArrayAdapter that can display the data out of our custom model class. In onCreateView(), we create a simple ListView that will display the model items.

In onResume(), we see how fragments can communicate with one another. This component asks the FragmentManager for an instance of the DataFragment we defined previously. If one exists, it obtains the latest data model list from that fragment. The fragment is found by referencing its tag value, and we will see shortly how that link is made.

This fragment also defines a custom listener interface that we will use to communicate back to the parent activity. In the onAttach() callback, we set the activity we attach to as the listener for this fragment. This is one of many patterns we could use to call back to the parent. If the fragment will always be attached to the same activity in your application, another common method is to simply call getActivity() and cast the result to access the methods you have written on your activity directly. We could have asked the MasterFragment to talk directly to the DetailsFragment in a similar fashion in which the DataFragment was accessed.

Whenever an item is selected in the list, the listener is notified. DialogFragment provides the getShowsDialog() method to determine whether the view is currently embedded in the activity or being shown as a dialog box. If the fragment is currently shown inside of a dialog, we also call dismiss() after the selection.

> **Tip** The dismiss() method technically does work even when the fragment is not shown as a dialog. This method just removes the view from its container. This behavior can be a bit awkward, so it is best to always check the mode first.

Now let's look at our last item, the detail view, in Listing 3-60.

Listing 3-60. Detail View Fragment

```
public class DetailFragment extends Fragment {

    private WebView mWebView;
```

```java
/*
 * Custom client to enable progress visibility. Adding a
 * client also sets the WebView to load all requests directly
 * rather than handing them off to the browser.
 */
private WebViewClient mWebViewClient = new WebViewClient() {
    @Override
    public void onPageStarted(WebView view, String url,
            Bitmap favicon) {
        getActivity()
                .setProgressBarIndeterminateVisibility(true);
    }

    public void onPageFinished(WebView view, String url) {
        getActivity()
                .setProgressBarIndeterminateVisibility(false);
    }
};

/*
 * Create and set up a basic WebView for the display
 */
@Override
public View onCreateView(LayoutInflater inflater,
        ViewGroup container, Bundle savedInstanceState) {
    mWebView = new WebView(getActivity());
    mWebView.getSettings().setJavaScriptEnabled(true);
    mWebView.setWebViewClient(mWebViewClient);

    return mWebView;
}

/*
 * External method to load a new site into the view
 */
public void loadUrl(String url) {
    mWebView.loadUrl(url);
}

}
```

This component is the simplest of the bunch. Here we just create a WebView that will load the contents of the URL passed to it. We also attach a WebViewClient to monitor the loading progress so we can display a progress indicator to the user. For more-detailed information about WebView and WebViewClient, check out the recipes in the next chapter.

Important   Because this application uses a WebView to access remote sites, you will need to declare the android.permission.INTERNET permission in your manifest.

Finally, take a look at the activity defined for the example in Listings 3-61 through 3-63.

Listing 3-61. res/layout/main.xml

```xml
<?xml version="1.0" encoding="utf-8"?>
<!-- Portrait Device Layout -->
<LinearLayout
    xmlns:android="http://schemas.android.com/apk/res/android"
    android:layout_width="match_parent"
    android:layout_height="match_parent"
    android:orientation="vertical" >
    <Button
        android:layout_width="match_parent"
        android:layout_height="wrap_content"
        android:text="Show List"
        android:onClick="onShowClick" />
    <fragment
        android:name="com.examples.fragmentsample.DetailFragment"
        android:id="@+id/fragment_detail"
        android:layout_width="match_parent"
        android:layout_height="match_parent" />
</LinearLayout>
```

Listing 3-62. res/layout-land/main.xml

```xml
<?xml version="1.0" encoding="utf-8"?>
<!-- Landscape Device Layout -->
<LinearLayout
    xmlns:android="http://schemas.android.com/apk/res/android"
    android:layout_width="match_parent"
    android:layout_height="match_parent"
    android:orientation="horizontal" >
    <FrameLayout
        android:id="@+id/fragment_master"
        android:layout_width="0dp"
        android:layout_height="match_parent"
        android:layout_weight="1" />
    <fragment
        android:name="com.examples.fragmentsample.DetailFragment"
        android:id="@+id/fragment_detail"
        android:layout_width="0dp"
        android:layout_height="match_parent"
        android:layout_weight="3" />
</LinearLayout>
```

Listing 3-63. Master Detail Activity

```java
public class MainActivity extends FragmentActivity implements
        MasterFragment.OnItemSelectedListener {

    private MasterFragment mMaster;
    private DetailFragment mDetail;
```

```java
@Override
protected void onCreate(Bundle savedInstanceState) {
    super.onCreate(savedInstanceState);

    // Enable a progress indicator on the window
    requestWindowFeature(Window.FEATURE_INDETERMINATE_PROGRESS);
    setContentView(R.layout.main);
    setProgressBarIndeterminateVisibility(false);

    // Load the data fragment. If an instance does not exist
    // in the FragmentManager, attach a new one.
    DataFragment fragment =
            (DataFragment) getSupportFragmentManager()
                    .findFragmentByTag(DataFragment.TAG);
    if (fragment == null) {
        fragment = DataFragment.newInstance();
        // We want to retain this instance so we get the same
        // one back on configuration changes.
        fragment.setRetainInstance(true);
        //Attach the fragment with a tag rather than a container id
        FragmentTransaction ft =
                getSupportFragmentManager().beginTransaction();
        ft.add(fragment, DataFragment.TAG);
        ft.commit();
    }

    // Get the details fragment
    mDetail = (DetailFragment) getSupportFragmentManager()
            .findFragmentById(R.id.fragment_detail);

    // Either embed the master fragment or hold onto it to
    // show as a dialog
    mMaster = MasterFragment.newInstance();
    // If the container view exists, embed the fragment
    View container = findViewById(R.id.fragment_master);
    if (container != null) {
        FragmentTransaction ft = getSupportFragmentManager()
                .beginTransaction();
        ft.add(R.id.fragment_master, mMaster);
        ft.commit();
    }
}

@Override
public void onDataItemSelected(DataItem selected) {
    //Pass the selected item to show in the detail view
    mDetail.loadUrl(selected.getUrl());
}

public void onShowClick(View v) {
    //When this button exists and is clicked, show the
    // DetailFragment as a dialog
```

```
            mMaster.show(getSupportFragmentManager(), null);
    }
}
```

We have created two different layouts for portrait (default) orientation and landscape orientation. In the portrait layout, we embed the DetailFragment directly into the UI by using the <fragment> tag. This will automatically create the fragment and attach it when the layout is inflated. In this orientation, the master list will not fit, so we add a button instead that will show the master list as a dialog. In the landscape layout, we have room to display both elements side by side. In this case, we embed the detail view again and then place an empty container view where we will eventually attach the master view.

When the activity is first created, the first thing we do is ensure that a DataFragment is attached to the FragmentManager; if not, we create a new instance and attach it. On this fragment specifically, we call setRetainInstance(), which tells FragmentManager to hold onto this even when a configuration change occurs. This allows the component responsible for the data model to exist only once and not be affected by changes to the user interface.

Fragments are added, removed, or replaced through a FragmentTransaction. This is because fragment operations are asynchronous. All the data associated with a particular operation, such as what operation to perform and whether that operation should be part of the BACK button stack, is set on a particular FragmentTransaction and that transaction is committed.

We obtain the DetailsFragment by using the findFragmentById() method on FragmentManager. Notice that this ID matches the value placed on the <fragment> tag in each layout. The MasterFragment is created in code, and then we decide what to do with it based on the state of the layout. If our empty container exists, we attach the fragment to the FragmentManager, referencing the ID of the container where we want the content view to display. This effectively embeds the MasterFragment into the view hierarchy. If the container view is not there, we do nothing further because the fragment will be shown later.

In a portrait layout, the user can press the Show List button, which will call show() on our MasterFragment, causing it to display inside a dialog. It is also at this point that the MasterFragment gets attached to the FragmentManager. Remember that, when a user clicks an option in the list, the listener interface method will be called. This activity forwards that selection on to the DetailsFragment for the content to be displayed in the WebView.

You can see in Figures 3-20 and 3-21 how the application displays in portrait and landscape orientation.

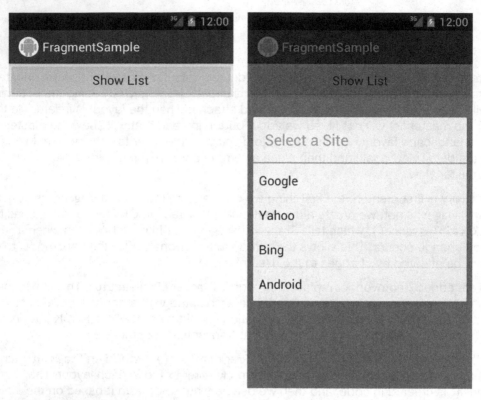

Figure 3-20. Portrait layout (left) and dialog display (right)

Figure 3-21. Landscape layout with fragments side by side

Fragments are a fantastic way to break up your code into modules that can be reorganized and reused in order to allow your application to scale easily to multiple device types while staying easy to maintain.

Summary

In this chapter, we explored a number of techniques that we can use to build a compelling user interface that conforms to the design guidelines that Google has set forth for the Android platform. We started out looking at how to effectively use the action bar interface elements in applications. We explored managing configuration changes such as device orientation in creative ways. You saw techniques for managing user input through text and touch handling. Finally, you were exposed to implementing common navigation patterns such as the drawer layout and swipe-paging views.

In the next chapter, we will look at using the SDK to communicate with the outside world by accessing network resources and talking to other devices by using technologies such as USB and Bluetooth.

4

Communications and Networking

The key to many successful mobile applications is their ability to connect and interact with remote data sources. Web services and APIs are abundant in today's world, allowing an application to interact with just about any service, from weather forecasts to personal financial information. Bringing this data into the palm of a user's hand and making it accessible from anywhere is one of the greatest powers of the mobile platform. Android builds on the web foundations that Google is known for and provides a rich toolset for communicating with the outside world.

4-1. Displaying Web Information

Problem

HTML or image data from the Web needs to be presented in the application without any modification or processing.

Solution

(API Level 1)

Display the information in a WebView. WebView is a view widget that can be embedded in any layout to display web content, both local and remote, in your application. WebView is based on the same open source WebKit technology that powers the Android Browser application, affording applications the same level of power and capability.

How It Works

WebView has some very desirable properties when displaying assets downloaded from the Web, not the least of which are two-dimensional scrolling (horizontal and vertical at the same time) and zoom controls. A WebView can be the perfect place to house a large image, such as a stadium map, in which the user may want to pan and zoom around. Here we will discuss how to do this with both local and remote assets.

Display a URL

The simplest case is displaying an HTML page or image by supplying the URL of the resource to the WebView. The following are a handful of practical uses for this technique in your applications:

- Provide access to your corporate site without leaving the application.

- Display a page of live content from a web server, such as an FAQ section, that can be changed without requiring an upgrade to the application.

- Display a large image resource that the user would want to interact with using pan/zoom.

Let's take a look at a simple example that loads a very popular web page inside the content view of an activity instead of within the browser (see Listings 4-1 and 4-2).

Listing 4-1. Activity Containing a WebView

```
public class MyActivity extends Activity {
    @Override
    public void onCreate(Bundle savedInstanceState) {
        super.onCreate(savedInstanceState);

        WebView webview = new WebView(this);
        //Enable JavaScript support
        webview.getSettings().setJavaScriptEnabled(true);
        webview.loadUrl("http://www.google.com/");

        setContentView(webview);
    }
}
```

> **Note**   By default, WebView has JavaScript support disabled. Be sure to enable JavaScript in the WebView.WebSettings object if the content you are displaying requires it.

Listing 4-2. AndroidManifest.xml Setting the Required Permissions

```xml
<?xml version="1.0" encoding="utf-8"?>
<manifest
    xmlns:android="http://schemas.android.com/apk/res/android"
    package="com.examples.webview"
    android:versionCode="1"
    android:versionName="1.0">

    <uses-permission android:name="android.permission.INTERNET" />

    <application android:icon="@drawable/icon"
        android:label="@string/app_name">
        <activity android:name=".MyActivity">
            <intent-filter>
                <action
                    android:name="android.intent.action.MAIN" />
                <category
                    android:name="android.intent.category.LAUNCHER" />
            </intent-filter>
        </activity>
    </application>
</manifest>
```

Important   If the content you are loading into WebView is remote, AndroidManifest.xml must declare that it uses the android.permission.INTERNET permission.

The result displays the HTML page in your activity (see Figure 4-1).

Figure 4-1. HTML page in a WebView

Local Assets

WebView is also quite useful in displaying local content to take advantage of either HTML/CSS formatting or the pan/zoom behavior it provides to its contents. You may use the assets directory of your Android project to store resources you would like to display in a WebView, such as large images or HTML files. To better organize the assets, you may also create subdirectories under assets to store files in.

WebView.loadUrl() can display files stored under assets by using the file:///android_asset/<resource path> URL schema. For example, if the file android.jpg was placed into the assets directory, it could be loaded into a WebView using the following URL:

file:///android_asset/android.jpg

If that same file were placed in a directory named images under assets, WebView could load it with the following URL:

file:///android_asset/images/android.jpg

In addition, WebView.loadData() will load raw HTML stored in a string resource or variable into the view. Using this technique, preformatted HTML text could be stored in res/values/strings.xml or downloaded from a remote API and displayed in the application.

Listings 4-3 and 4-4 show an example activity with two WebView widgets stacked vertically on top of one another. The upper view is displaying a large image file stored in the assets directory, and the lower view is displaying an HTML string stored in the application's string resources.

Listing 4-3. res/layout/main.xml

```
<LinearLayout
  xmlns:android="http://schemas.android.com/apk/res/android"
  android:layout_width="match_parent"
  android:layout_height="match_parent"
  android:orientation="vertical">
  <WebView
    android:id="@+id/upperview"
    android:layout_width="match_parent"
    android:layout_height="match_parent"
    android:layout_weight="1"
  />
  <WebView
    android:id="@+id/lowerview"
    android:layout_width="match_parent"
    android:layout_height="match_parent"
    android:layout_weight="1"
  />
</LinearLayout>
```

Listing 4-4. Activity to Display Local Web Content

```
public class MyActivity extends Activity {
    @Override
    public void onCreate(Bundle savedInstanceState) {
        super.onCreate(savedInstanceState);
        setContentView(R.layout.main);

        WebView upperView = (WebView)findViewById(R.id.upperview);
        //Zoom feature must be enabled
        upperView.getSettings().setBuiltInZoomControls(true);
        upperView.loadUrl("file:///android_asset/android.jpg");

        WebView lowerView = (WebView)findViewById(R.id.lowerview);
        String htmlString =
                "<h1>Header</h1><p>This is HTML text<br />"
                + "<i>Formatted in italics</i></p>";
        lowerView.loadData(htmlString, "text/html", "utf-8");
    }
}
```

When the activity is displayed, each WebView occupies half of the screen's vertical space. The HTML string is formatted as expected, while the large image can be scrolled both horizontally and vertically; the user may even zoom in or out (see Figure 4-2).

Header

This is HTML text
Formatted in italics

Figure 4-2. Two WebViews displaying local resources

4-2. Intercepting WebView Events

Problem

Your application is using a WebView to display content, but it also needs to listen and respond to users clicking links on the page.

Solution

(API Level 1)

Implement a WebViewClient and attach it to the WebView. WebViewClient and WebChromeClient are two WebKit classes that allow an application to get event callbacks and customize the behavior of the WebView. By default, WebView will pass a URL to the ActivityManager to be handled if no WebViewClient is present, which usually results in any clicked link loading in the Browser application instead of the current WebView.

How It Works

In Listing 4-5, we create an activity with a WebView that will handle its own URL loading.

Listing 4-5. Activity with a WebView That Handles URLs

```java
public class MyActivity extends Activity {
    @Override
    public void onCreate(Bundle savedInstanceState) {
        super.onCreate(savedInstanceState);

        WebView webview = new WebView(this);
        webview.getSettings().setJavaScriptEnabled(true);
        //Add a client to the view
        webview.setWebViewClient(new WebViewClient());
        webview.loadUrl("http://www.google.com");
        setContentView(webview);
    }
}
```

In this example, simply providing a plain vanilla WebViewClient to WebView allows it to handle any URL requests itself, instead of passing them up to the ActivityManager, so clicking a link will load the requested page inside the same view. This is because the default implementation simply returns false for shouldOverrideUrlLoading(), which tells the client to pass the URL to the WebView and not to the application.

In this next case, we will take advantage of the WebViewClient.shouldOverrideUrlLoading() callback to intercept and monitor user activity (see Listing 4-6).

Listing 4-6. Activity That Intercepts WebView URLs

```java
public class MyActivity extends Activity {
    @Override
    public void onCreate(Bundle savedInstanceState) {
        super.onCreate(savedInstanceState);

        WebView webview = new WebView(this);
        webview.getSettings().setJavaScriptEnabled(true);
        //Add a client to the view
        webview.setWebViewClient(mClient);
        webview.loadUrl("http://www.google.com");
        setContentView(webview);
    }

    private WebViewClient mClient = new WebViewClient() {
        @Override
        public boolean shouldOverrideUrlLoading(WebView view,
                String url) {
            Uri request = Uri.parse(url);
```

```
            if(TextUtils.equals(request.getAuthority(),
                    "www.google.com")) {
                //Allow the load
                return false;
            }

            Toast.makeText(MyActivity.this,
                    "Sorry, buddy",
                    Toast.LENGTH_SHORT).show();
            return true;
        }
    };
}
```

In this example, shouldOverrideUrlLoading() determines whether to load the content back
in this WebView based on the URL it was passed, keeping the user from leaving Google's site.
Uri.getAuthority() returns the hostname portion of a URL, and we use that to check whether
the link the user clicked is on Google's domain (www.google.com). If we can verify that the link is to
another Google page, returning false allows the WebView to load the content. If not, we notify the
user and, returning true, tell the WebViewClient that the application has taken care of this URL and
not to allow the WebView to load it.

This technique can be more sophisticated, enabling the application to actually handle the URL by
doing something interesting. A custom schema could even be developed to create a full interface
between your application and the WebView content.

4-3. Accessing WebView with JavaScript

Problem

Your application needs access to the raw HTML of the current contents displayed in a WebView,
either to read or modify specific values.

Solution

(API Level 1)

Create a JavaScript interface to bridge between the WebView and application code.

How It Works

WebView.addJavascriptInterface() binds a Java object to JavaScript so that its methods can then
be called within the WebView. Using this interface, JavaScript can be used to marshal data between
your application code and the WebView's HTML.

> **Caution** Allowing JavaScript to control your application can inherently present a security threat, allowing remote execution of application code. This interface should be utilized with that possibility in mind.

Let's look at an example of this in action. Listing 4-7 presents a simple HTML form to be loaded into the WebView from the local assets directory. Listing 4-8 is an activity that uses two JavaScript functions to exchange data between the activity preferences and content in the WebView.

Listing 4-7. assets/form.html

```html
<!DOCTYPE HTML PUBLIC "-//W3C//DTD HTML 4.01//EN"
    "http://www.w3.org/TR/html4/strict.dtd">
<html>

<form name="input" action="form.html" method="get">
Enter Email: <input type="text" id="emailAddress" />
<input type="submit" value="Submit" />
</form>

</html>
```

Listing 4-8. Activity with JavaScript Bridge Interface

```java
public class MyActivity extends Activity {
    @Override
    public void onCreate(Bundle savedInstanceState) {
        super.onCreate(savedInstanceState);

        WebView webview = new WebView(this);
        //JavaScript is not enabled by default
        webview.getSettings().setJavaScriptEnabled(true);
        webview.setWebViewClient(mClient);
        //Attach the custom interface to the view
        webview.addJavascriptInterface(new MyJavaScriptInterface(), "BRIDGE");

        setContentView(webview);

        webview.loadUrl("file:///android_asset/form.html");
    }

    private static final String JS_SETELEMENT =
            "javascript:document.getElementById('%s').value='%s'";
    private static final String JS_GETELEMENT =
            "javascript:window.BRIDGE"
            + ".storeElement('%s',document.getElementById('%s').value)";
    private static final String ELEMENTID = "emailAddress";
```

```
    private WebViewClient mClient = new WebViewClient() {
        @Override
        public boolean shouldOverrideUrlLoading(WebView view, String url) {
            //Before leaving the page, attempt to retrieve the email
            // using JavaScript
            executeJavascript(view,
                    String.format(JS_GETELEMENT, ELEMENTID, ELEMENTID) );
            return false;
        }

        @Override
        public void onPageFinished(WebView view, String url) {
            //When page loads, inject address into page using JavaScript
            SharedPreferences prefs = getPreferences(Activity.MODE_PRIVATE);
            executeJavascript(view, String.format(JS_SETELEMENT, ELEMENTID,
                    prefs.getString(ELEMENTID, "")) );
        }
    };

    private void executeJavascript(WebView view, String script) {
        if (Build.VERSION.SDK_INT >= Build.VERSION_CODES.KITKAT) {
            view.evaluateJavascript(script, null);
        } else {
            view.loadUrl(script);
        }
    }

    private class MyJavaScriptInterface {
        //Store an element in preferences
        @JavascriptInterface
        public void storeElement(String id, String element) {
            SharedPreferences.Editor edit =
                    getPreferences(Activity.MODE_PRIVATE).edit();
            edit.putString(id, element);
            edit.commit();
            //If element is valid, raise a Toast
            if(!TextUtils.isEmpty(element)) {
                Toast.makeText(MyActivity.this, element, Toast.LENGTH_SHORT)
                        .show();
            }
        }
    }
}
```

In this somewhat contrived example, a single element form is created in HTML and displayed in a WebView. In the activity code, we look for a form value in the WebView with the ID of emailAddress, and its value is saved to SharedPreferences every time a link is clicked on the page (in this case, the Submit button of the form) through the shouldOverrideUrlLoading() callback. Whenever the page finished loading (that is, onPageFinished() is called), we attempt to inject the current value from SharedPreferences back into the web form.

> **Note**   JavaScript is not enabled by default in WebView. In order to inject or even simply render JavaScript, we must call WebSettings.setJavaScriptEnabled(true) when initializing the view.

A Java class is created called MyJavaScriptInterface, which defines the method storeElement(). When the view is created, we call the WebView.addJavascriptInterface() method to attach this object to the view and give it the name BRIDGE. When calling this method, the string parameter is a name used to reference the interface inside JavaScript code.

We have defined two JavaScript methods as constant strings here: JS_GETELEMENT and JS_SETELEMENT. Prior to Android 4.4, we executed these methods on the WebView by calling the same loadUrl() method we've seen before. However, in API Level 19 and beyond, we have a new method on WebView named evaluateJavascript() for this purpose. The example code verifies the API level currently in use and calls the appropriate method.

Notice that JS_GETELEMENT is a reference to calling our custom interface function (referenced as BRIDGE.storeElement), which will call that method on MyJavaScriptInterface and store the form element's value in preferences. If the value retrieved from the form is not blank, a Toast will also be raised.

Any JavaScript may be executed on the WebView in this manner, and it does not need to be a method included as part of the custom interface. JS_SETELEMENT, for example, uses pure JavaScript to set the value of the form element on the page.

One popular application of this technique is to remember form data that a user may need to enter in the application, but the form must be web based, such as a reservation form or payment form for a web application that doesn't have a lower-level API to access.

4-4. Downloading an Image File

Problem

Your application needs to download and display an image from the Web or another remote server.

Solution

(API Level 3)

Use AsyncTask to download the data in a background thread. AsyncTask is a wrapper class that makes threading long-running operations into the background painless and simple; it also manages concurrency with an internal thread pool. In addition to handling the background threading, callback methods are provided before, during, and after the operation executes, allowing you to make any updates required on the main UI thread.

How It Works

In the context of downloading an image, let's create a subclass of ImageView called WebImageView, which will lazily load an image from a remote source and display it as soon as it is available. The downloading will be performed inside an AsyncTask operation (see Listing 4-9).

Listing 4-9. WebImageView

```java
public class WebImageView extends ImageView {

    private Drawable mPlaceholder, mImage;

    public WebImageView(Context context) {
        this(context, null);
    }

    public WebImageView(Context context, AttributeSet attrs) {
        this(context, attrs, 0);
    }

    public WebImageView(Context context, AttributeSet attrs,
            int defStyle) {
        super(context, attrs, defaultStyle);
    }

    public void setPlaceholderImage(Drawable drawable) {
        mPlaceholder = drawable;
        if(mImage == null) {
            setImageDrawable(mPlaceholder);
        }
    }

    public void setPlaceholderImage(int resid) {
        mPlaceholder = getResources().getDrawable(resid);
        if(mImage == null) {
            setImageDrawable(mPlaceholder);
        }
    }

    public void setImageUrl(String url) {
        DownloadTask task = new DownloadTask();
        task.execute(url);
    }

    private class DownloadTask extends
            AsyncTask<String, Void, Bitmap> {
        @Override
        protected Bitmap doInBackground(String... params) {
            String url = params[0];
            try {
                URLConnection connection =
                        (new URL(url)).openConnection();
```

```
            InputStream is = connection.getInputStream();
            BufferedInputStream bis =
                    new BufferedInputStream(is);

            ByteArrayBuffer baf = new ByteArrayBuffer(50);
            int current = 0;
            while ((current = bis.read()) != -1) {
                baf.append((byte)current);
            }
            byte[] imageData = baf.toByteArray();
            return BitmapFactory.decodeByteArray(imageData, 0,
                    imageData.length);
        } catch (Exception exc) {
            return null;
        }
    }

    @Override
    protected void onPostExecute(Bitmap result) {
        mImage = new BitmapDrawable(result);
        if(mImage != null) {
            setImageDrawable(mImage);
        }
    }
  };
}
```

As you can see, WebImageView is a simple extension of the Android ImageView widget. The setPlaceholderImage() methods allow a local drawable to be set as the display image until the remote content is finished downloading. The bulk of the interesting work begins after the view has been given a remote URL using setImageUrl(), at which point the custom AsyncTask begins work.

Notice that an AsyncTask is strongly typed with three values for the input parameter, progress value, and result. In this case, a string is passed to the task's execute() method and the background operation should return a Bitmap. The middle value, the progress, we are not using in this example, so it is set as Void. When extending AsyncTask, the only required method to implement is doInBackground(), which defines the chunk of work to be run on a background thread. In the previous example, this is where a connection is made to the remote URL provided, and the image is downloaded. Upon completion, we attempt to create a Bitmap from the downloaded data. If an error occurs at any point, the operation will abort and return null.

The other callback methods defined in AsyncTask, such as onPreExecute(), onPostExecute(), and onProgressUpdate(), are called on the main thread for the purposes of updating the user interface. In the previous example, onPostExecute() is used to update the view's image with the result data.

Important   Android UI classes are not thread-safe. Be sure to use one of the callback methods that occur on the main thread to make any updates to the UI. Do not update views from within doInBackground().

Listings 4-10 and 4-11 show simple examples of using this class in an activity. Because this class is not part of the `android.widget` or `android.view` packages, we must write the fully qualified package name when using it in XML.

Listing 4-10. `res/layout/main.xml`

```xml
<?xml version="1.0" encoding="utf-8"?>
<LinearLayout
    xmlns:android="http://schemas.android.com/apk/res/android"
    android:layout_width="match_parent"
    android:layout_height="match_parent"
    android:orientation="vertical">
    <com.examples.WebImageView
        android:id="@+id/webImage"
        android:layout_width="wrap_content"
        android:layout_height="wrap_content" />
</LinearLayout>
```

Listing 4-11. Example Activity

```java
public class WebImageActivity extends Activity {
    @Override
    public void onCreate(Bundle savedInstanceState) {
        super.onCreate(savedInstanceState);
        setContentView(R.layout.main);

        WebImageView imageView =
                (WebImageView) findViewById(R.id.webImage);
        imageView.setPlaceholderImage(R.drawable.icon);
        imageView.setImageUrl(
          "http://apress.com/resource/weblogo/Apress_120x90.gif");
    }
}
```

In this example, we first set a local image (the application icon) as the `WebImageView` placeholder. This image is displayed immediately to the user. We then tell the view to fetch an image of the Apress logo from the Web. As noted previously, this downloads the image in the background and, when it is complete, replaces the placeholder image in the view. It is this simplicity in creating background operations that has led the Android team to refer to `AsyncTask` as *painless threading*.

4-5. Downloading Completely in the Background

Problem

The application must download a large resource to the device, such as a movie file, that must not require the user to keep the application active.

Solution

(API Level 9)

Use the `DownloadManager` API. The `DownloadManager` is a service added to the SDK with API Level 9 that allows a long-running download to be handed off and managed completely by the system. The primary advantage of using this service is that `DownloadManager` will continue attempting to download the resource despite failures, connection changes, and even device reboots.

How It Works

Listing 4-12 is a sample activity that uses `DownloadManager` to handle the download of a large image file. When complete, the image is displayed in an `ImageView`. Whenever you utilize `DownloadManager` to access content from the Web, be sure to declare you are using the `android.permission.INTERNET` in the application's manifest.

Listing 4-12. DownloadManager Sample Activity

```java
public class DownloadActivity extends Activity {

    private static final String DL_ID = "downloadId";
    private SharedPreferences prefs;

    private DownloadManager dm;
    private ImageView imageView;

    @Override
    public void onCreate(Bundle savedInstanceState) {
        super.onCreate(savedInstanceState);
        imageView = new ImageView(this);
        setContentView(imageView);

        prefs =
            PreferenceManager.getDefaultSharedPreferences(this);
        dm = (DownloadManager)getSystemService(DOWNLOAD_SERVICE);
    }

    @Override
    public void onResume() {
        super.onResume();

        if(!prefs.contains(DL_ID)) {
            //Start the download
            Uri resource = Uri.parse(
                    "http://www.bigfoto.com/dog-animal.jpg");
            DownloadManager.Request request =
                    new DownloadManager.Request(resource);
            //Set allowed connections to process download
            request.setAllowedNetworkTypes(Request.NETWORK_MOBILE
                    | Request.NETWORK_WIFI);
            request.setAllowedOverRoaming(false);
```

```java
            //Display in the notification bar
            request.setTitle("Download Sample");
            long id = dm.enqueue(request);
            //Save the unique id
            prefs.edit().putLong(DL_ID, id).commit();
        } else {
            //Download already started, check status
            queryDownloadStatus();
        }

        registerReceiver(receiver, new IntentFilter(
                DownloadManager.ACTION_DOWNLOAD_COMPLETE));
    }

    @Override
    public void onPause() {
        super.onPause();
        unregisterReceiver(receiver);
    }

    private BroadcastReceiver receiver = new BroadcastReceiver() {
        @Override
        public void onReceive(Context context, Intent intent) {
            queryDownloadStatus();
        }
    };

    private void queryDownloadStatus() {
        DownloadManager.Query query = new DownloadManager.Query();
        query.setFilterById(prefs.getLong(DL_ID, 0));
        Cursor c = dm.query(query);

        if(c.moveToFirst()) {
            int status = c.getInt(
                c.getColumnIndex(DownloadManager.COLUMN_STATUS));

            switch(status) {
            case DownloadManager.STATUS_PAUSED:
            case DownloadManager.STATUS_PENDING:
            case DownloadManager.STATUS_RUNNING:
                //Do nothing, still in progress
                break;
            case DownloadManager.STATUS_SUCCESSFUL:
                //Done, display the image
                try {
                    ParcelFileDescriptor file =
                        dm.openDownloadedFile(
                            prefs.getLong(DL_ID, 0) );
                    FileInputStream fis = new ParcelFileDescriptor
                        .AutoCloseInputStream(file);
```

```
        imageView.setImageBitmap(
            BitmapFactory.decodeStream(fis));
    } catch (Exception e) {
        e.printStackTrace();
    }
    break;
case DownloadManager.STATUS_FAILED:
    //Clear the download and try again later
    dm.remove(prefs.getLong(DL_ID, 0));
    prefs.edit().clear().commit();
    break;
    }
  }
 }
}
```

Important As of this book's publishing date, there is a bug in the SDK that throws an Exception claiming `android.permission.ACCESS_ALL_DOWNLOADS` is required to use `DownloadManager`. This Exception is actually thrown when `android.permission.INTERNET` is not in your manifest.

This example does all of its useful work in the `Activity.onResume()` method so the application can determine the status of the download each time the user returns to the activity. Downloads within the manager can be references using a long ID value that is returned when `DownloadManager.enqueue()` is called. In the example, we persist that value in the application's preferences in order to monitor and retrieve the downloaded content at any time.

Upon the first launch of the example application, a `DownloadManager.Request` object is created to represent the content to download. At a minimum, this request needs the `Uri` of the remote resource. However, there are many useful properties to set on the request as well to control its behavior. Some of the useful properties include the following:

- `Request.setAllowedNetworkTypes()`: Set specific network types over which the download may be retrieved.

- `Request.setAllowedOverRoaming()`: Set if the download is allowed to occur while the device is on a roaming connection.

- `Request.setDescription()`: Set a description to be displayed in the system notification for the download.

- `Request.setTitle()`: Set a title to be displayed in the system notification for the download.

Once an ID has been obtained, the application uses that value to check the status of the download. By registering a `BroadcastReceiver` to listen for the `ACTION_DOWNLOAD_COMPLETE` broadcast, the application will react to the download finishing by setting the image file on the activity's `ImageView`. If the activity is paused while the download completes, upon the next resume the status will be checked and the `ImageView` content will be set.

It is important to note that `ACTION_DOWNLOAD_COMPLETE` is a broadcast sent by the `DownloadManager` for every download it may be managing. Because of this, we still must check that the download ID we are interested in is really ready.

Destinations

In Listing 4-12, we never told the `DownloadManager` where to place the file. Instead, when we wanted to access the file, we used the `DownloadManager.openDownloadedFile()` method with the ID value stored in preferences to get a `ParcelFileDescriptor`, which can be turned into a stream the application can read from. This is a simple and straightforward way to gain access to the downloaded content, but it has some caveats to be aware of.

Without a specific destination, files are downloaded to the shared download cache, where the system retains the right to delete them at any time to reclaim space. Downloading in this fashion is a convenient way to get data quickly, but if your needs for the download are more long-term, a permanent destination should be specified on external storage by using one of the `DownloadManager.Request` methods:

- `Request.setDestinationInExternalFilesDir()`: Set the destination to a hidden directory on external storage.

- `Request.setDestinationInExternalPublicDir()`: Set the destination to a public directory on external storage.

- `Request.setDestinationUri()`: Set the destination to a file `Uri` located on external storage.

> **Note**   All destination methods writing to external storage will require your application to declare use of `android.permission.WRITE_EXTERNAL_STORAGE` in the manifest.

Files without an explicit destination also often get removed when `DownloadManager.remove()` gets called to clear the entry from the manager list or the user clears the downloads list; files downloaded to external storage will not be removed by the system under these conditions.

4-6. Accessing a REST API
Problem

Your application needs to access a RESTful API over HTTP to interact with the web services of a remote host.

> **Note**   *REST* stands for *Representational State Transfer*. It is a common architectural style for web services today. RESTful APIs are typically built using standard HTTP verbs to create requests of the remote resource, and the responses are typically returned in a structured document format, such as XML, JSON, or comma-separated values (CSV).

Solution

There are two recommended ways to use HTTP to send and receive data over a network connection in Android: the first is the Apache HttpClient, and the second is the Java HttpURLConnection. The decision about which to use in your application should be based primarily on what versions of Android you aim to support.

(API Level 3)

If you are targeting earlier Android versions, use the Apache HTTP classes inside an AsyncTask. Android includes the Apache HTTP components library, which provides a robust method of creating connections to remote APIs. The Apache library includes classes to create GET, POST, PUT, and DELETE requests with ease, as well as providing support for Secure Sockets Layer (SSL), cookie storage, authentication, and other HTTP requirements that your specific API may have in its HttpClient.

The other primary advantage of this approach is the level of abstraction provided by the Apache library. Applications require very little code to do most network operations over HTTP. Much of the lower-level transaction code is hidden away from the developer.

One major disadvantage is that the version of the Apache components bundled with Android does not include MultipartEntity, a class that is necessary to do binary or multipart form data POST transactions. If you need this functionality and want to use HttpClient, you must pull in a newer version of the components library as an external JAR.

(API Level 9)

Use the Java HttpURLConnection class inside an AsyncTask. This class has been part of the Android framework since API Level 1 but has been the recommended method for network I/O only since the release of Android 2.3. The primary reason for this is that there were a few bugs in its implementation prior to that, which made HttpClient a more stable choice. However, moving forward, HttpURLConnection is where the Android team will continue to make performance and stability enhancements, so it is the recommended implementation choice.

The biggest advantage to using HttpURLConnection is performance. The classes are lightweight, and newer versions of Android have response compression and other enhancements built in. Its API is also lower level, so it is more ubiquitous, and implementing any type of HTTP transaction is possible. The drawback to this is that it requires more coding by the developer (but isn't that why you bought this book?).

How It Works

HttpClient

Let's look first at using HTTP with the Apache `HttpClient`. Listing 4-13 is an `AsyncTask` that can process any `HttpUriRequest` and return the string response.

Listing 4-13. AsyncTask Processing HttpRequest

```
public class RestTask extends
        AsyncTask<HttpUriRequest, Void, Object> {
    private static final String TAG = "RestTask";

    public interface ResponseCallback {
        public void onRequestSuccess(String response);
        public void onRequestError(Exception error);
    }

    private AbstractHttpClient mClient;

    private WeakReference<ResponseCallback> mCallback;

    public RestTask() {
        this(new DefaultHttpClient());
    }

    public RestTask(AbstractHttpClient client) {
        mClient = client;
    }

    public void setResponseCallback(ResponseCallback callback) {
        mCallback = new WeakReference<ResponseCallback>(callback);
    }

    @Override
    protected Object doInBackground(HttpUriRequest… params) {
        try{
            HttpUriRequest request = params[0];
            HttpResponse serverResponse =
                    mClient.execute(request);

            BasicResponseHandler handler =
                    new BasicResponseHandler();
            String response =
                    handler.handleResponse(serverResponse);
            return response;
        } catch (Exception e) {
            Log.w(TAG, e);
            return e;
        }
    }
}
```

```
    @Override
    protected void onPostExecute(Object result) {
        if (mCallback != null && mCallback.get() != null) {
            final ResponseCallback callback = mCallback.get();
            if (result instanceof String) {
                callback.onRequestSuccess((String) result);
            } else if (result instanceof Exception) {
                callback.onRequestError((Exception) result);
            } else {
                callback.onRequestError(new IOException(
                        "Unknown Error Contacting Host") );
            }
        }
    }
}

}
```

The RestTask can be constructed with or without an HttpClient parameter. The reason for allowing this is so multiple requests can use the same client object. This is extremely useful if your API requires cookies to maintain a session or if there is a specific set of required parameters that are easier to set up once (for example, SSL stores). The task takes an HttpUriRequest parameter to process (of which HttpGet, HttpPost, HttpPut, and HttpDelete are all subclasses) and executes it.

A BasicResponseHandler processes the response, which is a convenience class that abstracts our task from needing to check the response for errors. BasicResponseHandler will return the HTTP response as a string if the response code is 1XX or 2XX, but it will throw an HttpResponseException if the response code is 300 or greater.

The final important piece of this class exists in onPostExecute(), after the interaction with the API is complete. RestTask has an optional callback interface that will be notified when the request is complete (with a string of the response data) or an error has occurred (with the exception that was triggered). This callback is stored in the form of a WeakReference so that we can safely use an activity or other system component as the callback, without worrying about a running task keeping that component from being removed if it gets paused or stopped. Now let's use this powerful new tool to create some basic API requests.

GET Example

In the following example, we utilize the Google Custom Search REST API. This API takes a few parameters for each request:

- ▓ key: Unique value to identify the application making the request
- ▓ cx: Identifier for the custom search engine you want to access
- ▓ q: String representing the search query you want to execute

> **Note**   Visit https://developers.google.com/custom-search/ to receive more information about this API.

A GET request is the simplest and most common request in many public APIs. Parameters that must be sent with the request are encoded into the URL string itself, so no additional data must be provided. Let's create a GET request to search for *Android* (see Listing 4-14).

Listing 4-14. Activity Executing API GET Request

```java
public class SearchActivity extends Activity implements
        ResponseCallback {

    private static final String SEARCH_URI =
            "https://www.googleapis.com/customsearch/v1"
            + "?key=%s&cx=%s&q=%s";
    private static final String SEARCH_KEY =
            "AIzaSyBbW-W1SHCK4eWOkK74VGMLJj_b-byNzkI";
    private static final String SEARCH_CX =
            "008212991319514020231:1mkouq8yagw";
    private static final String SEARCH_QUERY = "Android";

    private TextView mResult;
    private ProgressDialog mProgress;

    @Override
    public void onCreate(Bundle savedInstanceState) {
        super.onCreate(savedInstanceState);
        ScrollView scrollView = new ScrollView(this);
        mResult = new TextView(this);
        scrollView.addView(mResult, new ViewGroup.LayoutParams(
                LayoutParams.MATCH_PARENT,
                LayoutParams.WRAP_CONTENT) );
        setContentView(scrollView);

        try{
            //Simple GET
            String url = String.format(SEARCH_URI, SEARCH_KEY,
                    SEARCH_CX, SEARCH_QUERY);
            HttpGet searchRequest = new HttpGet(url);

            RestTask task = new RestTask();
            task.setResponseCallback(this);
            task.execute(searchRequest);

            //Display progress to the user
            mProgress = ProgressDialog.show(this, "Searching",
                    "Waiting For Results…", true);
        } catch (Exception e) {
            mResult.setText(e.getMessage());
        }
    }
}
```

```java
    @Override
    public void onRequestSuccess(String response) {
        //Clear progress indicator
        if(mProgress != null) {
            mProgress.dismiss();
        }

        //Process the response data (here we just display it)
        mResult.setText(response);
    }

    @Override
    public void onRequestError(Exception error) {
        //Clear progress indicator
        if(mProgress != null) {
            mProgress.dismiss();
        }

        //Process the response data (here we just display it)
        mResult.setText(error.getMessage());
    }
}
```

In the example, we create the type of HTTP request that we need with the URL that we want to connect to (in this case, a GET request to googleapis.com). The URL is stored as a constant format string, and the required parameters for the Google API are added at runtime just before the request is created.

A RestTask is created with the activity set as its callback, and the task is executed. When the task is complete, either onRequestSuccess() or onRequestError() will be called and, in the case of a success, the API response can be unpacked and processed. We will discuss parsing structured XML and JSON responses like this one in Recipes 4-7 and 4-8, so for now the example simply displays the raw response to the user interface.

POST Example

Many times, APIs require that you provide some data as part of the request, perhaps an authentication token or the contents of a search query. The API will require you to send the request over HTTP POST so these values may be encoded into the request body instead of the URL. To demonstrate a working POST, we will be sending a request to httpbin.org, which is a development site designed to read and validate the contents of a request and echo them back (see Listing 4-15).

Listing 4-15. Activity Executing API POST Request

```java
public class SearchActivity extends Activity implements
        ResponseCallback {

    private static final String POST_URI =
            "http://httpbin.org/post";

    private TextView mResult;
    private ProgressDialog mProgress;
```

```java
@Override
public void onCreate(Bundle savedInstanceState) {
    super.onCreate(savedInstanceState);
    ScrollView scrollView = new ScrollView(this);
    mResult = new TextView(this);
    scrollView.addView(mResult, new ViewGroup.LayoutParams(
            LayoutParams.MATCH_PARENT,
            LayoutParams.WRAP_CONTENT));
    setContentView(scrollView);

    try{
        //Simple POST
        HttpPost postRequest =
                new HttpPost( new URI(POST_URI) );
        List<NameValuePair> parameters =
                new ArrayList<NameValuePair>();
        parameters.add(new BasicNameValuePair("title",
                "Android Recipes") );
        parameters.add(new BasicNameValuePair("summary",
                "Learn Android Quickly") );
        parameters.add(new BasicNameValuePair("author",
                "Smith"));
        postRequest.setEntity(
                new UrlEncodedFormEntity(parameters));

        RestTask task = new RestTask();
        task.setResponseCallback(this);
        task.execute(postRequest);

        //Display progress to the user
        mProgress = ProgressDialog.show(this, "Searching",
                "Waiting For Results…", true);
    } catch (Exception e) {
        mResult.setText(e.getMessage());
    }
}

@Override
public void onRequestSuccess(String response) {
    //Clear progress indicator
    if(mProgress != null) {
        mProgress.dismiss();
    }

    //Process the response data (here we just display it)
    mResult.setText(response);
}
```

```
    @Override
    public void onRequestError(Exception error) {
        //Clear progress indicator
        if(mProgress != null) {
            mProgress.dismiss();
        }

        //Process the response data (here we just display it)
        mResult.setText(error.getMessage());
    }
}
```

Notice in this example that the parameters passed to the API are encoded into an HttpEntity instead of passed directly in the request URL. The request created in this case is an HttpPost instance, which is still a subclass of HttpUriRequest (like HttpGet), so we can use the same RestTask to run the operation. As with the GET example, we will discuss parsing structured XML and JSON responses like this one in Recipes 4-7 and 4-8, so for now the example simply displays the raw response to the user interface.

> **Reminder**   The Apache library bundled with the Android SDK does not include support for multipart HTTP POSTs. However, MultipartEntity, from the publicly available org.apache.http.mime library, is compatible and can be brought in to your project as an external source.

Basic Authorization

Another common requirement for working with an API is some form of authentication. Standards are emerging for REST API authentication such as OAuth 2.0, but a common authentication method is still a basic username and password authorization over HTTP. In Listing 4-16, we modify the RestTask to enable authentication in the HTTP header per request.

Listing 4-16. RestTask with Basic Authorization

```
public class RestAuthTask extends
        AsyncTask<HttpUriRequest, Void, Object> {
    private static final String TAG = "RestTask";

    private static final String AUTH_USER = "user@mydomain.com";
    private static final String AUTH_PASS = "password";

    public interface ResponseCallback {
        public void onRequestSuccess(String response);

        public void onRequestError(Exception error);
    }

    private AbstractHttpClient mClient;
    private WeakReference<ResponseCallback> mCallback;
```

```java
    public RestAuthTask(boolean authenticate) {
        this(new DefaultHttpClient(), authenticate);

    }

    public RestAuthTask(AbstractHttpClient client,
            boolean authenticate) {
        mClient = client;
        if(authenticate) {
            UsernamePasswordCredentials creds =
                    new UsernamePasswordCredentials(
                            AUTH_USER, AUTH_PASS);
            mClient.getCredentialsProvider()
                    .setCredentials(AuthScope.ANY, creds);
        }
    }

    @Override
    protected Object doInBackground(HttpUriRequest… params) {
        try{
            HttpUriRequest request = params[0];
            HttpResponse serverResponse =
                    mClient.execute(request);

            BasicResponseHandler handler =
                    new BasicResponseHandler();
            String response =
                    handler.handleResponse(serverResponse);
            return response;
        } catch (Exception e) {
            Log.w(TAG, e);
            return e;
        }
    }

    @Override
    protected void onPostExecute(Object result) {
        if (mCallback != null && mCallback.get() != null) {
            final ResponseCallback callback = mCallback.get();
            if (result instanceof String) {
                callback.onRequestSuccess((String) result);
            } else if (result instanceof Exception) {
                callback.onRequestError((Exception) result);
            } else {
                callback.onRequestError(new IOException(
                        "Unknown Error Contacting Host") );
            }
        }
    }

}
```

Basic authentication is added to the `HttpClient` in the Apache paradigm. Because our example task allows for a specific client object to be passed in for use, which may already have the necessary authentication credentials, we have only modified the case where a default client is created. In this case, a `UsernamePasswordCredentials` instance is created with the username and password strings, and then set on the client's `CredentialsProvider`.

HttpUrlConnection

Now let's take a look at making HTTP requests with the preferred method for newer applications, `HttpUrlConnection`. We'll start off by defining our same `RestTask` implementation in Listing 4-17, with a helper class in Listing 4-18.

Listing 4-17. RestTask Using HttpUrlConnection

```java
public class RestTask extends AsyncTask<Void, Integer, Object> {
    private static final String TAG = "RestTask";

    public interface ResponseCallback {
        public void onRequestSuccess(String response);

        public void onRequestError(Exception error);
    }

    public interface ProgressCallback {
        public void onProgressUpdate(int progress);
    }

    private HttpURLConnection mConnection;
    private String mFormBody;
    private File mUploadFile;
    private String mUploadFileName;

    //Activity callbacks. Use WeakReferences to avoid blocking
    // operations causing linked objects to stay in memory
    private WeakReference<ResponseCallback> mResponseCallback;
    private WeakReference<ProgressCallback> mProgressCallback;

    public RestTask(HttpURLConnection connection) {
        mConnection = connection;
    }

    public void setFormBody(List<NameValuePair> formData) {
        if (formData == null) {
            mFormBody = null;
            return;
        }

        StringBuilder sb = new StringBuilder();
        for (int i = 0; i < formData.size(); i++) {
            NameValuePair item = formData.get(i);
            sb.append( URLEncoder.encode(item.getName()) );
```

```java
            sb.append("=");
            sb.append( URLEncoder.encode(item.getValue()) );
            if (i != (formData.size() - 1)) {
                sb.append("&");
            }
        }

        mFormBody = sb.toString();
    }

    public void setUploadFile(File file, String fileName) {
        mUploadFile = file;
        mUploadFileName = fileName;
    }

    public void setResponseCallback(ResponseCallback callback) {
        mResponseCallback =
                new WeakReference<ResponseCallback>(callback);
    }

    public void setProgressCallback(ProgressCallback callback) {
        mProgressCallback =
                new WeakReference<ProgressCallback>(callback);
    }

    private void writeMultipart(String boundary,
            String charset,
            OutputStream output,
            boolean writeContent) throws IOException {

        BufferedWriter writer = null;
        try {
            writer = new BufferedWriter(
                    new OutputStreamWriter(output,
                            Charset.forName(charset)), 8192);
            // Post Form Data Component
            if (mFormBody != null) {
                writer.write("--" + boundary);
                writer.write("\r\n");
                writer.write(
                        "Content-Disposition: form-data;"
                        + " name=\"parameters\"");
                writer.write("\r\n");
                writer.write("Content-Type: text/plain; charset="
                        + charset);
                writer.write("\r\n");
                writer.write("\r\n");
```

```java
    if (writeContent) {
        writer.write(mFormBody);
    }
    writer.write("\r\n");
    writer.flush();
}

// Send binary file.
writer.write("--" + boundary);
writer.write("\r\n");
writer.write("Content-Disposition: form-data; name=\""
        + mUploadFileName + "\"; filename=\""
        + mUploadFile.getName() + "\"");
writer.write("\r\n");
writer.write("Content-Type: "
        + URLConnection.guessContentTypeFromName(
        mUploadFile.getName()));
writer.write("\r\n");
writer.write("Content-Transfer-Encoding: binary");
writer.write("\r\n");
writer.write("\r\n");
writer.flush();
if (writeContent) {
    InputStream input = null;
    try {
        input = new FileInputStream(mUploadFile);
        byte[] buffer = new byte[1024];
        for (int length = 0;
                (length = input.read(buffer)) > 0;) {
            output.write(buffer, 0, length);
        }
        // Don't close the OutputStream yet
        output.flush();
    } catch (IOException e) {
        Log.w(TAG, e);
    } finally {
        if (input != null) {
            try {
                input.close();
            } catch (IOException e) {
            }
        }
    }
}
// This CRLF signifies the end of the binary chunk
writer.write("\r\n");
writer.flush();

// End of multipart/form-data.
writer.write("--" + boundary + "--");
```

```
                writer.write("\r\n");
                writer.flush();
        } finally {
            if (writer != null) {
                writer.close();
            }
        }
    }

    private void writeFormData(String charset,
            OutputStream output) throws IOException {
        try {
            output.write(mFormBody.getBytes(charset));
            output.flush();
        } finally {
            if (output != null) {
                output.close();
            }
        }
    }

    @Override
    protected Object doInBackground(Void… params) {
        //Generate random string for boundary
        String boundary =
                Long.toHexString(System.currentTimeMillis());
        String charset = Charset.defaultCharset().displayName();

        try {
            // Set up output if applicable
            if (mUploadFile != null) {
                //We must do a multipart request
                mConnection.setRequestProperty("Content-Type",
                        "multipart/form-data; boundary="
                        + boundary);

                //Calculate the size of the extra metadata
                ByteArrayOutputStream bos =
                        new ByteArrayOutputStream();
                writeMultipart(boundary, charset, bos, false);
                byte[] extra = bos.toByteArray();
                int contentLength = extra.length;
                //Add the file size to the length
                contentLength += mUploadFile.length();
                //Add the form body, if it exists
                if (mFormBody != null) {
                    contentLength += mFormBody.length();
                }
```

```
        mConnection
            .setFixedLengthStreamingMode(contentLength);
    } else if (mFormBody != null) {
        //In this case, it is just form data to post
        mConnection.setRequestProperty("Content-Type",
            "application/x-www-form-urlencoded; charset="
            + charset);
        mConnection.setFixedLengthStreamingMode(
            mFormBody.length() );
    }

    //This is the first call on URLConnection that
    // actually does Network IO.  Even openConnection() is
    // still just doing local operations.
    mConnection.connect();

    // Do output if applicable (for a POST)
    if (mUploadFile != null) {
        OutputStream out = mConnection.getOutputStream();
        writeMultipart(boundary, charset, out, true);
    } else if (mFormBody != null) {
        OutputStream out = mConnection.getOutputStream();
        writeFormData(charset, out);
    }

    // Get response data
    int status = mConnection.getResponseCode();
    if (status >= 300) {
        String message = mConnection.getResponseMessage();
        return new HttpResponseException(status, message);
    }

    InputStream in = mConnection.getInputStream();
    String encoding = mConnection.getContentEncoding();
    int contentLength = mConnection.getContentLength();
    if (encoding == null) {
        encoding = "UTF-8";
    }
    BufferedReader reader = new BufferedReader(
            new InputStreamReader(in, encoding));
    char[] buffer = new char[4096];

    StringBuilder sb = new StringBuilder();
    int downloadedBytes = 0;
    int len1 = 0;
    while ((len1 = reader.read(buffer)) > 0) {
        downloadedBytes += len1;
        publishProgress(
                (downloadedBytes * 100) / contentLength);
        sb.append(buffer);
    }
```

```
            return sb.toString();
        } catch (Exception e) {
            Log.w(TAG, e);
            return e;
        } finally {
            if (mConnection != null) {
                mConnection.disconnect();
            }
        }
    }

    @Override
    protected void onProgressUpdate(Integer... values) {
        // Update progress UI
        if (mProgressCallback != null
                && mProgressCallback.get() != null) {
            mProgressCallback.get().onProgressUpdate(values[0]);
        }
    }

    @Override
    protected void onPostExecute(Object result) {
        if (mResponseCallback != null
                && mResponseCallback.get() != null) {
            final ResponseCallback cb = mResponseCallback.get();
            if (result instanceof String) {
                cb.onRequestSuccess((String) result);
            } else if (result instanceof Exception) {
                cb.onRequestError((Exception) result);
            } else {
                cb.onRequestError(new IOException(
                        "Unknown Error Contacting Host"));
            }
        }
    }
}
```

Listing 4-18. Util Class to Create Requests

```
public class RestUtil {

    public static final RestTask obtainGetTask(String url)
            throws MalformedURLException, IOException {
        HttpURLConnection connection =
                (HttpURLConnection) (new URL(url))
                .openConnection();

        connection.setReadTimeout(10000);
        connection.setConnectTimeout(15000);
        connection.setDoInput(true);
```

```java
        RestTask task = new RestTask(connection);
        return task;
    }

    public static final RestTask obtainFormPostTask(String url,
            List<NameValuePair> formData)
            throws MalformedURLException, IOException {
        HttpURLConnection connection =
                (HttpURLConnection) (new URL(url))
                .openConnection();

        connection.setReadTimeout(10000);
        connection.setConnectTimeout(15000);
        connection.setDoOutput(true);

        RestTask task = new RestTask(connection);
        task.setFormBody(formData);

        return task;
    }

    public static final RestTask obtainMultipartPostTask(
            String url, List<NameValuePair> formPart,
            File file, String fileName)
            throws MalformedURLException, IOException {
        HttpURLConnection connection =
                (HttpURLConnection) (new URL(url))
                .openConnection();

        connection.setReadTimeout(10000);
        connection.setConnectTimeout(15000);
        connection.setDoOutput(true);

        RestTask task = new RestTask(connection);
        task.setFormBody(formPart);
        task.setUploadFile(file, fileName);

        return task;
    }
}
```

The first thing you probably noticed is that this example requires a lot more code to implement certain requests, due to the low-level nature of the API. We have written a RestTask that is capable of handling GET, simple POST, and multipart POST requests, and we define the parameters of the request dynamically based on the components added to RestTask.

As before, we can attach an optional callback to be notified when the request has completed. However, in addition to that, we have added a progress callback interface that the task will call to update any visible UI of the progress while downloading response content. This is simpler to implement using HttpUrlConnection, rather than HttpClient, because we are interacting directly with the data streams.

In this example, an application would create an instance of RestTask through the RestUtil helper class. This subdivides the setup required on HttpURLConnection, which doesn't actually do any network I/O from the portions that connect and interact with the host. The helper class creates the connection instance and also sets up any time-out values and the HTTP request method.

> **Note**   By default, any URLConnection will have its request method set to GET. Calling setDoOutput() implicitly sets that method to POST. If you need to set that value to any other HTTP verb, use setRequestMethod().

If there is any body content, in the case of a POST, those values are set directly on our custom task to be written when the task executes.

Once a RestTask is executed, it goes through and determines whether there is any body data attached that it needs to write. If we have attached form data (as name-value pairs) or a file for upload, it takes that as a trigger to construct a POST body and send it. With HttpURLConnection, we are responsible for all aspects of the connection, including telling the server the amount of data that is coming. Therefore, RestTask takes the time to calculate how much data will be posted and calls setFixedLengthStreamingMode() to construct a header field telling the server how large our content is. In the case of a simple form post, this calculation is trivial, and we just pass the length of the body string.

A multipart POST that may include file data is more complex, however. Multipart has lots of extra data in the body to designate the boundaries between each part of the POST, and all those bytes must be accounted for in the length we set. In order to accomplish this, writeMultipart() is constructed in such a way that we can pass a local OutputStream (in this case, a ByteArrayOutputStream) to write all the extra data into it so we can measure it. When the method is called in this way, it skips over the actual content pieces, such as the file and form data, as those can be added in later by calling their respective length() methods, and we don't want to waste time loading them into memory.

> **Note**   If you do not know how big the content is that you want to POST, HttpURLConnection also supports chunked uploads via setChunkedStreamingMode(). In this case, you need only to pass the size of the data chunks you will be sending.

Once the task has written any POST data to the host, it is time to read the response content. If the initial request was a GET request, the task skips directly to this step because there was no additional data to write. The task first checks the value of the response code to make sure there were no server-side errors, and it then downloads the contents of the response into a StringBuilder. The download reads in chunks of data roughly 4KB at a time, notifying the progress callback handler with a percentage downloaded as a fraction of the total response content length. When all the content is downloaded, the task completes by handing back the resulting response as a string.

GET Example

Let's take a look at our same Google Custom Search example, but this time let's use the new and improved RestTask (see Listing 4-19).

Listing 4-19. Activity Executing API GET Request

```java
public class SearchActivity extends Activity implements
        RestTask.ProgressCallback, RestTask.ResponseCallback {

    private static final String SEARCH_URI =
            "https://www.googleapis.com/customsearch/v1"
            + "?key=%s&cx=%s&q=%s";
    private static final String SEARCH_KEY =
            "AIzaSyBbW-W1SHCK4eWOkK74VGMLJj_b-byNzkI";
    private static final String SEARCH_CX =
            "008212991319514020231:1mkouq8yagw";
    private static final String SEARCH_QUERY = "Android";

    private TextView mResult;
    private ProgressDialog mProgress;

    @Override
    public void onCreate(Bundle savedInstanceState) {
        super.onCreate(savedInstanceState);
        ScrollView scrollView = new ScrollView(this);
        mResult = new TextView(this);
        scrollView.addView(mResult, new ViewGroup.LayoutParams(
                LayoutParams.MATCH_PARENT,
                LayoutParams.WRAP_CONTENT));
        setContentView(scrollView);

        //Create the request
        try{
            //Simple GET
            String url = String.format(SEARCH_URI, SEARCH_KEY,
                    SEARCH_CX, SEARCH_QUERY);
            RestTask getTask = RestUtil.obtainGetTask(url);
            getTask.setResponseCallback(this);
            getTask.setProgressCallback(this);

            getTask.execute();

            //Display progress to the user
            mProgress = ProgressDialog.show(this, "Searching",
                    "Waiting For Results…", true);
        } catch (Exception e) {
            mResult.setText(e.getMessage());
        }
    }
```

```
    @Override
    public void onProgressUpdate(int progress) {
        if (progress >= 0) {
            if (mProgress != null) {
                mProgress.dismiss();
                mProgress = null;
            }
            //Update user of progress
            mResult.setText( String.format(
                    "Download Progress: %d%%", progress));
        }
    }

    @Override
    public void onRequestSuccess(String response) {
        //Clear progress indicator
        if(mProgress != null) {
            mProgress.dismiss();
        }
        //Process the response data (here we just display it)
        mResult.setText(response);
    }

    @Override
    public void onRequestError(Exception error) {
        //Clear progress indicator
        if(mProgress != null) {
            mProgress.dismiss();
        }
        //Process the response data (here we just display it)
        mResult.setText("An Error Occurred: "+error.getMessage());
    }
}
```

The example is almost identical to our previous iteration. We still construct the URL out of the necessary query parameters and obtain a RestTask instance. We then set this activity as the callback for the request and execute.

You can see, however, that we have added ProgressCallback to the list of interfaces this activity implements so it can be notified of how the download is going. Not all web servers return a valid content length for requests, instead returning −1, which makes progress based on the percentage difficult to do. In those cases, our callback simply leaves the indeterminate progress dialog box visible until the download is complete. However, in cases where valid progress can be determined, the dialog box is dismissed and the percentage of progress is displayed on the screen.

Once the download is complete, the activity receives a callback with the resulting JSON string. We will discuss parsing structured XML and JSON responses like this one in Recipes 4-7 and 4-8, so for now the example simply displays the raw response to the user interface.

POST Example

Listing 4-20 illustrates doing a simple form data POST using the new RestTask. The endpoint will be httpbin.org once again, so the resulting data displayed on the screen will be an echo back to the form parameters we passed in.

Listing 4-20. Activity Executing API POST Request

```
public class SearchActivity extends Activity implements
        RestTask.ProgressCallback, RestTask.ResponseCallback {

    private static final String POST_URI =
            "http://httpbin.org/post";

    private TextView mResult;
    private ProgressDialog mProgress;

    @Override
    public void onCreate(Bundle savedInstanceState) {
        super.onCreate(savedInstanceState);
        ScrollView scrollView = new ScrollView(this);
        mResult = new TextView(this);
        scrollView.addView(mResult, new ViewGroup.LayoutParams(
                LayoutParams.MATCH_PARENT,
                LayoutParams.WRAP_CONTENT));
        setContentView(scrollView);

        //Create the request
        try{
            //Simple POST
            List<NameValuePair> parameters =
                    new ArrayList<NameValuePair>();
            parameters.add(new BasicNameValuePair("title",
                    "Android Recipes"));
            parameters.add(new BasicNameValuePair("summary",
                    "Learn Android Quickly"));
            parameters.add(new BasicNameValuePair("author",
                    "Smith"));
            RestTask postTask = RestUtil.obtainFormPostTask(
                    POST_URI, parameters);
            postTask.setResponseCallback(this);
            postTask.setProgressCallback(this);

            postTask.execute();

            //Display progress to the user
            mProgress = ProgressDialog.show(this, "Searching",
                    "Waiting For Results…", true);
        } catch (Exception e) {
            mResult.setText(e.getMessage());
        }
    }
}
```

```
@Override
public void onProgressUpdate(int progress) {
    if (progress >= 0) {
        if (mProgress != null) {
            mProgress.dismiss();
            mProgress = null;
        }
        //Update user of progress
        mResult.setText( String.format(
                "Download Progress: %d%%", progress));
    }
}

@Override
public void onRequestSuccess(String response) {
    //Clear progress indicator
    if(mProgress != null) {
        mProgress.dismiss();
    }
    //Process the response data (here we just display it)
    mResult.setText(response);
}

@Override
public void onRequestError(Exception error) {
    //Clear progress indicator
    if(mProgress != null) {
        mProgress.dismiss();
    }
    //Process the response data (here we just display it)
    mResult.setText("An Error Occurred: "+error.getMessage());
}
}
```

It should be noted here that the progress callbacks are related only to the download of the response, and not the upload of the POST data, though that is certainly possible for the developer to implement.

Upload Example

Listing 4-21 illustrates something we cannot do natively with the Apache components in the Android framework: multipart POST.

Listing 4-21. Activity Executing API Multipart POST Request

```
public class SearchActivity extends Activity implements
        RestTask.ProgressCallback, RestTask.ResponseCallback {

    private static final String POST_URI =
            "http://httpbin.org/post";

    private TextView mResult;
    private ProgressDialog mProgress;
```

```java
@Override
public void onCreate(Bundle savedInstanceState) {
    super.onCreate(savedInstanceState);
    ScrollView scrollView = new ScrollView(this);
    mResult = new TextView(this);
    scrollView.addView(mResult, new ViewGroup.LayoutParams(
            LayoutParams.MATCH_PARENT,
            LayoutParams.WRAP_CONTENT));
    setContentView(scrollView);

    //Create the request
    try{
        //File POST
        Bitmap image = BitmapFactory.decodeResource(
                getResources(),
                R.drawable.ic_launcher);
        File imageFile = new File(
                getExternalCacheDir(), "myImage.png");
        FileOutputStream out =
                new FileOutputStream(imageFile);
        image.compress(CompressFormat.PNG, 0, out);
        out.flush();
        out.close();
        List<NameValuePair> fileParameters =
                new ArrayList<NameValuePair>();
        fileParameters.add(new BasicNameValuePair("title",
                "Android Recipes"));
        fileParameters.add(new BasicNameValuePair("desc",
                "Image File Upload"));
        RestTask uploadTask =
                RestUtil.obtainMultipartPostTask(
                        POST_URI, fileParameters,
                        imageFile, "avatarImage");
        uploadTask.setResponseCallback(this);
        uploadTask.setProgressCallback(this);

        uploadTask.execute();

        //Display progress to the user
        mProgress = ProgressDialog.show(this, "Searching",
                "Waiting For Results…", true);
    } catch (Exception e) {
        mResult.setText(e.getMessage());
    }
}

@Override
public void onProgressUpdate(int progress) {
    if (progress >= 0) {
        if (mProgress != null) {
            mProgress.dismiss();
            mProgress = null;
        }
```

```
            //Update user of progress
            mResult.setText( String.format(
                    "Download Progress: %d%%", progress));
        }
    }

    @Override
    public void onRequestSuccess(String response) {
        //Clear progress indicator
        if(mProgress != null) {
            mProgress.dismiss();
        }
        //Process the response data (here we just display it)
        mResult.setText(response);
    }

    @Override
    public void onRequestError(Exception error) {
        //Clear progress indicator
        if(mProgress != null) {
            mProgress.dismiss();
        }
        //Process the response data (here we just display it)
        mResult.setText("An Error Occurred: "+error.getMessage());
    }
}
```

In this example, we construct a POST request that has two distinct parts: a form data part (made up of name-value pairs) and a file part. For the purposes of the example, we take the application's icon and quickly write it out to external storage as a PNG file to use for the upload.

In this case, the JSON response from httpbin will echo back both the form data elements as well as a Base64-encoded representation of the PNG image.

Basic Authorization

Adding basic authorization to the new RestTask is fairly straightforward. It can be done in one of two ways: either directly on each request or globally using a class called Authenticator. First let's take a look at attaching basic authorization to an individual request. Listing 4-22 modifies RestUtil to include methods that attach a username and password in the proper format.

Listing 4-22. RestUtil with Basic Authorization

```
public class RestUtil {

    public static final RestTask obtainGetTask(String url)
            throws MalformedURLException, IOException {
        HttpURLConnection connection =
                (HttpURLConnection) (new URL(url))
                .openConnection();
```

```java
        connection.setReadTimeout(10000);
        connection.setConnectTimeout(15000);
        connection.setDoInput(true);

        RestTask task = new RestTask(connection);
        return task;
    }

    public static final RestTask obtainAuthenticatedGetTask(
            String url, String username, String password)
            throws MalformedURLException, IOException {
        HttpURLConnection connection =
                (HttpURLConnection) (new URL(url))
                .openConnection();

        connection.setReadTimeout(10000);
        connection.setConnectTimeout(15000);
        connection.setDoInput(true);

        attachBasicAuthentication(connection, username, password);

        RestTask task = new RestTask(connection);
        return task;
    }

    public static final RestTask obtainAuthenticatedFormPostTask(
            String url, List<NameValuePair> formData,
            String username, String password)
            throws MalformedURLException, IOException {
        HttpURLConnection connection =
                (HttpURLConnection) (new URL(url))
                .openConnection();

        connection.setReadTimeout(10000);
        connection.setConnectTimeout(15000);
        connection.setDoOutput(true);

        attachBasicAuthentication(connection, username, password);

        RestTask task = new RestTask(connection);
        task.setFormBody(formData);

        return task;
    }

    private static void attachBasicAuthentication(
            URLConnection connection,
            String username, String password) {
        //Add Basic Authentication Headers
        String userpassword = username + ":" + password;
```

```
        String encodedAuthorization = Base64.encodeToString(
                userpassword.getBytes(), Base64.NO_WRAP);
        connection.setRequestProperty("Authorization", "Basic "
                + encodedAuthorization);
    }

}
```

Basic authorization is added to an HTTP request as a header field with the name `Authorization` and the value of `Basic` followed by a Base64-encoded string of your username and password. The helper method `attachBasicAuthentication()` applies this property to the `URLConnection` before it is given to `RestTask`. The `Base64.NO_WRAP` flag is added to ensure that the encoder doesn't add any extra new lines, which will create an invalid value.

This is a really nice way of applying authentication to requests if not all your requests need to be authenticated in the same way. However, sometimes it's easier to just set your credentials once and let all your requests use them. This is where `Authenticator` comes in. `Authenticator` allows you to globally set the username and password credentials for the requests in your application process. Let's take a look at Listing 4-23, which shows how this can be done.

Listing 4-23. Activity Using Authenticator

```
public class AuthActivity extends Activity implements
        ResponseCallback {

    private static final String URI =
            "http://httpbin.org/basic-auth/android/recipes";
    private static final String USERNAME = "android";
    private static final String PASSWORD = "recipes";

    private TextView mResult;
    private ProgressDialog mProgress;

    @Override
    protected void onCreate(Bundle savedInstanceState) {
        super.onCreate(savedInstanceState);
        mResult = new TextView(this);
        setContentView(mResult);

        Authenticator.setDefault(new Authenticator() {
            @Override
            protected PasswordAuthentication
                    getPasswordAuthentication() {
                return new PasswordAuthentication(USERNAME,
                        PASSWORD.toCharArray());
            }
        });

        try {
            RestTask task = RestUtil.obtainGetTask(URI);
            task.setResponseCallback(this);
```

```
            task.execute();
        } catch (Exception e) {
            mResult.setText(e.getMessage());
        }
    }

    @Override
    public void onRequestSuccess(String response) {
        if (mProgress != null) {
            mProgress.dismiss();
            mProgress = null;
        }
        mResult.setText(response);
    }

    @Override
    public void onRequestError(Exception error) {
        if (mProgress != null) {
            mProgress.dismiss();
            mProgress = null;
        }
        mResult.setText(error.getMessage());
    }

}
```

This example connects to httpbin again, this time to an endpoint used to validate credentials. The username and password the host will require are coded into the URL path, and if those credentials are not properly supplied, the response from the host will be UNAUTHORIZED.

With a single call to Authenticator.setDefault(), passing in a new Authenticator instance, all subsequent requests will use the provided credentials for authentication challenges. So we pass the correct username and password to Authenticator by creating a new PasswordAuthentication instance whenever asked, and all URLConnection instances in our process will make use of that. Notice that in this example, our request does not have credentials attached to it, but when the request is made, we will get an authenticated response.

Caching Responses

(API Level 13)

One final platform enhancement you can take advantage of when you use HttpURLConnection is response caching with HttpResponseCache. A great way to speed up the response of your application is to cache responses coming back from the remote host so your application can load frequent requests from the cache rather than hitting the network each time. Installing and removing a cache in your application requires just a few simple lines of code:

```
//Installing a response cache
try {
    File httpCacheDir = new File(context.getCacheDir(), "http");
    long httpCacheSize = 10 * 1024 * 1024; // 10 MiB
```

```
    HttpResponseCache.install(httpCacheDir, httpCacheSize);
catch (IOException e) {
    Log.i(TAG, "HTTP response cache installation failed:" + e);
}

//Clearing a response cache
HttpResponseCache cache = HttpResponseCache.getInstalled();
if (cache != null) {
    cache.flush();
}
```

> **Note**   HttpResponseCache works with only HttpURLConnection variants. It will not work if you are using Apache HttpClient.

4-7. Parsing JSON

Problem

Your application needs to parse responses from an API or other source that is formatted in JavaScript Object Notation (JSON).

Solution

(API Level 1)

Use the org.json parser classes that are baked into Android. The SDK comes with a very efficient set of classes for parsing JSON-formatted strings in the org.json package. Simply create a new JSONObject or JSONArray from the formatted string data and you'll be armed with a set of accessor methods to get primitive data or nested JSONObjects and JSONArrays from within.

How It Works

This JSON parser is strict by default, meaning that it will halt with an exception when encountering invalid JSON data or an invalid key. Accessor methods that prefix with get will throw a JSONException if the requested value is not found. In some cases this behavior is not ideal, and for that there is a companion set of methods that are prefixed with opt. These methods will return null instead of throwing an exception when a value for the requested key is not found. In addition, many of them have an overloaded version that also takes a fallback parameter to return instead of null.

Let's look at an example of how to parse a JSON string into useful pieces. Consider the JSON in Listing 4-24.

Listing 4-24. Example JSON

```json
{
    "person": {
        "name": "John",
        "age": 30,
        "children": [
            {
                "name": "Billy"
                "age": 5
            },
            {
                "name": "Sarah"
                "age": 7
            },
            {
                "name": "Tommy"
                "age": 9
            }
        ]
    }
}
```

This defines a single object with three values: name (string), age (integer), and children. The parameter entitled children is an array of three more objects, each with its own name and age. If we were to use org.json to parse this data and display some elements in TextViews, it would look like the examples in Listings 4-25 and 4-26.

Listing 4-25. res/layout/main.xml

```xml
<?xml version="1.0" encoding="utf-8"?>
<LinearLayout
    xmlns:android="http://schemas.android.com/apk/res/android"
    android:layout_width="match_parent"
    android:layout_height="match_parent"
    android:orientation="vertical">
    <TextView
        android:id="@+id/line1"
        android:layout_width="match_parent"
        android:layout_height="wrap_content" />
    <TextView
        android:id="@+id/line2"
        android:layout_width="match_parent"
        android:layout_height="wrap_content" />
    <TextView
        android:id="@+id/line3"
        android:layout_width="match_parent"
        android:layout_height="wrap_content" />
</LinearLayout>
```

Listing 4-26. Sample JSON Parsing Activity

```
public class MyActivity extends Activity {
    private static final String JSON_STRING =
            "{\"person\":"
            + "{\"name\":\"John\",\"age\":30,\"children\":["
            + "{\"name\":\"Billy\",\"age\":5},"
            + "{\"name\":\"Sarah\",\"age\":7},"
            + "{\"name\":\"Tommy\",\"age\":9}"
            + "] } }";
    @Override
    public void onCreate(Bundle savedInstanceState) {
        super.onCreate(savedInstanceState);
        setContentView(R.layout.main);

        TextView line1 = (TextView)findViewById(R.id.line1);
        TextView line2 = (TextView)findViewById(R.id.line2);
        TextView line3 = (TextView)findViewById(R.id.line3);
        try {
            JSONObject person = (new JSONObject(JSON_STRING))
                    .getJSONObject("person");
            String name = person.getString("name");
            line1.setText("This person's name is " + name);
            line2.setText(name + " is " + person.getInt("age")
                    + " years old.");
            line3.setText(name + " has "
                    + person.getJSONArray("children").length()
                    + " children.");
        } catch (JSONException e) {
            e.printStackTrace();
        }
    }
}
```

For this example, the JSON string has been hard-coded as a constant. When the activity is created, the string is turned into a JSONObject, at which point all its data can be accessed as key-value pairs, just as if it were stored in a map or dictionary. All the business logic is wrapped in a try block because we are using the strict methods for accessing data.

Functions such as JSONObject.getString() and JSONObject.getInt() are used to read primitive data out and place it in the TextView; the getJSONArray() method pulls out the nested children array. JSONArray has the same set of accessor methods as JSONObject to read data, but they take an index into the array as a parameter instead of the name of the key. In addition, a JSONArray can return its length, which we used in the example to display the number of children the person had.

The result of the sample application is shown in Figure 4-3.

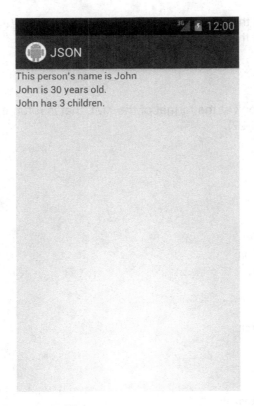

Figure 4-3. Display of parsed JSON data in the Activity

Debugging Trick

JSON is a very efficient notation; however, it can be difficult for humans to read a raw JSON string, which can make it hard to debug parsing issues. Quite often the JSON you are parsing is coming from a remote source or is not completely familiar to you, and you need to display it for debugging purposes. Both JSONObject and JSONArray have an overloaded toString() method that takes an integer parameter for pretty-printing the data in a returned and indented fashion, making it easier to decipher. Often adding something like myJsonObject.toString(2) to a troublesome section can save you time and a headache.

4-8. Parsing XML

Problem

Your application needs to parse responses, from an API or other source, that are formatted as XML.

Solution

(API Level 1)

Implement a subclass of org.xml.sax.helpers.DefaultHandler to parse the data using event-based SAX (Simple API for XML). Android has three primary methods you can use to parse XML data: DOM (Document Object Model), SAX, and Pull. The simplest of these to implement, and the most memory-efficient, is the SAX parser. SAX parsing works by traversing the XML data and generating callback events at the beginning and end of each element.

How It Works

To describe this further, let's look at the format of the XML that is returned when requesting an RSS/Atom news feed (see Listing 4-27).

Listing 4-27. RSS Basic Structure

```
<rss version="2.0">
  <channel>
    <item>
      <title></title>
      <link></link>
      <description></description>
    </item>
    <item>
      <title></title>
      <link></link>
      <description></description>
    </item>
    <item>
      <title></title>
      <link></link>
      <description></description>
    </item>
    ...
  </channel>
</rss>
```

Between each set of <title>, <link>, and <description> tags is the value associated with each item. Using SAX, we can parse this data out into an array of items that the application could then display to the user in a list (see Listing 4-28).

Listing 4-28. Custom Handler to Parse RSS

```
public class RSSHandler extends DefaultHandler {

    public class NewsItem {
        public String title;
        public String link;
        public String description;

        @Override
        public String toString() {
            return title;
        }
    }
```

```java
private StringBuffer buf;
private ArrayList<NewsItem> feedItems;
private NewsItem item;

private boolean inItem = false;

public ArrayList<NewsItem> getParsedItems() {
    return feedItems;
}

//Called at the head of each new element
@Override
public void startElement(String uri, String name,
        String qName, Attributes attrs) {
    if("channel".equals(name)) {
        feedItems = new ArrayList<NewsItem>();
    } else if("item".equals(name)) {
        item = new NewsItem();
        inItem = true;
    } else if("title".equals(name) && inItem) {
        buf = new StringBuffer();
    } else if("link".equals(name) && inItem) {
        buf = new StringBuffer();
    } else if("description".equals(name) && inItem) {
        buf = new StringBuffer();
    }
}

//Called at the tail of each element end
@Override
public void endElement(String uri, String name,
        String qName) {
    if("item".equals(name)) {
        feedItems.add(item);
        inItem = false;
    } else if("title".equals(name) && inItem) {
        item.title = buf.toString();
    } else if("link".equals(name) && inItem) {
        item.link = buf.toString();
    } else if("description".equals(name) && inItem) {
        item.description = buf.toString();
    }

    buf = null;
}

//Called with character data inside elements
@Override
public void characters(char ch[], int start, int length) {
    //Don't bother if buffer isn't initialized
```

```
            if(buf != null) {
                for (int i=start; i<start+length; i++) {
                    buf.append(ch[i]);
                }
            }
        }
    }
}
```

The RSSHandler is notified at the beginning and end of each element via startElement() and endElement(). In between, the characters that make up the element's value are passed into the characters() callback. As the parser moves through the document, the following steps occur:

1. When the parser encounters the first element, the list of items is initialized.

2. When each item element is encountered, a new NewsItem model is initialized.

3. Inside each item element, data elements are captured in a StringBuffer and inserted into the members of the NewsItem.

4. When the end of each item is reached, the NewsItem is added to the list.

5. When parsing is complete, feedItems is a complete list of all the items in the feed.

Let's look at this in action by using some of the tricks from the API example in Recipe 4-6 to download the latest Google News in RSS form (see Listing 4-29).

Listing 4-29. Activity That Parses the XML and Displays the Items

```java
public class FeedActivity extends Activity implements ResponseCallback {
    private static final String TAG = "FeedReader";
    private static final String FEED_URI =
            "http://news.google.com/?output=rss";

    private ListView mList;
    private ArrayAdapter<NewsItem> mAdapter;
    private ProgressDialog mProgress;

    @Override
    public void onCreate(Bundle savedInstanceState) {
        super.onCreate(savedInstanceState);

        mList = new ListView(this);
        mAdapter = new ArrayAdapter<NewsItem>(this,
                android.R.layout.simple_list_item_1,
                android.R.id.text1);
        mList.setAdapter(mAdapter);
        mList.setOnItemClickListener(
                new AdapterView.OnItemClickListener() {
            @Override
            public void onItemClick(AdapterView<?> parent, View v,
                    int position, long id) {
                NewsItem item = mAdapter.getItem(position);
```

```java
                Intent intent = new Intent(Intent.ACTION_VIEW);
                intent.setData(Uri.parse(item.link));
                startActivity(intent);
            }
        });

        setContentView(mList);
    }

    @Override
    public void onResume() {
        super.onResume();
        //Retrieve the RSS feed
        try{
            HttpGet feedRequest = new HttpGet(new URI(FEED_URI));
            RestTask task = new RestTask();
            task.setResponseCallback(this);
            task.execute(feedRequest);
            mProgress = ProgressDialog.show(this, "Searching",
                    "Waiting For Results…", true);
        } catch (Exception e) {
            Log.w(TAG, e);
        }
    }

    @Override
    public void onRequestSuccess(String response) {
        if (mProgress != null) {
            mProgress.dismiss();
            mProgress = null;
        }
        //Process the response data
        try {
            SAXParserFactory factory =
                    SAXParserFactory.newInstance();
            SAXParser p = factory.newSAXParser();
            RSSHandler parser = new RSSHandler();
            p.parse(new InputSource(new StringReader(response)),
                    parser);

            mAdapter.clear();
            for(NewsItem item : parser.getParsedItems()) {
                mAdapter.add(item);
            }
            mAdapter.notifyDataSetChanged();
        } catch (Exception e) {
            Log.w(TAG, e);
        }
    }
}
```

```
    @Override
    public void onRequestError(Exception error) {
        if (mProgress != null) {
            mProgress.dismiss();
            mProgress = null;
        }
        //Display the error
        mAdapter.clear();
        mAdapter.notifyDataSetChanged();
        Toast.makeText(this, error.getMessage(),
                Toast.LENGTH_SHORT).show();
    }
}
```

The example has been modified to display a ListView, which will be populated by the parsed items from the RSS feed. In the example, we add an OnItemClickListener to the list that will launch the news item's link in the browser.

Once the data is returned from the API in the response callback, Android's built-in SAX parser handles the job of traversing the XML string. SAXParser.parse() uses an instance of our RSSHandler to process the XML, which results in the handler's feedItems list being populated. The receiver then iterates through all the parsed items and adds them to an ArrayAdapter for display in the ListView.

XmlPullParser

The XmlPullParser provided by the framework is another efficient way of parsing incoming XML data. Like SAX, the parsing is stream based; it does not require much memory to parse large document feeds because the entire XML data structure does not need to be loaded before parsing can begin. Let's see an example of using XmlPullParser to parse our RSS feed data. Unlike with SAX, however, we must manually advance the parser through the data stream every step of the way, even over the tag elements we aren't interested in.

Listing 4-30 contains a factory class that iterates over the feed to construct model elements.

Listing 4-30. Factory Class to Parse XML into Model Objects

```
public class NewsItemFactory {

    /* Data Model Class */
    public static class NewsItem {
        public String title;
        public String link;
        public String description;

        @Override
        public String toString() {
            return title;
        }
    }
```

```java
/*
 * Parse the RSS feed out into a list of NewsItem elements
 */
public static List<NewsItem> parseFeed(XmlPullParser parser)
        throws XmlPullParserException, IOException {
    List<NewsItem> items = new ArrayList<NewsItem>();

    while (parser.next() != XmlPullParser.END_TAG) {
        if (parser.getEventType() != XmlPullParser.START_TAG){
            continue;
        }

        if (parser.getName().equals("rss") ||
                parser.getName().equals("channel")) {
            //Skip these items, but allow to drill inside
        } else if (parser.getName().equals("item")) {
            NewsItem newsItem = readItem(parser);
            items.add(newsItem);
        } else {
            //Skip any other elements and their children
            skip(parser);
        }
    }

    //Return the parsed list
    return items;
}

/*
 * Parse each <item> element in the XML into a NewsItem
 */
private static NewsItem readItem(XmlPullParser parser) throws
        XmlPullParserException, IOException {
    NewsItem newsItem = new NewsItem();

    //Must start with an <item> element to be valid
    parser.require(XmlPullParser.START_TAG, null, "item");
    while (parser.next() != XmlPullParser.END_TAG) {
        if (parser.getEventType() != XmlPullParser.START_TAG){
            continue;
        }

        String name = parser.getName();
        if (name.equals("title")) {
            parser.require(XmlPullParser.START_TAG,
                    null, "title");
            newsItem.title = readText(parser);
            parser.require(XmlPullParser.END_TAG,
                    null, "title");
        } else if (name.equals("link")) {
            parser.require(XmlPullParser.START_TAG,
                    null, "link");
```

```
                    newsItem.link = readText(parser);
                    parser.require(XmlPullParser.END_TAG,
                            null, "link");
            } else if (name.equals("description")) {
                    parser.require(XmlPullParser.START_TAG,
                            null, "description");
                    newsItem.description = readText(parser);
                    parser.require(XmlPullParser.END_TAG,
                            null, "description");
            } else {
                //Skip any other elements and their children
                skip(parser);
            }
        }
    }

    return newsItem;
}

/*
 * Read the text content of the current element, which is the
 * data contained between the start and end tag
 */
private static String readText(XmlPullParser parser) throws
        IOException, XmlPullParserException {
    String result = "";
    if (parser.next() == XmlPullParser.TEXT) {
        result = parser.getText();
        parser.nextTag();
    }
    return result;
}

/*
 * Helper method to skip over the current element and any
 * children it may have underneath it
 */
private static void skip(XmlPullParser parser) throws
        XmlPullParserException, IOException {
    if (parser.getEventType() != XmlPullParser.START_TAG) {
        throw new IllegalStateException();
    }

    /*
     * For every new tag, increase the depth counter.
     * Decrease it for each tag's end and return when we
     * have reached an end tag that matches the one we
     * started with.
     */
```

```
        int depth = 1;
        while (depth != 0) {
            switch (parser.next()) {
            case XmlPullParser.END_TAG:
                depth--;
                break;
            case XmlPullParser.START_TAG:
                depth++;
                break;
            }
        }
    }
}
```

Pull parsing works by processing the data stream as a series of events. The application advances the parser to the next event by calling the next() method or one of the specialized variations. The following are the event types the parser will advance within:

- START_DOCUMENT: The parser will return this event when it is first initialized. It will be in this state only until the first call to next(), nextToken(), or nextTag().

- START_TAG: The parser has just read a start tag element. The tag name can be retrieved with getName(), and any attributes that were present can be read with getAttributeValue() and associated methods.

- TEXT: Character data inside the tag element was read and can be obtained with getText().

- END_TAG: The parser has just read an end tag element. The tag name of the matching start tag can be retrieved with getName().

- END_DOCUMENT: The end of the data stream has been reached.

Because we must advance the parser ourselves, we have created a helper skip() method to assist in moving the parser past tags we aren't interested in. This method walks from the current position through all nested child elements until the matching end tag is reached, skipping over them. It does this through a depth counter that increments for each start tag and decrements for each end tag. When the depth counter reaches zero, we have reached the matching end tag for the initial position.

The parser in this example starts iterating through the tags in the stream, looking for <item> tags that it can parse into a NewsItem when the parseFeed() method is called. Every element that is not one of these is skipped over, with the exception of two: <rss> and <channel>. All the items are nested within these two tags, so although we aren't interested in them directly, we cannot hand them off to skip(), or all our items will be skipped as well.

The task of parsing each <item> element is handled by readItem(), where a new NewsItem is constructed and filled in by the data found within. The method begins by calling require(), which is a security check to ensure the XML is formatted as we expect. The method will quietly return if the current parser event matches the namespace and tag name passed in; otherwise, it will throw an exception. As we iterate through the child elements, we look specifically for the title, link, and description tags so we can read their values into the model data. After finding each tag, readText() advances the parser and pulls the enclosed character data out. Again, there are other elements inside <item> that we aren't parsing, so we call skip() in the case of any tag we don't need.

You can see that XmlPullParser is extremely flexible because you control every step of the process, but this also requires more code to accomplish the same result. Listing 4-31 shows our feed display activity reworked to use the new parser.

Listing 4-31. Activity Displaying Parsed XML Feed

```java
public class PullFeedActivity extends Activity implements
        ResponseCallback {
    private static final String TAG = "FeedReader";
    private static final String FEED_URI =
            "http://news.google.com/?output=rss";

    private ListView mList;
    private ArrayAdapter<NewsItem> mAdapter;
    private ProgressDialog mProgress;

    @Override
    public void onCreate(Bundle savedInstanceState) {
        super.onCreate(savedInstanceState);

        mList = new ListView(this);
        mAdapter = new ArrayAdapter<NewsItem>(this,
                android.R.layout.simple_list_item_1,
                android.R.id.text1);
        mList.setAdapter(mAdapter);
        mList.setOnItemClickListener(
                new AdapterView.OnItemClickListener() {
            @Override
            public void onItemClick(AdapterView<?> parent, View v,
                    int position, long id) {
                NewsItem item = mAdapter.getItem(position);
                Intent intent = new Intent(Intent.ACTION_VIEW);
                intent.setData(Uri.parse(item.link));
                startActivity(intent);
            }
        });

        setContentView(mList);
    }

    @Override
    public void onResume() {
        super.onResume();
        //Retrieve the RSS feed
        try{
            HttpGet feedRequest = new HttpGet(new URI(FEED_URI));
            RestTask task = new RestTask();
            task.setResponseCallback(this);
            task.execute(feedRequest);
```

```java
                mProgress = ProgressDialog.show(this, "Searching",
                        "Waiting For Results...", true);
        } catch (Exception e) {
            Log.w(TAG, e);
        }
    }

    @Override
    public void onRequestSuccess(String response) {
        if (mProgress != null) {
            mProgress.dismiss();
            mProgress = null;
        }
        //Process the response data
        try {
            XmlPullParser parser = Xml.newPullParser();
            parser.setInput(new StringReader(response));
            //Jump to the first tag
            parser.nextTag();

            mAdapter.clear();
            for(NewsItem i : NewsItemFactory.parseFeed(parser)) {
                mAdapter.add(i);
            }
            mAdapter.notifyDataSetChanged();
        } catch (Exception e) {
            Log.w(TAG, e);
        }
    }

    @Override
    public void onRequestError(Exception error) {
        if (mProgress != null) {
            mProgress.dismiss();
            mProgress = null;
        }
        //Display the error
        mAdapter.clear();
        mAdapter.notifyDataSetChanged();
        Toast.makeText(this, error.getMessage(),
                Toast.LENGTH_SHORT).show();
    }
}
```

A fresh XmlPullParser can be instantiated using Xml.newPullParser(), and the input data source can be a Reader or InputStream instance passed to setInput(). In our case, the response data from the web service is already in a String, so we wrap that in a StringReader to have the parser consume. We can pass the parser to NewsItemFactory, which will then return a list of NewsItem elements that we can add to the ListAdapter and display just as we did before.

> **Tip**　You can also use XmlPullParser to parse local XML data you may want to bundle in your application. By placing your raw XML into resources (such as res/xml/), you can use Resources.getXml() to instantiate an XmlResourceParser preloaded with your local data.

4-9. Receiving SMS

Problem

Your application must react to incoming SMS messages, commonly called text messages.

Solution

(API Level 1)

Register a BroadcastReceiver to listen for incoming messages, and process them in onReceive(). The operating system will fire a broadcast Intent with the android.provider.Telephony.SMS_ RECEIVED action whenever there is an incoming SMS message. Your application can register a BroadcastReceiver to filter for this Intent and process the incoming data.

> **Note**　Receiving this broadcast does not prevent the rest of the system's applications from receiving it as well. The default messaging application will still receive and display any incoming SMS.

How It Works

In previous recipes, we defined BroadcastReceivers as private internal members to an activity. In this case, it is probably best to define the receiver separately and register it in AndroidManifest.xml by using the <receiver> tag. This will allow your receiver to process the incoming events even when your application is not active. Listings 4-32 and 4-33 show an example of a receiver that monitors all incoming SMS and raises a Toast when one arrives from the party of interest.

Listing 4-32. Incoming SMS BroadcastReceiver

```
public class SmsReceiver extends BroadcastReceiver {
    private static final String SHORTCODE = "55443";

    @Override
    public void onReceive(Context context, Intent intent) {
        Bundle bundle = intent.getExtras();

        Object[] messages = (Object[])bundle.get("pdus");
        SmsMessage[] sms = new SmsMessage[messages.length];
```

```
        //Create messages for each incoming PDU
        for(int n=0; n < messages.length; n++) {
            sms[n] =
                SmsMessage.createFromPdu((byte[]) messages[n]);
        }

        for(SmsMessage msg : sms) {
            //Verify if the message came from our known sender
            if(TextUtils.equals(
                    msg.getOriginatingAddress(), SHORTCODE)) {
                //Keep other apps from processing this message
                abortBroadcast();

                //Display our own notification
                Toast.makeText(context,
                    "Received message from the mothership: "
                    + msg.getMessageBody(),
                    Toast.LENGTH_SHORT).show();
            }
        }
    }
}
```

Listing 4-33. Partial AndroidManifest.xml

```xml
<?xml version="1.0" encoding="utf-8"?>
<manifest ...>

    <uses-permission
        android:name="android.permission.RECEIVE_SMS" />

  <application ...>
    <receiver android:name=".SmsReceiver">
      <!-- Add a priority to catch the ordered broadcast -->
      <intent-filter android:priority="5">
        <action
          android:name="android.provider.Telephony.SMS_RECEIVED"
        />
      </intent-filter>
    </receiver>
  </application>

</manifest>
```

> **Important**   Receiving SMS messages requires that the android.permission.RECEIVE_SMS permission be declared in the manifest!

Incoming SMS messages are passed via the extras of the broadcast Intent as an Object array of byte arrays, each byte array representing an SMS protocol data unit (PDU). SmsMessage.createFromPdu() is a convenience method allowing us to create SmsMessage objects from the raw PDU data. With the setup work complete, we can inspect each message to determine whether there is something interesting to handle or process. In the example, we compare the originating address of each message against a known short code, and the user is notified when one arrives.

The broadcast triggered by the framework is an ordered broadcast message, which means that each registered receiver will receive the message in order and will have an opportunity to modify the broadcast before it is handed to the next receiver or to cancel it and stop any lower-priority receivers from receiving it at all.

In the AndroidManifest.xml entry for the <intent-filter>, we had added an arbitrary priority value to insert our receiver above the core system Messages application (which uses the default priority of zero). This allows our application to process the SMS message first.

> **Note**   With an ordered broadcast, receivers that are registered at the same priority will receive the Intent at the "same time," such that the order between them is not determined. Additionally, one receiver cannot cancel the broadcast from being delivered to the other(s) of the same priority.

Then, once we verify that the message we are looking at came from the sender we are tracking, a call to abortBroadcast() terminates the responder chain. This keeps the SMS messages we are processing from displaying to the user and cluttering up their SMS inbox.

> **Important**   There is no external method of verifying what other apps on the system may also be registered to handle this broadcast and have a very high priority (or at least, higher than your app). Your application is at the mercy of a higher-priority application not aborting the broadcast for the message you want to process.

At the point in the example where the Toast is raised, you may wish to provide something more useful to the user. Perhaps the SMS message includes an offer code for your application, and you could launch the appropriate activity to display this information to the user within the application.

> **DEFAULT SMS APPLICATIONS**

Starting with Android 4.4, the behavior of applications using SMS has changed. The device's Settings application now provides the user with a Default SMS App option that selects the application the user would prefer to use for SMS. At the framework level, this augments some of the behaviors around sending and receiving messages.

Applications that are not selected as the default may still send outgoing SMS and monitor incoming messages by using the same ordered broadcast described in this recipe. However, two new broadcast actions have been added for the default SMS app to receive messages:

- `android.provider.telephony.SMS_DELIVER`
- `android.provider.telephony.WAP_PUSH_DELIVER`

The framework will broadcast incoming SMS/MMS message data to the default SMS app separately from other applications using these two actions. Although the original `SMS_RECEIVED` action is still an ordered broadcast, aborting that broadcast can no longer be used as a technique to intercept certain messages from being delivered to that application. However, aborting the broadcast will still interrupt the chain from going to any other third-party app that is monitoring incoming SMS.

Additionally, an SMS application marked as the default is responsible for writing all SMS data received on the device to the device's internal content provider exposed publicly in API Level 19 via `android.provider.Telephony`. This application is the only one on the system with privileges to write data to the SMS provider, regardless of an application's request to obtain the `android.permission.WRITE_SMS` permission.

Other applications may still read the SMS provider data if they have obtained the `android.permission.READ_SMS` permission. We will look in more detail at reading the SMS provider in Chapter 7.

4-10. Sending an SMS Message

Problem

Your application must issue outgoing SMS messages.

Solution

(API Level 4)

Use the `SMSManager` to send text and data SMS messages. `SMSManager` is a system service that handles sending SMS and providing feedback to the application about the status of the operation. `SMSManager` provides methods to send text messages by using `SmsManager.sendTextMessage()` and `SmsManager.sendMultipartTextMessage()`, or data messages by using `SmsManager.sendDataMessage()`. Each of these methods takes `PendingIntent` parameters to deliver status for the send operation and the message delivery back to a requested destination.

How It Works

Let's take a look at a simple example activity that sends an SMS message and monitors its status (see Listing 4-34).

Listing 4-34. Activity to Send SMS Messages

```java
public class SmsActivity extends Activity {
    private static final String SHORTCODE = "55443";
    private static final String ACTION_SENT =
            "com.examples.sms.SENT";
    private static final String ACTION_DELIVERED =
            "com.examples.sms.DELIVERED";

    @Override
    public void onCreate(Bundle savedInstanceState) {
        super.onCreate(savedInstanceState);

        Button sendButton = new Button(this);
        sendButton.setText("Hail the Mothership");
        sendButton.setOnClickListener(new View.OnClickListener() {
            @Override
            public void onClick(View v) {
                sendSMS("Beam us up!");
            }
        });

        setContentView(sendButton);
    }

    private void sendSMS(String message) {
        PendingIntent sIntent = PendingIntent.getBroadcast(
            this, 0, new Intent(ACTION_SENT), 0);
        PendingIntent dIntent = PendingIntent.getBroadcast(
            this, 0, new Intent(ACTION_DELIVERED), 0);
         //Monitor status of the operation
        registerReceiver(sent, new IntentFilter(ACTION_SENT));
        registerReceiver(delivered,
                new IntentFilter(ACTION_DELIVERED));
         //Send the message
        SmsManager manager = SmsManager.getDefault();
        manager.sendTextMessage(SHORTCODE, null, message,
                sIntent, dIntent);
    }

    private BroadcastReceiver sent = new BroadcastReceiver(){
        @Override
        public void onReceive(Context context, Intent intent) {
            switch (getResultCode()) {
            case Activity.RESULT_OK:
                //Handle sent success
                break;
```

```
        case SmsManager.RESULT_ERROR_GENERIC_FAILURE:
        case SmsManager.RESULT_ERROR_NO_SERVICE:
        case SmsManager.RESULT_ERROR_NULL_PDU:
        case SmsManager.RESULT_ERROR_RADIO_OFF:
            //Handle sent error
            break;
        }

        unregisterReceiver(this);
    }
};

private BroadcastReceiver delivered = new BroadcastReceiver(){
    @Override
    public void onReceive(Context context, Intent intent) {
        switch (getResultCode()) {
        case Activity.RESULT_OK:
            //Handle delivery success
            break;
        case Activity.RESULT_CANCELED:
            //Handle delivery failure
            break;
        }

        unregisterReceiver(this);
    }
};
}
```

> **Important** Sending SMS messages requires that the android.permission.SEND_SMS permission be declared in the manifest!

In the example, an SMS message is sent out via the SMSManager whenever the user taps the button. Because SMSManager is a system service, the static SMSManager.getDefault() method must be called to get a reference to it. sendTextMessage() takes the destination address (number), service center address, and message as parameters. The service center address should be null to allow SMSManager to use the system default.

Two BroadcastReceivers are registered to receive the callback Intents that will be sent: one for status of the send operation and the other for status of the delivery. The receivers are registered only while the operations are pending, and they unregister themselves as soon as the Intent is processed.

4-11. Communicating over Bluetooth

Problem

You want to leverage Bluetooth communication to transmit data between devices in your application.

Solution

(API Level 5)

Use the Bluetooth APIs introduced in API Level 5 to create a peer-to-peer connection over the Radio frequency communications (RFCOMM) protocol interface. Bluetooth is a very popular wireless radio technology that is in almost all mobile devices today. Many users think of Bluetooth as a way for their mobile devices to connect with a wireless headset or integrate with a vehicle's stereo system. However, Bluetooth can also be a simple and effective way for developers to create peer-to-peer connections in their applications.

How It Works

> **Important**   Bluetooth is not currently supported in the Android emulator. In order to execute the code in this example, Bluetooth must be run on an Android device. Furthermore, to appropriately test the functionality, you need two devices running the application simultaneously.

Bluetooth Peer-to-Peer

Listings 4-35 through 4-37 illustrate an example that uses Bluetooth to find other users nearby and quickly exchange contact information (in this case, just an email address). Connections are made over Bluetooth by discovering available "services" and connecting to them by referencing their unique 128-bit UUID value. The UUID of the service you want to use must either be discovered or known ahead of time.

In this example, the same application is running on both devices on each end of the connection, so we have the freedom to define the UUID in code as a constant because both devices will have a reference to it.

> **Note**   To ensure that the UUID you choose is unique, use one of the many free UUID generators available on the Web or tools such as uuidgen on Mac/Linux.

Listing 4-35. AndroidManifest.xml

```xml
<?xml version="1.0" encoding="utf-8"?>
<manifest
    xmlns:android="http://schemas.android.com/apk/res/android"
    android:versionCode="1"
    android:versionName="1.0"
    package="com.examples.bluetooth">

    <uses-sdk android:minSdkVersion="5" />

    <uses-permission android:name="android.permission.BLUETOOTH"/>
    <uses-permission
        android:name="android.permission.BLUETOOTH_ADMIN"/>

    <application android:icon="@drawable/icon"
        android:label="@string/app_name">
        <activity android:name=".ExchangeActivity"
            android:label="@string/app_name">
            <intent-filter>
                <action
                    android:name="android.intent.action.MAIN" />
                <category
                    android:name="android.intent.category.LAUNCHER" />
            </intent-filter>
        </activity>
    </application>
</manifest>
```

> **Important**   Remember that `android.permission.BLUETOOTH` must be declared in the manifest to use these APIs. In addition, `android.permission.BLUETOOTH_ADMIN` must be declared to make changes to preferences such as discoverability and to enable/disable the adapter.

Listing 4-36. res/layout/main.xml

```xml
<?xml version="1.0" encoding="utf-8"?>
<RelativeLayout
    xmlns:android="http://schemas.android.com/apk/res/android"
    android:layout_width="match_parent"
    android:layout_height="match_parent">
    <TextView
        android:id="@+id/label"
        android:layout_width="wrap_content"
        android:layout_height="wrap_content"
        android:textAppearance="?android:attr/textAppearanceLarge"
        android:text="Enter Your Email:" />
```

```
        <EditText
            android:id="@+id/emailField"
            android:layout_width="match_parent"
            android:layout_height="wrap_content"
            android:layout_below="@id/label"
            android:singleLine="true"
            android:inputType="textEmailAddress" />
        <Button
            android:id="@+id/scanButton"
            android:layout_width="match_parent"
            android:layout_height="wrap_content"
            android:layout_alignParentBottom="true"
            android:text="Connect and Share" />
        <Button
            android:id="@+id/listenButton"
            android:layout_width="match_parent"
            android:layout_height="wrap_content"
            android:layout_above="@id/scanButton"
            android:text="Listen for Sharers" />
</RelativeLayout>
```

The user interface for this example consists of an EditText for users to enter an email address, and two buttons to initiate communication. The Listen for Sharers button puts the device into listen mode. In this mode, the device will accept and communicate with any device that attempts to connect with it. The Connect and Share button puts the device into search mode. In this mode, the device searches for any device that is currently listening and makes a connection (see Listing 4-37).

Listing 4-37. Bluetooth Exchange Activity

```
public class ExchangeActivity extends Activity {

    // Unique UUID for this application (generated from the web)
    private static final UUID MY_UUID =
        UUID.fromString("321cb8fa-9066-4f58-935e-ef55d1ae06ec");
    //Friendly name to match while discovering
    private static final String SEARCH_NAME = "bluetooth.recipe";

    BluetoothAdapter mBtAdapter;
    BluetoothSocket mBtSocket;
    Button listenButton, scanButton;
    EditText emailField;

    @Override
    public void onCreate(Bundle savedInstanceState) {
        super.onCreate(savedInstanceState);
        requestWindowFeature(
                Window.FEATURE_INDETERMINATE_PROGRESS);
        setContentView(R.layout.main);
```

```java
    //Check the system status
    mBtAdapter = BluetoothAdapter.getDefaultAdapter();
    if(mBtAdapter == null) {
        Toast.makeText(this, "Bluetooth is not supported.",
            Toast.LENGTH_SHORT).show();
        finish();
        return;
    }
    if (!mBtAdapter.isEnabled()) {
        Intent enableIntent = new Intent(
                BluetoothAdapter.ACTION_REQUEST_ENABLE);
        startActivityForResult(enableIntent, REQUEST_ENABLE);
    }

    emailField = (EditText)findViewById(R.id.emailField);
    listenButton = (Button)findViewById(R.id.listenButton);
    listenButton.setOnClickListener(
            new View.OnClickListener() {
        @Override
        public void onClick(View v) {
            //Make sure the device is discoverable first
            if (mBtAdapter.getScanMode() != BluetoothAdapter
                    .SCAN_MODE_CONNECTABLE_DISCOVERABLE) {
                Intent discoverableIntent = new Intent(
                        BluetoothAdapter
                            .ACTION_REQUEST_DISCOVERABLE);
                discoverableIntent.putExtra(BluetoothAdapter.
                        EXTRA_DISCOVERABLE_DURATION, 300);
                startActivityForResult(discoverableIntent,
                        REQUEST_DISCOVERABLE);
                return;
            }
            startListening();
        }
    });
    scanButton = (Button)findViewById(R.id.scanButton);
    scanButton.setOnClickListener(new View.OnClickListener() {
        @Override
        public void onClick(View v) {
            mBtAdapter.startDiscovery();
            setProgressBarIndeterminateVisibility(true);
        }
    });
}

@Override
public void onResume() {
    super.onResume();
    //Register the activity for broadcast intents
    IntentFilter filter = new IntentFilter(
            BluetoothDevice.ACTION_FOUND);
    registerReceiver(mReceiver, filter);
```

```java
        filter = new IntentFilter(
                BluetoothAdapter.ACTION_DISCOVERY_FINISHED);
        registerReceiver(mReceiver, filter);
    }

    @Override
    public void onPause() {
        super.onPause();
        unregisterReceiver(mReceiver);
    }

    @Override
    public void onDestroy() {
        super.onDestroy();
        try {
            if(mBtSocket != null) {
                mBtSocket.close();
            }
        } catch (IOException e) {
            e.printStackTrace();
        }
    }

    private static final int REQUEST_ENABLE = 1;
    private static final int REQUEST_DISCOVERABLE = 2;

    @Override
    protected void onActivityResult(int requestCode,
            int resultCode, Intent data) {
        switch(requestCode) {
        case REQUEST_ENABLE:
            if(resultCode != Activity.RESULT_OK) {
                Toast.makeText(this, "Bluetooth Not Enabled.",
                    Toast.LENGTH_SHORT).show();
                finish();
            }
            break;
        case REQUEST_DISCOVERABLE:
            if(resultCode == Activity.RESULT_CANCELED) {
                Toast.makeText(this, "Must be discoverable.",
                    Toast.LENGTH_SHORT).show();
            } else {
                startListening();
            }
            break;
        default:
            break;
        }
    }
```

```java
//Start a server socket and listen
private void startListening() {
    AcceptTask task = new AcceptTask();
    task.execute(MY_UUID);
    setProgressBarIndeterminateVisibility(true);
}

//AsyncTask to accept incoming connections
private class AcceptTask extends
        AsyncTask<UUID, Void, BluetoothSocket> {

    @Override
    protected BluetoothSocket doInBackground(UUID... params) {
        String name = mBtAdapter.getName();
        try {
            //While listening, set the discovery name to
            // a specific value
            mBtAdapter.setName(SEARCH_NAME);
            BluetoothServerSocket socket = mBtAdapter
                    .listenUsingRfcommWithServiceRecord(
                        "BluetoothRecipe", params[0]);
            BluetoothSocket connected = socket.accept();
            //Reset the BT adapter name
            mBtAdapter.setName(name);
            return connected;
        } catch (IOException e) {
            e.printStackTrace();
            mBtAdapter.setName(name);
            return null;
        }
    }

    @Override
    protected void onPostExecute(BluetoothSocket socket) {
        if(socket == null) {
            return;
        }
        mBtSocket = socket;
        ConnectedTask task = new ConnectedTask();
        task.execute(mBtSocket);
    }

}

//AsyncTask to receive a single line of data and post
private class ConnectedTask extends
        AsyncTask<BluetoothSocket,Void,String> {

    @Override
    protected String doInBackground(
            BluetoothSocket... params) {
        InputStream in = null;
```

```
            OutputStream out = null;
            try {
                //Send your data
                out = params[0].getOutputStream();
                String email = emailField.getText().toString();
                out.write(email.getBytes());
                //Receive the other's data
                in = params[0].getInputStream();
                byte[] buffer = new byte[1024];
                in.read(buffer);
                //Create a clean string from results
                String result = new String(buffer);
                //Close the connection
                mBtSocket.close();
                return result.trim();
            } catch (Exception exc) {
                return null;
            }
        }

        @Override
        protected void onPostExecute(String result) {
            Toast.makeText(ExchangeActivity.this, result,
                    Toast.LENGTH_SHORT).show();
            setProgressBarIndeterminateVisibility(false);
        }
    }

    // The BroadcastReceiver that listens for discovered devices
    private BroadcastReceiver mReceiver =
            new BroadcastReceiver() {
        @Override
        public void onReceive(Context context, Intent intent) {
            String action = intent.getAction();

            // When discovery finds a device
            if (BluetoothDevice.ACTION_FOUND.equals(action)) {
                // Get the BluetoothDevice object from the Intent
                BluetoothDevice device =
                    intent.getParcelableExtra(
                        BluetoothDevice.EXTRA_DEVICE);
                if(TextUtils.equals(device.getName(),
                        SEARCH_NAME)) {
                    //Matching device found, connect
                    mBtAdapter.cancelDiscovery();
                    try {
                        mBtSocket = device
                            .createRfcommSocketToServiceRecord(
                                MY_UUID);
                        mBtSocket.connect();
                        ConnectedTask task = new ConnectedTask();
```

```
                    task.execute(mBtSocket);
                } catch (IOException e) {
                    e.printStackTrace();
                }
            }
        //When discovery is complete
        } else if (BluetoothAdapter.ACTION_DISCOVERY_FINISHED
                .equals(action)) {
            setProgressBarIndeterminateVisibility(false);
        }


        }
    };
}
```

When the application first starts up, it runs some basic checks on the Bluetooth status of the device. If `BluetoothAdapter.getDefaultAdapter()` returns `null`, it is an indication that the device does not have Bluetooth support, and the application will go no further. Even with Bluetooth on the device, it must be enabled for the application to use it. If Bluetooth is disabled, the preferred method for enabling the adapter is to send an Intent to the system with `BluetoothAdapter.ACTION_REQUEST_ENABLE` as the action. This notifies the user of the issue, and that user can then enable Bluetooth. A `BluetoothAdapter` can be manually enabled with the `enable()` method, but we strongly discourage you from doing this unless you have requested the user's permission another way.

With Bluetooth validated, the application waits for user input. As mentioned previously, the example can be put into one of two modes on each device: listen mode or search mode. Let's look at the path each mode takes.

Listen Mode

Tapping the Listen for Sharers button starts the application listening for incoming connections. In order for a device to accept incoming connections from devices it may not know, it must be set as discoverable. The application verifies this by checking whether the adapter's scan mode is equal to `SCAN_MODE_CONNECTABLE_DISCOVERABLE`. If the adapter does not meet this requirement, another Intent is sent to the system to notify the user that they should allow the device to be discoverable, similar to the method used to request that Bluetooth be enabled. If the user accepts this request, the activity will return a result equal to the length of time they allowed the device to be discoverable; if they cancel the request, the activity will return `Activity.RESULT_CANCELED`. Our example monitors for a user canceling in `onActivityResult()`, and finishes under those conditions.

If the user allows discovery, or if the device was already discoverable, an `AcceptTask` is created and executed. This task creates a listener socket for the specified UUID of the service we defined, and it blocks the calling thread while waiting for an incoming connection request. Once a valid request is received, it is accepted, and the application moves into connected mode.

During the period of time while the device is listening, its Bluetooth name is set to a known unique value (`SEARCH_NAME`) to speed up the discovery process (you'll see more about why in the "Search Mode" section). Once the connection is established, the default name given to the adapter is restored.

Search Mode

Tapping the Connect and Share button tells the application to begin searching for another device to connect with. It does this by starting a Bluetooth discovery process and handling the results in a BroadcastReceiver. When a discovery is started via BluetoothAdapter.startDiscovery(), Android will asynchronously call back with broadcasts under two conditions: when another device is found, and when the process is complete.

The private receiver mReceiver is registered at all times when the activity is visible to the user, and it will receive a broadcast with each new discovered device. Recall from the discussion on listen mode that the device name of a listening device was set to a unique value. Upon each discovery made, the receiver checks that the device name matches our known value, and it attempts to connect when one is found. This is important to the speed of the discovery process, because otherwise the only way to validate each device is to attempt a connection to the specific service UUID and see whether the operation is successful. The Bluetooth connection process is heavyweight and slow and should be done only when necessary to keep things performing well.

This method of matching devices also relieves the user of the need to select manually which device they want to connect to. The application is smart enough to find another device that is running the same application and in a listening mode to complete the transfer. Removing the user also means that this value should be unique and obscure so as to avoid finding other devices that may accidentally have the same name.

With a matching device found, we cancel the discovery process (as it is also heavyweight and will slow down the connection) and then make a connection to the service's UUID. With a successful connection made, the application moves into connected mode.

Connected Mode

Once connected, the application on both devices will create a ConnectedTask to send and receive the user contact information. The connected BluetoothSocket has an InputStream and an OutputStream available to do data transfer. First, the current value of the e-mail text field is packaged up and written to the OutputStream. Then, the InputStream is read to receive the remote device's information. Finally, each device takes the raw data it received and packages this into a clean string to display for the user.

The ConnectedTask.onPostExecute() method is tasked with displaying the results of the exchange to the user; currently, this is done by raising a Toast with the received contents. After the transaction, the connection is closed, and both devices are in the same mode and ready to execute another exchange.

For more information on this topic, take a look at the BluetoothChat sample application provided with the Android SDK. This application provides a great demonstration of making a long-lived connection for users to send chat messages between devices.

Bluetooth Beyond Android

As we mentioned in the beginning of this section, Bluetooth is found in many wireless devices besides mobile phones and tablets. RFCOMM interfaces also exist in devices such as Bluetooth modems and serial adapters. The same APIs that were used to create the peer-to-peer connection between Android devices can also be used to connect to other embedded Bluetooth devices for the purposes of monitoring and control.

The key to establishing a connection with these embedded devices is obtaining the UUID of the RFCOMM services they support. Bluetooth services that are part of a profile standard, and their identifiers, are defined by the Bluetooth Special Interest Group (SIG); so you may be able to obtain the UUID you require for a given device from the documentation provided on www.bluetooth.org. However, if your device manufacturer has defined a device-specific UUID for a custom service type and it is not readily documented, we must have a way to discover it. As with the previous example, with the proper UUID we can create a BluetoothSocket and transmit data.

The capability to do this exists in the SDK, although prior to Android 4.0.3 (API Level 15) it was not part of the public SDK. There are two methods on BluetoothDevice that will provide this information; fetchUuidsWithSdp() and getUuids(). The latter simply returns the cached instances for the device found during discovery, while the former asynchronously connects to the device and does a fresh query. Because of this, when using fetchUuidsWithSdp(), you must register a BroadcastReceiver that will receive Intents set with the BluetoothDevice.ACTION_UUID action string to discover the UUID values.

Discover a UUID

A quick glance at the source code for BluetoothDevice (thanks to Android's open source roots) points out that these methods to return UUID information for a remote device have existed for a while. If necessary, we can use reflection to call them in earlier Android versions now that they are part of the public API and won't change in the future. The simplest to use is the synchronous (blocking) method getUuids(), which returns an array of ParcelUuid objects referring to each service. Here is an example method for reading the UUIDs of service records from a remote device using reflection:

```
public ParcelUuid servicesFromDevice(BluetoothDevice device) {
    try {
        Class cl =
            Class.forName("android.bluetooth.BluetoothDevice");
        Class[] par = {};
        Method method = cl.getMethod("getUuids", par);
        Object[] args = {};
        ParcelUuid[] retval =
            (ParcelUuid[]) method.invoke(device, args);
        return retval;
    } catch (Exception e) {
        e.printStackTrace();
        return null;
    }
}
```

You may also call fetchUuidsWithSdp()in the same fashion, but there were some variations in the Intent structure that was returned in early versions, so we would not recommend doing so for earlier Android versions.

4-12. Querying Network Reachability

Problem

Your application needs to be aware of changes in network connectivity.

Solution

(API Level 1)

Keep tabs on the device's connectivity with ConnectivityManager. One of the paramount issues to consider in mobile application design is that the network is not always available for use. As people move about, the speeds and capabilities of networks are subject to change. An application that uses network resources should always be able to detect whether those resources are reachable and then notify the user when they are not.

In addition to reachability, ConnectivityManager can provide the application with information about the connection type. This allows you to make decisions such as whether to download a large file because the user is currently roaming and it may cost the user a fortune.

How It Works

Listing 4-38 creates a wrapper method you can place in your code to check for network connectivity.

Listing 4-38. ConnectivityManager Wrapper

```
public static boolean isNetworkReachable() {
    final ConnectivityManager mManager =
            (ConnectivityManager)context.getSystemService(
                    Context.CONNECTIVITY_SERVICE);
    NetworkInfo current = mManager.getActiveNetworkInfo();
    if(current == null) {
        return false;
    }
    return (current.getState() == NetworkInfo.State.CONNECTED);
}
```

ConnectivityManager does pretty much all the work in checking the network status, and this wrapper method is more to simplify having to check all possible network paths each time. Note that ConnectivityManager.getActiveNetworkInfo() will return null if there is no active data connection available, so we must check for that case first. If there is an active network, we can inspect its state, which will return one of the following:

- DISCONNECTED
- CONNECTING
- CONNECTED
- DISCONNECTING

When the state returns as CONNECTED, the network is considered stable and we can utilize it to access remote resources.

Verifying a Route

Mobile devices have multiple connectivity routes (WiFi, 3G/4G, and so forth), and it is common for a device to be connected to a network that doesn't have a route to the external Web; this is especially common with WiFi networks. ConnectivityManager alone simply notifies you of whether or not your device has associated with a particular network, but says nothing of that network's ability to access an outside IP address. Add to this the fact that when a device attempts to connect through a network that is "connected" but has no valid route, the time the network stack can take to time out and fail properly can be minutes.

You may find yourself in a situation where it is smarter to check for a valid Internet connection rather than just an association with a network. Listing 4-39 builds on the previous reachability check to do just that.

Listing 4-39. Smarter ConnectivityManager Wrapper

```java
public static boolean hasNetworkConnection(Context context) {
        final ConnectivityManager connectivityManager =
                (ConnectivityManager) context.getSystemService(
                        Context.CONNECTIVITY_SERVICE);
        final NetworkInfo activeNetworkInfo =
                connectivityManager.getActiveNetworkInfo();

        //If we aren't even associated with a network, we're done
        boolean connected = (null != activeNetworkInfo)
                && activeNetworkInfo.isConnected();
        if (!connected) return false;

        //Check if we can access a remote server
        boolean routeExists;
        try {
            //Check Google Public DNS
            InetAddress host = InetAddress.getByName("8.8.8.8");

            Socket s = new Socket();
            s.connect(new InetSocketAddress(host, 53), 5000);
            //It exists if no exception is thrown
            routeExists = true;
            s.close();
        } catch (IOException e) {
            routeExists = false;
        }

        return (connected && routeExists);
}
```

After verifying the same reachability condition as before, Listing 4-39 goes a step further and attempts to open a socket to the well-known standard IPv4 address for the Google Public DNS (8.8.8.8) with a 5-second time-out. If a connection to this host succeeds, we can have a relatively high level of confidence that the device can access any active Internet resource. The advantage to this approach over attempting to fully connect directly to your remote server is that this code will fail faster, forcing up to only a 5-second delay before telling the user they really don't have the Internet connection they think they do.

It is considered good practice to call a reachability check whenever a network request fails and to notify the user that their request failed because of a lack of connectivity. Listing 4-40 is an example of doing this when a network access fails.

Listing 4-40. Notify User of Connectivity Failure

```
try {
    //Attempt to access network resource. May throw
    // HttpResponseException or some other IOException on failure
} catch (Exception e) {
    if( !isNetworkReachable() ) {
        AlertDialog.Builder builder =
                new AlertDialog.Builder(context);
        builder.setTitle("No Network Connection");
        builder.setMessage("The Network is unavailable."
                + " Please try your request again later.");
        builder.setPositiveButton("OK",null);
        builder.create().show();
    }
}
```

Determining Connection Type

In cases where it is also essential to know whether the user is connected to a network that charges for bandwidth, we can call NetworkInfo.getType() on the active network connection (see Listing 4-41).

Listing 4-41. ConnectivityManager Bandwidth Checking

```
public boolean isWifiReachable() {
    ConnectivityManager mManager =
            (ConnectivityManager)context.getSystemService(
                    Context.CONNECTIVITY_SERVICE);
    NetworkInfo current = mManager.getActiveNetworkInfo();
    if(current == null) {
        return false;
    }
    return (current.getType() == ConnectivityManager.TYPE_WIFI);
}
```

This modified version of the reachability check determines whether the user is attached to a WiFi connection, typically indicating that the user has a faster connection where bandwidth isn't tariffed.

4-13. Transferring Data with NFC

Problem

You have an application that must quickly transfer small data packets between two Android devices with minimal setup.

Solution

(API Level 16)

Use the Near field communications (NFC) Beam APIs. NFC communication was originally added to the SDK in Android 2.3 and was expanded in 4.0 to make short-message transfer between devices painless through a process called Android Beam. In Android 4.1, even more was added to make the Beam APIs fully mature for transferring data between two devices.

One of the major additions in 4.1 was the ability to transfer large data over alternate connections. NFC is a great method of discovering devices and setting up an initial connection, but it is low bandwidth and inefficient for sending large data packets such as full-color images. Previously, developers could use NFC to connect two devices but would need to manually negotiate a second connection over WiFi Direct or Bluetooth to transfer the file data. In Android 4.1, the framework now handles that entire process, and any application can share large files over any available connection with a single API call.

How It Works

Depending on the size of the content you wish to push, there are two mechanisms available to transfer data from one device to another.

Beaming with Foreground Push

If you want to send simple content between devices over NFC, you can use the foreground push mechanism to create an `NfcMessage` containing one or more `NfcRecord` instances. Listings 4-42 and 4-43 illustrate creating a simple `NfcMessage` to push to another device.

Listing 4-42. AndroidManifest.xml

```xml
<manifest
    xmlns:android="http://schemas.android.com/apk/res/android"
    package="com.examples.nfcbeam"
    android:versionCode="1"
    android:versionName="1.0" >

    <uses-sdk
        android:minSdkVersion="16"
        android:targetSdkVersion="16" />
```

```xml
<uses-permission android:name="android.permission.NFC" />
<application
    android:icon="@drawable/ic_launcher"
    android:label="NfcBeam">
    <activity
        android:name=".NfcActivity"
        android:label="NfcActivity"
        android:launchMode="singleTop">
        <intent-filter>
            <action android:name="android.intent.action.MAIN" />
            <category android:name="android.intent.category.LAUNCHER" />
        </intent-filter>
        <intent-filter>
            <action android:name="android.nfc.action.NDEF_DISCOVERED" />
            <category android:name="android.intent.category.DEFAULT" />
            <data android:mimeType=
                "application/com.example.androidrecipes.beamtext"/>
        </intent-filter>
    </activity>
</application>
</manifest>
```

First notice that android.permission.NFC is required to work with the NFC service. Second, note the custom <intent-filter> placed on our activity. This is how Android will know which application to launch in response to the content it receives.

Listing 4-43. Activity Generating an NFC Foreground Push

```java
public class NfcActivity extends Activity implements
        CreateNdefMessageCallback, OnNdefPushCompleteCallback {
    private static final String TAG = "NfcBeam";
    private NfcAdapter mNfcAdapter;
    private TextView mDisplay;

    @Override
    public void onCreate(Bundle savedInstanceState) {
        super.onCreate(savedInstanceState);
        mDisplay = new TextView(this);
        setContentView(mDisplay);

        // Check for available NFC Adapter
        mNfcAdapter = NfcAdapter.getDefaultAdapter(this);
        if (mNfcAdapter == null) {
          mDisplay.setText("NFC not available on this device.");
        } else {
            // Register callback to set NDEF message. Setting
            // this makes NFC data push active while the Activity
            // is in the foreground.
            mNfcAdapter.setNdefPushMessageCallback(this, this);
```

```java
        // Register callback for message-sent success
        mNfcAdapter.setOnNdefPushCompleteCallback(this, this);
    }
}

@Override
public void onResume() {
    super.onResume();
    // Check to see if a Beam launched this Activity
    if (NfcAdapter.ACTION_NDEF_DISCOVERED
            .equals(getIntent().getAction())) {
        processIntent(getIntent());
    }
}

@Override
public void onNewIntent(Intent intent) {
    // onResume gets called after this to handle the intent
    setIntent(intent);
}

void processIntent(Intent intent) {
    Parcelable[] rawMsgs = intent.getParcelableArrayExtra(
            NfcAdapter.EXTRA_NDEF_MESSAGES);
    // only one message sent during the beam
    NdefMessage msg = (NdefMessage) rawMsgs[0];
    // record 0 contains the MIME type
    mDisplay.setText(new String(
            msg.getRecords()[0].getPayload()) );
}

@Override
public NdefMessage createNdefMessage(NfcEvent event) {
    String text = String.format(
            "Sending A Message From Android Recipes at %s",
            DateFormat.getTimeFormat(this)
                    .format(new Date()) );
    NdefMessage msg = new NdefMessage(NdefRecord.createMime(
            "application/com.example.androidrecipes.beamtext",
            text.getBytes()) );
    return msg;
}

@Override
public void onNdefPushComplete(NfcEvent event) {
    //This callback happens on a binder thread, don't update
    // the UI directly from this method.
    Log.i(TAG, "Message Sent!");
}
}
```

This example application encompasses both the sending and receiving of an NFC push, so the same application should be installed on both devices: the one that is sending and the one that is receiving the data. The activity registers itself for foreground push by using the setNdefPushMessageCallback() method on the NfcAdapter. This call does two things simultaneously. It tells the NFC service to call this activity at the moment a transfer is initiated to receive the message it needs to send, and it also activates NFC push whenever this activity is in the foreground. There is also an alternate version of this called setNdefPushMessage() that takes the message directly rather than implementing a callback.

The callback method constructs an NdefMessage containing a single NFC Data Exchange Format (NDEF) MIME record (created with the NdefRecord.createMime() method). MIME records are simple ways of passing application-specific data. The createMime() method takes both a string for the MIME type and a byte array for the raw data. The information can be anything from a text string to a small image; your application is responsible for packing and unpacking it. Notice that the MIME type here matches the type defined in the manifest's <intent-filter>.

In order for the push to work, the sending device must have this activity active in the foreground, and the receiving device must not be locked. When the user touches the two devices together, the sending screen shows Android's Touch to Beam UI, and a tap of the screen sends the message to the other device. As soon as the message is received, the application launches on the receiving device, and the sending device's onNdefPushComplete() callback is triggered.

On the receiving device, the activity is launched with the ACTION_NDEF_DISCOVERED Intent, so our example will inspect the Intent for the NdefMessage and unpack the payload, turning it back from bytes into a string. This method of using Intent matching to send NFC data is the most flexible, but sometimes you want your application to be explicitly called. This is where Android Application Records come in.

Android Application Records

Your application can provide an additional NdefRecord inside an NdefMessage that directs Android to call a specific package name on the receiving device. To include this in our previous example, we would simply modify the CreateNdefMessageCallback like so:

```
@Override
public NdefMessage createNdefMessage(NfcEvent event) {
    String text = String.format(
            "Sending A Message From Android Recipes at %s",
            DateFormat.getTimeFormat(this)
                    .format(new Date()) );
    NdefMessage msg = new NdefMessage(NdefRecord.createMime(
            "application/com.example.androidrecipes.beamtext",
            text.getBytes()),
            NdefRecord
                .createApplicationRecord("com.examples.nfcbeam"));
    return msg;
}
```

With the addition of NdefRecord.createApplicationRecord(), this push message is now guaranteed to launch only our com.examples.nfcbeam package. The text information is still the first record in the message, so our unpacking of the received message remains unchanged.

Beaming Larger Content

We mentioned at the beginning of this recipe that sending large content blobs over NFC is not a great idea. However, Android Beam has the capability to handle that as well. Have a look at Listings 4-44 and 4-45 for examples of sending large image files over Beam.

Listing 4-44. AndroidManifest.xml

```xml
<manifest
    xmlns:android="http://schemas.android.com/apk/res/android"
    package="com.examples.nfcbeam"
    android:versionCode="1"
    android:versionName="1.0" >

    <uses-sdk
        android:minSdkVersion="16"
        android:targetSdkVersion="16" />

    <uses-permission android:name="android.permission.NFC" />
    <application
        android:icon="@drawable/ic_launcher"
        android:label="NfcBeam">
        <activity
            android:name=".BeamActivity"
            android:label="BeamActivity"
            android:launchMode="singleTop">
            <intent-filter>
                <action android:name="android.intent.action.MAIN" />
                <category
                    android:name="android.intent.category.LAUNCHER" />
            </intent-filter>
            <intent-filter>
                <action android:name="android.intent.action.VIEW" />
                <data android:mimeType="image/*" />
            </intent-filter>
        </activity>
    </application>

</manifest>
```

Listing 4-45. Activity to Transfer an Image File

```java
public class BeamActivity extends Activity implements
        CreateBeamUrisCallback, OnNdefPushCompleteCallback {
    private static final String TAG = "NfcBeam";
    private static final int PICK_IMAGE = 100;

    private NfcAdapter mNfcAdapter;
    private Uri mSelectedImage;
```

```java
private TextView mUriName;
private ImageView mPreviewImage;

@Override
protected void onCreate(Bundle savedInstanceState) {
    super.onCreate(savedInstanceState);
    setContentView(R.layout.main);

    mUriName = (TextView) findViewById(R.id.text_uri);
    mPreviewImage =
            (ImageView) findViewById(R.id.image_preview);

    // Check for available NFC Adapter
    mNfcAdapter = NfcAdapter.getDefaultAdapter(this);
    if (mNfcAdapter == null) {
        mUriName.setText("NFC not available on this device.");
    } else {
        // Register callback to set NDEF message
        mNfcAdapter.setBeamPushUrisCallback(this, this);
        // Register callback for message-sent success
        mNfcAdapter.setOnNdefPushCompleteCallback(this, this);
    }
}

@Override
protected void onActivityResult(int requestCode,
        int resultCode, Intent data) {
    if (requestCode == PICK_IMAGE && resultCode == RESULT_OK
            && data != null) {
        mUriName.setText( data.getData().toString() );
        mSelectedImage = data.getData();
    }
}

@Override
public void onResume() {
    super.onResume();
    //Check to see that the Activity started due to
    // an Android Beam
    if (Intent.ACTION_VIEW.equals(getIntent().getAction())) {
        processIntent(getIntent());
    }
}

@Override
public void onNewIntent(Intent intent) {
    // onResume gets called after this to handle the intent
    setIntent(intent);
}
```

```
void processIntent(Intent intent) {
    Uri data = intent.getData();
    if(data != null) {
        mPreviewImage.setImageURI(data);
    } else {
        mUriName.setText("Received Invalid Image Uri");
    }
}

public void onSelectClick(View v) {
    Intent intent = new Intent(Intent.ACTION_GET_CONTENT);
    intent.setType("image/*");
    startActivityForResult(intent, PICK_IMAGE);
}

@Override
public Uri[] createBeamUris(NfcEvent event) {
    if (mSelectedImage == null) {
        return null;
    }
    return new Uri[] {mSelectedImage};
}

@Override
public void onNdefPushComplete(NfcEvent event) {
    //This callback happens on a binder thread, don't update
    // the UI directly from this method. This is a good time
    // to tell your user they don't need to hold
    // their phones together anymore!
    Log.i(TAG, "Push Complete!");
}
}
```

This example uses CreateBeamUrisCallback, which allows an application to construct an array of Uri instances pointing to content you would like to transmit. Android will do the work of negotiating the initial connection over NFC but will then drop to a more suitable connection such as Bluetooth or WiFi Direct to finish the larger transfers.

In this case, the data on the receiving device is launched using the system's standard Intent. ACTION_VIEW action, so it is not necessary to load the application on both devices. However, our application does filter for ACTION_VIEW so the receiving device could use it to view the received image content if the user prefers.

Here, the user is asked to select an image from the device to transfer, and then the Uri of that content is displayed once selected. As soon as the user touches that device to another, the same Touch to Beam UI (see Figure 4-4) displays, and the transfer begins when the screen is tapped.

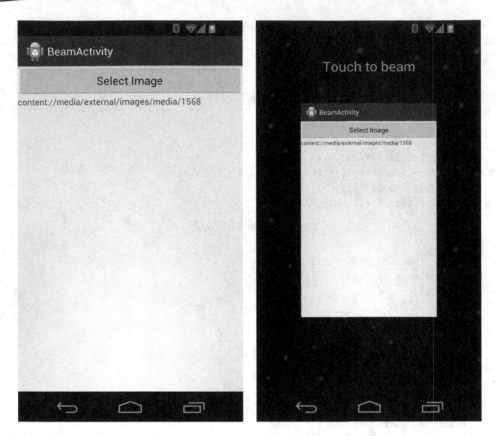

Figure 4-4. Activity with Touch to Beam activated

Once the NFC portion of the transfer is complete, the onNdefPushComplete() method is called on the sending device. At this point, the transfer has moved to another connection, so the users don't need to hold their phones together anymore.

The receiving device will display a progress notification in the system's window shade while the file is transferring. When the transfer is complete, the user can tap on the notification to view the content. If this application is chosen as the content viewer, the image will be shown in our application's ImageView. One possible disadvantage to registering your application with such a generic Intent is that every application on the device can then ask your application to view images, so choose your filters wisely!

4-14. Connecting over USB

Problem

Your application needs to communicate with a USB device for the purposes of control or transferring data.

Solution

(API Level 12)

Android has built-in support for devices that contain USB Host circuitry to allow them to enumerate and communicate with connected USB devices. USBManager is the system service that provides applications access to any external devices connected via USB, and we are going to see how you can use that service to establish a connection from your application.

USB Host circuitry is becoming more common on devices, but it is still rare. Initially, only tablet devices had this capability, but it is growing rapidly and may soon become a commonplace interface on commercial Android handsets as well. However, because of this you will certainly want to include the following element in your application manifest:

```
<uses-feature android:name="android.hardware.usb.host" />
```

This will limit your application to devices that have the available hardware to do the communications.

The APIs provided by Android are pretty much direct mirrors of the USB specification, without much in the way of higher-level abstraction. This means that if you would like to use them, you will need at least a basic knowledge of USB and how devices communicate.

USB Overview

Before looking at an example of how Android interacts with USB devices, let's take a moment to define some USB terms:

- *Endpoint*: The smallest building block of a USB device. These are what your application eventually connects to for the purpose of sending and receiving data. They can take the form of four main types:

    - *Control*: Used for configuration and status commands. Every device has at least one control endpoint, called *endpoint 0*, that is not attached to any interface.

    - *Interrupt*: Used for small, high-priority control commands.

    - *Bulk*: Large data transfer. Commonly found in bidirectional pair (1 IN and 1 OUT).

    - *Isochronous*: Used for real-time data transfer such as audio. Not supported by the latest Android SDK as of this writing.

- *Interface*: A collection of endpoints to represent a "logical" device.

  - Physical USB devices can manifest themselves to the host as multiple logical devices, and they do this by exposing multiple interfaces.

- *Configuration*: Collection of one or more interfaces. The USB protocol enforces that only one configuration can be active at any one time on a device. In fact, most devices have only one configuration at all. Think of this as the device's operating mode.

How It Works

Listings 4-46 and 4-47 show examples that use `UsbManager` to inspect devices connected over USB and then uses control transfers to further query the configuration.

Listing 4-46. `res/layout/main.xml`

```xml
<LinearLayout
    xmlns:android="http://schemas.android.com/apk/res/android"
    android:layout_width="match_parent"
    android:layout_height="match_parent"
    android:orientation="vertical" >
    <Button
        android:id="@+id/button_connect"
        android:layout_width="match_parent"
        android:layout_height="wrap_content"
        android:text="Connect"
        android:onClick="onConnectClick" />
    <TextView
        android:id="@+id/text_status"
        android:layout_width="match_parent"
        android:layout_height="wrap_content" />
    <TextView
        android:id="@+id/text_data"
        android:layout_width="match_parent"
        android:layout_height="wrap_content" />

</LinearLayout>
```

Listing 4-47. Activity on USB Host Querying Devices

```java
public class USBActivity extends Activity {
    private static final String TAG = "UsbHost";

    TextView mDeviceText, mDisplayText;
    Button mConnectButton;

    UsbManager mUsbManager;
    UsbDevice mDevice;
    PendingIntent mPermissionIntent;
```

```java
@Override
public void onCreate(Bundle savedInstanceState) {
    super.onCreate(savedInstanceState);
    setContentView(R.layout.main);

    mDeviceText = (TextView) findViewById(R.id.text_status);
    mDisplayText = (TextView) findViewById(R.id.text_data);
    mConnectButton =
        (Button) findViewById(R.id.button_connect);

    mUsbManager =
        (UsbManager) getSystemService(Context.USB_SERVICE);
}

@Override
protected void onResume() {
    super.onResume();
    mPermissionIntent =
        PendingIntent.getBroadcast(this, 0,
            new Intent(ACTION_USB_PERMISSION), 0);
    IntentFilter filter =
        new IntentFilter(ACTION_USB_PERMISSION);
    registerReceiver(mUsbReceiver, filter);

    //Check currently connected devices
    updateDeviceList();
}

@Override
protected void onPause() {
    super.onPause();
    unregisterReceiver(mUsbReceiver);
}

public void onConnectClick(View v) {
    if (mDevice == null) {
        return;
    }
    mDisplayText.setText("---");

    //This will either prompt the user with a grant permission
    // dialog, or immediately fire the ACTION_USB_PERMISSION
    // broadcast if the user has already granted it to us.
    mUsbManager.requestPermission(mDevice, mPermissionIntent);
}

/*
 * Receiver to catch user permission responses, which are
 * required in order to actually interact with a connected
 * device.
 */
```

```java
private static final String ACTION_USB_PERMISSION =
        "com.android.recipes.USB_PERMISSION";
private final BroadcastReceiver mUsbReceiver =
        new BroadcastReceiver() {
    public void onReceive(Context context, Intent intent) {
        String action = intent.getAction();
        if (ACTION_USB_PERMISSION.equals(action)) {
            UsbDevice device =
                (UsbDevice) intent.getParcelableExtra(
                    UsbManager.EXTRA_DEVICE);

            if (intent.getBooleanExtra(
                UsbManager.EXTRA_PERMISSION_GRANTED, false)
                && device != null) {
                    //Query the device's descriptor
                    getDeviceStatus(device);
            } else {
                Log.d(TAG, "permission denied for " + device);
            }
        }
    }
};

//Type: Indicates whether this is a read or write
// Matches USB_ENDPOINT_DIR_MASK for either IN or OUT
private static final int REQUEST_TYPE = 0x80;
//Request: GET_CONFIGURATION_DESCRIPTOR = 0x06
private static final int REQUEST = 0x06;
//Value: Descriptor Type (High) and Index (Low)
// Configuration Descriptor = 0x2
// Index = 0x0 (First configuration)
private static final int REQ_VALUE = 0x200;
private static final int REQ_INDEX = 0x00;
private static final int LENGTH = 64;

/*
 * Initiate a control transfer to request the first
 * configuration descriptor of the device.
 */
private void getDeviceStatus(UsbDevice device) {
    UsbDeviceConnection connection =
            mUsbManager.openDevice(device);
    //Create a sufficiently large buffer for incoming data
    byte[] buffer = new byte[LENGTH];
    connection.controlTransfer(REQUEST_TYPE, REQUEST,
            REQ_VALUE, REQ_INDEX, buffer, LENGTH, 2000);
    //Parse received data into a description
    String description = parseConfigDescriptor(buffer);

    mDisplayText.setText(description);
    connection.close();
}
```

```java
/*
 * Parse the USB configuration descriptor response per the
 * USB Specification.  Return a printable description of
 * the connected device.
 */
private static final int DESC_SIZE_CONFIG = 9;
private String parseConfigDescriptor(byte[] buffer) {
    StringBuilder sb = new StringBuilder();
    //Parse configuration descriptor header
    int totalLength = (buffer[3] &0xFF) << 8;
    totalLength += (buffer[2] & 0xFF);
    //Interface count
    int numInterfaces = (buffer[5] & 0xFF);
    //Configuration attributes
    int attributes = (buffer[7] & 0xFF);
    //Power is given in 2mA increments
    int maxPower = (buffer[8] & 0xFF) * 2;

    sb.append("Configuration Descriptor:\n");
    sb.append("Length: " + totalLength + " bytes\n");
    sb.append(numInterfaces + " Interfaces\n");
    sb.append(String.format("Attributes:%s%s%s\n",
        (attributes & 0x80) == 0x80 ? " BusPowered" : "",
        (attributes & 0x40) == 0x40 ? " SelfPowered" : "",
        (attributes & 0x20) == 0x20 ? " RemoteWakeup" : ""));
    sb.append("Max Power: " + maxPower + "mA\n");

    //The rest of the descriptor is interfaces and endpoints
    int index = DESC_SIZE_CONFIG;
    while (index < totalLength) {
        //Read length and type
        int len = (buffer[index] & 0xFF);
        int type = (buffer[index+1] & 0xFF);
        switch (type) {
        case 0x04: //Interface Descriptor
            int intfNumber = (buffer[index+2] & 0xFF);
            int numEndpoints = (buffer[index+4] & 0xFF);
            int intfClass = (buffer[index+5] & 0xFF);

            sb.append( String.format(
                    "- Interface %d, %s, %d Endpoints\n",
                    intfNumber,
                    nameForClass(intfClass),
                    numEndpoints) );
            break;
        case 0x05: //Endpoint Descriptor
            int endpointAddr = ((buffer[index+2] & 0xFF));
            //Number is lower 4 bits
            int endpointNum = (endpointAddr & 0x0F);
            //Direction is high bit
            int direction = (endpointAddr & 0x80);
```

```
                int endpointAttrs = (buffer[index+3] & 0xFF);
                //Type is the lower two bits
                int endpointType = (endpointAttrs & 0x3);

                sb.append(String.format("-- Endpoint %d, %s %s\n",
                        endpointNum,
                        nameForEndpointType(endpointType),
                        nameForDirection(direction) ));
                break;
            }
            //Advance to next descriptor
            index += len;
        }

        return sb.toString();
    }

    private void updateDeviceList() {
        HashMap<String, UsbDevice> connectedDevices =
                mUsbManager.getDeviceList();
        if (connectedDevices.isEmpty()) {
            mDevice = null;
            mDeviceText.setText("No Devices Currently Connected");
            mConnectButton.setEnabled(false);
        } else {
            StringBuilder builder = new StringBuilder();
            for (UsbDevice device : connectedDevices.values()) {
                //Use the last device detected (if multiple)
                // to open
                mDevice = device;
                builder.append(readDevice(device));
                builder.append("\n\n");
            }
            mDeviceText.setText(builder.toString());
            mConnectButton.setEnabled(true);
        }
    }

    /*
     * Enumerate the endpoints and interfaces on the connected
     * device. We do not need permission to do anything here, it
     * is all "publicly available" until we try to connect to
     * an actual device.
     */
    private String readDevice(UsbDevice device) {
        StringBuilder sb = new StringBuilder();
        sb.append("Device Name: " + device.getDeviceName()
                + "\n");
        sb.append( String.format(
                "Device Class: %s -> Subclass: 0x%02x -> "
                    + "Protocol: 0x%02x\n",
                nameForClass(device.getDeviceClass()),
```

```java
                device.getDeviceSubclass(),
                device.getDeviceProtocol())
    );

    for (int i = 0; i < device.getInterfaceCount(); i++) {
        UsbInterface intf = device.getInterface(i);
        sb.append( String.format(
                "+--Interface %d Class: %s -> "
                    + "Subclass: 0x%02x -> Protocol: 0x%02x\n",
                intf.getId(),
                nameForClass(intf.getInterfaceClass()),
                intf.getInterfaceSubclass(),
                intf.getInterfaceProtocol())
        );

        for (int j = 0; j < intf.getEndpointCount(); j++) {
            UsbEndpoint endpoint = intf.getEndpoint(j);
            sb.append( String.format(
                    "   +---Endpoint %d: %s %s\n",
                    endpoint.getEndpointNumber(),
                    nameForEndpointType(endpoint.getType()),
                    nameForDirection(endpoint.getDirection()))
            );
        }
    }

    return sb.toString();
}

/* Helper Methods to Provide Readable Names for USB Constants
 */

private String nameForClass(int classType) {
    switch (classType) {
    case UsbConstants.USB_CLASS_APP_SPEC:
        return String.format(
                "Application Specific 0x%02x", classType);
    case UsbConstants.USB_CLASS_AUDIO:
        return "Audio";
    case UsbConstants.USB_CLASS_CDC_DATA:
        return "CDC Control";
    case UsbConstants.USB_CLASS_COMM:
        return "Communications";
    case UsbConstants.USB_CLASS_CONTENT_SEC:
        return "Content Security";
    case UsbConstants.USB_CLASS_CSCID:
        return "Content Smart Card";
    case UsbConstants.USB_CLASS_HID:
        return "Human Interface Device";
    case UsbConstants.USB_CLASS_HUB:
        return "Hub";
```

```
            case UsbConstants.USB_CLASS_MASS_STORAGE:
                return "Mass Storage";
            case UsbConstants.USB_CLASS_MISC:
                return "Wireless Miscellaneous";
            case UsbConstants.USB_CLASS_PER_INTERFACE:
                return "(Defined Per Interface)";
            case UsbConstants.USB_CLASS_PHYSICA:
                return "Physical";
            case UsbConstants.USB_CLASS_PRINTER:
                return "Printer";
            case UsbConstants.USB_CLASS_STILL_IMAGE:
                return "Still Image";
            case UsbConstants.USB_CLASS_VENDOR_SPEC:
                return String.format(
                        "Vendor Specific 0x%02x", classType);
            case UsbConstants.USB_CLASS_VIDEO:
                return "Video";
            case UsbConstants.USB_CLASS_WIRELESS_CONTROLLER:
                return "Wireless Controller";
            default:
                return String.format("0x%02x", classType);
        }
    }

    private String nameForEndpointType(int type) {
        switch (type) {
        case UsbConstants.USB_ENDPOINT_XFER_BULK:
            return "Bulk";
        case UsbConstants.USB_ENDPOINT_XFER_CONTROL:
            return "Control";
        case UsbConstants.USB_ENDPOINT_XFER_INT:
            return "Interrupt";
        case UsbConstants.USB_ENDPOINT_XFER_ISOC:
            return "Isochronous";
        default:
            return "Unknown Type";
        }
    }

    private String nameForDirection(int direction) {
        switch (direction) {
        case UsbConstants.USB_DIR_IN:
            return "IN";
        case UsbConstants.USB_DIR_OUT:
            return "OUT";
        default:
            return "Unknown Direction";
        }
    }
}
```

When the activity first comes into the foreground, it registers a BroadcastReceiver with a custom action (which we'll discuss in more detail shortly), and it queries the list of currently connected devices by using UsbManager.getDeviceList(), which returns a HashMap of UsbDevice items that we can iterate over and interrogate. For each device connected, we query each interface and endpoint, building a description string to print to the user about what this device is. We then print all that data to the user interface.

> **Note**   This application, as it stands, does not require any manifest permissions. We do not need to declare a permission simply to query information about devices connected to the host.

You can see that UsbManager provides APIs to inspect just about every piece of information you would need to discover if a connected device is the one you are interested in communicating with. All standard definitions for device classes, endpoint types, and transfer directions are also defined in UsbConstants, so you can match the types you want without defining all of this yourself.

So, what about that BroadcastReceiver we registered? The remainder of this example code takes action when the user presses the Connect button on the screen. At this point, we would like to talk to the connected device, which is an operation that does require user permission. Here, when the user clicks the button, we call UsbManager.requestPermission() to ask the user if we can connect. If permission has not yet been granted, the user will see a dialog box asking him or her to grant permission to connect.

Upon saying yes, the PendingIntent passed along to the method will get fired. In our example, that Intent was a broadcast with a custom action string we defined, so this will trigger onReceive() in that BroadcastReceiver; any subsequent calls to requestPermission() will immediately trigger the receiver as well. Inside the receiver, we check to make sure that the result was a permission-granted response, and we attempt to open a connection to the device with UsbManager.openDevice(), which returns a UsbDeviceConnection instance when successful.

With a valid connection made, we request some more detailed information about the device by requesting its configuration descriptor via a control transfer. Control transfers are requests always made on endpoint 0 of the device. A configuration descriptor contains information about the configuration as well as each interface and endpoint, so its length is variable. We allocate a decent-sized buffer to ensure we capture everything.

Upon returning from controlTransfer(), the buffer is filled with the response data. Our application then processes the bytes, determining some more information about the device, including its maximum power draw and whether the device is configured to be powered from the USB post (bus-powered) or by an external source (self-powered). This example parses out only a fraction of the useful information that can be found inside these descriptors. Once again, all the parsed data is put into a string report and displayed to the user interface.

Much of the data read in the first section from the framework APIs and in the second section directly from the device is the same and should match up 1:1 between the two text reports displayed on the screen. One thing to note is that this application works only if the device is already connected when the application runs: it will not be notified if a connection happens while it is in the foreground. We will look at how to handle that scenario in the next section.

Getting Notified of Device Connections

In order for Android to notify your application when a particular device is connected, you need to register the device types you are interested in with an `<intent-filter>` in the manifest. Take a look at Listings 4-48 and 4-49 to see how this is done.

Listing 4-48. Partial `AndroidManifest.xml`

```xml
<activity
    android:name=".USBActivity"
    android:label="@string/title_activity_usb" >
    <intent-filter>
        <action android:name="android.intent.action.MAIN" />
        <category android:name="android.intent.category.LAUNCHER" />
    </intent-filter>
    <intent-filter>
        <action android:name=
            "android.hardware.usb.action.USB_DEVICE_ATTACHED" />
    </intent-filter>

    <meta-data android:name=
        "android.hardware.usb.action.USB_DEVICE_ATTACHED"
        android:resource="@xml/device_filter" />
</activity>
```

Listing 4-49. `res/xml/device_filter.xml`

```xml
<?xml version="1.0" encoding="utf-8"?>
<resources>
    <usb-device vendor-id="5432" product-id="9876" />
</resources>
```

The activity you want to launch with a connection has a filter added to it with the USB_DEVICE_ATTACHED action string and with some XML metadata describing the devices you are interested in. There are several device attribute fields you can place into `<usb-device>` to filter which connection events notify your application:

- vendor-id
- product-id
- class
- subclass
- protocol

You can define as many of these as necessary to fit your application. For example, if you want to communicate with only one specific device, you might define both vendor-id and product-id as the example code did. If you are more interested in all devices of a given type (say, all mass-storage devices), you might define only the class attribute. It is even allowable to define *no* attributes, and have your application match on *any* device connected!

Summary

Connecting an Android application to the Web and web services is a great way to add user value in today's connected world. Android's framework for connecting to the Web and other remote hosts makes adding this functionality straightforward. We've explored how to bring the standards of the Web into your application, using HTML and JavaScript to interact with the user, but within a native context. You also saw how to use Android to download content from remote servers and consume it in your application. We also showed that a web server is not the only host worth connecting to, by using Bluetooth, NFC, and SMS to communicate directly from one device to another. In the next chapter, we will look at using the tools that Android provides to interact with a device's hardware resources.

Interacting with Device Hardware and Media

Integrating application software with device hardware presents opportunities to create unique user experiences that only the mobile platform can provide. Capturing media by using the microphone and camera allows applications to incorporate a personal touch through a photo or recorded greeting. Integration of sensor and location data can help you develop applications to answer relevant questions such as "Where am I?" and "What am I looking at?"

In this chapter, we are going to investigate how to leverage the location, media, and sensor APIs provided by Android to add that unique value the mobile device brings into your applications.

5-1. Integrating Device Location

Problem

You want to leverage the device's ability to report its current physical position in an application.

Solution

(API Level 1)

Utilize the background services provided by the Android `LocationManager`. One of the most powerful benefits that a mobile application can often provide to the user is the ability to add context by including information based on where that user is currently located. Applications may ask the `LocationManager` to provide updates of a device's location either regularly or just when it is detected that the device has moved a significant distance.

When working with the Android location services, some care should be taken to respect both the device battery and the user's wishes. Obtaining a fine-grained location fix by using a device's GPS is a power-intensive process, and this can quickly drain the battery in the user's device if left on continuously. For this reason, among others, Android allows the user to disable certain sources of location data, such as the device's GPS. These settings must be observed when your application decides how it will obtain location.

Each location source also comes with a trade-off degree of accuracy. The GPS will return a more exact location (within a few meters) but will take longer to fix and use more power, whereas the network location will usually be accurate to a few kilometers but is returned much faster and uses less power. Consider the requirements of the application when deciding which sources to access; if your application wishes to display information about only the local city, perhaps GPS fixes are not necessary.

> **Important**   When using location services in an application, keep in mind that android.permission.ACCESS_COARSE_LOCATION or android.permission.ACCESS_FINE_LOCATION must be declared in the application manifest. If you declare android.permission.ACCESS_FINE_LOCATION, you do not need both because it includes coarse permissions as well.

How It Works

When creating a simple monitor for user location in an activity or service, there are a few actions that we need to consider:

1. Determine whether the source we want to use is enabled. If it's not, decide whether to ask the user to enable it or to try another source.

2. Register for updates using reasonable values for a minimum distance and update interval.

3. Unregister for updates when they are no longer needed to conserve device power.

In Listing 5-1, we register an activity to listen for location updates while it is visible to the user and to display that location onscreen.

Listing 5-1. Activity Monitoring Location Updates

```
public class MainActivity extends Activity {

    private LocationManager mManager;
    private Location mCurrentLocation;

    private TextView mLocationView;

    @Override
    public void onCreate(Bundle savedInstanceState) {
        super.onCreate(savedInstanceState);
        mLocationView = new TextView(this);
        setContentView(mLocationView);
```

```java
    mManager = (LocationManager)
            getSystemService(Context.LOCATION_SERVICE);
}

@Override
public void onResume() {
    super.onResume();
    if(!mManager
            .isProviderEnabled(LocationManager.GPS_PROVIDER)) {
        //Ask the user to enable GPS
        AlertDialog.Builder builder =
                new AlertDialog.Builder(this);
        builder.setTitle("Location Manager");
        builder.setMessage(
                "We would like to use your location, "
                + "but GPS is currently disabled.\n"
                + "Would you like to change these settings "
                + "now?");
        builder.setPositiveButton("Yes",
                new DialogInterface.OnClickListener() {
            @Override
            public void onClick(DialogInterface dialog,
                    int which) {
                //Launch settings, allowing user to change
                Intent i = new Intent(Settings
                        .ACTION_LOCATION_SOURCE_SETTINGS);
                startActivity(i);
            }
        });
        builder.setNegativeButton("No",
                new DialogInterface.OnClickListener() {
            @Override
            public void onClick(DialogInterface dialog,
                    int which) {
                //No location service, no Activity
                finish();
            }
        });
        builder.create().show();
    }
    //Get a cached location, if it exists
    mCurrentLocation = mManager.getLastKnownLocation(
            LocationManager.GPS_PROVIDER);
    updateDisplay();
    //Register for updates
    int minTime = 5000;
    float minDistance = 0;
    mManager.requestLocationUpdates(
            LocationManager.GPS_PROVIDER,
            minTime,
```

```
                minDistance,
                mListener);
    }

    @Override
    public void onPause() {
        super.onPause();
        //Disable updates when we are not in the foreground
        mManager.removeUpdates(mListener);
    }

    private void updateDisplay() {
        if(mCurrentLocation == null) {
            mLocationView.setText("Determining Your Location...");
        } else {
            mLocationView.setText(
                    String.format("Your Location:\n%.2f, %.2f",
                            mCurrentLocation.getLatitude(),
                            mCurrentLocation.getLongitude()));
        }
    }

    private LocationListener mListener = new LocationListener() {
        //New location event
        @Override
        public void onLocationChanged(Location location) {
            mCurrentLocation = location;
            updateDisplay();
        }

        //The requested provider was disabled in settings
        @Override
        public void onProviderDisabled(String provider) { }

        //The requested provider was enabled in settings
        @Override
        public void onProviderEnabled(String provider) { }

        //Availability changes in the requested provider
        @Override
        public void onStatusChanged(String provider,
                int status, Bundle extras) { }

    };
}
```

This example chooses to work strictly with the device's GPS to get location updates. Because it is a key element to the functionality of this activity, the first major task undertaken after each resume is to check whether the LocationManager.GPS_PROVIDER is still enabled. If, for any reason, the user has disabled this feature, we provide the opportunity to rectify this by asking whether the user would like to enable GPS. An application does not have the ability to do this for the user, so if the user agrees, we launch an activity by using the Intent action `Settings.ACTION_LOCATION_SOURCE_SETTINGS`, which brings up the device settings for enabling GPS.

EMULATING LOCATION CHANGES

If you are testing your application inside of the Android emulator, your application will not be able to receive real location data from any of the system providers. Using the DDMS tool in the SDK, however, you are able to inject location change events for the `GPS_PROVIDER` manually.

With DDMS active, select the Emulator Control tab and find the Location Controls section. A tabbed interface allows you to enter a latitude/longitude pair directly, or have series of them read from common file formats.

When entering a single value manually, a valid latitude and longitude must be entered in the text boxes. You may then click the Send button to inject that location as an event inside the selected emulator. Any applications registered to listen to location changes will also receive an update with this location value.

Once GPS is active and available, the activity registers a `LocationListener` to be notified of location updates. The `LocationManager.requestLocationUpdates()` method takes two major parameters of interest in addition to the provider type and destination listener:

- `minTime`: The minimum time interval between updates, in milliseconds

  - Setting this to nonzero allows the location provider to rest for approximately the specified period before updating again.

  - This is a parameter to conserve power, and it should not be set to a value any lower than the minimum acceptable update rate.

- `minDistance`: The distance the device must move before another update will be sent, in meters

  - Setting this to nonzero will block updates until it is determined that the device has moved at least this much.

In the example, we request that updates be sent no more often than every 5 seconds, with no regard for whether the location has changed significantly. When these updates arrive, the `onLocationChanged()` method of the registered listener is called. Notice that a `LocationListener` will also be notified when the status of different providers changes, although we are not utilizing those callbacks here.

Note If you are receiving updates in a service or other background operation, Google recommends that the minimum time interval should be no less than 60,000 (60 seconds).

The example keeps a running reference to the latest location it received. Initially, this value is set to the last known location that the provider has cached by calling `getLastKnownLocation()`, which may return `null` if the provider does not have a cached location value. With each incoming update, the location value is reset and the user interface display is updated to reflect the new change.

5-2. Mapping Locations

Problem

You would like to display one or more locations on a map for the user. Additionally, you would like to display the user's own location on that same map.

Solution

(API Level 8)

The simplest way to show the user a map is to create an Intent with the location data and pass it to the Android system to launch in a mapping application. We'll look more in depth at this method for doing various tasks in Chapter 7. You can embed maps within your application by using `MapView` and `MapFragment`, provided by the Google Maps v2 library component of the Google Play Services library.

> **Important**   Google Maps v2 is distributed as part of the Google Play Services library; it is not part of the native SDK at any platform level. However, any application targeting API Level 8 or later and devices inside the Google Play ecosystem can use the mapping library. For more information on including Google Play Services in your project, reference our guide in Chapter 1.

Obtaining an API Key

To get started with Maps v2, you will need to create an API project, enable the Maps v2 service inside of that project, and generate an API key to include in your application code. Without an API key, the mapping classes may be utilized, but no map tiles will be returned to the application. Follow these steps:

1. Visit `https://code.google.com/apis/console/` and log in with your Google account to access the Google API console,

2. Select Create Project to make a new project for your maps. If you already have an existing project, you can add the Maps v2 service and keys to that if you prefer. In that case, select the project where you would like to add Maps v2.

3. In the navigation panel, select Services , scroll down to Google Maps Android API v2, and enable the service.

4. Select API Access in the navigation panel, and select Create new Android Key.

5. Follow the onscreen instructions to add keystore signature/application package pairs to your key for the apps you want to use. In our case, the package name for the sample application is `com.androidrecipes.mapper`, and the signature comes from the debug key on your development machine, usually located at `<USERHOME>/.android/debug.keystore`.

> **Note**   For more information on the SDK, and the most up-to-date instructions on getting an API key, visit `https://developers.google.com/maps/documentation/android/start`.

If you are running code in an emulator to test, that emulator must be built using an SDK target of Android 4.3 or later that includes the Google APIs for mapping to operate properly. Previous versions of the SDK bundled in the Maps v1 library rather than Google Play Services, so they will not work for testing.

If you create emulators from the command line, these targets are named Google Inc.:Google APIs:X, where *X* is the API version indicator. If you create emulators from inside an IDE (such as Eclipse), the target has a similar naming convention of Google APIs (Google Inc.) – X, where *X* is the API version indicator.

Meeting Manifest Requirements

Once you have obtained a valid API key, we need to include it in our `AndroidManifest.xml` file. The following code block must be inside the `<application>` element:

```
<meta-data
    android:name="com.google.android.maps.v2.API_KEY"
    android:value="YOUR_KEY_HERE" />
```

Additionally, Maps v2 has a device requirement of at least OpenGL ES 2.0. We can require this as a device feature by adding the following block inside your `<manifest>` element, typically placed just above the `<application>` element:

```
<!-- Maps v2 requires OpenGL ES 2.0 -->
<uses-feature
    android:glEsVersion="0x00020000"
    android:required="true" />
```

Finally, Maps v2 requires a set of permissions to talk to Google Play Services and render the map tiles. So we must add one more block inside the `<manifest>` element, typically placed just above the `<application>` element:

```
<!-- Permissions Required to Display a Map -->
<uses-permission android:name="android.permission.INTERNET" />
<uses-permission
```

```
    android:name="android.permission.ACCESS_NETWORK_STATE" />
<uses-permission
    android:name="android.permission.WRITE_EXTERNAL_STORAGE"
/>
<uses-permission android:name=
    "com.google.android.providers.gsf.permission.READ_GSERVICES"
/>
```

Altogether, your manifest should look something like Listing 5-2.

Listing 5-2. Partial AndroidManifest.xml

```xml
<manifest xmlns:android="http://schemas.android.com/apk/res/android"
    package="com.androidrecipes.mapper"
    android:versionCode="1"
    android:versionName="1.0" >

    <uses-sdk android:minSdkVersion="8"
        android:targetSdkVersion="16" />

    <!-- Permissions Required to Display a Map -->
    <uses-permission android:name="android.permission.INTERNET" />
    <uses-permission
      android:name="android.permission.ACCESS_NETWORK_STATE" />
    <uses-permission
      android:name="android.permission.WRITE_EXTERNAL_STORAGE"
    />
    <uses-permission android:name=
      "com.google.android.providers.gsf.permission.READ_GSERVICES"
    />

    <!-- Maps v2 requires OpenGL ES 2.0 -->
    <uses-feature
        android:glEsVersion="0x00020000"
        android:required="true" />

    <application
        android:icon="@drawable/ic_launcher"
        android:label="@string/app_name"
        android:theme="@style/AppTheme" >

        <!-- Activities, Services, Providers, and such -->

        <meta-data
            android:name="com.google.android.maps.v2.API_KEY"
            android:value="YOUR_KEY_HERE" />
    </application>

</manifest>
```

With the API key in hand and a suitable test platform in place, you are ready to begin.

How It Works

To display a map, simply create an instance of `MapView` or `MapFragment`. The API key is global to your application, so any instance of these elements will use this value. You do not need to add the key to each instance, as was the case with Maps v1.

> **Note** In addition to the permissions described previously, we must also add `android.permission.ACCESS_FINE_LOCATION` for this example. This is required only because this example is hooking back up to the `LocationManager` to get the cached location value.

Now, let's look at an example that puts the last-known user location on a map and displays it. See Listing 5-3.

Listing 5-3. res/layout/main.xml

```xml
<?xml version="1.0" encoding="utf-8"?>
<LinearLayout
    xmlns:android="http://schemas.android.com/apk/res/android"
    android:layout_width="match_parent"
    android:layout_height="match_parent"
    android:orientation="vertical" >
    <TextView
        android:layout_width="match_parent"
        android:layout_height="wrap_content"
        android:gravity="center_horizontal"
        android:text="Map Of Your Location" />
    <RadioGroup
        android:id="@+id/group_maptype"
        android:layout_width="match_parent"
        android:layout_height="wrap_content"
        android:orientation="horizontal" >
        <RadioButton
            android:id="@+id/type_normal"
            android:layout_width="0dp"
            android:layout_height="wrap_content"
            android:layout_weight="1"
            android:text="Normal Map" />
        <RadioButton
            android:id="@+id/type_satellite"
            android:layout_width="0dp"
            android:layout_height="wrap_content"
            android:layout_weight="1"
            android:text="Satellite Map" />
    </RadioGroup>
```

```
<fragment
    class="com.google.android.gms.maps.SupportMapFragment"
    android:id="@+id/map"
    android:layout_width="match_parent"
    android:layout_height="match_parent"/>
</LinearLayout>
```

> **Note**   When adding `MapView` or `MapFragment` to an XML layout, the fully qualified package name must be included, because the class does not exist in `android.view` or `android.widget`.

Here we have created a simple layout that includes a selector to toggle the map type displayed alongside a `MapFragment` instance. Listing 5-4 reveals the activity code to control the map.

Listing 5-4. Activity Displaying Cached Location

```java
public class BasicMapActivity extends FragmentActivity implements
        RadioGroup.OnCheckedChangeListener {

    private SupportMapFragment mMapFragment;
    private GoogleMap mMap;

    @Override
    public void onCreate(Bundle savedInstanceState) {
        super.onCreate(savedInstanceState);
        setContentView(R.layout.main);

        //Check if Google Play Services is up-to-date.
        switch (GooglePlayServicesUtil
                .isGooglePlayServicesAvailable(this)) {
            case ConnectionResult.SUCCESS:
                //Do nothing, move on
                break;
            case ConnectionResult.SERVICE_VERSION_UPDATE_REQUIRED:
                Toast.makeText(this,
                        "Maps service requires an update, "
                        + "please open Google Play.",
                        Toast.LENGTH_SHORT).show();
                finish();
                return;
            default:
                Toast.makeText(this,
                        "Maps are not available on this device.",
                        Toast.LENGTH_SHORT).show();
                finish();
                return;
        }
```

```
    mMapFragment =
            (SupportMapFragment) getSupportFragmentManager()
                    .findFragmentById(R.id.map);
    mMap = mMapFragment.getMap();

    //See if our last known user location is valid, and center
    // the map around that point.  If not, use a default.
    LocationManager manager = (LocationManager)
            getSystemService(Context.LOCATION_SERVICE);
    Location location = manager.getLastKnownLocation(
            LocationManager.GPS_PROVIDER);

    LatLng mapCenter;
    if(location != null) {
        mapCenter = new LatLng(location.getLatitude(),
                location.getLongitude());
    } else {
        //Use a default location
        mapCenter = new LatLng(37.4218,  -122.0840);
    }

    //Center and zoom the map simultaneously
    CameraUpdate newCamera =
            CameraUpdateFactory.newLatLngZoom(mapCenter, 13);
    mMap.moveCamera(newCamera);

    // Wire up the map type selector UI
    RadioGroup typeSelect =
            (RadioGroup) findViewById(R.id.group_maptype);
    typeSelect.setOnCheckedChangeListener(this);
    typeSelect.check(R.id.type_normal);
}

@Override
public void onResume() {
    super.onResume();
    //Enable user location display on the map
    mMap.setMyLocationEnabled(true);
}

@Override
public void onPause() {
    super.onResume();
    //Disable user location when not visible
    mMap.setMyLocationEnabled(false);
}

/** OnCheckedChangeListener Methods */

@Override
public void onCheckedChanged(RadioGroup group,
        int checkedId) {
```

```
        switch (checkedId) {
            case R.id.type_satellite:
                //Show the satellite map view
                mMap.setMapType(GoogleMap.MAP_TYPE_SATELLITE);
                break;
            case R.id.type_normal:
            default:
                //Show the normal map view
                mMap.setMapType(GoogleMap.MAP_TYPE_NORMAL);
                break;
        }
    }
}
```

Our first order of business is to verify that the correct version of Google Play Services is installed on this device. Google manages the Google Play Services library automatically as the user of the device interacts with Google applications such as Google Play. Play Services is automatically updated in the background, so we need to verify at runtime that the user has what we need by using methods from GooglePlayServicesUtil. The result we receive from isGooglePlayServicesAvailable() will tell us whether the services are the correct version, need an update, or are even installed at all.

This activity takes the latest user location and centers the map on that point. All control of the map is done through a GoogleMap instance, which we obtain by calling MapFragment.getMap(). In this example, we use the map's moveCamera()method to adjust the map display with a CameraUpdate object.

A CameraUpdate allows you to make adjustments to one or more components of the map display at once, such as modifying the zoom as well as the center point. The map's zoom level is a discrete value between 2.0 and 21.0, with the lowest value making the entire world approximately 1,024dp wide, and each increasing level doubling the width of the world on the display.

When the user selects a different radio button, the map type is toggled between satellite view and the traditional map view. In addition to the values used in the example, other allowable map types are as follows:

- MAP_TYPE_HYBRID: Displays map data (for example, streets and points of interest) over the top of the satellite view

- MAP_TYPE_TERRAIN: Displays a map with terrain elevation contour lines

Finally, to enable the user location display and controls, we simply need to call setMyLocationEnabled() on the map. Because this method will enable location tracking and likely turn on elements such as the GPS, it should also be disabled when no longer needed (when the view is not visible). Figure 5-1 shows our basic map with the user location visible.

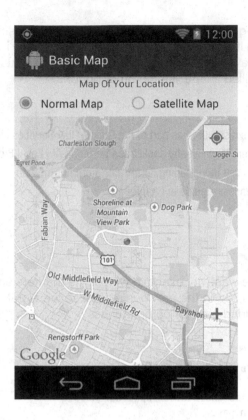

Figure 5-1. Map of user location

This is a great start, but perhaps a little boring. To bring in some more interactivity, Recipe 5-3 will create markers and other annotations to the map, and show you how to customize them.

5-3. Annotating Maps

Problem

In addition to displaying a map centered on a specific location, your application needs to put an annotation down to mark a location more explicitly.

Solution

(API Level 8)

Add Marker objects and shape elements such as Circle and Polygon to the map. Marker objects are interactive objects defined by an icon that displays over a given location. That location can be fixed, or you can set the Marker to be dragged by the user to any point they wish. Each Marker can also respond to touch events such as taps and long-presses. Additionally, a Marker can be given metadata including a title and text snippet that should be displayed in a pop-up info window when the marker is tapped. These windows themselves are also customizable in their display.

Maps v2 also supports drawing discrete shape elements. These elements are not inherently interactive, though we will see it is not difficult to add the capability to interact with a shape. This feature can also be used to draw routes onto a map by using the `Polyline` shape, which does not attempt to draw as a closed, filled shape like the other options.

Important   Google Maps v2 is distributed as part of the Google Play Services library; it is not part of the native SDK at any platform level. However, any application targeting API Level 8 or later and devices inside the Google Play ecosystem can use the mapping library. For more information on including Google Play Services in your project, reference our guide in Chapter 1.

How It Works

Listings 5-5 and 5-6 show a new activity example with some markers added to the map. The XML layout is the same as we used in the previous recipe, so we won't spend time dissecting its components again, but it is added here for completeness.

Listing 5-5. res/layout/main.xml

```xml
<?xml version="1.0" encoding="utf-8"?>
<LinearLayout
    xmlns:android="http://schemas.android.com/apk/res/android"
    android:layout_width="match_parent"
    android:layout_height="match_parent"
    android:orientation="vertical" >
    <TextView
        android:layout_width="match_parent"
        android:layout_height="wrap_content"
        android:gravity="center_horizontal"
        android:text="Map Of Your Location" />
    <RadioGroup
        android:id="@+id/group_maptype"
        android:layout_width="match_parent"
        android:layout_height="wrap_content"
        android:orientation="horizontal" >
        <RadioButton
            android:id="@+id/type_normal"
            android:layout_width="0dp"
            android:layout_height="wrap_content"
            android:layout_weight="1"
            android:text="Normal Map" />
        <RadioButton
            android:id="@+id/type_satellite"
            android:layout_width="0dp"
            android:layout_height="wrap_content"
            android:layout_weight="1"
            android:text="Satellite Map" />
    </RadioGroup>
```

```
    <fragment
        class="com.google.android.gms.maps.SupportMapFragment"
        android:id="@+id/map"
        android:layout_width="match_parent"
        android:layout_height="match_parent"/>
</LinearLayout>
```

Listing 5-6. Activity Showing Map with Markers

```java
public class MarkerMapActivity extends FragmentActivity implements
        RadioGroup.OnCheckedChangeListener,
        GoogleMap.OnMarkerClickListener,
        GoogleMap.OnMarkerDragListener,
        GoogleMap.OnInfoWindowClickListener,
        GoogleMap.InfoWindowAdapter {

    private SupportMapFragment mMapFragment;
    private GoogleMap mMap;

    @Override
    protected void onCreate(Bundle savedInstanceState) {
        super.onCreate(savedInstanceState);
        setContentView(R.layout.main);

        // Check if Google Play Services is up-to-date.
        switch (GooglePlayServicesUtil
                .isGooglePlayServicesAvailable(this)) {
            case ConnectionResult.SUCCESS:
                // Do nothing, move on
                break;
            case ConnectionResult.SERVICE_VERSION_UPDATE_REQUIRED:
                Toast.makeText(this,
                        "Maps service requires an update, "
                        + "please open Google Play.",
                        Toast.LENGTH_SHORT).show();
                finish();
                return;
            default:
                Toast.makeText(this,
                        "Maps are not available on this device.",
                        Toast.LENGTH_SHORT).show();
                finish();
                return;
        }

        mMapFragment =
                (SupportMapFragment) getSupportFragmentManager()
                        .findFragmentById(R.id.map);
        mMap = mMapFragment.getMap();
```

```java
        // Monitor interaction with marker elements
        mMap.setOnMarkerClickListener(this);
        mMap.setOnMarkerDragListener(this);
        // Set our application to serve views for the info windows
        mMap.setInfoWindowAdapter(this);
        // Monitor click events on info windows
        mMap.setOnInfoWindowClickListener(this);

        // Google HQ 37.427,-122.099
        Marker marker = mMap.addMarker(new MarkerOptions()
                .position(new LatLng(37.4218, -122.0840))
                .title("Google HQ")
                // Show an image resource from our app as the marker
                .icon(BitmapDescriptorFactory
                        .fromResource(R.drawable.logo))
                //Reduce the opacity
                .alpha(0.6f));
        //Make this marker draggable on the map
        marker.setDraggable(true);

        // Subtract 0.01 degrees
        mMap.addMarker(new MarkerOptions()
                .position(new LatLng(37.4118, -122.0740))
                .title("Neighbor #1")
                .snippet("Best Restaurant in Town")
                // Show a default marker, in the default color
                .icon(BitmapDescriptorFactory.defaultMarker()));

        // Add 0.01 degrees
        mMap.addMarker(new MarkerOptions()
                .position(new LatLng(37.4318, -122.0940))
                .title("Neighbor #2")
                .snippet("Worst Restaurant in Town")
                // Show a default marker, with a blue tint
                .icon(BitmapDescriptorFactory
                        .defaultMarker(
                            BitmapDescriptorFactory.HUE_AZURE)));

        // Center and zoom the map simultaneously
        LatLng mapCenter = new LatLng(37.4218, -122.0840);
        CameraUpdate newCamera = CameraUpdateFactory
                .newLatLngZoom(mapCenter, 13);
        mMap.moveCamera(newCamera);

        // Wire up the map type selector UI
        RadioGroup typeSelect =
                (RadioGroup) findViewById(R.id.group_maptype);
        typeSelect.setOnCheckedChangeListener(this);
        typeSelect.check(R.id.type_normal);
    }
```

```java
/** OnCheckedChangeListener Methods */

@Override
public void onCheckedChanged(RadioGroup group,
        int checkedId) {
    switch (checkedId) {
        case R.id.type_satellite:
            mMap.setMapType(GoogleMap.MAP_TYPE_SATELLITE);
            break;
        case R.id.type_normal:
        default:
            mMap.setMapType(GoogleMap.MAP_TYPE_NORMAL);
            break;
    }
}

/** OnMarkerClickListener Methods */

@Override
public boolean onMarkerClick(Marker marker) {
    // Return true to disable auto-center and info pop-up
    return false;
}

/** OnMarkerDragListener Methods */

@Override
public void onMarkerDrag(Marker marker) {
    // Do something while the marker is moving
}

@Override
public void onMarkerDragEnd(Marker marker) {
    Log.i("MarkerTest", "Drag " + marker.getTitle()
            + " to " + marker.getPosition());
}

@Override
public void onMarkerDragStart(Marker marker) {
    Log.d("MarkerTest", "Drag " + marker.getTitle()
            + " from " + marker.getPosition());
}

/** OnInfoWindowClickListener Methods */

@Override
public void onInfoWindowClick(Marker marker) {
    // Act on the event, here we just close the window
    marker.hideInfoWindow();
}
```

```
/** InfoWindowAdapter Methods */

/*
 * Return a content view to be placed inside a standard
 * info window. Only called if getInfoWindow() returns null.
 */
@Override
public View getInfoContents(Marker marker) {
    return null;
}

/*
 * Return the entire info window to be displayed.
 * Returning null here also will show default info window.
 */
@Override
public View getInfoWindow(Marker marker) {
    return null;
}

/*
 * Private helper method to construct the content view
 */
private View createInfoView(Marker marker) {
    // We have no parent for layout, so pass null
    View content = getLayoutInflater().inflate(
            R.layout.info_window, null);
    ImageView image = (ImageView) content
            .findViewById(R.id.image);
    TextView text = (TextView) content
            .findViewById(R.id.text);

    image.setImageResource(R.drawable.ic_launcher);
    text.setText(marker.getTitle());

    return content;
}
}
```

Disclaimer   We have not visited the locations on this map to know if they are actually restaurants, or if their customer ratings qualify them for the subtitles we've placed here!

We've added some new listener interfaces to our activity, which is now set up to monitor for click-and-drag events on each `Marker`, as well as click events on the pop-up info window shown from a `Marker` tap. Additionally, we have implemented `InfoWindowAdapter`, which will allow us to customize the pop-up windows eventually, but let's table that for now.

Markers are added to the map by passing a `MarkerOptions` instance into `GoogleMap.addMarker()`. `MarkerOptions` works like a builder, in that you can simply chain all the information you want to apply right off the constructor (which is what we have done). Basic information such as the marker location, display icon, and title are set here. You will also find additional options available for modifying the marker display, such as alpha, rotation, and anchor point. We've chosen to add a marker at Google HQ in Mountain View, and two others nearby.

There are a host of supported methods for creating a `Marker` icon. These are applied using a `BitmapDescriptor` object, and `BitmapDescriptorFactory` provides methods for creating all of them. For two of our elements, we have chosen `defaultMarker()`, which creates a standard Google pin to display. We can also pass in one of several constants to control the display color of the pin.

The marker at Google HQ has been customized to display as an icon we have in our application resources using `fromResource()`. You may also apply images that may be in our assets directory with a separate factory method. Additionally, we have set this marker to be draggable by the user. This means if the user were to long-press on this icon, it would be picked up from its current location and they could drag and drop the pin anywhere they like somewhere else on the map. The `OnMarkerDragListener` we implemented provides callbacks as to where the marker is being placed.

If the user taps one of the markers, the standard info window will show above the icon. That window will show the title and snippet applied to that marker. We have implemented an `OnInfoWindowClickListener` that closes this window when it is tapped, which is not the default behavior.

Note we do not need to implement `OnMarkerClickListener` in order to get this described behavior; but if we want to override it, we will. By default, the info window will display and the map will center on a selected marker. If we return `true` from `onMarkerClick()`, we can disable this and provide our own behavior.

When run, this activity produces the display shown in Figure 5-2.

Figure 5-2. Map with `ItemizedOverlay`

Customizing the Info Window

To see how we can customize the info window that pops up on a marker tap, let's add some custom UI for the window (see Listings 5-7 and 5-8) and modify the `InfoWindowAdapter` methods implemented in our activity to look like Listing 5-9.

Listing 5-7. res/layout/info_window.xml

```xml
<?xml version="1.0" encoding="utf-8"?>
<LinearLayout
    xmlns:android="http://schemas.android.com/apk/res/android"
    android:layout_width="wrap_content"
    android:layout_height="wrap_content"
    android:orientation="vertical" >
    <ImageView
        android:id="@+id/image"
        android:layout_width="35dp"
        android:layout_height="35dp"
        android:layout_gravity="center_horizontal"
        android:scaleType="fitCenter" />
```

```xml
        <TextView
            android:id="@+id/text"
            android:layout_width="wrap_content"
            android:layout_height="wrap_content" />
</LinearLayout>
```

Listing 5-8. res/drawable/background.xml

```xml
<?xml version="1.0" encoding="utf-8"?>
<shape xmlns:android="http://schemas.android.com/apk/res/android"
    android:shape="rectangle">
    <corners
        android:radius="10dp"/>
    <solid
        android:color="#CCC"/>
    <padding
        android:left="10dp"
        android:right="10dp"
        android:top="10dp"
        android:bottom="10dp"/>
</shape>
```

Listing 5-9. InfoWindowAdapter Methods

```java
/*
 * Return a content view to be placed inside a standard info
 * window. Only called if getInfoWindow() returns null.
 */
@Override
public View getInfoContents(Marker marker) {
    //Try returning createInfoView() here instead
    return null;
}


/*
 * Return the entire info window to be displayed.
 */
@Override
public View getInfoWindow(Marker marker) {
    View content = createInfoView(marker);
    content.setBackgroundResource(R.drawable.background);
    return content;
}


/*
 * Private helper method to construct the content view
 */
private View createInfoView(Marker marker) {
    // We have no parent for layout, so pass null
    View content = getLayoutInflater().inflate(
            R.layout.info_window, null);
```

```
    ImageView image = (ImageView) content
            .findViewById(R.id.image);
    TextView text = (TextView) content
            .findViewById(R.id.text);

    image.setImageResource(R.drawable.ic_launcher);
    text.setText(marker.getTitle());

    return content;
}
```

By returning a valid View from getInfoContents(), the view will be used as the content inside the standard window background display. Returning the same View from getInfoWindow() will display it as a fully custom window with no standard components. We have abstracted the creation of our pop-up into a helper method so you can easily try it both ways.

Working with Shapes

Let's talk about adding shape elements to a map. In the next example, we've created a custom class called ShapeAdapter that creates and adds circular or rectangular shapes on the map to describe map regions. It also uses the OnMapClickListener of GoogleMap to validate when a user has tapped a certain region to select it. Listing 5-10 shows the adapter code.

Listing 5-10. ShapeAdapter to Map Shapes

```
public class ShapeAdapter implements OnMapClickListener {

    private static final float STROKE_SELECTED = 6.0f;
    private static final float STROKE_NORMAL = 2.0f;
    /* Colors for the drawn regions */
    private static final int COLOR_STROKE = Color.RED;
    private static final int COLOR_FILL =
            Color.argb(127, 0, 0, 255);

    /*
     * External interface to notify listeners of a change in
     * the selected region based on user taps
     */
    public interface OnRegionSelectedListener {
        //User selected one of our tracked regions
        public void onRegionSelected(Region selectedRegion);
        //User selected an area where we have no regions
        public void onNoRegionSelected();
    }

    /*
     * Base definition of an interactive region on the map.
     * Defines methods to change display and check user taps
     */
    public static abstract class Region {
```

```java
    private String mRegionName;
    public Region(String regionName) {
        mRegionName = regionName;
    }

    public String getName() {
        return mRegionName;
    }
    //Check if a location is inside this region
    public abstract boolean hitTest(LatLng point);
    //Change display of the region based on selection
    public abstract void setSelected(boolean isSelected);
}

/*
 * Implementation of a region drawn as a circle
 */
private static class CircleRegion extends Region {
    private Circle mCircle;

    public CircleRegion(String name, Circle circle) {
        super(name);
        mCircle = circle;
    }

    @Override
    public boolean hitTest(LatLng point) {
        final LatLng center = mCircle.getCenter();
        float[] result = new float[1];
        Location.distanceBetween(center.latitude,
                center.longitude,
                point.latitude,
                point.longitude,
                result);

        return (result[0] < mCircle.getRadius());
    }

    @Override
    public void setSelected(boolean isSelected) {
        mCircle.setStrokeWidth(isSelected ?
                STROKE_SELECTED : STROKE_NORMAL);
    }

}

/*
 * Implementation of a region drawn as a rectangle
 */
private static class RectRegion extends Region {
    private Polygon mRect;
    private LatLngBounds mRectBounds;
```

```java
    public RectRegion(String name, Polygon rect,
            LatLng southwest, LatLng northeast) {
        super(name);
        mRect = rect;
        mRectBounds = new LatLngBounds(southwest, northeast);
    }

    @Override
    public boolean hitTest(LatLng point) {
        return mRectBounds.contains(point);
    }

    @Override
    public void setSelected(boolean isSelected) {
        mRect.setStrokeWidth(isSelected ?
                STROKE_SELECTED : STROKE_NORMAL);
    }
}

private GoogleMap mMap;

private OnRegionSelectedListener mRegionSelectedListener;
private ArrayList<Region> mRegions;
private Region mCurrentRegion;

public ShapeAdapter(GoogleMap map) {
    //Internally track regions for selection validation
    mRegions = new ArrayList<Region>();

    mMap = map;
    mMap.setOnMapClickListener(this);
}

public void setOnRegionSelectedListener(
        OnRegionSelectedListener listener) {
    mRegionSelectedListener = listener;
}

/*
 * Construct and add a new circular region around the
 * given point.
 */
public void addCircularRegion(String name, LatLng center,
        double radius) {
    CircleOptions options = new CircleOptions()
            .center(center)
            .radius(radius);
    //Set display properties of the shape
    options
        .strokeWidth(STROKE_NORMAL)
        .strokeColor(COLOR_STROKE)
        .fillColor(COLOR_FILL);
```

```java
        Circle c = mMap.addCircle(options);
        mRegions.add(new CircleRegion(name, c));
}

/*
 * Construct and add a new rectangular region with the
 * given boundaries.
 */
public void addRectangularRegion(String name,
        LatLng southwest, LatLng northeast) {
    PolygonOptions options = new PolygonOptions().add(
            new LatLng(southwest.latitude,
                    southwest.longitude),
            new LatLng(southwest.latitude,
                    northeast.longitude),
            new LatLng(northeast.latitude,
                    northeast.longitude),
            new LatLng(northeast.latitude,
                    southwest.longitude));

    //Set display properties of the shape
    options
        .strokeWidth(STROKE_NORMAL)
        .strokeColor(COLOR_STROKE)
        .fillColor(COLOR_FILL);


    Polygon p = mMap.addPolygon(options);
    mRegions.add(new RectRegion(name, p,
            southwest, northeast));
}

/*
 * Handle incoming tap events from the map object.
 * Determine which region element may have been selected.
 * If regions overlap at this point, the first added will
 * be selected.
 */
@Override
public void onMapClick(LatLng point) {
    Region newSelection = null;
    //Find and select the tapped region
    for (Region region : mRegions) {
        if (region.hitTest(point) && newSelection == null) {
            region.setSelected(true);
            newSelection = region;
        } else {
            region.setSelected(false);
        }
    }
```

```
        if (mCurrentRegion != newSelection) {
            //Notify and update the change
            if (newSelection != null
                    && mRegionSelectedListener != null) {
                mRegionSelectedListener
                        .onRegionSelected(newSelection);
            } else if (mRegionSelectedListener != null) {
                mRegionSelectedListener.onNoRegionSelected();
            }

            mCurrentRegion = newSelection;
        }
    }
}
```

This class defines an abstract type called `Region` that we can use to define common patterns
between our shape types. Primarily, each region must define the logic for whether a map location is
inside the given region, and what to do when that region is selected. We then define implementations
of this for a `Circle` shape and a `Polygon`, which we will use to draw a rectangle. A center point
and a radius define the circular region, while the rectangular region is defined by its southwest and
northeast point. We construct the rectangle by constructing a `Polygon` out of a list of the four corner
points that make up the shape.

Tap events will come in through the `onMapClick()` method of the listener interface, and the Maps
library gives us the tap location as a `LatLng` location. We can validate that these events are inside a
circular region simply enough by checking whether the distance between the center and the tap is
larger than the radius. `Location` has a convenience method for calculating direct distance between
two map points. For a rectangular region, we use the `LatLngBounds` class that is part of the Maps
library because it can directly validate whether a given point is inside or outside our shape.

For each tap event, we iterate over our list of regions to find the first one that considers this location
a hit. If we find no regions, the selected region is set to `null`. We then determine whether the
selection has changed, and call back one of the methods on our custom `OnRegionSelectedListener`
interface that higher-level objects can use to be notified of these events.

Listing 5-11 shows how we can use this adapter inside an activity.

Listing 5-11. Activity Integrating ShapeAdapter

```
public class ShapeMapActivity extends FragmentActivity implements
        RadioGroup.OnCheckedChangeListener,
        ShapeAdapter.OnRegionSelectedListener {

    private SupportMapFragment mMapFragment;
    private GoogleMap mMap;

    @Override
    protected void onCreate(Bundle savedInstanceState) {
        super.onCreate(savedInstanceState);
        setContentView(R.layout.main);
```

```java
// Check if Google Play Services is up-to-date.
switch (GooglePlayServicesUtil
        .isGooglePlayServicesAvailable(this)) {
    case ConnectionResult.SUCCESS:
        // Do nothing, move on
        break;
    case ConnectionResult.SERVICE_VERSION_UPDATE_REQUIRED:
        Toast.makeText(this,
                "Maps service requires an update, "
                + "please open Google Play.",
                Toast.LENGTH_SHORT).show();
        finish();
        return;
    default:
        Toast.makeText(this,
                "Maps are not available on this device.",
                Toast.LENGTH_SHORT).show();
        finish();
        return;
}

mMapFragment =
        (SupportMapFragment) getSupportFragmentManager()
                .findFragmentById(R.id.map);
mMap = mMapFragment.getMap();

ShapeAdapter adapter = new ShapeAdapter(mMap);
adapter.setOnRegionSelectedListener(this);

//Add our previous markers as shape regions
adapter.addRectangularRegion("Google HQ",
        new LatLng(37.4168, -122.0890),
        new LatLng(37.4268, -122.0790));
adapter.addCircularRegion("Neighbor #1",
        new LatLng(37.4118, -122.0740), 400);
adapter.addCircularRegion("Neighbor #2",
        new LatLng(37.4318, -122.0940), 400);

//Center and zoom map simultaneously
LatLng mapCenter = new LatLng(37.4218,  -122.0840);
CameraUpdate newCamera =
        CameraUpdateFactory.newLatLngZoom(mapCenter, 13);
mMap.moveCamera(newCamera);

//Wire up the map type selector UI
RadioGroup typeSelect =
        (RadioGroup) findViewById(R.id.group_maptype);
typeSelect.setOnCheckedChangeListener(this);
typeSelect.check(R.id.type_normal);
}
```

```
/** OnCheckedChangeListener Methods */

@Override
public void onCheckedChanged(RadioGroup group,
        int checkedId) {
    switch (checkedId) {
        case R.id.type_satellite:
            mMap.setMapType(GoogleMap.MAP_TYPE_SATELLITE);
            break;
        case R.id.type_normal:
        default:
            mMap.setMapType(GoogleMap.MAP_TYPE_NORMAL);
            break;
    }
}


/** OnRegionSelectedListener Methods */

@Override
public void onRegionSelected(Region selectedRegion) {
    Toast.makeText(this, selectedRegion.getName(),
            Toast.LENGTH_SHORT).show();
}

@Override
public void onNoRegionSelected() {
    Toast.makeText(this, "No Region",
            Toast.LENGTH_SHORT).show();
}
}
```

Here we have added the same locations from our previous example, but this time as shape regions using our new ShapeAdapter. Google HQ is added as a rectangular region, and the other two as circles. When the user makes a selection change affecting any of these regions, either of the methods onRegionSelected() or onNoRegionSelected() will be called and a message displayed. Figure 5-3 shows our region selector in action.

Figure 5-3. Map overlay with custom markers

5-4. Monitoring Location Regions

Problem

You need your application to provide contextual information to your users when they enter or exit specific location areas.

Solution

(API Level 8)

Use the geofencing features available as part of Google Play Services. With these features, your application can define circular areas around a particular point for which you want to receive callbacks when the user moves into or out of that region. Your application can create multiple Geofence instances that are either tracked indefinitely, or automatically removed for you after an expiration time.

Using region-based monitoring of a user's location can be a significantly more power-efficient method of tracking that user's arrival at a location that you find important. Allowing the services framework to track location and call you back in this manner will often result in much better battery life than your application continuously tracking user location to find out when they reach a given destination.

> **Important**   The geofencing features described here are part of the Google Play Services library; they are
> not part of the native SDK at any platform level. However, any application targeting API Level 8 or later and
> devices inside the Google Play ecosystem can use the mapping library. For more information on including
> Google Play Services in your project, reference our guide in Chapter 1.

How It Works

We are going to create an application that consists of a simple activity to allow the user to set a
geofence around their current location, and then explicitly start or stop monitoring. Once monitoring
is enabled, a background service will be activated to respond to events related to the user's location
transitioning into or out of the geofence area. The service component allows us to respond to these
events without the need for our application's UI to be in the foreground.

> **Important**   Because we are accessing the user's location in this example, we need to request the
> `android.permission.ACCESS_FINE_LOCATION` permission in our `AndroidManifest.xml`.

Let's start with Listing 5-12, which describes the layout of the activity.

Listing 5-12. res/layout/activity_main.xml

```xml
<?xml version="1.0" encoding="utf-8"?>
<LinearLayout
    xmlns:android="http://schemas.android.com/apk/res/android"
    android:layout_width="match_parent"
    android:layout_height="match_parent"
    android:orientation="vertical">

    <TextView
        android:id="@+id/status"
        android:layout_width="match_parent"
        android:layout_height="wrap_content" />
    <SeekBar
        android:id="@+id/radius"
        android:layout_width="match_parent"
        android:layout_height="wrap_content"
        android:max="1000"/>
    <TextView
        android:id="@+id/radius_text"
        android:layout_width="match_parent"
        android:layout_height="wrap_content" />
    <Button
        android:layout_width="match_parent"
        android:layout_height="wrap_content"
```

```
        android:text="Set Geofence at My Location"
        android:onClick="onSetGeofenceClick" />

    <!-- Spacer -->
    <View
        android:layout_width="match_parent"
        android:layout_height="0dp"
        android:layout_weight="1" />

    <Button
        android:layout_width="match_parent"
        android:layout_height="wrap_content"
        android:text="Start Monitoring"
        android:onClick="onStartMonitorClick" />
    <Button
        android:layout_width="match_parent"
        android:layout_height="wrap_content"
        android:text="Stop Monitoring"
        android:onClick="onStopMonitorClick" />
</LinearLayout>
```

The layout contains a SeekBar that enables the user to slide a finger to select the desired radius value. The user can lock in the new geofence by tapping the uppermost button, and start or stop monitoring by using the buttons at the bottom. Figure 5-4 illustrates what the UI should look like.

Figure 5-4. RegionMonitor's control activity

Listing 5-13 shows the activity code to manage the geofence monitoring.

Listing 5-13. Activity to Set a Geofence

```
public class MainActivity extends Activity implements
        OnSeekBarChangeListener,
        GooglePlayServicesClient.ConnectionCallbacks,
        GooglePlayServicesClient.OnConnectionFailedListener,
        LocationClient.OnAddGeofencesResultListener,
        LocationClient.OnRemoveGeofencesResultListener {
    private static final String TAG = "RegionMonitorActivity";

    //Unique identifier for our single geofence
    private static final String FENCE_ID =
            "com.androidrecipes.FENCE";

    private LocationClient mLocationClient;
    private SeekBar mRadiusSlider;
    private TextView mStatusText, mRadiusText;

    private Geofence mCurrentFence;
    private Intent mServiceIntent;
    private PendingIntent mCallbackIntent;

    @Override
    protected void onCreate(Bundle savedInstanceState) {
        super.onCreate(savedInstanceState);
        setContentView(R.layout.activity_main);

        //Wire up the UI connections
        mStatusText = (TextView) findViewById(R.id.status);
        mRadiusText = (TextView) findViewById(R.id.radius_text);
        mRadiusSlider = (SeekBar) findViewById(R.id.radius);
        mRadiusSlider.setOnSeekBarChangeListener(this);
        updateRadiusDisplay();

        //Check if Google Play Services is up-to-date.
        switch (GooglePlayServicesUtil
                .isGooglePlayServicesAvailable(this)) {
        case ConnectionResult.SUCCESS:
            //Do nothing, move on
            break;
        case ConnectionResult.SERVICE_VERSION_UPDATE_REQUIRED:
            Toast.makeText(this,
                    "Geofencing service requires an update,"
                    + " please open Google Play.",
                    Toast.LENGTH_SHORT).show();
            finish();
            return;
```

```
        default:
            Toast.makeText(this,
                    "Geofencing service is not available.",
                    Toast.LENGTH_SHORT).show();
            finish();
            return;
    }
    //Create a client for Google Services
    mLocationClient = new LocationClient(this, this, this);
    //Create an Intent to trigger our service
    mServiceIntent = new Intent(this,
            RegionMonitorService.class);
    //Create a PendingIntent for Google Services callbacks
    mCallbackIntent = PendingIntent.getService(this, 0,
            mServiceIntent,
            PendingIntent.FLAG_UPDATE_CURRENT);
}

@Override
protected void onResume() {
    super.onResume();
    //Connect to all services
    if (!mLocationClient.isConnected()
            && !mLocationClient.isConnecting()) {
        mLocationClient.connect();
    }
}

@Override
protected void onPause() {
    super.onPause();
    //Disconnect when not in the foreground
    mLocationClient.disconnect();
}

public void onSetGeofenceClick(View v) {
    //Obtain the last location from services and radius
    // from the UI
    Location current = mLocationClient.getLastLocation();
    int radius = mRadiusSlider.getProgress();

    //Create a new Geofence using the Builder
    Geofence.Builder builder = new Geofence.Builder();
    mCurrentFence = builder
        //Unique to this geofence
        .setRequestId(FENCE_ID)
        //Size and location
        .setCircularRegion(
            current.getLatitude(),
            current.getLongitude(),
            radius)
```

```java
            //Events both in and out of the fence
            .setTransitionTypes(Geofence.GEOFENCE_TRANSITION_ENTER
                    | Geofence.GEOFENCE_TRANSITION_EXIT)
            //Keep alive
            .setExpirationDuration(Geofence.NEVER_EXPIRE)
            .build();

        mStatusText.setText(String.format(
                "Geofence set at %.3f, %.3f",
                current.getLatitude(),
                current.getLongitude()) );
    }

    public void onStartMonitorClick(View v) {
        if (mCurrentFence == null) {
            Toast.makeText(this, "Geofence Not Yet Set",
                    Toast.LENGTH_SHORT).show();
            return;
        }

        //Add the fence to start tracking, the PendingIntent will
        // be triggered with new updates
        ArrayList<Geofence> geofences = new ArrayList<Geofence>();
        geofences.add(mCurrentFence);
        mLocationClient.addGeofences(geofences,
                mCallbackIntent, this);
    }

    public void onStopMonitorClick(View v) {
        //Remove to stop tracking
        mLocationClient.removeGeofences(mCallbackIntent, this);
    }

    /** SeekBar Callbacks */

    @Override
    public void onProgressChanged(SeekBar seekBar, int progress,
            boolean fromUser) {
        updateRadiusDisplay();
    }

    @Override
    public void onStartTrackingTouch(SeekBar seekBar) { }

    @Override
    public void onStopTrackingTouch(SeekBar seekBar) { }

    private void updateRadiusDisplay() {
        mRadiusText.setText(mRadiusSlider.getProgress()
                + " meters");
    }
```

```java
/** Google Services Connection Callbacks */

@Override
public void onConnected(Bundle connectionHint) {
    Log.v(TAG, "Google Services Connected");
}

@Override
public void onDisconnected() {
    Log.w(TAG, "Google Services Disconnected");
}

@Override
public void onConnectionFailed(ConnectionResult result) {
    Log.w(TAG, "Google Services Connection Failure");
}

/** LocationClient Callbacks */

/*
 * Called when the asynchronous geofence add is complete.
 * When this happens, we start our monitoring service.
 */
@Override
public void onAddGeofencesResult(int statusCode,
        String[] geofenceRequestIds) {
    if (statusCode == LocationStatusCodes.SUCCESS) {
        Toast.makeText(this,
                "Geofence Added Successfully",
                Toast.LENGTH_SHORT).show();
    }

    Intent startIntent = new Intent(mServiceIntent);
    startIntent.setAction(RegionMonitorService.ACTION_INIT);
    startService(mServiceIntent);
}

/*
 * Called when the asynchronous geofence remove is complete.
 * The version called depends on whether you requested the
 * removal via PendingIntent or request Id.
 * When this happens, we stop our monitoring service.
 */
@Override
public void onRemoveGeofencesByPendingIntentResult(
        int statusCode, PendingIntent pendingIntent) {
    if (statusCode == LocationStatusCodes.SUCCESS) {
        Toast.makeText(this, "Geofence Removed Successfully",
                Toast.LENGTH_SHORT).show();
    }

    stopService(mServiceIntent);
}
```

```
    @Override
    public void onRemoveGeofencesByRequestIdsResult(
            int statusCode, String[] geofenceRequestIds) {
        if (statusCode == LocationStatusCodes.SUCCESS) {
            Toast.makeText(this, "Geofence Removed Successfully",
                    Toast.LENGTH_SHORT).show();
        }

        stopService(mServiceIntent);
    }
}
```

Our first order of business after the activity has been created is to verify that Google Play Services exists and is up-to-date. If not, we need to encourage the user to visit Google Play to trigger the latest automatic update.

With that out of the way, we make a connection to the location services through a `LocationClient` instance. We want to stay connected to this only while in the foreground, so the connection calls are balanced between `onResume()` and `onPause()`. This connection is asynchronous, so we must wait for the `onConnected()` method before doing anything further. In our case, we need to access the `LocationClient` only when the user presses a button, so there is nothing of specific interest to do in this method.

> **Tip**   *Asynchronous* doesn't have to mean *slow*. Just because a method call is asynchronous doesn't mean we should expect it to take a long time. It simply means we cannot access the object immediately after the function returns. In most cases, these callbacks are still triggered long before the activity is fully visible.

Once the user has selected the desired radius and taps the Set Geofence button, we obtain the last-known location from the `LocationClient` and the selected radius to build our geofence. `Geofence` instances are created using the `Geofence.Builder`, which allows us to set the location of the geofence, a unique identifier, and any additional properties we may need.

With `setTransitionTypes()`, we control which transitions generate notifications. There are two possible values for transitions: `GEOFENCE_TRANSITION_ENTER` and `GEOFENCE_TRANSITION_EXIT`. You may request callbacks on one or both events; we've chosen both.

The expiration time, when positive, represents a time in the future from when the `Geofence` is added that it should be automatically removed. Setting the value to `NEVER_EXPIRE` allows us to track this region indefinitely until we remove it manually.

At any point in the future when the user taps the Start Monitoring button, we will request updates for this region by calling `LocationClient.addGeofences()` with both the `Geofence` and a `PendingIntent` that the framework will fire for each new monitoring event. Notice in our case that `PendingIntent` points to a service. This request is also asynchronous, and we will receive a callback via `onAddGeofencesResult()` when the operation is finished. At this point, a start command is sent to our background service, which we will discuss in more detail shortly.

Finally, when the user taps the Stop Monitoring button, the geofence will be removed and new updates will cease. We reference which element(s) to remove by using the same PendingIntent that was passed to the original request. Geofences can also be removed by using the unique identifier they were originally built with. Once the asynchronous remove is complete, a stop command is sent to our background service.

In both the start and stop cases, we are sending an Intent to the service with a unique action string so the service can differentiate between these requests and the updates it will receive from location services. Listing 5-14 reveals this background service that we've been hearing so much about.

Listing 5-14. Region Monitor Service

```java
public class RegionMonitorService extends Service {
    private static final String TAG = "RegionMonitorService";

    private static final int NOTE_ID = 100;
    //Unique action to identify start requests vs. events
    public static final String ACTION_INIT =
            "com.androidrecipes.regionmonitor.ACTION_INIT";

    private NotificationManager mNoteManager;

    @Override
    public void onCreate() {
        super.onCreate();
        mNoteManager = (NotificationManager) getSystemService(
                NOTIFICATION_SERVICE);
        //Post a system notification when the service starts
        NotificationCompat.Builder builder =
                new NotificationCompat.Builder(this);
        builder.setSmallIcon(R.drawable.ic_launcher);
        builder.setContentTitle("Geofence Service");
        builder.setContentText("Waiting for transition...");
        builder.setOngoing(true);

        Notification note = builder.build();
        mNoteManager.notify(NOTE_ID, note);
    }

    @Override
    public int onStartCommand(Intent intent, int flags,
                int startId) {
        //Nothing to do yet, just starting the service
        if (ACTION_INIT.equals(intent.getAction())) {
            //We don't care if this service dies unexpectedly
            return START_NOT_STICKY;
        }
```

```java
        if (LocationClient.hasError(intent)) {
            //Log any errors
            Log.w(TAG, "Error monitoring region: "
                    + LocationClient.getErrorCode(intent));
        } else {
            //Update the ongoing notification from the new event
            NotificationCompat.Builder builder =
                    new NotificationCompat.Builder(this);
            builder.setSmallIcon(R.drawable.ic_launcher);
            builder.setDefaults(Notification.DEFAULT_SOUND
                    | Notification.DEFAULT_LIGHTS);
            builder.setOngoing(true);

            int transitionType =
                    LocationClient.getGeofenceTransition(intent);
            //Check whether we entered or exited the region
            if (transitionType ==
                    Geofence.GEOFENCE_TRANSITION_ENTER) {
                builder.setContentTitle("Geofence Transition");
                builder.setContentText("Entered your Geofence");
            } else if (transitionType ==
                    Geofence.GEOFENCE_TRANSITION_EXIT) {
                builder.setContentTitle("Geofence Transition");
                builder.setContentText("Exited your Geofence");
            }

            Notification note = builder.build();
            mNoteManager.notify(NOTE_ID, note);
        }

        //We don't care if this service dies unexpectedly
        return START_NOT_STICKY;
    }

    @Override
    public void onDestroy() {
        super.onDestroy();
        //When the service dies, cancel our ongoing notification
        mNoteManager.cancel(NOTE_ID);
    }

    /* We are not binding to this service */
    @Override
    public IBinder onBind(Intent intent) {
        return null;
    }
}
```

The primary role of this service is to receive updates from the location services about our monitored region and post them to a notification in the status bar so the user can see the change. We will talk in more detail about how notifications work and how to create them in a later chapter.

When the service is first created (which will happen when the start command is sent after our button press), an initial notification is created and posted to the status bar. This will be followed by the first onStartCommand(), where we find our unique action string and do nothing further.

Relatively immediately after this occurs, the first region monitoring event will come into this service, calling onStartCommand() again. This first event is a transition that indicates the initial state of the device location with respect to the Geofence. In this case, we check to see whether the Intent contains an error message, and if it is a successful tracking event, we construct an updated notification based on the transition information contained within and post the update to the status bar.

This process will repeat for each new event we receive while the region monitoring is active. When the user finally returns to our activity and presses Stop Monitoring, that stop command will cause onDestroy() to be called in the service. It is here that we remove the notification from the status bar to signify to the user that monitoring is no longer active.

Note   If you have activated multiple Geofence instances by using the same PendingIntent, you can use the additional method LocationClient.getTriggeringGeofences() to determine which regions were part of any given event.

5-5. Capturing Images and Video

Problem

Your application needs to use the device's camera in order to capture media, whether it be still images or short video clips.

Solution

(API Level 3)

Send an Intent to Android to transfer control to the Camera application and to return the image the user captured. Android does contain APIs for directly accessing the camera hardware, previewing, and taking snapshots or videos. However, if your only goal is to simply get the media content by using the camera with an interface the user is familiar with, there is no better solution than a handoff.

How It Works

Let's take a look at how to use the Camera application to take both still images and video clips.

Image Capture

Let's take a look at an example activity that will activate the Camera application when the Take a Picture button is pressed; you will receive the result of this operation as a Bitmap. See Listings 5-15 and 5-16.

Listing 5-15. res/layout/main.xml

```xml
<?xml version="1.0" encoding="utf-8"?>
<LinearLayout
    xmlns:android="http://schemas.android.com/apk/res/android"
    android:orientation="vertical"
    android:layout_width="match_parent"
    android:layout_height="match_parent">
    <Button
        android:id="@+id/capture"
        android:layout_width="match_parent"
        android:layout_height="wrap_content"
        android:text="Take a Picture" />
    <ImageView
        android:id="@+id/image"
        android:layout_width="match_parent"
        android:layout_height="match_parent"
        android:scaleType="centerInside" />
</LinearLayout>
```

Listing 5-16. Activity to Capture an Image

```java
public class MyActivity extends Activity {

    private static final int REQUEST_IMAGE = 100;

    Button captureButton;
    ImageView imageView;

    @Override
    public void onCreate(Bundle savedInstanceState) {
        super.onCreate(savedInstanceState);
        setContentView(R.layout.main);

        captureButton = (Button)findViewById(R.id.capture);
        captureButton.setOnClickListener(listener);

        imageView = (ImageView)findViewById(R.id.image);
    }

    @Override
    protected void onActivityResult(int requestCode,
            int resultCode, Intent data) {
        if(requestCode == REQUEST_IMAGE
                && resultCode == Activity.RESULT_OK) {
            //Process and display the image
            Bitmap userImage =
                    (Bitmap)data.getExtras().get("data");
            imageView.setImageBitmap(userImage);
        }
    }
```

```
    private View.OnClickListener listener =
            new View.OnClickListener() {
        @Override
        public void onClick(View v) {
            try {
                Intent intent =
                        new Intent(MediaStore.ACTION_IMAGE_CAPTURE);
                startActivityForResult(intent, REQUEST_IMAGE);
            } catch (ActivityNotFoundException e) {
                //Handle if no application exists
            }
        }
    };
}
```

In this example, we construct an Intent to activate the Camera application and capture an image. While it is unlikely, we want to be prepared for the case that a Camera application does not exist on the device. In this case, the call to `startActivity()` will throw an `ActivityNotFoundException`, so we have wrapped the call in a `try` block in order to handle this case gracefully.

> **Tip** You can also query whether camera hardware is present with the `PackageManager.hasSystemFeature()` method, passing in `PackageManager.FEATURE_CAMERA` as the parameter.

This method captures the image and returns a scaled-down `Bitmap` as an extra in the `data` field. If you need to capture the full-sized image, insert a `Uri` for the image destination into the `MediaStore.EXTRA_OUTPUT` field of the Intent before starting the capture, and the image will be saved at that location. See Listing 5-17.

Listing 5-17. Full-Size Image Capture to File

```
public class MyActivity extends Activity {

    private static final int REQUEST_IMAGE = 100;

    Button captureButton;
    ImageView imageView;
    File destination;

    @Override
    public void onCreate(Bundle savedInstanceState) {
        super.onCreate(savedInstanceState);
        setContentView(R.layout.main);

        captureButton = (Button)findViewById(R.id.capture);
        captureButton.setOnClickListener(listener);
```

```java
        imageView = (ImageView)findViewById(R.id.image);

        destination = new File(Environment
                .getExternalStorageDirectory(), "image.jpg");
    }

    @Override
    protected void onActivityResult(int requestCode,
            int resultCode, Intent data) {
        if(requestCode == REQUEST_IMAGE
                && resultCode == Activity.RESULT_OK) {
            try {
                FileInputStream in =
                        new FileInputStream(destination);
                BitmapFactory.Options options =
                        new BitmapFactory.Options();
                options.inSampleSize = 10; //Downsample by 10x

                Bitmap userImage = BitmapFactory
                        .decodeStream(in, null, options);
                imageView.setImageBitmap(userImage);
            } catch (Exception e) {
                e.printStackTrace();
            }
        }
    }

    private View.OnClickListener listener =
            new View.OnClickListener() {
        @Override
        public void onClick(View v) {
            try {
                Intent intent =
                        new Intent(MediaStore.ACTION_IMAGE_CAPTURE);
                //Add extra to save full-image somewhere
                intent.putExtra(MediaStore.EXTRA_OUTPUT,
                        Uri.fromFile(destination));
                startActivityForResult(intent, REQUEST_IMAGE);
            } catch (ActivityNotFoundException e) {
                //Handle if no application exists
            }
        }
    };
}
```

This method will instruct the Camera application to store the image elsewhere (in this case, on the device's SD card as image.jpg), and the result will not be scaled down. When going to retrieve the image after the operation returns, we now go directly to the file location where we told the camera to store the image.

> **Tip**   The documentation states that only one image output should be expected. If no `Uri` exists, a small
> image is returned as data. Otherwise, the image is saved to the `Uri` location. You should not expect to receive
> both, even if some devices in the market behave this way.

Using `BitmapFactory.Options`, however, we do still scale the image down prior to displaying to the
screen to avoid loading the full-size `Bitmap` into memory at once. Also note that this example chose
a file location that was on the device's external storage, which requires the `android.permission.`
`WRITE_EXTERNAL_STORAGE` permission to be declared in API Levels 4 and above. If your final solution
writes the file elsewhere, this may not be necessary.

Video Capture

Capturing video clips by using this method is just as straightforward, although the results produced
are slightly different. There is no case under which the actual video-clip data is returned directly in
the Intent extras, and it is always saved to a destination file location. The following two parameters
may be passed along as extras:

- `MediaStore.EXTRA_VIDEO_QUALITY`: Integer value to describe the quality level
  used to capture the video. Allowed values are 0 for low quality and 1 for high
  quality.

- `MediaStore.EXTRA_OUTPUT`: `Uri` destination of where to save the video content. If
  this is not present, the video will be saved in a standard location for the device.

When the video recording is complete, the actual location where the data was saved is returned
as a `Uri` in the data field of the result Intent. Let's take a look at a similar example that allows the
user to record and save their videos and then display the saved location back to the screen. See
Listings 5-18 and 5-19.

Listing 5-18. `res/layout/main.xml`

```xml
<?xml version="1.0" encoding="utf-8"?>
<LinearLayout
    xmlns:android="http://schemas.android.com/apk/res/android"
    android:orientation="vertical"
    android:layout_width="match_parent"
    android:layout_height="match_parent">
    <Button
        android:id="@+id/capture"
        android:layout_width="match_parent"
        android:layout_height="wrap_content"
        android:text="Take a Video" />
    <TextView
        android:id="@+id/file"
        android:layout_width="match_parent"
        android:layout_height="match_parent" />
</LinearLayout>
```

Listing 5-19. Activity to Capture a Video Clip

```java
public class MyActivity extends Activity {

    private static final int REQUEST_VIDEO = 100;

    Button captureButton;
    TextView text;
    File destination;

    @Override
    public void onCreate(Bundle savedInstanceState) {
        super.onCreate(savedInstanceState);
        setContentView(R.layout.main);

        captureButton = (Button)findViewById(R.id.capture);
        captureButton.setOnClickListener(listener);

        text = (TextView)findViewById(R.id.file);

        destination = new File(Environment
                .getExternalStorageDirectory(), "myVideo");
    }

    @Override
    protected void onActivityResult(int requestCode,
            int resultCode, Intent data) {
        if(requestCode == REQUEST_VIDEO
                && resultCode == Activity.RESULT_OK) {
            String location = data.getData().toString();
            text.setText(location);
        }
    }

    private View.OnClickListener listener =
            new View.OnClickListener() {
        @Override
        public void onClick(View v) {
            try {
                Intent intent =
                        new Intent(MediaStore.ACTION_VIDEO_CAPTURE);
                //Add (optional) extra to save video to our file
                intent.putExtra(MediaStore.EXTRA_OUTPUT,
                        Uri.fromFile(destination));
                //Optional extra to set video quality
                intent.putExtra(MediaStore.EXTRA_VIDEO_QUALITY, 0);
                startActivityForResult(intent, REQUEST_VIDEO);
```

```
        } catch (ActivityNotFoundException e) {
            //Handle if no application exists
        }
    }
};
}
```

This example, like the previous example saving an image, puts the recorded video on the device's SD card (which requires the `android.permission.WRITE_EXTERNAL_STORAGE` permission for API Levels 4+). To initiate the process, we send an Intent with the `MediaStore.ACTION_VIDEO_CAPTURE` action string to the system. Android will launch the default Camera application to handle recording the video and return with an OK result when recording is complete. We retrieve the location where the data was stored as a `Uri` by calling `Intent.getData()` in the `onActivityResult()` callback method, and then display that location to the user.

This example requests explicitly that the video be shot using the low-quality setting, but this parameter is optional. If `MediaStore.EXTRA_VIDEO_QUALITY` is not present in the request Intent, the device will usually choose to shoot using high quality.

In cases where `MediaStore.EXTRA_OUTPUT` is provided, the `Uri` returned should match the location you requested, unless an error occurs that keeps the application from writing to that location. If this parameter is not provided, the returned value will be a `content://` `Uri` to retrieve the media from the system's MediaStore Content Provider.

Later, in Recipe 5-10, we will look at practical ways to play this media back in your application.

5-6. Making a Custom Camera Overlay
Problem

Many applications need more-direct access to the camera, either for the purposes of overlaying a custom user interface (UI) for controls or displaying metadata about what is visible through information based on location and direction sensors (augmented reality).

Solution

(API Level 5)

Attach directly to the camera hardware in a custom activity. Android provides APIs to directly access the device's camera for the purposes of obtaining the preview feed and taking photos. We can access these when the needs of the application grow beyond simply snapping and returning a photo for display.

> **Note**   Because we are taking a more direct approach to the camera here, the `android.permission.` `CAMERA` permission must be declared in the manifest.

How It Works

We start by creating a SurfaceView, a dedicated view for live drawing where we will attach the camera's preview stream. This provides us with a live preview inside a view that we can lay out any way we choose inside an activity. From there, it's simply a matter of adding other views and controls that suit the context of the application. Let's take a look at the code (see Listings 5-20 and 5-21).

> **Note**   The Camera class used here is android.hardware.Camera, not to be confused with android. graphics.Camera. Ensure that you have imported the correct reference within your application.

Listing 5-20. res/layout/main.xml

```xml
<?xml version="1.0" encoding="utf-8"?>
<RelativeLayout
    xmlns:android="http://schemas.android.com/apk/res/android"
    android:layout_width="match_parent"
    android:layout_height="match_parent">
    <SurfaceView
        android:id="@+id/preview"
        android:layout_width="match_parent"
        android:layout_height="match_parent" />
</RelativeLayout>
```

Listing 5-21. Activity Displaying Live Camera Preview

```java
import android.hardware.Camera;

public class PreviewActivity extends Activity implements
        SurfaceHolder.Callback {

    Camera mCamera;
    SurfaceView mPreview;

    @Override
    public void onCreate(Bundle savedInstanceState) {
        super.onCreate(savedInstanceState);
        setContentView(R.layout.main);

        mPreview = (SurfaceView)findViewById(R.id.preview);
        mPreview.getHolder().addCallback(this);
        //Needed for support prior to Android 3.0
        mPreview.getHolder()
                .setType(SurfaceHolder.SURFACE_TYPE_PUSH_BUFFERS);

        mCamera = Camera.open();
    }
```

```java
@Override
public void onPause() {
    super.onPause();
    mCamera.stopPreview();
}

@Override
public void onDestroy() {
    super.onDestroy();
    mCamera.release();
}

//Surface Callback Methods
@Override
public void surfaceChanged(SurfaceHolder holder, int format,
        int width, int height) {
    Camera.Parameters params = mCamera.getParameters();
    //Get the device's supported sizes and pick the first,
    // which is the largest
    List<Camera.Size> sizes =
            params.getSupportedPreviewSizes();
    Camera.Size selected = sizes.get(0);
    params.setPreviewSize(selected.width,selected.height);
    mCamera.setParameters(params);

    mCamera.startPreview();
}

@Override
public void surfaceCreated(SurfaceHolder holder) {
    try {
        mCamera.setPreviewDisplay(mPreview.getHolder());
    } catch (Exception e) {
        e.printStackTrace();
    }
}

@Override
public void surfaceDestroyed(SurfaceHolder holder) { }
}
```

Note If you are testing on an emulator, there may not be a camera to preview. Newer versions of the SDK have started to use cameras built into some host machines, but this is not universal. Where a camera is unavailable, the emulator displays a fake preview that looks slightly different depending on the version you are running. To verify that this code is working properly, open the Camera application on your specific emulator and take note of what the preview looks like. The same display should appear in this sample. It is always best to test code that integrates with device hardware on an actual device.

In the example, we create a `SurfaceView` that fills the window and tells it that our activity is to be notified of all the `SurfaceHolder` callbacks. The camera cannot begin displaying preview information on the surface until it is fully initialized, so we wait until `surfaceCreated()` gets called to attach the `SurfaceHolder` of our view to the `Camera` instance. Similarly, we wait to size the preview and start drawing until the surface has been given its size, which occurs when `surfaceChanged()` is called.

The camera hardware resources are opened and claimed for this application by calling `Camera.open()`. There is an alternate version of this method introduced in Android 2.3 (API Level 9) that takes an integer parameter (valid values being from 0 to `getNumberOfCameras()-1`) to determine which camera you would like to access for devices that have more than one. On these devices, the version that takes no parameters will always default to the rear-facing camera.

> **Important**   Some newer devices, such as Google's Nexus 7 tablet, do not have a rear-facing camera, and so the old implementation of `Camera.open()` will return `null`. If you have a Camera application that supports older versions of Android, you will want to branch your code and use the newer API where available to get whatever camera the device has to offer.

Calling `Parameters.getSupportedPreviewSizes()` returns a list of all the sizes the device will accept, and they are typically ordered largest to smallest. In the example, we pick the first (and, thus, largest) preview resolution and use it to set the size.

> **Note**   In versions earlier than 2.0 (API Level 5), it was acceptable to directly pass the height and width parameters from this method as to `Parameters.setPreviewSize()`; but in 2.0, and later, the camera will set its preview to only one of the supported resolutions of the device. Attempts otherwise will result in an exception.

`Camera.startPreview()` begins the live drawing of camera data on the surface. Notice that the preview always displays in a landscape orientation. Prior to Android 2.2 (API Level 8), there was no official way to adjust the rotation of the preview display. For that reason, it is recommended that an activity using the camera preview have its orientation fixed with `android:screenOrientation="landsc ape"` in the manifest to match if you must support devices running older versions.

The Camera service can be accessed by only one application at a time. For this reason, it is important that you call `Camera.release()` as soon as the camera is no longer needed. In the example, we no longer need the camera when the activity is finished, so this call takes place in `onDestroy()`.

Changing Capture Orientation

(API Level 8)

Starting with Android 2.2, the ability to rotate the actual camera preview was added. Applications can now call `Camera.setDisplayOrientation()` to rotate the incoming data to match the orientation of their activity. Valid values are degrees of 0, 90, 180, and 270; 0 will map to the default landscape orientation. This method affects primarily how the preview data is drawn on the surface before the capture.

To rotate the output data from the camera, use the method `setRotation()` on `Camera.Parameters`. This method's implementation depends on the device; it will either rotate the actual image output, update the EXIF data with a rotation parameter, or both.

Overlaying the Preview

We can now add on to the previous example any controls or views that are appropriate to display on top of the camera preview. Let's modify the preview to include a Cancel button and a Snap Photo button. See Listings 5-22 and 5-23.

Listing 5-22. res/layout/main.xml

```xml
<?xml version="1.0" encoding="utf-8"?>
<RelativeLayout
    xmlns:android="http://schemas.android.com/apk/res/android"
    android:layout_width="match_parent"
    android:layout_height="match_parent">
    <SurfaceView
        android:id="@+id/preview"
        android:layout_width="match_parent"
        android:layout_height="match_parent" />
    <RelativeLayout
        android:layout_width="match_parent"
        android:layout_height="100dip"
        android:layout_alignParentBottom="true"
        android:gravity="center_vertical"
        android:background="#A000">
        <Button
            android:layout_width="100dip"
            android:layout_height="wrap_content"
            android:text="Cancel"
            android:onClick="onCancelClick" />
        <Button
            android:layout_width="100dip"
            android:layout_height="wrap_content"
            android:layout_alignParentRight="true"
            android:text="Snap Photo"
            android:onClick="onSnapClick" />
    </RelativeLayout>
</RelativeLayout>
```

Listing 5-23. Activity with Photo Controls Added

```java
public class PreviewActivity extends Activity implements
        SurfaceHolder.Callback, Camera.ShutterCallback, Camera.PictureCallback {

    Camera mCamera;
    SurfaceView mPreview;

    @Override
    public void onCreate(Bundle savedInstanceState) {
        super.onCreate(savedInstanceState);
        setContentView(R.layout.main);

        mPreview = (SurfaceView)findViewById(R.id.preview);
        mPreview.getHolder().addCallback(this);
        //Neede for support prior to Android 3.0
        mPreview.getHolder()
                .setType(SurfaceHolder.SURFACE_TYPE_PUSH_BUFFERS);

        mCamera = Camera.open();
    }

    @Override
    public void onPause() {
        super.onPause();
        mCamera.stopPreview();
    }

    @Override
    public void onDestroy() {
        super.onDestroy();
        mCamera.release();
        Log.d("CAMERA","Destroy");
    }

    public void onCancelClick(View v) {
        finish();
    }

    public void onSnapClick(View v) {
        //Snap a photo
        mCamera.takePicture(this, null, null, this);
    }

    //Camera Callback Methods
    @Override
    public void onShutter() {
        Toast.makeText(this, "Click!", Toast.LENGTH_SHORT).show();
    }
```

```java
@Override
public void onPictureTaken(byte[] data, Camera camera) {

    //Store the picture off somewhere
    //Here, we chose to save to internal storage
    try {
        FileOutputStream out =
                openFileOutput("picture.jpg", Activity.MODE_PRIVATE);
        out.write(data);
        out.flush();
        out.close();
    } catch (FileNotFoundException e) {
        e.printStackTrace();
    } catch (IOException e) {
        e.printStackTrace();
    }

    //Must restart preview
    camera.startPreview();
}

//Surface Callback Methods
@Override
public void surfaceChanged(SurfaceHolder holder, int format,
        int width, int height) {
    Camera.Parameters params = mCamera.getParameters();
    List<Camera.Size> sizes = params.getSupportedPreviewSizes();
    Camera.Size selected = sizes.get(0);
    params.setPreviewSize(selected.width,selected.height);
    mCamera.setParameters(params);

    mCamera.setDisplayOrientation(90);
    mCamera.startPreview();
}

@Override
public void surfaceCreated(SurfaceHolder holder) {
    try {
        mCamera.setPreviewDisplay(mPreview.getHolder());
    } catch (Exception e) {
        e.printStackTrace();
    }
}

@Override
public void surfaceDestroyed(SurfaceHolder holder) { }
}
```

Here we have added a simple, partially transparent overlay to include a pair of controls for camera operation. The action taken by Cancel is nothing to speak of; we simply finish the activity. However, Snap Photo introduces more of the Camera API in manually taking and returning a photo to the application. A user action will initiate the `Camera.takePicture()` method, which takes a series of callback pointers.

Notice that the activity in this example implements two more interfaces: `Camera.ShutterCallback` and `Camera.PictureCallback`. The former is called as near as possible to the moment when the image is captured (when the "shutter" closes), while the latter can be called at multiple instances when different forms of the image are available.

The parameters of `takePicture()` are a single `ShutterCallback` and up to three `PictureCallback` instances. The `PictureCallbacks` will be called at the following times (in the order they appear as parameters):

- After the image is captured with RAW image data. This may return `null` on devices with limited memory.

- After the image is processed with scaled image data (known as the `POSTVIEW` image). This may return `null` on devices with limited memory.

- After the image is compressed with JPEG image data.

This example cares to be notified only when the JPEG is ready. Consequently, that is also the last callback made and the point in time when the preview must be started back up again. If `startPreview()` is not called again after a picture is taken, then preview on the surface will remain frozen at the captured image.

Tip   If you would like to guarantee that your application is downloaded only on devices that have the appropriate hardware, you can use the market filter for the camera in your manifest with the following line: `<uses-feature android:name="android.hardware.camera"/>`.

5-7. Recording Audio

Problem

You have an application that needs to use the device microphone to record audio input.

Solution

(API Level 1)

Use the `MediaRecorder` to capture the audio and store it out to a file.

How It Works

MediaRecorder is quite simple to use. All you need to provide is some basic information about the file format to use for encoding and where to store the data. Listings 5-24 and 5-25 provide examples of how to record an audio file to the device's SD card, monitoring user actions for when to start and stop.

> **Important**   In order to use MediaRecorder to record audio input, you must also declare the android.permission.RECORD_AUDIO permission in the application manifest.

Listing 5-24. res/layout/main.xml

```xml
<?xml version="1.0" encoding="utf-8"?>
<LinearLayout
    xmlns:android="http://schemas.android.com/apk/res/android"
    android:orientation="vertical"
    android:layout_width="match_parent"
    android:layout_height="match_parent">
    <Button
        android:id="@+id/startButton"
        android:layout_width="match_parent"
        android:layout_height="wrap_content"
        android:text="Start Recording" />
    <Button
        android:id="@+id/stopButton"
        android:layout_width="match_parent"
        android:layout_height="wrap_content"
        android:text="Stop Recording"
        android:enabled="false" />
</LinearLayout>
```

Listing 5-25. Activity for Recording Audio

```java
public class RecordActivity extends Activity {

    private MediaRecorder recorder;
    private Button start, stop;
    File path;

    @Override
    public void onCreate(Bundle savedInstanceState) {
        super.onCreate(savedInstanceState);
        setContentView(R.layout.main);

        start = (Button)findViewById(R.id.startButton);
        start.setOnClickListener(startListener);
        stop = (Button)findViewById(R.id.stopButton);
        stop.setOnClickListener(stopListener);
```

```java
        recorder = new MediaRecorder();
        path = new File(Environment.getExternalStorageDirectory(),
                "myRecording.3gp");

        resetRecorder();
    }

    @Override
    public void onDestroy() {
        super.onDestroy();
        recorder.release();
    }

    private void resetRecorder() {
        recorder.setAudioSource(MediaRecorder.AudioSource.MIC);
        recorder.setOutputFormat(
                MediaRecorder.OutputFormat.THREE_GPP);
        recorder.setAudioEncoder(
                MediaRecorder.AudioEncoder.DEFAULT);
        recorder.setOutputFile(path.getAbsolutePath());
        try {
            recorder.prepare();
        } catch (Exception e) {
            e.printStackTrace();
        }
    }

    private View.OnClickListener startListener =
            new View.OnClickListener() {
        @Override
        public void onClick(View v) {
            try {
                recorder.start();

                start.setEnabled(false);
                stop.setEnabled(true);
            } catch (Exception e) {
                e.printStackTrace();
            }
        }
    };

    private View.OnClickListener stopListener =
            new View.OnClickListener() {
        @Override
        public void onClick(View v) {
            recorder.stop();
            resetRecorder();
```

```
                start.setEnabled(true);
                stop.setEnabled(false);
            }
        };
    }
```

The UI for this example is very basic. There are two buttons, and their uses alternate based on the recording state. When the user presses Start, we enable the Stop button and begin recording. When the user presses Stop, we re-enable the Start button and reset the recorder to run again.

MediaRecorder setup is just as straightforward. We create a file on the SD card entitled myRecording.3gp and pass the path in setOutputFile(). The remaining setup methods tell the recorder to use the device microphone as input (AudioSource.MIC), and it will create a 3GP file format for the output using the default encoder.

For now, you could play this audio file by using any of the device's file browser or media player applications. Later, in Recipe 5-10, we will point out how to play audio back through the application as well.

5-8. Capturing Custom Video

Problems

Your application requires video capture, but you need more control over the video recording process than Recipe 5-5 provides.

Solution

(API Level 8)

Use MediaRecorder and Camera directly in concert with each other to create your own video-capture activity. This is slightly more complex than working with MediaRecorder in an audio-only context as we did with the previous recipe. We want the user to be able to see the camera preview even during the times that we aren't recording video, and to do this, we must manage the access to the camera between the two objects.

How It Works

Listings 5-26 through 5-28 illustrate an example of recording video to the device's external storage.

Listing 5-26. Partial AndroidManifest.xml

```xml
<uses-permission android:name="android.permission.RECORD_AUDIO" />
<uses-permission android:name="android.permission.CAMERA" />
<uses-permission
    android:name="android.permission.WRITE_EXTERNAL_STORAGE" />
```

...

```
<activity
    android:name=".VideoCaptureActivity"
    android:screenOrientation="portrait" >
    <intent-filter>
        <action android:name="android.intent.action.MAIN" />
        <category
            android:name="android.intent.category.LAUNCHER" />
    </intent-filter>
</activity>
```

The key element to point out in the manifest is that we have set our activity orientation to be fixed in portrait. There is also a small host of permissions required to access the camera and to make a recording that includes the audio track.

Listing 5-27. res/layout/main.xml

```
<RelativeLayout
    xmlns:android="http://schemas.android.com/apk/res/android"
    android:layout_width="match_parent"
    android:layout_height="match_parent" >

    <Button
        android:id="@+id/button_record"
        android:layout_width="match_parent"
        android:layout_height="wrap_content"
        android:layout_alignParentBottom="true"
        android:onClick="onRecordClick" />

    <SurfaceView
        android:id="@+id/surface_video"
        android:layout_width="match_parent"
        android:layout_height="match_parent"
        android:layout_above="@id/button_record" />
</RelativeLayout>
```

Listing 5-28. Activity Capturing Video

```
public class VideoCaptureActivity extends Activity implements
        SurfaceHolder.Callback {

    private Camera mCamera;
    private MediaRecorder mRecorder;

    private SurfaceView mPreview;
    private Button mRecordButton;

    private boolean mRecording = false;

    @Override
    public void onCreate(Bundle savedInstanceState) {
        super.onCreate(savedInstanceState);
        setContentView(R.layout.main);
```

```java
    mRecordButton = (Button) findViewById(R.id.button_record);
    mRecordButton.setText("Start Recording");

    mPreview = (SurfaceView) findViewById(R.id.surface_video);
    mPreview.getHolder().addCallback(this);
    mPreview.getHolder()
            .setType(SurfaceHolder.SURFACE_TYPE_PUSH_BUFFERS);

    mCamera = Camera.open();
    //Rotate the preview display to match portrait
    mCamera.setDisplayOrientation(90);
    mRecorder = new MediaRecorder();
}

@Override
protected void onDestroy() {
    mCamera.release();
    mCamera = null;
    super.onDestroy();
}

public void onRecordClick(View v) {
    updateRecordingState();
}

/*
 * Initialize the camera and recorder.
 * The order of these methods is important because MediaRecorder is
 * a strict state machine that moves through states as each method
 * is called.
 */
private void initializeRecorder() throws
        IllegalStateException, IOException {
    //Unlock the camera to let MediaRecorder use it
    mCamera.unlock();
    mRecorder.setCamera(mCamera);
    //Update the source settings
    mRecorder.setAudioSource(
            MediaRecorder.AudioSource.CAMCORDER);
    mRecorder.setVideoSource(
            MediaRecorder.VideoSource.CAMERA);
    //Update the output settings
    File recordOutput = new File(
            Environment.getExternalStorageDirectory(),
            "recorded_video.mp4");
    if (recordOutput.exists()) {
        recordOutput.delete();
    }
    CamcorderProfile cpHigh = CamcorderProfile.get(
            CamcorderProfile.QUALITY_HIGH);
```

```java
            mRecorder.setProfile(cpHigh);
            mRecorder.setOutputFile(recordOutput.getAbsolutePath());
            //Attach the surface to the recorder to allow
            // preview while recording
            mRecorder.setPreviewDisplay(
                    mPreview.getHolder().getSurface());

            //Optionally, set limit values on recording
            mRecorder.setMaxDuration(50000); // 50 seconds
            mRecorder.setMaxFileSize(5000000); // Approximately 5MB

            mRecorder.prepare();
    }

    private void updateRecordingState() {
        if (mRecording) {
            mRecording = false;
            //Reset the recorder state for the next recording
            mRecorder.stop();
            mRecorder.reset();
            //Take the camera back to let preview continue
            mCamera.lock();
            mRecordButton.setText("Start Recording");
        } else {
            try {
                //Reset the recorder for the next session
                initializeRecorder();
                //Start recording
                mRecording = true;
                mRecorder.start();
                mRecordButton.setText("Stop Recording");
            } catch (Exception e) {
                //Error occurred initializing recorder
                e.printStackTrace();
            }
        }
    }

    @Override
    public void surfaceCreated(SurfaceHolder holder) {
        //When we get a surface, immediately start camera preview
        try {
            mCamera.setPreviewDisplay(holder);
            mCamera.startPreview();
        } catch (IOException e) {
            e.printStackTrace();
        }
    }
```

```
@Override
public void surfaceChanged(SurfaceHolder holder, int format,
        int width, int height) { }

@Override
public void surfaceDestroyed(SurfaceHolder holder) { }
}
```

When this activity is first created, it obtains an instance of the device's camera and sets its display orientation to match the portrait orientation we defined in the manifest. This call will affect how only the preview content is displayed, not the recorded output; we will talk more about this later in the section. When the activity becomes visible, we will receive the surfaceCreated() callback, at which point the Camera begins sending preview data.

When the user decides to press the button and start recording, the Camera is unlocked and handed over to MediaRecorder for use. The recorder is then set up with the proper sources and formats that it should use to capture video, including both a time and file-size limit to keep users from overloading their storage.

> **Note**   It is possible to record video with MediaRecorder without having to manage the Camera directly, but you will be unable to modify the display orientation and the application will display only preview frames while recording is taking place.

Once recording is finished, the file is automatically saved to external storage and we reset the recorder instance to be ready if the user wants to record again. We also regain control of the Camera so that preview frames will continue to draw.

Output Format Orientation

(API Level 9)

In our example, we used Camera.setDisplayOrientation() to match the preview display orientation to our portrait activity. However, in some cases, if you play this video back on your computer, the playback will still be in landscape. To fix this problem, we can use the setOrientationHint() method on MediaRecorder. This method takes a value in degrees that would match up with our display orientation and applies that value to the metadata of the video container file (that is, the 3GP or MP4 file) to notify other video player applications that the video should be oriented a certain way.

This may not be necessary because some video players determine orientation based on which dimension of the video size is smaller. It is for this reason, and to keep compatibility with API Level 8, that we have not added it to the example here.

5-9. Adding Speech Recognition

Problem

Your application needs speech-recognition technology in order to interpret voice input.

Solution

(API Level 3)

Use the classes of the android.speech package to leverage the built-in speech-recognition technology of every Android device. Every Android device that is equipped with voice search (available since Android 1.5) provides applications with the ability to use the built-in SpeechRecognizer to process voice input.

To activate this process, the application needs only to send a RecognizerIntent to the system, where the recognition service will handle recording the voice input and processing it; then it returns to you a list of strings indicating what the recognizer thought it heard.

How It Works

Let's examine this technology in action. See Listing 5-29.

Listing 5-29. Activity Launching and Processing Speech Recognition

```
public class RecognizeActivity extends Activity {

    private static final int REQUEST_RECOGNIZE = 100;

    TextView tv;

    @Override
    public void onCreate(Bundle savedInstanceState) {
        super.onCreate(savedInstanceState);
        tv = new TextView(this);
        setContentView(tv);

        Intent intent = new Intent(
                RecognizerIntent.ACTION_RECOGNIZE_SPEECH);
        intent.putExtra(RecognizerIntent.EXTRA_LANGUAGE_MODEL,
                RecognizerIntent.LANGUAGE_MODEL_FREE_FORM);
        intent.putExtra(RecognizerIntent.EXTRA_PROMPT,
                "Tell Me Your Name");
        try {
            startActivityForResult(intent, REQUEST_RECOGNIZE);
        } catch (ActivityNotFoundException e) {
            //If no recognizer exists, download from Google Play
            showDownloadDialog();
        }
    }
}
```

```java
private void showDownloadDialog() {
    AlertDialog.Builder builder =
            new AlertDialog.Builder(this);
    builder.setTitle("Not Available");
    builder.setMessage(
        "There is no recognition application installed."
        + "  Would you like to download one?");
    builder.setPositiveButton("Yes",
            new DialogInterface.OnClickListener() {
        @Override
        public void onClick(DialogInterface dialog,
                int which) {
            //Download, for example, Google Voice Search
            Intent marketIntent =
                    new Intent(Intent.ACTION_VIEW);
            marketIntent.setData(
                Uri.parse("market://details?"
                    + "id=com.google.android.voicesearch") );
        }
    });
    builder.setNegativeButton("No", null);
    builder.create().show();
}

@Override
protected void onActivityResult(int requestCode,
        int resultCode, Intent data) {
    if(requestCode == REQUEST_RECOGNIZE &&
            resultCode == Activity.RESULT_OK) {
        ArrayList<String> matches =
            data.getStringArrayListExtra(RecognizerIntent.EXTRA_RESULTS);
        StringBuilder sb = new StringBuilder();
        for(String piece : matches) {
            sb.append(piece);
            sb.append('\n');
        }
        tv.setText(sb.toString());
    } else {
        Toast.makeText(this, "Operation Canceled",
                Toast.LENGTH_SHORT).show();
    }
}
}
```

Note   If you are testing your application in the emulator, beware that neither Google Play nor any voice recognizers will likely be installed. It is best to test the operation of this example on a device.

This example automatically starts the speech-recognition activity upon launch of the application and asks the user, "Tell Me Your Name." Upon receiving speech from the user and processing the result, the activity returns with a list of possible items the user could have said. This list is in order of probability, and so in many cases, it would be prudent to simply call matches.get(0) as the best possible choice and move on. However, this activity takes all the returned values and displays them on the screen for entertainment purposes.

When starting up the SpeechRecognizer, there are a number of extras that can be passed in the Intent to customize the behavior. This example uses the two that are most common:

- EXTRA_LANGUAGE_MODEL: A value to help fine-tune the results from the speech processor.

  - Typical speech-to-text queries should use the LANGUAGE_MODEL_FREE_FORM option.

  - If shorter request-type queries are being made, LANGUAGE_MODEL_WEB_SEARCH may produce better results.

- EXTRA_PROMPT: This string value displays as the prompt for user speech.

In addition to these, a handful of other parameters may be useful to pass along:

- EXTRA_MAX_RESULTS: This integer sets the maximum number of returned results.

- EXTRA_LANGUAGE: This requests that results be returned in a language other than the current system default. The string value is a valid IETF tag, such as en-US or es.

5-10. Playing Back Audio/Video

Problem

An application needs to play audio or video content, either local or remote, on the device.

Solution

(API Level 1)

Use the MediaPlayer to play local or streamed media. Whether the content is audio or video, local or remote, MediaPlayer will connect, prepare, and play the associated media efficiently. In this recipe, we will also explore using MediaController and VideoView as simple ways to include interaction and video play in an activity layout.

How It Works

> **Note**   Before expecting a specific media clip or stream to play, please read the "Android Supported Media Formats" section of the developer documentation to verify support.

Audio Playback

Let's look at a simple example of just using `MediaPlayer` to play a sound. See Listing 5-30.

Listing 5-30. Activity Playing Local Sound

```java
public class PlayActivity extends Activity implements
        MediaPlayer.OnCompletionListener {

    private Button mPlay;
    private MediaPlayer mPlayer;

    @Override
    public void onCreate(Bundle savedInstanceState) {
        super.onCreate(savedInstanceState);

        mPlay = new Button(this);
        mPlay.setText("Play Sound");
        mPlay.setOnClickListener(playListener);

        setContentView(mPlay);
    }

    @Override
    public void onDestroy() {
        super.onDestroy();
        if(mPlayer != null) {
            mPlayer.release();
        }
    }

    private View.OnClickListener playListener =
        new View.OnClickListener() {
        @Override
        public void onClick(View v) {
            if(mPlayer == null) {
                try {
                    mPlayer = MediaPlayer.create(PlayActivity.this,
                            R.raw.sound);
                    mPlayer.start();
                } catch (Exception e) {
                    e.printStackTrace();
                }
            } else {
                mPlayer.stop();
                mPlayer.release();
                mPlayer = null;
            }
        }
    };
```

```
//OnCompletionListener Methods
@Override
public void onCompletion(MediaPlayer mp) {
    mPlayer.release();
    mPlayer = null;
}

}
```

This example uses a button to start and stop playback of a local sound file that is stored in the res/raw directory of a project. MediaPlayer.create() is a convenience method with several forms, intended to construct and prepare a player object in one step. The form used in this example takes a reference to a local resource ID, but create() can also be used to access and play a remote resource using MediaPlayer.create(Context context, Uri uri).

Once created, the example starts playing the sound immediately. While the sound is playing, the user may press the button again to stop play. The activity also implements the MediaPlayer. OnCompletionListener interface, so it receives a callback when the playing operation completes normally.

In either case, after play is stopped, the MediaPlayer instance is released. This method allows the resources to be retained only as long as they are in use, and the sound may be played multiple times. To be sure resources are not unnecessarily retained, the player is also released when the activity is destroyed if it still exists.

If your application needs to play many different sounds, you may consider calling reset() instead of release() when playback is over. Remember, though, to still call release() when the player is no longer needed (or the activity goes away).

Audio Player

Beyond just simple playback, what if the application needs to create an interactive experience for the user to be able to play, pause, and seek through the media? There are methods available on MediaPlayer to implement all these functions with custom UI elements, but Android also provides the MediaController view so you don't have to. See Listings 5-31 and 5-32.

Listing 5-31. res/layout/main.xml

```xml
<?xml version="1.0" encoding="utf-8"?>
<LinearLayout
    xmlns:android="http://schemas.android.com/apk/res/android"
    android:id="@+id/root"
    android:orientation="vertical"
    android:layout_width="match_parent"
    android:layout_height="match_parent">
    <TextView
        android:layout_width="wrap_content"
        android:layout_height="wrap_content"
        android:layout_gravity="center_horizontal"
        android:text="Now Playing..." />
```

```
    <ImageView
        android:id="@+id/coverImage"
        android:layout_width="match_parent"
        android:layout_height="match_parent"
        android:scaleType="centerInside" />
</LinearLayout>
```

Listing 5-32. Activity Playing Audio with a MediaController

```
public class PlayerActivity extends Activity implements
        MediaController.MediaPlayerControl,
        MediaPlayer.OnBufferingUpdateListener {

    MediaController mController;
    MediaPlayer mPlayer;
    ImageView coverImage;

    int bufferPercent = 0;

    @Override
    public void onCreate(Bundle savedInstanceState) {
        super.onCreate(savedInstanceState);
        setContentView(R.layout.main);

        coverImage = (ImageView)findViewById(R.id.coverImage);

        mController = new MediaController(this);
        mController.setAnchorView(findViewById(R.id.root));
    }

    @Override
    public void onResume() {
        super.onResume();
        mPlayer = new MediaPlayer();
        //Set the audio data source
        try {
            mPlayer.setDataSource(this,
                    Uri.parse("<URI_TO_REMOTE_AUDIO>"));
            mPlayer.prepare();
        } catch (Exception e) {
            e.printStackTrace();
        }
        //Set an image for the album cover
        coverImage.setImageResource(R.drawable.icon);

        mController.setMediaPlayer(this);
        mController.setEnabled(true);
    }

    @Override
    public void onPause() {
        super.onPause();
```

```java
        mPlayer.release();
        mPlayer = null;
    }

    @Override
    public boolean onTouchEvent(MotionEvent event) {
        mController.show();
        return super.onTouchEvent(event);
    }

    //MediaPlayerControl Methods
    @Override
    public int getBufferPercentage() {
        return bufferPercent;
    }

    @Override
    public int getCurrentPosition() {
        return mPlayer.getCurrentPosition();
    }

    @Override
    public int getDuration() {
        return mPlayer.getDuration();
    }

    @Override
    public boolean isPlaying() {
        return mPlayer.isPlaying();
    }

    @Override
    public void pause() {
        mPlayer.pause();
    }

    @Override
    public void seekTo(int pos) {
        mPlayer.seekTo(pos);
    }

    @Override
    public void start() {
        mPlayer.start();
    }

    //BufferUpdateListener Methods
    @Override
    public void onBufferingUpdate(MediaPlayer mp, int percent) {
        bufferPercent = percent;
    }
```

```
//Android 2.0+ Target Callbacks
public boolean canPause() {
    return true;
}

public boolean canSeekBackward() {
    return true;
}

public boolean canSeekForward() {
    return true;
}
}
```

This example creates a simple audio player that displays an image for the artist or cover art associated with the audio being played (we just set it to the application icon here). The example still uses a MediaPlayer instance, but this time we are not creating it by using the create() convenience method. Instead we use setDataSource() after the instance is created to set the content. When attaching the content in this manner, the player is not automatically prepared, so we must also call prepare() to ready the player for use.

At this point, the audio is ready to start. We would like the MediaController to handle all playback controls, but MediaController can attach to only objects that implement the MediaController. MediaPlayerControl interface. Strangely, MediaPlayer alone does not implement this interface, so we appoint the activity to do that job instead. Six of the seven methods included in the interface are actually implemented by MediaPlayer, so we just call down to those directly.

LATE ADDITIONS

If your application is targeting API Level 5 or later, there are three additional methods to implement in the MediaController.MediaPlayerControl interface:

canPause()

canSeekBackward()

canSeekForward()

These methods simply tell the system whether we want to allow these operations to occur inside this control, so our example returns true for all three. These methods are not required if you target a lower API level (which is why we didn't provide @Override annotations above them), but you may implement them for best results when running on later versions.

The final method required to use MediaController is getBufferPercentage(). To obtain this data, the activity is also tasked with implementing MediaPlayer.OnBufferingUpdateListener, which updates the buffer percentage as it changes.

MediaController has one trick to its implementation. It is designed as a widget that floats above an active view in its own window and it is visible for only a few seconds at a time. As a result, we do not instantiate the widget in the XML layout of the content view, but rather in code. The link is made between the MediaController and the content view by calling setAnchorView(), which also determines where the controller will show up onscreen. In this example, we anchor it to the root layout object, so it will display at the bottom of the screen when visible. If the MediaController is anchored to a child view in the hierarchy, it will display next to that child instead.

Also, because of the controller's separate window, MediaController.show() must not be called from within onCreate(), and doing so will cause a fatal exception. MediaController is designed to be hidden by default and activated by the user. In this example, we override the onTouchEvent() method of the activity to show the controller whenever the user taps the screen. Unless show() is called with a parameter of 0, it will fade out after the amount of time noted by the parameter. Calling show() without any parameter tells it to fade out after the default timeout, which is around 3 seconds. See Figure 5-5.

Figure 5-5. Activity using MediaController

Now all features of the audio playback are handled by the standard controller widget. The version of setDataSource() used in this example takes a Uri, making it suitable for loading audio from a ContentProvider or a remote location. Keep in mind that all of this works just as well with local audio files and resources using the alternate forms of setDataSource().

Video Player

When playing video, typically a full set of playback controls is required to play, pause, and seek through the content. In addition, MediaPlayer must have a reference to a SurfaceHolder onto which it can draw the frames of the video. As we mentioned in the previous example, Android provides APIs to do all of this and create a custom video-playing experience. However, in many cases the most efficient path forward is to let the classes provided with the SDK, namely MediaController and VideoView, do all the heavy lifting.

Let's take a look at an example of creating a video player in an activity. See Listing 5-33.

Listing 5-33. Activity to Play Video Content

```
public class VideoActivity extends Activity {

    VideoView videoView;
    MediaController controller;

    @Override
    public void onCreate(Bundle savedInstanceState) {
        super.onCreate(savedInstanceState);
        videoView = new VideoView(this);

        videoView.setVideoURI( Uri.parse("URI_TO_REMOTE_VIDEO") );
        controller = new MediaController(this);
        videoView.setMediaController(controller);
        videoView.start();

        setContentView(videoView);
    }

    @Override
    public void onDestroy() {
        super.onDestroy();
        videoView.stopPlayback();
    }
}
```

This example passes the URI of a remote video location to VideoView and tells it to handle the rest. VideoView can be embedded in larger XML layout hierarchies as well, although often it is the only thing and is displayed as full-screen, so setting it in code as the only view in the layout tree is not uncommon.

With VideoView, interaction with MediaController is much simpler. VideoView implements the MediaController.MediaPlayerControl interface, so no additional glue logic is required to make the controls functional. VideoView also internally handles the anchoring of the controller to itself, so it displays onscreen in the proper location.

Handling Redirects

We have one final note about using the MediaPlayer classes to handle remote content. Many media content servers on the Web today do not publicly expose a direct URL to the video container. Either for the purposes of tracking or security, public media URLs can often redirect one or more times before ending up at the true media content. MediaPlayer does not handle this redirect process, and it will return an error when presented with a redirected URL.

If you are unable to directly retrieve locations of the content you want to display in an application, that application must trace the redirect path before handing the URL to MediaPlayer. Listing 5-34 is an example of a simple AsyncTask tracer that will do the job.

Listing 5-34. RedirectTracerTask

```
public class RedirectTracerTask extends AsyncTask<Uri, Void, Uri> {

    private VideoView mVideo;
    private Uri initialUri;

    public RedirectTracerTask(VideoView video) {
        super();
        mVideo = video;
    }

    @Override
    protected Uri doInBackground(Uri... params) {
        initialUri = params[0];
        String redirected = null;
        try {
          URL url = new URL(initialUri.toString());
          HttpURLConnection connection =
                    (HttpURLConnection)url.openConnection();
          //Once connected, see where you ended up
          redirected = connection.getHeaderField("Location");

          return Uri.parse(redirected);
        } catch (Exception e) {
          e.printStackTrace();
          return null;
        }
    }

    @Override
    protected void onPostExecute(Uri result) {
        if(result != null) {
            mVideo.setVideoURI(result);
        } else {
            mVideo.setVideoURI(initialUri);
        }
    }

}
```

This helper class tracks down the final location by retrieving it out of the HTTP headers. If there were no redirects in the supplied `Uri`, the background operation will end up returning `null`, in which case the original `Uri` is passed to the `VideoView`. With this helper class, you can now pass the locations to the view as follows:

```
VideoView videoView = new VideoView(this);
RedirectTracerTask task = new RedirectTracerTask(videoView);
Uri location = Uri.parse("URI_TO_REMOTE_VIDEO");

task.execute(location);
```

5-11. Playing Sound Effects

Problem

Your application requires a handful of short sound effects that need to be played in response to user interaction with very low latency.

Solution

(API Level 1)

Use `SoundPool` to buffer load your sound files into memory and play them back quickly in response to the user's actions. The Android framework provides `SoundPool` as a way to decode small sound files and hold them in memory for rapid and repeated playback. It also has some added features where the volume and playback speed of each sound can be controlled at runtime. The sounds themselves can be housed in assets, resources, or just in the device's filesystem.

How It Works

Let's take a look at how to use `SoundPool` to load up some sounds and attach them to `Button` clicks. See Listings 5-35 and 5-36.

Listing 5-35. res/layout/main.xml

```xml
<?xml version="1.0" encoding="utf-8"?>
<LinearLayout
    xmlns:android="http://schemas.android.com/apk/res/android"
    android:layout_width="match_parent"
    android:layout_height="match_parent"
    android:orientation="vertical" >
    <Button
        android:id="@+id/button_beep1"
        android:layout_width="match_parent"
        android:layout_height="wrap_content"
        android:text="Play Beep 1" />
    <Button
        android:id="@+id/button_beep2"
        android:layout_width="match_parent"
```

```
        android:layout_height="wrap_content"
        android:text="Play Beep 2" />
<Button
        android:id="@+id/button_beep3"
        android:layout_width="match_parent"
        android:layout_height="wrap_content"
        android:text="Play Beep 3" />
</LinearLayout>
```

Listing 5-36. Activity with SoundPool

```
public class SoundPoolActivity extends Activity implements
        View.OnClickListener {

    private AudioManager mAudioManager;
    private SoundPool mSoundPool;
    private SparseIntArray mSoundMap;

    @Override
    protected void onCreate(Bundle savedInstanceState) {
        super.onCreate(savedInstanceState);
        setContentView(R.layout.main);

        //Get the AudioManager system service
        mAudioManager =
                (AudioManager) getSystemService(AUDIO_SERVICE);
        //Set up pool to only play one sound at a time over the
        // standard speaker output.
        mSoundPool =
                new SoundPool(1, AudioManager.STREAM_MUSIC, 0);

        findViewById(R.id.button_beep1).setOnClickListener(this);
        findViewById(R.id.button_beep2).setOnClickListener(this);
        findViewById(R.id.button_beep3).setOnClickListener(this);

        //Load each sound and save their streamId into a map
        mSoundMap = new SparseIntArray();
        AssetManager manager = getAssets();
        try {
            int streamId;
            streamId = mSoundPool.load(
                    manager.openFd("Beep1.ogg"), 1);
            mSoundMap.put(R.id.button_beep1, streamId);

            streamId = mSoundPool.load(
                    manager.openFd("Beep2.ogg"), 1);
            mSoundMap.put(R.id.button_beep2, streamId);

            streamId = mSoundPool.load(
                    manager.openFd("Beep3.ogg"), 1);
```

```
            mSoundMap.put(R.id.button_beep3, streamId);
    } catch (IOException e) {
        Toast.makeText(this, "Error Loading Sound Effects",
                Toast.LENGTH_SHORT).show();
    }
}

@Override
public void onDestroy() {
    super.onDestroy();
    mSoundPool.release();
    mSoundPool = null;
}

@Override
public void onClick(View v) {
    //Retrieve the appropriate sound ID
    int streamId = mSoundMap.get(v.getId());
    if (streamId > 0) {
        float streamVolumeCurrent = mAudioManager
                .getStreamVolume(AudioManager.STREAM_MUSIC);
        float streamVolumeMax = mAudioManager
                .getStreamMaxVolume(AudioManager.STREAM_MUSIC);
        float volume = streamVolumeCurrent / streamVolumeMax;

        //Play the sound at the specified volume, with no loop
        // and at the standard playback rate
        mSoundPool.play(streamId, volume, volume, 1, 0, 1.0f);
    }
}
}
```

This example is fairly straightforward. The activity initially loads three sound files from the application's `assets` directory into the `SoundPool`. This step decodes them into raw PCM audio and buffers them in memory. Each time a sound is loaded into the pool with `load()`, a stream identifier is returned that will be used to play the sound later. We attach each sound to play with a particular button by storing them together as a key/value pair inside of a `SparseIntArray`.

> **Note** `SparseIntArray` (and its sibling `SparseBooleanArray`) is a key/value store similar to a Map. However, it is significantly more efficient at storing primitive data such as integers because it avoids unnecessary object creation caused by auto-boxing. Whenever possible, these classes should be chosen over Map for best performance.

When the user presses one of the buttons, the stream identifier to play and call `SoundPool` again to play the audio is retrieved. Because the `maxStreams` property of the `SoundPool` constructor was set to 1, if the user taps multiple buttons in quick succession, new sounds will cause older ones to stop. If this value is increased, multiple sounds can be played together.

The parameters of the play() method allow the sound to be configured with each access. Features such as looping the sound or playing it back slower or faster than the original source can be controlled from here.

- Looping supports any finite number of loops, or the value can be set to –1 to loop infinitely.

- Rate control supports any value between 0.5 and 2.0 (half-speed to double-speed).

If you want to use SoundPool to dynamically change which sounds are loaded into memory at a given time, without re-creating the pool, you can use the unload() method to remove items from the pool in order to load() more in. When you are completely done with a SoundPool, call release() to relinquish its native resources.

5-12. Creating a Tilt Monitor

Problem

Your application requires feedback from the device's accelerometer that goes beyond just understanding whether the device is oriented in portrait or landscape.

Solution

(API Level 3)

Use SensorManager to receive constant feedback from the accelerometer sensor. SensorManager provides a generic abstracted interface for working with sensor hardware on Android devices. The accelerometer is just one of many sensors that an application can register to receive regular updates from.

How It Works

> **Important**   Device sensors such as the accelerometer do not exist in the emulator. It is best to test SensorManager code on an Android device.

This example activity registers with SensorManager for accelerometer updates and displays the data onscreen. The raw X/Y/Z data is displayed in a TextView at the bottom of the screen, but in addition the device's "tilt" is visualized through a simple graph of four views in a TableLayout. See Listings 5-37 and 5-38.

> **Note**   It is also recommended that you add android:screenOrientation="portrait" or android:
> screenOrientation="landscape" to the application's manifest to keep the activity from trying to rotate
> as you move and tilt the device.

Listing 5-37. res/layout/main.xml

```xml
<?xml version="1.0" encoding="utf-8"?>
<RelativeLayout
    xmlns:android="http://schemas.android.com/apk/res/android"
    android:layout_width="match_parent"
    android:layout_height="match_parent">
    <TableLayout
        android:layout_width="match_parent"
        android:layout_height="match_parent"
        android:stretchColumns="0,1,2">
        <TableRow
            android:layout_weight="1">
            <View
                android:id="@+id/top"
                android:layout_column="1" />
        </TableRow>
        <TableRow
            android:layout_weight="1">
            <View
                android:id="@+id/left"
                android:layout_column="0" />
            <View
                android:id="@+id/right"
                android:layout_column="2" />
        </TableRow>
        <TableRow
            android:layout_weight="1">
            <View
                android:id="@+id/bottom"
                android:layout_column="1" />
        </TableRow>
    </TableLayout>
    <TextView
        android:id="@+id/values"
        android:layout_width="match_parent"
        android:layout_height="wrap_content"
        android:layout_alignParentBottom="true" />
</RelativeLayout>
```

Listing 5-38. Tilt Monitoring Activity

```java
public class TiltActivity extends Activity implements
        SensorEventListener {

    private SensorManager mSensorManager;
    private Sensor mAccelerometer;
    private TextView valueView;
    private View mTop, mBottom, mLeft, mRight;

    public void onCreate(Bundle savedInstanceState) {
        super.onCreate(savedInstanceState);
        setContentView(R.layout.main);

        mSensorManager =
                (SensorManager)getSystemService(SENSOR_SERVICE);
        mAccelerometer = mSensorManager.getDefaultSensor(
                Sensor.TYPE_ACCELEROMETER);

        valueView = (TextView)findViewById(R.id.values);
        mTop = findViewById(R.id.top);
        mBottom = findViewById(R.id.bottom);
        mLeft = findViewById(R.id.left);
        mRight = findViewById(R.id.right);
    }

    protected void onResume() {
        super.onResume();
        mSensorManager.registerListener(this, mAccelerometer,
            SensorManager.SENSOR_DELAY_UI);
    }

    protected void onPause() {
        super.onPause();
        mSensorManager.unregisterListener(this);
    }

    public void onAccuracyChanged(Sensor sensor, int accuracy) { }

    public void onSensorChanged(SensorEvent event) {
        final float[] values = event.values;
        float x = values[0] / 10;
        float y = values[1] / 10;
        int scaleFactor;

        if(x > 0) {
            scaleFactor = (int)Math.min(x * 255, 255);
            mRight.setBackgroundColor(Color.TRANSPARENT);
```

```
        mLeft.setBackgroundColor(
                Color.argb(scaleFactor, 255, 0, 0));
    } else {
        scaleFactor = (int)Math.min(Math.abs(x) * 255, 255);
        mRight.setBackgroundColor(
                Color.argb(scaleFactor, 255, 0, 0));
        mLeft.setBackgroundColor(Color.TRANSPARENT);
    }

    if(y > 0) {
        scaleFactor = (int)Math.min(y * 255, 255);
        mTop.setBackgroundColor(Color.TRANSPARENT);
        mBottom.setBackgroundColor(
                Color.argb(scaleFactor, 255, 0, 0));
    } else {
        scaleFactor = (int)Math.min(Math.abs(y) * 255, 255);
        mTop.setBackgroundColor(
                Color.argb(scaleFactor, 255, 0, 0));
        mBottom.setBackgroundColor(Color.TRANSPARENT);
    }
    //Display the raw values
    valueView.setText(String.format(
            "X: %1$1.2f, Y: %2$1.2f, Z: %3$1.2f",
            values[0], values[1], values[2]));
    }
}
```

The orientation of the three axes on the device accelerometer is as follows, from the perspective of looking at the device screen, upright in portrait:

- X: Horizontal axis with positive pointing to the right
- Y: Vertical axis with positive pointing up
- Z: Perpendicular axis with positive pointing back at you

When the activity is visible to the user (between onResume() and onPause()), it registers with SensorManager to receive updates about the accelerometer. When registering, the last parameter to registerListener() defines the update rate. The chosen value, SENSOR_DELAY_UI, is the fastest recommended rate to receive updates and still directly modify the UI with each update.

With each new sensor value, the onSensorChanged() method of our registered listener is called with a SensorEvent value; this event contains the X/Y/Z acceleration values.

Quick science note   An accelerometer measures the acceleration due to forces applied. When a device is at rest, the only force operating on it is the force of gravity (~9.8 m/s2). The output value on each axis is the product of this force (pointing down to the ground) and each orientation vector. When the two are parallel, the value will be at its maximum (~9.8–10). When the two are perpendicular, the value will be at its minimum (~0.0). Therefore, a device lying flat on a table will read ~0.0 for both X and Y, and ~9.8 for Z.

The example application displays the raw acceleration values for each axis in the TextView at the bottom of the screen. In addition, there is a grid of four Views arranged in a top/bottom/left/right pattern, and we proportionally adjust the background color of this grid based on the orientation. When the device is perfectly flat, both X and Y should be close to zero and the entire screen will be black. As the device tilts, the squares on the low side of the tilt will start to glow red until they are completely red once the device orientation reaches upright in either position.

> **Tip**   Try modifying this example with some of the other rate values, such as SENSOR_DELAY_NORMAL. Notice how the change affects the update rate in the example.

In addition, you can shake the device and see alternating grid boxes highlight as the device accelerates in each direction.

SENSOR BATCHING

In Android 4.4 and later, applications can request that the sensors they interact with run in *batch mode* to reduce overall power consumption when you need to monitor the sensor for an extended period of time. In this mode, sensor events may be queued up in hardware buffers for a period without waking up the application processor each time.

In order to enable batch mode for a sensor, simply utilize a version of SensorManager.registerListener() that takes a maxBatchReportLatencyUs parameter. This parameter tells the hardware how long events can be queued before the batch is sent to the application.

Additionally, if the application needs to get the current batch prior to the next interval, a flush() can be called on the SensorManager to force the sensor to deliver what it has to the listener.

Not all sensors will support batching on all devices, and in these cases the implementation will fall back to the default continuous operation mode.

5-13. Monitoring Compass Orientation

Problem

Your application wants to know which major direction the user is facing by monitoring the device's compass sensor.

Solution

(API Level 3)

SensorManager comes to the rescue once again. Android doesn't provide a "compass" sensor exactly; instead it includes the necessary methods to infer where the device is pointing based on other sensor data. In this case, the device's magnetic field sensor will be used with the accelerometer to ascertain in which direction the user is facing.

We can then ask SensorManager for the user's orientation with respect to the Earth using getOrientation().

How It Works

> **Important**   Device sensors such as the accelerometer do not exist in the emulator. It is best to test SensorManager code on an Android device.

As with the previous accelerometer example, we use SensorManager to register for updates on all sensors of interest (in this case, there are two) and to then process the results in onSensorChanged(). This example calculates and displays the user orientation from the device camera's point of view, as it would be required for an application such as augmented reality. See Listings 5-39 and 5-40.

Listing 5-39. res/layout/main.xml

```xml
<?xml version="1.0" encoding="utf-8"?>
<RelativeLayout
    xmlns:android="http://schemas.android.com/apk/res/android"
    android:layout_width="match_parent"
    android:layout_height="match_parent">
    <TextView
        android:id="@+id/direction"
        android:layout_width="wrap_content"
        android:layout_height="wrap_content"
        android:layout_centerInParent="true"
        android:textSize="64dip"
        android:textStyle="bold" />
    <TextView
        android:id="@+id/values"
        android:layout_width="wrap_content"
        android:layout_height="wrap_content"
        android:layout_alignParentBottom="true" />
</RelativeLayout>
```

Listing 5-40. Activity Monitoring User Orientation

```java
public class CompassActivity extends Activity implements SensorEventListener {

    private SensorManager mSensorManager;
    private Sensor mAccelerometer, mField;
    private TextView valueView, directionView;

    private float[] mGravity = new float[3];
    private float[] mMagnetic = new float[3];
```

```java
public void onCreate(Bundle savedInstanceState) {
    super.onCreate(savedInstanceState);
    setContentView(R.layout.main);

    mSensorManager = (SensorManager)getSystemService(SENSOR_SERVICE);
    mAccelerometer =
            mSensorManager.getDefaultSensor(Sensor.TYPE_ACCELEROMETER);
    mField =
            mSensorManager.getDefaultSensor(Sensor.TYPE_MAGNETIC_FIELD);

    valueView = (TextView)findViewById(R.id.values);
    directionView = (TextView)findViewById(R.id.direction);
}

protected void onResume() {
    super.onResume();
    mSensorManager.registerListener(this, mAccelerometer,
            SensorManager.SENSOR_DELAY_UI);
    mSensorManager.registerListener(this, mField,
            SensorManager.SENSOR_DELAY_UI);
}

protected void onPause() {
    super.onPause();
    mSensorManager.unregisterListener(this);
}

//Allocate data arrays once and reuse
float[] temp = new float[9];
float[] rotation = new float[9];
float[] values = new float[3];

private void updateDirection() {
    //Load rotation matrix into R
    SensorManager.getRotationMatrix(temp, null, mGravity, mMagnetic);
    //Remap to camera's point of view
    SensorManager.remapCoordinateSystem(temp,
            SensorManager.AXIS_X, SensorManager.AXIS_Z, rotation);
    //Return the orientation values
    SensorManager.getOrientation(rotation, values);
    //Convert to degrees
    for (int i=0; i < values.length; i++) {
        Double degrees = (values[i] * 180) / Math.PI;
        values[i] = degrees.floatValue();
    }
    //Display the compass direction
    directionView.setText( getDirectionFromDegrees(values[0]) );
```

```
        //Display the raw values
        valueView.setText(
                String.format("Azimuth: %1$1.2f, Pitch: %2$1.2f, Roll: %3$1.2f",
                values[0], values[1], values[2]));
    }

    private String getDirectionFromDegrees(float degrees) {
        if(degrees >= -22.5 && degrees < 22.5) { return "N"; }
        if(degrees >= 22.5 && degrees < 67.5) { return "NE"; }
        if(degrees >= 67.5 && degrees < 112.5) { return "E"; }
        if(degrees >= 112.5 && degrees < 157.5) { return "SE"; }
        if(degrees >= 157.5 || degrees < -157.5) { return "S"; }
        if(degrees >= -157.5 && degrees < -112.5) { return "SW"; }
        if(degrees >= -112.5 && degrees < -67.5) { return "W"; }
        if(degrees >= -67.5 && degrees < -22.5) { return "NW"; }

        return null;
    }

    public void onAccuracyChanged(Sensor sensor, int accuracy) { }

    public void onSensorChanged(SensorEvent event) {
        //Copy the latest values into the correct array
        switch(event.sensor.getType()) {
        case Sensor.TYPE_ACCELEROMETER:
            System.arraycopy(event.values, 0,
                    mGravity, 0,
                    event.values.length);
            break;
        case Sensor.TYPE_MAGNETIC_FIELD:
            System.arraycopy(event.values, 0,
                    mMagnetic, 0,
                    event.values.length);
            break;
        default:
            return;
        }

        if(mGravity != null && mMagnetic != null) {
            updateDirection();
        }
    }
}
```

This example activity displays the three raw values returned by the sensor calculation at the bottom of the screen in real time. In addition, the compass direction associated with where the user is currently facing is converted and displayed center-stage. As updates are received from the sensors, local copies of the latest values from each are maintained. As soon as we have received at least one reading from both sensors of interest, we allow the UI to begin updating.

updateDirection() is where all the heavy lifting takes place. SensorManager.getOrientation() provides the output information we require to display direction. The method returns no data, and instead an empty float array is passed in for the method to fill in three angle values, and they represent (in order):

- *Azimuth*: Angle of rotation about an axis pointing directly into the Earth. This is the value of interest in the example.

- *Pitch*: Angle of rotation about an axis pointing west.

- *Roll*: Angle of rotation about an axis pointing at magnetic north.

One of the parameters passed to getOrientation() is a float array representing a rotation matrix. The rotation matrix is a representation of how the current coordinate system of the devices is oriented, so the method may provide appropriate rotation angles based on its reference coordinates. The rotation matrix for the device orientation is obtained by using getRotationMatrix(), which takes the latest values from the accelerometer and magnetic field sensor as input. Like getOrientation(), it also returns void; an empty float array of length 9 or 16 (to represent a 3x3 or 4x4 matrix) must be passed in as the first parameter for the method to fill in.

Finally, we want the output of the orientation calculation to be specific to the camera's point of view. To further transform the obtained rotation, we use the remapCoordinateSystem() method. This method takes four parameters (in order):

1. Input array representing the matrix to transform

2. Which axis of the world (globe) is aligned with the device's x axis

3. Which axis of the world (globe) is aligned with the device's y axis

4. Empty array to fill in the result

In our example, we want to leave the x axis untouched, so we map X to X. However, we would like to align the device's y axis (vertical axis) to the world's z axis (the one pointing into the Earth). This orients the rotation matrix we receive to match up with the device being held vertically upright as if the user is using the camera and looking at the preview on the screen.

With the angular data calculated, we do some data conversion and display the result on the screen. The unit output of getOrientation() is radians, so we first have to convert each result to degrees before displaying it. In addition, we need to convert the azimuth value to a compass direction; getDirectionFromDegrees() is a helper method to return the proper direction based on the range the current reading falls within. Going in a full clockwise circle, the azimuth will read from 0 to 180 degrees from north to south. Continuing around the circle, the azimuth will read −180 to 0 degrees rotating from south to north.

5-14. Retrieving Metadata from Media Content

Problem

Your application needs to gather thumbnail screenshots or other metadata from media content on the device.

Solution

(API Level 10)

Use MediaMetadataRetriever to read media files and return useful information. This class can read and track information such as album and artist data or data about the content itself, such as the size of a video. In addition, you can use it to grab a screenshot of any frame within a video file, either at a specific time or just any frame that Android considers representative.

MediaMetadataRetriever is a great option for applications that work with lots of media content from the device and that need to display extra data about the media to enrich the user interface.

How It Works

Listings 5-41 and 5-42 show how to access this extra metadata on the device.

Listing 5-41. res/layout/main.xml

```xml
<RelativeLayout
    xmlns:android="http://schemas.android.com/apk/res/android"
    android:layout_width="match_parent"
    android:layout_height="match_parent" >
    <Button
        android:id="@+id/button_select"
        android:layout_width="match_parent"
        android:layout_height="wrap_content"
        android:text="Pick Video"
        android:onClick="onSelectClick" />
    <TextView
        android:id="@+id/text_metadata"
        android:layout_width="wrap_content"
        android:layout_height="wrap_content"
        android:layout_below="@id/button_select"
        android:layout_margin="15dp" />
    <ImageView
        android:id="@+id/image_frame"
        android:layout_width="wrap_content"
        android:layout_height="wrap_content"
        android:layout_alignParentBottom="true"
        android:layout_centerHorizontal="true"
        android:layout_margin="10dp" />
</RelativeLayout>
```

Listing 5-42. Activity with MediaMetadataRetriever

```java
public class MetadataActivity extends Activity {
    private static final int PICK_VIDEO = 100;

    private ImageView mFrameView;
    private TextView mMetadataView;

    @Override
    public void onCreate(Bundle savedInstanceState) {
        super.onCreate(savedInstanceState);
        setContentView(R.layout.main);

        mFrameView = (ImageView) findViewById(R.id.image_frame);
        mMetadataView =
                (TextView) findViewById(R.id.text_metadata);
    }

    @Override
    protected void onActivityResult(int requestCode,
            int resultCode, Intent data) {
        if (requestCode == PICK_VIDEO
                && resultCode == RESULT_OK
                && data != null) {
            Uri video = data.getData();
            MetadataTask task = new MetadataTask(this, mFrameView,
                    mMetadataView);
            task.execute(video);
        }
    }

    public void onSelectClick(View v) {
        Intent intent = new Intent(Intent.ACTION_GET_CONTENT);
        intent.setType("video/*");
        startActivityForResult(intent, PICK_VIDEO);
    }

    public static class MetadataTask
            extends AsyncTask<Uri, Void, Bundle> {
        private Context mContext;
        private ImageView mFrame;
        private TextView mMetadata;
        private ProgressDialog mProgress;

        public MetadataTask(Context context, ImageView frame,
                TextView metadata) {
            mContext = context;
            mFrame = frame;
            mMetadata = metadata;
        }
```

```java
@Override
protected void onPreExecute() {
    mProgress = ProgressDialog.show(mContext, "",
            "Analyzing Video File...", true);
}

@Override
protected Bundle doInBackground(Uri... params) {
    Uri video = params[0];
    MediaMetadataRetriever retriever =
            new MediaMetadataRetriever();
    retriever.setDataSource(mContext, video);

    Bitmap frame = retriever.getFrameAtTime();

    String date = retriever.extractMetadata(
        MediaMetadataRetriever.METADATA_KEY_DATE);
    String duration = retriever.extractMetadata(
        MediaMetadataRetriever.METADATA_KEY_DURATION);
    String width = retriever.extractMetadata(
        MediaMetadataRetriever.METADATA_KEY_VIDEO_WIDTH);
    String height = retriever.extractMetadata(
        MediaMetadataRetriever.METADATA_KEY_VIDEO_HEIGHT);

    Bundle result = new Bundle();
    result.putParcelable("frame", frame);
    result.putString("date", date);
    result.putString("duration", duration);
    result.putString("width", width);
    result.putString("height", height);

    return result;
}

@Override
protected void onPostExecute(Bundle result) {
    if (mProgress != null) {
        mProgress.dismiss();
        mProgress = null;
    }

    Bitmap frame = result.getParcelable("frame");
    mFrame.setImageBitmap(frame);
    String metadata = String.format("Video Date: %s\n"
            + "Video Duration: %s\nVideo Size: %s x %s",
            result.getString("date"),
            result.getString("duration"),
```

```
                    result.getString("width"),
                    result.getString("height") );
            mMetadata.setText(metadata);
        }
    }
}
```

In this example, the user can select a video file from the device to process. Upon receipt of a valid video Uri, the activity starts an AsyncTask to parse some metadata out of the video. We create an AsyncTask for this purpose because the process can take a few seconds or more to complete, and we don't want to block the UI thread while this is going on.

The background task creates a new MediaMetadataRetriever and sets the selected video as its data source. We then call the method getFrameAtTime() to return a Bitmap image of a frame in the video. This method is useful for creating thumbnails for a video in your UI. The version we call takes no parameters, and the frame it returns is semirandom. If you are more interested in a specific frame, there is an alternate version of the method that takes the presentation time (in microseconds) of the where you would like a frame. In this case, it will return a key frame in the video that is closest to the requested time.

In addition to the frame image, we also gather some basic information about the video, including when it was created, how long it is, and how big it is. All the resulting data is packaged into a bundle and passed back from the background thread. The onPostExecute() method of the task is called on the main thread, so we use it to update the UI with the data we retrieved.

5-15. Detecting User Motion
Problem

You would like your application to respond to changes in user behavior, such as whether the device is sitting still, or if the user is currently active and in motion.

Solution
(API Level 8)

Google Play Services includes features to monitor user activity via the ActivityRecognitionClient. The user activity tracking service is a low-power method of receiving regular updates about what a user is doing. The service periodically monitors local sensor data on the device in short bursts rather than relying on high-power means like web services or GPS.

Using this API, applications will receive updates for one of the following events:

- IN_VEHICLE: The user is likely driving or riding in a vehicle, such as a car, bus, or train.

- ON_BICYCLE: The user is likely on a bicycle.

- ON_FOOT: The user is likely walking or running.

- STILL: The user, or at least the device, is currently sitting still.

- TILTING: The device has recently been tilted. This can happen when the device is picked up from rest or an orientation change occurs.

- UNKNOWN: There is not enough data to determine with significant confidence what the user is currently doing.

When working with ActivityRecognitionClient, an application initiates periodic updates by calling requestActivityUpdates(). The parameters this method takes define the frequency of updates to the application and a PendingIntent that will be used to trigger each event.

An application can pass any frequency interval, in milliseconds, that they wish; passing a value of zero will send updates as fast as possible to the application. This rate is not guaranteed by Google Play Services; samples can be delayed if the service requires more sensor samples to make a particular determination. In addition, if multiple applications are requesting activity updates, Google Play Services will deliver updates to all applications and the fastest rate requested.

Each event includes a list of DetectedActivity instances, which wrap the activity type (one of the options described previously) and the level of confidence the service has in its prediction. The list is sorted by confidence so the most probable user activity is first.

Important   User activity tracking is part of the Google Play Services library; it is not part of the native SDK at any platform level. However, any application targeting API Level 8 or later and devices inside the Google Play ecosystem can use the mapping library. For more information on including Google Play Services in your project, reference our guide in Chapter 1.

How It Works

Let's take a look at a basic example application that monitors user activity changes, logs them to the display, and includes a safety precaution that locks the user out from the application if the user attempts to access it while in a car or on a bicycle. We'll start with Listing 5-43, which is a snippet of the AndroidManfest.xml that reveals the permissions we need to work with this service.

Listing 5-43. Partial AndroidManifest.xml

```
<manifest
    xmlns:android="http://schemas.android.com/apk/res/android"
    package="com.androidrecipes.usermotionactivity"
    android:versionCode="1"
    android:versionName="1.0" >

    <uses-sdk
        android:minSdkVersion="8"
        android:targetSdkVersion="18" />
```

```
<!-- Required permission to User Activity Recognition -->
<uses-permission android:name=
    "com.google.android.gms.permission.ACTIVITY_RECOGNITION"
/>

<application ...>

    <!-- Activity, Service, Provider elements -->

</application>
</manifest>
```

You can see that we must declare a custom permission in the manifest specifically to read activity recognition data from Google Play Services. Listings 5-44 and 5-45 describe the activity we will use.

Listing 5-44. res/layout/activity_main.xml

```
<FrameLayout
    xmlns:android="http://schemas.android.com/apk/res/android"
    android:layout_width="match_parent"
    android:layout_height="match_parent">
    <!-- List with transcript enabled to autoscroll content -->
    <ListView
        android:id="@+id/list"
        android:layout_width="match_parent"
        android:layout_height="match_parent"
        android:stackFromBottom="true"
        android:transcriptMode="normal" />

    <!-- Safety Blocking View -->
    <!-- Clickable to consume touch events when visible -->
    <TextView
        android:id="@+id/blocker"
        android:layout_width="match_parent"
        android:layout_height="match_parent"
        android:gravity="center"
        android:clickable="true"
        android:textSize="32dp"
        android:textColor="#F55"
        android:text="Do not operate your device in a vehicle!"
        android:background="#C333"
        android:visibility="gone" />
</FrameLayout>
```

Listing 5-45. Activity Displaying User Motion

```
public class MainActivity extends Activity implements
        ServiceConnection,
        UserMotionService.OnActivityChangedListener,
        GooglePlayServicesClient.ConnectionCallbacks,
```

```java
        GooglePlayServicesClient.OnConnectionFailedListener {
    private static final String TAG = "UserActivity";

    private Intent mServiceIntent;
    private PendingIntent mCallbackIntent;
    private UserMotionService mService;

    private ActivityRecognitionClient mRecognitionClient;
    //Custom list adapter to display results
    private ActivityAdapter mListAdapter;

    private View mBlockingView;

    @Override
    protected void onCreate(Bundle savedInstanceState) {
        super.onCreate(savedInstanceState);
        setContentView(R.layout.activity_main);

        mBlockingView = findViewById(R.id.blocker);

        //Construct a simple list adapter that will display all
        // incoming activity change events from the service.
        ListView list = (ListView) findViewById(R.id.list);

        mListAdapter = new ActivityAdapter(this);
        list.setAdapter(mListAdapter);

        //When the list is clicked, display all the probable
        // activities
        list.setOnItemClickListener(
                new AdapterView.OnItemClickListener() {
            @Override
            public void onItemClick(AdapterView<?> parent, View v,
                    int position, long id) {
                showDetails(mListAdapter.getItem(position));
            }
        });

        //Check if Google Play Services is up-to-date.
        switch (GooglePlayServicesUtil
                .isGooglePlayServicesAvailable(this)) {
            case ConnectionResult.SUCCESS:
                //Do nothing, move on
                break;
            case ConnectionResult.SERVICE_VERSION_UPDATE_REQUIRED:
                Toast.makeText(this,
                        "Activity service requires an update, "
                        + "please open Google Play.",
                        Toast.LENGTH_SHORT).show();
                finish();
                return;
```

```
            default:
                Toast.makeText(this,
                        "Activity service is not available.",
                        Toast.LENGTH_SHORT).show();
                finish();
                return;
        }

        //Create a client instance for talking to Google Services
        mRecognitionClient = new ActivityRecognitionClient(
                this,    //Context
                this,    //ConnectionCallbacks
                this);   //OnConnectionFailedListener

        //Create an Intent to bind to the service
        mServiceIntent =
                new Intent(this, UserMotionService.class);

        //Create a PendingIntent for Google Services callbacks
        mCallbackIntent = PendingIntent.getService(this, 0,
                mServiceIntent,
                PendingIntent.FLAG_UPDATE_CURRENT);
    }

@Override
protected void onResume() {
    super.onResume();
    //Connect to Google Services and our Service
    mRecognitionClient.connect();
    bindService(mServiceIntent, this, BIND_AUTO_CREATE);
}

@Override
protected void onPause() {
    super.onPause();
    //Disconnect from all services
    mRecognitionClient.removeActivityUpdates(mCallbackIntent);
    mRecognitionClient.disconnect();

    disconnectService();
    unbindService(this);
}

/** ServiceConnection Methods */

public void onServiceConnected(ComponentName name,
        IBinder service) {
    //Attach ourselves to our Service as a callback for events
    mService = ((LocalBinder) service).getService();
    mService.setOnActivityChangedListener(this);
}
```

```java
@Override
public void onServiceDisconnected(ComponentName name) {
    disconnectService();
}

private void disconnectService() {
    if (mService != null) {
        mService.setOnActivityChangedListener(null);
    }
    mService = null;
}

/** Google Services Connection Callbacks */

@Override
public void onConnected(Bundle connectionHint) {
    //We must wait until the services are connected
    // to request any updates.
    // Request updates at 5 second intervals.
    mRecognitionClient.requestActivityUpdates(5000,
            mCallbackIntent);
}

@Override
public void onDisconnected() {
    Log.w(TAG, "Google Services Disconnected");
}

@Override
public void onConnectionFailed(ConnectionResult result) {
    Log.w(TAG, "Google Services Connection Failure");
}

/** OnActivityChangedListener Methods */

@Override
public void onUserActivityChanged(int bestChoice,
        int bestConfidence,
        ActivityRecognitionResult newActivity) {
    //Add latest event to the list
    mListAdapter.add(newActivity);
    mListAdapter.notifyDataSetChanged();

    //Determine user action based on our custom algorithm
    switch (bestChoice) {
        case DetectedActivity.IN_VEHICLE:
        case DetectedActivity.ON_BICYCLE:
            mBlockingView.setVisibility(View.VISIBLE);
            break;
```

```
        case DetectedActivity.ON_FOOT:
        case DetectedActivity.STILL:
            mBlockingView.setVisibility(View.GONE);
            break;
        default:
            //Ignore other states
            break;
    }
}

/*
 * Utility that builds a simple Toast with all the probable
 * activity choices with their confidence values
 */
private void showDetails(ActivityRecognitionResult activity) {
    StringBuilder sb = new StringBuilder();
    sb.append("Details:");
    for(DetectedActivity element :
            activity.getProbableActivities()) {
        sb.append("\n"
                + UserMotionService.getActivityName(element)
                + ", " + element.getConfidence() + "% sure");
    }

    Toast.makeText(this, sb.toString(),
            Toast.LENGTH_SHORT).show();
}

/*
 * ListAdapter to display each activity result we receive
 * from the service
 */
private static class ActivityAdapter extends
        ArrayAdapter<ActivityRecognitionResult> {

    public ActivityAdapter(Context context) {
        super(context, android.R.layout.simple_list_item_1);
    }

    @Override
    public View getView(int position, View convertView,
            ViewGroup parent) {
        if (convertView == null) {
            convertView =
                LayoutInflater.from(getContext()).inflate(
                    android.R.layout.simple_list_item_1,
                    parent,
                    false);
        }
```

```
        //Display the most probable activity with its
        // confidence in the list
        TextView tv = (TextView) convertView;
        ActivityRecognitionResult result = getItem(position);
        DetectedActivity newActivity =
                result.getMostProbableActivity();
        String entry =
            DateFormat.format("hh:mm:ss", result.getTime())
            + ": " +
            UserMotionService.getActivityName(newActivity)
            + ", " + newActivity.getConfidence()
            + "% confidence";
        tv.setText(entry);

        return convertView;
    }
  }
}
```

In this example, our first order of business is to check whether Google Play Services is available on the device and is up-to-date. With that verified, we can create our ActivityRecognitionClient, an Intent we will need to connect to our service (which we haven't seen yet), and the PendingIntent that we will give the recognition services to use in calling us back.

> **Note** Do not confuse Activity, the application component that displays UI, with *activity* as it is used in this context to describe a user's physical activity. The word is thrown around a lot in this API, so keep in mind the difference.

When the application is brought to the foreground, we make a connection request to the recognition service. This process is asynchronous, and we will later receive a call in onConnected() when the connection is complete. To ensure that we don't drain unnecessary power, we remove these updates when going into the background.

During those same events, we bind and unbind with our own service so that binding is active only while we are in the foreground. We will see shortly the significance this service will have in the overall application.

> **Tip** With bound services, onServiceDisconnected() is called only if the service crashes or disconnects unexpectedly. Any cleanup you wish to do when disconnecting explicitly must also be done alongside unbindService().

Once the recognition service is connected to us, we initiate updates using
requestActivityUpdates() with an interval of 5 seconds and our PendingIntent, which describes
where the updates will go. In our case, the PendingIntent is set to trigger the UserMotionService,
and the code for this service is in Listing 5-46.

Listing 5-46. Service Receiving Motion Updates

```java
public class UserMotionService extends IntentService {
    private static final String TAG = "UserMotionService";

    /*
     * Callback interface for detected activity type changes
     */
    public interface OnActivityChangedListener{
        public void onUserActivityChanged(int bestChoice,
                int bestConfidence,
                ActivityRecognitionResult newActivity);
    }

    /* Last detected activity type */
    private DetectedActivity mLastKnownActivity;

    /*
     * Marshals requests from the background thread so the
     * callbacks can be made on the main (UI) thread.
     */
    private CallbackHandler mHandler;
    private static class CallbackHandler extends Handler {
        /* Callback for activity changes */
        private OnActivityChangedListener mCallback;

        public void setCallback(
                OnActivityChangedListener callback) {
            mCallback = callback;
        }

        @Override
        public void handleMessage(Message msg) {
            if (mCallback != null) {
                //Read payload data out of the message and
                // fire callback
                ActivityRecognitionResult newActivity =
                        (ActivityRecognitionResult) msg.obj;
                mCallback.onUserActivityChanged(
                        msg.arg1,
                        msg.arg2,
                        newActivity);
            }
        }
    }
}
```

```java
public UserMotionService() {
    //String is used to name the background thread created
    super("UserMotionService");
    mHandler = new CallbackHandler();
}

public void setOnActivityChangedListener(
        OnActivityChangedListener listener) {
    mHandler.setCallback(listener);
}

@Override
public void onDestroy() {
    super.onDestroy();
    Log.w(TAG, "Service is stopping...");
}

/*
 * Incoming action events from the framework will come
 * in here.  This is called on a background thread, so
 * we can do long processing here if we wish.
 */
@Override
protected void onHandleIntent(Intent intent) {
    if (ActivityRecognitionResult.hasResult(intent)) {
        //Extract the result from the Intent
        ActivityRecognitionResult result =
                ActivityRecognitionResult.extractResult(intent);
        DetectedActivity activity =
                result.getMostProbableActivity();
        Log.v(TAG, "New User Activity Event");

        //If the highest probability is UNKNOWN, but the
        // confidence is low, check if another exists and
        // select it instead.
        if (activity.getType() == DetectedActivity.UNKNOWN
                && activity.getConfidence() < 60
                && result.getProbableActivities().size() > 1){
            //Select the next probable element
            activity = result.getProbableActivities().get(1);
        }

        //On a change in activity, alert the callback
        if (mLastKnownActivity == null
                || mLastKnownActivity.getType()
                        != activity.getType()
                || mLastKnownActivity.getConfidence()
                        != activity.getConfidence()) {
            //Pass the results to the main thread in a Message
            Message msg = Message.obtain(null,
                    0,                          //what
                    activity.getType(),         //arg1
```

```
                        activity.getConfidence(),  //arg2
                        result);                   //obj
                mHandler.sendMessage(msg);
            }
            mLastKnownActivity = activity;
        }
    }

    /*
     * This is called when the Activity wants to bind to the
     * service.  We have to provide a wrapper around this instance
     * to pass it back.
     */
    @Override
    public IBinder onBind(Intent intent) {
        return mBinder;
    }

    /*
     * This is a simple wrapper that we can pass to the Activity
     * to allow it direct access to this service.
     */
    private LocalBinder mBinder = new LocalBinder();
    public class LocalBinder extends Binder {
        public UserMotionService getService() {
            return UserMotionService.this;
        }
    }

    /*
     * Utility to get a good display name for each state
     */
    public static String getActivityName(
            DetectedActivity activity) {
        switch(activity.getType()) {
            case DetectedActivity.IN_VEHICLE:
                return "Driving";
            case DetectedActivity.ON_BICYCLE:
                return "Biking";
            case DetectedActivity.ON_FOOT:
                return "Walking";
            case DetectedActivity.STILL:
                return "Not Moving";
            case DetectedActivity.TILTING:
                return "Tilting";
            case DetectedActivity.UNKNOWN:
            default:
                return "No Clue";
        }
    }
}
```

UserMotionService is an IntentService, which is a service that forwards all Intent commands to a background thread it creates and processes them in the onHandleIntent() method. Its primary advantage is a built-in mechanism to queue up Intent requests and process them in order, in the background, via this method.

When the activity binds to this service, it will be automatically started and returned via onBind() to the caller. The activity will receive the service instance in onServiceConnected(), where we will register the activity as a callback for user activity change events determined in the service. Once the activity unbinds from the service, it will automatically stop itself as well.

Once the point is reached where the activity has registered for update events from Google Play Services, the framework will start triggering the PendingIntent on a regular basis, which results in onHandleIntent() in our service.

For each event, we use the utility methods on ActivityRecognitionResult to unpack the data from the incoming Intent. We then determine what the most probable user activity was. We have customized the algorithm a little bit, in that if the most probable activity is UNKNOWN, but the confidence in that decision is low, we will pick the next best option to return instead. This pattern will work well for any additional custom decision logic you would like to put into your application as well.

Once we have selected the user activity to compare, we check whether this is the same activity type or a change in activity has occurred. In the case of a change, we want to post a callback to the activity that registered itself when we were bound. We use a Handler instead of calling the method directly because onHandleIntent() is running on a background thread, and we want to post our callback on the main thread in case the activity (or other listeners) want to do any work that involves updating the UI.

Summary

This collection of recipes exposed how to integrate maps, user location, and device sensor data about the user's surroundings into your Android applications. You learned about the many additional APIs that Google provides to Android devices that exist within the Google Play ecosystem. We also discussed how to utilize the device's camera and microphone, allowing users to capture, and sometimes interpret, what's around them. Finally, using the media APIs, you learned how to take media content, either captured locally by the user or downloaded remotely from the Web, and play it back from within your applications. In the next chapter, we will discuss how to use Android's many persistence techniques to store nonvolatile data on the device.

Persisting Data

Even in the midst of grand architectures designed to shift as much user data into the cloud as possible, the transient nature of mobile applications will always require that at least some user data be persisted locally on the device. This data may range from cached responses from a web service guaranteeing offline access to preferences that the user has set for specific application behaviors. Android provides a series of helpful frameworks to take the pain out of using files and databases to persist information.

6-1. Making a Preference Screen

Problem

You need to create a simple way to store, change, and display user preferences and settings within your application.

Solution

(API Level 1)

Use the `PreferenceActivity` and an XML `Preference` hierarchy to provide the user interface, key/value combinations, and persistence all at once. Using this method will create a user interface that is consistent with the Settings application on Android devices, and it will keep users' experiences consistent with what they expect.

Within the XML, an entire set of one or more screens can be defined with the associated settings displayed and grouped into categories by using the `PreferenceScreen`, `PreferenceCategory`, and associated `Preference` elements. The activity can then load this hierarchy for the user by using very little code.

How It Works

Listings 6-1 and 6-2 show the basic settings for an Android application. The XML defines two screens with a variety of all the common preference types that this framework supports. Notice that one screen is nested inside the other; the internal screen will be displayed when the user clicks on its associated list item from the root screen.

Listing 6-1. res/xml/settings.xml

```xml
<?xml version="1.0" encoding="utf-8"?>
<PreferenceScreen xmlns:android="http://schemas.android.com/apk/res/android">
    <EditTextPreference
        android:key="namePref"
        android:title="Name"
        android:summary="Tell Us Your Name"
        android:defaultValue="Apress" />
    <CheckBoxPreference
        android:key="morePref"
        android:title="Enable More Settings"
        android:defaultValue="false" />
    <PreferenceScreen
        android:key="moreScreen"
        android:title="More Settings"
        android:dependency="morePref">
        <ListPreference
            android:key="colorPref"
            android:title="Favorite Color"
            android:summary="Choose your favorite color"
            android:entries="@array/color_names"
            android:entryValues="@array/color_values"
            android:defaultValue="GRN" />
        <PreferenceCategory
            android:title="Location Settings">
            <CheckBoxPreference
                android:key="gpsPref"
                android:title="Use GPS Location"
                android:summary="Use GPS to Find You"
                android:defaultValue="true" />
            <CheckBoxPreference
                android:key="networkPref"
                android:title="Use Network Location"
                android:summary="Use Network to Find You"
                android:defaultValue="true" />
        </PreferenceCategory>
    </PreferenceScreen>
</PreferenceScreen>
```

Listing 6-2. res/values/arrays.xml

```xml
<?xml version="1.0" encoding="utf-8"?>
<resources>
    <string-array name="color_names">
        <item>Black</item>
        <item>Red</item>
        <item>Green</item>
    </string-array>
    <string-array name="color_values">
        <item>BLK</item>
        <item>RED</item>
        <item>GRN</item>
    </string-array>
</resources>
```

Notice first the convention used to create the XML file. Although this resource could be inflated from any directory (such as `res/layout`), the convention is to put them into a generic directory for the project titled simply `xml`.

Also, notice that we provide an `android:key` attribute for each `Preference` object instead of `android:id`. When each stored value is referenced elsewhere in the application through a `SharedPreferences` object, it will be accessed using the key. In addition, `PreferenceActivity` includes the `findPreference()` method for obtaining a reference to an inflated `Preference` in Java code, which is more efficient than using `findViewById()`; `findPreference()` also takes the key as a parameter.

When inflated, the root `PreferenceScreen` presents a list with the following three options (in order):

1. Name: This is an instance of `EditTextPreference`, which stores a string value. Tapping this item will present a text box so that the user can type a new preference value.

2. Enable More Settings: This is an instance of `CheckBoxPreference`, which stores a boolean value. Tapping this item will toggle the checked status of the check box.

3. More Settings: Tapping this item will load another `PreferenceScreen` with more items.

When the user taps the More Settings item, a second screen is displayed with three more items: a `ListPreference` item and two more `CheckBoxPreferences` grouped together by a `PreferenceCategory`. `PreferenceCategory` is simply a way to create section breaks and headers in the list for grouping actual preference items.

The `ListPreference` is the final preference type used in the example. This item requires two array parameters (although they can both be set to the same array) that represent a set of choices the user may pick from. The `android:entries` array is the list of human-readable items to display, while the `android:entryValues` array represents the actual value to be stored.

All the preference items may optionally have a default value set for them as well. This value is not automatically loaded, however. It will load the first time this XML file is inflated when the PreferenceActivity is displayed *or* when a call to PreferenceManager.setDefaultValues() is made.

Now let's take a look at how a PreferenceActivity would load and manage this. See Listing 6-3.

Listing 6-3. PreferenceActivity in Action

```
public class SettingsActivity extends PreferenceActivity {

    @Override
    public void onCreate(Bundle savedInstanceState) {
        super.onCreate(savedInstanceState);
        //Load preference data from XML
        addPreferencesFromResource(R.xml.settings);
    }
}
```

All that is required to display the preferences and allow the user to make changes is a call to addPreferencesFromResource(). There is no need to call setContentView() when we extend PreferenceActivity; addPreferencesFromResource() inflates the XML and manages displaying the content in a list. However a custom layout may be provided as long as it contains a ListView with the android:id="@android:id/list" attribute set, which is where PreferenceActivity will load the preference items.

Preference items can also be placed in the list for the sole purpose of controlling access. In the example, we put the Enable More Settings item in the list just to allow the user to enable or disable access to the second PreferenceScreen. In order to accomplish this, our nested PreferenceScreen includes the android:dependency attribute, which links its enabled state to the state of another preference. Whenever the referenced preference is either not set or false, this preference will be disabled.

When this activity loads, you see something like Figure 6-1.

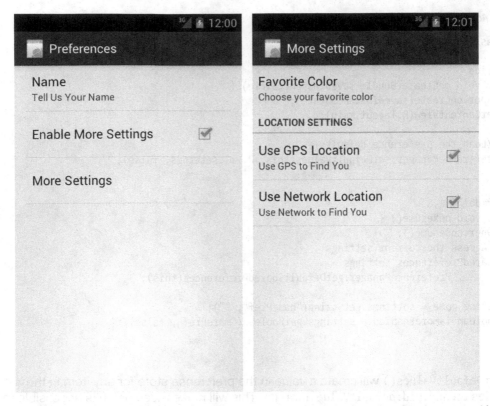

Figure 6-1. The root PreferenceScreen (left) displays first. If the user taps More Settings, the secondary screen (right) displays

Loading Defaults and Accessing Preferences

Typically, a PreferenceActivity such as this one is not the root of an application. Often, if default values are set, they may need to be accessed by the rest of the application before the user ever visits Settings (the first case under which the defaults will load). Therefore, it can be helpful to put a call to the following method elsewhere in your application to ensure that the defaults are loaded prior to being used.

```
PreferenceManager.setDefaultValues(Context context, int resId, boolean readAgain);
```

This method may be called multiple times, and the defaults will not get loaded over again. It may be placed in the main activity so it is called on first launch, or perhaps it could be in a common place where the application can call it before any access to shared preferences.

Preferences that are stored by using this mechanism are put into the default shared preferences object, which can be accessed with any Context pointer by using the following:

```
PreferenceManager.getDefaultSharedPreferences(Context context);
```

An example activity that would load the defaults set in our previous example and access some of the current values stored would look like Listing 6-4.

Listing 6-4. *Activity Loading Preference Defaults*

```
public class HomeActivity extends Activity {

    @Override
    public void onCreate(Bundle savedInstanceState) {
        super.onCreate(savedInstanceState);
        setContentView(R.layout.main);

        //Load the preference defaults
        PreferenceManager.setDefaultValues(this, R.xml.settings, false);
    }

    @Override
    public void onResume() {
        super.onResume();
        //Access the current settings
        SharedPreferences settings =
                PreferenceManager.getDefaultSharedPreferences(this);

        String name = settings.getString("namePref", "");
        boolean isMoreEnabled = settings.getBoolean("morePref", false);
    }
}
```

Calling setDefaultValues() will create a value in the preference store for any item in the XML file that includes an android:defaultValue attribute. This will make those defaults accessible to the application, even if the user has not yet visited the settings screen.

These values can then be accessed using a set of typed accessor functions on the SharedPreferences object. Each of these accessor methods requires both the name of the preference key and a default value to be returned if a value for the preference key does not yet exist.

PreferenceFragment

(API Level 11)

Starting with Android 3.0, a new method of creating preference screens was introduced in the form of PreferenceFragment. This class is not in the Support Library, so it can be used only as a replacement for PreferenceActivity if your application targets a minimum of API Level 11. Listings 6-5 and 6-6 modify the previous example to use PreferenceFragment instead.

Listing 6-5. *Activity Containing Fragments*

```
public class MainActivity extends Activity {

    @Override
    protected void onCreate(Bundle savedInstanceState) {
        super.onCreate(savedInstanceState);
```

```
        FragmentTransaction ft = getFragmentManager().beginTransaction();
        ft.add(android.R.id.content, new PreferenceFragment());
        ft.commit();
    }
}
```

Listing 6-6. New PreferenceFragment

```
public class SettingsFragment extends PreferenceFragment {

    @Override
    public void onCreate(Bundle savedInstanceState) {
        super.onCreate(savedInstanceState);
        //Load preference data from XML
        addPreferencesFromResource(R.xml.settings);
    }
}
```

Now the preferences themselves are housed inside a PreferenceFragment, which manages them in the same way as before. The other required change is that a fragment cannot live on its own; it must be contained inside an activity, so we have created a new root activity where the fragment is attached.

The Android framework has moved to Fragments for preferences in order to more easily allow multiple preference hierarchies (perhaps representing different top-level categories of settings) to be easily displayed inside a single activity rather than forcing the user to jump in and out of each category with multiple activity instances.

KITKAT SECURITY

As of Android 4.4, a PreferenceActivity must override the isValidFragment() method in applications targeting SDK Level 19 or higher. This method prevents external applications from performing fragment injection by supplying an incorrect class name in the Intent extras directed at an exported PreferenceActivity that hosts PreferenceFragment instances.

In applications with a lower SDK target, this method will always return true for compatibility, which also leaves the security hole open. It is prudent for developers to update their target to 19+ and implement this method to validate that only Fragments you expect can be instantiated. If isValidFragment() is not overridden on an app with an updated target SDK, an exception will be thrown.

6-2. Displaying Custom Preferences
Problem

The Preference elements provided by the framework are not flexible enough, and you need to add a more specific UI for modifying the value.

Solution

(API Level 1)

Extend Preference, or one of its subclasses, to integrate a new type into a PreferenceActivity or PreferenceFragment. When creating a new preference type, there are two major objectives you need to keep in mind: how to provide an interface to the user for modifying the preference, and how to persist their selection back into SharedPreferences.

With regards to the user interface, there are several callback methods you may want to override. Notice that they use a similar pattern to the adapters we see in ListView:

- onCreateView(): Construct a new layout to be used for this preference element in the list. This is called the first time an instance of this preference is needed. If multiple elements of the same type exist, these views will be recycled when possible. If you don't override this, the default view with a title and summary will be displayed.

- onBindView(): Attach the data for this current preference to the view constructed in onCreateView(), which is passed into this method as a parameter. This will be called every time the preference is about to be displayed.

- getSummary(): Override the summary value displayed in the standard UI layout. This is only useful if you don't override onCreateView()/onBindView().

- onClick(): Handle an event when the user taps on this item in the list.

Basic preferences in the framework, such as CheckBoxPreference, simply toggle the persisted state on each click. Other preferences, such as EditTextPreference or ListPreference, are subclasses of DialogPreference, which use the click event to display a dialog to provide a more complex UI for updating the given setting.

The second set of overrides you may have in a custom Preference deal with retrieving and persisting data:

- onGetDefaultValue(): This method will be called to allow you to read the android:defaultValue attribute from the preference's XML definition. You will receive the TypedArray where the attributes live and the index necessary to obtain the value using whichever typed method makes sense for the preference value.

- onSetInitialValue(): Locally set the value of this preference instance. The restorePersistedValue flag indicates whether the value should come from SharedPreferences, or from the default value. The default value parameter is the instance returned from onGetDefaultValue().

Anytime that your preference needs to read the current value saved in SharedPreferences, you can invoke one of the typed getPersistedXxx() methods to return the value type your preference is persisting (integer, boolean, string, and so forth). Conversely, when the preference needs to save a new value, you can use the typed persistXxx() methods to update SharedPreferences.

How It Works

In the following example, we create a ColorPreference: a simple extension of DialogPreference that provides the user interface to select a color as three sliders that provide the RGB values discretely. Similar to ListPreference, an AlertDialog will display when the preference is selected from the list. This is where the user will make their selection and save or cancel the change, rather than in the list UI directly (as with CheckBoxPreference, for example). Listing 6-7 shows the layout for our custom dialog box, followed by Listing 6-8, which reveals our ColorPreference implementation.

Listing 6-7. res/layout/preference_color.xml

```xml
<?xml version="1.0" encoding="utf-8"?>
<LinearLayout xmlns:android="http://schemas.android.com/apk/res/android"
    android:layout_width="wrap_content"
    android:layout_height="wrap_content"
    android:padding="16dp"
    android:minWidth="300dp"
    android:orientation="vertical" >
    <TextView
        android:layout_width="wrap_content"
        android:layout_height="wrap_content"
        android:text="Red" />
    <SeekBar
        android:id="@+id/selector_red"
        android:layout_width="match_parent"
        android:layout_height="wrap_content"
        android:max="255" />

    <TextView
        android:layout_width="wrap_content"
        android:layout_height="wrap_content"
        android:text="Green" />
    <SeekBar
        android:id="@+id/selector_green"
        android:layout_width="match_parent"
        android:layout_height="wrap_content"
        android:max="255" />

    <TextView
        android:layout_width="wrap_content"
        android:layout_height="wrap_content"
        android:text="Blue" />
    <SeekBar
        android:id="@+id/selector_blue"
        android:layout_width="match_parent"
        android:layout_height="wrap_content"
        android:max="255" />
</LinearLayout>
```

Listing 6-8. Custom Preference Definition

```java
public class ColorPreference extends DialogPreference {

    private static final int DEFAULT_COLOR = Color.WHITE;
    /* Local copy of the current color setting */
    private int mCurrentColor;
    /* Sliders to set color components */
    private SeekBar mRedLevel, mGreenLevel, mBlueLevel;

    public ColorPreference(Context context, AttributeSet attrs) {
        super(context, attrs);
    }

    /*
     * Called to construct a new dialog to show when the preference
     * is clicked.  We create and set up a new content view for
     * each instance.
     */
    @Override
    protected void onPrepareDialogBuilder(Builder builder) {
        //Create the dialog's content view
        View rootView =
                LayoutInflater.from(getContext()).inflate(R.layout.preference_color, null);
        mRedLevel = (SeekBar) rootView.findViewById(R.id.selector_red);
        mGreenLevel = (SeekBar) rootView.findViewById(R.id.selector_green);
        mBlueLevel = (SeekBar) rootView.findViewById(R.id.selector_blue);

        mRedLevel.setProgress(Color.red(mCurrentColor));
        mGreenLevel.setProgress(Color.green(mCurrentColor));
        mBlueLevel.setProgress(Color.blue(mCurrentColor));

        //Attach the content view
        builder.setView(rootView);
        super.onPrepareDialogBuilder(builder);
    }

    /*
     * Called when the dialog is closed with the result of
     * the button tapped by the user.
     */
    @Override
    protected void onDialogClosed(boolean positiveResult) {
        if (positiveResult) {
            //When OK is pressed, obtain and save the color value
            int color = Color.rgb(
                    mRedLevel.getProgress(),
                    mGreenLevel.getProgress(),
                    mBlueLevel.getProgress());
            setCurrentValue(color);
        }
    }
```

```java
/*
 * Called by the framework to obtain the default value
 * passed in the preference XML definition
 */
@Override
protected Object onGetDefaultValue(TypedArray a, int index) {
    //Return the default value from XML as a color int
    ColorStateList value = a.getColorStateList(index);
    if (value == null) {
        return DEFAULT_COLOR;
    }
    return value.getDefaultColor();
}

/*
 * Called by the framework to set the initial value of the
 * preference, either from its default or the last persisted
 * value.
 */
@Override
protected void onSetInitialValue(boolean restorePersistedValue, Object defaultValue) {
    setCurrentValue( restorePersistedValue ?
            getPersistedInt(DEFAULT_COLOR) : (Integer)defaultValue );
}

/*
 * Return a custom summary based on the current setting
 */
@Override
public CharSequence getSummary() {
    //Construct the summary with the color value in hex
    int color = getPersistedInt(DEFAULT_COLOR);
    String content = String.format("Current Value is 0x%02X%02X%02X",
            Color.red(color), Color.green(color), Color.blue(color));
    //Return the summary text as a Spannable, colored by the selection
    Spannable summary = new SpannableString (content);
    summary.setSpan(new ForegroundColorSpan(color), 0, summary.length(), 0);
    return summary;
}

private void setCurrentValue(int value) {
    //Update latest value
    mCurrentColor = value;

    //Save new value
    persistInt(value);
    //Notify preference listeners
    notifyDependencyChange(shouldDisableDependents());
    notifyChanged();
}

}
```

When the `ColorPreference` is first created from XML, `onGetDefaultValue()` will be called with the `android:defaultValue` attribute (if one was added) so we can parse it. We want to allow any color attribute to be used, so we read the attribute's value using `getColorStateList()`, which supports reading color strings and references to color resources, and return the result (which will be an integer).

Later, when the preference is attached to the activity, `onSetInitialValue()` will tell us whether we should read that default value in or use a value already saved in `SharedPreferences`. On the first run, we will choose the default, while each attempt after that will read the saved value using `getPersistedInt()`. The parameter to `getPersistedInt()` is the default value we should use if the persisted value doesn't exist or can't be read as an integer.

For the user interface, rather than monitoring `onClick()`, we have two new callbacks provided by `DialogPreference`: `onPrepareDialogBuilder()` and `onDialogClosed()`. The former is triggered with an `AlertDialog.Builder` instance so we can customize the dialog box to be shown when a user clicks the preference; this will happen on each new click. We are using this method to inflate and attach our dialog box layout containing the three sliders—one each for the red, green, and blue components.

When we receive `onDialogClosed()`, we are told whether the user selected OK to save the preference or Cancel to revert the change. In the positive case, we want to create the new color from the UI sliders and persist the value using `persistInt()`. In the negative case, we take no action to change the current setting.

Finally, whenever a new change is persisted, we call `notifyDependencyChange()` and `notifyChanged()` to alert any preference listeners of the update. This also alerts the `PreferenceActivity` to update the list display.

We have made one final customization using `getSummary()`. In this example, we didn't provide a completely new layout, but rather we are customizing the summary display to include the current color selection (as a hex string) and that text will be colored with the selection. We can do this because `getSummary()` returns a `CharSequence` (instead of a pure `String`) allowing styled `Spannable` types to be returned.

With our new preference constructed, we can simply add it to an XML definition of a `<PreferenceScreen>` alongside other standard preferences, just as we saw in the previous recipe (see Listings 6-9 and 6-10).

Listing 6-9. `res/xml/settings.xml`

```xml
<?xml version="1.0" encoding="utf-8"?>
<PreferenceScreen xmlns:android="http://schemas.android.com/apk/res/android">
    <CheckBoxPreference
        android:key="dummyPref"
        android:title="CheckBox Select"
        android:summary="Standard preference element"
        android:defaultValue="false" />
    <com.androidrecipes.custompreference.ColorPreference
        android:key="colorPref"
        android:title="Select Color"
        android:defaultValue="@android:color/black" />
</PreferenceScreen>
```

Listing 6-10. PreferenceActivity with New Settings

```java
public class CustomPreferenceActivity extends PreferenceActivity {

    @Override
    protected void onCreate(Bundle savedInstanceState) {
        super.onCreate(savedInstanceState);
        addPreferencesFromResource(R.xml.settings);
    }
}
```

We have set the default value of our color preference to a framework resource for black, which will be read by our onGetDefaultValue() override. You can see in Listing 6-10 that inflating this new preference hierarchy requires no modifications to the existing PreferenceActivity code we saw in the previous recipe. Figure 6-2 shows our results.

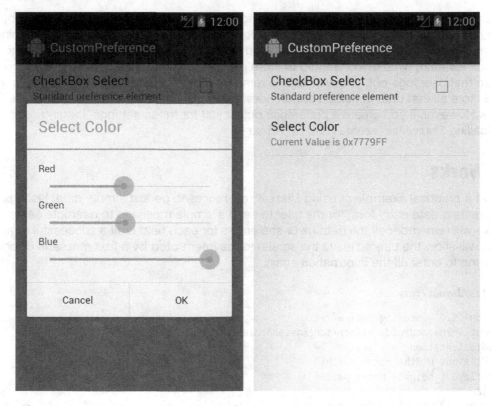

Figure 6-2. PreferenceScreen with our custom ColorPreference

6-3. Persisting Simple Data

Problem

Your application needs a simple, low-overhead method of storing basic data such as numbers and strings in persistent storage.

Solution

(API Level 1)

Using SharedPreferences objects, applications can quickly create one or more persistent stores where data can be saved and retrieved at a later time. Underneath the hood, these objects are actually stored as XML files in the application's user data area. However, unlike directly reading and writing data from files, SharedPreferences provide an efficient framework for persisting basic data types.

Creating multiple SharedPreferences as opposed to dumping all your data in the default object can be a good habit to get into, especially if the data you are storing will have a shelf life. Keeping in mind that all preferences stored using the XML and PreferenceActivity framework are also stored in the default location, what if you wanted to store a group of items related to, say, a logged-in user? When that user logs out, you will need to remove all the persisted data that goes along with that. If you store all that data in default preferences, you will most likely need to remove each item individually. However, if you create a preference object just for those settings, logging out can be as simple as calling SharedPreferences.Editor.clear().

How It Works

Let's look at a practical example of using SharedPreferences to persist simple data. Listings 6-11 and 6-12 create a data entry form for the user to send a simple message to a remote server. To aid the user, we will remember all the data he or she enters for each field until a successful request is made. This will allow the user to leave the screen (or be interrupted by a text message or phone call) without having to enter all the information again.

Listing 6-11. res/layout/form.xml

```xml
<?xml version="1.0" encoding="utf-8"?>
<LinearLayout xmlns:android="http://schemas.android.com/apk/res/android"
    android:orientation="vertical"
    android:layout_width="match_parent"
    android:layout_height="match_parent">
    <TextView
        android:layout_width="match_parent"
        android:layout_height="wrap_content"
        android:text="Email:"
        android:padding="5dip" />
    <EditText
        android:id="@+id/email"
        android:layout_width="match_parent"
        android:layout_height="wrap_content"
        android:singleLine="true" />
```

```xml
    <CheckBox
        android:id="@+id/age"
        android:layout_width="match_parent"
        android:layout_height="wrap_content"
        android:text="Are You Over 18?" />
    <TextView
        android:layout_width="match_parent"
        android:layout_height="wrap_content"
        android:text="Message:"
        android:padding="5dip" />
    <EditText
        android:id="@+id/message"
        android:layout_width="match_parent"
        android:layout_height="wrap_content"
        android:minLines="3"
        android:maxLines="3" />
    <Button
        android:id="@+id/submit"
        android:layout_width="match_parent"
        android:layout_height="wrap_content"
        android:text="Submit" />
</LinearLayout>
```

Listing 6-12. Entry Form with Persistence

```java
public class FormActivity extends Activity implements View.OnClickListener {

    EditText email, message;
    CheckBox age;
    Button submit;

    SharedPreferences formStore;

    boolean submitSuccess = false;

    @Override
    public void onCreate(Bundle savedInstanceState) {
        super.onCreate(savedInstanceState);
        setContentView(R.layout.form);

        email = (EditText)findViewById(R.id.email);
        message = (EditText)findViewById(R.id.message);
        age = (CheckBox)findViewById(R.id.age);

        submit = (Button)findViewById(R.id.submit);
        submit.setOnClickListener(this);

        //Retrieve or create the preferences object
        formStore = getPreferences(Activity.MODE_PRIVATE);
    }
```

```java
    @Override
    public void onResume() {
        super.onResume();
        //Restore the form data
        email.setText(formStore.getString("email", ""));
        message.setText(formStore.getString("message", ""));
        age.setChecked(formStore.getBoolean("age", false));
    }

    @Override
    public void onPause() {
        super.onPause();
        if(submitSuccess) {
            //Editor calls can be chained together
            formStore.edit().clear().commit();
        } else {
            //Store the form data
            SharedPreferences.Editor editor = formStore.edit();
            editor.putString("email", email.getText().toString());
            editor.putString("message", message.getText().toString());
            editor.putBoolean("age", age.isChecked());
            editor.commit();
        }
    }

    @Override
    public void onClick(View v) {

        //DO SOME WORK SUBMITTING A MESSAGE

        //Mark the operation successful
        submitSuccess = true;
        //Close
        finish();
    }
}
```

We start with a typical user form containing two simple EditText entry fields and a check box. When the activity is created, we gather a SharedPreferences object using Activity.getPreferences(), and this is where all the persisted data will be stored. If at any time the activity is paused for a reason other than a successful submission (controlled by the boolean member), the current state of the form will be quickly loaded into the preferences and persisted.

> **Note**   When saving data into SharedPreferences using an Editor, always remember to call commit() or apply() after the changes are made. Otherwise, your changes will not be saved.

Conversely, whenever the activity becomes visible, onResume() loads the user interface with the latest information stored in the preferences object. If no preferences exist, either because they were cleared or never created (first launch), then the form is set to blank.

When a user presses Submit and the fake form submits successfully, the subsequent call to onPause() will clear any stored form data in preferences. Because all these operations were done on a private preferences object, clearing the data does not affect any user settings that may have been stored using other means.

> **Note** Methods called from an Editor always return the same Editor object, allowing them to be chained together in places where doing so makes your code more readable.

Creating Common SharedPreferences

The previous example illustrated how to use a single SharedPreferences object within the context of a single activity with an object obtained from Activity.getPreferences(). Truth be told, this method is really just a convenience wrapper for Context.getSharedPreferences(), in which it passes the activity name as the preference store name. If the data you are storing are best shared between two or more activity instances, it might make sense to call getSharedPreferences() instead and pass a more common name so the data can be accessed easily from different places in code. See Listing 6-13.

Listing 6-13. Two Activities Using the Same Preferences

```
public class ActivityOne extends Activity {
    public static final String PREF_NAME = "myPreferences";
    private SharedPreferences mPreferences;

    @Override
    public void onCreate(Bundle savedInstanceState) {
        super.onCreate(savedInstanceState);
        mPreferences = getSharedPreferences(PREF_NAME, Activity.MODE_PRIVATE);
    }
}

public class ActivityTwo extends Activity {

    private SharedPreferences mPreferences;

    @Override
    public void onCreate(Bundle savedInstanceState) {
        super.onCreate(savedInstanceState);
        mPreferences = getSharedPreferences(ActivityOne.PREF_NAME,
            Activity.MODE_PRIVATE);
    }

}
```

In this example, both activity classes retrieve the SharedPreferences object using the same name (defined as a constant string): thus they will be accessing the same set of preference data. Furthermore, both references are even pointing at the same *instance* of preferences, as the framework creates a singleton object for each set of SharedPreferences (a set being defined by its name). This means that changes made on one side will immediately be reflected on the other.

A NOTE ABOUT MODE

Context.getSharedPreferences() also takes a mode parameter. Passing 0 or MODE_PRIVATE provides the default behavior of allowing only the application that created the preferences (or another application with the same user ID) to gain read/write access. This method supports two more mode parameters: MODE_WORLD_READABLE and MODE_WORLD_WRITEABLE. These modes allow other applications to gain access to these preferences by setting the user permissions on the file it creates appropriately. However, the external application still requires a valid Context pointing back to the package where the preference file was created.

For example, let's say you created SharedPreferences with world-readable permission in an application with the package com.examples.myfirstapplication. In order to access those preferences from a second application, the second application would obtain them using the following code:

Context otherContext = createPackageContext("com.examples.myfirstapplication", 0);

SharedPreferences externalPreferences = otherContext.getSharedPreferences(PREF_NAME, 0);

Caution   If you choose to use the mode parameter to allow external access, be sure that you are consistent in the mode you provide everywhere getSharedPreferences() is called. This mode is used only the first time the preference file gets created, so calling up SharedPreferences with different mode parameters at different times will only lead to confusion on your part.

6-4. Reading and Writing Files

Problem

Your application needs to read data in from an external file or write more-complex data out for persistence.

Solution

(API Level 1)

Sometimes, there is no substitute for working with a filesystem. Working with files allows your application to read and write data that does not lend itself well to other persistence options such as key/value preferences and databases. Android also provides a number of cache locations for files you can use to place data that you need to persist on a temporary basis.

Android supports all the standard Java file I/O APIs for create, read, update, and delete (CRUD) operations, along with some additional helpers to make accessing those files in specific locations a little more convenient. There are three main locations in which an application can work with files:

- *Internal storage*: Protected directory space to read and write file data.

- *External storage*: Externally mountable space to read and write file data. Requires the WRITE_EXTERNAL_STORAGE permission in API Level 4+. Often, this is a physical SD card in the device.

- *Assets*: Protected read-only space inside the APK bundle. Good for local resources that can't or shouldn't be compiled.

While the underlying mechanism to work with file data remains the same, we will look at the details that make working with each destination slightly different.

How It Works

As we stated earlier, the traditional Java FileInputStream and FileOutputStream classes constitute the primary method of accessing file data. In fact, you can create a File instance at any time with an absolute path location and use one of these streams to read and write data. However, with root paths varying on different devices and certain directories being protected from your application, we recommend some slightly more efficient ways to work with files.

Internal Storage

In order to create or modify a file's location on internal storage, utilize the Context.openFileInput() and Context.openFileOutput() methods. These methods require only the name of the file as a parameter, instead of the entire path, and will reference the file in relation to the application's protected directory space, regardless of the exact path on the specific device. See Listing 6-14.

Listing 6-14. CRUD a File on Internal Storage

```
public class InternalActivity extends Activity {

    private static final String FILENAME = "data.txt";

    @Override
    public void onCreate(Bundle savedInstanceState) {
        super.onCreate(savedInstanceState);
        TextView tv = new TextView(this);
        setContentView(tv);

        //Create a new file and write some data
        try {
            FileOutputStream mOutput = openFileOutput(FILENAME, Activity.MODE_PRIVATE);
            String data = "THIS DATA WRITTEN TO A FILE";
            mOutput.write(data.getBytes());
            mOutput.flush();
            mOutput.close();
```

```
        } catch (FileNotFoundException e) {
            e.printStackTrace();
        } catch (IOException e) {
            e.printStackTrace();
        }

        //Read the created file and display to the screen
        try {
            FileInputStream mInput = openFileInput(FILENAME);
            byte[] data = new byte[128];
            mInput.read(data);
            mInput.close();

            String display = new String(data);
            tv.setText(display.trim());
        } catch (FileNotFoundException e) {
            e.printStackTrace();
        } catch (IOException e) {
            e.printStackTrace();
        }

        //Delete the created file
        deleteFile(FILENAME);
    }
}
```

This example uses `Context.openFileOutput()` to write some simple string data out to a file. When using this method, the file will be created if it does not already exist. It takes two parameters: a file name and an operating mode. In this case, we use the default operation by defining the mode as `MODE_PRIVATE`. This mode will overwrite the file with each new write operation; use `MODE_APPEND` if you prefer that each write append to the end of the existing file.

After the write is complete, the example uses `Context.openFileInput()`, which requires only the file name again as a parameter to open an `InputStream` and read the file data. The data will be read into a byte array and displayed to the user interface through a `TextView`. Upon completing the operation, `Context.deleteFile()` is used to remove the file from storage.

Note   Data is written to the file streams as bytes, so higher-level data (even strings) must be converted into and out of this format.

This example leaves no traces of the file behind, but we encourage you to try the same example without running `deleteFile()` at the end in order to keep the file in storage. Using the SDK's DDMS tool with an emulator or unlocked device, you may view the filesystem and can find the file this application creates in its respective application data folder.

Because these methods are a part of Context, and not bound to an activity, this type of file access can occur anywhere in an application that you require, such as a BroadcastReceiver or even a custom class. Many system constructs either are a subclass of Context or will pass a reference to one in their callbacks. This allows the same open/close/delete operations to take place anywhere.

External Storage

The key differentiator between internal and external storage lies in the fact that external storage is mountable. This means that the user can connect his or her device to a computer and have the option of mounting that external storage as a removable disk on the PC. Often, the storage itself is physically removable (such as an SD card), but this is not a requirement of the platform.

> **Important** Writing to the external storage of the device will require that you add a declaration for android.permission.WRITE_EXTERNAL_STORAGE to the application manifest.

During periods where the device's external storage is either mounted externally or physically removed, it is not accessible to an application. Because of this, it is always prudent to check whether external storage is ready by checking Environment.getExternalStorageState().

Let's modify the file example to do the same operation with the device's external storage. See Listing 6-15.

Listing 6-15. CRUD a File on External Storage

```java
public class ExternalActivity extends Activity {

    private static final String FILENAME = "data.txt";

    @Override
    public void onCreate(Bundle savedInstanceState) {
        super.onCreate(savedInstanceState);
        TextView tv = new TextView(this);
        setContentView(tv);

        //Create the file reference
        File dataFile = new File(Environment.getExternalStorageDirectory(), FILENAME);

        //Check if external storage is usable
        if(!Environment.getExternalStorageState().equals(Environment.MEDIA_MOUNTED)) {
            Toast.makeText(this, "Cannot use storage.", Toast.LENGTH_SHORT).show();
            finish();
            return;
        }
```

```java
        //Create a new file and write some data
        try {
            FileOutputStream mOutput = new FileOutputStream(dataFile, false);
            String data = "THIS DATA WRITTEN TO A FILE";
            mOutput.write(data.getBytes());
            mOutput.flush();
            //With external files, it is often good to sync the file
            mOutput.getFD().sync();
            mOutput.close();
        } catch (FileNotFoundException e) {
            e.printStackTrace();
        } catch (IOException e) {
            e.printStackTrace();
        }

        //Read the created file and display to the screen
        try {
            FileInputStream mInput = new FileInputStream(dataFile);
            byte[] data = new byte[128];
            mInput.read(data);
            mInput.close();

            String display = new String(data);
            tv.setText(display.trim());
        } catch (FileNotFoundException e) {
            e.printStackTrace();
        } catch (IOException e) {
            e.printStackTrace();
        }

        //Delete the created file
        dataFile.delete();
    }
}
```

With external storage, we utilize a little more of the traditional Java file I/O. The key to working with external storage is calling `Environment.getExternalStorageDirectory()` to retrieve the root path to the device's external storage location.

Before any operations can take place, the status of the device's external storage is first checked with `Environment.getExternalStorageState()`. If the value returned is anything other than `Environment.MEDIA_MOUNTED`, we do not proceed because the storage cannot be written to, so the activity is closed. Otherwise, a new file can be created and the operations may commence.

The input and output streams must now use default Java constructors, as opposed to the `Context` convenience methods. The default behavior of the output stream will be to overwrite the current file or to create it if it does not exist. If your application must append to the end of the existing file with each write, change the boolean parameter in the `FileOutputStream` constructor to `true`.

Often, it makes sense to create a special directory on external storage for your application's files. We can accomplish this simply by using more of Java's file API. See Listing 6-16.

Listing 6-16. CRUD a File Inside New Directory

```java
public class ExternalActivity extends Activity {

    private static final String FILENAME = "data.txt";
    private static final String DNAME = "myfiles";

    @Override
    public void onCreate(Bundle savedInstanceState) {
        super.onCreate(savedInstanceState);
        TextView tv = new TextView(this);
        setContentView(tv);

        //Create a new directory on external storage
        File rootPath = new File(Environment.getExternalStorageDirectory(), DNAME);
        if(!rootPath.exists()) {
            rootPath.mkdirs();
        }
        //Create the file reference
        File dataFile = new File(rootPath, FILENAME);

        //Create a new file and write some data
        try {
            FileOutputStream mOutput = new FileOutputStream(dataFile, false);
            String data = "THIS DATA WRITTEN TO A FILE";
            mOutput.write(data.getBytes());
            mOutput.flush();
            //With external files, it is often good to wait for the write
            mOutput.getFD().sync();

            mOutput.close();
        } catch (FileNotFoundException e) {
            e.printStackTrace();
        } catch (IOException e) {
            e.printStackTrace();
        }

        //Read the created file and display to the screen
        try {
            FileInputStream mInput = new FileInputStream(dataFile);
            byte[] data = new byte[128];
            mInput.read(data);
            mInput.close();

            String display = new String(data);
            tv.setText(display.trim());
        } catch (FileNotFoundException e) {
            e.printStackTrace();
        } catch (IOException e) {
            e.printStackTrace();
        }
```

```
        //Delete the created file
        dataFile.delete();
    }
}
```

In this example we created a new directory path within the external storage directory and used that new location as the root location for the data file. Once the file reference is created using the new directory location, the remainder of the example is the same.

A NOTE ABOUT WRITING FILES

Android applications run inside the Dalvik virtual machine environment. This has some effects to be aware of when working with certain aspects of the system, such as the filesystem. Java APIs like `FileOutputStream` do not share a 1:1 relationship with the native file descriptor inside the kernel. Typically, when data is written to the stream by using the `write()` method, that data is written directly into a memory buffer for the file and asynchronously written out to disk. In most cases, as long as your file access is strictly within the Dalvik VM, you will never see this implementation detail. A file you just wrote could be opened and immediately read without issue, for example.

However, when dealing with removeable storage such as an SD card on a mobile handset or tablet, we may often need to guarantee that the file data has made it all the way to the filesystem before returning some operation to the user since the user has the ability to physically remove the storage medium. The following is a good standard code block to use when writing external files:

```
//Write the data
out.write();
//Clear the stream buffers
out.flush();
//Sync all data to the filesystem
out.getFD().sync();
//Close the stream
out.close();
```

The `flush()` method on an OutputStream is designed to ensure that all the data resident in the stream is written out the VM's memory buffer. In the direct case of `FileOutputStream`, this method actually does nothing. However, in cases where that stream may be wrapped inside another (such as a `BufferedOutputStream`), this method can be essential in clearing out internal buffers, so it is a good habit to get into by calling it on every file write before closing the stream.

Additionally, with external files, we can issue a `sync()` to the underlying `FileDescriptor`. This method will block until all the data has been successfully written to the underlying filesystem, so it is the best indicator of when a user could safely remove physical storage media without file corruption.

External System Directories

(API Level 8)

There are additional methods in Environment and Context that provide standard locations on external storage where specific files can be written. Some of these locations have additional properties as well.

- Environment.getExternalStoragePublicDirectory(String type)

  - Returns a common directory where all applications store media files. The contents of these directories are visible to users and other applications. In particular, the media placed here will likely be scanned and inserted into the device's MediaStore for applications such as the Gallery.

  - Valid type values include DIRECTORY_PICTURES, DIRECTORY_MUSIC, DIRECTORY_MOVIES, and DIRECTORY_RINGTONES.

- Context.getExternalFilesDir(String type)

  - Returns a directory on external storage for media files that are specific to the application. Media placed here will not be considered public, however, and won't show up in MediaStore.

  - This is external storage, however, so it is still possible for users and other applications to see and edit the files directly: there is no security enforced.

  - Files placed here will be removed when the application is uninstalled, so it can be a good location in which to place large content files the application needs that one may not want on internal storage.

  - Valid type values include DIRECTORY_PICTURES, DIRECTORY_MUSIC, DIRECTORY_MOVIES, and DIRECTORY_RINGTONES.

- Context.getExternalCacheDir()

  - Returns a directory on internal storage for app-specific temporary files. The contents of this directory are visible to users and other applications.

  - Files placed here will be removed when the application is uninstalled, so it can be a good location in which to place large content files the application needs that one may not want on internal storage.

6-5. Using Files as Resources

Problem

Your application must utilize resource files that are in a format Android cannot compile into a resource ID.

Solution

(API Level 1)

Use the `assets` directory to house files your application needs to read from, such as local HTML, comma-separated values (CSV), or proprietary data. The `assets` directory is a protected resource location for files in an Android application. The files placed in this directory will be bundled with the final APK but will not be processed or compiled. Like all other application resources, the files in `assets` are read-only.

How It Works

There are a few specific instances that we've seen already in this book, where `assets` can be used to load content directly into widgets, such as `WebView` and `MediaPlayer`. However, in most cases, `assets` is best accessed through a traditional `InputStream`. Listings 6-17 and 6-18 provide an example in which a private CSV file is read from `assets` and displayed onscreen.

Listing 6-17. assets/data.csv

```
John,38,Red
Sally,42,Blue
Rudy,31,Yellow
```

Listing 6-18. Reading from an Asset File

```
public class AssetActivity extends Activity {

    @Override
    public void onCreate(Bundle savedInstanceState) {
        super.onCreate(savedInstanceState);
        TextView tv = new TextView(this);
        setContentView(tv);

        try {
            //Access application assets
            AssetManager manager = getAssets();
            //Open our data file
            InputStream in = manager.open("data.csv");

            //Parse the CSV data and display
            ArrayList<Person> cooked = parse(in);
            StringBuilder builder = new StringBuilder();
            for(Person piece : cooked) {
                builder.append(String.format("%s is %s years old, and likes the color %s",
                        piece.name, piece.age, piece.color));
                builder.append('\n');
            }
            tv.setText(builder.toString());
        } catch (FileNotFoundException e) {
            e.printStackTrace();
```

```
        } catch (IOException e) {
            e.printStackTrace();
        }

    }

    /* Simple CSV Parser */
    private static final int COL_NAME = 0;
    private static final int COL_AGE = 1;
    private static final int COL_COLOR = 2;

    private ArrayList<Person> parse(InputStream in) throws IOException {
        ArrayList<Person> results = new ArrayList<Person>();

        BufferedReader reader = new BufferedReader(new InputStreamReader(in));
        String nextLine = null;
        while ((nextLine = reader.readLine()) != null) {
            String[] tokens = nextLine.split(",");
            if (tokens.length != 3) {
                Log.w("CSVParser", "Skipping Bad CSV Row");
                continue;
            }

            //Add new parsed result
            Person current = new Person();
            current.name = tokens[COL_NAME];
            current.color = tokens[COL_COLOR];
            current.age = tokens[COL_AGE];

            results.add(current);
        }

        in.close();

        return results;
    }

    private class Person {
        public String name;
        public String age;
        public String color;

        public Person() { }
    }
}
```

The key to accessing files in assets lies in using AssetManager, which will allow the application to open any resource currently residing in the assets directory. Passing the name of the file we are interested in to AssetManager.open() returns an InputStream for us to read the file data. Once the stream is read into memory, the example passes the raw data off to a parsing routine and displays the results to the user interface.

Parsing the CSV

This example also illustrates a simple method of taking data from a CSV file and parsing it into a model object (called Person in this case). The method used here takes the entire file and reads it into a byte array for processing as a single string. This method is not the most memory efficient when the amount of data to be read is quite large, but for small files like this one it works just fine.

The raw string is passed into a StringTokenizer instance, along with the required characters to use as breakpoints for the tokens: comma and new line. At this point, each individual chunk of the file can be processed in order. Using a basic state machine approach, the data from each line is inserted into new Person instances and loaded into the resulting list.

6-6. Managing a Database

Problem

Your application needs to persist data that can later be queried or modified as subsets or individual records.

Solution

(API Level 1)

Create an SQLiteDatabase with the assistance of an SQLiteOpenHelper to manage your data store. SQLite is a fast and lightweight database technology that utilizes SQL syntax to build queries and manage data. Support for SQLite is baked in to the Android SDK, making it very easy to set up and use in your applications.

How It Works

Customizing SQLiteOpenHelper allows you to manage the creation and modification of the database schema itself. It is also an excellent place to insert any initial or default values you may want into the database while it is created. Listing 6-19 is an example of how to customize the helper in order to create a database with a single table that stores basic information about people.

Listing 6-19. Custom SQLiteOpenHelper

```
public class MyDbHelper extends SQLiteOpenHelper {

    private static final String DB_NAME = "mydb";
    private static final int DB_VERSION = 1;

    public static final String TABLE_NAME = "people";
    public static final String COL_NAME = "pName";
    public static final String COL_DATE = "pDate";
    private static final String STRING_CREATE =
        "CREATE TABLE "+TABLE_NAME+" (_id INTEGER PRIMARY KEY AUTOINCREMENT, "
        + COL_NAME + " TEXT, " + COL_DATE + " DATE);";
```

```java
public MyDbHelper(Context context) {
    super(context, DB_NAME, null, DB_VERSION);
}

@Override
public void onCreate(SQLiteDatabase db) {
    //Create the database table
    db.execSQL(STRING_CREATE);

    //You may also load initial values into the database here
    ContentValues cv = new ContentValues(2);
    cv.put(COL_NAME, "John Doe");
    //Create a formatter for SQL date format
    SimpleDateFormat dateFormat = new SimpleDateFormat("yyyy-MM-dd HH:mm:ss");
    cv.put(COL_DATE, dateFormat.format(new Date())); //Insert 'now' as the date
    db.insert(TABLE_NAME, null, cv);
}

@Override
public void onUpgrade(SQLiteDatabase db, int oldVersion, int newVersion) {
    //For now, clear the database and re-create
    db.execSQL("DROP TABLE IF EXISTS "+TABLE_NAME);
    onCreate(db);
}
}
```

They key pieces of information you will need for your database are a name and version number. Creating and upgrading an SQLiteDatabase does require some light knowledge of SQL, so we recommend glancing at an SQL reference briefly if you are unfamiliar with some of the syntax. The helper will call onCreate() anytime this particular database is accessed, using either SQLiteOpenHelper.getReadableDatabase() or SQLiteOpenHelper.getWritableDatabase(), if it does not already exist.

The example abstracts the table and column names as constants for external use (a good practice to get into). Here is the actual SQL create string that is used in onCreate() to make our table:

CREATE TABLE people (_id INTEGER PRIMARY KEY AUTOINCREMENT, pName TEXT, pAge INTEGER, pDate DATE);

When using SQLite in Android, there is a small amount of formatting that the database must have in order for it to work properly with the framework. Most of it is created for you, but one piece that the tables you create must have is a column for _id. The remainder of this string creates two more columns for each record in the table:

- A text field for the person's name
- A date field for the date this record was entered

Data is inserted into the database by using ContentValues objects. The example illustrates how to use ContentValues to insert some default data into the database when it is created. SQLiteDatabase. insert() takes a table name, null column hack, and ContentValues representing the record to insert as parameters.

The null column hack is not used here but serves a purpose that may be vital to your application. SQL cannot insert an entirely empty value into the database, and attempting to do so will cause an error. If there is a chance that your implementation may pass an empty ContentValues to insert(), the null column hack is used to instead insert a record where the value of the referenced column is NULL.

A Note About Upgrading

SQLiteOpenHelper also does a great job of assisting you with migrating your database schema in future versions of the application. Whenever the database is accessed, but the version on disk does not match the current version (meaning the version passed in the constructor), onUpgrade() will be called.

In our example, we took the lazy way out and simply dropped the existing database and re-created it. In practice, this may not be a suitable method if the database contains user-entered data; a user probably won't be too happy to see it disappear. So let's digress for a moment and look at an example of onUpgrade() that may be more useful. Take, for example, the following three databases used throughout the lifetime of an application:

- *Version 1*: First release of the application

- *Version 2*: Application upgrade to include phone-number field

- *Version 3*: Application upgrade to include date entry inserted

We can leverage onUpgrade() to alter the existing database instead of erasing all the current information in place. See Listing 6-20.

Listing 6-20. Sample of onUpgrade()

```
@Override
public void onUpgrade(SQLiteDatabase db, int oldVersion, int newVersion) {
    //Upgrade from v1. Adding phone number
    if(oldVersion <= 1) {
        db.execSQL("ALTER TABLE "+TABLE_NAME+" ADD COLUMN phone_number INTEGER;");
    }
    //Upgrade from v2. Add entry date
    if(oldVersion <= 2) {
        db.execSQL("ALTER TABLE "+TABLE_NAME+" ADD COLUMN entry_date DATE;");
    }
}
```

In this example, if the user's existing database version is 1, both statements will be called to add columns to the database. If a user already has version 2, just the latter statement is called to add the entry date column. In both cases, any existing data in the application database is preserved.

Using the Database

Looking back to our original sample, let's take a look at how an activity would utilize the database we've created. See Listings 6-21 and 6-22.

Listing 6-21. res/layout/main.xml

```xml
<?xml version="1.0" encoding="utf-8"?>
<LinearLayout xmlns:android="http://schemas.android.com/apk/res/android"
    android:orientation="vertical"
    android:layout_width="match_parent"
    android:layout_height="match_parent">
    <EditText
        android:id="@+id/name"
        android:layout_width="match_parent"
        android:layout_height="wrap_content" />
    <Button
        android:id="@+id/add"
        android:layout_width="match_parent"
        android:layout_height="wrap_content"
        android:text="Add New Person" />
    <ListView
        android:id="@+id/list"
        android:layout_width="match_parent"
        android:layout_height="match_parent" />
</LinearLayout>
```

Listing 6-22. Activity to View and Manage Database

```java
public class DbActivity extends Activity implements View.OnClickListener,
        AdapterView.OnItemClickListener {

    EditText mText;
    Button mAdd;
    ListView mList;

    MyDbHelper mHelper;
    SQLiteDatabase mDb;
    Cursor mCursor;
    SimpleCursorAdapter mAdapter;

    @Override
    public void onCreate(Bundle savedInstanceState) {
        super.onCreate(savedInstanceState);
        setContentView(R.layout.main);

        mText = (EditText)findViewById(R.id.name);
        mAdd = (Button)findViewById(R.id.add);
        mAdd.setOnClickListener(this);
        mList = (ListView)findViewById(R.id.list);
        mList.setOnItemClickListener(this);

        mHelper = new MyDbHelper(this);
    }
```

```java
@Override
public void onResume() {
    super.onResume();
    //Open connections to the database
    mDb = mHelper.getWritableDatabase();
    String[] columns = new String[] {"_id", MyDbHelper.COL_NAME, MyDbHelper.COL_DATE};
    mCursor = mDb.query(MyDbHelper.TABLE_NAME, columns, null, null, null, null,
            null);
    //Refresh the list
    String[] headers = new String[] {MyDbHelper.COL_NAME, MyDbHelper.COL_DATE};
    mAdapter = new SimpleCursorAdapter(this, android.R.layout.two_line_list_item,
            mCursor, headers, new int[]{android.R.id.text1, android.R.id.text2});
    mList.setAdapter(mAdapter);
}

@Override
public void onPause() {
    super.onPause();
    //Close all connections
    mDb.close();
    mCursor.close();
}

@Override
public void onClick(View v) {
    //Add a new value to the database
    ContentValues cv = new ContentValues(2);
    cv.put(MyDbHelper.COL_NAME, mText.getText().toString());
    //Create a formatter for SQL date format
    SimpleDateFormat dateFormat = new SimpleDateFormat("yyyy-MM-dd HH:mm:ss");
    //Insert 'now' as the date
    cv.put(MyDbHelper.COL_DATE, dateFormat.format(new Date()));
    mDb.insert(MyDbHelper.TABLE_NAME, null, cv);
    //Refresh the list
    mCursor.requery();
    mAdapter.notifyDataSetChanged();
    //Clear the edit field
    mText.setText(null);
}

@Override
public void onItemClick(AdapterView<?> parent, View v, int position, long id) {
    //Delete the item from the database
    mCursor.moveToPosition(position);
     //Get the id value of this row
    String rowId = mCursor.getString(0); //Column 0 of the cursor is the id
    mDb.delete(MyDbHelper.TABLE_NAME, "_id = ?", new String[]{rowId});
    //Refresh the list
    mCursor.requery();
    mAdapter.notifyDataSetChanged();
}
}
```

In this example, we utilize our custom `SQLiteOpenHelper` to give us access to a database instance, and it displays each record in that database as a list to the user interface. Information from the database is returned in the form of a `Cursor`, an interface designed to read, write, and traverse the results of a query.

When the activity becomes visible, a database query is made to return all records in the `people` table. An array of column names must be passed to the query to tell the database which values to return. The remaining parameters of `query()` are designed to narrow the selection data set, and we will investigate this further in the next recipe. It is important to close all database and cursor connections when they are no longer needed. In the example, we do this in `onPause()`, when the activity is no longer in the foreground.

`SimpleCursorAdapter` is used to map the data from the database to the standard Android two-line list item view. The string and int array parameters constitute the mapping; the data from each item in the string array will be inserted into the view with the corresponding ID value in the int array. The list of column names passed here is slightly different than the array passed to the query. This is because we will need to know the record ID for other operations, but it is not necessary in mapping the data to the user interface.

The user may enter a name in the text field and then press the Add New Person button to create a new `ContentValues` instance and insert it into the database. At that point, in order for the UI to display the change, we call `Cursor.requery()` and `ListAdapter.notifyDataSetChanged()`.

Conversely, tapping on an item in the list will remove that specified item from the database. In order to accomplish this, we must construct a simple SQL statement telling the database to remove only records where the `_id` value matches this selection. At that point, the cursor and list adapter are refreshed again.

The `_id` value of the selection is obtained by moving the cursor to the selected position and calling `getString(0)` to get the value of column index zero. This request returns the `_id` because the first parameter (`index 0`) passed in the columns list to the query was `_id`. The `delete` statement is composed of two parameters: the statement string and the arguments. An argument from the passed array will be inserted in the statement for each question mark that appears in the string.

6-7. Querying a Database

Problem

Your application uses an `SQLiteDatabase`, and you need to return specific subsets of the data contained therein.

Solution

(API Level 1)

Using fully structured SQL queries, it is very simple to create filters for specific data and return those subsets from the database. There are several overloaded forms of SQLiteDatabase.query() to gather information from the database. We'll examine the most verbose of them here:

```
public Cursor query(String table, String[] columns,
        String selection,
        String[] selectionArgs,
        String groupBy,
        String having,
        String orderBy,
        String limit)
```

The first two parameters simply define the table in which to query data, as well as the columns for each record that we would like to have access to. The remaining parameters define how we will narrow the scope of the results.

- selection: SQL WHERE clause for the given query.

- selectionArgs: If question marks are in the selection, these items fill in those fields.

- groupBy: SQL GROUP BY clause for the given query.

- having: SQL ORDER BY clause for the given query.

- orderBy: SQL ORDER BY clause for the given query.

- limit: Maximum number of results returned from the query.

As you can see, all of these parameters are designed to provide the full power of SQL to the database queries.

How It Works

Let's look at some example queries that can be constructed to accomplish some common practical queries:

- Return all rows where the value matches a given parameter.

```
String[] COLUMNS = new String[] {COL_NAME, COL_DATE};
String selection = COL_NAME+" = ?";
String[] args = new String[] {"NAME_TO_MATCH"};
Cursor result = db.query(TABLE_NAME, COLUMNS, selection, args, null, null, null, null);
```

This query is fairly straightforward. The selection statement just tells the database to match any data in the name column with the argument supplied (which is inserted in place of ? in the selection string).

- Return the last 10 rows inserted into the database.

```
String orderBy = "_id DESC";
String limit = "10";
Cursor result = db.query(TABLE_NAME, COLUMNS, null, null, null, null, orderBy, limit);
```

This query has no special selection criteria but instead tells the database to order the results by the auto-incrementing _id value, with the newest (highest _id) records first. The limit clause sets the maximum number of returned results to 10.

- Return rows where a date field is within a specified range (within the year 2000, in this example).

```
String[] COLUMNS = new String[] {COL_NAME, COL_DATE};
String selection = "datetime("+COL_DATE+") > datetime(?)"+
        " AND datetime("+COL_DATE+") < datetime(?)";
String[] args = new String[] {"2000-1-1 00:00:00","2000-12-31 23:59:59"};
Cursor result = db.query(TABLE_NAME, COLUMNS, selection, args, null, null, null, null);
```

SQLite does not reserve a specific data type for dates, although they allow DATE as a declaration type when creating a table. However, the standard SQL date and time functions can be used to create representations of the data as TEXT, INTEGER, or REAL. Here, we compare the return values of datetime() for both the value in the database and a formatted string for the start and end dates of the range.

- Return rows where an integer field is within a specified range (between 7 and 10 in the example).

```
String[] COLUMNS = new String[] {COL_NAME, COL_AGE};
String selection = COL_AGE+" > ? AND "+COL_AGE+" < ?";
String[] args = new String[] {"7","10"};
Cursor result = db.query(TABLE_NAME, COLUMNS, selection, args, null, null, null, null);
```

This is similar to the previous example but is much less verbose. Here, we simply have to create the selection statement to return values greater than the low limit, but less than the high limit. Both limits are provided as arguments to be inserted so they can be dynamically set in the application.

6-8. Backing Up Data

Problem

Your application persists data on the device, and you need to provide users with a way to back up and restore this data in cases where they change devices or are forced to reinstall the application.

Solution

(API Level 1)

Use the device's external storage as a safe location to copy databases and other files. External storage is often physically removable, allowing the user to place it in another device and do a restore. Even in cases where this is not possible, external storage can always be mounted when the user connects his or her device to a computer, allowing data transfer to take place.

How It Works

Listing 6-23 shows an implementation of AsyncTask that copies a database file back and forth between the device's external storage and its location in the application's data directory. It also defines an interface for an activity to implement to get notified when the operation is complete. File operations such as copy can take some time to complete, so you can implement this by using an AsyncTask so it can happen in the background and not block the main thread.

Listing 6-23. AsyncTask for Backup and Restore

```java
public class BackupTask extends AsyncTask<String,Void,Integer> {

    public interface CompletionListener {
        void onBackupComplete();
        void onRestoreComplete();
        void onError(int errorCode);
    }

    public static final int BACKUP_SUCCESS = 1;
    public static final int RESTORE_SUCCESS = 2;
    public static final int BACKUP_ERROR = 3;
    public static final int RESTORE_NOFILEERROR = 4;

    public static final String COMMAND_BACKUP = "backupDatabase";
    public static final String COMMAND_RESTORE = "restoreDatabase";

    private Context mContext;
    private CompletionListener listener;

    public BackupTask(Context context) {
        super();
        mContext = context;
    }

    public void setCompletionListener(CompletionListener aListener) {
        listener = aListener;
    }

    @Override
    protected Integer doInBackground(String... params) {

        //Get a reference to the database
        File dbFile = mContext.getDatabasePath("mydb");
        //Get a reference to the directory location for the backup
        File exportDir =
                new File(Environment.getExternalStorageDirectory(), "myAppBackups");
        if (!exportDir.exists()) {
            exportDir.mkdirs();
        }
        File backup = new File(exportDir, dbFile.getName());
```

```java
        //Check the required operation
        String command = params[0];
        if(command.equals(COMMAND_BACKUP)) {
            //Attempt file copy
            try {
                backup.createNewFile();
                fileCopy(dbFile, backup);

                return BACKUP_SUCCESS;
            } catch (IOException e) {
                return BACKUP_ERROR;
            }
        } else if(command.equals(COMMAND_RESTORE)) {
            //Attempt file copy
            try {
                if(!backup.exists()) {
                    return RESTORE_NOFILEERROR;
                }
                dbFile.createNewFile();
                fileCopy(backup, dbFile);
                return RESTORE_SUCCESS;
            } catch (IOException e) {
                return BACKUP_ERROR;
            }
        } else {
            return BACKUP_ERROR;
        }
    }

    @Override
    protected void onPostExecute(Integer result) {

        switch(result) {
        case BACKUP_SUCCESS:
            if(listener != null) {
                listener.onBackupComplete();
            }
            break;
        case RESTORE_SUCCESS:
            if(listener != null) {
                listener.onRestoreComplete();
            }
            break;
        case RESTORE_NOFILEERROR:
            if(listener != null) {
                listener.onError(RESTORE_NOFILEERROR);
            }
            break;
        default:
            if(listener != null) {
                listener.onError(BACKUP_ERROR);
            }
        }
    }
}
```

```
private void fileCopy(File source, File dest) throws IOException {
    FileChannel inChannel = new FileInputStream(source).getChannel();
    FileChannel outChannel = new FileOutputStream(dest).getChannel();
    try {
        inChannel.transferTo(0, inChannel.size(), outChannel);
    } finally {
        if (inChannel != null)
            inChannel.close();
        if (outChannel != null)
            outChannel.close();
    }
}
}
```

As you can see, BackupTask operates by copying the current version of a named database to a specific directory in external storage when COMMAND_BACKUP is passed to execute(), and it copies the file back when COMMAND_RESTORE is passed.

Once executed, the task uses Context.getDatabasePath() to retrieve a reference to the database file we need to back up. This line could easily be replaced with a call to Context.getFilesDir(), accessing a file on the system's internal storage to back up instead. A reference to a backup directory we've created on external storage is also obtained.

The files are copied using traditional Java file I/O, and if all is successful, the registered listener is notified. During the process, any exceptions thrown are caught and an error is returned to the listener instead. Now let's take a look at an activity that utilizes this task to back up a database (see Listing 6-24).

Listing 6-24. Activity Using BackupTask

```
public class BackupActivity extends Activity implements BackupTask.CompletionListener {

    @Override
    public void onCreate(Bundle savedInstanceState) {
        super.onCreate(savedInstanceState);
        setContentView(R.layout.main);
        //Dummy example database
        SQLiteDatabase db = openOrCreateDatabase("mydb", Activity.MODE_PRIVATE, null);
        db.close();
    }

    @Override
    public void onResume() {
        super.onResume();
        if( Environment.getExternalStorageState().equals(Environment.MEDIA_MOUNTED) ) {
            BackupTask task = new BackupTask(this);
            task.setCompletionListener(this);
            task.execute(BackupTask.COMMAND_RESTORE);
        }
    }
```

```
    @Override
    public void onPause() {
        super.onPause();
        if( Environment.getExternalStorageState().equals(Environment.MEDIA_MOUNTED) ) {
            BackupTask task = new BackupTask(this);
            task.execute(BackupTask.COMMAND_BACKUP);
        }
    }

    @Override
    public void onBackupComplete() {
        Toast.makeText(this, "Backup Successful", Toast.LENGTH_SHORT).show();
    }

    @Override
    public void onError(int errorCode) {
        if(errorCode == BackupTask.RESTORE_NOFILEERROR) {
            Toast.makeText(this, "No Backup Found to Restore",
                Toast.LENGTH_SHORT).show();
        } else {
            Toast.makeText(this, "Error During Operation: "+errorCode,
                Toast.LENGTH_SHORT).show();
        }
    }

    @Override
    public void onRestoreComplete() {
        Toast.makeText(this, "Restore Successful", Toast.LENGTH_SHORT).show();
    }
}
```

The activity implements the CompletionListener defined by BackupTask, so it may be notified when operations are finished or an error occurs. For the purposes of the example, a dummy database is created in the application's database directory. We call openOrCreateDatabase() only to allow a file to be created, so the connection is immediately closed afterward. Under normal circumstances, this database would already exist and these lines would not be necessary.

The example does a restore operation each time the activity is resumed, registering itself with the task so it can be notified and raise a Toast to the user of the status result. Notice that the task of checking whether external storage is usable falls to the activity as well, and no tasks are executed if external storage is not accessible. When the activity is paused, a backup operation is executed, this time without registering for callbacks. This is because the activity is no longer interesting to the user, so we won't need to raise a toast to point out the operation results.

Extra Credit

This background task could be extended to save the data to a cloud-based service for maximum safety and data portability. There are many options available to accomplish this, including Google's own set of web APIs, and we recommend you give this a try.

Android, as of API Level 8, also includes an API for backing up data to a cloud-based service. This API may suit your purposes; however, we will not discuss it here. The Android framework cannot guarantee that this service will be available on all Android devices, and there is no API as of this writing to determine whether the device the user has will support the Android backup, so it is not recommended for critical data.

6-9. Sharing Your Database

Problem

Your application would like to provide the database content it maintains to other applications on the device.

Solution

(API Level 4)

Create a `ContentProvider` to act as an external interface for your application's data. `ContentProvider` exposes an arbitrary set of data to external requests through a database-like interface of `query()`, `insert()`, `update()`, and `delete()`, though the implementer is free to design how the interface maps to the actual data model. Creating a `ContentProvider` to expose the data from an `SQLiteDatabase` is straightforward and simple. With some minor exceptions, the developer needs only to pass calls from the provider down to the database.

Arguments about which data set to operate on are typically encoded in the `Uri` passed to the `ContentProvider`. For example, sending a query `Uri` such as

```
content://com.examples.myprovider/friends
```

would tell the provider to return information from the `friends` table within its data set, while

```
content://com.examples.myprovider/friends/15
```

would instruct just the record ID 15 to return from the query. It should be noted that these are only the conventions used by the rest of the system, and that you are responsible for making the `ContentProvider` you create behave in this manner. There is nothing inherent about `ContentProvider` that provides this functionality for you.

How It Works

First of all, to create a `ContentProvider` that interacts with a database, we must have a database in place to interact with. Listing 6-25 is a sample `SQLiteOpenHelper` implementation that we will use to create and access the database itself.

Listing 6-25. Sample SQLiteOpenHelper

```java
public class ShareDbHelper extends SQLiteOpenHelper {

    private static final String DB_NAME = "frienddb";
    private static final int DB_VERSION = 1;

    public static final String TABLE_NAME = "friends";
    public static final String COL_FIRST = "firstName";
    public static final String COL_LAST = "lastName";
    public static final String COL_PHONE = "phoneNumber";

    private static final String STRING_CREATE =
        "CREATE TABLE "+TABLE_NAME+" (_id INTEGER PRIMARY KEY AUTOINCREMENT, "
        +COL_FIRST+" TEXT, "+COL_LAST+" TEXT, "+COL_PHONE+" TEXT);";

    public ShareDbHelper(Context context) {
        super(context, DB_NAME, null, DB_VERSION);
    }

    @Override
    public void onCreate(SQLiteDatabase db) {
        //Create the database table
        db.execSQL(STRING_CREATE);

        //Inserting example values into database
        ContentValues cv = new ContentValues(3);
        cv.put(COL_FIRST, "John");
        cv.put(COL_LAST, "Doe");
        cv.put(COL_PHONE, "8885551234");
        db.insert(TABLE_NAME, null, cv);
        cv = new ContentValues(3);
        cv.put(COL_FIRST, "Jane");
        cv.put(COL_LAST, "Doe");
        cv.put(COL_PHONE, "8885552345");
        db.insert(TABLE_NAME, null, cv);
        cv = new ContentValues(3);
        cv.put(COL_FIRST, "Jill");
        cv.put(COL_LAST, "Doe");
        cv.put(COL_PHONE, "8885553456");
        db.insert(TABLE_NAME, null, cv);
    }

    @Override
    public void onUpgrade(SQLiteDatabase db, int oldVersion, int newVersion) {
        //For now, clear the database and re-create
        db.execSQL("DROP TABLE IF EXISTS "+TABLE_NAME);
        onCreate(db);
    }
}
```

Overall, this helper is fairly simple, creating a single table to keep a list of our friends with just three columns for housing text data. For the purposes of this example, three row values are inserted. Now let's take a look at a `ContentProvider` that will expose this database to other applications: see Listings 6-26 and 6-27.

Listing 6-26. Manifest Declaration for `ContentProvider`

```
<manifest xmlns:android="http://schemas.android.com/apk/res/android" ...>
    <application ...>
      <provider android:name=".FriendProvider"
          android:authorities="com.examples.sharedb.friendprovider">
      </provider>
    </application>
</manifest>
```

Listing 6-27. ContentProvider for a Database

```
public class FriendProvider extends ContentProvider {

    public static final Uri CONTENT_URI =
            Uri.parse("content://com.examples.sharedb.friendprovider/friends");

    public static final class Columns {
        public static final String _ID = "_id";
        public static final String FIRST = "firstName";
        public static final String LAST = "lastName";
        public static final String PHONE = "phoneNumber";
    }

    /* Uri Matching */
    private static final int FRIEND = 1;
    private static final int FRIEND_ID = 2;

    private static final UriMatcher matcher = new UriMatcher(UriMatcher.NO_MATCH);
    static {
        matcher.addURI(CONTENT_URI.getAuthority(), "friends", FRIEND);
        matcher.addURI(CONTENT_URI.getAuthority(), "friends/#", FRIEND_ID);
    }

    SQLiteDatabase db;

    @Override
    public int delete(Uri uri, String selection, String[] selectionArgs) {
        int result = matcher.match(uri);
        switch(result) {
        case FRIEND:
            return db.delete(ShareDbHelper.TABLE_NAME, selection, selectionArgs);
        case FRIEND_ID:
            return db.delete(ShareDbHelper.TABLE_NAME, "_ID = ?",
                    new String[]{uri.getLastPathSegment()});
```

```java
        default:
            return 0;
        }
    }

    @Override
    public String getType(Uri uri) {
        return null;
    }

    @Override
    public Uri insert(Uri uri, ContentValues values) {
        long id = db.insert(ShareDbHelper.TABLE_NAME, null, values);
        if(id >= 0) {
            return Uri.withAppendedPath(uri, String.valueOf(id));
        } else {
            return null;
        }
    }

    @Override
    public boolean onCreate() {
        ShareDbHelper helper = new ShareDbHelper(getContext());
        db = helper.getWritableDatabase();
        return true;
    }

    @Override
    public Cursor query(Uri uri, String[] projection, String selection,
        String[] selectionArgs, String sortOrder) {
        int result = matcher.match(uri);
        switch(result) {
        case FRIEND:
            return db.query(ShareDbHelper.TABLE_NAME, projection, selection,
selectionArgs, null, null, sortOrder);
        case FRIEND_ID:
            return db.query(ShareDbHelper.TABLE_NAME, projection, "_ID = ?",
                    new String[]{uri.getLastPathSegment()}, null, null, sortOrder);
        default:
            return null;
        }
    }

    @Override
    public int update(Uri uri, ContentValues values, String selection,
        String[] selectionArgs) {
        int result = matcher.match(uri);
        switch(result) {
        case FRIEND:
            return db.update(ShareDbHelper.TABLE_NAME, values, selection,
                selectionArgs);
```

```
        case FRIEND_ID:
            return db.update(ShareDbHelper.TABLE_NAME, values, "_ID = ?",
                    new String[]{uri.getLastPathSegment()});
        default:
            return 0;
        }
    }

}
```

A `ContentProvider` must be declared in the application's manifest with the authority string that it represents. This allows the provider to be accessed from external applications, but the declaration is still required even if you use the provider only internally within your application. The authority is what Android uses to match `Uri` requests to the provider, so it should match the authority portion of the public `CONTENT_URI`.

The six required methods to override when extending `ContentProvider` are `query()`, `insert()`, `update()`, `delete()`, `getType()`, and `onCreate()`. The first four of these methods have direct counterparts in `SQLiteDatabase`, so the database method is simply called with the appropriate parameters. The primary difference between the two is that the `ContentProvider` method passes in a `Uri`, which the provider should inspect to determine which portion of the database to operate on.

These four primary CRUD methods are called on the provider when an activity or other system component calls the corresponding method on its internal `ContentResolver` (you see this in action in Listing 6-27).

To adhere to the `Uri` convention mentioned in the first part of this recipe, `insert()` returns a `Uri` object created by appending the newly created record ID onto the end of the path. This `Uri` should be considered by its requester to be a direct reference back to the record that was just created.

The remaining methods (`query()`, `update()`, and `delete()`) adhere to the convention by inspecting the incoming `Uri` to see whether it refers to a specific record or to the whole table. This task is accomplished with the help of the `UriMatcher` convenience class. The `UriMatcher.match()` method compares a `Uri` to a set of supplied patterns and returns the matching pattern as an int, or `UriMatcher.NO_MATCH` if one is not found. If a `Uri` is supplied with a record ID appended, the call to the database is modified to affect only that specific row.

A `UriMatcher` should be initialized by supplying a set of patterns with `UriMatcher.addURI()`; Google recommends that this all be done in a static context within the `ContentProvider`, so it will be initialized the first time the class is loaded into memory. Each pattern added is also given a constant identifier that will be the return value when matches are made. There are two wildcard characters that may be placed in the supplied patterns: the pound (#) character will match any number, and the asterisk (*) will match any text.

Our example has created two patterns to match. The initial pattern matches the supplied `CONTENT_URI` directly, and it is taken to reference the entire database table. The second pattern looks for an appended number to the path, which will be taken to reference just the record at that ID.

Access to the database is obtained through a reference given by the `ShareDbHelper` in `onCreate()`. The size of the database that is used should be considered when deciding whether this method will be appropriate for your application. Our database is quite small when it is created, but larger databases may take a long time to create, in which case the main thread should not be tied up while this operation is taking place; getWritableDatabase() may need to be wrapped in an AsyncTask and done in the background in these cases. Now let's take a look at a sample activity accessing the data: see Listings 6-28 and 6-29.

Listing 6-28. AndroidManifest.xml

```xml
<?xml version="1.0" encoding="utf-8"?>
<manifest xmlns:android="http://schemas.android.com/apk/res/android"
    package="com.examples.sharedb" android:versionCode="1" android:versionName="1.0">
    <uses-sdk android:minSdkVersion="4" />
    <application android:icon="@drawable/icon" android:label="@string/app_name">
        <activity android:name=".ShareActivity" android:label="@string/app_name">
            <intent-filter>
                <action android:name="android.intent.action.MAIN" />
                <category android:name="android.intent.category.LAUNCHER" />
            </intent-filter>
        </activity>
        <provider android:name=".FriendProvider"
            android:authorities="com.examples.sharedb.friendprovider">
        </provider>
    </application>
</manifest>
```

Listing 6-29. Activity Accessing the ContentProvider

```java
public class ShareActivity extends FragmentActivity implements
    LoaderManager.LoaderCallbacks<Cursor>, AdapterView.OnItemClickListener {
    private static final int LOADER_LIST = 100;
    SimpleCursorAdapter mAdapter;

    @Override
    public void onCreate(Bundle savedInstanceState) {
        super.onCreate(savedInstanceState);
        getSupportLoaderManager().initLoader(LOADER_LIST, null, this);

        mAdapter = new SimpleCursorAdapter(this,
                android.R.layout.simple_list_item_1, null,
                new String[]{FriendProvider.Columns.FIRST},
                new int[]{android.R.id.text1}, 0);

        ListView list = new ListView(this);
        list.setOnItemClickListener(this);
        list.setAdapter(mAdapter);

        setContentView(list);
    }
```

```java
@Override
public void onItemClick(AdapterView<?> parent, View v, int position, long id) {
    Cursor c = mAdapter.getCursor();
    c.moveToPosition(position);

    Uri uri = Uri.withAppendedPath(FriendProvider.CONTENT_URI, c.getString(0));
    String[] projection = new String[]{FriendProvider.Columns.FIRST,
            FriendProvider.Columns.LAST,
            FriendProvider.Columns.PHONE};
    //Get the full record
    Cursor cursor = getContentResolver().query(uri, projection, null, null, null);
    cursor.moveToFirst();

    String message = String.format("%s %s, %s", cursor.getString(0),
            cursor.getString(1), cursor.getString(2));
    Toast.makeText(this, message, Toast.LENGTH_SHORT).show();
    cursor.close();
}

@Override
public Loader<Cursor> onCreateLoader(int id, Bundle args) {
    String[] projection = new String[]{FriendProvider.Columns._ID,
            FriendProvider.Columns.FIRST};
    return new CursorLoader(this, FriendProvider.CONTENT_URI,
            projection, null, null, null);
}

@Override
public void onLoadFinished(Loader<Cursor> loader, Cursor data) {
    mAdapter.swapCursor(data);
}

@Override
public void onLoaderReset(Loader<Cursor> loader) {
    mAdapter.swapCursor(null);
}
}
```

> **Important**   This example requires the Support Library to provide access to the Loader pattern in Android 1.6 and above. If you are targeting Android 3.0+ in your application, you may replace FragmentActivity with Activity and getSupportLoaderManager() with getLoaderManager().

This example queries the FriendsProvider for all its records and places them into a list, displaying only the first-name column. In order for the Cursor to adapt properly into a list, our projection must include the ID column, even though it is not displayed.

If the user taps any of the items in the list, another query is made of the provider using a Uri constructed with the record ID appended to the end, forcing the provider to return only that one record. In addition, an expanded projection is provided to get all the column data about this friend.

The returned data is placed into a Toast and raised for the user to see. Individual fields from the cursor are accessed by their *column index*, corresponding to the index in the projection passed to the query. The Cursor.getColumnIndex() method may also be used to query the cursor for the index associated with a given column name.

A Cursor should always be closed when it is no longer needed, as we do with the Cursor created after a user click. The only exceptions to this are Cursor instances created and managed by the Loader.

Figure 6-3 shows the result of running this sample to display the provider content.

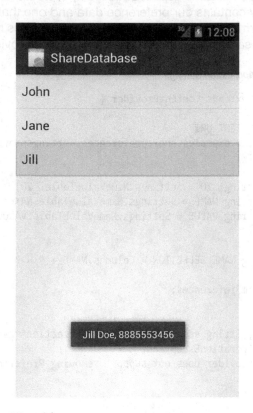

Figure 6-3. *Information from a* ContentProvider

6-10. Sharing Your SharedPreferences

Problem

You would like your application to provide the settings values it has stored in SharedPreferences to other applications of the system and even to allow those applications to modify those settings if they have permission to do so.

Solution

(API Level 1)

Create a ContentProvider to interface your application's SharedPreferences to the rest of the system. The settings data will be delivered using a MatrixCursor, which is an implementation that can be used for data that does not reside in a database. The ContentProvider will be protected by separate permissions to read/write the data within so that only permitted applications will have access.

How It Works

To properly demonstrate the permissions aspect of this recipe, we need to create two separate applications: one that actually contains our preference data and one that wants to read and modify it through the ContentProvider interface. This is because Android does not enforce permissions on anything operating within the same application. Let's start with the provider, shown in Listing 6-30.

Listing 6-30. ContentProvider for Application Settings

```
public class SettingsProvider extends ContentProvider {

    public static final Uri CONTENT_URI =
        Uri.parse("content://com.examples.sharepreferences.settingsprovider/settings");

    public static class Columns {
        public static final String _ID = Settings.NameValueTable._ID;
        public static final String NAME = Settings.NameValueTable.NAME;
        public static final String VALUE = Settings.NameValueTable.VALUE;
    }

    private static final String NAME_SELECTION = Columns.NAME + " = ?";

    private SharedPreferences mPreferences;

    @Override
    public int delete(Uri uri, String selection, String[] selectionArgs) {
        throw new UnsupportedOperationException(
                "This ContentProvider does not support removing Preferences");
    }

    @Override
    public String getType(Uri uri) {
        return null;
    }

    @Override
    public Uri insert(Uri uri, ContentValues values) {
        throw new UnsupportedOperationException(
                "This ContentProvider does not support adding new Preferences");
    }
```

```java
@Override
public boolean onCreate() {
    mPreferences = PreferenceManager.getDefaultSharedPreferences(getContext());
    return true;
}

@Override
public Cursor query(Uri uri, String[] projection, String selection,
        String[] selectionArgs, String sortOrder) {
    MatrixCursor cursor = new MatrixCursor(projection);
    Map<String, ?> preferences = mPreferences.getAll();
    Set<String> preferenceKeys = preferences.keySet();

    if(TextUtils.isEmpty(selection)) {
        //Get all items
        for(String key : preferenceKeys) {
            //Insert only the columns they requested
            MatrixCursor.RowBuilder builder = cursor.newRow();
            for(String column : projection) {
                if(column.equals(Columns._ID)) {
                    //Generate a unique id
                    builder.add(key.hashCode());
                }
                if(column.equals(Columns.NAME)) {
                    builder.add(key);
                }
                if(column.equals(Columns.VALUE)) {
                    builder.add(preferences.get(key));
                }
            }
        }
    } else if (selection.equals(NAME_SELECTION)) {
        //Parse the key value and check if it exists
        String key = selectionArgs == null ? "" : selectionArgs[0];
        if(preferences.containsKey(key)) {
            //Get the requested item
            MatrixCursor.RowBuilder builder = cursor.newRow();
            for(String column : projection) {
                if(column.equals(Columns._ID)) {
                    //Generate a unique id
                    builder.add(key.hashCode());
                }
                if(column.equals(Columns.NAME)) {
                    builder.add(key);
                }
                if(column.equals(Columns.VALUE)) {
                    builder.add(preferences.get(key));
                }
            }
        }
    }
}
```

```
        return cursor;
    }

    @Override
    public int update(Uri uri, ContentValues values, String selection,
            String[] selectionArgs) {
        //Check if the key exists, and update its value
        String key = values.getAsString(Columns.NAME);
        if (mPreferences.contains(key)) {
            Object value = values.get(Columns.VALUE);
            SharedPreferences.Editor editor = mPreferences.edit();
            if (value instanceof Boolean) {
                editor.putBoolean(key, (Boolean)value);
            } else if (value instanceof Number) {
                editor.putFloat(key, ((Number)value).floatValue());
            } else if (value instanceof String) {
                editor.putString(key, (String)value);
            } else {
                //Invalid value, do not update
              return 0;
            }
            editor.commit();
            //Notify any observers
            getContext().getContentResolver().notifyChange(CONTENT_URI, null);
            return 1;
        }
        //Key not in preferences
        return 0;
    }
}
```

Upon creation of this ContentProvider, we obtain a reference to the application's default SharedPreferences rather than opening up a database connection as in the previous example. We support only two methods in this provider—query() and update()—and throw exceptions for the rest. This allows read/write access to the preference values without allowing any ability to add or remove new preference types.

Inside the query() method, we check the selection string to determine whether we should return all preference values or just the requested value. There are three fields defined for each preference: _id, name, and value. The value of _id may not be related to the preference itself, but if the client of this provider wants to display the results in a list by using CursorAdapter, this field will need to exist and have a unique value for each record, so we generate one. Notice that we obtain the preference value as an Object to insert in the cursor; we want to minimize the amount of knowledge the provider should have about the types of data it contains.

The cursor implementation used in this provider is a MatrixCursor, which is a cursor designed to be built around data not held inside a database. The example iterates through the list of columns requested (the projection) and builds each row according to these columns it contains. Each row is created by calling MatrixCursor.newRow(), which also returns a Builder instance that will be used to add the column data. Care should always be taken to match the order of the column data that is added to the order of the requested projection. They should always match.

The implementation of update() inspects only the incoming ContentValues for the preference it needs to update. Because this is enough to describe the exact item we need, we don't implement any further logic using the selection arguments. If the name value of the preference already exists, the value for it is updated and saved. Unfortunately, there is no method to simply insert an Object back into SharedPreferences, so you must inspect it based on the valid types that ContentValues can return and call the appropriate setter method to match. Finally, we call notifyObservers() so any registered ContentObserver objects will be notified of the data change.

You may have noticed that there is no code in the ContentProvider to manage the read/write permissions we promised to implement! This is actually handled by Android for us: we just need to update the manifest appropriately. Have a look at Listing 6-31.

Listing 6-31. AndroidManifest.xml

```xml
<manifest xmlns:android="http://schemas.android.com/apk/res/android"
    package="com.examples.sharepreferences"
    android:versionCode="1"
    android:versionName="1.0" >

    <uses-sdk ... />

    <permission
        android:name="com.examples.sharepreferences.permission.READ_PREFERENCES"
        android:label="Read Application Settings"
        android:protectionLevel="normal" />
    <permission
        android:name="com.examples.sharepreferences.permission.WRITE_PREFERENCES"
        android:label="Write Application Settings"
        android:protectionLevel="dangerous" />

    <uses-permission
        android:name="com.examples.sharepreferences.permission.READ_PREFERENCES" />
    <uses-permission
        android:name="com.examples.sharepreferences.permission.WRITE_PREFERENCES" />

    <application ... >
        <activity android:name=".SettingsActivity" >
            <intent-filter>
                <action android:name="android.intent.action.MAIN" />
                <category android:name="android.intent.category.LAUNCHER" />
            </intent-filter>
            <intent-filter>
                <action android:name="com.examples.sharepreferences.ACTION_SETTINGS" />
                <category android:name="android.intent.category.DEFAULT" />
            </intent-filter>
        </activity>

        <provider
            android:name=".SettingsProvider"
            android:authorities="com.examples.sharepreferences.settingsprovider"
```

```
            android:readPermission=
                    "com.examples.sharepreferences.permission.READ_PREFERENCES"
            android:writePermission=
                    "com.examples.sharepreferences.permission.WRITE_PREFERENCES" >
        </provider>
    </application>

</manifest>
```

Here you can see two custom `<permission>` elements declared and attached to our `<provider>` declaration. This is the only code we need to add, and Android knows to enforce the read permissions for operations such as query(), and the write permission for insert(), update(), and delete(). We have also declared a custom `<intent-filter>` on the activity in this application, which will come in handy for any external applications that may want to launch the settings UI directly. Listings 6-32 through 6-34 define the rest of this example.

Listing 6-32. res/xml/preferences.xml

```
<?xml version="1.0" encoding="utf-8"?>
<PreferenceScreen xmlns:android="http://schemas.android.com/apk/res/android" >
    <CheckBoxPreference
        android:key="preferenceEnabled"
        android:title="Set Enabled"
        android:defaultValue="true"/>
    <EditTextPreference
        android:key="preferenceName"
        android:title="User Name"
        android:defaultValue="John Doe"/>
    <ListPreference
        android:key="preferenceSelection"
        android:title="Selection"
        android:entries="@array/selection_items"
        android:entryValues="@array/selection_items"
        android:defaultValue="Four"/>
</PreferenceScreen>
```

Listing 6-33. res/values/arrays.xml

```
<?xml version="1.0" encoding="utf-8"?>
<resources>
    <string-array name="selection_items">
        <item>One</item>
        <item>Two</item>
        <item>Three</item>
        <item>Four</item>
    </string-array>
</resources>
```

Listing 6-34. Preferences Activity

```
//Note the package for this application
package com.examples.sharepreferences;

public class SettingsActivity extends PreferenceActivity {

    @Override
    protected void onCreate(Bundle savedInstanceState) {
        super.onCreate(savedInstanceState);
        //Load the preferences defaults on first run
        PreferenceManager.setDefaultValues(this, R.xml.preferences, false);

        addPreferencesFromResource(R.xml.preferences);
    }
}
```

The settings values for this example application are manageable directly via a simple `PreferenceActivity`, whose data are defined in the `preferences.xml` file.

Note `PreferenceActivity` was deprecated in Android 3.0 in favor of `PreferenceFragment`, but at the time of this book's publication, `PreferenceFragment` has not yet been added to the Support Library. Therefore, we use it here to allow support for earlier versions of Android.

Usage Example

Next let's take a look at Listings 6-35 through 6-37, which define a second application that will attempt to access our preferences data by using this `ContentProvider` interface.

Listing 6-35. AndroidManifest.xml

```
<manifest xmlns:android="http://schemas.android.com/apk/res/android"
    package="com.examples.accesspreferences"
    android:versionCode="1"
    android:versionName="1.0">

    <uses-sdk ... />

    <uses-permission
        android:name="com.examples.sharepreferences.permission.READ_PREFERENCES" />
    <uses-permission
        android:name="com.examples.sharepreferences.permission.WRITE_PREFERENCES" />

    <application ... >
        <activity android:name=".MainActivity" >
            <intent-filter>
                <action android:name="android.intent.action.MAIN" />
                <category android:name="android.intent.category.LAUNCHER" />
```

```
        </intent-filter>
      </activity>
    </application>

</manifest>
```

The key point here is that this application declares the use of both our custom permissions as `<uses-permission>` elements. This is what allows it to have access to the external provider. Without these, a request through ContentResolver would result in a SecurityException.

Listing 6-36. `res/layout/main.xml`

```xml
<RelativeLayout xmlns:android="http://schemas.android.com/apk/res/android"
    android:layout_width="match_parent"
    android:layout_height="match_parent" >
    <Button
        android:id="@+id/button_settings"
        android:layout_width="match_parent"
        android:layout_height="wrap_content"
        android:text="Show Settings"
        android:onClick="onSettingsClick" />
    <CheckBox
        android:id="@+id/checkbox_enable"
        android:layout_width="wrap_content"
        android:layout_height="wrap_content"
        android:layout_below="@id/button_settings"
        android:text="Set Enable Setting"/>
    <LinearLayout
        android:layout_width="wrap_content"
        android:layout_height="wrap_content"
        android:layout_centerInParent="true"
        android:orientation="vertical">
        <TextView
            android:id="@+id/value_enabled"
            android:layout_width="wrap_content"
            android:layout_height="wrap_content" />
        <TextView
            android:id="@+id/value_name"
            android:layout_width="wrap_content"
            android:layout_height="wrap_content" />
        <TextView
            android:id="@+id/value_selection"
            android:layout_width="wrap_content"
            android:layout_height="wrap_content" />
    </LinearLayout>
</RelativeLayout>
```

Listing 6-37. Activity Interacting with the Provider

```
//Note the package as this is a different application
package com.examples.accesspreferences;
```

```java
public class MainActivity extends Activity implements OnCheckedChangeListener {
    public static final String SETTINGS_ACTION =
        "com.examples.sharepreferences.ACTION_SETTINGS";
    public static final Uri SETTINGS_CONTENT_URI =
        Uri.parse("content://com.examples.sharepreferences.settingsprovider/settings");
    public static class SettingsColumns {
        public static final String _ID = Settings.NameValueTable._ID;
        public static final String NAME = Settings.NameValueTable.NAME;
        public static final String VALUE = Settings.NameValueTable.VALUE;
    }

    TextView mEnabled, mName, mSelection;
    CheckBox mToggle;

    private ContentObserver mObserver = new ContentObserver(new Handler()) {
        public void onChange(boolean selfChange) {
            updatePreferences();
        }
    };

    @Override
    public void onCreate(Bundle savedInstanceState) {
        super.onCreate(savedInstanceState);
        setContentView(R.layout.main);

        mEnabled = (TextView) findViewById(R.id.value_enabled);
        mName = (TextView) findViewById(R.id.value_name);
        mSelection = (TextView) findViewById(R.id.value_selection);
        mToggle = (CheckBox) findViewById(R.id.checkbox_enable);
        mToggle.setOnCheckedChangeListener(this);
    }

    @Override
    protected void onResume() {
        super.onResume();
        //Get the latest provider data
        updatePreferences();
        //Register an observer for changes that will
        // happen while we are active
        getContentResolver().registerContentObserver(SETTINGS_CONTENT_URI,
                false, mObserver);
    }

    @Override
    public void onCheckedChanged(CompoundButton buttonView, boolean isChecked) {
        ContentValues cv = new ContentValues(2);
        cv.put(SettingsColumns.NAME, "preferenceEnabled");
        cv.put(SettingsColumns.VALUE, isChecked);
```

```
        //Update the provider, which will trigger our observer
        getContentResolver().update(SETTINGS_CONTENT_URI, cv, null, null);
    }

    public void onSettingsClick(View v) {
        try {
            Intent intent = new Intent(SETTINGS_ACTION);
            startActivity(intent);
        } catch (ActivityNotFoundException e) {
            Toast.makeText(this,
                    "You do not have the Android Recipes Settings App installed.",
                    Toast.LENGTH_SHORT).show();
        }
    }

    private void updatePreferences() {
        Cursor c = getContentResolver().query(SETTINGS_CONTENT_URI,
                new String[] {SettingsColumns.NAME, SettingsColumns.VALUE},
                null, null, null);
        if (c == null) {
            return;
        }

        while (c.moveToNext()) {
            String key = c.getString(0);
            if ("preferenceEnabled".equals(key)) {
                mEnabled.setText( String.format("Enabled Setting = %s",
                    c.getString(1)) );
                mToggle.setChecked( Boolean.parseBoolean(c.getString(1)) );
            } else if ("preferenceName".equals(key)) {
                mName.setText( String.format("User Name Setting = %s",
                    c.getString(1)) );
            } else if ("preferenceSelection".equals(key)) {
                mSelection.setText( String.format("Selection Setting = %s",
                    c.getString(1)) );
            }
        }

        c.close();
    }
}
```

Because this is a separate application, it may not have access to the constants defined in the first (unless you control both applications and use a library project or some other method), so we have redefined them here for this example. If you were producing an application with an external provider you would like other developers to use, it would be prudent to also provide a JAR library that contains the constants necessary to access the Uri and column data in the provider, similar to the API provided by ContactsContract and CalendarContract.

In this example, the activity queries the provider for the current values of the settings each time it returns to the foreground and displays them in a TextView. The results are returned in a Cursor with two values in each row: the preference name and its value. The activity also registers a ContentObserver so that if the values change while this activity is active, the displayed values can be updated as well. When the user changes the value of the CheckBox onscreen, this calls the provider's update() method, which will trigger this observer to update the display.

Finally, if desired, the user could launch the SettingsActivity from the external application directly by clicking the Show Settings button. This calls startActivity() with an Intent containing the custom action string for which SettingsActivity is set to filter.

6-11. Sharing Your Other Data

Problem

You would like your application to provide the files or other private data it maintains to applications on the device.

Solution

(API Level 3)

Create a ContentProvider to act as an external interface for your application's data. ContentProvider exposes an arbitrary set of data to external requests through a database-like interface of query(), insert(), update(), and delete(), though the implementation is free to design how the data passes to the actual model from these methods.

ContentProvider can be used to expose any type of application data, including the application's resources and assets, to external requests.

How It Works

Let's take a look at a ContentProvider implementation that exposes two data sources: an array of strings located in memory, and a series of image files stored in the application's assets directory. As before, we must declare our provider to the Android system by using a <provider> tag in the manifest. See Listings 6-38 and 6-39.

Listing 6-38. Manifest Declaration for ContentProvider

```xml
<?xml version="1.0" encoding="utf-8"?>
<manifest xmlns:android="http://schemas.android.com/apk/res/android" ...>
    <application ...>
      <provider android:name=".ImageProvider"
          android:authorities="com.examples.share.imageprovider">
      </provider>
    </application>
</manifest>
```

Listing 6-39. Custom ContentProvider Exposing Assets

```java
public class ImageProvider extends ContentProvider {

    public static final Uri CONTENT_URI =
        Uri.parse("content://com.examples.share.imageprovider");

    public static final String COLUMN_NAME = "nameString";
    public static final String COLUMN_IMAGE = "imageUri";

    private String[] mNames;

    @Override
    public int delete(Uri uri, String selection, String[] selectionArgs) {
        throw new UnsupportedOperationException("This ContentProvider is read-only");
    }

    @Override
    public String getType(Uri uri) {
        return null;
    }

    @Override
    public Uri insert(Uri uri, ContentValues values) {
        throw new UnsupportedOperationException("This ContentProvider is read-only");
    }

    @Override
    public boolean onCreate() {
        mNames = new String[] {"John Doe", "Jane Doe", "Jill Doe"};
        return true;
    }

    @Override
    public Cursor query(Uri uri, String[] projection, String selection,
        String[] selectionArgs, String sortOrder) {
        MatrixCursor cursor = new MatrixCursor(projection);
        for(int i = 0; i < mNames.length; i++) {
            //Insert only the columns they requested
            MatrixCursor.RowBuilder builder = cursor.newRow();
            for(String column : projection) {
                if(column.equals("_id")) {
                    //Use the array index as a unique id
                    builder.add(i);
                }
                if(column.equals(COLUMN_NAME)) {
                    builder.add(mNames[i]);
                }
                if(column.equals(COLUMN_IMAGE)) {
                    builder.add(Uri.withAppendedPath(CONTENT_URI, String.valueOf(i)));
                }
```

```
            }
        }
        return cursor;
    }

    @Override
    public int update(Uri uri, ContentValues values, String selection,
        String[] selectionArgs) {
        throw new UnsupportedOperationException("This ContentProvider is read-only");
    }

    @Override
    public AssetFileDescriptor openAssetFile(Uri uri, String mode) throws
        FileNotFoundException {
        int requested = Integer.parseInt(uri.getLastPathSegment());
        AssetFileDescriptor afd;
        AssetManager manager = getContext().getAssets();
        //Return the appropriate asset for the requested item
        try {
            switch(requested) {
            case 0:
                afd = manager.openFd("logo1.png");
                break;
            case 1:
                afd = manager.openFd("logo2.png");
                break;
            case 2:
                afd = manager.openFd("logo3.png");
                break;
            default:
                afd = manager.openFd("logo1.png");
            }
            return afd;
        } catch (IOException e) {
            e.printStackTrace();
            return null;
        }
    }
}
```

As you may have guessed, the example exposes three logo image assets. The images we have chosen for this example are shown in Figure 6-4.

Figure 6-4. Examples of logo1.png (left), logo2.png (center), and logo3.png (right) stored in assets

Because we are exposing read-only content in the assets directory, there is no need to support the inherited methods insert(), update(), or delete(), so we have these methods simply throw an UnsupportedOperationException.

When the provider is created, the string array that holds people's names is created and onCreate() returns true; this signals to the system that the provider was created successfully. The provider exposes constants for its Uri and all readable column names. These values will be used by external applications to make requests for data.

This provider supports only a query for all the data within it. To support conditional queries for specific records or a subset of all the content, an application can process the values passed in to query() for selection and selectionArgs. In this example, any call to query() will build a cursor with all three elements contained within.

The cursor implementation used in this provider is a MatrixCursor, which is a cursor designed to be built around data that is not held inside a database. The example iterates through the list of columns requested (the projection) and builds each row according to these columns it contains. Each row is created by calling MatrixCursor.newRow(), which also returns a Builder instance that will be used to add the column data. Care should always be taken to match the order that the column data is added to the order of the requested projection. They should always match.

The value in the name column is the respective string in the local array, and the _id value, which Android requires to utilize the returned cursor with most ListAdapters, is simply returned as the array index. The information presented in the image column for each row is actually a content Uri representing the image file for each row, created with the provider's content Uri as the base, with the array index appended to it.

When an external application actually goes to retrieve this content, through ContentResolver.openInputStream(), a call will be made to openAssetFile(), which has been overridden to return an AssetFileDescriptor pointing to one of the image files in the assets directory. This implementation determines which image file to return by deconstructing the content Uri once again and retrieving the appended index value from the end.

Usage Example

Let's take a look at how this provider should be implemented and accessed in the context of the Android application. See Listing 6-40.

Listing 6-40. AndroidManifest.xml

```xml
<?xml version="1.0" encoding="utf-8"?>
<manifest xmlns:android="http://schemas.android.com/apk/res/android"
    package="com.examples.share"
    android:versionCode="1"
    android:versionName="1.0">
    <uses-sdk android:minSdkVersion="3" />

    <application android:icon="@drawable/icon" android:label="@string/app_name">
        <activity android:name=".ShareActivity"
                android:label="@string/app_name">
            <intent-filter>
```

```
            <action android:name="android.intent.action.MAIN" />
            <category android:name="android.intent.category.LAUNCHER" />
        </intent-filter>
    </activity>
    <provider android:name=".ImageProvider"
        android:authorities="com.examples.share.imageprovider">
    </provider>
    </application>
</manifest>
```

To implement this provider, the manifest of the application that owns the content must declare a <provider> tag pointing out the ContentProvider name and the authority to match when requests are made. The authority value should match the base portion of the exposed content Uri. The provider must be declared in the manifest so the system can instantiate and run it, even when the owning application is not running. See Listings 6-41 and 6-42.

Listing 6-41. `res/layout/main.xml`

```xml
<?xml version="1.0" encoding="utf-8"?>
<LinearLayout xmlns:android="http://schemas.android.com/apk/res/android"
  android:orientation="vertical"
  android:layout_width="match_parent"
  android:layout_height="match_parent">
  <TextView
    android:id="@+id/name"
    android:layout_width="wrap_content"
    android:layout_height="20dip"
    android:layout_gravity="center_horizontal"
  />
  <ImageView
    android:id="@+id/image"
    android:layout_width="wrap_content"
    android:layout_height="50dip"
    android:layout_gravity="center_horizontal"
  />
  <ListView
    android:id="@+id/list"
    android:layout_width="match_parent"
    android:layout_height="match_parent"
  />
</LinearLayout>
```

Listing 6-42. *Activity Reading from* `ImageProvider`

```java
public class ShareActivity extends FragmentActivity implements
        LoaderManager.LoaderCallbacks<Cursor>, AdapterView.OnItemClickListener {
    private static final int LOADER_LIST = 100;
    SimpleCursorAdapter mAdapter;
```

```java
@Override
public void onCreate(Bundle savedInstanceState) {
    super.onCreate(savedInstanceState);
    getSupportLoaderManager().initLoader(LOADER_LIST, null, this);
    setContentView(R.layout.main);

    mAdapter = new SimpleCursorAdapter(this, android.R.layout.simple_list_item_1,
            null, new String[]{ImageProvider.COLUMN_NAME},
            new int[]{android.R.id.text1}, 0);

    ListView list = (ListView)findViewById(R.id.list);
    list.setOnItemClickListener(this);
    list.setAdapter(mAdapter);
}

@Override
public void onItemClick(AdapterView<?> parent, View v, int position, long id) {
    //Seek the cursor to the selection
    Cursor c = mAdapter.getCursor();
    c.moveToPosition(position);

    //Load the name column into the TextView
    TextView tv = (TextView)findViewById(R.id.name);
    tv.setText(c.getString(1));

    ImageView iv = (ImageView)findViewById(R.id.image);
    try {
        //Load the content from the image column into the ImageView
        InputStream in =
                getContentResolver().openInputStream(Uri.parse(c.getString(2)));
        Bitmap image = BitmapFactory.decodeStream(in);
        iv.setImageBitmap(image);
    } catch (FileNotFoundException e) {
        e.printStackTrace();
    }
}

@Override
public Loader<Cursor> onCreateLoader(int id, Bundle args) {
    String[] projection = new String[]{"_id",
            ImageProvider.COLUMN_NAME,
            ImageProvider.COLUMN_IMAGE};
    return new CursorLoader(this, ImageProvider.CONTENT_URI,
            projection, null, null, null);
}

@Override
public void onLoadFinished(Loader<Cursor> loader, Cursor data) {
    mAdapter.swapCursor(data);
}
```

```
    @Override
    public void onLoaderReset(Loader<Cursor> loader) {
        mAdapter.swapCursor(null);
    }
}
```

> **Important**   This example requires the Support Library to provide access to the Loader pattern in Android 1.6 and above. If you are targeting Android 3.0+ in your application, you may replace FragmentActivity with Activity and getSupportLoaderManager() with getLoaderManager().

In this example, a managed cursor is obtained from the custom ContentProvider, referencing the exposed Uri and column names for the data. The data is then connected to a ListView through a SimpleCursorAdapter to display only the name value.

When the user taps any of the items in the list, the cursor is moved to that position and the respective name and image are displayed above. This is where the activity calls ContentResolver.openInputStream() to access the asset images through the Uri that was stored in the column field.

Figure 6-5 displays the result of running this application and selecting the last item in the list (Jill Doe).

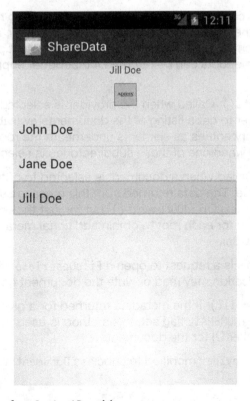

Figure 6-5. Activity drawing resources from ContentProvider

Note that we have not closed the connection to the Cursor explicitly. Since the Loader created the Cursor, it is also the job of the Loader to manage its life cycle.

DocumentsProvider

(API Level 19)

The DocumentsProvider is a specialized ContentProvider API that applications can use to expose their contents to the common documents picker interface in Android 4.4 and later. The advantage to using this framework is that it allows applications that manage access to storage services to expose the files and documents they own by using a common interface throughout the system. It also includes the ability for client applications to create and save new documents inside these applications (we will look more at the client side of this API in the next chapter).

A custom DocumentsProvider must identify all the files and directories it would like to expose by using a unique document ID string. This value does not need to match any specific format, but it must be unique and cannot change after it is reported to the system. The framework will persist these values for permissions purposes, so even across reboots the document IDs you provide (and later expect) must be consistent for any resource.

When subclassing DocumentsProvider, we will be implementing a different set of callbacks than the basic CRUD methods we used in the bare ContentProvider. The system's document picker interface will trigger the following methods on the provider as the user explores:

- queryRoots(): First called when the picker UI is launched to request basic information about the top-level "document" in your provider, as well as some basic metadata such as the name and icon to display. Most providers have only one root, but multiple roots can be returned if that better supports the provider's use case.

- queryChildDocuments(): Called when the provider is selected with the root's document ID in order to get a listing of the documents available under this root. If you return directory entries as elements underneath the root, the same method will be called again when one of those subdirectories is selected.

- queryDocument(): Called when a document is selected to obtain metadata about that specific instance. The data returned from this message should mirror what was returned from queryChildDocuments(), but for just the one element. This method is also called for each root to obtain additional metadata of the top-level directory in the provider.

- openDocument(): This is a request to open a FileDescriptor to the document so that the client application may read or write the document contents.

- openDocumentThumbnail(): If the metadata returned for a given document has the FLAG_SUPPORTS_THUMBNAIL flag set, this method is used to obtain a thumbnail to display in the picker UI for the document.

Listing 6-43 shows our ImageProvider modified to subclass DocumentProvider instead.

Listing 6-43. ImageProvider as a DocumentsProvider

```java
public class ImageProvider extends DocumentsProvider {
    private static final String TAG = "ImageProvider";

    /* Cached recent selection */
    private static String sLastFilename;
    private static String sLastTitle;

    /* Default projection for a root when none supplied */
    private static final String[] DEFAULT_ROOT_PROJECTION = {
        Root.COLUMN_ROOT_ID, Root.COLUMN_MIME_TYPES,
        Root.COLUMN_FLAGS, Root.COLUMN_ICON, Root.COLUMN_TITLE,
        Root.COLUMN_SUMMARY, Root.COLUMN_DOCUMENT_ID,
        Root.COLUMN_AVAILABLE_BYTES
    };
    /* Default projection for documents when none supplied */
    private static final String[] DEFAULT_DOCUMENT_PROJECTION = {
        Document.COLUMN_DOCUMENT_ID, Document.COLUMN_MIME_TYPE,
        Document.COLUMN_DISPLAY_NAME, Document.COLUMN_LAST_MODIFIED,
        Document.COLUMN_FLAGS, Document.COLUMN_SIZE
    };

    private ArrayMap<String, String> mDocuments;

    @Override
    public boolean onCreate() {
        //Dummy data for our documents
        mDocuments = new ArrayMap<String, String>();
        mDocuments.put("logo1.png", "John Doe");
        mDocuments.put("logo2.png", "Jane Doe");
        mDocuments.put("logo3.png", "Jill Doe");

        //Dump asset images onto internal storage
        writeAssets(mDocuments.keySet());
        return true;
    }

    /*
     * Helper method to stream some dummy files out to the
     * internal storage directory
     */
    private void writeAssets(Set<String> filenames) {
        for(String name : filenames) {
            try {
                Log.d("ImageProvider", "Writing "+name+" to storage");
                InputStream in = getContext().getAssets().open(name);
                FileOutputStream out = getContext().openFileOutput(name, Context.MODE_PRIVATE);
```

```
                int size;
                byte[] buffer = new byte[1024];
                while ((size = in.read(buffer, 0, 1024)) >= 0) {
                    out.write(buffer, 0, size);
                }
                out.flush();
                out.close();
            } catch (IOException e) {
                Log.w(TAG, e);
            }
        }
    }

    /* Helper method to construct documentId from a file name */
    private String getDocumentId(String filename) {
        return "root:" + filename;
    }

    /*
     * Helper method to extract file name from a documentId.
     * Returns empty string for the "root" document.
     */
    private String getFilename(String documentId) {
        int split = documentId.indexOf(":");
        if (split < 0) {
            return "";
        }
        return documentId.substring(split+1);
    }

    /*
     * Called by the system to determine how many "providers" are
     * hosted here.  It is most common to return only one, via a
     * Cursor that has only one result row.
     */
    @Override
    public Cursor queryRoots(String[] projection) throws FileNotFoundException {
        if (projection == null) {
            projection = DEFAULT_ROOT_PROJECTION;
        }
        MatrixCursor result = new MatrixCursor(projection);
        //Add the single root for this provider
        MatrixCursor.RowBuilder builder = result.newRow();

        builder.add(Root.COLUMN_ROOT_ID, "root");
        builder.add(Root.COLUMN_TITLE, "Android Recipes");
        builder.add(Root.COLUMN_SUMMARY, "Android Recipes Documents Provider");
        builder.add(Root.COLUMN_ICON, R.drawable.ic_launcher);

        builder.add(Root.COLUMN_DOCUMENT_ID, "root:");
```

```java
        builder.add(Root.COLUMN_FLAGS,
                //Results will come from only the local filesystem
                Root.FLAG_LOCAL_ONLY
                //We support showing recently selected items
                | Root.FLAG_SUPPORTS_RECENTS);
        builder.add(Root.COLUMN_MIME_TYPES, "image/*");
        builder.add(Root.COLUMN_AVAILABLE_BYTES, 0);

        return result;
}

/*
 * Called by the system to determine the child items for a given
 * parent.  Will be called for the root, and for each subdirectory
 * defined within.
 */
@Override
public Cursor queryChildDocuments(String parentDocumentId, String[] projection,
        String sortOrder) throws FileNotFoundException {

    if (projection == null) {
        projection = DEFAULT_DOCUMENT_PROJECTION;
    }
    MatrixCursor result = new MatrixCursor(projection);

    try {
        for(String key : mDocuments.keySet()) {
            addImageRow(result, mDocuments.get(key), key);
        }
    } catch (IOException e) {
        return null;
    }

    return result;
}

/*
 * Return the same information provided via queryChildDocuments(), but
 * just for the single documentId requested.
 */
@Override
public Cursor queryDocument(String documentId, String[] projection)
        throws FileNotFoundException {

    if (projection == null) {
        projection = DEFAULT_DOCUMENT_PROJECTION;
    }

    MatrixCursor result = new MatrixCursor(projection);
```

```java
        try {
            String filename = getFilename(documentId);
            if (TextUtils.isEmpty(filename)) {
                //This is a query for root
                addRootRow(result);
            } else {
                addImageRow(result, mDocuments.get(filename), filename);
            }
        } catch (IOException e) {
            return null;
        }

        return result;
    }

    /*
     * Called to populate any recently used items from this
     * provider in the Recents picker UI.
     */
    @Override
    public Cursor queryRecentDocuments(String rootId, String[] projection)
            throws FileNotFoundException {

        if (projection == null) {
            projection = DEFAULT_DOCUMENT_PROJECTION;
        }

        MatrixCursor result = new MatrixCursor(projection);

        if (sLastFilename != null) {
            try {
                addImageRow(result, sLastTitle, sLastFilename);
            } catch (IOException e) {
                Log.w(TAG, e);
            }
        }
        Log.d(TAG, "Recents: "+result.getCount());
        //We'll return the last selected result to a recents query
        return result;
    }

    /*
     * Helper method to write the root into the supplied
     * Cursor
     */
    private void addRootRow(MatrixCursor cursor) {
        final MatrixCursor.RowBuilder row = cursor.newRow();

        row.add(Document.COLUMN_DOCUMENT_ID, "root:");
        row.add(Document.COLUMN_DISPLAY_NAME, "Root");
        row.add(Document.COLUMN_SIZE, 0);
        row.add(Document.COLUMN_MIME_TYPE, Document.MIME_TYPE_DIR);
```

```java
        long installed;
        try {
            installed = getContext().getPackageManager()
                    .getPackageInfo(getContext().getPackageName(), 0)
                    .firstInstallTime;
        } catch (NameNotFoundException e) {
            installed = 0;
        }
        row.add(Document.COLUMN_LAST_MODIFIED, installed);
        row.add(Document.COLUMN_FLAGS, 0);
    }

    /*
     * Helper method to write a specific image file into
     * the supplied Cursor
     */
    private void addImageRow(MatrixCursor cursor, String title, String filename)
            throws IOException {

        final MatrixCursor.RowBuilder row = cursor.newRow();

        AssetFileDescriptor afd = getContext().getAssets().openFd(filename);

        row.add(Document.COLUMN_DOCUMENT_ID, getDocumentId(filename));
        row.add(Document.COLUMN_DISPLAY_NAME, title);
        row.add(Document.COLUMN_SIZE, afd.getLength());
        row.add(Document.COLUMN_MIME_TYPE, "image/*");

        long installed;
        try {
            installed = getContext().getPackageManager()
                    .getPackageInfo(getContext().getPackageName(), 0)
                    .firstInstallTime;
        } catch (NameNotFoundException e) {
            installed = 0;
        }
        row.add(Document.COLUMN_LAST_MODIFIED, installed);
        row.add(Document.COLUMN_FLAGS, Document.FLAG_SUPPORTS_THUMBNAIL);
    }

    /*
     * Return a reference to an image asset the framework will use
     * in the items list for any document with the FLAG_SUPPORTS_THUMBNAIL
     * flag enabled.  This method is safe to block while downloading content.
     */
    @Override
    public AssetFileDescriptor openDocumentThumbnail(String documentId, Point sizeHint,
            CancellationSignal signal) throws FileNotFoundException {
```

```
        //We will load the thumbnail from the version on storage
        String filename = getFilename(documentId);
        //Create a file reference to the image on internal storage
        final File file = new File(getContext().getFilesDir(), filename);
        //Return a file descriptor wrapping the file reference
        final ParcelFileDescriptor pfd =
                ParcelFileDescriptor.open(file, ParcelFileDescriptor.MODE_READ_ONLY);
        return new AssetFileDescriptor(pfd, 0, AssetFileDescriptor.UNKNOWN_LENGTH);
    }

    /*
     * Return a file descriptor to the document referenced by the supplied
     * documentId.  The client will use this descriptor to read the contents
     * directly.  This method is safe to block while downloading content.
     */
    @Override
    public ParcelFileDescriptor openDocument(String documentId, String mode,
            CancellationSignal signal) throws FileNotFoundException {

        //We will load the document itself from assets
        try {
            String filename = getFilename(documentId);
            //Return the file descriptor directly from APK assets
            AssetFileDescriptor afd = getContext().getAssets().openFd(filename);

            //Save this as the last selected document
            sLastFilename = filename;
            sLastTitle = mDocuments.get(filename);

            return afd.getParcelFileDescriptor();
        } catch (IOException e) {
            Log.w(TAG, e);
            return null;
        }
    }

    /*
     * This method is invoked when openDocument() receives a file descriptor
     * from assets.  Documents opened from standard files will not invoke
     * this method.
     */
    @Override
    public AssetFileDescriptor openAssetFile(Uri uri, String mode)
            throws FileNotFoundException {

        //Last segment of Uri is the documentId
        String filename = getFilename(uri.getLastPathSegment());

        AssetManager manager = getContext().getAssets();
        try {
            //Return the appropriate asset for the requested item
            AssetFileDescriptor afd = manager.openFd(filename);
```

```
        //Save this as the last selected document
        sLastFilename = filename;
        sLastTitle = mDocuments.get(filename);

        return afd;
    } catch (IOException e) {
        Log.w(TAG, e);
        return null;
    }
  }
 }
}
```

In this example, we show how to serve the same three logo image files used previously from the assets directory of our APK and from internal storage to indicate the method of opening a resource from both locations. In order to do this, when the provider is created, we read the image files out of assets and copy them to internal storage.

We have created a simple structure of converting file names into document IDs. In our case, root is the virtual top-level directory where our logo images live, and we create each ID as a pseudo-path to that file by using colon separators. The methods getDocumentId() and getFilename() are helpers to convert back and forth between our published ID and the actual image file name.

> **Tip** Document IDs will be embedded in a content Uri by the framework, so if you are converting directory paths to IDs, you must use characters that are not otherwise considered a path separator by the Uri class.

Inside queryRoots(), we return a MatrixCursor that includes the basic metadata of the single provider root. Notice that the query methods of the provider should respect the column projection passed in, and return only the data requested. We are using an updated version of the add() method as well that takes the column name for each item. This version is convenient, as it monitors the projection passed into the MatrixCursor constructor, and silently ignores attempts to add columns not in the projection, thus eliminating the looping we did before to add elements.

The title, summary, and icon columns deal with the provider display in the picker UI. We have also defined the following:

- COLUMN_DOCUMENT_ID: Provides the ID we will be handed back later to reference this top-level root element.

- COLUMN_MIME_TYPES: Reports the document types this root contains. We have image files, so we are using image/*.

In addition, COLUMN_FLAGS reports additional features the root item may support. The options are as follows:

- FLAG_LOCAL_ONLY: Results are on the device, and don't require network requests.

- FLAG_SUPPORTS_CREATE: The root allows client applications to create a new document inside this provider. We will discuss how to do this on the client side in the next chapter.

- FLAG_SUPPORTS_RECENTS: Tells the framework we can participate in the recent documents UI with results. This will result in calls to queryRecentDocuments() to obtain this metadata.

- FLAG_SUPPORTS_SEARCH: Similar to recents, tells the framework we can handle search queries via querySearchDocuments().

We have set the local and recents flags in our example. Once this method returns, the framework will call queryDocument() with the document ID of the root to get more information. Inside addRootRow() we populate the cursor with the necessary fields. For COLUMN_MIME_TYPE we use the constant MIME_TYPE_DIR to indicate this element is a directory containing other documents. This same definition should be applied to any subdirectories in the hierarchy you create for the provider. Also, since all the files we are providing have existed since we installed the application, we provide the APK install date as the COLUMN_LAST_MODIFIED value; for a more dynamic filesystem, this could just be the modified date of the file on disk.

When the provider is selected by the user, we receive a call to queryChildDocuments() to list all the files in the root. For us, this includes adding a row to the cursor for each logo image file we have. The addImageRow() method constructs the appropriate column data with similar elements to the previous iterations.

We want to allow each image to be represented by a thumbnail image in the picker UI, so we set the FLAG_SUPPORTS_THUMBNAIL for COLUMN_FLAGS on each image row. This will trigger openDocumentThumbnail() for each element as they are displayed in the picker. In this method, we've shown how to open a FileDescriptor from internal storage and return it. If this technique were used for openDocument(), the last step of wrapping the ParcelFileDescriptor in an AssetFileDescriptor would not be necessary.

The sizeHint parameter should be used to ensure you don't return a thumbnail that is too large for display in the picker's list. Our images are all small to begin with, so we haven't checked this parameter here. It is safe, if necessary, to block and download content inside this method. For this case, a CancellationSignal is provided, which should be checked regularly in case the framework cancels the load before it is finished.

When a document is finally selected, queryDocument() will be called again with the ID of the logo image supplied. In this case, we must simply return the same results from addImageRow() for the single document requested. This will trigger a call to openDocument(), where we must return a valid ParcelFileDescriptor that the client can use to access the resource.

In our specific example, we return the file from assets directly. When the framework realizes we have returned a FileDescriptor from inside our APK, the secondary method openAssetFile() will be called to obtain the raw AssetFileDescriptor. In most cases where your content lives on other storage, this is not necessary. However, if you choose to expose files in assets, you must implement openAssetFile() as well, or the loading will fail.

The definition for our provider in the manifest also looks a bit different from before. Since the provider will be queried directly by the framework, we must define some specific filters and permissions (see Listing 6-44).

Listing 6-44. AndroidManifest.xml DocumentsProvider Snippet

```
<provider
    android:name="com.androidrecipes.sharedocuments.ImageProvider"
    android:authorities="com.androidrecipes.sharedocuments.images"
```

```
    android:grantUriPermissions="true"
    android:exported="true"
    android:permission="android.permission.MANAGE_DOCUMENTS">
    <!-- Unique filter the system will use to find published providers -->
    <intent-filter>
        <action android:name="android.content.action.DOCUMENTS_PROVIDER" />
    </intent-filter>
</provider>
```

First, the provider must be exported so external applications can access it. This is usually the default behavior with a provider that has an `<intent-filter>` attached, but it's good to be explicit here. The filter must include the DOCUMENTS_PROVIDER action, which is how the framework will find installed providers it can access. Next, the provider must be protected by the MANAGE_DOCUMENTS permission. This is a system-level permission that only system applications can obtain, so this protects your provider from being exploited by other apps. Finally, the grantUriPermissions attribute should be enabled. This allows the framework to provide access permissions to client applications on a document-by-document basis, rather than giving each client access to the whole provider.

This example application doesn't really have a user interface to launch, but with the application installed, you can invoke the new provider by going to any system application that requires you to pick an image; the Contacts application is a good choice. When creating a new contact, you can add a photo, and selecting an existing image invokes the system picker UI. You can see in Figure 6-6 what this would look like for our example.

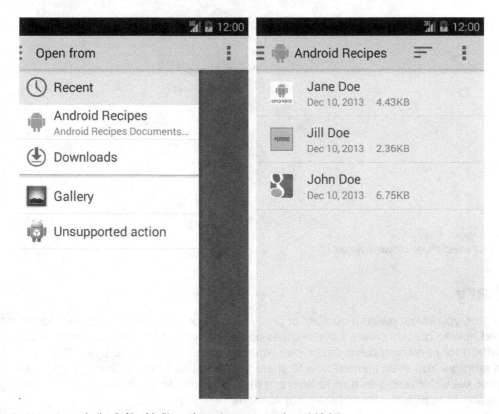

Figure 6-6. Provider shown in list (left) with file options shown once selected (right)

Recent Documents

Remember in our example that we set the FLAG_SUPPORTS_RECENTS in the root metadata. We also provided an implementation of queryRecentDocuments() to react to these inquiries. There is no inherent limit to the number of recent documents any provider can return here, but you will want to pick something that is relevant and contextual to the user. Here, we return only the last selected logo image from our provider (something that we save on each open request in a static variable). The metadata here is the same as any other documents query, so the same addImageRow() method is invoked to populate the cursor.

With this in place, when we access the Recent section of our provider (as shown in Figure 6-7), we can see the last image selection made.

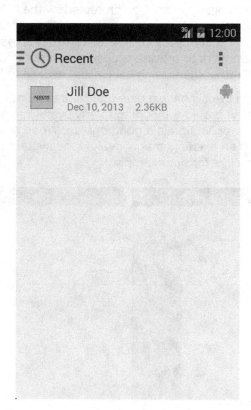

Figure 6-7. *Last select image shown in Recent UI*

Summary

In this chapter, you investigated a number of practical methods to persist data on Android devices. You learned how to quickly create a preferences screen as well as how to use preferences and a simple method for persisting basic data types. You saw how and where to place files, for reference as well as storage. You even learned how to share your persisted data with other applications. In the next chapter, we will investigate how to leverage the operating system's services to do background operations and to communicate between applications.

7

Interacting with the System

The Android operating system provides a number of useful services that applications can leverage. Many of these services are designed to allow your application to function within the mobile system in ways beyond just interacting briefly with a user. Applications can schedule themselves for alarms, run background services, and send messages to each other—all of which allows an Android application to integrate to the fullest extent with the mobile device. In addition, Android provides a set of standard interfaces that are designed to expose all the data collected by its core applications to your software. Through these interfaces, any application may integrate with, add to, and improve upon the core functionality of the platform, thereby enhancing the experience for the user.

7-1. Notifying from the Background

Problem

Your application is running in the background, with no currently visible interface to the user, but must notify the user of an important event that has occurred.

Solution

(API Level 4)

Use `NotificationManager` to post a status bar notification. Notifications provide an unobtrusive way of indicating that you want the user's attention. Perhaps new messages have arrived, an update is available, or a long-running job is complete; notifications are perfect for accomplishing these tasks.

How It Works

A notification can be posted to the NotificationManager from just about any system component, such as a Service, BroadcastReceiver, or Activity. In Listing 7-1, we will look at an activity that posts a series of different notification types when the user leaves the activity and goes to the home screen.

Listing 7-1. Activity Firing a Notification

```
public class NotificationActivity extends Activity {

    //Unique notification id values
    public static final int NOTE_BASIC = 100;
    public static final int NOTE_BIGTEXT = 200;
    public static final int NOTE_PICTURE = 300;
    public static final int NOTE_INBOX = 400;

    @Override
    public void onCreate(Bundle savedInstanceState) {
        super.onCreate(savedInstanceState);
        TextView tv = new TextView(this);
        tv.setText("When You Leave Here, Notifications Will Post");
        tv.setGravity(Gravity.CENTER);

        setContentView(tv);
    }

    @Override
    public void onStop() {
        super.onStop();

        NotificationManager manager =
                (NotificationManager) getSystemService(Context.NOTIFICATION_SERVICE);

        //Post 4 unique notifications
        Notification note = buildNotification(NOTE_BASIC);
        manager.notify(NOTE_BASIC, note);
        note = buildNotification(NOTE_BIGTEXT);
        manager.notify(NOTE_BIGTEXT, note);
        note = buildNotification(NOTE_PICTURE);
        manager.notify(NOTE_PICTURE, note);
        note = buildNotification(NOTE_INBOX);
        manager.notify(NOTE_INBOX, note);
    }

    private Notification buildNotification(int type) {
        Intent launchIntent =
                new Intent(this, NotificationActivity.class);
        PendingIntent contentIntent =
                PendingIntent.getActivity(this, 0, launchIntent, 0);
```

```java
// Create notification using a builder
NotificationCompat.Builder builder = new NotificationCompat.Builder(
        NotificationActivity.this);


builder.setSmallIcon(R.drawable.ic_launcher)
        .setTicker("Something Happened")
        .setWhen(System.currentTimeMillis())
        .setAutoCancel(true)
        .setDefaults(Notification.DEFAULT_SOUND)
        .setContentTitle("We're Finished!")
        .setContentText("Click Here!")
        .setContentIntent(contentIntent);

switch (type) {
    case NOTE_BASIC:
        //Return the simple notification
        return builder.build();
    case NOTE_BIGTEXT:
        //Include two actions
        builder.addAction(android.R.drawable.ic_menu_call,
                "Call", contentIntent);
        builder.addAction(android.R.drawable.ic_menu_recent_history,
                "History", contentIntent);
        //Use the BigTextStyle when expanded
        NotificationCompat.BigTextStyle textStyle =
                new NotificationCompat.BigTextStyle(builder);
        textStyle.bigText(
                "Here is some additional text to be displayed when the notification is "
                +"in expanded mode.  I can fit so much more content into this giant view!");

        return textStyle.build();
    case NOTE_PICTURE:
        //Add one additional action
        builder.addAction(android.R.drawable.ic_menu_compass,
                "View Location", contentIntent);
        //Use the BigPictureStyle when expanded
        NotificationCompat.BigPictureStyle pictureStyle =
                new NotificationCompat.BigPictureStyle(builder);
        pictureStyle.bigPicture(BitmapFactory.decodeResource(getResources(), R.drawable.dog));

        return pictureStyle.build();
    case NOTE_INBOX:
        //Use the InboxStyle when expanded
        NotificationCompat.InboxStyle inboxStyle =
                new NotificationCompat.InboxStyle(builder);
        inboxStyle.setSummaryText("4 New Tasks");
        inboxStyle.addLine("Make Dinner");
        inboxStyle.addLine("Call Mom");
        inboxStyle.addLine("Call Wife First");
        inboxStyle.addLine("Pick up Kids");
```

```
                    return inboxStyle.build();
            default:
                throw new IllegalArgumentException("Unknown Type");
        }
    }
}
```

A series of new notification elements are created using `Notification.Builder` when the user leaves the activity. We will discuss the expanded types shortly, and just focus on the basic type for now. An icon resource and title string may be provided, and these items will display in the status bar at the time the notification occurs. In addition, we pass a time value (in milliseconds) to display in the notification list as the event time. Here, we are setting that value to the time the notification fired, but it may take on a different meaning in your application.

> **Important**   We using `NotificationCompat.Builder` in this example, which is part of the Support Library and allows us to use the new API, which was introduced in Android 3.0 (API Level 11), going back to Android 1.6. If you are targeting Android 3.0+ only, you can replace `NotificationCompat.Builder` with `Notification.Builder` within the code.

Prior to creating the notification, we can fill it out with some other useful parameters, such as more-detailed text to be displayed in the notifications list when the user pulls down the status bar.

One of the parameters passed to the builder is a `PendingIntent` that points back to our activity. This Intent makes the notification interactive, allowing the user to tap it in the list and launch the activity.

> **Note**   This Intent will launch a new activity with each event. If you would rather an existing instance of the activity respond to the launch, if one exists in the stack, be sure to include Intent flags and manifest parameters appropriately to accomplish this, such as `Intent.FLAG_ACTIVITY_CLEAR_TOP` and `android:launchMode="singleTop"`.

To enhance the notification beyond the visual animation in the status bar, the notification defaults are modified to include that the system's default notification sound be played when the notification fires. Values such as `Notification.DEFAULT_VIBRATION` and `Notification.DEFAULT_LIGHTS` may also be added.

> **Tip**   If you would like to customize the sound played with a notification, set the `Notification.sound` parameter to a `Uri` that references a file or `ContentProvider` to read from.

We finally add a series of flags to the notification for further customization. This example uses `setAutoCancel()` in the builder to enable `Notification.FLAG_AUTO_CANCEL`, which cancels or removes the notification from the list as soon as the user selects it. Without this flag, the notification remains in the list until it is manually dismissed or canceled programmatically by calling NotificationManager.cancel() or NotificationManager.cancelAll(). Another helpful flag to set with the builder is setOngoing(), which disables any user ability to remove the notification. It can be cancelled only programmatically. This is useful for notifying the user of background operations currently running, such as music playing or location tracking underway.

Additionally, here are some other useful flags to apply that do not have methods inside the builder. These flags can be set directly on the notification after it is constructed:

- FLAG_INSISTENT: Repeats the notification sounds until the user responds.

- FLAG_NO_CLEAR: Does not allow the notification to be cleared with the user's Clear Notifications button, but only through a call to cancel(). Once the notification is prepared, it is posted to the user with NotificationManager.notify(), which takes an ID parameter as well. Each notification type in your application should have a unique ID. The manager will allow only one notification with the same ID in the list at a time, and new instances with the same ID will take the place of those existing. In addition, the ID is required to cancel a specific notification manually.

When we run this example, an activity displays with instructions to leave the application immediately. Upon leaving, you can see the notification set post sometime later, even though the activity is no longer visible (see Figure 7-1).

Figure 7-1. Notification that is occurring (left) and being displayed in the list (right)

Expanded Notification Styles

(API Level 16)

Starting with Android 4.1, notifications have the capability to display additional rich information with interactivity directly in the notification view. These are known as notification styles. Any notification that is currently at the top of the window shade is expanded by default, and the user can expand any other notification with a two-finger gesture. Therefore, expanded views don't replace the traditional view; rather, they enhance the experience at certain times.

There are three default styles (implementations of `Notification.Style`) provided by the platform:

- `BigTextStyle`: Displays an extended amount of text, such as the full contents of a message or post

- `BigPictureStyle`: Displays a large, full-color image

- `InboxStyle`: Provides a list of items, similar to the inbox view from an application such as Gmail

You are not limited to using these, however. `Notification.Style` is an interface that your application can implement to display any custom expanded layout that may best fit your needs.

In addition to styles, Android 4.1 added inline actions for an expanded notification. This means that you can add multiple action items for the user to take directly from the window shade view rather than just the single callback Intent when the user clicks the whole notification item. These items will show up on top of the expanded view, lined up at the bottom. Listing 7-2 shows the code from the previous example to add a `BigTextStyle` expanded notification collected together, and Figure 7-2 shows the result.

Listing 7-2. BigTextStyle Notification

```
//Create notification with the time it was fired
NotificationCompat.Builder builder =
        new NotificationCompat.Builder(NotificationActivity.this);

builder.setSmallIcon(R.drawable.icon)
        .setTicker("Something Happened")
        .setWhen(System.currentTimeMillis())
        .setAutoCancel(true)
        .setDefaults(Notification.DEFAULT_SOUND)
        .setContentTitle("We're Finished!")
        .setContentText("Click Here!")
        .setContentIntent(contentIntent);

//Add some custom actions
builder.addAction(android.R.id.drawable.ic_menu_call, "Call Back", contentIntent);
builder.addAction(android.R.id.drawable.ic_menu_recent_history,
        "Call History", contentIntent);

//Apply an expanded style
NotificationCompat.BigTextStyle expandedStyle =
        new NotificationCompat.BigTextStyle(builder);
expandedStyle.bigText("Here is some additional text to be displayed when"
```

```
        + " the notification is in expanded mode.  "
        + " I can fit so much more content into this giant view!");

Notification note = expandedStyle.build();
```

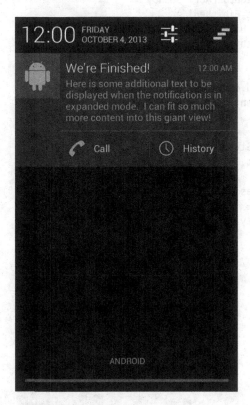

Figure 7-2. `BigTextStyle` in the window shade

You can attach custom actions by using the `addAction()` method on the builder. You can see here how the actions that are added lay out with respect to the overall view. In this example, each action goes to the same place, but you can attach any `PendingIntent` to each action to make them travel to different places in your application.

The only necessary modification to the previous example is that we wrap our existing `Builder` object in the `BigTextStyle` and apply any specific customizations there. In this case, the only additional piece of information is setting `bigText()` with the text to display in expanded mode. Then the notification is created from the `build()` method on the style, rather than the builder.

Let's take a look at `BigPictureStyle` in Listing 7-3 and Figure 7-3.

Listing 7-3. `BigPictureStyle` Notification

```
//Create notification with the time it was fired
NotificationCompat.Builder builder =
        new NotificationCompat.Builder(NotificationActivity.this);
```

```
builder.setSmallIcon(R.drawable.icon)
        .setTicker("Something Happened")
        .setWhen(System.currentTimeMillis())
        .setAutoCancel(true)
        .setDefaults(Notification.DEFAULT_SOUND)
        .setContentTitle("We're Finished!")
        .setContentText("Click Here!")
        .setContentIntent(contentIntent);

//Add some custom actions
builder.addAction(android.R.id.drawable.ic_menu_compass,
        "View Location", contentIntent);

//Apply an expanded style
NotificationCompat.BigPictureStyle expandedStyle =
        new NotificationCompat.BigPictureStyle(builder);
expandedStyle.bigPicture(
        BitmapFactory.decodeResource(getResources(), R.drawable.icon) );

Notification note = expandedStyle.build();
```

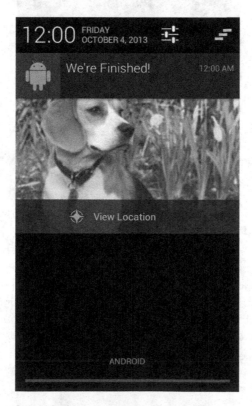

Figure 7-3. BigPictureStyle *in the window shade*

This code is almost identical to BigTextStyle, except that here we use the bigPicture() method to pass in the Bitmap that will be used as the full-color image. Finally, take a look at InboxStyle in Listing 7-4 and Figure 7-4.

Listing 7-4. InboxStyle Notification

```
//Create notification with the time it was fired
NotificationCompat.Builder builder =
        new NotificationCompat.Builder(NotificationActivity.this);

builder.setSmallIcon(R.drawable.icon)
        .setTicker("Something Happened")
        .setWhen(System.currentTimeMillis())
        .setAutoCancel(true)
        .setDefaults(Notification.DEFAULT_SOUND)
        .setContentTitle("We're Finished!")
        .setContentText("Click Here!")
        .setContentIntent(contentIntent);

//Apply an expanded style
NotificationCompat.InboxStyle expandedStyle =
        new NotificationCompat.InboxStyle(builder);
expandedStyle.setSummaryText("4 New Tasks");
expandedStyle.addLine("Make Dinner");
expandedStyle.addLine("Call Mom");
expandedStyle.addLine("Call Wife First");
expandedStyle.addLine("Pick up Kids");

Notification note = expandedStyle.build();
```

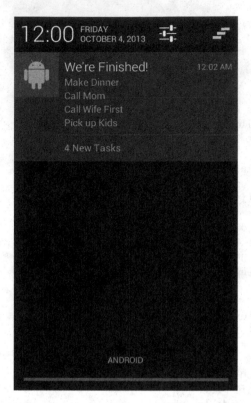

Figure 7-4. InboxStyle in the window shade

With `Notification.InboxStyle`, multiple items are added to the list by using the `addLine()` method. We also topped off the example with a summary line noting the number of items with `setSummaryText()`, a method that is available for use with all the previous styles as well.

As before, we've used the Support Library's `NotificationCompat` class, which allows us to call all these methods in an application running back to API Level 4. If your application is targeting Android 4.1 as the minimum platform, you can replace this with the native `Notification.Builder`.

One of the real powers of the Support Library is shown in this particular case. We are calling methods that are not available until API Level 16, but the Support Library takes care of version checking for us under the hood and simply ignores methods that a certain platform doesn't support; we don't have to branch our code to use new APIs.

As a result, when this same code is used on a device running Android 4.0 or earlier, the traditional notification will simply appear as if we hadn't taken advantage of the new features.

> **Note**   One of the great powers of the Support Library is that you can use new APIs in applications running on older Android devices, and you don't have to branch your own code to do so.

NotificationListenerService

(API Level 18)

As of Android 4.3, a new service is available to applications that wish to monitor the status of all the notifications on the device. Applications can extend `NotificationListenerService` to receive updates whenever any application posts a new notification or when the user clears an existing notification. In addition, the application can programmatically cancel any specific notification, or clear all of them at once.

ENABLING NOTIFICATION ACCESS

Because this service provides your application global access to the active notifications list, permission must first be granted. However, in this case, your application cannot declare this as a standard permission it would like to obtain. Instead, the user must explicitly grant access from the Security section of the device's Settings application. There is a section for Notification Access, which will list all installed applications that have an exported `NotificationListenerService` for the user to enable or disable this feature.

Figure 7-5 shows what the Notification Access section of Settings looks like on a Nexus device, along with the prompt that a user will see after tapping your application item to enable access to this information.

Figure 7-5. InboxStyle *in the window shade*

It is up to your application to guide the user to Settings to enable this service to receive events; the framework will not do it for you. You can take the user directly to the appropriate screen in Settings by firing an Intent with the `android.settings.ACTION_NOTIFICATION_LISTENER_SETTINGS` action string to start the activity. As of Android 4.3, this string is not public in the SDK, so be aware that it may change in future versions.

Listing 7-5 shows a simple extension of `NotificationListenerService`.

Listing 7-5. NotificationListenerService Example

```java
public class MonitorService extends NotificationListenerService {
    private static final String TAG = "RecipesMonitorService";

    @Override
    public void onNotificationPosted(StatusBarNotification sbn) {
        //Validate the notification came from this application
        if (!TextUtils.equals(sbn.getPackageName(), getPackageName())) {
            return;
        }

        Log.i(TAG, "Notification "+sbn.getId()+" Posted");
    }

    @Override
    public void onNotificationRemoved(StatusBarNotification sbn) {
        //Validate the notification came from this application
        if (!TextUtils.equals(sbn.getPackageName(), getPackageName())) {
            return;
        }
        //We are looking for the basic notification
        if (NotificationActivity.NOTE_BASIC != sbn.getId()) {
            return;
        }

        //If the basic notification cancels, dismiss all of ours
        for (StatusBarNotification note : getActiveNotifications()) {
            if (TextUtils.equals(note.getPackageName(), getPackageName())) {
                cancelNotification(note.getPackageName(),
                        note.getTag(),
                        note.getId());
            }
        }
    }

}
```

There are two abstract methods you must implement: onNotificationPosted() and onNotificationRemoved(). These will be called by the framework when a new notification comes in or another is dismissed, respectively. The content passed in is a StatusBarNotification instance, which is just a basic wrapper around the original notification with some additional metadata (for example, the package name of the application that posted it and the ID or tag applied). The original notification is also still accessible as a parameter.

In this example, when a notification is added, we simply log the event if the notification came from our application. If a notification is removed, we check whether it was the basic style notification element and, if so, dismiss all the notifications posted from our application that are still active. The getActiveNotifications() method is helpful in obtaining everything currently visible to the user. We can verify which notifications came from us by comparing the package names of each one. When the package matches, we call cancelNotification() with the metadata from the notification element to remove it programmatically. You can also call cancelAllNotifications() to clear the entire window shade without any regard for where the active elements came from.

Listing 7-6 shows the AndroidManifest.xml snippet you will need to add.

Listing 7-6. NotificationListenerService Manifest Element

```xml
<service android:name=".MonitorService"
    android:permission="android.permission.BIND_NOTIFICATION_LISTENER_SERVICE">
    <intent-filter>
        <action android:name="android.service.notification.NotificationListenerService" />
    </intent-filter>
</service>
```

The two required elements here are the action string of the <intent-filter> and the declared permission. The framework will look for both of these when determining which NotificationListenerService elements it can bind to.

7-2. Creating Timed and Periodic Tasks

Problem

Your application needs to run an operation on a timer, such as updating the UI on a scheduled basis.

Solution

(API Level 1)

Use the timed operations provided by Handler. With Handler, operations can efficiently be scheduled to occur at a specific time or after a specified delay.

How It Works

Let's look at an example activity that displays the current time in a TextView. See Listing 7-7.

Listing 7-7. Activity Updated with a Handler

```java
public class TimingActivity extends Activity {

    TextView mClock;
```

```java
@Override
public void onCreate(Bundle savedInstanceState) {
    super.onCreate(savedInstanceState);
    mClock = new TextView(this);
    setContentView(mClock);
}

private Handler mHandler = new Handler();
private Runnable timerTask = new Runnable() {
    @Override
    public void run() {
        Calendar now = Calendar.getInstance();
        mClock.setText(String.format("%02d:%02d:%02d",
                now.get(Calendar.HOUR),
                now.get(Calendar.MINUTE),
                now.get(Calendar.SECOND)) );
        //Schedule the next update in one second
        mHandler.postDelayed(timerTask,1000);
    }
};

@Override
public void onResume() {
    super.onResume();
    mHandler.post(timerTask);
}

@Override
public void onPause() {
    super.onPause();
    mHandler.removeCallbacks(timerTask);
}
}
```

Here we've wrapped up the operation of reading the current time and updating the UI into a Runnable named timerTask, which will be triggered by the Handler that has also been created. When the activity becomes visible, the task is executed as soon as possible with a call to Handler.post(). After the TextView has been updated, the final operation of timerTask is to invoke the Handler to schedule another execution 1 second (1,000 milliseconds) from now by using Handler.postDelayed().

As long as the activity remains uninterrupted, this cycle will continue, with the UI being updated every second. As soon as the activity is paused (the user leaves or something else grabs his or her attention), Handler.removeCallbacks() removes all pending operations and ensures the task will not be called further until the activity becomes visible once more.

> **Tip**   In this example, we are safe to update the UI because the Handler was created on the main thread. A Handler will always execute operations on the thread in which it was created, unless a Looper from another thread is passed explicitly to its constructor. We will see how this can be used for background queues in a later recipe, but it is also worth noting here that you can create a Handler from a background thread that posts to the main thread by passing it the result of Looper.getMainLooper(), which is a static reference to the Looper of the main UI thread.

7-3. Scheduling a Periodic Task

Problem

Your application needs to register to run a task periodically, such as checking a server for updates or reminding the user to do something.

Solution

(API Level 1)

Utilize the AlarmManager to manage and execute your task. AlarmManager is useful for scheduling future single or repeated operations that need to occur even if your application is not running. AlarmManager is handed a PendingIntent to fire whenever an alarm is scheduled. This Intent can point to any system component, such as an Activity, BroadcastReceiver, or Service, that can be executed when the alarm triggers.

It should be noted that this method is best suited to operations that need to occur even when the application code may not be running. The AlarmManager requires too much overhead to be useful for simple timing operations that may be needed while an application is in use. These are better handled using the postAtTime() and postDelayed() methods of a Handler.

How It Works

Let's take a look at how AlarmManager can be used to trigger a BroadcastReceiver on a regular basis. See Listings 7-8 through 7-10.

Listing 7-8. BroadcastReceiver to Be Triggered

```
public class AlarmReceiver extends BroadcastReceiver {
    @Override
    public void onReceive(Context context, Intent intent) {
        //Perform an interesting operation, we'll just display the current time
        Calendar now = Calendar.getInstance();
        DateFormat formatter = SimpleDateFormat.getTimeInstance();
        Toast.makeText(context, formatter.format(now.getTime()),
            Toast.LENGTH_SHORT).show();
    }
}
```

> **Reminder** BroadcastReceiver (AlarmReceiver, in this case) must be declared in the manifest with a `<receiver>` tag in order for AlarmManager to be able to trigger it. Be sure to include one within your `<application>` tag like so:
>
> ```xml
> <application>
> ...
> <receiver android:name=".AlarmReceiver" />
> </application>
> ```

Listing 7-9. res/layout/main.xml

```xml
<?xml version="1.0" encoding="utf-8"?>
<LinearLayout xmlns:android="http://schemas.android.com/apk/res/android"
    android:orientation="vertical"
    android:layout_width="match_parent"
    android:layout_height="match_parent">
    <Button
        android:id="@+id/start"
        android:layout_width="match_parent"
        android:layout_height="wrap_content"
        android:text="Start Alarm" />
    <Button
        android:id="@+id/stop"
        android:layout_width="match_parent"
        android:layout_height="wrap_content"
        android:text="Cancel Alarm" />
</LinearLayout>
```

Listing 7-10. Activity to Register/Unregister Alarms

```java
public class AlarmActivity extends Activity implements View.OnClickListener {

    private PendingIntent mAlarmIntent;

    @Override
    public void onCreate(Bundle savedInstanceState) {
        super.onCreate(savedInstanceState);
        setContentView(R.layout.main);
        //Attach the listener to both buttons
        findViewById(R.id.start).setOnClickListener(this);
        findViewById(R.id.stop).setOnClickListener(this);
        //Create the launch sender
        Intent launchIntent = new Intent(this, AlarmReceiver.class);
        mAlarmIntent = PendingIntent.getBroadcast(this, 0, launchIntent, 0);
    }

    @Override
    public void onClick(View v) {
        AlarmManager manager = (AlarmManager)getSystemService(Context.ALARM_SERVICE);
        long interval = 5*1000; //5 seconds
```

```
    switch(v.getId()) {
    case R.id.start:
        Toast.makeText(this, "Scheduled", Toast.LENGTH_SHORT).show();
        manager.setRepeating(AlarmManager.ELAPSED_REALTIME,
                SystemClock.elapsedRealtime()+interval,
                interval,
                mAlarmIntent);
        break;
    case R.id.stop:
        Toast.makeText(this, "Canceled", Toast.LENGTH_SHORT).show();
        manager.cancel(mAlarmIntent);
        break;
    default:
        break;
    }
  }
}
```

In this example, we have provided a very basic BroadcastReceiver that, when triggered, will simply display the current time as a Toast. That receiver must be registered in the application's manifest with a <receiver> tag. Otherwise, AlarmManager—which is external to your application—will not be aware of how to trigger it. The sample activity presents two buttons: one to begin firing regular alarms, and the other to cancel them.

The operation to trigger is referenced by a PendingIntent, which will be used to both set and cancel the alarms. We create an Intent referencing the application's BroadcastReceiver directly, and then we wrap that Intent inside a PendingIntent obtained with getBroadcast() (because we are creating a reference to a BroadcastReceiver).

> **Reminder**   PendingIntent has the creator methods getActivity() and getService() as well. Be sure to reference the correct application component you are triggering when creating this piece.

When the Start button is pressed, the activity registers a repeating alarm by using AlarmManager.setRepeating(). In addition to PendingIntent, this method takes some parameters to determine when to trigger the alarms. The first parameter defines the alarm type, in terms of the units of time to use and whether the alarm should occur when the device is in sleep mode. In the example, we chose ELAPSED_REALTIME, which indicates a value (in milliseconds) since the last device boot. In addition, there are three other modes that may be used:

- ELAPSED_REALTIME_WAKEUP: The alarm times are referenced to time elapsed and will wake the device to trigger if it is asleep.

- RTC: The alarm times are referenced to UTC time.

- RTC_WAKEUP: The alarm times are referenced to UTC time and will wake the device to trigger if it is asleep. The remaining parameters (respectively) refer to the first time the alarm will trigger and the interval on which it should repeat. Because the chosen alarm type is ELAPSED_REALTIME, the start time must also be relative to elapsed time; SystemClock.elapsedRealtime() provides the current time in this format.

The alarm in the example is registered to trigger 5 seconds after the button is pressed, and then every 5 seconds after that. Every 5 seconds, a Toast will come onscreen with the current time value, even if the application is no longer running or in front of the user. When the user displays the activity and presses the Stop button, any pending alarms matching our PendingIntent are immediately canceled and will stop the flow of Toasts.

A More Precise Example

What if we wanted to schedule an alarm to occur at a specific time? Perhaps once per day at 9:00 AM? Setting AlarmManager with some slightly different parameters could accomplish this. See Listing 7-11.

Listing 7-11. Precision Alarm

```
long oneDay = 24*3600*1000; //24 hours
long firstTime;

//Get a Calendar (defaults to today)
//Set the time to 09:00:00
Calendar startTime = Calendar.getInstance();
startTime.set(Calendar.HOUR_OF_DAY, 9);
startTime.set(Calendar.MINUTE, 0);
startTime.set(Calendar.SECOND, 0);

//Get a Calendar at the current time
Calendar now = Calendar.getInstance();

if(now.before(startTime)) {
    //It's not 9AM yet, start today
    firstTime = startTime.getTimeInMillis();
} else {
    //Start 9AM tomorrow
    startTime.add(Calendar.DATE, 1);
    firstTime = startTime.getTimeInMillis();
}

//Set the alarm
 manager.setRepeating(AlarmManager.RTC_WAKEUP,
                firstTime,
                oneDay,
                mAlarmIntent);
```

This example uses an alarm that is referenced to real time. A determination is made whether the next occurrence of 9:00 AM will be today or tomorrow, and that value is returned as the initial trigger time for the alarm. The calculated value of 24 hours in terms of milliseconds is then passed as the interval so that the alarm triggers once per day from that point forward.

> **Important**   Alarms do not persist through a device reboot. If a device is powered off and then back on, any previously registered alarms must be rescheduled.

7-4. Creating Sticky Operations

Problem

Your application needs to execute one or more background operations that will run to completion even if the user suspends the application.

Solution

(API Level 3)

Create an IntentService to handle the work. IntentService is a wrapper around Android's base service implementation, the key component to doing work in the background without interaction from the user. IntentService queues incoming work (expressed using Intents), processing each request in turn, and then stops itself when the queue is empty.

IntentService also handles creation of the worker thread needed to do the work in the background, so it is not necessary to use AsyncTask or Java threads to ensure that the operation is properly in the background.

This recipe provides an example of using IntentService to create a central manager of background operations. In the example, the manager will be invoked externally with calls to Context.startService(). The manager will queue up all requests received, and process them individually with a call to onHandleIntent().

How It Works

Let's take a look at how to construct a simple IntentService implementation to handle a series of background operations. See Listing 7-12.

Listing 7-12. IntentService Handling Operations

```java
public class OperationsManager extends IntentService {

    public static final String ACTION_EVENT = "ACTION_EVENT";
    public static final String ACTION_WARNING = "ACTION_WARNING";
    public static final String ACTION_ERROR = "ACTION_ERROR";
    public static final String EXTRA_NAME = "eventName";

    private static final String LOGTAG = "EventLogger";

    private IntentFilter matcher;

    public OperationsManager() {
        super("OperationsManager");
        //Create the filter for matching incoming requests
        matcher = new IntentFilter();
        matcher.addAction(ACTION_EVENT);
        matcher.addAction(ACTION_WARNING);
        matcher.addAction(ACTION_ERROR);
    }
```

```java
@Override
protected void onHandleIntent(Intent intent) {
    //Check for a valid request
    if(!matcher.matchAction(intent.getAction())) {
        Toast.makeText(this, "OperationsManager: Invalid Request",
                Toast.LENGTH_SHORT).show();
        return;
    }

    //Handle each request directly in this method. Don't create more threads.
    if(TextUtils.equals(intent.getAction(), ACTION_EVENT)) {
        logEvent(intent.getStringExtra(EXTRA_NAME));
    }
    if(TextUtils.equals(intent.getAction(), ACTION_WARNING)) {
        logWarning(intent.getStringExtra(EXTRA_NAME));
    }
    if(TextUtils.equals(intent.getAction(), ACTION_ERROR)) {
        logError(intent.getStringExtra(EXTRA_NAME));
    }
}

private void logEvent(String name) {
    try {
        //Simulate a long network operation by sleeping
        Thread.sleep(5000);
        Log.i(LOGTAG, name);
    } catch (InterruptedException e) {
        e.printStackTrace();
    }
}

private void logWarning(String name) {
    try {
        //Simulate a long network operation by sleeping
        Thread.sleep(5000);
        Log.w(LOGTAG, name);
    } catch (InterruptedException e) {
        e.printStackTrace();
    }
}

private void logError(String name) {
    try {
        //Simulate a long network operation by sleeping
        Thread.sleep(5000);
        Log.e(LOGTAG, name);
    } catch (InterruptedException e) {
        e.printStackTrace();
    }
}
}
```

IntentService does not have a default constructor (one that takes no parameters), so a custom implementation must implement a constructor that calls through to super with a service name. This name is of little technical importance, as it is useful only for debugging; Android uses the name provided to name the worker thread that it creates.

All requests are processed by the service through the onHandleIntent() method. This method is called on the provided worker thread, so all work should be done directly here; no new threads or operations should be created. When onHandleIntent() returns, this is the signal to the IntentService to begin processing the next request in the queue.

This example provides three logging operations that can be requested using different action strings on the request Intents. For demonstration purposes, each operation writes the provided message out to the device log by using a specific logging level (INFO, WARNING, or ERROR). Note that the message itself is passed as an extra of the request Intent. Use the data and extra fields of each Intent to hold any parameters for the operation, leaving the action field to define the operation type.

The service in the example maintains an IntentFilter, which is used for convenience to determine whether a valid request has been made. All of the valid actions are added to the filter when the service is created, allowing us to call IntentFilter.matchAction() on any incoming request to determine whether it includes an action we can process here.

Listings 7-13 and 7-14 reveal an example including an activity calling in to this service to perform work.

Listing 7-13. AndroidManifest.xml

```xml
<?xml version="1.0" encoding="utf-8"?>
<manifest xmlns:android="http://schemas.android.com/apk/res/android"
    package="com.examples.sticky"
    android:versionCode="1"
    android:versionName="1.0">
    <uses-sdk android:minSdkVersion="3" />

    <application android:icon="@drawable/icon" android:label="@string/app_name">
        <activity android:name=".ReportActivity"
                android:label="@string/app_name">
            <intent-filter>
                <action android:name="android.intent.action.MAIN" />
                <category android:name="android.intent.category.LAUNCHER" />
            </intent-filter>
        </activity>
        <service android:name=".OperationsManager"></service>
    </application>
</manifest>
```

Reminder   The package attribute in **AndroidManifest.xml** must match the package you have chosen for your application; "com.examples.sticky" is simply the chosen package for our example here.

> **Note**   Because `IntentService` is invoked as a service, it must be declared in the application manifest
> with a `<service>` tag.

Listing 7-14. Activity Calling IntentService

```java
public class ReportActivity extends Activity {

    @Override
    public void onCreate(Bundle savedInstanceState) {
        super.onCreate(savedInstanceState);
        logEvent("CREATE");
    }

    @Override
    public void onStart() {
        super.onStart();
        logEvent("START");
    }

    @Override
    public void onResume() {
        super.onResume();
        logEvent("RESUME");
    }

    @Override
    public void onPause() {
        super.onPause();
        logWarning("PAUSE");
    }

    @Override
    public void onStop() {
        super.onStop();
        logWarning("STOP");
    }

    @Override
    public void onDestroy() {
        super.onDestroy();
        logWarning("DESTROY");
    }

    private void logEvent(String event) {
        Intent intent = new Intent(this, OperationsManager.class);
        intent.setAction(OperationsManager.ACTION_EVENT);
        intent.putExtra(OperationsManager.EXTRA_NAME, event);
```

```
        startService(intent);
    }

    private void logWarning(String event) {
        Intent intent = new Intent(this, OperationsManager.class);
        intent.setAction(OperationsManager.ACTION_WARNING);
        intent.putExtra(OperationsManager.EXTRA_NAME, event);

        startService(intent);
    }
}
```

This activity isn't much to look at, as all the interesting events are sent out through the device log instead of to the user interface. Nevertheless, it helps illustrate the queue-processing behavior of the service we created in the previous example. As the activity becomes visible, it will call through all of its normal life-cycle methods, resulting in three requests made of the logging service. As each request is processed, a line will output to the log and the service will move on.

> **Tip**   These log statements are visible through the `logcat` tool provided with the SDK. The `logcat` output from a device or emulator is visible from within most development environments (including Eclipse) or from the command line by typing `adb logcat`.

Notice also that when the service is finished with all three requests, a notification is logged out that the service has been stopped. `IntentServices` are around in memory for only as long as required to complete the job; this is a very useful feature for your services to have, making them good citizens of the system.

Pressing either the HOME or BACK buttons will cause more of the life-cycle methods to generate requests of the service, and the Pause/Stop/Destroy portion calls a separate operation in the service, causing their messages to be logged as warnings; simply setting the action string of the request Intent to a different value controls this.

Notice that messages continue to be output to the log, even after the application is no longer visible (or even if another application is opened instead). This is the power of the Android service component at work. These operations are protected from the system until they are complete, regardless of user behavior.

A Possible Drawback

In each of the operation methods, a 5-second delay has been placed to simulate the time required for an actual request to be made of a remote API or some similar operation. When running this example, it also helps to illustrate that `IntentService` handles all requests sent to it in a serial fashion with a single worker thread. The example queues multiple requests in succession from each life-cycle method; however, the result will still be a log message every 5 seconds, because `IntentService` does not start a new request until the current one is complete (essentially, when `onHandleIntent()` returns).

If your application requires concurrency from sticky background tasks, you may need to create a more customized service implementation that uses a pool of threads to execute work. The beauty of Android being an open source project is that you can go directly to the source code for `IntentService` and use it as a starting point for such an implementation, minimizing the amount of time and custom code required.

7-5. Running Persistent Background Operations

Problem

Your application has a component that must be running in the background indefinitely, performing some operation or monitoring certain events to occur.

Solution

(API Level 1)

Build the component into a service. Services are designed as background components that an application may start and leave running for an indefinite amount of time. Services are also given elevated status above other background processes in terms of protection from being killed in low-memory conditions.

Services may be started and stopped explicitly for operations that do not require a direct connection to another component (like an activity). However, if the application must interact directly with the service, a binding interface is provided to pass data. In these instances, the service may be started and stopped implicitly by the system as is required to fulfill its requested bindings.

The key thing to remember with service implementations is to always be user-friendly. An indefinite operation most likely should not be started unless the user explicitly requests it. The overall application should probably contain an interface or setting that allows the user to control enabling or disabling such a service.

How It Works

Listing 7-15 is an example of a persisted service that is used to track and log the user's location over a certain period.

Listing 7-15. Persistent Tracking Service

```
public class TrackerService extends Service implements LocationListener {

    private static final String LOGTAG = "TrackerService";

    private LocationManager manager;
    private ArrayList<Location> storedLocations;

    private boolean isTracking = false;
```

```java
/* Service Setup Methods */
@Override
public void onCreate() {
    manager = (LocationManager)getSystemService(LOCATION_SERVICE);
    storedLocations = new ArrayList<Location>();
    Log.i(LOGTAG, "Tracking Service Running...");
}

@Override
public void onDestroy() {
    manager.removeUpdates(this);
    Log.i(LOGTAG, "Tracking Service Stopped...");
}

public void startTracking() {
    if(!manager.isProviderEnabled(LocationManager.GPS_PROVIDER)) {
        return;
    }
    Toast.makeText(this, "Starting Tracker", Toast.LENGTH_SHORT).show();
    manager.requestLocationUpdates(LocationManager.GPS_PROVIDER, 30000, 0, this);

    isTracking = true;
}

public void stopTracking() {
    Toast.makeText(this, "Stopping Tracker", Toast.LENGTH_SHORT).show();
    manager.removeUpdates(this);
    isTracking = false;
}

public boolean isTracking() {
    return isTracking;
}

/* Service Access Methods */
public class TrackerBinder extends Binder {
    TrackerService getService() {
        return TrackerService.this;
    }
}

private final IBinder binder = new TrackerBinder();

@Override
public IBinder onBind(Intent intent) {
    return binder;
}

public int getLocationsCount() {
    return storedLocations.size();
}
```

```
public ArrayList<Location> getLocations() {
    return storedLocations;
}

/* LocationListener Methods */
@Override
public void onLocationChanged(Location location) {
    Log.i("TrackerService", "Adding new location");
    storedLocations.add(location);
}

@Override
public void onProviderDisabled(String provider) { }

@Override
public void onProviderEnabled(String provider) { }

@Override
public void onStatusChanged(String provider, int status, Bundle extras) { }
}
```

This service monitors and tracks the updates it receives from the LocationManager. When the service is created, it prepares a blank list of Location items and waits to begin tracking. An external component, such as an activity, can call startTracking() and stopTracking() to enable and disable the flow of location updates to the service. In addition, methods are exposed to access the list of locations that the service has logged.

Because this service requires direct interaction from an activity or other component, a Binder interface is required. The Binder concept can get complex when a service has to communicate across process boundaries, but for instances like this, where everything is local to the same process, a very simple Binder is created with one method, getService(), to return the service instance itself to the caller. We'll look at this in more detail from the activity's perspective in a moment.

When tracking is enabled on the service, it registers for updates with LocationManager, and it stores every update received in its locations list. Notice that requestLocationUpdates() was called with a minimum time of 30 seconds. Because this service is expected to be running for a long time, it is prudent to space out the updates to give the GPS (and consequently the battery) a little rest.

Now let's take a look at a simple activity that allows the user access into this service. See Listings 7-16 through 7-18.

Listing 7-16. AndroidManifest.xml

```xml
<?xml version="1.0" encoding="utf-8"?>
<manifest xmlns:android="http://schemas.android.com/apk/res/android"
    package="com.examples.service"
    android:versionCode="1"
    android:versionName="1.0">
    <uses-sdk android:minSdkVersion="1" />
    <application android:icon="@drawable/icon" android:label="@string/app_name">
        <activity android:name=".ServiceActivity"
                    android:label="@string/app_name">
```

```
            <intent-filter>
                <action android:name="android.intent.action.MAIN" />
                <category android:name="android.intent.category.LAUNCHER" />
            </intent-filter>
        </activity>
        <service android:name=".TrackerService"></service>
    </application>
    <uses-permission android:name="android.permission.ACCESS_FINE_LOCATION"/>
</manifest>
```

Reminder   The service must be declared in the application manifest by using a `<service>` tag so Android knows how and where to call on it. Also, for this example, the permission `android.permission.ACCESS_FINE_LOCATION` is required because we are working with the GPS.

Listing 7-17. res/layout/main.xml

```xml
<?xml version="1.0" encoding="utf-8"?>
<LinearLayout xmlns:android="http://schemas.android.com/apk/res/android"
    android:orientation="vertical"
    android:layout_width="match_parent"
    android:layout_height="match_parent">
    <Button
        android:id="@+id/enable"
        android:layout_width="match_parent"
        android:layout_height="wrap_content"
        android:text="Start Tracking" />
    <Button
        android:id="@+id/disable"
        android:layout_width="match_parent"
        android:layout_height="wrap_content"
        android:text="Stop Tracking" />
    <TextView
        android:id="@+id/status"
        android:layout_width="match_parent"
        android:layout_height="wrap_content" />
</LinearLayout>
```

Listing 7-18. Activity Interacting with Service

```java
public class ServiceActivity extends Activity implements View.OnClickListener {

    Button enableButton, disableButton;
    TextView statusView;

    TrackerService trackerService;
    Intent serviceIntent;

    @Override
    public void onCreate(Bundle savedInstanceState) {
        super.onCreate(savedInstanceState);
```

```java
    setContentView(R.layout.main);
    enableButton = (Button)findViewById(R.id.enable);
    enableButton.setOnClickListener(this);
    disableButton = (Button)findViewById(R.id.disable);
    disableButton.setOnClickListener(this);
    statusView = (TextView)findViewById(R.id.status);

    serviceIntent = new Intent(this, TrackerService.class);
}

@Override
public void onResume() {
    super.onResume();
    //Starting the service makes it stick, regardless of bindings
    startService(serviceIntent);
    //Bind to the service
    bindService(serviceIntent, serviceConnection, Context.BIND_AUTO_CREATE);
}

@Override
public void onPause() {
    super.onPause();
    if(!trackerService.isTracking()) {
        //Stopping the service lets it die once unbound
        stopService(serviceIntent);
    }
    //Unbind from the service
    unbindService(serviceConnection);
}

@Override
public void onClick(View v) {
    switch(v.getId()) {
    case R.id.enable:
        trackerService.startTracking();
        break;
    case R.id.disable:
        trackerService.stopTracking();
        break;
    default:
        break;
    }
    updateStatus();
}

private void updateStatus() {
    if(trackerService.isTracking()) {
        statusView.setText(
            String.format("Tracking enabled. %d locations
                logged.",trackerService.getLocationsCount()));
    } else {
```

```
                statusView.setText("Tracking not currently enabled.");
            }
        }

        private ServiceConnection serviceConnection = new ServiceConnection() {
            public void onServiceConnected(ComponentName className, IBinder service) {
                trackerService = ((TrackerService.TrackerBinder)service).getService();
                updateStatus();
            }

            public void onServiceDisconnected(ComponentName className) {
                trackerService = null;
            }
        };
    }
```

Figure 7-6 displays the basic activity with two buttons for the user to enable and disable location-tracking behavior, and a text display for the current service status.

Figure 7-6. ServiceActivity layout

While the activity is visible, it is bound to the TrackerService. This is done with the help of the ServiceConnection interface, which provides callback methods when the binding and unbinding operations are complete. With the service bound to the activity, you can now make direct calls on all the public methods exposed by the service.

However, bindings alone will not allow the service to run for the long term; accessing the service solely through its Binder interface causes it to be created and destroyed automatically along with the life cycle of this activity. In this case, we want the service to persist beyond when this activity is in memory. In order to accomplish this, the service is explicitly started via startService() before it is bound. There is no harm in sending start commands to a service that is already running, so we can safely do this in onResume() as well.

The service will now continue running in memory, even after the activity unbinds itself. In onPause(), the example always checks whether the user has activated tracking, and if not, it stops the service first. This allows the service to die if it is not required for tracking, which keeps the service from perpetually hanging out in memory if it has no real work to do.

Running this example and pressing the Start Tracking button will spin up the persisted service and the LocationManager. The user may leave the application at this point, and the service will remain running, all the while logging all incoming location updates from the GPS. Upon returning to this application, the user can see that the service is still running, and the current number of stored location points is displayed. Pressing Stop Tracking will end the process and allow the service to die as soon as the user leaves the activity once more.

7-6. Launching Other Applications
Problem

Your application requires a specific function that another application on the device is already programmed to do. Instead of overlapping functionality, you would like to launch the other application for the job instead.

Solution

(API Level 1)

Use an implicit Intent to tell the system what you are looking to do, and determine whether any applications exist to meet the need. Most often, developers use Intents in an explicit fashion to start another activity or service, like so:

```
Intent intent = new Intent(this, NewActivity.class);
startActivity(intent);
```

By declaring the specific component we want to launch, the Intent is very explicit in its delivery. We also have the power to define an Intent in terms of its action, category, data, and type to define a more implicit requirement of what task we want to accomplish.

External applications are always launched within the same Android task as your application when fired in this fashion, so once the operation is complete (or if the user backs out), the user is returned to your application. This keeps the experience seamless, allowing multiple applications to act as one from the user's perspective.

How It Works

When defining Intents in this fashion, it can be unclear what information you must include, because there is no published standard and it is possible for two applications offering the same service (reading a PDF file, for example) to define slightly different filters to listen for incoming Intents. You want to make sure to provide enough information for the system (or the user) to pick the best application to handle the required task.

The core piece of information to define on almost any implicit Intent is the action: a string value that is passed either in the constructor or via `Intent.setAction()`. This value tells Android what you want to do, whether it is to view a piece of content, send a message, select a choice, and so on. From there, the fields provided are scenario specific, and often multiple combinations can arrive at the same result. Let's take a look at some useful examples.

Read a PDF File

Components to display PDF documents are not included in the core SDK, although almost every consumer Android device on the market today ships with a PDF reader application, and many more are available through Google Play. Because of this, it may not make sense to go through the trouble of embedding PDF display capabilities in your application.

Instead, Listing 7-19 illustrates how to find and launch another app to view the PDF.

Listing 7-19. Method to View PDF

```
private void viewPdf(Uri file) {
        Intent intent;
        intent = new Intent(Intent.ACTION_VIEW);
        intent.setDataAndType(file, "application/pdf");
        try {
            startActivity(intent);
        } catch (ActivityNotFoundException e) {
            //No application to view, ask to download one
            AlertDialog.Builder builder = new AlertDialog.Builder(this);
            builder.setTitle("No Application Found");
            builder.setMessage("We could not find an application to view PDFs."
                    +"  Would you like to download one from Android Market?");
            builder.setPositiveButton("Yes, Please",
                new DialogInterface.OnClickListener() {
                @Override
                public void onClick(DialogInterface dialog, int which) {
                    Intent marketIntent = new Intent(Intent.ACTION_VIEW);
                    marketIntent.setData(
```

```
                        Uri.parse("market://details?id=com.adobe.reader"));
                startActivity(marketIntent);
            }
        });
        builder.setNegativeButton("No, Thanks", null);
        builder.create().show();
    }
}
```

This example will open any local PDF file on the device (internal or external storage) by using the best application found. If no application is found on the device to view PDFs, a message will encourage the user to go to Google Play and download one.

The Intent we create for this is constructed with the generic `Intent.ACTION_VIEW` action string, telling the system we want to view the data provided in the Intent. The data file itself and its MIME type are also set to tell the system what kind of data we want to view.

Tip   `Intent.setData()` and `Intent.setType()` clear each other's previous values when used. If you need to set both simultaneously, use `Intent.setDataAndType()`, as in the example.

If `startActivity()` fails with an `ActivityNotFoundException`, it means that no application is installed on the user's device that can view PDFs. We want users to have the full experience, so if this happens, a dialog box indicates the problem and asks whether the user would like to go to Market and get a reader. If the user presses Yes, another implicit Intent will request that Google Play be opened directly to the application page for Adobe Reader, a free application the user may download to view PDF files. We'll discuss the `Uri` scheme used for this Intent in the next recipe.

Notice that the example method takes a `Uri` parameter to the local file. Here is an example of how to retrieve a `Uri` for files located on internal storage:

```
String filename = NAME_OF_YOUR_FILE;
File internalFile = getFileStreamPath(filename);
Uri internal = Uri.fromFile(internalFile);
```

The method `getFileStreamPath()` is called from a `Context`, so if this code is not in an activity, you must have reference to a `Context` object to call on. Here's how to create a `Uri` for files located on external storage:

```
String filename = NAME_OF_YOUR_FILE;
File externalFile = new File(Environment.getExternalStorageDirectory(), filename);
Uri external = Uri.fromFile(externalFile);
```

This same example will work for any other document type as well by simply changing the MIME type attached to the Intent.

Share with Friends

Another popular feature for developers to include in their applications is a method of sharing the application content with others, either through e-mail, text messaging, or prominent social networks. All Android devices include applications for e-mail and text messaging, and most users who wish to share via a social network (for example, Facebook or Twitter) also have those mobile applications on their devices.

As it turns out, this task can also be accomplished using an implicit Intent because most of these applications respond to the `Intent.ACTION_SEND` action string in some way. Listing 7-20 is an example of allowing a user to post to any medium with a single Intent request.

Listing 7-20. Sharing Intent

```
private void shareContent(String update) {
    Intent intent = new Intent(Intent.ACTION_SEND);
    intent.setType("text/plain");
    intent.putExtra(Intent.EXTRA_TEXT, update);
    startActivity(Intent.createChooser(intent, "Share..."));
}
```

Here, we tell the system that we have a piece of text that we would like to send, passed in as an extra. This is a very generic request, and we expect more than one application to be able to handle it. By default, Android will present the user with a list of applications that the user can select to open. In addition, some devices provide the user with a check box to set a selection as a default so the list is never shown again.

We would prefer to have a little more control over this process because we also expect multiple results every time. Therefore, instead of passing the Intent directly to `startActivity()`, we first pass it through `Intent.createChooser()`, which allows us to customize the title and guarantee the selection list will always be displayed.

When the user selects a choice, that specific application will launch with the EXTRA_TEXT prepopulated into the message entry box, ready for sharing!

Use ShareActionProvider

(API Level 14)

Starting with Android 4.0, a new widget was introduced to assist applications in sharing content by using a common mechanism called `ShareActionProvider`. It is designed to be added to an item in the options menu to show up either on the Action Bar or in the overflow. It also has an added feature for the users in that, by default, it ranks the share options it provides by usage. Options that users click most frequently will always be at the top of the list.

Implementing `ShareActionProvider` in a menu is quite simple, and it requires only a few more lines of code than creating the share Intent itself. Listing 7-21 shows how to attach the provider to a menu item.

Listing 7-21. res/menu/options.xml

```
<menu xmlns:android="http://schemas.android.com/apk/res/android">
    <item android:id="@+id/menu_share"
        android:showAsAction="ifRoom"
        android:title="Share"
        android:actionProviderClass="android.widget.ShareActionProvider"/>
</menu>
```

> **Note**   If you do not define your Menu in XML, you can still attach the ShareActionProvider by calling setActionProvider() inside your Java code.

Listing 7-22 shows how to attach the share Intent to the provider widget inside an activity.

Listing 7-22. Providing the Share Intent

```
@Override
public boolean onCreateOptionsMenu(Menu menu) {
    //Inflate the menu
    getMenuInflater().inflate(R.menu.options, menu);

    //Find the item and set the share Intent
    MenuItem item = menu.findItem(R.id.menu_share);
    ShareActionProvider provider = (ShareActionProvider) item.getActionProvider();

    Intent intent = new Intent(Intent.ACTION_SEND);
    intent.setType("text/plain");
    intent.putExtra(Intent.EXTRA_TEXT, update);
    provider.setShareIntent(intent);

    return true;
}
```

And that's it! The provider handles all the user interaction so your application doesn't even need to handle the user selection events for that MenuItem.

7-7. Launching System Applications

Problem

Your application requires a specific function that one of the system applications on the device is already programmed to do. Instead of overlapping functionality, you would like to launch the system application for the job instead.

Solution

(API Level 1)

Use an implicit Intent to tell the system which application you are interested in. Each system application subscribes to a custom Uri scheme that can be inserted as data into an implicit Intent to signify the specific application you need to launch.

External applications are always launched in the same task as your application when fired in this fashion, so once the task is complete (or if the user backs out), the user is returned to your application. This keeps the experience seamless, allowing multiple applications to act as one from the user's perspective.

How It Works

All of the following examples will construct Intents that can be used to launch system applications in various states. Once constructed, you should launch these applications by passing the Intent to startActivity().

Browser

The Browser application may be launched to display a web page or run a web search.

To display a web page, construct and launch the following Intent:

```
Intent pageIntent = new Intent();
pageIntent.setAction(Intent.ACTION_VIEW);
pageIntent.setData(Uri.parse("http://WEB_ADDRESS_TO_VIEW"));

startActivity(pageIntent);
```

This replaces the Uri in the data field with the page you would like to view. To launch a web search inside the Browser, construct and launch the following Intent:

```
Intent searchIntent = new Intent();
searchIntent.setAction(Intent.ACTION_WEB_SEARCH);
searchIntent.putExtra(SearchManager.QUERY, STRING_TO_SEARCH);

startActivity(searchIntent);
```

This places the search query you want to execute as an extra in the Intent.

Phone Dialer

The Dialer application may be launched to place a call to a specific number by using the following Intent:

```
Intent dialIntent = new Intent();
dialIntent.setAction(Intent.ACTION_DIAL);
dialIntent.setData(Uri.Parse("tel:8885551234"));

startActivity(dialIntent);
```

This replaces the phone number in the data Uri with the number to call.

> **Note**   This action just brings up the Dialer; it does not place the call. Intent.ACTION_CALL can be used to place the call directly, although Google discourages using this in most cases. Using ACTION_CALL will also require that the android.permission.CALL_PHONE permission be declared in the manifest.

Maps

The Maps application on the device can be launched to display a location or to provide directions between two points. If you know the latitude and longitude of the location you want to map, then create the following Intent:

```
Intent mapIntent = new Intent();
mapIntent.setAction(Intent.ACTION_VIEW);
mapIntent.setData(Uri.parse("geo:latitude,longitude"));

startActivity(mapIntent);
```

This replaces the coordinates for latitude and longitude of your location. For example, the Uri

```
"geo:37.422,122.084"
```

would map the location of Google's headquarters. If you know the address of the location to display, then create the following Intent:

```
Intent mapIntent = new Intent();
mapIntent.setAction(Intent.ACTION_VIEW);
mapIntent.setData(Uri.parse("geo:0,0?q=ADDRESS"));

startActivity(mapIntent);
```

This inserts the address you would like to map. For example, the Uri

```
"geo:0,0?q=1600 Amphitheatre Parkway, Mountain View, CA 94043"
```

would map the address of Google's headquarters.

> **Tip** The Maps application will also accept a Uri that uses the + character to replace spaces in the Address query. If you are having trouble encoding a string with spaces in it, try replacing them with + instead.

If you would like to display directions between two locations, create the following Intent:

```
Intent mapIntent = new Intent();
mapIntent.setAction(Intent.ACTION_VIEW);
mapIntent.setData(Uri.parse("http://maps.google.com/maps?saddr=lat,lng&daddr=lat,lng"));

startActivity(mapIntent);
```

This inserts the locations for the start and end addresses.

You also can include only one of the parameters if you want to open the Maps application with one address being open-ended. For example, the Uri

```
"http://maps.google.com/maps?&daddr=37.422,122.084"
```

would display the Maps application with the destination location prepopulated, but it would allow users to enter their own start address.

E-mail

Any e-mail application on the device can be launched into compose mode by using the following Intent:

```
Intent mailIntent = new Intent();
mailIntent.setAction(Intent.ACTION_SEND);
mailIntent.setType("message/rfc822");
mailIntent.putExtra(Intent.EXTRA_EMAIL, new String[] {"recipient@gmail.com"});
mailIntent.putExtra(Intent.EXTRA_CC, new String[] {"carbon@gmail.com"});
mailIntent.putExtra(Intent.EXTRA_BCC, new String[] {"blind@gmail.com"});
mailIntent.putExtra(Intent.EXTRA_SUBJECT, "Email Subject");
mailIntent.putExtra(Intent.EXTRA_TEXT, "Body Text");
mailIntent.putExtra(Intent.EXTRA_STREAM, URI_TO_FILE);

startActivity(mailIntent);
```

In this scenario, the action and type fields are the only required pieces to bring up a blank e-mail message. All the remaining extras prepopulate specific fields of the e-mail message. Notice that EXTRA_EMAIL (which fills the To field), EXTRA_CC, and EXTRA_BCC are passed string arrays, even if there is only one recipient to be placed there. File attachments may also be specified in the Intent by using EXTRA_STREAM. The value passed here should be a Uri pointing to the local file to be attached.

If you need to attach more than one file to an e-mail, the requirements change slightly to the following:

```
Intent mailIntent = new Intent();
mailIntent.setAction(Intent.ACTION_SEND_MULTIPLE);
mailIntent.setType("message/rfc822");
mailIntent.putExtra(Intent.EXTRA_EMAIL, new String[] {"recipient@gmail.com"});
mailIntent.putExtra(Intent.EXTRA_CC, new String[] {"carbon@gmail.com"});
mailIntent.putExtra(Intent.EXTRA_BCC, new String[] {"blind@gmail.com"});
mailIntent.putExtra(Intent.EXTRA_SUBJECT, "Email Subject");
mailIntent.putExtra(Intent.EXTRA_TEXT, "Body Text");

ArrayList<Uri> files = new ArrayList<Uri>();
files.add(URI_TO_FIRST_FILE);
files.add(URI_TO_SECOND_FILE);
//...Repeat add() as often as necessary to add all the files you need
mailIntent.putParcelableArrayListExtra(Intent.EXTRA_STREAM, files);

startActivity(mailIntent);
```

Notice that the Intent's action string is now ACTION_SEND_MULTIPLE. All the primary fields remain the same as before, except for the data that gets added as the EXTRA_STREAM. This example creates a list of Uri elements pointing to the files you want to attach and adds them by using putParcelableArrayListExtra().

It is not uncommon for users to have multiple applications on their devices that can handle this content, so it is usually prudent to wrap either of these constructed Intents with Intent.createChooser() before passing it on to startActivity().

SMS (Messages)

The Messages application can be launched into compose mode for a new SMS message by using the following Intent:

```
Intent smsIntent = new Intent();
smsIntent.setAction(Intent.ACTION_VIEW);
smsIntent.setType("vnd.android-dir/mms-sms");
smsIntent.putExtra("address", "8885551234");
smsIntent.putExtra("sms_body", "Body Text");

startActivity(smsIntent);
```

As with composing e-mail, you must set the action and type at a minimum to launch the application with a blank message. Including the address and sms_body extras allows the application to prepopulate the recipient (address) and body text (sms_body) of the message.

Neither of these keys has a constant defined in the Android framework, which means that they are subject to change in the future. However, as of this writing, the keys behave as expected on all versions of Android.

Contact Picker

An application may launch the default contact picker, enabling a selection from the user's Contacts database, by using the following Intent:

```
static final int REQUEST_PICK = 100;

Intent pickIntent = new Intent();
pickIntent.setAction(Intent.ACTION_PICK);
pickIntent.setData(URI_TO_CONTACT_TABLE);

startActivityForResult(pickIntent, REQUEST_PICK);
```

This Intent requires the `CONTENT_URI` of the Contacts table you are interested in to be passed in the data field. Because of the major changes to the Contacts API in API Level 5 (Android 2.0) and later, this may not be the same `Uri` if you are supporting versions across that boundary.

For example, to pick a person from the contacts list on a device previous to 2.0, we would pass

```
android.provider.Contacts.People.CONTENT_URI
```

However, in 2.0 and later, similar data would be gathered by passing

```
android.provider.ContactsContract.Contacts.CONTENT_URI
```

Be sure to consult the API documentation with regards to the contact data you need to access. This activity is also designed to return a `Uri` representing the selection the user made, so you will want to launch this by using `startActivityForResult()`.

Google Play

Google Play can be launched from within an application to display a specific application's details page or to run a search for specific keywords. To launch a specific application's page, use the following Intent:

```
Intent marketIntent = new Intent();
marketIntent.setAction(Intent.ACTION_VIEW);
marketIntent.setData(Uri.parse("market://details?id=PACKAGE_NAME_HERE"));

startActivity(marketIntent);
```

This inserts the unique package name (such as `com.adobe.reader`) of the application you want to display. If you would like to open Google Play with a search query, use this Intent:

```
Intent marketIntent = new Intent();
marketIntent.setAction(Intent.ACTION_VIEW);
marketIntent.setData(Uri.parse("market://search?q=SEARCH_QUERY"));

startActivity(marketIntent);
```

This will insert the query string you would like to search on. The search query itself can take one of three main forms:

- q=<simple text string here>: In this case, the search will be a keyword-style search of the market.

- q=pname:<package name here>: In this case, the package names will be searched, and only exact matches will be returned.

- q=pub:<developer name here>: In this case, the developer name field will be searched, and only exact matches will be returned.

7-8. Letting Other Applications Launch Your Application

Problem

You've created an application that is absolutely the best at doing a specific task, and you would like to expose an interface for other applications on the device to be able to run your application.

Solution

(API Level 1)

Create an IntentFilter on the activity or service you would like to expose. Then publicly document the actions, data types, and extras that are required to access it properly. Recall that the action, category, and data/type of an Intent can all be used as criteria to match requests to your application. Any additional required or optional parameters should be passed in as extras.

How It Works

Let's say you have created an application that includes an activity to play a video and will marquee the video's title at the top of the screen during playback. You want to allow other applications to play video using your application, so we need to define a useful Intent structure for applications to pass in the required data and then create an IntentFilter on the activity in the application's manifest to match.

This hypothetical activity requires two pieces of data to do its job:

- The Uri of a video, either local or remote
- A string representing the video's title

If the application specializes in a certain type of video, we could define that a generic action (such as ACTION_VIEW) be used and filter more specifically on the data type of the video content we want to handle. Listing 7-23 is an example of how the activity would be defined in the manifest to filter Intents in this manner.

Listing 7-23. AndroidManifest.xml <activity> Element with Data Type Filter

```
<activity android:name=".PlayerActivity">
    <intent-filter>
    <action android:name="android.intent.action.VIEW" />
    <category android:name="android.intent.category.DEFAULT" />
    <data android:mimeType="video/h264" />
    </intent-filter>
</activity>
```

This filter will match any Intent with Uri data that is either explicitly declared as an H.264 video clip or is determined to be H.264 upon inspecting the Uri file. An external application would then be able to call on this activity to play a video by using the following lines of code:

```
Uri videoFile = A_URI_OF_VIDEO_CONTENT;
Intent playIntent = new Intent(Intent.ACTION_VIEW);
playIntent.setDataAndType(videoFile, "video/h264");
playIntent.putExtra(Intent.EXTRA_TITLE, "My Video");
startActivity(playIntent);
```

In some cases, it may be more useful for an external application to directly reference this player as the target, regardless of the type of video they want to pass in. In this case, we would create a unique custom action string for Intents to implement. The filter attached to the activity in the manifest would then need to match only the custom action string. See Listing 7-24.

Listing 7-24. AndroidManifest.xml <activity> Element with Custom Action Filter

```
<activity android:name=".PlayerActivity">
    <intent-filter>
    <action android:name="com.examples.myplayer.PLAY" />
    <category android:name="android.intent.category.DEFAULT" />
    </intent-filter>
</activity>
```

An external application could call on this activity to play a video by using the following code:

```
Uri videoFile = A_URI_OF_VIDEO_CONTENT;
Intent playIntent = new Intent("com.examples.myplayer.PLAY");
playIntent.setData(videoFile);
playIntent.putExtra(Intent.EXTRA_TITLE, "My Video");
startActivity(playIntent);
```

Processing a Successful Launch

Regardless of how the Intent is matched to the activity, once it is launched, we want to inspect the incoming Intent for the two pieces of data the activity needs to complete its intended purpose. See Listing 7-25.

Listing 7-25. Activity Inspecting Intent

```java
public class PlayerActivity extends Activity {

    public static final String ACTION_PLAY = "com.examples.myplayer.PLAY";

    @Override
    public void onCreate(Bundle savedInstanceState) {
        super.onCreate(savedInstanceState);
        setContentView(R.layout.main);

        //Inspect the Intent that launched us
        Intent incoming = getIntent();
        //Get the video URI from the data field
        Uri videoUri = incoming.getData();
        //Get the optional title extra, if it exists
        String title;
        if(incoming.hasExtra(Intent.EXTRA_TITLE)) {
            title = incoming.getStringExtra(Intent.EXTRA_TITLE);
        } else {
            title = "";
        }

        /* Begin playing the video and displaying the title */
    }

    /* Remainder of the Activity Code */

}
```

When the activity is launched, the calling Intent can be retrieved with `Activity.getIntent()`. Because the `Uri` for the video content is passed in the data field of the Intent, it is unpacked by calling `Intent.getData()`. The video's title is an optional value for calling Intents, so we check the extras bundle to first see whether the caller decided to pass it in; if it exists, that value is unpacked from the Intent as well.

Notice that the `PlayerActivity` in this example did define the custom action string as a constant, but it was not referenced in the sample Intent we constructed to launch the activity. Since this call is coming from an external application, it does not have access to the shared public constants defined in this application.

For this reason, it is also a good idea to reuse the Intent extra keys already in the SDK whenever possible, as opposed to defining new constants. In this example, we chose the standard `Intent.EXTRA_TITLE` to define the optional extra to be passed instead of creating a custom key for this value.

7-9. Interacting with Contacts

Problem

Your application needs to interact directly with the `ContentProvider` exposed by Android to the user's contacts to add, view, change, or remove information from the database.

Solution

(API Level 5)

Use the interface exposed by ContactsContract to access the data. ContactsContract is a vast ContentProvider API that attempts to aggregate the contact information stored in the system from multiple user accounts into a single data store. The result is a maze of Uris, tables, and columns, from which data may be accessed and modified.

The Contact structure is a hierarchy with three tiers: Contacts, RawContacts, and Data:

- A Contact conceptually represents a person, and it is an aggregation of all RawContacts believed by Android to represent that same person.

- RawContacts represents a collection of data stored in the device from a specific device account, such as the user's e-mail address book or Facebook account.

- Data elements are the specific pieces of information attached to RawContacts, such as an e-mail address, phone number, or postal address.

The complete API has too many combinations and options for us to cover them all here, so consult the SDK documentation for all possibilities. We will investigate how to construct the basic building blocks for performing queries and making changes to the Contacts data set.

How It Works

The Android Contacts API boils down to a complex database with multiple tables and joins. Therefore, the methods for accessing the data are no different than those used to access any other SQLite database from an application.

Listing/Viewing Contacts

Let's look at an example activity that lists all contact entries in the database and that displays more detail when an item is selected. See Listing 7-26.

> **Important**   In order to display information from the Contacts API in your application, you will need to declare `android.permission.READ_CONTACTS` in the application manifest.

Listing 7-26. Activity Displaying Contacts

```
public class ContactsActivity extends FragmentActivity {

    private static final int ROOT_ID = 100;

    @Override
    protected void onCreate(Bundle savedInstanceState) {
        super.onCreate(savedInstanceState);
        FrameLayout rootView = new FrameLayout(this);
        rootView.setId(ROOT_ID);
```

```java
        setContentView(rootView);

        //Create and add a new list fragment
        getSupportFragmentManager().beginTransaction()
            .add(ROOT_ID, ContactsFragment.newInstance())
            .commit();
    }

    public static class ContactsFragment extends ListFragment
            implements AdapterView.OnItemClickListener, LoaderManager.LoaderCallbacks<Cursor> {

        public static ContactsFragment newInstance() {
            return new ContactsFragment();
        }

        private SimpleCursorAdapter mAdapter;

        @Override
        public void onActivityCreated(Bundle savedInstanceState) {
            super.onActivityCreated(savedInstanceState);

            // Display all contacts in a ListView
            mAdapter = new SimpleCursorAdapter(getActivity(),
                    android.R.layout.simple_list_item_1, null,
                    new String[] { ContactsContract.Contacts.DISPLAY_NAME },
                    new int[] { android.R.id.text1 },
                    0);
            setListAdapter(mAdapter);
            // Listen for item selections
            getListView().setOnItemClickListener(this);

            getLoaderManager().initLoader(0, null, this);
        }

        @Override
        public Loader<Cursor> onCreateLoader(int id, Bundle args) {
            // Return all contacts, ordered by name
            String[] projection = new String[] {
                    ContactsContract.Contacts._ID,
                    ContactsContract.Contacts.DISPLAY_NAME
            };

            return new CursorLoader(getActivity(),
                    ContactsContract.Contacts.CONTENT_URI,
                    projection, null, null,
                    ContactsContract.Contacts.DISPLAY_NAME);
        }

        @Override
        public void onLoadFinished(Loader<Cursor> loader, Cursor data) {
            mAdapter.swapCursor(data);
        }
```

```java
@Override
public void onLoaderReset(Loader<Cursor> loader) {
    mAdapter.swapCursor(null);
}

@Override
public void onItemClick(AdapterView<?> parent, View v,
        int position, long id) {
    final Cursor contacts = mAdapter.getCursor();
    if (contacts.moveToPosition(position)) {
        int selectedId = contacts.getInt(0); // _ID column
        // Gather email data from email table
        Cursor email = getActivity().getContentResolver()
                .query(ContactsContract.CommonDataKinds.Email.CONTENT_URI,
                        new String[] {ContactsContract.CommonDataKinds.Email.DATA},
                        ContactsContract.Data.CONTACT_ID
                                + " = " + selectedId,
                        null, null);
        // Gather phone data from phone table
        Cursor phone = getActivity().getContentResolver()
                .query(ContactsContract.CommonDataKinds.Phone.CONTENT_URI,
                        new String[] {ContactsContract.CommonDataKinds.Phone.NUMBER},
                        ContactsContract.Data.CONTACT_ID
                                + " = " + selectedId,
                        null, null);
        // Gather addresses from address table
        Cursor address = getActivity().getContentResolver()
                .query(ContactsContract.CommonDataKinds.StructuredPostal.CONTENT_URI,
                        new String[] {ContactsContract.CommonDataKinds
                                .StructuredPostal.FORMATTED_ADDRESS},
                        ContactsContract.Data.CONTACT_ID
                                + " = " + selectedId,
                        null, null);

        // Build the dialog message
        StringBuilder sb = new StringBuilder();
        sb.append(email.getCount() + " Emails\n");
        if (email.moveToFirst()) {
            do {
                sb.append("Email: " + email.getString(0));
                sb.append('\n');
            } while (email.moveToNext());
            sb.append('\n');
        }
        sb.append(phone.getCount() + " Phone Numbers\n");
        if (phone.moveToFirst()) {
            do {
                sb.append("Phone: " + phone.getString(0));
                sb.append('\n');
            } while (phone.moveToNext());
            sb.append('\n');
        }
```

```
                    sb.append(address.getCount() + " Addresses\n");
                    if (address.moveToFirst()) {
                        do {
                            sb.append("Address:\n"
                                    + address.getString(0));
                        } while (address.moveToNext());
                        sb.append('\n');
                    }

                    AlertDialog.Builder builder = new AlertDialog.Builder(getActivity());
                    builder.setTitle(contacts.getString(1)); // Display name
                    builder.setMessage(sb.toString());
                    builder.setPositiveButton("OK", null);
                    builder.create().show();

                    // Finish temporary cursors
                    email.close();
                    phone.close();
                    address.close();
                }
            }
        }
    }
```

As you can see, referencing all the tables and columns in this API can result in very verbose code. All of the references to Uri elements, tables, and columns in this example are inner classes stemming off of ContactsContract. It is important to verify when interacting with the Contacts API that you are referencing the proper classes, as any Contacts classes not stemming from ContactsContract are deprecated and incompatible.

When the fragment containing the UI for the activity is created, we construct a simple query on the core Contacts table through a CursorLoader referencing Contacts.CONTENT_URI, requesting only the columns we need to wrap the cursor in a ListAdapter. The resulting cursor is displayed in a list on the user interface. The example leverages the convenience behavior of ListFragment to provide a ListView as the content view so that we do not have to manage these components.

At this point, the user can scroll through all the contact entries on the device, and can tap one to get more information. When a list item is selected, the ID value of that particular contact is recorded and the application goes out to the other ContactsContract.Data tables to gather more-detailed information. Notice that the information for this single contact is spread across multiple tables (e-mails in an e-mail table, phone numbers in a phone table, and so on), requiring multiple queries to obtain.

Each CommonDataKinds table has a unique CONTENT_URI for the query to reference, as well as a unique set of column aliases for requesting the data. All of the rows in these data tables are linked to the specific contact through the Data.CONTACT_ID, so each cursor asks to return only rows where the values match.

With all the data collected for the selected contact, we iterate through the results to display in a dialog to the user. Because the data in these tables are an aggregation of multiple sources, it is not uncommon for all of these queries to return multiple results. With each cursor, we display the number of results, and then append each value included. When all the data is composed, the dialog is created and shown to the user.

As a final step, all temporary and unmanaged cursors are closed as soon as they are no longer required.

Running the Application

The first thing that you may notice when running this application on a device that has any number of accounts set up is that the list seems insurmountably long, certainly much longer than what shows up when running the Contacts application bundled with the device. The Contacts API allows for the storage of grouped entries that may be hidden from the user and are used for internal purposes. Gmail often uses this to store incoming e-mail addresses for quick access, even if an address is not associated with a true contact.

In the next example, we will show how to filter this list, but for now marvel at the amount of data truly stored in the Contacts table.

Changing/Adding Contacts

Now let's look at an example activity that manipulates the data for a specific contact. See Listing 7-27.

Listing 7-27. Activity Writing to Contacts API

```
public class ContactsEditActivity extends FragmentActivity {

    private static final String TEST_EMAIL = "tester@email.com";
    private static final int ROOT_ID = 100;

    @Override
    protected void onCreate(Bundle savedInstanceState) {
        super.onCreate(savedInstanceState);
        FrameLayout rootView = new FrameLayout(this);
        rootView.setId(ROOT_ID);

        setContentView(rootView);

        //Create and add a new list fragment
        getSupportFragmentManager().beginTransaction()
            .add(ROOT_ID, ContactsEditFragment.newInstance())
            .commit();
    }

    public static class ContactsEditFragment extends ListFragment implements
            AdapterView.OnItemClickListener,
            DialogInterface.OnClickListener,
            LoaderManager.LoaderCallbacks<Cursor> {

        public static ContactsEditFragment newInstance() {
            return new ContactsEditFragment();
        }

        private SimpleCursorAdapter mAdapter;
        private Cursor mEmail;
        private int selectedContactId;
```

```java
@Override
public void onActivityCreated(Bundle savedInstanceState) {
    super.onActivityCreated(savedInstanceState);

    // Display all contacts in a ListView
    mAdapter = new SimpleCursorAdapter(getActivity(),
            android.R.layout.simple_list_item_1, null,
            new String[] { ContactsContract.Contacts.DISPLAY_NAME },
            new int[] { android.R.id.text1 },
            0);
    setListAdapter(mAdapter);
    // Listen for item selections
    getListView().setOnItemClickListener(this);

    getLoaderManager().initLoader(0, null, this);
}

@Override
public Loader<Cursor> onCreateLoader(int id, Bundle args) {
    // Return all contacts, ordered by name
    String[] projection = new String[] { ContactsContract.Contacts._ID,
            ContactsContract.Contacts.DISPLAY_NAME };
    //List only contacts visible to the user
    return new CursorLoader(getActivity(),
            ContactsContract.Contacts.CONTENT_URI,
            projection, ContactsContract.Contacts.IN_VISIBLE_GROUP+" = 1",
            null,
            ContactsContract.Contacts.DISPLAY_NAME);
}

@Override
public void onLoadFinished(Loader<Cursor> loader, Cursor data) {
    mAdapter.swapCursor(data);
}

@Override
public void onLoaderReset(Loader<Cursor> loader) {
    mAdapter.swapCursor(null);
}

@Override
public void onItemClick(AdapterView<?> parent, View v, int position, long id) {
    final Cursor contacts = mAdapter.getCursor();
    if (contacts.moveToPosition(position)) {
        selectedContactId = contacts.getInt(0); // _ID column
        // Gather email data from email table
        String[] projection = new String[] {
                ContactsContract.Data._ID,
                ContactsContract.CommonDataKinds.Email.DATA };
```

```java
        mEmail = getActivity().getContentResolver().query(
                ContactsContract.CommonDataKinds.Email.CONTENT_URI,
                projection,
                ContactsContract.Data.CONTACT_ID + " = " + selectedContactId,
                null,
                null);

        AlertDialog.Builder builder = new AlertDialog.Builder(getActivity());
        builder.setTitle("Email Addresses");
        builder.setCursor(mEmail, this, ContactsContract.CommonDataKinds.Email.DATA);
        builder.setPositiveButton("Add", this);
        builder.setNegativeButton("Cancel", null);
        builder.create().show();
    }
}

@Override
public void onClick(DialogInterface dialog, int which) {
    //Data must be associated with a RAW contact, retrieve the first raw ID
    Cursor raw = getActivity().getContentResolver().query(
            ContactsContract.RawContacts.CONTENT_URI,
            new String[] { ContactsContract.Contacts._ID },
            ContactsContract.Data.CONTACT_ID + " = " + selectedContactId, null, null);
    if(!raw.moveToFirst()) {
        return;
    }

    int rawContactId = raw.getInt(0);
    ContentValues values = new ContentValues();
    switch(which) {
        case DialogInterface.BUTTON_POSITIVE:
            //User wants to add a new email
            values.put(ContactsContract.CommonDataKinds.Email.RAW_CONTACT_ID, rawContactId);
            values.put(ContactsContract.Data.MIMETYPE, ContactsContract
                    .CommonDataKinds.Email.CONTENT_ITEM_TYPE);
            values.put(ContactsContract.CommonDataKinds.Email.DATA, TEST_EMAIL);
            values.put(ContactsContract.CommonDataKinds.Email.TYPE,
                    ContactsContract.CommonDataKinds.Email.TYPE_OTHER);
            getActivity().getContentResolver()
                    .insert(ContactsContract.Data.CONTENT_URI, values);
            break;
        default:
            //User wants to edit selection
            values.put(ContactsContract.CommonDataKinds.Email.DATA, TEST_EMAIL);
            values.put(ContactsContract.CommonDataKinds.Email.TYPE,
                    ContactsContract.CommonDataKinds.Email.TYPE_OTHER);
            getActivity().getContentResolver()
                    .update(ContactsContract.Data.CONTENT_URI, values,
                            ContactsContract.Data._ID+" = "+mEmail.getInt(0), null);
            break;
    }
```

```
            //Don't need the email cursor anymore
            mEmail.close();
        }
    }
}
```

> **Important**   In order to interact with the Contacts API in your application, you must declare `android.`
> `permission.READ_CONTACTS` and `android.permission.WRITE_CONTACTS` in the application manifest.

In this example, we start out as before, performing a query for all entries in the Contacts database. This time, we provide a single selection criterion:

`ContactsContract.Contacts.IN_VISIBLE_GROUP+" = 1"`

The effect of this line is to limit the returned entries to only those that are visible to the user through the Contacts user interface. This will (drastically, in some cases) reduce the size of the list displayed in the activity and will make it more closely match the list displayed in the Contacts application.

When the user selects a contact from this list, a dialog is displayed with a list of all the e-mail entries attached to that contact. If a specific address is selected from the list, that entry is edited; if the Add button is pressed, a new e-mail address entry is added. For the purposes of simplifying the example, we do not provide an interface to enter a new e-mail address. Instead, a constant value is inserted, either as a new record or as an update to the selected one.

Data elements, such as e-mail addresses, can be associated only with a `RawContact`. Therefore, when we want to add a new e-mail address, we must obtain the ID of one of the `RawContacts` represented by the higher-level contact that the user selected. For the purposes of the example, we aren't terribly interested in which one, so we retrieve the ID of the first `RawContact` that matches. This value is required only for doing an insert, because the update references the distinct row ID of the e-mail record already present in the table.

The `Uri` provided in `CommonDataKinds` that was used as an alias to read this data cannot be used to make updates and changes. Inserts and updates must be called directly on the `ContactsContract.Data Uri`. What this means (besides referencing a different `Uri` in the operation method) is that an extra piece of metadata, the `MIMETYPE`, must also be specified. Without setting the `MIMETYPE` field for inserted data, subsequent queries made may not recognize it as a contact's e-mail address.

Aggregating at Work

Because this example updates records by adding or editing e-mail addresses with the same value, it offers a unique opportunity to see Android's aggregation operations in real time. As you run this example application, you may notice that adding or editing contacts to give them the same e-mail address often triggers Android to start thinking that previously separate contacts are now the same people. Even in this sample application, as the managed query attached to the core Contacts table updates, notice that certain contacts will disappear as they become aggregated together.

> **Note**   Contact aggregation behavior is not implemented fully on the Android emulator. To see this effect in full, you will need to run the code on a real device.

Maintaining a Reference

The Android Contacts API introduces one more concept that can be important, depending on the scope of the application. Because of this aggregation process that occurs, the distinct row ID that refers to a contact becomes quite volatile; a certain contact may receive a new _ID when it is aggregated together with another one.

If your application requires a long-standing reference to a specific contact, it is recommended that your application persist the `ContactsContract.Contacts.LOOKUP_KEY` instead of the row ID. When querying for a contact by using this key, a special `Uri` is also provided as the `ContactsContract.Contacts.CONTENT_LOOKUP_URI`. Using these values to query records over the long term will protect your application from getting confused by the automatic aggregation process.

7-10. Reading Device Media and Documents
Problem

Your application needs to import a user-selected document item (such as a text file, audio, video, or image) for display or playback.

Solution

(API Level 1)

Use an implicit Intent targeted with `Intent.ACTION_GET_CONTENT` to bring up a picker interface from a specific application. Firing this Intent with a matching content type for the media of interest (audio, video, or image are the most common) will present the user with a picker interface to select an item, and the Intent result will include a content `Uri` pointing to the selection the user made.

(API Level 19)

Use an implicit Intent targeted with `Intent.ACTION_OPEN_DOCUMENT` to bring up the system's document picker interface. This is a single common interface where all applications that support the requested content type will list the items the user may select. The content that populates this interface comes from applications that expose `DocumentProvider` for the requested type. These provider elements can come from the system or other applications. We will look at how to create one of your own later in this chapter.

> **Tip**   ACTION_GET_CONTENT can still be used with API Level 19+, and it will launch the standard document picker into a compatibility mode that includes the newer integrated providers along with the options to pick a single application's picker interface.

How It Works

Let's take a look at this technique used in the context of an example activity. See Listings 7-28 and 7-29.

Listing 7-28. res/layout/main.xml

```xml
<?xml version="1.0" encoding="utf-8"?>
<LinearLayout xmlns:android="http://schemas.android.com/apk/res/android"
    android:orientation="vertical"
    android:layout_width="match_parent"
    android:layout_height="match_parent">
    <Button
        android:id="@+id/imageButton"
        android:layout_width="match_parent"
        android:layout_height="wrap_content"
        android:text="Images" />
    <Button
        android:id="@+id/videoButton"
        android:layout_width="match_parent"
        android:layout_height="wrap_content"
        android:text="Video" />
    <Button
        android:id="@+id/audioButton"
        android:layout_width="match_parent"
        android:layout_height="wrap_content"
        android:text="Audio" />
</LinearLayout>
```

Listing 7-29. Activity to Pick Media

```java
public class MediaActivity extends Activity implements View.OnClickListener {

    private static final int REQUEST_AUDIO = 1;
    private static final int REQUEST_VIDEO = 2;
    private static final int REQUEST_IMAGE = 3;

    @Override
    public void onCreate(Bundle savedInstanceState) {
        super.onCreate(savedInstanceState);
        setContentView(R.layout.main);

        Button images = (Button)findViewById(R.id.imageButton);
        images.setOnClickListener(this);
```

```java
        Button videos = (Button)findViewById(R.id.videoButton);
        videos.setOnClickListener(this);
        Button audio = (Button)findViewById(R.id.audioButton);
        audio.setOnClickListener(this);

    }

    @Override
    protected void onActivityResult(int requestCode, int resultCode, Intent data) {

        if(resultCode == Activity.RESULT_OK) {
            //Uri to user selection returned in the Intent
            Uri selectedContent = data.getData();

            if(requestCode == REQUEST_IMAGE) {
                //Pass an InputStream to BitmapFactory
            }
            if(requestCode == REQUEST_VIDEO) {
                //Pass the Uri or a FileDescriptor to MediaPlayer
            }
            if(requestCode == REQUEST_AUDIO) {
                //Pass the Uri or a FileDescriptor to MediaPlayer
            }
        }
    }

    @Override
    public void onClick(View v) {
        Intent intent = new Intent();
        //Use the proper Intent action
        if (Build.VERSION.SDK_INT >= Build.VERSION_CODES.KITKAT) {
            intent.setAction(Intent.ACTION_OPEN_DOCUMENT);
        } else {
            intent.setAction(Intent.ACTION_GET_CONTENT);
        }
        //Only return files to which we can open a stream
        intent.addCategory(Intent.CATEGORY_OPENABLE);

        //Set correct MIME type and launch
        switch(v.getId()) {
        case R.id.imageButton:
            intent.setType("image/*");
            startActivityForResult(intent, REQUEST_IMAGE);
            return;
        case R.id.videoButton:
            intent.setType("video/*");
            startActivityForResult(intent, REQUEST_VIDEO);
            return;
```

```
        case R.id.audioButton:
            intent.setType("audio/*");
            startActivityForResult(intent, REQUEST_AUDIO);
            return;
        default:
            return;
        }
    }
}
```

This example has three buttons for the user to press, each targeting a specific type of media. When the user presses any one of these buttons, an Intent with the appropriate action for the platform level is fired to the system. On devices running 4.4 and later, this will display the system document picker. Previous devices will launch the proper picker activity from the necessary application, showing a chooser if multiple applications can handle the content type. We have also included CATEGORY_OPENABLE to this Intent, which indicates to the system that only items our application can open a stream to will be displayed in the picker.

If the user selects a valid item, a content Uri pointing to that item is returned in the result Intent with a status of RESULT_OK. If the user cancels or otherwise backs out of the picker, the status will be RESULT_CANCELED and the Intent's data field will be null.

With the Uri of the media received, the application is now free to play or display the content as deemed appropriate. Classes such as MediaPlayer and VideoView will take a Uri directly to play media content, while most others will take either an InputStream or a FileDescriptor reference. Both of these can be obtained from the Uri by using ContentResolver.openInputStream() and ContentResolver.openFileDescriptor(), respectively.

7-11. Saving Device Media and Documents
Problem

Your application would like to create new documents or media and insert them into the device's global providers so that they are visible to all applications.

Solution

(API Level 1)

Utilize the ContentProvider interface exposed by MediaStore to perform inserts or media content. In addition to the media content itself, this interface allows you to insert metadata to tag each item, such as a title, description, or time created. The result of the ContentProvider insert operation is a Uri that the application may use as a destination for the new media.

(API Level 19)

On Android 4.4+ devices, we can also trigger an implicit Intent targeted with Intent.ACTION_CREATE_ DOCUMENT to save a new document in any of the device's registered DocumentProvider instances. This can be any type of document content, including (but not restricted to) media files. However, it is not meant to supersede MediaStore, which is still the best method for saving directly to the system's core ContentProvider. If you instead need to involve the user more directly in saving the content (including media), the document framework is a better path here.

How It Works

Let's take a look at an example of inserting an image or video clip into MediaStore. See Listings 7-30 and 7-31.

Listing 7-30. res/layout/save.xml

```xml
<?xml version="1.0" encoding="utf-8"?>
<LinearLayout xmlns:android="http://schemas.android.com/apk/res/android"
    android:layout_width="fill_parent"
    android:layout_height="fill_parent"
    android:orientation="vertical" >
    <Button
        android:id="@+id/imageButton"
        android:layout_width="fill_parent"
        android:layout_height="wrap_content"
        android:text="Images" />
    <Button
        android:id="@+id/videoButton"
        android:layout_width="fill_parent"
        android:layout_height="wrap_content"
        android:text="Video" />
    <Button
        android:id="@+id/textButton"
        android:layout_width="fill_parent"
        android:layout_height="wrap_content"
        android:text="Text Document" />

</LinearLayout>
```

Listing 7-31. Activity Saving Data in the MediaStore

```java
public class StoreActivity extends Activity implements View.OnClickListener {

    private static final int REQUEST_CAPTURE = 100;
    private static final int REQUEST_DOCUMENT = 101;

    @Override
    public void onCreate(Bundle savedInstanceState) {
        super.onCreate(savedInstanceState);
        setContentView(R.layout.save);

        Button images = (Button) findViewById(R.id.imageButton);
        images.setOnClickListener(this);
        Button videos = (Button) findViewById(R.id.videoButton);
        videos.setOnClickListener(this);
```

```java
        //We can only create new documents above API Level 19
        Button text = (Button) findViewById(R.id.textButton);
        if (Build.VERSION.SDK_INT >= Build.VERSION_CODES.KITKAT) {
            text.setOnClickListener(this);
        } else {
            text.setVisibility(View.GONE);
        }
    }

    @Override
    protected void onActivityResult(int requestCode, int resultCode, Intent data) {
        if (requestCode == REQUEST_CAPTURE && resultCode == Activity.RESULT_OK) {
            Toast.makeText(this, "All Done!", Toast.LENGTH_SHORT).show();
        }
        if (requestCode == REQUEST_DOCUMENT && resultCode == Activity.RESULT_OK) {
            //Once the user has selected where to save the new document,
            // we can write the contents into it
            Uri document = data.getData();
            writeDocument(document);
        }
    }

    private void writeDocument(Uri document) {
        try {
            ParcelFileDescriptor pfd = getContentResolver().openFileDescriptor(document, "w");
            FileOutputStream out = new FileOutputStream(pfd.getFileDescriptor());
            //Construct some content for our file
            StringBuilder sb = new StringBuilder();
            sb.append("Android Recipes Log File:");
            sb.append("\n");
            sb.append("Last Written at: ");
            sb.append(DateFormat.getLongDateFormat(this).format(new Date()));

            out.write(sb.toString().getBytes());

            // Let the document provider know you're done by closing the stream.
            out.flush();
            out.close();
            // Close our file handle
            pfd.close();
        } catch (FileNotFoundException e) {
            Log.w("AndroidRecipes", e);
        } catch (IOException e) {
            Log.w("AndroidRecipes", e);
        }
    }

    @Override
    public void onClick(View v) {
        ContentValues values;
        Intent intent;
        Uri storeLocation;
        final long nowMillis = System.currentTimeMillis();
```

```java
switch(v.getId()) {
case R.id.imageButton:
    //Create any metadata for image
    values = new ContentValues(5);
    values.put(MediaStore.Images.ImageColumns.DATE_TAKEN, nowMillis);
    values.put(MediaStore.Images.ImageColumns.DATE_ADDED, nowMillis / 1000);
    values.put(MediaStore.Images.ImageColumns.DATE_MODIFIED, nowMillis / 1000);
    values.put(MediaStore.Images.ImageColumns.DISPLAY_NAME, "Android Recipes Image Sample");
    values.put(MediaStore.Images.ImageColumns.TITLE, "Android Recipes Image Sample");

    //Insert metadata and retrieve Uri location for file
    storeLocation = getContentResolver()
            .insert(MediaStore.Images.Media.EXTERNAL_CONTENT_URI, values);
    //Start capture with new location as destination
    intent = new Intent(MediaStore.ACTION_IMAGE_CAPTURE);
    intent.putExtra(MediaStore.EXTRA_OUTPUT, storeLocation);
    startActivityForResult(intent, REQUEST_CAPTURE);
    return;
case R.id.videoButton:
    //Create any metadata for video
    values = new ContentValues(7);
    values.put(MediaStore.Video.VideoColumns.DATE_TAKEN, nowMillis);
    values.put(MediaStore.Video.VideoColumns.DATE_ADDED, nowMillis / 1000);
    values.put(MediaStore.Video.VideoColumns.DATE_MODIFIED, nowMillis / 1000);
    values.put(MediaStore.Video.VideoColumns.DISPLAY_NAME, "Android Recipes Video Sample");
    values.put(MediaStore.Video.VideoColumns.TITLE, "Android Recipes Video Sample");
    values.put(MediaStore.Video.VideoColumns.ARTIST, "Yours Truly");
    values.put(MediaStore.Video.VideoColumns.DESCRIPTION, "Sample Video Clip");

    //Insert metadata and retrieve Uri location for file
    storeLocation = getContentResolver()
            .insert(MediaStore.Video.Media.EXTERNAL_CONTENT_URI, values);
    //Start capture with new location as destination
    intent = new Intent(MediaStore.ACTION_VIDEO_CAPTURE);
    intent.putExtra(MediaStore.EXTRA_OUTPUT, storeLocation);
    startActivityForResult(intent, REQUEST_CAPTURE);
    return;
case R.id.textButton:
    //Create a new document
    intent = new Intent(Intent.ACTION_CREATE_DOCUMENT);
    intent.addCategory(Intent.CATEGORY_OPENABLE);

    //This is a text document
    intent.setType("text/plain");
    //Optional title to pre-set on document
    intent.putExtra(Intent.EXTRA_TITLE, "Android Recipes");
    startActivityForResult(intent, REQUEST_DOCUMENT);
default:
    return;
    }
  }
}
```

> **Note**   Because this example interacts with the Camera hardware, you should run it on a real device to get the full effect. Emulators will execute the code appropriately, but without real hardware, the example is less interesting.

In this example, when the user clicks the Image or Video button, metadata associated with the media are inserted into a `ContentValues` instance. Some of the more common metadata columns to both image and video are the following:

- `TITLE`: String value for the content title. Displayed in the gallery applications as the content name.

- `DISPLAY_NAME`: Name displayed in most selection interfaces such as the system document picker.

- `DATE_TAKEN`: Integer value describing the date the media item was captured. Note this value is in milliseconds.

- `DATE_ADDED`: Integer value describing when the media was added to `MediaStore`. Note this value is in seconds, not milliseconds.

- `DATE_MODIFIED`: Integer value describing the last change to the media. This is used to sort items in the system document picker. Note this value is also in seconds.

The `ContentValues` are then inserted into the `MediaStore` by using the appropriate `CONTENT_URI` reference. Notice that the metadata are inserted before the media item itself is actually captured. The return value from a successful insert is a fully qualified `Uri` that the application may use as the destination for the media content.

In the previous example, we are using the simplified methods from Chapter 5 of capturing audio and video by requesting that the system applications handle this process. Recall from Chapter 5 that both the audio and video capture Intent can be passed with an extra, declaring the destination for the result. This is where we pass the `Uri` that was returned from the insert.

Upon a successful return from the capture activity, there is nothing more for the application to do. The external application has saved the captured image or video into the location referenced by our `MediaStore` insert. This data is now visible to all applications, including the system's Gallery application.

Creating Documents

Notice the third button, labeled Text Document, is visible and enabled only if we are running on a device with Android 4.4 or later. If the user clicks this button, we construct an Intent request using `ACTION_CREATE_DOCUMENT` to launch the system's document interface. However, in this case, the interface is launched, allowing the user to select where the new file should be saved (that is, which provider application) and what its title should be. Along with this request, we set the MIME type to indicate the document type we want to create, which is plain text in our example. Finally, we can suggest a title by passing `EXTRA_TITLE` along with the Intent, but the user is always given the right to change it later.

Once the user has selected where to save the new document, we are given a content `Uri` in `onActivityResult()` and we can open a stream and write our document's data to storage. The `writeDocument()` method of the example opens a `FileDescriptor` from the `Uri` and writes some basic text content into the new document. Closing the stream and descriptor signal to the owning provider that the document update is complete.

> **Tip** ACTION_CREATE_DOCUMENT is used to make a new document that you want to save. For editing an existing document in place, use ACTION_OPEN_DOCUMENT from the previous example to obtain a working Uri to an existing file. Keep in mind, however, that not all providers support writing. You will need to check the permissions of the Uri you are given before attempting to edit a document received in this way.

7-12. Reading Messaging Data

Problem

You need to query the ContentProvider of locally saved information on the device for sent and received SMS/MMS messages.

Solution

(API Level 19)

Use the contract interface exposed via the Telephony framework. The inner classes of Telephony define all the Uris and data columns used to read SMS messages, MMS messages, and additional metadata.

> **Important** You must request android.permission.READ_SMS in the manifest in order to gain read access to the Telephony provider.

The Telephony provider exposes an interface for the following blocks of data:

- Telephony.Sms: Contains the message content and recipient/delivery metadata for all SMS messages.

- Telephony.Mms: Contains the message content and recipient/delivery metadata for all MMS messages.

- Telephony.MmsSms: Contains the combined messages for SMS and MMS. Also includes custom Uris for requesting a list of conversations, drafts, and searching messages.

- Telephony.Threads: Provides additional metadata about conversations, such as the message count and read status of the conversation thread.

Text-based SMS messages are relatively straightforward, with their entire content housed within a few columns in the Telephony.Sms tables. Even if a message has multiple recipients, those are broken up into multiple messages with the same text content. MMS messages, however, are composed of multiple parts that are all stored separately in individual tables:

- `Mms.Addr`: Contains metadata about all the recipients involved in each MMS message. Each message can have a unique group of recipients.

- `Mms.Part`: Contains the contents of each piece included in the MMS message. The message text is stored as one part with any image, video, or other attachments stored as additional pieces. A MIME string designates the content type of each part.

Displaying a single SMS message can be done with a single query to the `Telephony.Sms` content Uri. Displaying a single MMS message, however, requires iterating through all of these subparts in `Telephony.Mms` to collect the data we need.

> **Tip**   SMS/MMS data will be present only on a device that has telephony hardware, so you will likely want to add a `<uses-feature android:name="android.hardware.telephony"/>` declaration to the manifest to filter out devices that don't have the proper capabilities.

WRITING TO THE TELEPHONY PROVIDER

Writing message data and metadata into the `Telephony` provider has some special rules associated with it. While any application can request the `WRITE_SMS` permission (and have it granted), only the application selected by the user as the Default Messaging Application in Settings will be allowed to write data into the content provider.

Nondefault applications sending SMS messages by using the mechanisms we described in Chapter 4 will have their message contents written into the provider automatically by the framework, but the default application (as the sole application with provider access) will be responsible for writing its own content directly.

In order for a messaging application to be considered for selection as the default, the following criteria must exist in the application's manifest:

- A broadcast receiver registered for the `android.provider.Telephony.SMS_DELIVER` action to receive new SMS messages.

- A broadcast receiver registered for the `android.provider.Telephony.WAP_PUSH_DELIVER` action to receive new MMS messages.

- An activity filtering for the `android.intent.action.SENDTO` action to send new SMS/MMS messages.

- A service filtering for the `android.intent.action.RESPOND_VIA_MESSAGE` action to send quick response messages to incoming callers.

If you are writing a messaging application that must have write access to the provider, the same Uri and column structure defined in the `Telephony` contract that we discuss in this recipe can be used to `insert()`, `update()`, or `delete()` the provider contents as well.

How It Works

In this example, we will create a simple messaging application that reads conversation data from the Telephony provider and displays it in a list. Let's start with the code to query and parse the data coming from the provider. In Listing 7-32, we've created a custom AsyncTaskLoader implementation that allows us to query the provider on a background thread and return the result easily to the UI.

Listing 7-32. Loader for Conversation Data

```java
public class ConversationLoader extends AsyncTaskLoader<List<MessageItem>> {

    public static final String[] PROJECTION = new String[] {
        //Determine if message is SMS or MMS
        MmsSms.TYPE_DISCRIMINATOR_COLUMN,
        //Base item ID
        BaseColumns._ID,
        //Conversation (thread) ID
        Conversations.THREAD_ID,
        //Date values
        Sms.DATE,
        Sms.DATE_SENT,
        // For SMS only
        Sms.ADDRESS,
        Sms.BODY,
        Sms.TYPE,
        // For MMS only
        Mms.SUBJECT,
        Mms.MESSAGE_BOX
    };

    //Thread ID of the conversation we are loading
    private long mThreadId;
    //This device's number
    private String mDeviceNumber;

    public ConversationLoader(Context context) {
        this(context, -1);
    }

    public ConversationLoader(Context context, long threadId) {
        super(context);
        mThreadId = threadId;
        //Obtain the phone number of this device, if available
        TelephonyManager manager =
                (TelephonyManager) context.getSystemService(Context.TELEPHONY_SERVICE);
        mDeviceNumber = manager.getLine1Number();
    }

    @Override
    protected void onStartLoading() {
        //Reload on every init request
        forceLoad();
    }
```

```java
@Override
public List<MessageItem> loadInBackground() {
    Uri uri;
    String[] projection;
    if (mThreadId < 0) {
        //Load all conversations
        uri = MmsSms.CONTENT_CONVERSATIONS_URI;
        projection = null;
    } else {
        //Load just the requested thread
        uri = ContentUris.withAppendedId(MmsSms.CONTENT_CONVERSATIONS_URI, mThreadId);
        projection = PROJECTION;
    }

    Cursor cursor = getContext().getContentResolver().query(
            uri,
            projection,
            null,
            null,
            null);

    return MessageItem.parseMessages(getContext(), cursor, mDeviceNumber);
    }
}
```

AysncTaskLoader is fairly simply to customize. You just need to provide an implementation of loadInBackground() to do the interesting work, and include some logic in onStartLoading() to get the process running. In the framework, results are usually cached, and forceLoad() is called only if the content has changed, but for simplicity we are loading data from the provider on every request.

Our ConversationLoader will be used to obtain two message lists: a list of all conversations present, and a list of all the messages for a selected conversation (or thread). So when ConversationLoader is instantiated, the ID of the conversation thread is either passed in or ignored to determine the output results. We also obtain the phone number of our device from TelephonyManager for use later. This step is not integral to reading the provider, but will help us clean up the display later.

> **Important**   When using TelephonyManager to get the device information, your application must also declare android.permission.READ_PHONE_STATE in the manifest.

In both request modes, we are making a query of the MmsSms.CONTENT_CONVERSATIONS_URI in the combined message table. This Uri is convenient for getting a conversation overview because it will return a list of all the known conversation threads by returning the latest message in each thread. This makes it easy to display the results directly to the user.

When listing all the conversations, we don't need to provide a customized projection, which will return all the columns. However, when looking at a specific thread, we pass in a specific column subset to inspect. This is mainly so we can obtain the MmsSms.TYPE_DISCRIMINATOR_COLUMN value, which tells us whether each message is SMS or MMS. This column is not available for the main conversations list, and it also isn't returned by default for a null projection.

SORTING COMBINED RESULTS

It is likely that you may want to sort the results by date for these queries. A common implementation would be to use the ordering clause in the provider query to sort the results returned. However, with a combined SMS/MMS query like what we have done here, this is not straightforward. The DATE and DATE_SENT fields of SMS messages present their timestamps in elapsed milliseconds from epoch, while those same fields for MMS messages show timestamps in elapsed seconds from epoch.

The simplest method for sorting combined results is to normalize the timestamps when parsing out into a model (such as MessageItem), and then use the sorting features of Collections to sort the resulting object list.

After we have successfully queried the provider, we want to parse the contents into a common model object that we can easily display in a list. To do this, we pass the result Cursor to a factory method in a MessageItem class we've created, which you can see in Listing 7-33.

Listing 7-33. MessageItem Model and Parsing

```java
public class MessageItem {
    /* Message Type Identifiers */
    private static final String TYPE_SMS = "sms";
    private static final String TYPE_MMS = "mms";

    static final String[] MMS_PROJECTION = new String[] {
        //Base item ID
        BaseColumns._ID,
        //MIME Type of the content for this part
        Mms.Part.CONTENT_TYPE,
        //Text content of a text/plain part
        Mms.Part.TEXT,
        //Path to binary content of a nontext part
        Mms.Part._DATA
    };

    /* Message Id */
    public long id;
    /* Thread (Conversation) Id */
    public long thread_id;
    /* Address string of message */
    public String address;
    /* Body string of message */
    public String body;
    /* Whether this message was sent or received on this device */
    public boolean incoming;
    /* MMS image attachment */
    public Uri attachment;

    /*
     * Construct a list of messages from the Cursor data
     * queried by the Loader
     */
```

```java
public static List<MessageItem> parseMessages(Context context, Cursor cursor,
        String myNumber) {

    List<MessageItem> messages = new ArrayList<MessageItem>();
    if (!cursor.moveToFirst()) {
        return messages;
    }
    //Parse each message based on the type identifiers
    do {
        String type = getMessageType(cursor);
        if (TYPE_SMS.equals(type)) {
            MessageItem item = parseSmsMessage(cursor);
            messages.add(item);
        } else if (TYPE_MMS.equals(type)) {
            MessageItem item = parseMmsMessage(context, cursor, myNumber);
            messages.add(item);
        } else {
            Log.w("TelephonyProvider", "Unknown Message Type");
        }
    } while (cursor.moveToNext());
    cursor.close();

    return messages;
}

/*
 * Read message type, if present in Cursor; otherwise
 * infer it from the column values present in the Cursor
 */
private static String getMessageType(Cursor cursor) {
    int typeIndex = cursor.getColumnIndex(MmsSms.TYPE_DISCRIMINATOR_COLUMN);
    if (typeIndex < 0) {
        //Type column not in projection, use another discriminator
        String cType = cursor.getString(cursor.getColumnIndex(Mms.CONTENT_TYPE));
        //If a content type is present, this is an MMS message
        if (cType != null) {
            return TYPE_MMS;
        } else {
            return TYPE_SMS;
        }
    } else {
        return cursor.getString(typeIndex);
    }
}

/*
 * Parse out a MessageItem with contents from an SMS message
 */
private static MessageItem parseSmsMessage(Cursor data) {
    MessageItem item = new MessageItem();
    item.id = data.getLong(data.getColumnIndexOrThrow(BaseColumns._ID));
    item.thread_id = data.getLong(data.getColumnIndexOrThrow(Conversations.THREAD_ID));
```

```
        item.address = data.getString(data.getColumnIndexOrThrow(Sms.ADDRESS));
        item.body = data.getString(data.getColumnIndexOrThrow(Sms.BODY));
        item.incoming = isIncomingMessage(data, true);
        return item;
}


/*
 * Parse out a MessageItem with contents from an MMS message
 */
private static MessageItem parseMmsMessage(Context context, Cursor data, String myNumber) {
    MessageItem item = new MessageItem();
    item.id = data.getLong(data.getColumnIndexOrThrow(BaseColumns._ID));
    item.thread_id = data.getLong(data.getColumnIndexOrThrow(Conversations.THREAD_ID));

    item.incoming = isIncomingMessage(data, false);

    long _id = data.getLong(data.getColumnIndexOrThrow(BaseColumns._ID));

    //Query the address information for this message
    Uri addressUri = Uri.withAppendedPath(Mms.CONTENT_URI, _id + "/addr");
    Cursor addr = context.getContentResolver().query(
            addressUri,
            null,
            null,
            null,
            null);
    HashSet<String> recipients = new HashSet<String>();
    while (addr.moveToNext()) {
        String address = addr.getString(addr.getColumnIndex(Mms.Addr.ADDRESS));
        //Don't add our own number to the displayed list
        if (myNumber == null || !address.contains(myNumber)) {
            recipients.add(address);
        }
    }
    item.address = TextUtils.join(", ", recipients);
    addr.close();

    //Query all the MMS parts associated with this message
    Uri messageUri = Uri.withAppendedPath(Mms.CONTENT_URI, _id + "/part");
    Cursor inner = context.getContentResolver().query(
            messageUri,
            MMS_PROJECTION,
            Mms.Part.MSG_ID + " = ?",
            new String[] {String.valueOf(data.getLong(data.getColumnIndex(Mms._ID)))},
            null);

    while(inner.moveToNext()) {
        String contentType = inner.getString(inner.getColumnIndex(Mms.Part.CONTENT_TYPE));
        if (contentType == null) {
            continue;
        } else if (contentType.matches("image/.*")) {
```

```
                //Find any part that is an image attachment
                long partId = inner.getLong(inner.getColumnIndex(BaseColumns._ID));
                item.attachment = Uri.withAppendedPath(Mms.CONTENT_URI, "part/" + partId);
            } else if (contentType.matches("text/.*")) {
                //Find any part that is text data
                item.body = inner.getString(inner.getColumnIndex(Mms.Part.TEXT));
            }
        }

        inner.close();
        return item;
    }

    /*
     * Validate if the message is incoming or outgoing by the
     * type/box information listed in the provider
     */
    private static boolean isIncomingMessage(Cursor cursor, boolean isSms) {
        int boxId;
        if (isSms) {
            boxId = cursor.getInt(cursor.getColumnIndexOrThrow(Sms.TYPE));
            return (boxId == TextBasedSmsColumns.MESSAGE_TYPE_INBOX ||
                    boxId == TextBasedSmsColumns.MESSAGE_TYPE_ALL) ?
                    true : false;
        } else {
            boxId = cursor.getInt(cursor.getColumnIndexOrThrow(Mms.MESSAGE_BOX));
            return (boxId == Mms.MESSAGE_BOX_INBOX || boxId == Mms.MESSAGE_BOX_ALL) ?
                    true : false;
        }
    }
}
```

The MessageItem itself is a standard placeholder object for the message identifiers, name, text content, and image attachment (for MMS messages). Inside parseMessages(), we iterate through the Cursor data and construct a new MessageItem from each row. SMS and MMS are parsed differently, so we must first determine the message type. When the TYPE_DISCRIMINATOR_COLUMN is present, this is simple and we just check the value. In other cases, we can infer the type based on the column entries for each message.

Parsing an SMS message is straightforward, as we just need to read the ID, thread ID, address, body, and incoming status as columns directly from the main Cursor. Parsing an MMS message is slightly more involved because the message contents are segmented into parts. We can read the ID, thread ID, and incoming status from the main Cursor, but the address and content information need to be retrieved from additional tables.

First, we need to get the recipient information from the Mms.Addr table. MMS messages can be sent to multiple recipients, and each one is represented by a row in this table with a MSG_ID that matches the MMS message. We iterate through these elements and construct a comma-separated list of the results to attach to the MessageItem. Notice also that we are checking for our own number in this list to avoid having it added as well. Each message will also have an Addr entry for the local device number, and we don't want to display that in our UI each time, so we are filtering it out.

Next we need to parse out the message contents. These values are stored in the Mms.Part table, keyed by the MSG_ID again. MMS messages can have many types of content associated with them (contact data, videos, images, and so forth) but we are interested in displaying only the text or image data that may be present. As we iterate through the parts, we validate the MIME string of the content type to find any text or image components to add to our MessageItem. For image attachments, we simply store the Uri pointing to the content rather than decoding the image and saving it here.

> **Note**   As of this writing, the SDK provides column constants for Mms.Addr and Mms.Part, but there is no exposed content Uri. This will likely change in the future, but for now we have to hard-code the paths off the base Mms.CONTENT_URI constant.

For both SMS and MMS messages, the status of whether the message is incoming or outgoing can be determined by looking at the message's box type. Messages that are marked in the Inbox or have no designation are considered incoming messages, while all other message box designations (Outbox, Sent, Drafts, and so forth) are considered outgoing.

Now that we have a parsed list of messages, let's take a look at Listings 7-34 and 7-35 to inspect the user interface implemented in this example.

Listing 7-34. Activity to Display SMS/MMS Messages

```
public class SmsActivity extends Activity
        implements OnItemClickListener, LoaderCallbacks<List<MessageItem>> {

    private MessagesAdapter mAdapter;

    @Override
    protected void onCreate(Bundle savedInstanceState) {
        super.onCreate(savedInstanceState);
        ListView list = new ListView(this);
        mAdapter = new MessagesAdapter(this);
        list.setAdapter(mAdapter);

        final Intent intent = getIntent();

        if (!intent.hasExtra("threadId")) {
            //Items are clickable if we are not showing a conversation
            list.setOnItemClickListener(this);
        }
        //Load the messages data
        getLoaderManager().initLoader(0, getIntent().getExtras(), this);

        setContentView(list);
    }

    @Override
    public void onItemClick(AdapterView<?> parent, View view, int position, long id) {
        final MessageItem item = mAdapter.getItem(position);
        long threadId = item.thread_id;
```

```
        //Launch a new instance to show this conversation
        Intent intent = new Intent(this, SmsActivity.class);
        intent.putExtra("threadId", threadId);
        startActivity(intent);
    }

    @Override
    public Loader<List<MessageItem>> onCreateLoader(int id, Bundle args) {
        if (args != null && args.containsKey("threadId")) {
            return new ConversationLoader(this, args.getLong("threadId"));
        } else {
            return new ConversationLoader(this);
        }
    }

    @Override
    public void onLoadFinished(Loader<List<MessageItem>> loader, List<MessageItem> data) {
        mAdapter.clear();
        mAdapter.addAll(data);
        mAdapter.notifyDataSetChanged();
    }

    @Override
    public void onLoaderReset(Loader<List<MessageItem>> loader) {
        mAdapter.clear();
        mAdapter.notifyDataSetChanged();
    }

    private static class MessagesAdapter extends ArrayAdapter<MessageItem> {

        int cacheSize = 4 * 1024 * 1024; // 4MiB
        private LruCache<String, Bitmap> bitmapCache = new LruCache<String, Bitmap>(cacheSize) {
            protected int sizeOf(String key, Bitmap value) {
                return value.getByteCount();
            }
        };

        public MessagesAdapter(Context context) {
            super(context, 0);
        }

        @Override
        public View getView(int position, View convertView, ViewGroup parent) {
            if (convertView == null) {
                convertView = LayoutInflater.from(getContext())
                        .inflate(R.layout.message_item, parent, false);
            }

            MessageItem item = getItem(position);

            TextView text1 = (TextView) convertView.findViewById(R.id.text1);
            TextView text2 = (TextView) convertView.findViewById(R.id.text2);
            ImageView image = (ImageView) convertView.findViewById(R.id.image);
```

```java
            text1.setText(item.address);
            text2.setText(item.body);
            //Set text style based on incoming/outgoing status
            Typeface tf = item.incoming ?
                    Typeface.defaultFromStyle(Typeface.ITALIC) : Typeface.DEFAULT;
            text2.setTypeface(tf);
            image.setImageBitmap(getAttachment(item));

            return convertView;
        }

        private Bitmap getAttachment(MessageItem item) {
            if (item.attachment == null) return null;

            final Uri imageUri = item.attachment;
            //Pull image thumbnail from cache if we have it
            Bitmap cached = bitmapCache.get(imageUri.toString());
            if (cached != null) {
                return cached;
            }

            //Decode the asset from the provider if we don't have it in cache
            try {
                BitmapFactory.Options options = new BitmapFactory.Options();
                options.inJustDecodeBounds = true;
                int cellHeight = getContext().getResources()
                        .getDimensionPixelSize(R.dimen.message_height);
                InputStream is = getContext().getContentResolver().openInputStream(imageUri);
                BitmapFactory.decodeStream(is, null, options);

                options.inJustDecodeBounds = false;
                options.inSampleSize = options.outHeight / cellHeight;
                is = getContext().getContentResolver().openInputStream(imageUri);
                Bitmap bitmap = BitmapFactory.decodeStream(is, null, options);

                bitmapCache.put(imageUri.toString(), bitmap);
                return bitmap;
            } catch (Exception e) {
                return null;
            }
        }
    }
}
```

Listing 7-35. res/layout/message_item.xml

```xml
<?xml version="1.0" encoding="utf-8"?>
<RelativeLayout xmlns:android="http://schemas.android.com/apk/res/android"
    android:layout_width="match_parent"
    android:layout_height="wrap_content"
    android:minHeight="@dimen/message_height">
```

```
<ImageView
    android:id="@+id/image"
    android:layout_width="@dimen/message_height"
    android:layout_height="@dimen/message_height"
    android:layout_alignParentRight="true"
    android:layout_centerVertical="true" />
<TextView
    android:id="@+id/text1"
    android:layout_width="match_parent"
    android:layout_height="wrap_content"
    android:layout_toLeftOf="@id/image"
    android:layout_marginLeft="6dp"
    android:textStyle="bold" />
<TextView
    android:id="@+id/text2"
    android:layout_width="match_parent"
    android:layout_height="wrap_content"
    android:layout_below="@id/text1"
    android:layout_toLeftOf="@id/image"
    android:layout_marginLeft="12dp" />
```

```
</RelativeLayout>
```

Our activity is used to display both types of message data. Upon creation, the activity calls initLoader() to construct a new ConversationLoader to query the provider. The arguments passed in are the extras received by the activity Intent. When the application first launches, there are no incoming Intent extras, so a ConversationLoader is constructed to load all conversation threads. Later, when the activity is launched with a specific thread ID, ConversationLoader will query all messages in that conversation.

Once the loading is complete, the data is presented in a ListView using our custom MessagesAdapter. This adapter inflates a custom item layout (from Listing 7-35) with two text rows and space for an image. The MessageItem address information is loaded into the top label, and the text content into the bottom label. If the message is MMS and an image attachment is present, we attempt to return the image via getAttachment() and insert it into the ImageView.

Loading these images from disk each time is expensive and a tad slow, so to improve scrolling performance in the list, we have added an LruCache to store recently loaded bitmaps in memory. The cache is set to 4MiB in size, so as to not overinflate the application's heap over time. Additionally, each image is downsampled when returned from BitmapFactory (via BitmapFactory.Options. inSampleSize) to avoid loading an image that is larger than the space available in the list row and wasting memory.

We now have a basic messaging application that presents a read-only window into the SMS/MMS on our device. When launched, this application will list all the conversations by showing the latest message for each thread. When a conversation is tapped, a new activity will display, showing all the individual messages within that thread. Pressing the Back button will return to the main list so the user can select another conversation to view.

7-13. Interacting with the Calendar

Problem

Your application needs to interact directly with the ContentProvider exposed by the Android framework to add, view, change, or remove calendar events on the device.

Solution

(API Level 14)

Use the CalendarContract interface to read/write data to the system's ContentProvider for event data. CalendarContract exposes the API that is necessary to gain access to the device's calendars, events, attendees, and reminders. Much like ContactsContract, this interface defines mostly the data that is necessary to perform queries. The methods used will be the same as when working with any other system ContentProvider.

How It Works

Working with CalendarContract is very similar to working with ContactsContract; they both provide identifiers for the Uri and column values you will need to construct queries through the ContentResolver. Listing 7-36 illustrates an activity that obtains and displays a list of the calendars present on the device.

Listing 7-36. Activity Listing Calendars on the Device

```
public class CalendarListActivity extends ListActivity implements
        LoaderManager.LoaderCallbacks<Cursor>, AdapterView.OnItemClickListener {
    private static final int LOADER_LIST = 100;

    SimpleCursorAdapter mAdapter;

    @Override
    public void onCreate(Bundle savedInstanceState) {
        super.onCreate(savedInstanceState);
        getLoaderManager().initLoader(LOADER_LIST, null, this);

        // Display all calendars in a ListView
        mAdapter = new SimpleCursorAdapter(this,
                android.R.layout.simple_list_item_2, null,
                new String[] {
                        CalendarContract.Calendars.CALENDAR_DISPLAY_NAME,
                        CalendarContract.Calendars.ACCOUNT_NAME },
                new int[] {
                        android.R.id.text1, android.R.id.text2 }, 0);
        setListAdapter(mAdapter);
        // Listen for item selections
        getListView().setOnItemClickListener(this);
    }
```

```java
@Override
public void onItemClick(AdapterView<?> parent, View view, int position,
        long id) {
    Cursor c = mAdapter.getCursor();
    if (c != null && c.moveToPosition(position)) {
        Intent intent = new Intent(this, CalendarDetailActivity.class);
        // Pass the _ID and TITLE of the selected calendar to the next
        // Activity
        intent.putExtra(Intent.EXTRA_UID, c.getInt(0));
        intent.putExtra(Intent.EXTRA_TITLE, c.getString(1));
        startActivity(intent);
    }
}

@Override
public Loader<Cursor> onCreateLoader(int id, Bundle args) {
    // Return all calendars, ordered by name
    String[] projection = new String[] { CalendarContract.Calendars._ID,
            CalendarContract.Calendars.CALENDAR_DISPLAY_NAME,
            CalendarContract.Calendars.ACCOUNT_NAME };

    return new CursorLoader(this, CalendarContract.Calendars.CONTENT_URI,
            projection, null, null,
            CalendarContract.Calendars.CALENDAR_DISPLAY_NAME);
}

@Override
public void onLoadFinished(Loader<Cursor> loader, Cursor data) {
    mAdapter.swapCursor(data);
}

@Override
public void onLoaderReset(Loader<Cursor> loader) {
    mAdapter.swapCursor(null);
}
}
```

In contrast to our contacts example, here we use Android's Loader pattern to query the data and load the resulting Cursor into the list. This pattern provides a lot of benefit over managedCursor(), primarily in that all queries are automatically made on background threads to keep the UI responsive. The Loader pattern also has built-in reuse, so multiple clients wanting the same data can actually gain access to the same Loader through the LoaderManager.

With Loaders, our activity receives a series of callback methods when new data is available. Under the hood, CursorLoader also registers as a ContentObserver, so we will get a callback with a new Cursor when the underlying data set changes without even having to request a reload. But back to the calendar...

To obtain a list of the device calendars, we construct a query to the Calendars.CONTENT_URI with the column names we are interested in (here, the record ID, calendar name, and owning account name). When the query is complete, onLoadFinished() is called with a new Cursor pointing to the result data, which we then pass to our list adapter. When the user taps on a particular calendar item, a new activity is initialized to look at the specific events it contains. We will see this in more detail in the next section.

Viewing/Modifying Calendar Events

Listing 7-37 shows the contents of the second activity in this example that displays a list of all the events for the selected calendar.

Listing 7-37. Activity Listing and Modifying Calendar Events

```java
public class CalendarDetailActivity extends ListActivity implements
        LoaderManager.LoaderCallbacks<Cursor>, AdapterView.OnItemClickListener,
        AdapterView.OnItemLongClickListener {
    private static final int LOADER_DETAIL = 101;

    SimpleCursorAdapter mAdapter;

    int mCalendarId;

    @Override
    protected void onCreate(Bundle savedInstanceState) {
        super.onCreate(savedInstanceState);

        mCalendarId = getIntent().getIntExtra(Intent.EXTRA_UID, -1);

        String title = getIntent().getStringExtra(Intent.EXTRA_TITLE);
        setTitle(title);

        getLoaderManager().initLoader(LOADER_DETAIL, null, this);

        // Display all events in a ListView
        mAdapter = new SimpleCursorAdapter(this,
                android.R.layout.simple_list_item_2, null,
                new String[] {
                        CalendarContract.Events.TITLE,
                        CalendarContract.Events.EVENT_LOCATION },
                new int[] {
                        android.R.id.text1, android.R.id.text2 }, 0);
        setListAdapter(mAdapter);
        // Listen for item selections
        getListView().setOnItemClickListener(this);
        getListView().setOnItemLongClickListener(this);
    }

    @Override
    public boolean onCreateOptionsMenu(Menu menu) {
        menu.add("Add Event")
            .setIcon(android.R.drawable.ic_menu_add)
            .setShowAsAction(MenuItem.SHOW_AS_ACTION_ALWAYS);

        return true;
    }
```

```java
@Override
public boolean onOptionsItemSelected(MenuItem item) {
    showAddEventDialog();
    return true;
}

// Display a dialog to add a new event
private void showAddEventDialog() {
    final EditText nameText = new EditText(this);
    AlertDialog.Builder builder = new AlertDialog.Builder(this);
    builder.setTitle("New Event");
    builder.setView(nameText);
    builder.setNegativeButton("Cancel", null);
    builder.setPositiveButton("Add Event",
            new DialogInterface.OnClickListener() {
                @Override
                public void onClick(DialogInterface dialog, int which) {
                    addEvent(nameText.getText().toString());
                }
            });
    builder.show();
}

// Add an event to the calendar with the specified name
// and the current time as the start date
private void addEvent(String eventName) {
    long start = System.currentTimeMillis();
    // End 1 hour from now
    long end = start + (3600 * 1000);

    ContentValues cv = new ContentValues(5);
    cv.put(CalendarContract.Events.CALENDAR_ID, mCalendarId);
    cv.put(CalendarContract.Events.TITLE, eventName);
    cv.put(CalendarContract.Events.DESCRIPTION,
            "Event created by Android Recipes");
    cv.put(CalendarContract.Events.EVENT_TIMEZONE,
            Time.getCurrentTimezone());
    cv.put(CalendarContract.Events.DTSTART, start);
    cv.put(CalendarContract.Events.DTEND, end);

    getContentResolver().insert(CalendarContract.Events.CONTENT_URI, cv);
}

// Remove the selected event from the calendar
private void deleteEvent(int eventId) {
    String selection = CalendarContract.Events._ID + " = ?";
    String[] selectionArgs = { String.valueOf(eventId) };
    getContentResolver().delete(CalendarContract.Events.CONTENT_URI,
            selection, selectionArgs);
}
```

```java
@Override
public void onItemClick(AdapterView<?> parent, View view, int position,
        long id) {
    Cursor c = mAdapter.getCursor();
    if (c != null && c.moveToPosition(position)) {
        // Show a dialog with more detailed data about the event when
        // clicked
        SimpleDateFormat sdf = new SimpleDateFormat("yyyy-MM-dd HH:mm:ss");
        StringBuilder sb = new StringBuilder();

        sb.append("Location: "
                + c.getString(
                        c.getColumnIndex(CalendarContract.Events.EVENT_LOCATION))
                + "\n\n");
        int startDateIndex = c.getColumnIndex(CalendarContract.Events.DTSTART);
        Date startDate = c.isNull(startDateIndex) ? null
                : new Date( Long.parseLong(c.getString(startDateIndex)) );
        if (startDate != null) {
            sb.append("Starts At: " + sdf.format(startDate) + "\n\n");
        }
        int endDateIndex = c.getColumnIndex(CalendarContract.Events.DTEND);
        Date endDate = c.isNull(endDateIndex) ? null
                : new Date( Long.parseLong(c.getString(endDateIndex)) );
        if (endDate != null) {
            sb.append("Ends At: " + sdf.format(endDate) + "\n\n");
        }

        AlertDialog.Builder builder = new AlertDialog.Builder(this);
        builder.setTitle(
                c.getString(c.getColumnIndex(CalendarContract.Events.TITLE)) );
        builder.setMessage(sb.toString());
        builder.setPositiveButton("OK", null);
        builder.show();
    }
}

@Override
public boolean onItemLongClick(AdapterView<?> parent, View view,
        int position, long id) {
    Cursor c = mAdapter.getCursor();
    if (c != null && c.moveToPosition(position)) {
        // Allow the user to delete the event on a long-press
        final int eventId = c.getInt(
                c.getColumnIndex(CalendarContract.Events._ID));
        String eventName = c.getString(
                c.getColumnIndex(CalendarContract.Events.TITLE));
        AlertDialog.Builder builder = new AlertDialog.Builder(this);
        builder.setTitle("Delete Event");
        builder.setMessage(String.format(
                "Are you sure you want to delete %s?",
                TextUtils.isEmpty(eventName) ? "this event" : eventName));
        builder.setNegativeButton("Cancel", null);
```

```
            builder.setPositiveButton("Delete Event",
                    new DialogInterface.OnClickListener() {
                        @Override
                        public void onClick(DialogInterface dialog, int which) {
                            deleteEvent(eventId);
                        }
                    });
            builder.show();
        }

        return true;
    }

    @Override
    public Loader<Cursor> onCreateLoader(int id, Bundle args) {
        // Return all calendars, ordered by name
        String[] projection = new String[] { CalendarContract.Events._ID,
                CalendarContract.Events.TITLE, CalendarContract.Events.DTSTART,
                CalendarContract.Events.DTEND,
                CalendarContract.Events.EVENT_LOCATION };
        String selection = CalendarContract.Events.CALENDAR_ID + " = ?";
        String[] selectionArgs = { String.valueOf(mCalendarId) };

        return new CursorLoader(this, CalendarContract.Events.CONTENT_URI,
                projection, selection, selectionArgs,
                CalendarContract.Events.DTSTART + " DESC");
    }

    @Override
    public void onLoadFinished(Loader<Cursor> loader, Cursor data) {
        mAdapter.swapCursor(data);
    }

    @Override
    public void onLoaderReset(Loader<Cursor> loader) {
        mAdapter.swapCursor(null);
    }
}
```

You can see that the code to query the list of events and display them is very similar; in this case, you query the Events.CONTENT_URI with the ID of the selected calendar as a selection parameter. After tapping an event, the user is presented with a simple dialog box with more details about the event itself. In addition, though, this activity includes a few more methods to create and delete events on this calendar.

To add a new event, an item is added to the options menu, which will show up in the overhead Action Bar if the device has one visible. When pressed, a dialog box appears, allowing the user to enter a name for this event. If the user elects to continue, a ContentValues object is created with the bare necessities required to create a new event. Because this event is nonrecurring, it must have both start and end times, as well as a valid time zone. We must also supply the ID of the calendar we are looking at so the event is properly attached. From there, the data is handed back to ContentResolver to be inserted into the Events table.

To delete an event, the user may long-press a particular item in the list and then confirm the deletion through a dialog box. In this case, all we need is the unique record ID of the selected event to pass in a selection string to ContentResolver.

Did you notice in both of these cases that we didn't write any code after the insert/delete to refresh the Cursor or the CursorAdapter? That's the power of the Loader pattern! Because the CursorLoader is observing the data set, when a change occurred, it automatically refreshed itself and handed a new Cursor to the adapter, which refreshes the display.

> **Note**   Loaders were introduced in Android 3.0 (API Level 11), but they are also part of the Support Library. You can use them in your applications supporting all the way back to Android 1.6.

7-14. Logging Code Execution
Problem

You need to place log statements into your code for debugging or testing purposes, and they should be removed before shipping the code to production.

Solution

(API Level 1)

Leverage the BuildConfig.DEBUG flag to protect statements in the Log class so they print only on debug builds of the application. It can be extremely convenient to keep logging statements in your code for future testing and development, even after the application has shipped to your users. But if those statements are unchecked, you might risk printing private information to the console on a user's device. By creating a simple wrapper class around Log that monitors BuildConfig.DEBUG, you can leave log statements in place without fear of what they will show in the field.

How It Works

Listing 7-38 illustrates a simple wrapper class around the default Android Log functionality.

Listing 7-38. Logger Wrapper

```
public class Logger {
    private static final String LOGTAG = "AndroidRecipes";

    private static String getLogString(String format, Object... args) {
        //Minor optimization, only call String.format if necessary
        if(args.length == 0) {
            return format;
        }
```

```
        return String.format(format, args);
    }

    /* The INFO, WARNING, ERROR log levels print always */

    public static void e(String format, Object... args) {
        Log.e(LOGTAG, getLogString(format, args));
    }

    public static void w(String format, Object... args) {
        Log.w(LOGTAG, getLogString(format, args));
    }

    public static void w(Throwable throwable) {
        Log.w(LOGTAG, throwable);
    }

    public static void i(String format, Object... args) {
        Log.i(LOGTAG, getLogString(format, args));
    }

    /* The DEBUG and VERBOSE log levels are protected by DEBUG flag */

    public static void d(String format, Object... args) {
        if(!BuildConfig.DEBUG) return;

        Log.d(LOGTAG, getLogString(format, args));
    }

    public static void v(String format, Object... args) {
        if(!BuildConfig.DEBUG) return;

        Log.v(LOGTAG, getLogString(format, args));
    }
}
```

This class provides a few simple optimizations around the framework's version to make logging a bit more civilized. First, it consolidates the log tag so your entire application prints under one consistent tag heading in logcat. Second, it takes input in the form of a format string so variables can be logged out cleanly without needing to break up the log string. The one additional optimization to this is that String.format() can be slow, so we want to call it only when there are actually parameters to format. Otherwise, we can just pass the raw string along directly.

Finally, it protects two of the five main log levels with the BuildConfig.DEBUG flag, so that log statements set to these levels print only in debug versions of the application. There are many cases where we want log statements to be output in the production application as well (such as error conditions), so it is prudent not to hide all the log levels behind the debug flag. Listing 7-39 quickly shows how this wrapper can take the place of traditional logging.

Listing 7-39. Activity Using Logger

```
public class LoggerActivity extends Activity {

    @Override
    public void onCreate(Bundle savedInstanceState) {
        super.onCreate(savedInstanceState);
        setContentView(R.layout.main);

        //This statement only printed in debug
        Logger.d("Activity Created");
    }

    @Override
    protected void onResume() {
        super.onResume();

        //This statement only printed in debug
        Logger.d("Activity Resume at %d", System.currentTimeMillis());
        //This statement always printed
        Logger.i("It is now %d", System.currentTimeMillis());
    }

    @Override
    protected void onPause() {
        super.onPause();

        //This statement only printed in debug
        Logger.d("Activity Pause at %d", System.currentTimeMillis());
        //This always printed
        Logger.w("No, don't leave!");
    }
}
```

7-15. Creating a Background Worker

Problem

You need to create a long-running background thread that sits waiting for work to execute and that can be terminated easily when it is no longer needed.

Solution

(API Level 1)

Let `HandlerThread` assist you in creating a background thread with a working `Looper` that can be attached to a `Handler` for processing work inside its `MessageQueue`. One of the most popular backgrounding methods in Android is `AsyncTask`, which is a fabulous class and should be used in your applications. However, it has some drawbacks that may make other implementations more efficient in certain cases. One of those drawbacks is that `AsyncTask` execution is one-shot and finite.

If you want to do the same task repeatedly or indefinitely for the life cycle of a component such as an activity or service, AsyncTask can be a bit heavyweight. Often, you will need to create multiple instances to accomplish that goal.

The advantage of HandlerThread in cases like this is we can create one worker object to accept multiple tasks to handle in the background and it will process them serially through the built-in queue that Looper maintains.

How It Works

Listing 7-40 contains an extension of HandlerThread used to do some simple manipulation of image data. Because modifying images can take some time, we want to task this to a background operation to keep the application UI responsive.

Listing 7-40. Background Worker Thread

```
public class ImageProcessor extends HandlerThread implements Handler.Callback {
    public static final int MSG_SCALE = 100;
    public static final int MSG_CROP = 101;

    private Context mContext;
    private Handler mReceiver, mCallback;

    public ImageProcessor(Context context) {
        this(context, null);
    }

    public ImageProcessor(Context context, Handler callback) {
        super("AndroidRecipesWorker");
        mCallback = callback;
        mContext = context;
    }

    @Override
    protected void onLooperPrepared() {
        mReceiver = new Handler(getLooper(), this);
    }

    @Override
    public boolean handleMessage(Message msg) {
        Bitmap source, result;
        //Retrieve arguments from the incoming message
        int scale = msg.arg1;
        switch (msg.what) {
        case MSG_SCALE:
            source = BitmapFactory.decodeResource(mContext.getResources(),
                    R.drawable.ic_launcher);
            //Create a new, scaled up image
            result = Bitmap.createScaledBitmap(source,
                    source.getWidth() * scale, source.getHeight() * scale, true);
            break;
```

```java
        case MSG_CROP:
            source = BitmapFactory.decodeResource(mContext.getResources(),
                    R.drawable.ic_launcher);
            int newWidth = source.getWidth() / scale;
            //Create a new, horizontally cropped image
            result = Bitmap.createBitmap(source,
                    (source.getWidth() - newWidth) / 2, 0,
                    newWidth, source.getHeight());
            break;
        default:
            throw new IllegalArgumentException("Unknown Worker Request");
        }

        // Return the image to the main thread
        if (mCallback != null) {
            mCallback.sendMessage(Message.obtain(null, 0, result));
        }
        return true;
    }

    //Add/Remove a callback handler
    public void setCallback(Handler callback) {
        mCallback = callback;
    }

    /* Methods to Queue Work */

    // Scale the icon to the specified value
    public void scaleIcon(int scale) {
        Message msg = Message.obtain(null, MSG_SCALE, scale, 0, null);
        mReceiver.sendMessage(msg);
    }

    //Crop the icon in the center and scale the result to the specified value
    public void cropIcon(int scale) {
        Message msg = Message.obtain(null, MSG_CROP, scale, 0, null);
        mReceiver.sendMessage(msg);
    }
}
```

The name HandlerThread may be a bit of a misnomer, as it does not actually contain a Handler that you can use to process input. Instead it is a thread designed to work externally with a Handler to create a background process. We have to still provide a customized implementation of Handler to execute the work we want done. In this example, our custom processor implements the Handler. Callback interface, which we pass into a new Handler owned by the thread. We do this simply to avoid the need to subclass Handler, which would have worked just as well. The receiver Handler is not created until the onLooperPrepared() callback because we need to have the Looper object that HandlerThread creates to send work to the background thread.

The external API we create to allow other objects to queue work all create a Message and send it to the receiver Handler to be processed in handleMessage(), which inspects the Message contents and creates the appropriate modified image. Any code that goes through handleMessage() is running on our background thread.

Once the work is complete, we need to have a second Handler attached to the main thread so we can send our results and modify the UI.

> **Reminder**   Any code that touches UI elements *must* be called from the main thread *only*. This cannot be overstated.

This callback Handler receives a second Message containing the Bitmap result from the image code. This is one of the great features about using the Message interface to pass data between threads; each instance can take with it two integer arguments as well as any arbitrary Object so no additional code is necessary to pass in parameters or access your results. In our case, one integer is passed in as a parameter for the scale value of the transformation, and the Object field is used to return the image as a Bitmap. To see how this is used in practice, take a look at the sample application in Listings 7-41 and 7-42.

Listing 7-41. res/layout/main.xml

```xml
<LinearLayout xmlns:android="http://schemas.android.com/apk/res/android"
    android:layout_width="match_parent"
    android:layout_height="match_parent"
    android:orientation="vertical" >

    <Button
        android:layout_width="match_parent"
        android:layout_height="wrap_content"
        android:text="Scale Icon"
        android:onClick="onScaleClick" />
    <Button
        android:layout_width="match_parent"
        android:layout_height="wrap_content"
        android:text="Crop Icon"
        android:onClick="onCropClick" />

    <ImageView
        android:id="@+id/image_result"
        android:layout_width="match_parent"
        android:layout_height="match_parent"
        android:scaleType="center" />
</LinearLayout>
```

Listing 7-42. Activity Interacting with Worker

```java
public class WorkerActivity extends Activity implements Handler.Callback {

    private ImageProcessor mWorker;
    private Handler mResponseHandler;

    private ImageView mResultView;

    @Override
    public void onCreate(Bundle savedInstanceState) {
        super.onCreate(savedInstanceState);
        setContentView(R.layout.main);

        mResultView = (ImageView) findViewById(R.id.image_result);
        //Handler to map background callbacks to this Activity
        mResponseHandler = new Handler(this);
    }

    @Override
    protected void onResume() {
        super.onResume();
        //Start a new worker
        mWorker = new ImageProcessor(this, mResponseHandler);
        mWorker.start();
    }

    @Override
    protected void onPause() {
        super.onPause();
        //Terminate the worker
        mWorker.setCallback(null);
        mWorker.quit();
        mWorker = null;
    }

    /*
     * Callback method for background results.
     * This is called on the UI thread.
     */
    @Override
    public boolean handleMessage(Message msg) {
        Bitmap result = (Bitmap) msg.obj;
        mResultView.setImageBitmap(result);
        return true;
    }

    /* Action Methods to Post Background Work */
```

```
public void onScaleClick(View v) {
    for(int i=1; i < 10; i++) {
        mWorker.scaleIcon(i);
    }
}

public void onCropClick(View v) {
    for(int i=1; i < 10; i++) {
        mWorker.cropIcon(i);
    }
}
```

This sample makes use of our worker by creating a single running instance while the activity is in the foreground and passing image requests to it when the user clicks the buttons. To further illustrate the scale of this pattern, we queue up several requests with each button click. The activity also implements Handler.Callback and owns a simple Handler (which is running on the main thread) to receive result messages from the worker.

To start the processor, we just have to call start() on the HandlerThread, which sets up the Looper and Handler, and it begins waiting for input. Terminating it is just as simple; calling quit() stops the Looper and immediately drops any unprocessed messages. We also set the callback to null just so that any work that may be in process currently doesn't try to call the activity after this point.

Run this application and you can see how the background work doesn't slow the UI no matter how fast or how often the buttons are pressed. Each request just gets added to the queue and processed if possible before the user leaves the activity. The visible result is that each created image will be displayed below the buttons as that request finishes.

7-16. Customizing the Task Stack
Problem

Your application allows external applications to launch certain Activities directly, and you need to implement the proper BACK vs. UP navigation patterns.

Solution

(API Level 4)

The NavUtils and TaskStackBuilder classes in the Support Library allow you to easily construct and launch the appropriate navigation stacks from within your application. The functionality of both these classes is actually native to the SDK in Android 4.1 and later, but for applications that need to target earlier platform versions as well, the Support Library implementation provides a compatible API that will still call the native methods whenever they are present.

BACK vs. UP

Android screen navigation provides for two specific user actions. The first is the action taken when the user presses the BACK button. The second is the action taken when the user presses the Home icon in the Action Bar, which is known as the UP action. For developers who are new to the platforms, the distinction can often be confusing, especially since in many cases both actions always perform the same function.

Conceptually, BACK should always navigate to the content screen that the user had been viewing prior to the current screen. The UP action, on the other hand, should navigate to the hierarchical parent screen of the current screen. For most applications where the user drills down from the home screen to subsequent screens with more-specific content, BACK and UP will go to the same place, and so their usefulness may be called into question.

Consider, though, an application where one or more activity elements can be launched directly by an external application. Say, for example, an activity is designed to view an image file. Or perhaps the application posts notification messages that allow the user to go directly to a lower-level activity when an event occurs. In these cases, the BACK action should take the user back to the application task he or she was using before jumping into your application. But the UP action provides a way to move back up your application's stack if the user decides to continue using this application rather than going back to the original task. In this instance, the entire stack of activity elements that your application normally has constructed to get to this point may not exist, and that is where `TaskStackBuilder` and some key attributes in your application's manifest can help.

How It Works

Let's define two applications to illustrate how this recipe works. First, look at Listing 7-43, which shows the `<application>` element of the manifest.

Listing 7-43. AndroidManifest.xml Application Tag

```xml
<application
    android:icon="@drawable/ic_launcher"
    android:label="TaskStack"
    android:theme="@style/AppTheme" >
    <activity
        android:name=".RootActivity"
        android:label="@string/title_activity_root" >
        <intent-filter>
            <action android:name="android.intent.action.MAIN" />
            <category android:name="android.intent.category.LAUNCHER" />
        </intent-filter>
    </activity>
    <activity android:name=".ItemsListActivity"
        android:parentActivityName=".RootActivity">
        <!-- Parent definition for the support library -->
        <meta-data android:name="android.support.PARENT_ACTIVITY"
            android:value=".RootActivity" />
    </activity>
    <activity android:name=".DetailsActivity"
```

```
            android:parentActivityName=".ItemsListActivity">
        <!-- Parent definition for the support library -->
        <meta-data android:name="android.support.PARENT_ACTIVITY"
            android:value=".ItemsListActivity" />
        <!-- Supply a filter to allow external launches -->
        <intent-filter>
            <action android:name="com.examples.taskstack.ACTION_NEW_ARRIVAL" />
            <category android:name="android.intent.category.DEFAULT" />
        </intent-filter>
    </activity>
</application>
```

The first step in defining ancestral navigation is to define the parent-child relationship hierarchy between each activity. In Android 4.1, the android:parentActivityName attribute was introduced to create this link. To support the same functionality in older platforms, the Support Library defines a <meta-data> value that can be attached to each activity to define the parent. Our example defines both attributes for each lower-level activity to work with both the native API and the Support Library.

We have also defined a custom <intent-filter> on the DetailsActivity, which will allow an external application to launch this activity directly.

> **Note**   If you are supporting only Android 4.1 and later with your application, you can stop here. All the remaining functionality to build the stack and navigate are built into Activity in these versions, and the default behavior happens without any extra code. In this case, you would need to implement only TaskStackBuilder if you want to somehow customize the task stack in certain situations.

With our hierarchy defined, we can create the code for each activity. See Listings 7-44 through 7-46.

Listing 7-44.   Root Activity

```java
public class RootActivity extends Activity implements View.OnClickListener {

    @Override
    public void onCreate(Bundle savedInstanceState) {
        super.onCreate(savedInstanceState);
        Button listButton = new Button(this);
        listButton.setText("Show Family Members");
        listButton.setOnClickListener(this);

        setContentView(listButton,
                new ViewGroup.LayoutParams(LayoutParams.MATCH_PARENT,
                        LayoutParams.WRAP_CONTENT));
    }
```

```java
    @Override
    public void onClick(View v) {
        //Launch the next Activity
        Intent intent = new Intent(this, ItemsListActivity.class);
        startActivity(intent);
    }
}
```

Listing 7-45. Second-Level Activity

```java
public class ItemsListActivity extends Activity implements OnItemClickListener {

    private static final String[] ITEMS = {"Mom", "Dad", "Sister", "Brother", "Cousin"};

    @Override
    protected void onCreate(Bundle savedInstanceState) {
        super.onCreate(savedInstanceState);
        //Enable ActionBar home button with up arrow
        getActionBar().setDisplayHomeAsUpEnabled(true);
        //Create and display a list of family members
        ListView list = new ListView(this);
        ArrayAdapter<String> adapter = new ArrayAdapter<String>(this,
                android.R.layout.simple_list_item_1, ITEMS);
        list.setAdapter(adapter);
        list.setOnItemClickListener(this);

        setContentView(list);
    }

    @Override
    public boolean onOptionsItemSelected(MenuItem item) {
        switch (item.getItemId()) {
        case android.R.id.home:
            //Create an intent for the parent Activity
            Intent upIntent = NavUtils.getParentActivityIntent(this);
            //Check if we need to create the entire stack
            if (NavUtils.shouldUpRecreateTask(this, upIntent)) {
                //This stack doesn't exist yet, so it must be synthesized
                TaskStackBuilder.create(this)
                        .addParentStack(this)
                        .startActivities();
            } else {
                //Stack exists, so just navigate up
                NavUtils.navigateUpFromSameTask(this);
            }
            return true;
        default:
            return super.onOptionsItemSelected(item);
        }
    }
}
```

```
    @Override
    public void onItemClick(AdapterView<?> parent, View v, int position, long id) {
        //Launch the final Activity, passing in the selected item name
        Intent intent = new Intent(this, DetailsActivity.class);
        intent.putExtra(Intent.EXTRA_TEXT, ITEMS[position]);
        startActivity(intent);
    }
}
```

Listing 7-46. Third-Level Activity

```
public class DetailsActivity extends Activity {
    //Custom Action String for external Activity launches
    public static final String ACTION_NEW_ARRIVAL =
            "com.examples.taskstack.ACTION_NEW_ARRIVAL";

    @Override
    protected void onCreate(Bundle savedInstanceState) {
        super.onCreate(savedInstanceState);
        //Enable ActionBar home button with up arrow
        getActionBar().setDisplayHomeAsUpEnabled(true);

        TextView text = new TextView(this);
        text.setGravity(Gravity.CENTER);
        String item = getIntent().getStringExtra(Intent.EXTRA_TEXT);
        text.setText(item);

        setContentView(text);
    }

    @Override
    public boolean onOptionsItemSelected(MenuItem item) {
        switch (item.getItemId()) {
        case android.R.id.home:
            //Create an intent for the parent Activity
            Intent upIntent = NavUtils.getParentActivityIntent(this);
            //Check if we need to create the entire stack
            if (NavUtils.shouldUpRecreateTask(this, upIntent)) {
                //This stack doesn't exist yet, so it must be synthesized
                TaskStackBuilder.create(this)
                    .addParentStack(this)
                    .startActivities();
            } else {
                //Stack exists, so just navigate up
                NavUtils.navigateUpFromSameTask(this);
            }
            return true;
        default:
            return super.onOptionsItemSelected(item);
        }
    }
}
```

This example application consists of three screens. The root screen just has a button to launch the next activity. The second activity contains a `ListView` with several options to select from. When any item in the list is selected, the third activity is launched, which displays the selection made in the center of the view. As you might expect, the user can use the BACK button to navigate back through this stack of screens. However, in this case, we have also enabled the UP action to provide the same navigation.

There is some common code in the two lower-level Activities that enables the UP navigation. The first is a call to `setDisplayHomeAsUpEnabled()` on `ActionBar`. This enables the home icon in the bar to be clickable and also to display with the default back arrow that indicates an UP action is possible. Whenever this item is clicked by the user, `onOptionsItemSelected()` will trigger and the item's ID will be `android.R.id.home`, so we use this information to filter out when the user taps requests to navigate UP.

When navigating UP, we have to determine whether the activity stack we need already exists, or we need to create it; the `shouldUpRecreateTask()` method does this for us. On platform versions prior to Android 4.1, it does this by checking whether the target Intent has a valid action string that isn't `Intent.ACTION_MAIN`. On Android 4.1 and later, it decides this by checking the `taskAffinity` of the target Intent against the rest of the application.

If the task stack does not exist, primarily because this activity was launched directly rather than being navigated to from within its own application, we must create it. `TaskStackBuilder` contains a host of methods to allow the stack to be created in any way that fits your application's needs. We are using the convenience method `addParentStack()`, which traverses all of the `parentActivityName` attributes (or `PARENT_ACTIVITY` on support platforms) and every Intent necessary to re-create the path from this activity to the root. With the stack built, we just need to call `startActivities()` to have it build the stack and navigate to the next level up.

If the stack already exists, we can call on `NavUtils` to take us up one level with `navigateUpFromSameTask()`. This is really just a convenience method for `navigateUpTo()` that constructs the target Intent by calling `getParentActivityIntent()` for us.

Now we have an application that is properly compliant with the BACK/UP navigation pattern, but how do we test it? Running this application as is will produce the same results for each BACK and UP action. Let's construct a simple second application to launch our `DetailsActivity` to better illustrate the navigation pattern. See Listings 7-47 and 7-48.

Listing 7-47. res/layout/main.xml

```xml
<?xml version="1.0" encoding="utf-8"?>
<LinearLayout xmlns:android="http://schemas.android.com/apk/res/android"
    android:layout_width="match_parent"
    android:layout_height="match_parent"
    android:orientation="vertical" >
    <Button
        android:id="@+id/button_nephew"
        android:layout_width="match_parent"
        android:layout_height="wrap_content"
        android:text="Add a New Nephew" />
    <Button
        android:id="@+id/button_niece"
        android:layout_width="match_parent"
```

```
                android:layout_height="wrap_content"
                android:text="Add a New Niece" />
        <Button
                android:id="@+id/button_twins"
                android:layout_width="match_parent"
                android:layout_height="wrap_content"
                android:text="Add Twin Nieces!" />
</LinearLayout>
```

Listing 7-48. Activity Launching into the Task Stack

```java
public class MainActivity extends Activity implements View.OnClickListener {
    //Custom Action String for external Activity launches
    public static final String ACTION_NEW_ARRIVAL =
            "com.examples.taskstack.ACTION_NEW_ARRIVAL";

    @Override
    protected void onCreate(Bundle savedInstanceState) {
        super.onCreate(savedInstanceState);
        setContentView(R.layout.main);
        //Attach the button listeners
        findViewById(R.id.button_nephew).setOnClickListener(this);
        findViewById(R.id.button_niece).setOnClickListener(this);
        findViewById(R.id.button_twins).setOnClickListener(this);
    }

    @Override
    public void onClick(View v) {
        String newArrival;
        switch(v.getId()) {
        case R.id.button_nephew:
            newArrival = "Baby Nephew";
            break;
        case R.id.button_niece:
            newArrival = "Baby Niece";
            break;
        case R.id.button_twins:
            newArrival = "Twin Nieces!";
            break;
        default:
            return;
        }

        Intent intent = new Intent(ACTION_NEW_ARRIVAL);
        intent.putExtra(Intent.EXTRA_TEXT, newArrival);
        startActivity(intent);
    }
}
```

This application provides a few options for name values to pass in, and it then launches our previous application's DetailActivity directly. In this case, we see different behavior exhibited between BACK and UP. Pressing the BACK button will take the user back to the options selection screen, because that is the activity that launched it. But pressing the UP action button will launch the user into the original application's task stack, so it will go to the screen with the ListView of items instead. From this point forward, the user's task has changed, so BACK button actions will now also traverse the original stack, thus matching subsequent UP actions. Figure 7-7 illustrates this use case.

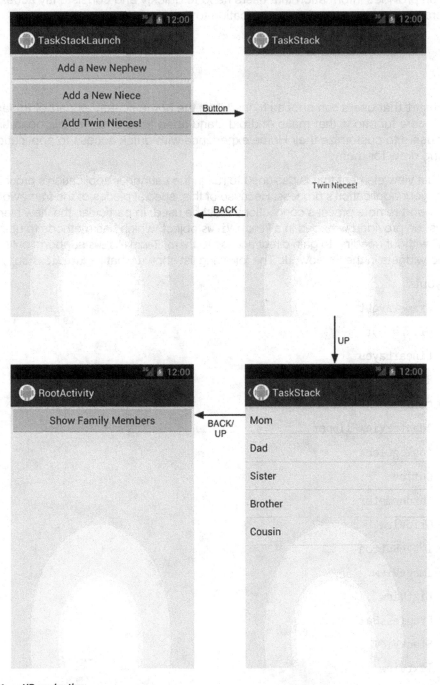

Figure 7-7. BACK vs. UP navigation

7-17. Implementing AppWidgets

Problem

Your application provides information that users need to quickly and consistently access. You want to add an interactive component of your application to the user's home screen.

Solution

(API Level 3)

Build an AppWidget that users can choose to install on the home screen as part of the application. AppWidgets are core functions that make Android stand apart from other mobile operating systems. The ability for users to customize their Home experience with quick access to applications they use most is a strong draw for many.

An AppWidget is a view element that is designed to run in the Launcher application's process but is controlled from your application's process. Because of this, special pieces of the framework that are designed to support remote process connections must be used. In particular, the view hierarchy of the widget must be provided wrapped in a RemoteViews object, which has methods to update view elements by ID without needing to gain direct access to them. RemoteViews supports only a subset of the layouts and widgets in the framework. The following list shows what RemoteViews supports currently:

- Layouts
  - FrameLayout
  - GridLayout
  - LinearLayout
  - RelativeLayout
- Widgets
  - AdapterViewFlipper
  - AnalogClock
  - Button
  - Chronometer
  - GridView
  - ImageButton
  - ImageView
  - ListView
  - ProgressBar
  - StackView
  - TextView
  - ViewFlipper

The view for your `AppWidget` must be composed of these objects only, or the view will not properly display.

Working in a remote process also means that most user interaction must be handled through `PendingIntent` instances, rather than traditional listener interfaces. The `PendingIntent` allows your application to freeze Intent action along with the `Context` that has permission to execute it so the action can be freely handed off to another process and be run at the specified time as if it had come directly from the originating application `Context`.

Sizing

Android Launcher screens on handsets are typically made from a 4×4 grid of spaces in which you can fit your `AppWidget`. While tablets will have considerably greater space, this should be the design metric to keep in mind when determining the minimum height or width of your widget. Android 3.1 introduced the ability for a user to also resize an `AppWidget` after it had been placed, but prior to that, a widget's size was fixed to these values. Taken from the Android documentation, Table 7-1 defines a good rule of thumb to use in determining how many cells a given minimum size will occupy.

Table 7-1. Home Screen Grid Cell Sizes

Number of Cells	Available Space
1	40dp
2	110dp
3	180dp
4	250dp
n	$(70 \times n) - 30$

So, as an example, if your widget needed to be at least 200dp × 48dp in size, it would require three columns and one row in order to display on the Launcher.

How It Works

Let's first take a look at constructing a simple `AppWidget` that can be updated from either the widget itself or the associated activity. This example constructs a random number generator (something I'm sure we all wish could be on our Launcher screen) that can be placed as an `AppWidget`. Let's start with the application's manifest in Listing 7-49.

Listing 7-49. AndroidManifest.xml

```
<application android:label="@string/app_name"
        android:icon="@drawable/ic_launcher">
    <!-- Simple AppWidget Components -->
    <activity android:name=".MainActivity">
        <intent-filter>
            <action android:name="android.intent.action.MAIN" />
            <category android:name="android.intent.category.LAUNCHER" />
```

```
            </intent-filter>
        </activity>

        <receiver android:name=".SimpleAppWidget">
            <intent-filter>
                <action android:name="android.appwidget.action.APPWIDGET_UPDATE" />
            </intent-filter>
            <!-- This data required to configure the AppWidget -->
            <meta-data android:name="android.appwidget.provider"
                android:resource="@xml/simple_appwidget" />
        </receiver>

        <service android:name=".RandomService" />
</application>
```

The only required component here to produce the AppWidget is the `<receiver>` marked
SimpleAppWidget. This element must point to a subclass of AppWidgetProvider, which, as you might
expect, is a customized BroadcastReceiver. It must register in the manifest for the APPWIDGET_UPDATE
broadcast action. There are several other broadcasts that it processes, but this is the only one that
must be declared in the manifest. You must also attach a `<meta-data>` element that points to an
`<appwidget-provider>`, which will eventually be inflated into AppWidgetProviderInfo. Let's have a
look at that element now in Listing 7-50.

Listing 7-50. res/xml/simple_appwidget.xml

```xml
<?xml version="1.0" encoding="utf-8"?>
<appwidget-provider xmlns:android="http://schemas.android.com/apk/res/android"
    android:minWidth="180dp"
    android:minHeight="40dp"
    android:updatePeriodMillis="86400000"
    android:initialLayout="@layout/simple_widget_layout"/>
```

These attributes define the configuration for the AppWidget. Besides the size metrics,
updatePeriodMillis defines the period on which Android should automatically call an update on this
widget to refresh it. Be judicious with this value, and do not set it higher than you need to. In many
cases, it is more efficient to have other services or observers notifying you of changes that require
an AppWidget update. In fact, Android will not deliver updates to an AppWidget more frequently than
30 seconds. We have set our AppWidget to update only once per day. This example also defines an
initialLayout attribute, which points to the layout that should be used for the AppWidget.

There are a number of other useful attributes you can apply here as well:

- android:configure provides an activity that should be launched to configure the
  AppWidget before it is added to the Launcher.

- android:icon references a resource to be displayed at the widget icon on the
  system's selection UI.

- android:previewImage references a resource to display a full-size preview of the
  AppWidget in the system's selection UI (API Level 11).

- android:resizeMode defines how the widget should be resizable on platforms
  that support it: horizontally, vertically, or both (API Level 12).

Listings 7-51 and 7-52 reveal what the AppWidget layout looks like.

Listing 7-51. res/layout/simple_widget_layout.xml

```xml
<?xml version="1.0" encoding="utf-8"?>
<LinearLayout xmlns:android="http://schemas.android.com/apk/res/android"
    android:layout_width="match_parent"
    android:layout_height="match_parent"
    android:background="@drawable/widget_background"
    android:orientation="horizontal"
    android:padding="10dp" >
    <LinearLayout
        android:id="@+id/container"
        android:layout_width="0dp"
        android:layout_height="wrap_content"
        android:layout_weight="1"
        android:layout_gravity="center_vertical"
        android:orientation="vertical">
        <TextView
            android:id="@+id/text_title"
            android:layout_width="wrap_content"
            android:layout_height="wrap_content"
            android:layout_gravity="center_horizontal"
            android:textAppearance="?android:attr/textAppearanceMedium"
            android:text="Random Number" />
        <TextView
            android:id="@+id/text_number"
            android:layout_width="wrap_content"
            android:layout_height="wrap_content"
            android:layout_gravity="center_horizontal"
            android:textStyle="bold"
            android:textAppearance="?android:attr/textAppearanceLarge"/>
    </LinearLayout>

    <ImageButton
        android:id="@+id/button_refresh"
        android:layout_width="55dp"
        android:layout_height="55dp"
        android:layout_gravity="center_vertical"
        android:background="@null"
        android:src="@android:drawable/ic_menu_rotate" />

</LinearLayout>
```

Listing 7-52. res/drawable/widget_background.xml

```xml
<?xml version="1.0" encoding="utf-8"?>
<shape xmlns:android="http://schemas.android.com/apk/res/android"
    android:shape="rectangle">
    <corners
        android:radius="10dp" />
    <solid
        android:color="#A333" />
```

```
    <stroke
        android:width="2dp"
        android:color="#333" />
</shape>
```

It is always good practice with an AppWidget, especially in later platform versions where they can be resized, to define layouts that easily stretch and adapt to a changing container size. In this case, we have defined the background for the widget as a semitransparent rounded rectangle in XML, which could fill any size necessary. The children of the layout are also defined by using weight, so they will fill excess space. This layout is made of two TextView elements and an ImageButton. We have applied android:id attributes to all of these views because there will be no other way to access them once wrapped in a RemoteViews instance later. Listing 7-53 reveals our AppWidgetProvider mentioned earlier.

Listing 7-53. AppWidgetProvider Instance

```
public class SimpleAppWidget extends AppWidgetProvider {

    /*
     * This method is called to update the widgets created by this provider.
     * Normally, this will get called:
     * 1. Initially when the widget is created
     * 2. When the updatePeriodMillis defined in the AppWidgetProviderInfo expires
     * 3. Manually when updateAppWidget() is called on AppWidgetManager
     */
    @Override
    public void onUpdate(Context context, AppWidgetManager appWidgetManager,
            int[] appWidgetIds) {
        //Start the background service to update the widget
        context.startService(new Intent(context, RandomService.class));
    }
}
```

The only required method to implement here is onUpdate(), which will get called initially when the user selects the widget to be added and subsequently when either the framework or your application requests another update. In many cases, you can create the views and update your AppWidget directly inside this method. Because AppWidgetProvider is a BroadcastReceiver, it is not considered good practice to do long operations inside of it. If you must do intensive work to set up your AppWidget, you should start a service instead and perhaps a background thread as well to do the work, which is what we have done here.

For convenience, this method is passed an AppWidgetManager instance, which is necessary for updating the AppWidget if you do so from this method. It is also possible to have multiple AppWidgets loaded on a single Launcher screen. The array of IDs references each individual AppWidget so you can update them all at once. Let's have a look at that service in Listing 7-54.

Listing 7-54. AppWidget Service

```
public class RandomService extends Service {
    /* Broadcast Action When Updates Complete */
    public static final String ACTION_RANDOM_NUMBER =
            "com.examples.appwidget.ACTION_RANDOM_NUMBER";
```

```java
/* Current Data Saved as a static value */
private static int sRandomNumber;
public static int getRandomNumber() {
    return sRandomNumber;
}

@Override
public int onStartCommand(Intent intent, int flags, int startId) {
    //Update the random number data
    sRandomNumber = (int)(Math.random() * 100);

    //Create the AppWidget view
    RemoteViews views = new RemoteViews(getPackageName(),
            R.layout.simple_widget_layout);
    views.setTextViewText(R.id.text_number, String.valueOf(sRandomNumber));

    //Set an Intent for the refresh button to start this service again
    PendingIntent refreshIntent = PendingIntent.getService(this, 0,
            new Intent(this, RandomService.class), 0);
    views.setOnClickPendingIntent(R.id.button_refresh, refreshIntent);

    //Set an Intent so tapping the widget text will open the Activity
    PendingIntent appIntent = PendingIntent.getActivity(this, 0,
            new Intent(this, MainActivity.class), 0);
    views.setOnClickPendingIntent(R.id.container, appIntent);

    //Update the widget
    AppWidgetManager manager = AppWidgetManager.getInstance(this);
    ComponentName widget = new ComponentName(this, SimpleAppWidget.class);
    manager.updateAppWidget(widget, views);

    //Fire a broadcast to notify listeners
    Intent broadcast = new Intent(ACTION_RANDOM_NUMBER);
    sendBroadcast(broadcast);

    //This service should not continue to run
    stopSelf();
    return START_NOT_STICKY;
}

/*
 * We are not binding to this Service, so this method should
 * just return null.
 */
@Override
public IBinder onBind(Intent intent) {
    return null;
}
}
```

This `RandomService` does two operations when started. First, it regenerates and saves the random number data into a static field. Second, it constructs a new view for our `AppWidget`. In this way, we can use this service to refresh our `AppWidget` on demand. We must first create a `RemoteViews` instance, passing in our widget layout. We use `setTextViewText()` to update a `TextView` in the layout with the new number, and `setOnClickPendingIntent()` attaches click listeners. The first `PendingIntent` is attached to the Refresh button on the `AppWidget`, and the Intent that it is set to fire will restart this same service. The second `PendingIntent` is attached to the main layout of the widget, allowing the user to click anywhere inside it, and it fires an Intent to launch the application's main activity.

The final step with our `RemoteViews` initialized is to update the `AppWidget`. We do this by obtaining the `AppWidgetManager` instance and calling `updateAppWidget()`. We do not have the ID values for each `AppWidget` attached to the provider here, which is one method of updating them. Instead, we can pass a `ComponentName` that references our `AppWidgetProvider` and this update will apply to all `AppWidgets` attached to that provider.

To finish up, we send a broadcast to any listeners that a new random number has been generated and we stop the service. At this point, we have all the code in place for our `AppWidget` to be live and working on a device. But let's add one more component and include an activity that interacts with the same data. See Listings 7-55 and 7-56.

Listing 7-55. `res/layout/main.xml`

```xml
<?xml version="1.0" encoding="utf-8"?>
<LinearLayout xmlns:android="http://schemas.android.com/apk/res/android"
    android:layout_width="match_parent"
    android:layout_height="match_parent"
    android:orientation="vertical" >
    <Button
        android:layout_width="match_parent"
        android:layout_height="wrap_content"
        android:text="Generate New Number"
        android:onClick="onRandomClick" />
    <TextView
        android:layout_width="wrap_content"
        android:layout_height="wrap_content"
        android:layout_gravity="center_horizontal"
        android:textAppearance="?android:attr/textAppearanceLarge"
        android:text="Current Random Number" />
    <TextView
        android:id="@+id/text_number"
        android:layout_width="wrap_content"
        android:layout_height="wrap_content"
        android:layout_gravity="center_horizontal"
        android:textSize="55dp"
        android:textStyle="bold" />

</LinearLayout>
```

Listing 7-56. Main Application Activity

```java
public class MainActivity extends Activity {

    private TextView mCurrentNumber;

    @Override
    protected void onCreate(Bundle savedInstanceState) {
        super.onCreate(savedInstanceState);
        setContentView(R.layout.main);

        mCurrentNumber = (TextView) findViewById(R.id.text_number);
    }

    @Override
    protected void onResume() {
        super.onResume();
        updateNumberView();
        //Register a receiver to receive updates when the service finishes
        IntentFilter filter = new IntentFilter(RandomService.ACTION_RANDOM_NUMBER);
        registerReceiver(mReceiver, filter);
    }

    @Override
    protected void onPause() {
        super.onPause();
        //Unregister our receiver
        unregisterReceiver(mReceiver);
    }

    public void onRandomClick(View v) {
        //Call the service to update the number data
        startService(new Intent(this, RandomService.class));
    }

    private void updateNumberView() {
        //Update the view with the latest number
        mCurrentNumber.setText(String.valueOf(RandomService.getRandomNumber()));
    }

    private BroadcastReceiver mReceiver = new BroadcastReceiver() {
        @Override
        public void onReceive(Context context, Intent intent) {
            //Update the view with the new number
            updateNumberView();
        }
    };
}
```

This activity displays the current value of the random number provided by our RandomService. It also responds to button clicks by starting the service to generate a new number. The nice side effect is that this will also update our AppWidget so the two will stay in sync. We also register a

BroadcastReceiver to listen for the event when the service has finished generating new data so that we can update the user interface here as well. Figure 7-8 shows the application activity, and the corresponding AppWidget added to the home screen.

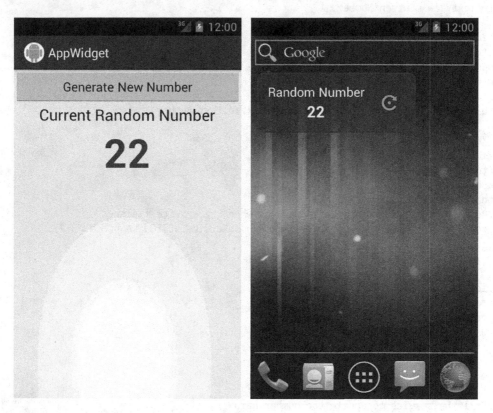

Figure 7-8. The Random Number Activity app (left) and AppWidget (right)

Collection-Based AppWidgets

(API Level 12)

Starting in Android 3.0, the things an AppWidget can display got a boost when collection views were added to the AppWidget framework. This allows applications to display information in a list, grid, or stack. In Android 3.1, AppWidgets also received the ability to be resized after being placed. Let's take a look at an example of an AppWidget that allows the user to see his or her media collection. Again, we'll start with the manifest in Listing 7-57.

Listing 7-57. AndroidManifest.xml

```
<application android:label="@string/app_name"
        android:icon="@drawable/ic_launcher">
    <!-- Collection AppWidget Components -->
    <activity android:name=".ListWidgetConfigureActivity">
        <intent-filter>
            <action android:name="android.appwidget.action.APPWIDGET_CONFIGURE"/>
```

```
        </intent-filter>
    </activity>

    <receiver android:name=".ListAppWidget">
        <intent-filter>
            <action android:name="android.appwidget.action.APPWIDGET_UPDATE" />
        </intent-filter>
        <meta-data android:name="android.appwidget.provider"
            android:resource="@xml/list_appwidget" />
    </receiver>

    <service android:name=".ListWidgetService"
        android:permission="android.permission.BIND_REMOTEVIEWS" />
    <service android:name=".MediaService" />
</application>
```

This example has a similar definition to the AppWidgetProvider, this time named ListAppWidget. We have defined a service with the special permission BIND_REMOTEVIEWS. You will see shortly that this is actually a RemoteViewsService, which the framework will use to provide data for the AppWidget's list, similar to how a ListAdapter works with ListView. Finally, we have defined an activity that will be used to configure the AppWidget before the user adds it. For this to take place, the activity must include an <intent-filter> for the APPWIDGET_CONFIGURE action. The AppWidgetProviderInfo attached to our AppWidget is defined in Listing 7-58.

Listing 7-58. res/xml/list_appwidget.xml

```xml
<?xml version="1.0" encoding="utf-8"?>
<appwidget-provider xmlns:android="http://schemas.android.com/apk/res/android"
    android:minWidth="110dp"
    android:minHeight="110dp"
    android:updatePeriodMillis="86400000"
    android:initialLayout="@layout/list_widget_layout"
    android:configure="com.examples.appwidget.ListWidgetConfigureActivity"
    android:resizeMode="horizontal|vertical"/>
```

In addition to the standard attributes we discussed in the previous example, we have added android:configure to point to our configuration activity, and android:resizeMode will enable this AppWidget to be resized in both directions. Listings 7-59 through 7-61 show the layouts we will use for both the AppWidget itself and for each row of the ListView.

Listing 7-59. res/layout/list_widget_layout.xml

```xml
<?xml version="1.0" encoding="utf-8"?>
<LinearLayout xmlns:android="http://schemas.android.com/apk/res/android"
    android:layout_width="match_parent"
    android:layout_height="match_parent"
    android:orientation="vertical"
    android:background="@drawable/list_widget_background">
    <TextView
        android:id="@+id/text_title"
        android:layout_width="match_parent"
        android:layout_height="45dp"
```

```
        android:gravity="center"
        android:textAppearance="?android:attr/textAppearanceMedium" />
    <FrameLayout
        android:layout_width="match_parent"
        android:layout_height="match_parent" >
        <ListView
            android:id="@+id/list"
            android:layout_width="match_parent"
            android:layout_height="match_parent" />
        <TextView
            android:id="@+id/list_empty"
            android:layout_width="wrap_content"
            android:layout_height="wrap_content"
            android:layout_gravity="center"
            android:text="No Items Available" />
    </FrameLayout>
</LinearLayout>
```

Listing 7-60. res/drawable/list_widget_background.xml

```
<?xml version="1.0" encoding="utf-8"?>
<shape xmlns:android="http://schemas.android.com/apk/res/android"
    android:shape="rectangle">
    <solid
        android:color="#A333" />
</shape>
```

Listing 7-61. res/layout/list_widget_item.xml

```
<?xml version="1.0" encoding="utf-8"?>
<LinearLayout xmlns:android="http://schemas.android.com/apk/res/android"
    android:id="@+id/list_widget_item"
    android:layout_width="match_parent"
    android:layout_height="?android:attr/listPreferredItemHeight"
    android:paddingLeft="10dp"
    android:gravity="center_vertical"
    android:orientation="vertical" >

    <TextView
        android:id="@+id/line1"
        android:layout_width="wrap_content"
        android:layout_height="wrap_content" />

    <TextView
        android:id="@+id/line2"
        android:layout_width="wrap_content"
        android:layout_height="wrap_content" />

</LinearLayout>
```

The layout of the AppWidget is a simple ListView with a TextView above it for a title. We have encapsulated the list into a FrameLayout so that we can also supply a sibling empty view as well.

> **Tip** Try as you might, you will be unsuccessful using most of the Android standard row layouts for
> `ListView` in an **AppWidget**, such as `android.R.id.simple_list_item_1`. This is because these
> elements typically contain views such as `CheckedTextView` that are not supported by `RemoteViews`. You
> will have to create your own layout for each row.

Before we look at the `AppWidgetProvider` for this example, let's first look at the configuration activity.
This is the first thing the user will see after dropping the `AppWidget` onto the home screen, but before
it is installed. The result from this activity will actually govern whether the `AppWidgetProvider` gets
called at all! See Listings 7-62 and 7-63.

Listing 7-62. res/layout/configure.xml

```xml
<?xml version="1.0" encoding="utf-8"?>
<RelativeLayout xmlns:android="http://schemas.android.com/apk/res/android"
    android:layout_width="match_parent"
    android:layout_height="match_parent">
    <TextView
        android:id="@+id/text_title"
        android:layout_width="wrap_content"
        android:layout_height="wrap_content"
        android:textAppearance="?android:attr/textAppearanceLarge"
        android:text="Select Media Type:" />
    <RadioGroup
        android:id="@+id/group_mode"
        android:layout_width="wrap_content"
        android:layout_height="wrap_content"
        android:layout_below="@id/text_title"
        android:orientation="vertical">
        <RadioButton
            android:id="@+id/mode_image"
            android:layout_width="wrap_content"
            android:layout_height="wrap_content"
            android:text="Images"/>
        <RadioButton
            android:id="@+id/mode_video"
            android:layout_width="wrap_content"
            android:layout_height="wrap_content"
            android:text="Videos"/>
    </RadioGroup>

    <Button
        android:layout_width="match_parent"
        android:layout_height="wrap_content"
        android:layout_alignParentBottom="true"
        android:text="Add Widget"
        android:onClick="onAddClick" />

</RelativeLayout>
```

Listing 7-63. Configuration Activity

```java
public class ListWidgetConfigureActivity extends Activity {

    private int mAppWidgetId;
    private RadioGroup mModeGroup;

    @Override
    protected void onCreate(Bundle savedInstanceState) {
        super.onCreate(savedInstanceState);
        setContentView(R.layout.configure);

        mModeGroup = (RadioGroup) findViewById(R.id.group_mode);

        mAppWidgetId = getIntent()
                .getIntExtra(AppWidgetManager.EXTRA_APPWIDGET_ID,
                        AppWidgetManager.INVALID_APPWIDGET_ID);

        setResult(RESULT_CANCELED);
    }

    public void onAddClick(View v) {
        SharedPreferences.Editor prefs =
                getSharedPreferences(String.valueOf(mAppWidgetId), MODE_PRIVATE)
                        .edit();
        RemoteViews views = new RemoteViews(getPackageName(),
                R.layout.list_widget_layout);
        switch (mModeGroup.getCheckedRadioButtonId()) {
        case R.id.mode_image:
            prefs.putString(ListWidgetService.KEY_MODE,
                    ListWidgetService.MODE_IMAGE).commit();
            views.setTextViewText(R.id.text_title, "Image Collection");
            break;
        case R.id.mode_video:
            prefs.putString(ListWidgetService.KEY_MODE,
                    ListWidgetService.MODE_VIDEO).commit();
            views.setTextViewText(R.id.text_title, "Video Collection");
            break;
        default:
            Toast.makeText(this, "Please Select a Media Type.",
                    Toast.LENGTH_SHORT).show();
            return;
        }

        Intent intent = new Intent(this, ListWidgetService.class);
        intent.putExtra(AppWidgetManager.EXTRA_APPWIDGET_ID, mAppWidgetId);
        intent.setData(Uri.parse(intent.toUri(Intent.URI_INTENT_SCHEME)));

        //Attach the adapter to populate the data for the list in
        //the form of an Intent that points to our RemoveViewsService
        views.setRemoteAdapter(mAppWidgetId, R.id.list, intent);
```

```
        //Set the empty view for the list
        views.setEmptyView(R.id.list, R.id.list_empty);

        Intent viewIntent = new Intent(Intent.ACTION_VIEW);
        PendingIntent pendingIntent = PendingIntent.getActivity(this, 0, viewIntent, 0);
        views.setPendingIntentTemplate(R.id.list, pendingIntent);

        AppWidgetManager manager = AppWidgetManager.getInstance(this);
        manager.updateAppWidget(mAppWidgetId, views);

        Intent data = new Intent();
        data.putExtra(AppWidgetManager.EXTRA_APPWIDGET_ID, mAppWidgetId);
        setResult(RESULT_OK, data);
        finish();
    }
}
```

The layout for this activity provides a single RadioGroup to choose between images and videos, which will be the selected media type that the AppWidget displays in its list and on an Add button. By convention, when we enter the activity, we immediately set the result to RESULT_CANCELED. This is because if the user ever leaves this activity without going through the process of hitting Add, we don't want the AppWidget to show up on the screen. The framework checks the result of this activity to decide whether to add the AppWidget. We are also passed the ID of this AppWidget by the framework, which we save for later.

Once the user had made a selection and clicks Add, that selection is saved in a specific SharedPreferences instance named by the AppWidget's ID. We want to be able to allow the application to handle multiple widgets, and we want their configuration values to be separate, so we avoid using the default SharedPreferences to persist this data.

> **Note**   In Android 4.1 the ability to pass configuration data to the **AppWidget** as a Bundle of options was introduced. However, to keep compatibility with previous versions, we can use the SharedPreferences approach instead.

We also can begin to construct the RemoteViews for this AppWidget, setting the title based on the user's type selection. For a collection-based AppWidget, we must construct an Intent that will launch an instance of RemoteViewsService to act as the adapter for the collection data, similar to a ListAdapter. This is attached to the RemoteViews with setRemoteAdapter(), which also takes the ID of the ListView we want the adapter to connect with. We also use setEmptyView() to attach the ID of our sibling TextView to display when the list is empty.

Each list item must have a PendingIntent attached to fire when the user clicks it. The framework is aware that you may need to supply specific information for every item, so it uses the pattern of a PendingIntent template that gets filled in by each item. Here we are creating the base Intent for each item to fill in as a simple ACTION_VIEW, and attaching it via setPendingIntentTemplate(); the data and extras fields will be filled in later.

With all this in place, we call updateAppWidget() on the AppWidgetManager. In this case, we called a version of this method that takes a single ID rather than a ComponentName because we want to update only this specific AppWidget. We then set the result to RESULT_OK and finish, allowing the framework to add the AppWidget to the screen. Let's look briefly now at the AppWidgetProvider, which is shown in Listing 7-64.

Listing 7-64. List AppWidgetProvider

```java
public class ListAppWidget extends AppWidgetProvider {

    /*
     * This method is called to update the widgets created by this provider.
     * Because we supplied a configuration Activity, this method will not get called
     * for the initial adding of the widget, but will still be called:
     * 1. When the updatePeriodMillis defined in the AppWidgetProviderInfo expires
     */
    @Override
    public void onUpdate(Context context, AppWidgetManager appWidgetManager,
            int[] appWidgetIds) {
        //Update each widget created by this provider
        for (int i=0; i < appWidgetIds.length; i++) {
            Intent intent = new Intent(context, ListWidgetService.class);
            intent.putExtra(AppWidgetManager.EXTRA_APPWIDGET_ID, appWidgetIds[i]);
            intent.setData(Uri.parse(intent.toUri(Intent.URI_INTENT_SCHEME)));

            RemoteViews views = new RemoteViews(context.getPackageName(),
                    R.layout.list_widget_layout);
            //Set the title view based on the widget configuration
            SharedPreferences prefs =
                    context.getSharedPreferences(String.valueOf(appWidgetIds[i]),
                        Context.MODE_PRIVATE);
            String mode = prefs.getString(ListWidgetService.KEY_MODE,
                    ListWidgetService.MODE_IMAGE);
            if (ListWidgetService.MODE_VIDEO.equals(mode)) {
                views.setTextViewText(R.id.text_title, "Video Collection");
            } else {
                views.setTextViewText(R.id.text_title, "Image Collection");
            }

            //Attach the adapter to populate the data for the list in
            //the form of an Intent that points to our RemoveViewsService
            views.setRemoteAdapter(appWidgetIds[i], R.id.list, intent);

            //Set the empty view for the list
            views.setEmptyView(R.id.list, R.id.list_empty);

            //Set the template Intent for item clicks that each item will fill-in
            Intent viewIntent = new Intent(Intent.ACTION_VIEW);
            PendingIntent pendingIntent = PendingIntent.getActivity(context, 0,
                    viewIntent, 0);
            views.setPendingIntentTemplate(R.id.list, pendingIntent);
```

```
            appWidgetManager.updateAppWidget(appWidgetIds[i], views);
        }
    }

    /*
     * Called when the first widget is added to the provider
     */
    @Override
    public void onEnabled(Context context) {
        //Start the service to monitor the MediaStore
        context.startService(new Intent(context, MediaService.class));
    }

    /*
     * Called when all widgets have been removed from this provider
     */
    @Override
    public void onDisabled(Context context) {
        //Stop the service that is monitoring the MediaStore
        context.stopService(new Intent(context, MediaService.class));
    }

    /*
     * Called when one or more widgets attached to this provider are removed
     */
    @Override
    public void onDeleted(Context context, int[] appWidgetIds) {
        //Remove the SharedPreferences we created for each widget removed
        for (int i=0; i < appWidgetIds.length; i++) {
            context.getSharedPreferences(String.valueOf(appWidgetIds[i]),
                    Context.MODE_PRIVATE)
                .edit()
                .clear()
                .commit();
        }

    }
}
```

The onUpdate() method of this provider is identical to the code found in the configuration activity, except that the provider is reading the current values of the user configuration settings rather than updating them. The code must be the same because we want to have the same AppWidget result from a subsequent update.

This provider also overrides onEnabled() and onDisabled(). These methods are called when the very first widget is added to the provider and after the very last widget is removed. The provider is using them to start and stop a long-running service that we will look at in more detail shortly, but its purpose is to monitor the MediaStore for changes so we can update our AppWidget. Finally, the onDeleted() callback is called for each AppWidget that gets removed. In our example, we use this to clear out the SharedPreferences we had created when the AppWidget was added.

Now look at Listing 7-65, which defines our RemoteViewsService for serving data to the AppWidget list.

Listing 7-65. RemoteViews Adapter

```java
public class ListWidgetService extends RemoteViewsService {

    public static final String KEY_MODE = "mode";
    public static final String MODE_IMAGE = "image";
    public static final String MODE_VIDEO = "video";

    @Override
    public RemoteViewsFactory onGetViewFactory(Intent intent) {
        return new ListRemoteViewsFactory(this, intent);
    }

    private class ListRemoteViewsFactory implements
            RemoteViewsService.RemoteViewsFactory {
        private Context mContext;
        private int mAppWidgetId;

        private Cursor mDataCursor;

        public ListRemoteViewsFactory(Context context, Intent intent) {
            mContext = context.getApplicationContext();
            mAppWidgetId = intent.getIntExtra(AppWidgetManager.EXTRA_APPWIDGET_ID,
                    AppWidgetManager.INVALID_APPWIDGET_ID);
        }

        @Override
        public void onCreate() {
            //Load preferences to get settings user set while adding the widget
            SharedPreferences prefs =
                    mContext.getSharedPreferences(String.valueOf(mAppWidgetId),
                            MODE_PRIVATE);
            //Get the user's config setting, defaulting to image mode
            String mode = prefs.getString(KEY_MODE, MODE_IMAGE);
            //Set the media type to query based on the user configuration setting
            if (MODE_VIDEO.equals(mode)) {
                //Query for video items in the MediaStore
                String[] projection = {MediaStore.Video.Media.TITLE,
                        MediaStore.Video.Media.DATE_TAKEN,
                        MediaStore.Video.Media.DATA};
                mDataCursor = MediaStore.Images.Media.query(getContentResolver(),
                        MediaStore.Video.Media.EXTERNAL_CONTENT_URI, projection);
            } else {
                //Query for image items in the MediaStore
                String[] projection = {MediaStore.Images.Media.TITLE,
                        MediaStore.Images.Media.DATE_TAKEN,
                        MediaStore.Images.Media.DATA};
                mDataCursor = MediaStore.Images.Media.query(getContentResolver(),
```

```
                        MediaStore.Images.Media.EXTERNAL_CONTENT_URI, projection);
    }
}

/*
 * This method gets called after onCreate(), but also if an external call
 * to AppWidgetManager.notifyAppWidgetViewDataChanged() indicates that the
 * data for a widget should be refreshed.
 */
@Override
public void onDataSetChanged() {
    //Refresh the Cursor data
    mDataCursor.requery();
}

@Override
public void onDestroy() {
    //Close the cursor when we no longer need it.
    mDataCursor.close();
    mDataCursor = null;
}

@Override
public int getCount() {
    return mDataCursor.getCount();
}

/*
 * If your data comes from the network or otherwise may take a while to load,
 * you can return a loading view here.  This view will be shown while
 * getViewAt() is blocked until it returns
 */
@Override
public RemoteViews getLoadingView() {
    return null;
}
/*
 * Return a view for each item in the collection.  You can safely perform long
 * operations in this method.  The loading view will be displayed until this
 * method returns.
 */
@Override
public RemoteViews getViewAt(int position) {
    mDataCursor.moveToPosition(position);

    RemoteViews views = new RemoteViews(getPackageName(),
            R.layout.list_widget_item);
    views.setTextViewText(R.id.line1, mDataCursor.getString(0));
    views.setTextViewText(R.id.line2, DateFormat.format("MM/dd/yyyy",
            mDataCursor.getLong(1)));
```

```
            SharedPreferences prefs = mContext
                .getSharedPreferences(String.valueOf(mAppWidgetId), MODE_PRIVATE);
            String mode = prefs.getString(KEY_MODE, MODE_IMAGE);
            String type;
            if (MODE_VIDEO.equals(mode)) {
                type = "video/*";
            } else {
                type = "image/*";
            }

            Uri data = Uri.fromFile(new File(mDataCursor.getString(2)));

            Intent intent = new Intent();
            intent.setDataAndType(data, type);
            views.setOnClickFillInIntent(R.id.list_widget_item, intent);

            return views;
        }

        @Override
        public int getViewTypeCount() {
            return 1;
        }

        @Override
        public boolean hasStableIds() {
            return false;
        }

        @Override
        public long getItemId(int position) {
            return position;
        }
    }
}
```

The RemoteViewsFactory implementation that RemoteViewsService must return looks very much like a ListAdapter. Many of the methods such as getCount() and getViewTypeCount() perform the same functions as they do for local lists. When the RemoteViewsFactory is first created, we check the setting value the user had selected during configuration, and we then retrieve the appropriate Cursor from the system's MediaStore content provider to display either images or videos. When the factory is destroyed because it's no longer needed, that is our opportunity to close the Cursor. When an external stimulus tells AppWidgetManager that the data need to be refreshed, onDataSetChanged() will be called. To refresh our data, all we need to do is requery() the Cursor.

The getViewAt() method is where we obtain a view for each row in the list. This method is safe to call long-running operations in (such as network I/O); the framework will display whatever is returned from getLoadingView() instead until getViewAt() returns. In the example, we update the RemoteViews version of our row layout with the title and a text representation of the date for the given item. We must then fill in the PendingIntent template that was set in our original update. We set the file path of the image or video and the appropriate MIME type as the data field. Combined with `ACTION_VIEW`, this will open the file in the device's Gallery app (or any other application capable of handling the media) when the item is clicked.

You may notice in this example we didn't use explicit column names when retrieving the Cursor data. This is primarily because the projections between the two types have different names, so it is more efficient to access them by index. Finally, look at Listing 7-66, which reveals the background service that was started and stopped by the AppWidgetProvider.

Listing 7-66. Update Monitoring Service

```java
public class MediaService extends Service {

    private ContentObserver mMediaStoreObserver;

    @Override
    public void onCreate() {
        super.onCreate();
        //Create and register a new observer on the MediaStore when this service begins
        mMediaStoreObserver = new ContentObserver(new Handler()) {
            @Override
            public void onChange(boolean selfChange) {
                //Update all the widgets currently attached to our AppWidgetProvider
                AppWidgetManager manager =
                        AppWidgetManager.getInstance(MediaService.this);
                ComponentName provider = new ComponentName(MediaService.this,
                        ListAppWidget.class);
                int[] appWidgetIds = manager.getAppWidgetIds(provider);
                //This method triggers onDataSetChanged() in the RemoteViewsService
                manager.notifyAppWidgetViewDataChanged(appWidgetIds, R.id.list);
            }
        };
        //Register for Images and Video
        getContentResolver().registerContentObserver(
            MediaStore.Images.Media.EXTERNAL_CONTENT_URI, true, mMediaStoreObserver);
        getContentResolver().registerContentObserver(
            MediaStore.Video.Media.EXTERNAL_CONTENT_URI, true, mMediaStoreObserver);
    }

    @Override
    public void onDestroy() {
        super.onDestroy();
        //Unregister the observer when the Service stops
        getContentResolver().unregisterContentObserver(mMediaStoreObserver);
    }

    /*
     * We are not binding to this Service, so this method should
     * just return null.
     */
```

```
    @Override
    public IBinder onBind(Intent intent) {
        return null;
    }

}
```

The purpose of this service is to register a ContentObserver with the MediaStore while any AppWidgets are active. This way, when a photo or video is added or removed, we can update the list of our widget to reflect that. Whenever the ContentObserver triggers, we will call notifyAppWidgetViewDataChanged() on AppWidgetManager for every widget currently attached. This will trigger the onDataSetChanged() callback in the RemoveViewsService to refresh the lists. You can see the result of all this working together in Figures 7-9 and 7-10.

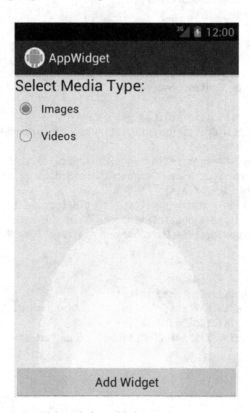

Figure 7-9. Configuration Activity prior to AppWidget being added

Figure 7-10. AppWidget added for both types (left) and after being resized (right)

You can see that by simply adding the resize attributes to the AppWidgetProviderInfo, the size of the AppWidget can be modified by the user. Each list can be scrolled, and a tap on any item will bring up the default viewing application to view the image or play the video.

7-18. Supporting Restricted Profiles

Problem

Your application targets an audience of various ages and abilities, and you need to provide the control to modify the app's behavior to suit each particular user.

Solution

(API Level 18)

UserManager provides some generic information about system-level features that may be unavailable to the user profile, via getUserRestrictions(), if that profile is set up to be restricted. Furthermore, applications can define custom feature sets that should be configurable in a restricted environment, and then obtain the current settings of the device from the UserManager by calling getApplicationRestrictions().

Each application can define a set of `RestrictionEntry` elements that the system will present the device owner in user settings to configure the app for the Restricted Profile. Each element defines the type of setting (Boolean, single selection, or multi-selection) and the data that should be visible in settings.

Android devices that support multiple user accounts provide the ability for the device owner (which is defined as the first account set up on the device) to create additional users or Restricted Profiles. Secondary users have their own applications, data spaces, and the same ability to administer the device just as the owner, with the exception of managing other user accounts.

Restricted Profiles were introduced in Android 4.3 as a way of providing restricted access to the applications and data that are part of the owner's account. These profiles do not have their own application space or associated data. Instead, they are a set of controls an owner can place on which of their own applications can be used and which features of those applications are accessible. The obvious use case for this is parental controls, but one could also use Restricted Profiles to put a device temporarily into a kiosk mode, for example.

> **Tip** Multiple user accounts are not typically enabled in emulator images, and are usually supported on only tablet devices. These types of features are not common on handsets.

How It Works

To illustrate an application that takes advantage of restricted user environments, we've constructed a simple drawing application for children and young adults. We will use application-level restrictions to remove and modify certain application features. Listing 7-67 contains the layout of the user interface.

Listing 7-67. res/layout/activity_main.xml

```xml
<?xml version="1.0" encoding="utf-8"?>
<FrameLayout xmlns:android="http://schemas.android.com/apk/res/android"
    android:layout_width="match_parent"
    android:layout_height="match_parent" >

    <com.androidrecipes.restrictedprofiles.DrawingView
        android:id="@+id/drawing_surface"
        android:layout_width="match_parent"
        android:layout_height="match_parent"/>

    <Button
        android:id="@+id/button_purchase"
        android:layout_width="wrap_content"
        android:layout_height="wrap_content"
        android:layout_gravity="right"
        android:text="$$$$"
        android:onClick="onPurchaseClick"/>
```

```xml
<SeekBar
    android:id="@+id/full_slider"
    android:layout_width="match_parent"
    android:layout_height="wrap_content"
    android:layout_gravity="bottom"
    android:max="45"/>
<RadioGroup
    android:id="@+id/simple_selector"
    android:layout_width="match_parent"
    android:layout_height="wrap_content"
    android:layout_gravity="bottom"
    android:orientation="horizontal">
    <RadioButton
        android:id="@+id/option_small"
        android:layout_width="0dp"
        android:layout_height="wrap_content"
        android:layout_weight="1"
        android:textColor="#555"
        android:text="Small" />
    <RadioButton
        android:id="@+id/option_medium"
        android:layout_width="0dp"
        android:layout_height="wrap_content"
        android:layout_weight="1"
        android:textColor="#555"
        android:text="Medium" />
    <RadioButton
        android:id="@+id/option_large"
        android:layout_width="0dp"
        android:layout_height="wrap_content"
        android:layout_weight="1"
        android:textColor="#555"
        android:text="Big" />
    <RadioButton
        android:id="@+id/option_xlarge"
        android:layout_width="0dp"
        android:layout_height="wrap_content"
        android:layout_weight="1"
        android:textColor="#555"
        android:text="Really Big" />
</RadioGroup>
</FrameLayout>
```

In this example, we have created a drawing surface where the user can paint with their finger (which is a custom view we will see shortly), a button that allows the user to purchase upgraded content (in our case, better colors) from our fake store, and some UI at the bottom of the screen to adjust the line width of the drawings (a slider and a set of radio buttons). We will be using application restrictions to control the latter two features. See Listing 7-68 for the activity element.

Listing 7-68. Restricted Profiles Activity

```java
public class MainActivity extends Activity implements
        OnSeekBarChangeListener, OnCheckedChangeListener {

    private Button mPurchaseButton;
    private DrawingView mDrawingView;
    private SeekBar mFullSlider;
    private RadioGroup mSimpleSelector;

    /* Profile Restriction Values */
    private boolean mHasPurchases;
    private int mMinAge;
    /* Content Purchase Flags */
    private boolean mHasCanvasColors = false;
    private boolean mHasPaintColors = false;

    @Override
    protected void onCreate(Bundle savedInstanceState) {
        super.onCreate(savedInstanceState);
        setContentView(R.layout.activity_main);

        mPurchaseButton = (Button) findViewById(R.id.button_purchase);
        mDrawingView = (DrawingView) findViewById(R.id.drawing_surface);
        mFullSlider = (SeekBar) findViewById(R.id.full_slider);
        mSimpleSelector = (RadioGroup) findViewById(R.id.simple_selector);

        mFullSlider.setOnSeekBarChangeListener(this);
        mSimpleSelector.setOnCheckedChangeListener(this);

        if (Build.VERSION.SDK_INT >= Build.VERSION_CODES.JELLY_BEAN_MR2) {
            UserManager manager = (UserManager) getSystemService(USER_SERVICE);
            //Check for system-level restrictions
            Bundle restrictions = manager.getUserRestrictions();
            if (restrictions != null && !restrictions.isEmpty()) {
                showSystemRestrictionsDialog(restrictions);
            }
        }
    }

    @Override
    protected void onStart() {
        super.onStart();
        /*
         * Restrictions may change while the app is in the background so we need
         * to check this each time we return
         */
        updateRestrictions();
        // Update UI based on restriction changes
        updateDisplay();
    }
```

```java
public void onPurchaseClick(View v) {
    AlertDialog.Builder builder =
            new AlertDialog.Builder(this);
    builder.setTitle("Content Upgrades")
            .setMessage(
                    "Tap any of the following items to add them.")
            .setPositiveButton("Canvas Colors $2.99",
                    mPurchaseListener)
            .setNeutralButton("Paint Colors $2.99",
                    mPurchaseListener)
            .setNegativeButton("Both Items $4.99",
                    mPurchaseListener).show();
}

private DialogInterface.OnClickListener mPurchaseListener =
        new DialogInterface.OnClickListener() {
    @Override
    public void onClick(DialogInterface dialog, int which) {
        switch (which) {
            case DialogInterface.BUTTON_POSITIVE:
                mHasCanvasColors = true;
                break;
            case DialogInterface.BUTTON_NEUTRAL:
                mHasPaintColors = true;
                break;
            case DialogInterface.BUTTON_NEGATIVE:
                mHasCanvasColors = true;
                mHasPaintColors = true;
                break;
        }
        Toast.makeText(getApplicationContext(), "Thank You For Your Purchase!",
                Toast.LENGTH_SHORT).show();
        updateDisplay();
    }
};

private void showSystemRestrictionsDialog(Bundle restrictions) {
    StringBuilder message = new StringBuilder();
    for (String key : restrictions.keySet()) {
        //Make sure the value of the restriction is true
        if (restrictions.getBoolean(key)) {
            message.append(RestrictionsReceiver.getNameForRestriction(key));
            message.append("\n");
        }
    }

    AlertDialog.Builder builder = new AlertDialog.Builder(this);
    builder.setTitle("System Restrictions")
        .setMessage(message.toString())
        .setPositiveButton("OK", null)
        .show();
}
```

```java
@Override
public void onCheckedChanged(RadioGroup group, int checkedId) {
    float width;
    switch(checkedId) {
        default:
        case R.id.option_small:
            width = 4f;
            break;
        case R.id.option_medium:
            width = 12f;
            break;
        case R.id.option_large:
            width = 25f;
            break;
        case R.id.option_xlarge:
            width = 45f;
            break;
    }
    mDrawingView.setStrokeWidth(width);
}

@Override
public void onProgressChanged(SeekBar seekBar, int progress,
        boolean fromUser) {
    mDrawingView.setStrokeWidth(progress);
}

@Override
public void onStartTrackingTouch(SeekBar seekBar) { }

@Override
public void onStopTrackingTouch(SeekBar seekBar) { }

private void updateDisplay() {
    //Show/hide purchase button
    mPurchaseButton.setVisibility(
            mHasPurchases ? View.VISIBLE : View.GONE);

    //Update age-restricted content
    mFullSlider.setVisibility(View.GONE);
    mSimpleSelector.setVisibility(View.GONE);
    switch (mMinAge) {
        case 18:
            //Full-range slider
            mFullSlider.setVisibility(View.VISIBLE);
            mFullSlider.setProgress(4);
            break;
        case 10:
            //Four options
            mSimpleSelector.setVisibility(View.VISIBLE);
            findViewById(R.id.option_medium).setVisibility(View.VISIBLE);
            findViewById(R.id.option_xlarge).setVisibility(View.VISIBLE);
```

```
                mSimpleSelector.check(R.id.option_medium);
                break;
            case 5:
                //Big/small option
                mSimpleSelector.setVisibility(View.VISIBLE);
                findViewById(R.id.option_medium).setVisibility(View.GONE);
                findViewById(R.id.option_xlarge).setVisibility(View.GONE);
                mSimpleSelector.check(R.id.option_small);
                break;
            case 3:
            default:
                //No selection
                break;
        }

        //Update display with purchases
        mDrawingView.setPaintColor(mHasPaintColors ? Color.BLUE : Color.GRAY);
        mDrawingView.setCanvasColor(mHasCanvasColors ? Color.GREEN : Color.BLACK);
    }

    private void updateRestrictions() {
        // Check for restrictions
        if (Build.VERSION.SDK_INT >= Build.VERSION_CODES.JELLY_BEAN_MR2) {
            UserManager manager = (UserManager) getSystemService(USER_SERVICE);
            Bundle restrictions = manager
                    .getApplicationRestrictions(getPackageName());
            if (restrictions != null) {
                // Read restriction settings
                mHasPurchases = restrictions.getBoolean(
                        RestrictionsReceiver.RESTRICTION_PURCHASE, true);
                try {
                    mMinAge = Integer.parseInt(restrictions.getString(
                            RestrictionsReceiver.RESTRICTION_AGERANGE, "18"));
                } catch (NumberFormatException e) {
                    mMinAge = 0;
                }
            } else {
                // We have no restrictions
                mHasPurchases = true;
                mMinAge = 18;
            }
        } else {
            // We are not on a system that supports restrictions
            mHasPurchases = true;
            mMinAge = 18;
        }
    }
}
```

System Feature Restrictions

When the activity is created, after verifying that we are running on a device with API Level 18 or later, we determine whether there are any system-level restrictions with UserManager. getUserRestrictions(). This returns a Bundle that will be empty if there are no restrictions (that is, when running as the device owner or another full user). However, if restrictions do exist, we collect descriptions about them together and show a dialog on the screen. A unique key and a Boolean value in the Bundle describe each restriction. For each possible key, if the value is true, that restriction applies; if the restriction does not apply, the value may be false or the key may not appear in the Bundle at all. Here is a list of the possible system restrictions:

- DISALLOW_CONFIG_BLUETOOTH: This profile cannot configure Bluetooth.

- DISALLOW_CONFIG_CREDENTIALS: This profile cannot configure system user credentials.

- DISALLOW_CONFIG_WIFI: This profile cannot modify the WiFi access point configuration.

- DISALLOW_INSTALL_APPS: This profile cannot install new applications.

- DISALLOW_INSTALL_UNKNOWN_SOURCES: This profile cannot enable Unknown Sources in device settings for installing applications.

- DISALLOW_MODIFY_ACCOUNTS: This profile cannot add or remove device accounts.

- DISALLOW_REMOVE_USER: This profile cannot remove other users.

- DISALLOW_SHARE_LOCATION: This profile cannot toggle location-sharing settings.

- DISALLOW_UNINSTALL_APPS: This profile cannot uninstall applications.

- DISALLOW_USB_FILE_TRANSFER: This profile cannot transfer files over USB.

The descriptions we display are pulled from a helper utility inside RestrictionsReceiver, which is a BroadcastReceiver that we have defined in Listing 7-69.

Listing 7-69. Restrictions Receiver

```
public class RestrictionsReceiver extends BroadcastReceiver {

    public static final String RESTRICTION_PURCHASE = "purchases";
    public static final String RESTRICTION_AGERANGE = "age_range";

    private static final String[] AGES = {"3+", "5+", "10+", "18+"};
    private static final String[] AGE_VALUES = {"3", "5", "10", "18"};

    @Override
    public void onReceive(Context context, Intent intent) {
        ArrayList<RestrictionEntry> restrictions = new ArrayList<RestrictionEntry>();

        RestrictionEntry purchase = new RestrictionEntry(RESTRICTION_PURCHASE, false);
        purchase.setTitle("Content Purchases");
        purchase.setDescription("Allow purchasing of content in the application.");
        restrictions.add(purchase);
```

```
        RestrictionEntry ages =
                new RestrictionEntry(RESTRICTION_AGERANGE, AGE_VALUES[0]);
        ages.setTitle("Age Level");
        ages.setDescription("Difficulty level for application content.");
        ages.setChoiceEntries(AGES);
        ages.setChoiceValues(AGE_VALUES);
        restrictions.add(ages);

        Bundle result = new Bundle();
        result.putParcelableArrayList(Intent.EXTRA_RESTRICTIONS_LIST, restrictions);

        setResultExtras(result);
    }

    /*
     * Utility to get readable strings from restriction keys
     */
    public static String getNameForRestriction(String key) {
        if (UserManager.DISALLOW_CONFIG_BLUETOOTH.equals(key)) {
            return "Unable to configure Bluetooth";
        }
        if (UserManager.DISALLOW_CONFIG_CREDENTIALS.equals(key)) {
            return "Unable to configure user credentials";
        }
        if (UserManager.DISALLOW_CONFIG_WIFI.equals(key)) {
            return "Unable to configure Wifi";
        }
        if (UserManager.DISALLOW_INSTALL_APPS.equals(key)) {
            return "Unable to install applications";
        }
        if (UserManager.DISALLOW_INSTALL_UNKNOWN_SOURCES.equals(key)) {
            return "Unable to enable unknown sources";
        }
        if (UserManager.DISALLOW_MODIFY_ACCOUNTS.equals(key)) {
            return "Unable to modify accounts";
        }
        if (UserManager.DISALLOW_REMOVE_USER.equals(key)) {
            return "Unable to remove users";
        }
        if (UserManager.DISALLOW_SHARE_LOCATION.equals(key)) {
            return "Unable to toggle location sharing";
        }
        if (UserManager.DISALLOW_UNINSTALL_APPS.equals(key)) {
            return "Unable to uninstall applications";
        }
        if (UserManager.DISALLOW_USB_FILE_TRANSFER.equals(key)) {
            return "Unable to transfer files";
        }

        return "Unknown Restriction: "+key;
    }
}
```

Application-Specific Restrictions

Beyond hosting our description utility method, the primary purpose of `RestrictionsReceiver` is to define the set of custom restrictions we want to expose to the device owner explicitly for this application. When looking for restrictions that are exposed, the framework will send an ordered broadcast Intent with the `android.intent.action.GET_RESTRICTION_ENTRIES` action string. It is then the responsibility of any receiver that filters this action to construct a list of `RestrictionEntry` elements and return that list in the result `Bundle`.

Tip   If your restriction settings are too complex to boil down to a handful of selectable items, or if you would simply prefer to better brand that experience, you may return an Intent in the receiver's result `Bundle` with `EXTRA_RESTRICTIONS_INTENT` as the key. The Intent should reference an activity you would like the device settings to launch in order to set up restrictions for the application. In this case, the key/value data for the restrictions should be returned via the activity's result.

We have defined two restriction settings we want to expose: one to allow the user to make purchases from within the application, and the other to modify the application experience based on the age level of the user. The first setting is created as a Boolean type with the default value of `false` (that is, this restriction's value is `false` by default), and the second is a single selection with options for ages from 3+ to 18+. Listing 7-70 shows the `<receiver>` snippet that must be in the manifest for this receiver to be published correctly.

Listing 7-70. Manifest Snippet for Restrictions Receiver

```
<receiver android:name=".RestrictionsReceiver">
    <intent-filter>
        <action android:name="android.intent.action.GET_RESTRICTION_ENTRIES"/>
    </intent-filter>
</receiver>
```

With this application installed, now these two settings will show up for the device owner to configure when setting up a restricted user profile.

In Listing 7-68, we see that when the activity starts up, the current set of application restrictions is checked by calling `UserManager.getApplicationRestrictions()` to get another `Bundle`. This `Bundle` contains the list of key/value pairs for the settings we defined in our receiver. We use the values in this `Bundle` to update the internal state of the activity, which controls how the user interface is displayed. If we have no restrictions (for example, we are the device owner), this method will return `null`.

Because this application is shared between the device owner and the restricted profile, we have to assume that these setting values can change while the activity is in the background, so for that reason these checks are done in `onStart()` rather than `onCreate()` or some other one-shot initialization routine.

The Purchases setting controls whether the Money button in the top corner is visible. If purchases are allowed, the user can tap this button and choose from our fake storefront to get a new line color, background color, or both to spice up their drawing.

The Age Level setting controls what the user can do to update the line width. For very young children, this setting will get in the way, so we keep a fixed line width and hide all the controls. As the children move up in age, we want to give them some options, so a set of radio buttons is provided with either two or four width selections. If the minimum age is set all the way up to 18+, then we replace this UI with a full slider element for the user to choose exactly the line width they want with single-pixel precision.

To finish off the example, Listing 7-71 reveals our custom finger-drawing view.

Listing 7-71. Finger-Drawing View

```java
public class DrawingView extends View {

    private Paint mFingerPaint;
    private Path mPath;

    public DrawingView(Context context) {
        super(context);
        init();
    }

    public DrawingView(Context context, AttributeSet attrs) {
        super(context, attrs);
        init();
    }

    public DrawingView(Context context, AttributeSet attrs,
            int defStyle) {
        super(context, attrs, defStyle);
        init();
    }

    private void init() {
        //Set up the paint brush
        mFingerPaint = new Paint(Paint.ANTI_ALIAS_FLAG);
        mFingerPaint.setStyle(Style.STROKE);
        mFingerPaint.setStrokeCap(Cap.ROUND);
        mFingerPaint.setStrokeJoin(Join.ROUND);
        //Default stroke width
        mFingerPaint.setStrokeWidth(8f);
    }

    public void setPaintColor(int color) {
        mFingerPaint.setColor(color);
    }

    public void setStrokeWidth(float width) {
        mFingerPaint.setStrokeWidth(width);
    }
```

```java
    public void setCanvasColor(int color) {
        setBackgroundColor(color);
    }

    @Override
    public boolean onTouchEvent(MotionEvent event) {
        switch (event.getActionMasked()) {
            case MotionEvent.ACTION_DOWN:
                mPath = new Path();
                //Start at the touch down
                mPath.moveTo(event.getX(), event.getY());
                //Re-draw
                invalidate();
                break;
            case MotionEvent.ACTION_MOVE:
                //Add all touch points between events
                for (int i=0; i < event.getHistorySize(); i++) {
                    mPath.lineTo(event.getHistoricalX(i),
                            event.getHistoricalY(i) );
                }
                //Re-draw
                invalidate();
                break;
            default:
                break;
        }
        return true;
    }

    @Override
    protected void onDraw(Canvas canvas) {
        //Draw the background
        super.onDraw(canvas);
        //Draw the paint stroke
        if (mPath != null) {
            canvas.drawPath(mPath, mFingerPaint);
        }
    }
}
```

This is a basic View implementation that tracks all touch events and converts them into a Path to be drawn. On each new touch gesture, the old Path is discarded and the initial touch point is added to a new Path. On each subsequent move event, while the finger is dragging, the Path is updated with a line that follows the trail of touch events and the view is invalidated (which triggers onDraw() again). Since we are discarding the old contents on each new gesture, the view draws only the current stroke, and the existing contents will clear when the view is touched again.

Additionally, we have added external setters to update the stroke width and color parameters from the selections made in the UI. These values are simply modifications of the Paint that is used to draw the resulting line. Figure 7-11 shows the application running on the device owner's account, with all features running unrestricted.

Figure 7-11. Drawing app UI for unrestricted user

If we create a restricted profile on this device, part of the configuration settings will be to enable our application for that profile, and then set the settings appropriately for the target user. See Figure 7-12 for an example of these settings from a Nexus 7 device.

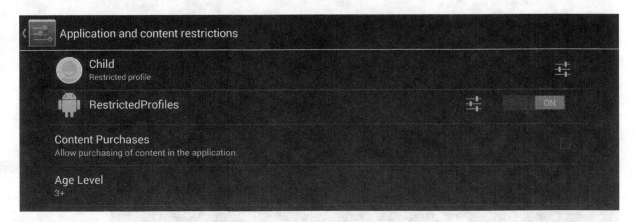

Figure 7-12. Content settings for a Restricted Profile

Finally, with the restrictions set as shown in Figure 7-12, Figure 7-13 shows the same application running under the restricted profile.

Figure 7-13. Dialog showing system restrictions (top), application UI in restricted mode (bottom)

First we see the dialog displayed with any system-level restrictions, followed by the main application UI. Notice in this case that the Purchase button is no longer visible and the stroke width control has been replaced with simpler choices.

Summary

In this chapter, you learned ways for your application to interact directly with the Android operating system. We discussed several methods of placing operations into the background for various lengths of time. You learned how applications share responsibility, launching each other to best accomplish the task at hand. Finally, we presented how the system exposes the content gathered by its core application suite for your application's use. In the next chapter, we will look at how you can use the wide array of publicly available Java libraries to further enhance your application.

Working with Android NDK and RenderScript

Developers typically write Android apps entirely in Java. However, situations arise where it's desirable (or even necessary) to express at least part of the code in another language (notably C or C++). Google addresses these situations by providing the Android Native Development Kit (NDK) and RenderScript.

Android NDK

The Android NDK complements the Android SDK by providing a tool set that lets you implement parts of your app by using native code languages such as C and C++. The NDK provides headers and libraries for building native activities, handling user input, using hardware sensors, and more.

The NDK exists primarily to boost app performance, but it is not without penalty. When invoking native code, execution transitions from the Dalvik virtual machine (VM) Java bytecode to compiled native code via the Java Native Interface (JNI). Calling methods across this interface adds overhead, which impacts performance, so it is best to use native code only in situations where this overhead will be negligible. Longer operations inside native methods along with fewer requests coming from the Java layer will help reduce the penalty.

> **Note** Code running inside Dalvik already experiences a performance boost thanks to the just-in-time compiler that was integrated with Dalvik in Android 2.2.

The NDK is used in the following scenarios:

■ Your app contains CPU-intensive code that doesn't allocate much memory. Code examples include physics simulation, signal processing, huge factorial calculations, and testing huge integers for primeness. RenderScript (discussed later in this chapter) is probably more appropriate for addressing at least some of these examples.

■ You want to ease the porting of existing C/C++-based source code to your app. Using the NDK can help to speed up app development by letting you keep most or all of your app's code in C/C++. Furthermore, working with the NDK can help you keep code changes synchronized between Android and non-Android projects.

> **Caution**   Think carefully about integrating native code into your app. Basing even part of an app on native code increases its complexity and makes it harder to debug.

Installing the NDK

If you believe that your app can benefit from being at least partly expressed in native code, you'll need to install the NDK. Before doing so, you need to be aware of the following software and system requirements:

■ A complete Android SDK installation (including all dependencies) is required. Version 1.5 or later of the SDK is supported.

■ The following operating systems are supported: Windows XP (32-bit), Windows Vista (32- or 64-bit), Windows 7 (32- or 64-bit), Mac OS X 10.4.8 or later (x86 only), and Linux (32- or 64-bit; Ubuntu 8.04, or other Linux distributions using glibc 2.7 or later).

■ For all platforms, GNU Make 3.81 or later is required. Earlier versions of GNU Make might work but have not been tested. Also, GNU Awk or Nawk is required.

■ For Windows platforms, Cygwin (1.7 or higher) is required to support debugging. Before Revision 7 of the NDK, Cygwin was also required to build projects by supplying Make and Awk tools.

■ The native libraries created by the Android NDK can be used only on devices running specific minimum Android platform versions. The minimum required platform version depends on the CPU architecture of the devices you are targeting. Table 8-1 details which Android platform versions are compatible with native code developed for specific CPU architectures.

Table 8-1. Mappings Between Native Code CPU Architectures and Compatible Android Platforms

Native Code CPU Architecture Used	Compatible Android Platforms
ARM, ARM NEON	Android 1.5 (API Level 3) and higher
x86	Android 2.3 (API Level 9) and higher
MIPS	Android 2.3 (API Level 9) and higher

These requirements mean that you can use native libraries created via the NDK in apps that are deployable to ARM-based devices running Android 1.5 or later. If you are deploying native libraries to x86- and MIPS-based devices, your app must target Android 2.3 or later.

■ To ensure compatibility, an app using a native library created via the NDK must declare a `<uses-sdk>` element in its manifest file, with an `android:minSdkVersion` attribute value of "3" or higher. For example:

```
<manifest>
  <uses-sdk android:minSdkVersion="3" />
  ...
</manifest>
```

■ If you use the NDK to create a native library that uses the OpenGL ES APIs, the app containing the library can be deployed only to devices running the minimum platform versions described in Table 8-2. To ensure compatibility, make sure that your app declares the proper `android:minSdkVersion` attribute value.

Table 8-2. Mappings Between OpenGL ES Versions, Compatible Android Platforms, and `uses-sdk`

OpenGL ES Version	Compatible Android Platforms	Required `uses-sdk` Attribute
OpenGL ES 1.1	Android 1.6 (API Level 4) and higher	`android:minSdkVersion="4"`
OpenGL ES 2.0	Android 2.0 (API Level 5) and higher	`android:minSdkVersion="5"`
OpenGL ES 3.0	Android 4.3 (API Level 18) and higher	`android:minSdkVersion="18"`

■ Additionally, an app using the OpenGL ES APIs should declare a `<uses-feature>` element in its manifest, with an `android:glEsVersion` attribute that specifies the minimum OpenGL ES version required by the app. This ensures that Google Play will show your app only to users whose devices can support your app. For example:

```
<manifest>
  <uses-feature android:glEsVersion="0x00020000" />
  ...
</manifest>
```

- If you use the NDK to create a native library that uses the Android API to access `android.graphics.Bitmap` pixel buffers, or utilizes native activities, the app containing the library can be deployed only to devices running Android 2.2 (API level 8) or higher. To ensure compatibility, make sure that your app declares a `<uses-sdk android:minSdkVersion="8" />` element in its manifest.

Point your browser to `http://developer.android.com/tools/sdk/ndk/index.html` and download one of the following NDK packages for your platform—Revision 9 is the latest version at the time of writing:

- `android-ndk-r9d-windows.zip` (Windows)

- `android-ndk-r9d-darwin-x86.tar.bz2` (Mac OS X: Intel)

- `android-ndk-r9d-linux-x86.tar.bz2` (Linux 32-/64-bit: x86)

After downloading your chosen package, unarchive it and move its `android- ndk-r9d` home directory to a more suitable location, perhaps to the same directory that contains the Android SDK's home directory.

Exploring the NDK

Now that you've installed the NDK on your platform, you might want to explore its home directory to discover what the NDK offers. The following list describes those directories and files that are located in the home directory for the Windows-based NDK:

- `build` contains the files that compose the NDK's build system.

- `docs` contains the NDK's HTML-based documentation files.

- `platforms` contains subdirectories that contain header files and shared libraries for each of the Android SDK's installed Android platforms.

- `prebuilt` contains binaries (notably `make.exe` and `awk.exe`) that let you build NDK source code without requiring Cygwin.

- `samples` contains various sample apps that demonstrate different aspects of the NDK.

- `sources` contains the source code and prebuilt binaries for various shared libraries, such as `cpufeatures` (to detect the target device's CPU family and the optional features it supports) and `stlport` (multiplatform C++ standard library). Android NDK 1.5 required that developers organize their native code library projects under this directory. Starting with Android NDK 1.6, native code libraries are stored in `jni` subdirectories of their Android app project directories.

- `tests` contains scripts and sources to perform automated testing of the NDK. They are useful for testing a custom-built NDK.

- `toolchains` contains compilers, linkers, and other tools for generating native ARM binaries on Linux, OS X, and Windows (with Cygwin) platforms.

- `documentation.html` is the entry point into the NDK's documentation.

- `GNUmakefile` is the default makefile used by GNU Make.

- `ndk-build` is a shell script that simplifies building machine code.

- `ndk-gdb` is a shell script that easily launches a native debugging session for your NDK-generated machine code. (Cygwin is required to run this script on Windows platforms.)

- `ndk-stack.exe` lets you filter stack traces as they appear in the output generated by `adb logcat` and replace any address inside a shared library with the corresponding values. In essence, it lets you observe more-readable crash dump information.

- `README.TXT` welcomes you to the NDK, and it refers you to various documentation files that inform you about changes in the current release (and more).

- `RELEASE.TXT` contains the NDK's release number (r9).

Each of the `platforms` directory's subdirectories contains header files that target stable native APIs. Google guarantees that all later platform releases will support the following APIs (see also http://developer.android.com/tools/sdk/ndk/overview.html#tools):

- Android logging (`liblog`)

- Android native app APIs

- C library (`libc`)

- C++ minimal support (`stlport`)

- JNI interface APIs

- Math library (`libm`)

- OpenGL ES 1.1, 2.0, and 3.0 (3D graphics libraries) APIs

- OpenSL ES native audio library APIs

- OpenMAX AL multimedia library APIs

- Pixel buffer access for Android 2.2 and above (`libjnigraphics`)

- Zlib compression (`libz`)

Caution Native system libraries that are not in this list are not stable and may change in future versions of the Android platform. Do not use them.

8-1. Developing Low-Level Native Activities
Problem

You want to learn how to develop low-level native activities, which are based on the
native_activity.h header file.

Solution

Create a low-level native activity project as if it were a regular Android app project. Then modify its
AndroidManifest.xml file appropriately, and introduce a jni subdirectory of the project directory that
contains the native activity's C/C++ source code along with an Android.mk makefile.

The modified AndroidManifest.xml file differs from the regular AndroidManifest.xml file in the
following ways:

- A <uses-sdk android:minSdkVersion="9"/> element precedes the
  <application> element; native activities require at least API Level 9.

- An android:hasCode="false" attribute appears in the <application> tag
  because native activities don't contain Java source code.

- The <activity> element's android:name attribute contains the value android.
  app.NativeActivity. When Android discovers this value, it locates the
  appropriate entry point in the native activity's library.

- A <meta-data> element specifies an android:name="android.app.lib_name"
  attribute and an android:value attribute whose value is the name of the native
  activity's library (without a lib prefix and a .so suffix).

Your native activity's C/C++ source file must define ANativeActivity_onCreate() as an entry point.
This method declares the following parameters:

- activity: This is the address of an ANativeActivity structure. ANativeActivity
  is defined in the NDK's native_activity.h header file, and it declares various
  members

  - callbacks: An array of pointers to callback functions; you can set these
    pointers to your own callbacks.

  - internalDataPath: The path to the app's internal data directory.

  - externalDataPath: The path to the app's external [removable/mountable]
    data directory.

  - sdkVersion: The platform's SDK version number.

  - assetManager: A pointer to an instance of the native equivalent of the app's
    android.content.res.AssetManager class for accessing binary assets
    bundled into the app's APK file.

- savedState: This is your activity's previously saved state. If the activity is being instantiated from a previously saved instance, savedState will be non-null and will point to the saved data. You must make a copy of this data when you need to access it later, because memory allocated to savedState will be released after you return from this function.

- savedStateSize: This is the size (in bytes) of the data pointed to by savedState.

> **Note**   When you launch an app that is based on a native activity, a NativeActivity instance is created. Its onCreate() method uses the JNI to call ANativeActivity_onCreate(ANativeActivity*, void*, size_t).

ANativeActivity_onCreate() should override any needed callbacks. It must also create a thread that promptly responds to input events in order to prevent an "Application Not Responding" error from occurring.

An NDK application has one additional required file that we haven't seen before, an Android.mk file. This is a makefile definition to tell the NDK how to build our C/C++ code into a shared library the framework can load. The components of an Android.mk are typically as follows:

- $(CLEAR_VARS): A macro that clears all the local variables from building any previous module. It is typically found as one of the first statements.

- LOCAL_MODULE: The name of the output module. Effectively, the built library files will be named as lib<LOCAL_MODULE>.so; so if the module name is "ndktest", the output file will be libndktest.so.

- LOCAL_SRC_FILES: List of all the C/C++ files you want to compile into the shared library.

- LOCAL_LD_LIBS: Additional libraries you may need to link in. Most of the stable NDK APIs you use will require a line to be added here.

- $(BUILD_SHARED_LIBRARY): A macro that tells the build system to execute the build once all the parameters are set. This is the last statement in a typical NDK makefile.

How It Works

Consider an LLNADemo project that demonstrates low-level native activities. All native code needs to be placed in a jni directory in your application project. This directory should be at the same level as src and res. Listing 8-1 presents the contents of this project's solitary llnademo.c source file.

Listing 8-1. jni/llnademo.c

```c
#include <android/log.h>
#include <android/native_activity.h>
#include <pthread.h>

#define LOGI(...) ((void)  android_log_print(ANDROID_LOG_INFO, "llnademo", VA_ARGS  ))

AInputQueue* _queue;
pthread_t thread;
pthread_cond_t cond;
pthread_mutex_t mutex;

static void onConfigurationChanged(ANativeActivity* activity)
{
    LOGI("ConfigurationChanged: %p\n", activity);
}

static void onDestroy(ANativeActivity* activity)
{
    LOGI("Destroy: %p\n", activity);
}

static void onInputQueueCreated(ANativeActivity* activity, AInputQueue* queue)
{
    LOGI("InputQueueCreated: %p -- %p\n", activity, queue);
    pthread_mutex_lock(&mutex);
    _queue = queue;
    pthread_cond_broadcast(&cond);
    pthread_mutex_unlock(&mutex);
}

static void onInputQueueDestroyed(ANativeActivity* activity, AInputQueue* queue)
{
    LOGI("InputQueueDestroyed: %p -- %p\n", activity, queue);
    pthread_mutex_lock(&mutex);
    _queue = NULL;
    pthread_mutex_unlock(&mutex);
}

static void onLowMemory(ANativeActivity* activity)
{
    LOGI("LowMemory: %p\n", activity);
}

static void onNativeWindowCreated(ANativeActivity* activity, ANativeWindow* window)
{
    LOGI("NativeWindowCreated: %p -- %p\n", activity, window);
}
```

```c
static void onNativeWindowDestroyed(ANativeActivity* activity, ANativeWindow* window)
{
    LOGI("NativeWindowDestroyed: %p -- %p\n", activity, window);
}

static void onPause(ANativeActivity* activity)
{
    LOGI("Pause: %p\n", activity);
}

static void onResume(ANativeActivity* activity)
{
    LOGI("Resume: %p\n", activity);
}

static void* onSaveInstanceState(ANativeActivity* activity, size_t* outLen)
{
    LOGI("SaveInstanceState: %p\n", activity);
    return NULL;
}

static void onStart(ANativeActivity* activity)
{
    LOGI("Start: %p\n", activity);
}

static void onStop(ANativeActivity* activity)
{
    LOGI("Stop: %p\n", activity);
}

static void onWindowFocusChanged(ANativeActivity* activity, int focused)
{
    LOGI("WindowFocusChanged: %p -- %d\n", activity, focused);
}

static void* process_input(void* param)
{
    while (1)
    {
        pthread_mutex_lock(&mutex);
        if (_queue == NULL)
            pthread_cond_wait(&cond, &mutex);
        AInputEvent* event = NULL;
        while (AInputQueue_getEvent(_queue, &event) >= 0)
        {
            if (AInputQueue_preDispatchEvent(_queue, event))
                break;
            AInputQueue_finishEvent(_queue, event, 0);
        }
        pthread_mutex_unlock(&mutex);
    }
}
```

```
void ANativeActivity_onCreate(ANativeActivity* activity,
                              void* savedState,
                              size_t savedStateSize)
{
    LOGI("Creating: %p\n", activity);
    LOGI("Internal data path: %s\n", activity->internalDataPath);



    LOGI("External data path: %s\n", activity->externalDataPath);
    LOGI("SDK version code: %d\n", activity->sdkVersion);
    LOGI("Asset Manager: %p\n", activity->assetManager);

    activity->callbacks->onConfigurationChanged = onConfigurationChanged;
    activity->callbacks->onDestroy = onDestroy;
    activity->callbacks->onInputQueueCreated = onInputQueueCreated;
    activity->callbacks->onInputQueueDestroyed = onInputQueueDestroyed;
    activity->callbacks->onLowMemory = onLowMemory;
    activity->callbacks->onNativeWindowCreated = onNativeWindowCreated;
    activity->callbacks->onNativeWindowDestroyed = onNativeWindowDestroyed;
    activity->callbacks->onPause = onPause;
    activity->callbacks->onResume = onResume;
    activity->callbacks->onSaveInstanceState = onSaveInstanceState;
    activity->callbacks->onStart = onStart;
    activity->callbacks->onStop = onStop;
    activity->callbacks->onWindowFocusChanged = onWindowFocusChanged;

    pthread_mutex_init(&mutex, NULL);
    pthread_cond_init(&cond, NULL);
    pthread_create(&thread, NULL, process_input, NULL);
}
```

Listing 8-1 begins with three #include directives that (before compilation) include the contents of three NDK header files for logging, native activities, and thread creation.

Listing 8-1 next declares a LOGI macro for logging information messages to the Android device's log (you can view this log by executing adb logcat). This macro refers to the android_log_print() function (prototyped in the log.h header file) that performs the actual writing. Each logged message must have a priority (such as ANDROID_LOG_INFO), a tag (such as "llnademo"), and a format string defining the message. Additional arguments are specified when the format string contains format specifiers (such as %d).

Listing 8-1 then declares a _queue variable of type AInputQueue*. (AInputQueue is defined in the input.h header file, which is included by the native_activity.h header file.) This variable is assigned a reference to the input queue when the queue is created, or it is assigned NULL when the queue is destroyed. The native activity must process all input events from this queue to avoid an "Application Not Responding" error.

Three thread global variables are now created: thread, cond, and mutex. The variable thread identifies the thread that is created later in the listing, and the variables cond and mutex are used to avoid busy waiting and to ensure synchronized access to the shared _queue variable, respectively.

A series of 'on'-prefixed callback functions follows. Each function is declared static to hide it from outside of its module. (The use of static isn't essential but is present for good form.)

Each 'on'-prefixed callback function is called on the main thread and logs some information for viewing in the device log. However, the onInputQueueCreated() and onInputQueueDestroyed() functions have a little more work to accomplish:

- onInputQueueCreated() must assign its queue argument address to the _queue variable. Because _queue is also accessed from a thread apart from the main thread, synchronization is required to ensure that there is no conflict between these threads. Synchronization is achieved by accessing _queue between pthread_mutex_lock() and pthread_mutex_unlock() calls. The former call locks a mutex (a program object used to prevent multiple threads from simultaneously accessing a shared variable); the latter call unlocks the mutex. Because the non-main thread waits until _queue contains a non-null value, a pthread_cond_broadcast() call is also present to wake up this waiting thread.

- onInputQueueDestroyed() is simpler, assigning NULL to _queue (within a locked region) when the input queue is destroyed.

The non-main thread executes the process_input() function. This function repeatedly executes AInputQueue_getEvent() to return the next input event. The integer return value is negative when no events are available or when an error occurs. When an event is returned, it is referenced by outEvent.

Assuming that an event has been returned, AInputQueue_preDispatchEvent() is called to send the event (if it is a keystroke-related event) to the current input method editor to be consumed before the app. This function returns 0 when the event was not predispatched, which means that you can process it right now.

When a nonzero value is returned, you must not process the current event so that the event can appear again in the event queue (assuming that it does not get consumed during predispatching).

At this point, you could do something with the event (when it is not predispatched). Regardless, you must finally call AInputQueue_finishEvent() to finish the dispatching of the given event. A 0 value is passed as the third parameter to indicate that the event has not been handled in your code.

Finally, Listing 8-1 declares ANativeActivity_onCreate(), which logs a message, overrides most of the default callbacks (you could also override the rest when desired), initializes the mutex and the condition variable, and finally creates and starts the thread that runs process_input().

The content of the project's AndroidManifest.xml file can be found in Listing 8-2.

Listing 8-2. AndroidManifest.xml

```
<?xml version="1.0" encoding="utf-8"?>
<manifest xmlns:android="http://schemas.android.com/apk/res/android"
    package="com.androidrecipes.lowlevelnative"
    android:versionCode="1"
    android:versionName="1.0">
```

```
<uses-sdk android:minSdkVersion="9"/>
<application android:label="@string/app_name" android:hasCode="false">
    <activity android:name="android.app.NativeActivity"
        android:label="@string/app_name"
        android:configChanges="orientation">
        <meta-data android:name="android.app.lib_name"
            android:value="llnademo"/>
        <intent-filter>
            <action android:name="android.intent.action.MAIN" />
            <category android:name="android.intent.category.LAUNCHER"/>
        </intent-filter>
    </activity>
</application>
</manifest>
```

An android:configChanges="orientation" attribute has been added to the <activity> tag so that onConfigurationChanged() is invoked when the device orientation changes (from portrait to landscape, for example). As an exercise, remove this attribute and observe how the log messages change. Listing 8-3 presents this project's Android.mk file.

Listing 8-3. jni/Android.mk

```
LOCAL_PATH := $(call my-dir)
include $(CLEAR_VARS)
LOCAL_MODULE    := llnademo
LOCAL_SRC_FILES := llnademo.c
LOCAL_LDLIBS := -llog -landroid include
$(BUILD_SHARED_LIBRARY)
```

This makefile presents a LOCAL_LDLIBS entry, which identifies the liblog.so and libandroid.so standard libraries that are to be linked against.

Building the Native Code

In order to run our application, we must first build the native components before we can execute the example on a device or in the emulator. This must be done using the NDK command-line tool ndk-build. On the command line, navigate to the top-level directory of your project and run the command:

```
$ /android-ndk-r9/ndk-build "APP_ABI := all"
```

The APP_ABI parameter tells the NDK to build the shared library for each supported CPU application binary interface (ABI). If we leave this parameter off, by default the NDK will build for only ARMv5. Additionally, we could have passed a subset list of just the architectures we want to build (for example, "APP_ABI := armeabi x86").

Tip You can also place this command in an Application.mk file in the same jni directory and not have to pass it on the command line each time.

If all goes well, you should see the following messages:

```
Compile thumb  : llnademo <= llnademo.c
SharedLibrary  : libllnademo.so
Install        : libllnademo.so => libs/armeabi-v7a/libllnademo.so
Compile thumb  : llnademo <= llnademo.c
SharedLibrary  : libllnademo.so
Install        : libllnademo.so => libs/armeabi/libllnademo.so
Compile x86    : llnademo <= llnademo.c
SharedLibrary  : libllnademo.so
Install        : libllnademo.so => libs/x86/libllnademo.so
Compile mips   : llnademo <= llnademo.c
SharedLibrary  : libllnademo.so
Install        : libllnademo.so => libs/mips/libllnademo.so
```

You should now see a subdirectory for each ABI the NDK supports, and also observe a libllnademo.so file in each subdirectory. If you run the application, the display will simply be black. However, if you interact with the display (tap on the screen) or rotate the device, you will see the log statements coming out from the NativeActivity code.

> **Note**   When the target SDK is set to API Level 13 or higher, and you haven't included screenSize with orientation in the value assigned to the configChanges attribute of the <activity> element (that is, "orientation|screenSize"), you will not see ConfigurationChanged messages in the log when you change the device orientation.

8-2. Developing High-Level Native Activities
Problem
You want to learn how to develop high-level native activities, which are based on the android_native_app_glue.h header file.

Solution
The development of a high-level native activity is very similar to that of a low-level native activity. However, a new source file and a new Android.mk file are required.

How It Works
Consider an HLNADemo project that demonstrates high-level native activities. Listing 8-4 presents the contents of this project's solitary hlnademo.c source file.

Listing 8-4. jni/hlnademo.c

```c
#include <android/log.h>
#include <android_native_app_glue.h>

#define LOGI(...) ((void)  android_log_print(ANDROID_LOG_INFO, "hlnademo", VA_ARGS))

static void handle_cmd(struct android_app* app, int32_t cmd)
{
    switch (cmd)
    {
        case APP_CMD_SAVE_STATE:
            LOGI("Save state");
            break;

        case APP_CMD_INIT_WINDOW:
            LOGI("Init window");
            break;

        case APP_CMD_TERM_WINDOW:
            LOGI("Terminate window");
            break;

        case APP_CMD_PAUSE:
            LOGI("Pausing");
            break;

        case APP_CMD_RESUME:
            LOGI("Resuming");
            break;

        case APP_CMD_STOP:
            LOGI("Stopping");
            break;

        case APP_CMD_DESTROY:
            LOGI("Destroying");
            break;

        case APP_CMD_LOST_FOCUS:
            LOGI("Lost focus");
            break;

        case APP_CMD_GAINED_FOCUS:
            LOGI("Gained focus");
    }
}
```

```
static int32_t handle_input(struct android_app* app, AInputEvent* event)
{
    if (AInputEvent_getType(event) == AINPUT_EVENT_TYPE_MOTION)
    {
        size_t pointerCount = AMotionEvent_getPointerCount(event);
        size_t i;
        for (i = 0; i < pointerCount; ++i)
        {
            LOGI("Received motion event from %zu: (%.2f, %.2f)", i,
                AMotionEvent_getX(event, i), AMotionEvent_getY(event, i));
        }
        return 1;
    }
    else if (AInputEvent_getType(event) == AINPUT_EVENT_TYPE_KEY)
    {
        LOGI("Received key event: %d", AKeyEvent_getKeyCode(event));
        if (AKeyEvent_getKeyCode(event) == AKEYCODE_BACK)
            ANativeActivity_finish(app->activity);
        return 1;
    }
    return 0;
}

void android_main(struct android_app* state)
{
    app_dummy(); // prevent glue from being stripped state->onAppCmd = &handle_cmd;

    state->onInputEvent = &handle_input;

    while(1)
    {
        int ident;
        int fdesc;
        int events;
        struct android_poll_source* source;

        while ((ident = ALooper_pollAll(0, &fdesc, &events, (void**)&source)) >= 0)
        {
            if (source)
                source->process(state, source);

            if (state->destroyRequested)
                return;
        }
    }
}
```

Listing 8-4 begins in a nearly identical fashion to Listing 8-1. However, the previous
native_activity.h header file has been replaced by android_native_app_glue.h, which includes
native_activity.h (along with pthread.h). A similar LOGI macro is also provided.

The handle_cmd() function is called (on a thread other than the main thread) in response to an activity command. The app parameter references an android_app struct (defined in android_native_app_glue.h) that provides access to app-related data, and the cmd parameter identifies a command.

> **Note**   Commands are integer values that correspond to the low-level native activity functions that were presented earlier, such as onDestroy(). The android_native_app_glue.h header file defines integer constants for these commands (APP_CMD_DESTROY, for example).

The handle_input() function is called (on a thread other than the main thread) in response to an input event. The event parameter references an AInputEvent struct (defined in input.h) that provides access to various kinds of event-related information.

The input.h header file declares several useful input functions, beginning with AInputEvent_getType(), which returns the type of the event. The return value is one of AINPUT_EVENT_TYPE_KEY for a key event and AINPUT_EVENT_TYPE_MOTION for a motion event.

For a motion event, the AMotionEvent_getPointerCount() function is called to return the number of pointers (active touch points) of data contained in this event (this value is greater than or equal to 1). This count is repeated, with each touch point's coordinates being obtained and logged.

> **Note**   Active touch points and AMotionEvent_getPointerCount() are related to multitouch. To learn more about this Android feature, check out "Making Sense of Multitouch" (http://android-developers.blogspot.com/2010/06/making-sense-of-multitouch.html).

For a key event, the AKeyEvent_getKeyCode() function returns the code of the physical key that was pressed. Physical key codes are defined in the keycodes.h header file. For example, AKEYCODE_BACK corresponds to the Back button on the device.

The key code is logged and is then compared with AKEYCODE_BACK to find out whether the user wants to terminate the activity (and, by extension, the single-activity app). If so, the ANativeActivity_finish() function (defined in native_activity.h) is invoked with app->activity referencing the activity to be finished.

After processing a mouse or key event, handle_input() returns 1 to indicate that it has handled the event. If the event was not handled (and should be handled by default processing in the background), this function returns 0.

> **Note**   You can modify handle_input() to simply return 0 when a key event is detected to cause the default processing to finish the activity when the Back button is pressed.

The android_main() function is the entry point. It first invokes a native glue function called app_dummy(), which does nothing. However, app_dummy() must be present to ensure that the Android build system includes the android_native_app_glue.o module in the library.

> **Note** See http://blog.beuc.net/posts/Make_sure_glue_isn__39__t_stripped/ to learn more about this behavior.

The android_app struct provides an onAppCmd field of type void (*onAppCmd)(struct android_app* app, int32_t cmd) and an onInputEvent field of type int32_t (*onInputEvent)(struct android_app* app, AInputEvent* event). The addresses of the aforementioned functions are assigned to these fields.

A pair of nested loops is now entered. The inner loop repeatedly invokes the ALooper_pollAll() function (defined in looper.h) to return the next event; this function returns a value greater than or equal to 0 when an event is ready for processing.

The event is recorded in an android_poll_source structure, whose address is stored in outData. Assuming that outData contains a non-NULL address, the void (*process)(struct android_app* app, struct android_poll_source* source) function pointer in android_poll_source is invoked to process the event. Behind the scenes, either handle_cmd() or handle_input() is invoked; it depends on which function is appropriate for handling the event.

Finally, the destroyRequested member of the android_app structure is set to a nonzero value, as a result of a call to ANativeActivity_finish() (or default processing in lieu of this function). This member is checked during each loop iteration to ensure that execution exits quickly from the nested loops and android_main(), because the app is ending. Failure to exit android_main() in a timely fashion can result in an "Application Not Responding" error.

Listing 8-5 presents this project's Android.mk file.

Listing 8-5. A Makefile for HLNADemo

```
LOCAL_PATH := $(call my-dir)
include $(CLEAR_VARS)
LOCAL_MODULE     := hlnademo
LOCAL_SRC_FILES := hlnademo.c
LOCAL_LDLIBS := -landroid
LOCAL_STATIC_LIBRARIES := android_native_app_glue
include $(BUILD_SHARED_LIBRARY)
$(call import-module,android/native_app_glue)
```

This makefile is similar to the makefile presented in Listing 8-3. However, there are some differences:

- The `LOCAL_LDLIBS` entry no longer contains `-llog` because the logging library is linked to the `android_native_app_glue` library when this library is built.

- A `LOCAL_STATIC_LIBRARIES` entry identifies `android_native_app_glue` as a library to be linked to the `hlnademo` module.

- A `$(call import-module,android/native_app_glue)` entry includes the `Android.mk` file associated with the `android_native_app_glue` module so that this library can be built.

Building the Native Code

Just as with the LLNADemo, we must first build the native components before we can execute the example on a device or in the emulator. This must be done using the NDK command-line tool `ndk-build`. On the command line, navigate to the top-level directory of your project and run the command:

```
$ /android-ndk-r9/ndk-build "APP_ABI := all"
```

If all goes well, we should see the following output:

```
Compile thumb  : hlnademo <= hlnademo.c
Compile thumb  : android_native_app_glue <= android_native_app_glue.c
StaticLibrary  : libandroid_native_app_glue.a
SharedLibrary  : libhlnademo.so
Install        : libhlnademo.so => libs/armeabi-v7a/libhlnademo.so
Compile thumb  : hlnademo <= hlnademo.c
Compile thumb  : android_native_app_glue <= android_native_app_glue.c
StaticLibrary  : libandroid_native_app_glue.a
SharedLibrary  : libhlnademo.so
Install        : libhlnademo.so => libs/armeabi/libhlnademo.so
Compile x86    : hlnademo <= hlnademo.c
Compile x86    : android_native_app_glue <= android_native_app_glue.c
StaticLibrary  : libandroid_native_app_glue.a
SharedLibrary  : libhlnademo.so
Install        : libhlnademo.so => libs/x86/libhlnademo.so
Compile mips   : hlnademo <= hlnademo.c
Compile mips   : android_native_app_glue <= android_native_app_glue.c
StaticLibrary  : libandroid_native_app_glue.a
SharedLibrary  : libhlnademo.so
Install        : libhlnademo.so => libs/mips/libhlnademo.so
```

The appropriate shared libraries should now be in placed in the `libs` directory of your project. Similar to the previous example, the display will be black when you run the application. However, interacting with the display and/or rotating the device will generate events that the native code can process and log out to `logcat`.

RenderScript

You can use the Android NDK to perform rendering and data-processing operations quickly. However, there are three major problems with this approach:

- *Lack of portability*: Your apps are constrained to run on only those devices that the native code targets. For example, a native library that runs on an ARM-based device won't run on an x86-based device.

- *Lack of performance*: Ideally, your code should run on multiple cores, be they CPU, GPU, or DSP cores. However, identifying cores, farming out work to them, and dealing with synchronization issues isn't easy.

- *Lack of usability*: Developing native code is harder than developing Java code. For example, you often need to create JNI glue code, which is a tedious process that can be a source of bugs.

Google's Android development team created RenderScript to address these problems, starting with lack of portability, then lack of performance, and finally lack of usability.

RenderScript consists of a language based on C99 (a modern dialect of the C language), a pair of compilers, and a runtime that collectively help you achieve high performance and visually compelling graphics via native code, but in a portable manner. You get native app speed along with SDK app portability, and you don't have to use the JNI.

RenderScript combines a graphics engine with a compute engine. The graphics engine helps you achieve fast 2D/3D rendering, and the compute engine helps you achieve fast data processing. Performance is achieved by running threads on multiple CPU, GPU, and DSP cores. (The compute engine is currently confined to CPU cores.)

> **Tip**   The compute engine is not limited to processing graphics data. For example, it could be used to model weather data.

Exploring RenderScript Architecture

RenderScript adopts an architecture in which the low-level RenderScript runtime is controlled by the higher-level Android framework. Figure 8-1 presents this architecture.

Figure 8-1. *RenderScript architecture is based on the Android framework and the RenderScript runtime*

The Android framework consists of Android apps running in the Dalvik VM that communicate with graphics or compute scripts running in the RenderScript runtime via instances of reflected layer classes. These classes serve as wrappers around their scripts that make this communication possible. The Android build tools automatically generate the classes for this layer during the build process. These classes eliminate the need to write JNI glue code, which is commonly done when working with the NDK.

Memory management is controlled at the VM level. The app is responsible for allocating memory and binding this memory to the RenderScript runtime so that the memory can be accessed by the script. The script can define simple (nonarray) fields for its own use, but that's about it.)

Apps make asynchronous calls to the RenderScript runtime (via the reflected layer classes) to make allocated memory available to start executing their scripts. They can subsequently obtain results from these scripts without having to worry about whether the scripts are still running.

When you build an APK, the LLVM (Low-Level Virtual Machine) front-end compiler compiles the script into a file of device-independent bitcode that is stored in the APK. (The reflected layer class is also created.) When the app launches, a small LLVM back-end compiler on the device compiles the bitcode into device-specific code, and it caches the code on the device so that it doesn't have to be recompiled each time you run the app. This is how portability is achieved.

Note   As of Android 4.1, the graphics engine has been deprecated. App developers told the Android development team that they prefer to use OpenGL directly because of its familiarity. Although the graphics engine is still supported, it will probably be removed in a future Android release. For this reason, the rest of this chapter focuses only on the compute engine.

Exploring Compute Engine-Based App Architecture

A compute engine-based app consists of Java code and an .rs file that defines the compute script. The Java code interacts with this script by using APIs defined in the android.renderscript package. Key classes in this package are RenderScript and Allocation:

- RenderScript defines a context that is used in further interactions with RenderScript APIs (and also the compute script's reflected layer class). A RenderScript instance is returned by invoking this class's static RenderScript.create() factory method.

- Allocation defines the means for moving data into and out of the compute script. Instances of this class are known as allocations, where an allocation combines an android.renderscript.Type instance with the memory needed to provide storage for user data and objects.

The Java code also interacts with the compute script by instantiating a reflected layer class. The name of the class begins with ScriptC_ and continues with the name of the .rs file containing the compute script. For example, if you had a file named gray.rs, the name of this class would be ScriptC_gray.

The C99-based .rs file begins with two #pragma directives that identify the RenderScript version number (currently 1) and the app's Java package name. Several additional items follow:

- rs_allocation directives that identify the input and output allocations created by the app and bound to the RenderScript code

- rs_script directive that provides a link to the app's ScriptC_script instance so that compute results can be returned to this instance

- Optional simple variable declarations whose values are supplied by the app

- A root() function that is called by each core to perform part of the overall computation

- A no-argument init() function with a void return type that's indirectly invoked from the Java code to execute root() on multiple CPU cores

At runtime, a Java-based activity creates a RenderScript context, creates input and output allocations, instantiates the ScriptC_-prefixed layer class, uses this object to bind the allocations and ScriptC_ instance, and invokes the compute script, which results in the script's init() function being invoked.

The init() function performs additional initialization (as necessary) and executes the rsForEach() function with the rs_script value and the rs_allocation input/output allocations. rsForEach() causes the root() function to be executed on the device's available CPU cores. Results are then sent back to the app via the output allocation.

Figure 8-2 illustrates this scenario.

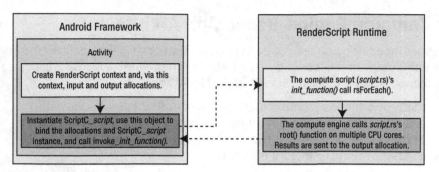

Figure 8-2. Compute engine–based app architecture can be partitioned into four major tasks

Using the RenderScript Support Package

RenderScript has been a public API only since Android 3.0 (API Level 11), but you may have noticed that the Android team at Google is fond of backporting their frameworks to allow developers to use them on older devices. The RenderScript support package allows applications to use its features on devices going back to Android 2.2 (FroYo).

To accomplish this, the build tools include a set of precompiled NDK libraries into your application's APK to install onto devices that don't natively support all the RenderScript features available in the support package.

> **Note**   Currently the RenderScript support package includes NDK libraries for only ARMv7, x86, and MIPS. There is no support for ARMv5 devices.

Using the RenderScript support package is a slightly different process than simply copying in additional Java libraries or resources at compile time. The build tools include hooks to copy the appropriate libraries after the build into the APK without needing to place them in your application source tree. To inform the build tools that this step needs to take place, we must add the following lines to the `project.properties` file:

```
renderscript.target=18
renderscript.support.mode=true
sdk.buildtools=18.1.0
```

You may set the `renderscript.target` and `sdk.buildtools` values to whatever your current version targets are, but the minimum target is API 18, and 18.1.0 is the minimum supported build tools version. Keep in mind that this doesn't mean the application must have its minimum SDK set to Android 4.3; but it does mean your application should have its target SDK set to at least that level.

With these parameters in place, the build tools will handle all the rest of the work for you. The only additional required step is to use the classes from the `android.support.v8.renderscript` package in your app rather than the native versions.

> **Important**   You must import `android.support.v8.renderscript.*` instead of the `android.renderscript` package in your Java code!

The remaining sections in this chapter that deal with RenderScript are structured to make use of the RenderScript support package. However, in most cases you only need to change the import statements included to move exclusively to the native versions instead.

8-3. Filtering Images with RenderScript
Problem
Your application needs a simply way to apply common filters to images.

Solution

RenderScript has a large collection of *script intrinsics*, or premade and encapsulated RenderScript kernels designed to do common tasks. You can use these intrinsics to do computation with RenderScript without even the need to write the script code! With each new Android release, new intrinsics are added, creating a library of useful functions to draw from. In this recipe, we are going to examine three of the most common intrinsics:

- `ScriptInstrinsicBlur`: Applies a Gaussian blur to each element in the input allocation. The radius of the blur is configurable on the script.

- `ScriptIntrinsicColorMatrix`: Applies a color matrix filter to each element in the input allocation. Similar to the `ColorFilter` applied to a `Drawable`. Has an additional convenience method for setting grayscale.

- `ScriptIntrinsicConvolve3x3`: Applies a 3×3 convolve matrix to each element in the input allocation. This matrix is commonly used to create photo filter effects such as sharpen, emboss, and edge detect.

How It Works

Let's explore an example application that uses RenderScript to apply filters to an image resource. In Listing 8-6, we find the layout for our activity, which is a simple grid of six `ImageView` instances.

Listing 8-6. res/layout/activity_main.xml

```xml
<?xml version="1.0" encoding="utf-8"?>
<TableLayout xmlns:android="http://schemas.android.com/apk/res/android"
    android:layout_width="match_parent"
    android:layout_height="match_parent"
    android:stretchColumns="*">
```

```xml
<TableRow>
    <ImageView
        android:id="@+id/image_normal"
        android:layout_weight="1"
        android:layout_margin="5dp"
        android:scaleType="fitCenter" />
    <ImageView
        android:id="@+id/image_blurred"
        android:layout_weight="1"
        android:layout_margin="5dp"
        android:scaleType="fitCenter" />
</TableRow>

<TableRow>
    <ImageView
        android:id="@+id/image_greyscale"
        android:layout_weight="1"
        android:layout_margin="5dp"
        android:scaleType="fitCenter" />
    <ImageView
        android:id="@+id/image_sharpen"
        android:layout_weight="1"
        android:layout_margin="5dp"
        android:scaleType="fitCenter" />
</TableRow>

<TableRow>
    <ImageView
        android:id="@+id/image_edge"
        android:layout_weight="1"
        android:layout_margin="5dp"
        android:scaleType="fitCenter" />
    <ImageView
        android:id="@+id/image_emboss"
        android:layout_weight="1"
        android:layout_margin="5dp"
        android:scaleType="fitCenter" />
</TableRow>

</TableLayout>
```

Each cell in this grid will be filled in with the same image, but with a different filter applied to it. In the first cell, we will display the base image without any filtering. The next two cells will be filtered using ScriptInstrinsicBlur and ScriptIntrinsicColorMatrix. The remaining cells will be filtered using various matrices and a ScriptIntrinsicConvolve3x3. In Listing 8-7, we find the activity code.

Listing 8-7. Image Filter Activity

```
import android.support.v8.renderscript.*;

public class MainActivity extends Activity {

    private enum ConvolutionFilter {
        SHARPEN, LIGHTEN, DARKEN, EDGE_DETECT, EMBOSS
    };

    @Override
    protected void onCreate(Bundle savedInstanceState) {
        super.onCreate(savedInstanceState);
        setContentView(R.layout.activity_main);
        //Create the source data, and a destination for the filtered results
        Bitmap inBitmap = BitmapFactory.decodeResource(getResources(), R.drawable.dog);
        Bitmap outBitmap = inBitmap.copy(inBitmap.getConfig(), true);
        //Show the normal image
        setImageInView(outBitmap.copy(outBitmap.getConfig(), false), R.id.image_normal);

        //Create the RenderScript context
        final RenderScript rs = RenderScript.create(this);
        //Create allocations for input and output data
        final Allocation input = Allocation.createFromBitmap(rs, inBitmap,
                Allocation.MipmapControl.MIPMAP_NONE,
                Allocation.USAGE_SCRIPT);
        final Allocation output = Allocation.createTyped(rs, input.getType());

        //Run blur script
        final ScriptIntrinsicBlur script = ScriptIntrinsicBlur
                .create(rs, Element.U8_4(rs));
        script.setRadius(4f);
        script.setInput(input);
        script.forEach(output);
        output.copyTo(outBitmap);
        setImageInView(outBitmap.copy(outBitmap.getConfig(), false), R.id.image_blurred);

        //Run grayscale script
        final ScriptIntrinsicColorMatrix scriptColor = ScriptIntrinsicColorMatrix
                .create(rs, Element.U8_4(rs));
        scriptColor.setGreyscale();
        scriptColor.forEach(input, output);
        output.copyTo(outBitmap);
        setImageInView(outBitmap.copy(outBitmap.getConfig(), false), R.id.image_greyscale);

        //Run sharpen script
        ScriptIntrinsicConvolve3x3 scriptC = ScriptIntrinsicConvolve3x3
                .create(rs, Element.U8_4(rs));
        scriptC.setCoefficients(getCoefficients(ConvolutionFilter.SHARPEN));
        scriptC.setInput(input);
        scriptC.forEach(output);
```

```java
        output.copyTo(outBitmap);
        setImageInView(outBitmap.copy(outBitmap.getConfig(), false), R.id.image_sharpen);

        //Run edge detect script
        scriptC = ScriptIntrinsicConvolve3x3.create(rs, Element.U8_4(rs));
        scriptC.setCoefficients(getCoefficients(ConvolutionFilter.EDGE_DETECT));
        scriptC.setInput(input);
        scriptC.forEach(output);
        output.copyTo(outBitmap);
        setImageInView(outBitmap.copy(outBitmap.getConfig(), false), R.id.image_edge);

        //Run emboss script
        scriptC = ScriptIntrinsicConvolve3x3.create(rs, Element.U8_4(rs));
        scriptC.setCoefficients(getCoefficients(ConvolutionFilter.EMBOSS));
        scriptC.setInput(input);
        scriptC.forEach(output);
        output.copyTo(outBitmap);
        setImageInView(outBitmap.copy(outBitmap.getConfig(), false), R.id.image_emboss);

        //Tear down the RenderScript context
        rs.destroy();
    }

    private void setImageInView(Bitmap bm, int viewId) {
        ImageView normalImage = (ImageView) findViewById(viewId);
        normalImage.setImageBitmap(bm);
    }

    /*
     * Helper to obtain matrix coefficients for each type of
     * convolution image filter.
     */
    private float[] getCoefficients(ConvolutionFilter filter) {
        switch (filter) {
            case SHARPEN:
                return new float[] {
                        0f, -1f, 0f,
                        -1f, 5f, -1f,
                        0f, -1f, 0f
                    };
            case LIGHTEN:
                return new float[] {
                        0f, 0f, 0f,
                        0f, 1.5f, 0f,
                        0f, 0f, 0f
                    };
            case DARKEN:
                return new float[] {
                        0f, 0f, 0f,
                        0f, 0.5f, 0f,
                        0f, 0f, 0f
                    };
```

```
        case EDGE_DETECT:
            return new float[] {
                    0f, 1f, 0f,
                    1f, -4f, 1f,
                    0f, 1f, 0f
                };
        case EMBOSS:
            return new float[] {
                -2f, -1f, 0f,
                -1f, 1f, 1f,
                0f, 1f, 2f
            };
        default:
            return null;
        }
    }
}
```

Before we can filter the images, we must initialize a RenderScript context with RenderScript.create(). We must also create two Allocation instances, one for the input data and one for the output result. These are the buffers that each RenderScript kernel will act on. There are convenience functions to create an Allocation from many common data structures in the framework, and in this case we have elected to make one directly from our input image Bitmap.

You can see each script follows a similar pattern. We must first create the script we want to run, initializing it with the data size to be used for the Allocation. We chose Element.U8_4() because our bitmap has ARGB pixel data, so each element (that is, pixel) is 4 unsigned bytes in size. We then must set up any parameters the script needs, and execute it by calling forEach(). Once the script execution is complete, we copy the results from the output Allocation into a new Bitmap to display in the ImageView.

For our blur filter, the radius is the only configurable parameter. The intrinsic accepts a radius value between 0 and 25. We use the color matrix filter to make a grayscale filter for our image by calling setGreyscale() during its setup. If we were to provide a distinct matrix, it would be passed using setColorMatrix() instead.

> **Tip** ScriptIntrinsicColorMatrix is also equipped to do color conversions between YUV and RGB color space.

Finally, we apply the remaining filters by obtaining a coefficients matrix for the given filter and passing them to the script via setCoefficients(). The 3×3 matrices for these filters are well known and easily obtainable on the Web. The values in the matrix define, as the script moves over each pixel in the allocation, how the value of the output pixel should be multiplied based on the current value of the input pixel and its neighbors. The value in the center of the matrix represents the current pixel, and the surrounding values represent the neighboring pixels.

For example, the darken filter decreases the value of the current pixel by half (0.5 multiplier), but otherwise the surrounding pixels do not affect the result. The sharpen filter magnifies the initial value five times, and then subtracts the value from the pixels above, below, and on each side to achieve the effect.

You can see the results of all the filters we applied in Figure 8-3.

Figure 8-3. RenderScript image filters (top to bottom, left to right): None, Greyscale, Edge Detect, Blur, Sharpen, Emboss)

Tip   When playing around with convolution matrices, the sum of all the matrix values should equal 1 to preserve the original brightness of the image. If the sum is larger, the image will be brighter, and if the sum is smaller, the image will be darker. The edge detect filter in the example has a net sum of zero, which is why that image is very dark.

8-4. Manipulating Images with RenderScript
Problem

You're intrigued by RenderScript and want to learn more about it. For example, you want to learn how to receive **rsForEach()**'s **usrData** value in the **root()** function.

Solution

The following resources will help you learn more about RenderScript:

- Romain Guy's and Chet Haase's "Learn about RenderScript" video (**http://youtube.com/watch?v=5jz0kSuR2j4**). This 1.5-hour video covers the graphics and compute sides of RenderScript, and it is well worth your time.

- The Android documentation's RenderScript page (**http://developer.android. com/guide/topics/renderscript/ index.html**) provides access to important compute information. It also provides access to RenderScript-oriented blog posts.

- The **android.renderscript** package documentation (**http://developer. android.com/reference/android/rendersc ript/package-summary.html**) can help you explore the various types, with emphasis on the **RenderScript** and **Allocation** classes.

- The RenderScript reference page (**http://developer.android.com/reference/ renderscript/ind ex.html**) provides documentation on all of the functions that RenderScript makes available to your compute script.

Regarding **root()**, this function is minimally declared with two parameters that identify the input/output allocations, as in **void root(const uchar4* v_in, uchar4* v_out)**. However, you can specify three more parameters to obtain a **usrData** value and the x/y coordinates of the value passed to **v_in** in the input allocation, as follows:

```
void root(const uchar4* v_in, uchar4* v_out, const void* usrData, uint32_t x,
        uint32_t y)
```

How It Works

Although the root() function may look a little intimidating, it's not hard to use. For example, Listing 8-8 presents source code to a compute script that uses this expanded function to give an image a wavy appearance as if being seen in water.

Listing 8-8. Waving an Image

```
#pragma version(1)
#pragma rs java_package_name(com.androidrecipes.imageprocessing)

rs_allocation in;
rs_allocation out;
rs_script script;
```

```
int height;

void root(const uchar4* v_in, uchar4* v_out, const void* usrData, uint32_t x, uint32_t y)
{
    float scaledy = y/(float) height;
    *v_out = *(uchar4*) rsGetElementAt(in, x,
            (uint32_t) ((scaledy+sin(scaledy*100)*0.03)*height) );
}

void filter()
{
    rsDebug("RS_VERSION = ", RS_VERSION);
#if !defined(RS_VERSION) || (RS_VERSION < 14)
    rsForEach(script, in, out, 0);
#else
    rsForEach(script, in, out);
#endif
}
```

The root() function ignores usrData (which isn't required), but it uses the values passed to x and y. It also uses the value passed to height, which represents the height of the image.

The function first uses height to scale the value passed to y to a floating-point value between 0 and 1. It then invokes RenderScript's rsGetElementAt() function to return the input allocation element that's located at position x and y, which is then assigned to v_out. This function takes three parameters: an input allocation, an x coordinate, and a y coordinate of the element to retrieve from the allocation.

The value passed to x, which happens to be the value in the x parameter of root(), is self-evident. However, the value passed to y may be a little harder to grasp. The idea is to vary the argument in a sinusoidal pattern so that returned pixels from the original image are chosen to yield a wavy appearance.

filter() first executes rsDebug("RS_VERSION = ", RS_VERSION) to output the value of the RS_VERSION constant to the log. You can invoke one of RenderScript's overloaded rsDebug() functions to output debugging information.

RS_VERSION is a special constant that is set to the SDK version number. filter() contains #if and #else directives that help the compiler choose a different version of rsForEach() to call based on this constant's existence and value.

Assuming that RS_VERSION exists and has a value less than 14, the simplest variant of rsForEach() that can be called is as follows:

```
void rsForEach(rs_script script, rs_allocation input, rs_allocation output, const void* usrData)
```

> **Note** usrData lets you pass a pointer to additional script-specific data to the root() function.

If RS_VERSION contains a value that is 14 or higher, the simplest variant of the rsForEach() function that can be called is as follows:

```
void rsForEach(rs_script script, rs_allocation input, rs_allocation output)
```

> **Note**   You will encounter rsForEach() call examples on the Internet that do not consult RS_VERSION. However, not testing this constant via #if and #else means that you may run into compiler warnings like the following:
>
> note: candidate function not viable: requires 4 arguments, but
>
> 3 were provided
>
> note: candidate function not viable: requires 5 arguments, but
>
> 3 were provided

Regardless of the rsForEach() function that is called, its first argument is a reference to the script object on the Java side; its second argument, in, corresponds to v_in; and its third argument, out, corresponds to v_out.

Listing 8-9 presents the source code to a WavyImage app that communicates with the compute script stored in wavy.rs.

Listing 8-9. Viewing Original and Watery Images of the Sun

```java
import android.support.v8.renderscript.*;

public class WavyImage extends Activity {
    boolean original = true;

    @Override
    public void onCreate(Bundle savedInstanceState) {
        super.onCreate(savedInstanceState);
        final ImageView iv = new ImageView(this);
        iv.setScaleType(ImageView.ScaleType.CENTER_CROP);
        iv.setImageResource(R.drawable.sol);
        setContentView(iv);
        iv.setOnClickListener(
                new View.OnClickListener() {
                    @Override
                    public void onClick(View v) {
                        if (original) {
                            drawWavy(iv, R.drawable.sol);
                        } else {
                            iv.setImageResource(R.drawable.sol);
                        }
                        original = !original;
                    }
                });
    }
```

```
private void drawWavy(ImageView iv, int imID) {
    Bitmap bmIn = BitmapFactory.decodeResource(getResources(), imID);
    Bitmap bmOut = Bitmap.createBitmap(bmIn.getWidth(), bmIn.getHeight(),
                                        bmIn.getConfig());
    RenderScript rs = RenderScript.create(this);
    Allocation allocIn;
    allocIn = Allocation.createFromBitmap(rs, bmIn,
            Allocation.MipmapControl.MIPMAP_NONE,
            Allocation.USAGE_SCRIPT);
    Allocation allocOut = Allocation.createTyped(rs, allocIn.getType());
    ScriptC_wavy script = new ScriptC_wavy(rs, getResources(), R.raw.wavy);
    script.set_in(allocIn);
    script.set_out(allocOut);
    script.set_script(script);
    script.set_height(bmIn.getHeight());
    script.invoke_filter();
    allocOut.copyTo(bmOut);

    iv.setImageBitmap(bmOut);
    }
}
```

In this example, the main content is set as an ImageView that we can tap on. Initially, the content is set to the unprocessed image, but when we tap on it, the drawWavy() method executes our RenderScript kernel to filter the image data.

The build tools take our wavy.rs RenderScript kernel and generate the ScriptC_wavy Java class that we will use to execute the script. Notice for each global parameter we defined in the script file (in, out, height, and so forth), a Java setter method has been reflected in the generated class. We use the set_in() and set_out() methods to apply the input and output Allocation, which are defined just as we described in the previous recipe. The set_height() method passes the bitmap's height to the script's height field so that the script can scale the y value.

To execute the script on our image, we then call filter() (reflected as invoke_filter() in Java), copy the results from the output Allocation into our output bitmap, and display it in the content view.

Note   If you do not do version checking in the script kernel as we did, the root() function of a RenderScript kernel is reflected as forEach_root() in the Java class and can be called directly.

If you were to build and run this app, and if you were to click the image of the Sun, you would see the result that's shown in Figure 8-4.

Figure 8-4. The Sun has a wavy (or possibly watery) appearance

8-5. Faking Translucent Overlays with Blur
Problem

You want to provide the illusion that one view is overlaying another with a partially transparent frosted or blurred effect.

Solution

We can call on `ScriptIntrinsicBlur` once again, along with some custom `View` and `Drawable` code to create a blurred copy of a background image, and apply that copy to provide the visual appearance of a partially transparent overlay. Rendering a live blurred overlay in real time is computationally expensive, and the performance of the application will suffer. So instead we are going to achieve the same effect by computing a blurred image of our background content ahead of time and using drawing tricks to implement the same effect while still keeping our application responsive.

How It Works

In this example, we have a ListView shown on top of a full-color background image. The ListView is equipped with a custom header view that offsets the list content such that the first item sits most of the way down the screen when scrolled to the top. As the list scrolls up, we will demonstrate two techniques for creating a blurred overlay: the first will gradually fade the image from clear to blurred, and the second will slide the blurred overlay up along with the list until it is fully covered.

To visualize where we are headed with this, have a look at Figures 8-5 and 8-6.

Figure 8-5. Fading blur example: initially clear (left) and partially blurred as we scroll (right)

Figure 8-6. Sliding blur example: blurred overlay follows the list

You can see in the fading blur example, the background starts completely clear initially. As the list content scrolls up, the blur becomes more visible and is uniform to the entire view. In the sliding blur example, the blurred overlay always follows the list item content; as more of the list items are shown, the blur takes up more of the view. Let's start by looking at the resources in this application. See Listings 8-10 and 8-11.

Listing 8-10. res/layout/activity_blur.xml

```xml
<?xml version="1.0" encoding="utf-8"?>
<FrameLayout xmlns:android="http://schemas.android.com/apk/res/android"
    android:layout_width="match_parent"
    android:layout_height="match_parent">
    <!-- Background Views for each blur type -->
    <com.androidrecipes.backgroundblur.BackgroundOverlayView
        android:id="@+id/background_slide"
        android:layout_width="match_parent"
        android:layout_height="match_parent"
        android:scaleType="centerCrop" />
    <ImageView
        android:id="@+id/background_fade"
        android:layout_width="match_parent"
```

```
            android:layout_height="match_parent"
            android:scaleType="centerCrop"
            android:visibility="gone" />

    <ListView
            android:id="@+id/list"
            android:layout_width="match_parent"
            android:layout_height="match_parent"
            android:cacheColorHint="@android:color/transparent"
            android:scrollbars="none"/>
</FrameLayout>
```

Listing 8-11. res/menu/blur.xml

```xml
<?xml version="1.0" encoding="utf-8"?>
<menu xmlns:android="http://schemas.android.com/apk/res/android" >
    <item android:id="@+id/menu_slide"
        android:title="Sliding Blur" />
    <item android:id="@+id/menu_fade"
        android:title="Fading Blur" />
</menu>
```

The layout for the application is simply a ListView on top of some image content. We have two views for the background to easily switch between the two blur type examples, so only one of these will be visible at any point in time. In this case, we are using the options menu to switch between the two modes, so we have also created a simple two-option <menu> element. Listing 8-12 shows our activity, where the RenderScript code will live.

Listing 8-12. Blurred Overlay Activity

```java
public class BlurActivity extends Activity implements
        AbsListView.OnScrollListener,
        AdapterView.OnItemClickListener {

    private static final String[] ITEMS = {
            "Item One", "Item Two", "Item Three", "Item Four", "Item Five",
            "Item Six", "Item Seven", "Item Eight", "Item Nine", "Item Ten",
            "Item Eleven", "Item Twelve", "Item Thirteen", "Item Fourteen", "Item Fifteen"};

    private BackgroundOverlayView mSlideBackground;
    private ImageView mFadeBackground;
    private ListView mListView;
    private View mHeader;

    @Override
    protected void onCreate(Bundle savedInstanceState) {
        super.onCreate(savedInstanceState);
        setContentView(R.layout.activity_blur);

        mSlideBackground = (BackgroundOverlayView) findViewById(R.id.background_slide);
        mFadeBackground = (ImageView) findViewById(R.id.background_fade);
        mListView = (ListView) findViewById(R.id.list);
```

```java
        //Apply a clear header view to shift the start position of the list elements down
        mHeader = new HeaderView(this);
        mListView.addHeaderView(mHeader, null, false);
        mListView.setAdapter(new ArrayAdapter<String>(this,
                android.R.layout.simple_list_item_1, ITEMS));

        mListView.setOnScrollListener(this);
        mListView.setOnItemClickListener(this);

        initializeImage();
    }

    @Override
    public boolean onCreateOptionsMenu(Menu menu) {
        getMenuInflater().inflate(R.menu.blur, menu);
        return true;
    }

    @Override
    public boolean onOptionsItemSelected(MenuItem item) {
        //Based on the selection, show the appropriate background view
        switch(item.getItemId()) {
            case R.id.menu_slide:
                mSlideBackground.setVisibility(View.VISIBLE);
                mFadeBackground.setVisibility(View.GONE);
                return true;
            case R.id.menu_fade:
                mSlideBackground.setVisibility(View.GONE);
                mFadeBackground.setVisibility(View.VISIBLE);
                return true;
            default:
                return super.onOptionsItemSelected(item);
        }
    }

    /*
     * The heart of our transparency tricks. We obtain a normal copy
     * and a pre-blurred copy of the background image.
     */
    private void initializeImage() {
        Bitmap inBitmap = BitmapFactory.decodeResource(getResources(), R.drawable.background);
        Bitmap outBitmap = inBitmap.copy(inBitmap.getConfig(), true);

        //Create the RenderScript context
        final RenderScript rs = RenderScript.create(this);
        //Create allocations for input and output data
        final Allocation input = Allocation.createFromBitmap(rs, inBitmap,
                Allocation.MipmapControl.MIPMAP_NONE,
                Allocation.USAGE_SCRIPT);
```

```java
        final Allocation output = Allocation.createTyped(rs, input.getType());
        //Run a blur at the maximum supported radius (25f)
        final ScriptIntrinsicBlur script = ScriptIntrinsicBlur.create(rs, Element.U8_4(rs));
        script.setRadius(25f);
        script.setInput(input);
        script.forEach(output);
        output.copyTo(outBitmap);

        //Tear down the RenderScript context
        rs.destroy();

        //Apply the two copies to our custom drawable for fading
        OverlayFadeDrawable drawable = new OverlayFadeDrawable(
                new BitmapDrawable(getResources(), inBitmap),
                new BitmapDrawable(getResources(), outBitmap));
        mFadeBackground.setImageDrawable(drawable);

        //Apply the two copies to our custom ImageView for sliding
        mSlideBackground.setImagePair(inBitmap, outBitmap);
    }

    @Override
    public void onItemClick(AdapterView<?> parent, View v, int position, long id) {
        //On a click event, animated scroll the list back to the top
        mListView.smoothScrollToPosition(0);
    }

    @Override
    public void onScroll(AbsListView view, int firstVisibleItem,
            int visibleItemCount, int totalItemCount) {
        //Make sure views have been measured first
        if (mHeader.getHeight() <= 0) return;

        //Adjust sliding effect clip point based on scroll position
        int topOffset;
        if (firstVisibleItem == 0) {
            //Header is still visible
            topOffset = mHeader.getTop() + mHeader.getHeight();
        } else {
            //Header has been detached, at this point we should be all the way up
            topOffset = 0;
        }
        mSlideBackground.setOverlayOffset(topOffset);

        //Adjust fading effect based on scroll position
        // Blur completely once 85% of the header is scrolled off
        float percent = Math.abs(mHeader.getTop()) / (mHeader.getHeight() * 0.85f);
        int level = Math.min((int)(percent * 10000), 10000);
        mFadeBackground.setImageLevel(level);
    }
```

```java
    @Override
    public void onScrollStateChanged(AbsListView view,
            int scrollState) { }
}
```

When the activity is created, we apply a very simple list adapter with some static data elements inside. We also apply a custom HeaderView as the header to our list; we see this implementation in Listing 8-13, and this is what shifts the list items down in the initial view of Figures 8-5 and 8-6.

Listing 8-13. Clear List Header View

```java
public class HeaderView extends View {

    public HeaderView(Context context) {
        super(context);
    }

    public HeaderView(Context context, AttributeSet attrs) {
        super(context, attrs);
    }

    public HeaderView(Context context, AttributeSet attrs, int defStyle) {
        super(context, attrs, defStyle);
    }

    /*
     * Measure this view's height to always be 85% of the
     * measured height from the parent view (ListView)
     */
    @Override
    protected void onMeasure(int widthMeasureSpec, int heightMeasureSpec) {
        View parent = (View) getParent();
        int parentHeight = parent.getMeasuredHeight();

        int height = Math.round(parentHeight * 0.85f);
        int width = MeasureSpec.getSize(widthMeasureSpec);

        setMeasuredDimension(width, height);
    }
}
```

There isn't much to this; it is simply a view designed to measure out its height to be 85 percent of the height of its parent (which in our case is always the ListView). This allows us to use it as a measured spacer, even though it contains no real content. This approach is more flexible to device screen differences than hard-coding a fixed view height.

Back in Listing 8-12, inside initializeImage(), we use the ScriptIntrinsicBlur function to create a blurred copy of our background image. As we discussed in the previous recipes on image filters, the blur radius determines the level of distortion, and can be a value greater than 0 and up to 25.

When RenderScript has completed the blur, we take the image pair (initial and blurred) and send them two places. The first is to a custom `OverlayFadeDrawable` instance, which we will use for our fade example. The second is a `BackgroundOverlayView`, which we will use for our slide example. We will take a look at these items shortly.

The activity is responsible for monitoring list scrolling and reporting those changes to the background views. The activity is registered as the `OnScrollListener` for the `ListView`, so as the view scrolls, the `onScroll()` method is called regularly. Inside this method, we calculate the offset position based on the header view, and feed that data into the two background views. Finally, the activity is also set to receive click events on individual list items. When this occurs, the list is scrolled back to the top with an animation.

To see how we draw the blur transitions, let's first have a look at the Drawable in Listing 8-14.

Listing 8-14. Overlay Fade Drawable

```java
public class OverlayFadeDrawable extends LayerDrawable {
    /*
     * Implementation of a Drawable container to hold our normal
     * and blurred images as layers
     */
    public OverlayFadeDrawable(Drawable base, Drawable overlay) {
        super(new Drawable[] {base, overlay});
    }

    /*
     * Force a redraw when the level value is externally changed
     */
    @Override
    protected boolean onLevelChange(int level) {
        invalidateSelf();
        return true;
    }

    @Override
    public void draw(Canvas canvas) {
        final Drawable base = getDrawable(0);
        final Drawable overlay = getDrawable(1);
        //Get the level as a percentage of the maximum value
        final float percent = getLevel() / 10000f;
        int setAlpha = Math.round(percent * 0xFF);

        //Optimize for end-cases to avoid overdraw
        if (setAlpha == 255) {
            overlay.draw(canvas);
            return;
        }
        if (setAlpha == 0) {
            base.draw(canvas);
            return;
        }
```

```
        //Draw composite if in-between
        base.draw(canvas);

        overlay.setAlpha(setAlpha);
        overlay.draw(canvas);
        overlay.setAlpha(0xFF);
    }
}
```

You may recall from Chapter 2 that a `Drawable` is just an abstraction of something to be displayed. We have chosen to extend the `LayerDrawable` in the framework, which is a container of N elements that are drawn in order as layers by default. We won't be leveraging the default drawing behavior, but using `LayerDrawable` as our base allows the framework to handle some of the other complex logic of invalidating each layer for us.

To update the state, we use the item's `level` parameter. Recall that this `Drawable` was set on an `ImageView`, and when the scroll position changed, we call `setImageLevel()` to update the background. That level is passed directly into this instance, and with each call to `draw()`, the level is inspected to determine how to blend the two images. We explicitly optimize for the two cases where the alpha is at 0 percent or 100 percent to minimize pixel overdraw (once either element is fully opaque, drawing the other is a waste). However, if the value is in the middle, we will draw the initial image first, with the partially visible blurred copy drawn on top. Now let's have a look at the drawing tricks for the sliding blur in Listing 8-15.

Listing 8-15. Background Overlay View

```java
public class BackgroundOverlayView extends ImageView {

    private Paint mPaint;
    private Bitmap mOverlayImage;
    private int mClipOffset;

    /*
     * Customization of ImageView to allow us to draw a
     * composite of two images, but still leverage all
     * the image scaling features of the framework.
     */
    public BackgroundOverlayView(Context context) {
        super(context);
        init();
    }

    public BackgroundOverlayView(Context context, AttributeSet attrs) {
        super(context, attrs);
        init();
    }

    public BackgroundOverlayView(Context context, AttributeSet attrs, int defStyle) {
        super(context, attrs, defStyle);
        init();
    }
```

```java
    private void init() {
        mPaint = new Paint(Paint.ANTI_ALIAS_FLAG);
    }

    /*
     * Set the normal and blurred image copies in our view
     */
    public void setImagePair(Bitmap base, Bitmap overlay) {
        mOverlayImage = overlay;

        /* Apply the normal image to the base ImageView, which
         * will allow it to apply our ScaleType for us and provide
         * a Matrix we can use to draw both images scaled accordingly
         * later on. This will also invalidate the view to trigger
         * a new draw.
         */
        setImageBitmap(base);
    }

    /*
     * Adjust the vertical point where the normal and blurred
     * copy should switch.
     */
    public void setOverlayOffset(int overlayOffset) {
        mClipOffset = overlayOffset;
        invalidate();
    }

    @Override
    protected void onDraw(Canvas canvas) {
        //Draw base image first, clipped to the top section
        // We clip the base image to avoid unnecessary overdraw in
        // the bottom section of the view.
        canvas.save();
        canvas.clipRect(getLeft(), getTop(), getRight(), mClipOffset);
        super.onDraw(canvas);
        canvas.restore();

        //Obtain the matrix used to scale the base image, and apply it
        // to the blurred overlay image so the two match up
        final Matrix matrix = getImageMatrix();
        canvas.save();
        canvas.clipRect(getLeft(), mClipOffset, getRight(), getBottom());
        canvas.drawBitmap(mOverlayImage, matrix, mPaint);
        canvas.restore();
    }
}
```

This is an extension of ImageView that does some custom drawing. We are using ImageView because it contains a lot of image scaling logic that we want to leverage. In our layout, we set the scaleType parameter to centerCrop so the view could take care of scaling and placing our background nicely. Notice when the activity sets the images on this view, the base image is passed directly to the base implementation as the main image. We do this for two reasons: primarily so the framework can do the image-scaling math, but also so we can easily draw the base image by just calling through to super.onDraw() later on.

With each scroll position change, the offset is passed into this view via setOverlayOffset(); which also invalidates the view, forcing a new draw pass. In the drawing portion of the view, we utilize that offset marker to create two clipping masks for the Canvas. The main purpose of this is to draw only the portion of the blurred overlay that we want to show to match the list position. However, we can use the same offset to clip off the base image drawing as well. This is again to eliminate pixel overdraw in our view, which will make the app perform much more smoothly. Even though the effect is that we are drawing a semitransparent overlay, we never actually draw any pixel in this view more than once.

As a final reminder of what we've created, Figure 8-7 shows the application with the list scrolled completely up and the blur overlay covering the complete view.

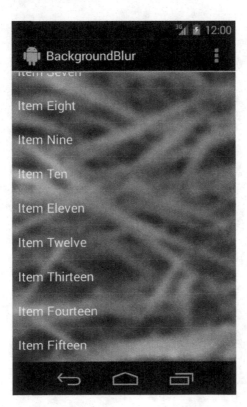

Figure 8-7. Blur overlay shown completely

Summary

The Android NDK complements the Android SDK by providing a tool set that lets you implement parts of your app by using native code languages such as C and C++. The NDK provides headers and libraries for building native activities, handling user input, using hardware sensors, and more.

RenderScript consists of a language based on C99 (a modern dialect of the C language), a collection of useful prebuilt script kernels, a pair of compilers, and a runtime that collectively help you achieve high-performance and visually compelling graphics via native code but in a portable manner. You get native app speed along with SDK app portability, and you don't have to use the JNI.

Index

T

X, Y, Z

Get the eBook for only $10!

> Now you can take the weightless companion with you anywhere, anytime. Your purchase of this book entitles you to 3 electronic versions for only $10.

This Apress title will prove so indispensible that you'll want to carry it with you everywhere, which is why we are offering the eBook in 3 formats for only $10 if you have already purchased the print book.

Convenient and fully searchable, the PDF version enables you to easily find and copy code—or perform examples by quickly toggling between instructions and applications. The MOBI format is ideal for your Kindle, while the ePUB can be utilized on a variety of mobile devices.

Go to www.apress.com/promo/tendollars to purchase your companion eBook.